Plans for Holy War

Writings of the Westminster Divines

Series Editors
John R. Bower, David C. Noe,
and Chad B. Van Dixhoorn

This series provides scholarly editions of texts by Westminster Assembly members and commissioners. Volumes will include new translations, previously unpublished manuscripts, and republications of rare editions. Carefully determined editorial standards will be used to ensure an authoritative product that is accessible to modern readers, while remaining reliable for students and scholars.

THE WESTMINSTER
ASSEMBLY PROJECT

Plans for Holy War

How the Spiritual Soldier Fights, Conquers, and Triumphs

John Arrowsmith

Translated by David C. Noe
Edited and introduced by Chad B. Van Dixhoorn

Reformation Heritage Books
Grand Rapids, Michigan

Reformation Heritage Books
3070 29th St. SE
Grand Rapids, MI 49512
616-977-0889
orders@heritagebooks.org
www.heritagebooks.org

Printed in the United States of America
24 25 26 27 28 29/10 9 8 7 6 5 4 3 2 1

Library of Congress Cataloging-in-Publication Data

Names: Arrowsmith, John, 1602-1659, author. | Noe, David C. (David Craig),
    translator. | Van Dixhoorn, Chad B., editor.
Title: Plans for holy war : how the spiritual soldier fights, conquers, and triumphs /
    John Arrowsmith ; translated by David C. Noe ; edited and introduced by Chad
    B. Van Dixhoorn.
Other titles: Tactica sacra. English
Description: Grand Rapids, Michigan : Reformation Heritage Books, [2024] |
    Series: Writings of the Westminster divines | Includes bibliographical references
    and index. | Summary: "An examination of spiritual warfare defining a Christian
    in terms of military duty, surveying his battle against the evil one, and recognizing
    how he is equipped for victory and triumph"-- Provided by publisher.
Identifiers: LCCN 2023047940 (print) | LCCN 2023047941 (ebook) |
    ISBN 9798886860887 (hardcover) | ISBN 9798886860894 (epub)
Subjects: LCSH: Spiritual warfare—Early works to 1800.
Classification: LCC BV4509.5.A753 T3313 2024 (print) | LCC BV4509.5.A753
    (ebook) | DDC 235/.4—dc23/eng/20231211
LC record available at https://lccn.loc.gov/2023047940
LC ebook record available at https://lccn.loc.gov/2023047941

Tarae et Aemiliae,
uxoribus nostris,
quae afficiunt nos bono, non autem malo,
omnibus diebus vitae nostrae.

Contents

PLANS FOR HOLY WAR

Plans for Holy War—Book I

Plans for Holy War—Book II

Plans for Holy War—Book III

Appendices

Indices

Acknowledgments

A project this size requires the talents of a great many individuals to bring it to a successful completion. We wish to thank the following persons from Calvin University, Westminster Theological Seminary, and Reformed Theological Seminary for their talented and generous contributions: Nell Colyn Duff and Amy Drake Silvasi provided much of the preliminary research assistance in identifying and formatting citations and references. Westminster assistants Zachary Herbster and Paul Woo hunted down difficult references, and Dr. Todd Rester spent hours puzzling over some of the last remaining citations that had stumped the editor. Together they have much improved the scholarly apparatus of this book.

Drs. Joseph A. Tipton and Patrick M. Owens were a constant reference for the translator, serving as a Latin advisory board and suggesting solutions to some of the construals he found more difficult. Dr. Tipton also read the whole work and improved its idiomacy and accuracy. Simon Hitchings's comments on the first chapter also led to improvements, for which we are grateful. Dr. Kirsten Macfarlane helped us track down and understand multiple Masoretic references.

A special debt of gratitude is reserved for Adrienne Ora, who worked with both editor and translator. Adrienne, working in multiple languages in order to offer substantive suggestions and corrections, has probably read the translation more carefully and thoroughly than anyone (save the two of us), and her tireless diligence and precision in reviewing texts and drafting notes materially improved the final product.

The Calvin Center for Christian Scholarship provided us with a large initial grant in 2014, which made possible all the research support just mentioned, as did the Craig Center for the Study of the Westminster Standards at Westminster Theological Seminary. Ligon Duncan, chancellor of Reformed Theological Seminary, provided a helpful grant for travel-related expenses.

We are grateful for the editorial and financial support we have received in this project. We are also deeply thankful, as we approach the age at which Arrowsmith wrote his final work, that we have been not only spared the painful losses experienced by Arrowsmith and his two spouses but also granted the blessings of good company and encouragement from our growing children. David thanks his children, Freddie, Jillian, Lucius, and Sophia, who helped occasionally with the wording, provided coffee and laughter, and endured patiently much more discussion of Arrowsmith and his work than they requested. Chad thanks Victoria, Caroline, Ashley, Peter, and even young Charlotte for ganging up on him to laugh down failed metaphors and poor turns of phrase. This is a better book because of all of you; it is dedicated to your mothers, and you, of all people, will best know why.

—David C. Noe
Chad B. Van Dixhoorn

Translator's Preface

This preface performs three tasks: First, I discuss what Arrowsmith considers his unique style of writing, particularly as his work is copious and diverse, and he claims to be presenting a new style. Next, I explain to the reader some of the metrical choices that were made in the translation of poetry, as Arrowsmith both quotes a large amount of Greek and Latin verse and includes at least one poem of his own composition. Then, I give some concluding evaluative comments on his value as a Latin stylist.

Arrowsmith's Style

At the beginning of his long treatise, Arrowsmith explains his choice of title. His comments are in keeping with the general conventions of literary prose stretching back to antiquity. Arrowsmith tells us he is borrowing the term *Tactica Sacra* from Aelian. This sounds an important note of general reliance on language and ideas from Greco-Roman antiquity, soon to be combined in *Tactica Sacra* with distinct theological categories from Scripture and the Christian tradition. Arrowsmith then explains that he will not use an ornamental style and singles out Cardinal Bembo for rhetorical extravagance, who substituted the rococo phrase "Muse of the western heaven" for "Holy Spirit." This extreme, florid bombast, Arrowsmith seeks to avoid. The other extreme, for which Arrowsmith cites Erasmus as his authority, is the Scholastic theologians' thorny style. And here he takes special aim at Duns Scotus. Instead, Arrowsmith will adopt a style he dubs *Scholastico-Pastoralis*. For him this means employing Scholastic terms when necessary, especially for polemic, but also using an elevated style for things that concern practical theology and philology (*practicam Theologiam vel Philologiam*). And he will do this with modesty, not in such a way as to appear that he is striving for effect—that is, to win his readers with pleasant language devoid of content. Yet it is very interesting to note that his definition of *pastoral* does not have to do exclusively with pious exhortation; it also has a strong philological element. This is especially interesting since the work was only intended for an audience, both English and Continental, that was fluent enough in Latin to appreciate his efforts and recognize his allusions. Though spending very little time describing what he means by a style that is *Scholastico-Pastoralis*, Arrowsmith goes to great lengths to demonstrate it.

As Arrowsmith promised, and as a reader might expect, the Scholastic portion of his style appears in places where he is engaged in polemic. A notable example is found in 2.7.7–8, where he is discussing Christ the mediator as the "proper and formal object of justifying faith." Here Arrowsmith gives a "huiusce theseos…brevem & scholasticam determinationem." It is not the mere inclusion of the adjective *Scholastic* that marks this section as belonging to that register of his style. It is instead the proliferation of standard Scholastic terminology that one might find in Aquinas, Bradwardine, Ockham, and Scotus (each of whom he quotes in this work). For example, there is a proliferation of qualifying adverbs, many of which are rare or unattested in classical authors. These include *specificative* (with respect to species), *reduplicative* (in a reduplicative sense), and *comprehensive* (comprehensively). The reader will note that in such instances, I have more often opted for translation by English derivative because of the lack of a precise equivalent in our target language. In addition to the sprouting of unusual adverbs, there is introducing the section a standard Scholastic division of the subject, where Arrowsmith defines his term thus: "Fides autem iustifican subire notionem triplicem." Such distributive, numerical adjectives as *duplex*, *triplex*, etc. are standard Scholastic terminology. As each idea based on the three adverbs already mentioned is fleshed out, moreover, we find a large proportion of Scholastic terms: *sumitur*, *obiectum principale*, *ut proprium*, *primario*, *fides…sumpta*, *pro obiecto formali*, *formalitatem*, *quoad gradum*, the privative *incomplexum*, etc. Equally interesting, however, is what is missing from these Scholastic sections as compared with the rest of the work: there is no poetry, and there are no classical allusions. The section concludes with a quotation from William Ames and discussion of contemporaries who wrote in a Scholastic style, Anthony Wotton and Thomas Gataker.

Though a clear reliance on Scholastic method and terminology emerges from time to time, the passages of the pastoral element are much more extended and developed. These include lengthy quotations from virtually every classical author in the canon, from church fathers, and from contemporaries. It will not be necessary for me to repeat here what Dr. Van Dixhoorn says so capably in the introduction. But I would note that some of these sayings are old saws, which Arrowsmith no doubt got from handbooks, similar to the way in which many people know snippets of Shakespeare without having ever read the poet directly. An interesting example is found at the beginning of his "Second Speech against Weigelianism," where he quotes from the Roman satirist Juvenal, explaining the difficulty in avoiding the genre of satire when all is corrupt. A more significant hallmark of the pastoral element than the mere quotation of authors his audience would have read as children is the developed and tactical use of the trope apostrophe. At moments of great emotion, Arrowsmith speaks directly to the audience, to God, to a character from history, or to an opponent—or just as often quotes one of his favorite authors who is addressing God or the enemy. In 1.1.3, for example, he speaks to Smalcius's tongue, rebuking it for its coldness and duplicity. In 1.3.2 he rebukes Ermolao Barbaro for the foolishness of the definition he gives for the word *soul*. In 1.2.10 he addresses Bernard as "most honey-tongued Father." And in 2.1.4 he breaks forth in prayer, addressing the "eternal father of our Lord Jesus Christ." This mode of address—speaking to a member of the audience, a part of the body, a part of a home, a historical individual, or even elements of nature—is very common in all Greco-Roman literature. It is present in Scripture as well (e.g., Isa. 1), but largely foreign to the English ear.

Because Arrowsmith is writing in this unique style—and because at points it seems as though he is staring at the bookshelf in his study, reaching for every last bit of wisdom and punch that he has encountered over a life of preaching and teaching—I have everywhere striven as a translator of Arrowsmith for idiomacy in style, and my own approach changed considerably over the course of several years of translating the work. Interrupted as I was by other obligations and opportunities, I learned Arrowsmith slowly. As time went on, and after a thorough final revision, I have everywhere sought to dress up the Latin in English garb rather than make it fit something ill suited, sticking out at the elbows. Examples include such simple efforts as changing impersonal verbs—*licet, videtur, pudet, piget, placet,* etc.—with datives, accusatives and so on, and rendering them actively. Thus, *mihi videtur* becomes "I thought"; *mihi placet*, "I like"; etc. Furthermore, I have everywhere endeavored to turn passive sentences in Latin into the active voice in English, such as is preferred in today's speech. Beyond that, I have often been compelled to break up very long sentences, which, though beautiful in Latin and composed of great intricacies of subordination and sophisticated assonance, nevertheless, through no fault of their own, can, like this sentence, weary the ear of the English speaker in a way that exceeds all reasonable measure. Everywhere the controlling principles were two: fidelity to Arrowsmith's meaning and clarity in the English expression. Fidelity requires a scrupulous maintenance of vocabulary, especially in the more theologically knotty sections in 2.7 on the nature of faith. So, important terms like πληροφορία, *fiducia*, and *certioratio* were translated identically in each occurrence so as, wherever possible and in keeping with the meaning, to represent Arrowsmith's thought accurately. When such terms were not under consideration, the principle of variety was followed. Generally speaking, Latin is not nearly as concerned with variety in adjectives or nouns as is English, being perfectly content to repeat a word within a short compass. Only the reader with knowledge of Latin and the ability to compare this translation to the original can judge the extent of my success, but that reader can take comfort in the knowledge that this translation was worked over meticulously and reviewed by several other very capable Latinists.

Arrowsmith's Poetry

Second, I must say something about the extensive poetry in the volume and how I decided to translate it. The fact most obvious to readers of *Plans for Holy War* in the original Latin is that while Arrowsmith quotes a fairly broad variety of meters, the English verse that I have rendered it into is primarily in a rhyming 8686 scheme. In 1.6.10, for example, Arrowsmith quotes two lines from Ovid's *Fasti*, written in elegiac couplets. I rendered this into two rhyming lines of fourteen syllables each, roughly trochaic. A little bit later, in 1.6.11, two lines and the first word of a third from Vergil's *Aeneid*—dactylic hexameters—are rendered in that same 8686 pattern. Quotations from epic poets, all in hexameters, have generally been rendered in this scheme, while occasionally I tried to reflect the original in English pentameters, rhyming where possible without sacrificing meaning. He also includes one couplet in 1.3.4 that appears to be original. Although its meaning is compelling, in my judgment, its scansion is not especially fluid.

By far the two most difficult poems to translate are found in the middle of the "Second Speech against Weigelianism" and at the very end of book 3 of *Plans for Holy War*. The first is challenging primarily because of the extensive list of philosophers' and theologians' names. I have set this into blank verse of alternating lines, fourteen and seven syllables in length. I am very satisfied with the accuracy in every instance of verse translation, but the reader will have to judge whether it pleases the ear. The second difficult poem is a verse adaptation of Psalm 36 by George Buchanan. It is a very free version of Psalm 36 (in places largely unrecognizable as based on that psalm). Lines alternate between dactylic pentameter and normal iambic trimeter. In a sense, it is unfortunate that Arrowsmith, my friend for many pages in many nights of study, chose to end his delightful essay with Buchanan's not very successful poem. I hope that my version is palatable, at least.

Arrowsmith as Latin Stylist

Now for the prose. As our author cites so many different primary sources, I have tried in each instance to let the unique nature of the Latin style speak for itself. This is not a new difficulty for Latin translators or for Latin writers. Aquinas sounds different from Augustine, who in turn does not sound like Cicero, try as he might (though Lactantius and Pico are much closer). Luther is not Suarez, and Melanchthon's Latin is almost nicer than Chrysostom's Greek. As a self-conscious communicator, Arrowsmith reserves highest praise for the brevity and sagacity of Calvin, for the clarity of Beza as an exegete, for Augustine's eloquence, and for the unrivaled sweetness of Bernard. For each of these men and their inimitable syntax and turn of phrase, each a master stylist in his own right, I have tried as a translator to imitate and respect those idiosyncrasies rather than flatten everything out and make it sound like schoolbook English, all written by the same individual. The refrain: we leave it to the reader to decide if this has been carried out successfully.

When Arrowsmith is not quoting but composing *de novo*, he is very successful. As I have previously worked to render in English the thought of men from the sixteenth century—Beza, Calvin, Junius, Vermigli, and others— I have for Arrowsmith a healthy point of comparison. The quality of his Latin seems to stand at a turning point. Some of his contemporaries— John Owen, for example—have a Latin style best deemed lifeless (I owe to Joseph Tipton the entirely apropos epithet for Owen, *exsanguis*). In other words, the lexemes, syntax, and grammar are all accurate in Owen, but it seems as though one is looking at a master-level school composition and not the natural growth of a mind in which Latin is as comfortable as English. Similarly, there does not seem to be in Arrowsmith as much breadth of vocabulary and fluidity as with Calvin or Melanchthon, generational talents fostered at the apex of Renaissance humanism. But nevertheless, there is nothing wooden or forced about his style either. He can write like Cicero occasionally but verges more toward the crabbed, pointed, and highly contrastive, nearly lapidary structure of Seneca. He clearly has extraordinary praise for Seneca as a wise pagan and seems to have imitated his style as well.

To conclude, I pray that, while you read this work, Arrowsmith will become your friend as he has become mine in the process of resurrecting his thought. His winsome, brilliant, and diligent appropriation of the Christian tradition, as well as his dedication to the truth, his affability, and his wit, are good models not only for students of theology but also for students of the ancient languages Arrowsmith loved and whose study he vigorously championed. May God in His providence arrange that someday John Arrowsmith can explain to me in person, in our resurrected bodies, in what ways I have unknowingly and unwillingly misrepresented his magnum opus. I hope that he will have a few words of praise for a student four hundred years his junior before we settle down for him to teach me the many finer points of the Latin language.

Editorial Conventions

This edition offers the reader a window into Arrowsmith's own practice of scholarly quotation and academic citation. Given the early modern priority of smooth prose over accurate repetition, Arrowsmith, like others in his day, would not uncommonly adjust the grammar of a quotation to better flow with his own sentences. Footnotes flag instances where we find these changes to be significant or indicative of a larger pattern in the work.

In attempting to identify works cited, we have sought to find editions of works printed prior to 1657, when Arrowsmith's book was completed. We have thus supplied the titles of texts that Arrowsmith used or may plausibly have used. Further, we have preferred where possible to use editions of works found in Trinity College Library, Cambridge, where Arrowsmith was master while writing his masterpiece. We do this in the hope of getting closer to the books he held in his own hands, even though we know that Arrowsmith enjoyed a significant personal library, was largely housebound, and would sometimes quote and cite texts from memory. Where we were unable to identify books in Trinity's collection, we employed the best sources available to us online, seeking the convenience of scholars around the world who may wish to read the larger context of a quotation. On rare occasions, we cite modern translations or editions, because of the exigencies of time or because travel restrictions during the pandemic inhibited access to early modern editions of works. Thankfully, copies of works contemporaneous to Arrowsmith are increasingly available in libraries and online, even to nonspecialists.

Readers attentive to our scholarly apparatus will see that wherever Arrowsmith offered a marginal note in *Tactica Sacra*, our editorial apparatus supplies the wording of his original note in our own footnote. Thus, "De Regno Persico lib. 2. p. 240, &c.]" The editorial note that almost invariably follows the lemma represents our attempt to identify the author, title, and a plausible publication. In supplying more and less complete information we employ the following conventions:

1. An incomplete note or the absence of a note signals that we could not find additional information about a work cited.

2. Where we could identify the author and title but could not view a copy of the volume (and thus verify Arrowsmith's own citation of pagination, etc.), the editorial note limits bibliographical info. Thus, "De Regno Persico lib. 2. p. 240, &c.] Barnabé Brisson, *De Regio Persarum principatu* ([Heidelberg], 1595)."

3. Where we could verify a correct citation with a physical or online copy, we offer full bibliographical info. Thus, "*Buxtorf.* Tiberias cap. 5. p. 23.] Johannes Buxtorf, Sr., *Tiberias* (Basel, 1620), ch. 5. p. 23."

4. Where we could verify Arrowsmith's citation with a physical or online copy, we also sometimes silently "correct" an erroneous citation. Thus, "*Alsted.* Chronolog. p. 415.] Johann Heinrich Alsted, *Thesaurus chronologiae* (Herborn, 1650), ch. 42, p. 432." Nonetheless, the editors are aware that, despite our attempts to consult multiple printings of a work, we may have failed to find the edition used by Arrowsmith, and, thus, our citation offers an alternative rather than a corrected citation.

The editorial apparatus identifies, in the first instance only, all persons mentioned and authors cited. Life dates are provided when known, as well as a short description of the person and, where available, a source of biographical information. All subsequent references to texts cite the author's surname. To conserve space, titles are rarely mentioned in full, even in the first instance, and all subsequent references to texts cite an abbreviated title only. Publication information, as is common in modern citations of early modern texts printed prior to 1700, cites the place and date of publication only and only in the first instance of a citation.

Scholars should note that this edition makes one minor change to the opening presentation of Arrowsmith's book. Both in the original edition and in this translated edition, the text of the three university speeches is followed by the text of the main volume, *Plans for Holy War*. Nonetheless, the table of contents in the original edition offers a structure that a twenty-first century reader would not anticipate, presenting a full table of contents for *Plans for Holy War*, then a table of contents for the three speeches, but then presenting the speeches prior to *Plans for Holy War*, contrary to the expected order in the table of contents. Here we have altered the table of contents to match the text (speeches and *Plans*) as presented both in the original edition and in this translation.

John Arrowsmith:
A Theological Life

Chad B. Van Dixhoorn

Student and Fellow

John Arrowsmith was born in Gateshead, Durham county, England, on March 29, 1602, in the dying years of Queen Elizabeth's reign.[1] Little is known of his parents, but a few breadcrumbs have been left behind, such as a plaque, a will, and matriculation and court records.

Arrowsmith's father was likely the Thomas Arrowsmith who died and was buried in Gateshead in 1632; his mother may have been named Mary.[2] Helpfully for historians, his family erected a memorial plaque in St. Mary's parish church in Gateshead, where he was buried. The memorial reads, in part,

Reader in that piece of earth in peace rests
Thomas ARROWSMITH
In peace he livd in peace went hence with God and man and conscience
Peace for other men he sought and peace with peeces some time bought
Pacific may others bee but *ex pace factus* hee[3]
Peace reader then doe not molest he is now possest
The God of peace for him in store hath joy and peace for evermore
Pangit plangit et amore dolore[4]

---

1. John Twigg, "John Arrowsmith," in *Oxford Dictionary of National Biography*, 60 vols. (Oxford: Oxford University Press, 2004). Hereafter cited as *ODNB*.

2. For the elder Thomas Arrowsmith's death date of September 27, 1632, see National Burial Index for England and Wales, accessed June 7, 2021, https://www.findmypast.com/transcript?id=BMD%2FNBI%2F02732578. Thomas likely married Mary Place in Cleasby, Yorkshire, in 1599. See Paver's Marriage Licenses from the Registry of York 1567–1614, p. 72, accessed June 7, 2021, htttps://www.findmypast.com/transcript?id=GBPRS%2FCOA%2FMARRLICENCE%2F00001835%2F1. The current pandemic has not, in every case, permitted me to view original records.

3. "But forged from peace was he."

4. For the memorial inscription at St. Mary's, Gateshead, see Northumberland and Durham Memorial Inscriptions, accessed June 7, 2021, https://www.findmypast.com/transcript?id=GBPRS%2FNORTHUMDURHAM%2FMIS%2F012342. "He is planted here and mourned

These are the words of a godly man with confidence in personal salvation. And there is more.

As John Arrowsmith's own last will and testament revealed, his father had bequeathed to him a Geneva Bible, testifying to the priority that his father placed on knowing the Scriptures. The same will reveals that John had a brother, Thomas, and a sister, Johan. Throughout his life, Arrowsmith appears to have been close to Thomas and Thomas's wife, both of whom remained in Gateshead; his sister, Johan, appears to have been widowed.[5]

Arrowsmith entered St. John's College, Cambridge, at age fourteen. It is there that the trail, gone cold since early childhood, warms once more. College records indicate that young Arrowsmith matriculated in 1616 as a pensioner but was made a scholar two years later.[6] (University students were admitted as either sizars or pensioners. Sizars worked their way through college, whereas pensioners—or "commoners"—paid their own way.) Arrowsmith's start as a pensioner is one more indication that, at least in 1616, his family was not poor. The 1618 scholarship tells us he was a precocious young man, and others recognized it.

But was this change in status—from a "paying customer" to a scholar whose fees were forgiven by the college—reflective of a change in his family's or his supporter's circumstances? It is hard to say. Other pensioners in the university contemporary with Arrowsmith were granted scholarships, so many of them that proof of financial hardship cannot have been a rigid requirement for the gift of a scholarship. Colleges could have awarded Arrowsmith and others scholarships based on academic merit alone. Nonetheless, a Thomas Arrowsmith in the county of Durham seems to have inherited some debts, and records show that he was often in court.[7] And four decades later, John Arrowsmith would passionately defend the importance of endowments for scholars from lower-income homes, even arguing that they, more than gentlemen, made the best use of the opportunity

---

with love and sorrow." The editor gratefully thanks David Noe for all translations appearing in the introduction.

5. Arrowsmith left three pounds for Thomas and his wife to purchase commemorative rings after his death, and he bequeathed the same sum for another couple, also close friends. Nonetheless, to his sister he bequeathed only thirty shillings, or one and a half pounds, suggesting that she was single. The scribal copy of the will renders her name as Johan Dawson, the change of surname indicating that she had been married. She must have been well cared for, as Arrowsmith left her little in his will. For the will, see Richmond upon Thames, National Archives (hereafter cited as NA), PROB 11/289/161, fols. 179r–180r.

6. J. A. Venn, ed., *Alumni Cantabrigienses*, 10 vols. (Cambridge: Cambridge University Press, 1922–1954), (hereafter cited as Venn); also accessible at venn.lib.cam.ac.uk.

7. E.g., NA E 134/41Eliz/Trin2.

afforded by a university education.[8] We may well wonder whether these comments were, in part, autobiographical and whether the unhappily indebted Thomas Arrowsmith was his father.

Having arrived in Cambridge, Arrowsmith would remain there, first as a student and then as a fellow, for the next fifteen years. Indeed, he would spend more than half of his life in the city, for after a stint in pastoral ministry, he would return to Cambridge for another fifteen years as a college master, professor, and vice-chancellor of the university. Along the way, Arrowsmith collected the appropriate degrees required of an early-modern academic: at St. John's College, he proceeded bachelor of arts in 1620 and master of arts in 1623, at which point he began a fellowship at St. Catherine's College.

For the first half of the seventeenth century and for some time thereafter, it was required that fellows be clergymen and, thus, if English, ordained in the Church of England. Conveniently, English canon law permitted fellows of colleges freedom in choosing which bishop they would approach to request ordination.[9] Arrowsmith sought ordination from George Mountain, the then bishop of London, and the ceremony took place at the bishop's palace. At first glance, Mountain seems an odd choice: the bishop was an advocate of ceremony over simplicity in worship and Arminianism over Calvinism in doctrine, and thus he was no obvious ally of a young Puritan. And yet, Mountain not only ordained the young man but—contrary to custom and canon law, which dictated that a year separate successive ordinations and that the minimum age for ordination be twenty-three for a deacon and twenty-four for a priest—Mountain ordained Arrowsmith first as deacon and then as priest on the same day in February 1624, while Arrowsmith was still twenty-one years old.[10]

Arrowsmith's ordination under such favorable conditions by a bishop so unsympathetic to Puritanism raises questions about the ordinand's ecclesiastical inclinations in his early twenties and the possibility that he was not

---

8. John Arrowsmith, *Tactica Sacra, Sive De Milite Spirituali Pugnante, Vincente, Et Triumphante Dissertatio, Tribus Libris Comprehensa* (Cambridge, 1657), translated here as "First Speech against Weigelianism," in *Plans for Holy War*. All references to Arrowsmith's *Tactica Sacra* will be to the text of this translation.

9. See the canons agreed upon by James I and VI but not by Parliament, *Constitutions and Canons Ecclesiastical* (London, 1604), canon XXXIV.

10. "Not that always every Deacon should be kept from the Ministry for a whole Year," but "no Bishop shall make any Person, of what Qualities or Gifts soever, a Deacon and a Minister both together upon one Day." *Constitutions and Canons Ecclesiastical*, canon XXXII. See also canon XXXIV, insisting that ordinands for deacon and priest be twenty-three and twenty-four "compleat."

yet a convert to the godly cause. After all, St. John's was hardly a hotbed of Puritanism, and nothing is actually known of Arrowsmith's theology or piety at this date. Also curious is the fact that, given his ability to choose whom he would approach for ordination, he did not choose his local prelate, Nicholas Felton, bishop of Ely. Felton, in the course of his career, would select George Walker as one of his chaplains and Edmund Calamy as an object of his patronage, both of whom became noted Puritan ministers and open opponents of Archbishop William Laud.[11]

Nonetheless, there is insufficient reason to doubt that Arrowsmith was already considered a godly young man at this early point. First, there were, in fact, adequate causes to induce Arrowsmith to ask for ordination from the bishop of London rather than his local overseer. The bishop of Ely, despite his friendliness or indifference toward Puritanism, did not usually live in his diocese and, thus, was no easier for Arrowsmith to access from Cambridge than was the bishop of London. Also, Mountain was not an illogical choice for a godly ordinand. He was reputed to be sloppy in his episcopal duties, and he might not have inquired too deeply into Arrowsmith's views about worship and the current state of the Church of England.[12] What is more, in a world where regional and institutional commitments mattered a great deal, Mountain had in common with Arrowsmith that he was a northerner and a Cambridge man.[13] There is also the chance that Mountain simply liked Arrowsmith, appreciating in a short time what he could see of the young man's abilities and the pleasantness of his character.

The young man's choice of bishop, therefore, does not raise an obstacle to affirming his godly orientation. Decisively in favor of Arrowsmith's godly leanings is the fact that Puritan fellows at St. Catherine's, including Thomas Goodwin, were eager to see Arrowsmith enter the college's fellowship.[14]

In keeping with its pre-Reformation purposes, the college principally existed to permit its own fellows to study, and Arrowsmith would have been provided a salary to do so from the college's many gifts and endowments. Following the Protestant Reformation, college fellows also usually supplemented their income by serving as a tutor, probably with the master doling out the students (and their fees) to various fellows. In some cases, and perhaps for a while in Arrowsmith's case, this income was further supplemented

---

11. Kenneth Fincham, "Nicholas Felton," *ODNB*.

12. Andrew Foster, "George Mountain," *ODNB*.

13. London, Guildhall Library 9535/2, Ordination Register (Clergy of the Church of England Database).

14. T. M. Lawrence, "Thomas Goodwin," *ODNB*.

by letting out a room in their gift to students in the college.[15] Actually, as a fellow, Arrowsmith would share a set of rooms with one other fellow; in the early days of his fellowship, he shared rooms with John Lothian, perhaps on the Mill Street side of the college.[16] Students were not required to attend lectures, and since the invention of the book, they were less likely to do so. But sessions with tutors and university and college sermons were mandatory, and thus a fellowship in a college allowed an opportunity not only for personal study but for significant service in shaping the theological and moral outlook of a rising generation.[17]

In 1626 Richard Sibbes was elected master of St. Catherine's College in what a historian has called "perhaps the most brilliant period" in its history. Fellows included Thomas Goodwin, William Strong, John Bond, William Spurstowe, Andrew Perne, and Arrowsmith—all of whom would find themselves at the assembly of divines at Westminster Abbey two decades later.[18] St. Catherine's thus offers the key to explaining many of Arrowsmith's lifelong friendships. His long stint at the college also reveals much about the man and his scholarly inclinations, and the depth of his later writings surely owes much to this prolonged period of study.

Curate and Vicar

In 1633, two years after having left the university for a curacy at St. Nicholas's Church in King's Lynn and for married life (a privilege forbidden to college fellows), Arrowsmith received his bachelor of divinity.[19] One foot was still in university life. Nonetheless, from 1631, Arrowsmith was a pastor and then a family man. He had married Elizabeth Ray early in 1632,[20] and their son John was born ten months later.[21] Robert came next, in the summer of 1634, but tragedy soon struck, for John died in the spring of 1635

---

15. W. H. S. Jones, *A History of St Catherine's College Cambridge* (Cambridge: Cambridge University Press, 1936), p. 227.

16. Jones, *History of St Catherine's College*, pp. 12, 227.

17. John Twigg, *The University of Cambridge and the English Revolution, 1625–1688* (Woodbridge: Boydell, 1990), pp. 1–4, 14–15.

18. Jones, *History of St Catherine's College*, p. 93.

19. The BD is a postgraduate degree awarded after a period of study—at that time, a minimum of seven years subsequent to the award of the MA. Arrowsmith would have been eligible to apply for that degree at the time that he left St. Catherine's, but perhaps, in leaving the university, he did not initially see its value. In modern times, the BD is still considered an earned degree and is senior to the PhD at the University of Cambridge.

20. For the marriage of Jan. 19, 1632, see Norfolk, Norfolk Record Office PD 39/83, p. 97 (the record office transcript errs in stating June 1631).

21. Bap. Nov. 30, 1632, Norfolk, Norfolk Record Office PD 39/83, p. 15.

at two and a half years of age.[22] Elizabeth was pregnant at the time, and Thomas was born a few months later.[23] Their fourth child, named Elizabeth, arrived on the date of their sixth wedding anniversary.[24]

St. Nicholas's had been a chapel of the nearby St. Margaret's for around two centuries. But in 1627 it gained permission to perform marriages and baptisms. The church building is unusually beautiful, filled with light, and large. Indeed, the designation "chapel" had always been somewhat misleading. St. Nicholas's was the largest chapel in England and, by any other name, is a very large church. It was the place of choice for the archdeacon of Norwich to try ecclesiastical cases, and a consistory court still survives in the building today.

As a curate of St. Nicholas, Arrowsmith preached frequently to a large congregation in the bustling town and conducted the full range of duties required of him. King's Lynn is a Norfolk seaside town and, in the early seventeenth century, was a contender for England's busiest port. Its docks saw the arrival of significant imports of iron and timber and were the major conduit in England's own export of grain. The port also supplied eastern towns with coal, salt, and fish.[25] The city was hit hard by plague in 1636 and, although a port town, managed to persuade King Charles I's government that the city's economy had been so devastated that its assessed payment of "ship money" should be reduced.[26] Arrowsmith and at least some members of his family survived the plague, and so did the shipping industry. Only after Arrowsmith's time at St. Nicholas would the port's importance clearly be eclipsed by western ports serving the Atlantic colonies and by the growth of London and the shipyards needed to serve the metropolis.

While ministering in Lynn, Arrowsmith maintained or grew his reputation for scholarship, fraternity, and perhaps peacemaking. Later in life, Arrowsmith noted in passing that, while in Lynn, he enjoyed the company of Johannes Willius of Elbing "as a guest for several months."[27] In the seventeenth century, Elbing was a town in Prussia—in theory, under the control of the Polish crown but, at key points in the Thirty Years' War, controlled by Sweden. In religion it was Lutheran, but English, Irish, and Scottish merchants had together established a Scottish Reformed church in the city.

----

22. Bap. Aug. 25, 1634, Norfolk, Norfolk Record Office PD 39/83, p. 21; buried Apr. 7, 1635, Norfolk, Norfolk Record Office PD 39/83, p. 291.

23. Bap. Aug. 7, 1635, Norfolk, Norfolk Record Office PD 39/83, p. 25.

24. Bap. Jan. 19, 1638, Norfolk, Norfolk Record Office PD 39/83, p. 34.

25. S. Yaxley, ed., *The Siege of King's Lynn, 1643* (Dereham, UK: Larks Press, 1993), i.

26. Kevin Sharpe, *The Personal Rule of Charles I* (New Haven: Yale University Press, 1995), p. 587.

27. Arrowsmith, *Plans for Holy War*, III.iii.6.

Significantly, not only would future fellow Westminster Assembly member Thomas Ford spend time in Elbing but so too would fellow member John Dury and his mentors in the ecumenical movement of the day, Johannes Amos Comenius and Samuel Hartlib (an Elbing native). That a foreign guest would stay in the home of Arrowsmith, neither a prestigious London minister nor an Oxbridge academic, suggests that he was good company and a good networker interested in the kind of efforts for which theologians in Elbing were becoming known.

Arrowsmith's initial connection to King's Lynn was likely Thomas Goodwin, his colleague at St. Catherine's. Goodwin had previously counseled a correspondent, Nicholas Price, a godly curate at St. Nicholas.[28] Arrowsmith himself was in time appointed vicar of the church, probably in 1637, when two new curates were ordained to serve at St. Nicholas. One of those curates, Lionel Gatford, was a complicated figure in a passing Puritan phase of life—a phase which he repudiated with energy at the outbreak of war some years after he had left King's Lynn.[29] Arrowsmith himself might have continued as vicar of St. Nicholas, pastoring his flock and preparing curates for their own pastoral charges, for the duration of his ministerial life if it were not for personal sorrows, and events brought about by the English Civil War.

By the early 1640s, Lynn had become for Arrowsmith a place marked by a long litany of sorrows. His little Elizabeth died less than three months after she was born.[30] Robert, almost five, was buried April 1, 1641.[31] Robert Ray, Arrowsmith's father-in-law, died in November 1641.[32] Then Elizabeth herself, after almost nine years of marriage and the loss of three of her four children, passed away in January 1642.[33] The bereaved father was left alone with Thomas and, no doubt, with sorrows that words cannot express.

All the while, storm clouds were gathering over the Atlantic Isles. The war that would eventually engulf Scotland, Ireland, and most of all England was the result of religious, political, and economic tensions in King Charles I's three kingdoms. And yet, in spite of the many grievances against the government of Charles, conflicts over the worship, government, and doctrine of the Church of England were arguably uppermost in the minds not only of most ministers but of most members of Parliament unhappy with the

---

28. Lawrence, "Thomas Goodwin."

29. Jason Mc Elligott, "Lionel Gatford," *ODNB*.

30. Buried Apr. 9, 1638, Norfolk, Norfolk Record Office PD 39/83, p. 303.

31. Buried Apr. 1, 1641, Norfolk, Norfolk Record Office PD 39/83, p. 320.

32. Buried Nov. 2, 1641, Norfolk, Norfolk Record Office PD 39/83, p. 322.

33. Buried Jan. 3, 1642, Norfolk, Norfolk Record Office PD 39/83, p. 323.

king's rule.[34] Efforts since the time of Queen Elizabeth to reform the church by appeals to monarchs and bishops had failed, and agitation had concentrated on increasingly restless parliaments since the late sixteenth century. Charles's attempt to lead England without parliaments in the 1630s, with an aggressive archbishop at the helm of the English church and a like-minded lieutenant in Ireland, led to an eventual collapse of order when the king decided to further advance his ceremonialist agenda in Scotland later that decade. The Scots declared, through a national covenant and a show of force, that they would no longer be led by their monarch without material change in Charles's mode of government.

Although the Scottish leadership was the first to revolt, the English Parliament was likewise exasperated and distrustful, and when war eventually broke out in 1641 between those loyal to the two houses of the English Parliament and strong forces loyal to the king, King's Lynn declared for Parliament and against Charles I. A year later the tide had turned, for in August 1642 (after careful Royalist planning and agitation), Lynn's mayor ordered the arrest of pro-Parliamentarians and house arrest for two Parliamentarian MPs. England's key port was now in Royalist hands and would remain so until mid-September.[35]

With the city in the king's possession, Arrowsmith himself would have been a marked man. There had been well-grounded speculation since 1642 that the rector of St. Nicholas would be invited to a Parliament-supported assembly of divines, and the invitation had been confirmed publicly in June 1643—a notice that would have made its way north to King's Lynn at some time in July or early August, while Royalists were still planning the overthrow of Lynn. More to the point, Arrowsmith had already traveled to Westminster and preached before the House of Commons. The sermon, in print sometime between February 9 and the end of March 1643, openly upheld the justice of Parliament's cause against the king.[36]

The sermon, preached on January 25, 1643, to the House of Commons, was entitled "The Covenant-Avenging Sword Brandished."[37] It was the first of six Arrowsmith works to be printed in two periods, beginning with three

---

34. John Morrill, *Nature of the English Revolution* (London: Longman, 1993), pp. 45–68.

35. Yaxley, *Siege of King's Lynn*, viii.

36. Samuel Man, the publisher, registered the book on February 9; the new year (1643) began on March 25, thus, its "1642" printing date requires it to have been printed between February 9 and March 24, 1643, in modern dating. See *A Transcript of the Registers of the Worshipful Company of Stationers, From 1640–1708, A.D.* (London, 1913; Gloucester, Mass.: Peter Smith, 1967), 1:54 (hereafter, *Stationers' Registers*).

37. John Arrowsmith, *The Covenant-Avenging Sword Brandished: In a Sermon, before the House of Commons, at Their Late Solemne Fast, Jan. 25* (London, 1642).

sermons preached before one or more house of Parliament in the 1640s. From its title page to its final applications, *The Covenant Avenging Sword* spelled out the necessity of Parliament's war against the king in order to "reconcile" Scotland, "reduce" Ireland, and "reform" England. Forthright, even affecting passages recounted the horrors of war (it is "hardly possible for the tonge of a sedentary Scholler to set forth the horrid works of a barbours souldiers hands") and of civil war in particular.[38] It has been suggested that he was deeply moved by the slaughter at Edgehill, although the battle had taken place three months earlier;[39] another scholar hears in the sermon a "despair" about the war more generally.[40] In any case, Arrowsmith urged peace as soon as practically possible.[41] The sermon as a whole explained that a nation in covenant with the Lord cannot be granted peace while ignoring known "quarrell-breeding sword-avenging violations of the Covenant." Arrowsmith listed six covenant quarrels that God evidently had with England, and he gave remedies for each. These, he argues, are the inescapable conclusions to be drawn from his text, Leviticus 26:25, which reads, "I will bring a sword upon you, that shall avenge the quarrel of my covenant."

The sermon reveals something of the preacher's magnetism, and readers of sermons preached before Parliament will not fail to note that Arrowsmith, even at his most confrontational, was suaver than most other preachers before the House of Lords or House of Commons. Indeed, Arrowsmith's aptitude for generating a good turn of phrase is already evident in this earliest work, as is his penchant for colorful stories—tales about kings and cardinals, the Duke of Burgundy, the Irish, the Hussites, and the Turks; moments from the life of Luther; anecdotes from Foxe's *Acts and Monuments*; and morsels from Ovid, Pliny, and Tacitus—all adding spice to a sermon, serving up meaty citations from the standard exegetes of the day, ranging from still-respected medieval figures to recent Reformed writers.

And yet it must be said that Arrowsmith's lifelong reputation as a pacific figure, a characteristic evidently marked in his own father, does not come from this first publication; indeed, modern readers will likely find the book jarring at points, although falling short of the "rich storehouse of Puritan invective" described by R. W. Ketton-Cremer.[42] Arrowsmith

---

38. Read "tongue" and "barbarous." Arrowsmith, *Covenant-Avenging Sword*, p. 8; see also pp. 9–10.

39. Twigg, *University of Cambridge*, p. 106n12.

40. James C. Spalding, "Sermons before Parliament (1640–1649) As a Public Puritan Diary," in *Church History* 36, no. 1 (Mar. 1967): p. 32.

41. Arrowsmith, *Covenant-Avenging Sword*, pp. 12–15.

42. R. W. Ketton-Cremer, *Norfolk in the Civil War: A Portrait of a Society in Conflict* (1969; Norwich: Giddon Books, 1985), p. 260.

himself acknowledges that his "harsh theme, requires rather keenessse than smoothnesse of stile."[43] Thus, while praising the Commons for its progress in reforming the ministry of the church (and while swerving from intimate encouragements from the Song of Songs all the way to dire warnings from the second Psalm!), the dedicatory epistle openly warns members of the lower house "to exalt the Ordinance of Christ above your own Priviledges, his Gospel above your Laws, his Glorie above your goods"[44] and urges them to properly "manage the publique affairs of Church or State."[45]

The sermon as printed is much of a piece with public sermons at times of war, and it is arguably more subtle than most. But it remained a militant sermon that brazenly puts all the right on Parliament's side, reinforcing the narrative of injury that pervaded all parliamentary sermons of the period. Presumably returning home after the sermon was delivered, Arrowsmith would also recognize in time that his public utterances would make a Royalist-controlled King's Lynn an uncomfortable place for him to continue ministering.

There were other reasons to think that Arrowsmith's center of gravity was shifting south, for a month after his London January 1643 sermon, the forty-year-old widower married Mary Percival in the London suburb of Middlesex.[46] For at least two months, Arrowsmith remained with Mary either in London or in King's Lynn or in Middlesex: eleven months after their marriage a son John was baptized in Middlesex, likely the site of Mary's family home.[47] If the preacher, or the preacher and his wife, had settled into life in Lynn, they must have slipped out of town and south to London prior to the Royalist takeover in August 1643. How else could Arrowsmith be heard making a speech at the assembly of divines in early September 1643 while Royalists (who surely would have imprisoned him if he were still in Lynn) were still in control of the port?[48]

---

43. Arrowsmith, *Covenant-Avenging Sword,* sig. A4v.

44. Arrowsmith, *Covenant-Avenging Sword,* sig. A4v.

45. Arrowsmith, *Covenant-Avenging Sword,* sig. A4r-v.

46. As with other transcripts of public records in this period, the marriage date of February 24, 1642, follows an Old-Style dating, with the new year beginning on March 25. In today's New-Style dating, we would reckon the year as 1643. See England Marriages 1598–1973, accessed June 7, 2021, https://www.findmypast.com/transcript?id=R_852990863. It is possible that this is the Mary Percival baptized March 29, 1618. See England Births and Baptisms 1538–1975, accessed June 7, 2021, https://www.findmypast.com/transcript?id=R_951945379.

47. John, bap. Jan. 12, 1644, Middlesex Baptisms, accessed June 7, 2021, https://www.findmypast.com/transcript?id=GBPRS%2FB%2F907192249%2F1.

48. *John Lightfoot's Journals of the Westminster Assembly,* ed. Chad Van Dixhoorn (Oxford: Oxford University Press, 2023), p. 79 (sess. 50).

The preacher may have officially retained his title as vicar of King's Lynn during his first year or two at the assembly; diocesan records break down in the 1640s and 1650s, and parliamentary records are incomplete.[49] But he was never to return as an active minister of St. Nicholas.[50] Even after Parliament regained control of its strategic port following a three-week siege, Arrowsmith would live in London and then Cambridge for the remainder of his life.

London Minister

Arrowsmith, like most of his Puritan colleagues, would speak against the practice of pluralism in the assembly of divines. Nonetheless, after leaving Lynn, events would lead him into a bi- and eventually trivocational ministry in three years' time. Indeed, while Arrowsmith was still active in the assembly, the Earl of Manchester, as chancellor of the University of Cambridge, selected Arrowsmith and a handful of other assembly members to serve in 1644 as college heads.

The college appointment appears to have been without prior consultation, perhaps even without prior *notice*, because two of the five appointees from the assembly, upon hearing the news, initially declined.[51] Arrowsmith, understandably, accepted. It must have been obvious that he should do so: he was built for academic life. It must also be acknowledged that there were often ulterior motives to accepting a mastership. For much of the seventeenth century, a college mastership offered a stepping-stone to even greater privilege. Twigg determined that "twenty of the 112 men who were elected or otherwise appointed to Cambridge masterships between 1600 and 1699 became bishops, and many others held other important or rewarding ecclesiastical posts as prebendaries and archdeacons." Thus, says Twigg, "Few expected to remain in their colleges for life."[52]

Such preferment would not have been envisaged in the 1640s, however, least of all for Arrowsmith and his friends who would side with Presbyterianism and thus find episcopal appointments, should they be retained in some form, of little attraction. The mastership of St. John's offered a place where

---

49. The handwriting in the parish registers is also inconclusive. The hand recording burials only changes in November 1642 (NRO PD 39/83, p. 325); the hand recording baptisms does not change during this period (NRO PD PD 39/1).

50. It was even less likely that he would return to Norfolk as it drifted toward opposition to parliament in the later 1640s. See Scott E. Hendrix, *Riot and Resistance in Country Norfolk, 1646–1650* (Lewiston, NY: Edwin Mellen Press, 2012).

51. *John Lightfoot's Journals*, p. 348 (sess. 178).

52. Twigg, *University of Cambridge*, p. 7.

much good could be done and where someone with pastoral and schol-arly impulses could happily finish out his days. Additionally, while the town leaned toward Parliament, the gown was for the king, and Arrowsmith, as master of St. John's, could help to create a more favorable atmosphere in the university on behalf of the godly cause.[53]

Arrowsmith entered the master's seat or stall in the college chapel on April 11, 1644, taking a perhaps personally constructed oath of office that referred to God, the Earl of Manchester, Parliament, and the assembly of divines. He promised "faithfully to promote piety and learning" agreeable to the (twice) mentioned Solemn League and Covenant, that all-important 1643 military alliance and religious bond between the English Parliament and their cobelligerents in Scotland. Following his example, the fellows of the college were to declare their own acceptance of the Solemn League and Covenant (but without an oath), thus committing them to the reform of the English church. The requirement resulted in the departure of four senior fellows and their replacement by men more pliable to Parliament's reformation. Conveniently, crosses and images had already been removed from the college chapel, and side-sepulchers turned into small apartments prior to Arrowsmith's arrival, apparently leaving little remaining for him to renovate other than the fellows and students themselves.[54] Nonetheless, a reforming master could always see worthy causes that needed furthering, and Arrowsmith found himself on more than one occasion down at West-minster Palace, delivering appeals or complaints to Parliament regarding college leadership or fellows or defending himself against accusations.[55]

While Arrowsmith formally took up his position at Cambridge, the assembly of divines managed to persuade Manchester that the master of St. John's should be excused from permanent residence in Cambridge for two years so that he could assist the assembly in drafting its Confession of Faith.[56] Arrowsmith honored this desire for the gathering to use his theo-logical gifts, and his services and attendance in the assembly seem to have been similar to that of other faithful members during the synod's most productive years.[57]

---

53. G. M. Trevelyan, *Trinity College: An Historical Sketch* (Cambridge: Cambridge Univer-sity Press, 1943), p. 35.

54. T. Baker, *History of the College of St. John the Evangelist, Cambridge,* ed. John E. B. Mayor (Cambridge: Cambridge University Press, 1869), 1:224–26.

55. Twigg, *University of Cambridge,* pp. 122n114, 123, 125–26.

56. Chad Van Dixhoorn, ed., *The Minutes and Papers of the Westminster Assembly, 1643–1652* (Oxford: Oxford University Press, 2012), 1:107 (hereafter cited as *MPWA*).

57. Whatever the jottings on the scribe's attendance record might have meant, his pres-ence on the three attendance lists approaches that of Burges, Valentine, Walker, and Maynard;

More difficult to explain, given his opposition to pastoral pluralism, is Arrowsmith's decision in 1645 to accept the rectorship of St. Martin Pomeroy in Ironmonger Lane, London, replacing the ejected Royalist minister, Edward Sparke. Perhaps Arrowsmith felt no need to rationalize his decision: the Cambridge position was academic, the Westminster Assembly post was temporary, and only the London ministry was explicitly pastoral. And yet there were financial motives too, even if one-fifth of the income from the living continued to be paid to Sparke's wife after Arrowsmith took up the charge. (Only in 1650 did Sparke surrender all claims to the parish, although he briefly regained the church a decade later and temporarily added it to his portfolio of benefices at the Restoration.)[58] Understandably, many assembly members had accepted pastoral positions for pecuniary reasons. The Long Parliament lacked follow-through on its promised payments to members for their daily service at the assembly,[59] and Arrowsmith had a growing family to care for: at the time of accepting the call to the London congregation, Arrowsmith's "most deare and helpful wife Mary" was caring for a nine-year-old stepson and one-year-old John and was carrying her second child.[60] Little Mary was baptized in St. Martin Pomeroy on May 13, 1645. (Her birth also conveniently sets an outside date for the arrival for the new pastor of the parish, for he would have begun his ministry there prior to that point.)[61]

Arrowsmith was not the only master and divine who preferred to be absent from his college to be present at the assembly.[62] Perhaps infrequent residence in Cambridge entailed less payment from the college. Perhaps the

---

Palmer, Bridge, Caryl, Burges, Vines, Cheynell; or, in the most complicated record of all, Taylor, Calamy, Seaman Young, Greenhill, and Cheynell. See *MPWA*, 2:260–61, 490–91; 3:4–5. Attendance can also be gleaned from speeches and committee appointments, as well as assignments to preach or pray for Parliament/committee for both kingdoms. See *MPWA*, 3:613, 700; 4:78–79, 344–45.

58. Sparke had edited the work of Josias Shute (invited to be an assembly member, although deceased) for a posthumous edition. Arnold Hunt, "Josias Shute," *ODNB*.

59. *MPWA*, 1:51–52.

60. NA PROB 11/289/161, fols. 179r–180r. Mary is referred to as his "deare wife" or "deare Mary" three times in the will.

61. See England Births and Christenings, 1538–1975, accessed June 7, 2021, https://www.familysearch.org/ark:/61903/1:1:JMQL-1M1. The regular timing of Mary's pregnancies makes it possible that another child was born to them and died in the period, as a Margery Arrowsmith was buried at Westminster on June 18, 1646. England Deaths & Burials 1538–1991, accessed June 7, 2021, https://www.findmypast.com/transcript?id=R_268607921. This was, perhaps, during a time when Arrowsmith had left St. Martin but had not yet moved his household to Cambridge. Nonetheless, there is also evidence that another Arrowsmith family may have lived in the area at that time.

62. For Palmer's absences from college, see Twigg, *University of Cambridge*, p. 113.

main perquisite of St. Martin Pomeroy was a residence within reach of the assembly, for Ironmonger Lane offered a home little more than a couple miles walk along the river from Westminster Abbey.

Theanthropos

It may have been as pastor of St. Martin Pomeroy that Arrowsmith began his first surviving systematic theological work. What he intended appears to have been a doctrinal exposition of the whole of the fourth gospel, one of the New Testament's most doctrinally dense books. Arrowsmith was unable to complete the series, perhaps because of increasing duties at Cambridge and the assembly, and the lectures or sermons he gave on the gospel were eventually published posthumously in 1660 as his final book, *Theanthropos; or, God-Man: Being an Exposition upon the First Eighteen Verses of the First Chapter of the Gospel According to John.*[63] It was delivered to the publishers by "T. A."—Thomas Arrowsmith, of course, for according to the stipulations of Arrowsmith's will, his eldest son was to have charge of all manuscripts except those "prepared for the presse," which *Theanthropos* decidedly was not.[64]

The deeply grieving son, still twenty-three years of age, initially prioritized publication speed over scholarly process, for in early August 1659, he offered no less than three works by his late father to London printers and publishers Humphrey Moseley and William Wilson: a collection of sermons on a call to vigilance in 1 Thessalonians 5:6; a collection of sermons on the account of the transfiguration in Luke 9; and the sermons that have survived on John 1.[65] Although in editing the sermons on the gospel of John, Thomas supplied no scholarly citations to support his father's many quotations and did little to help the exposition in its transition from lecture to book, he may still have underestimated the work involved in readying a book for the press. Seven months later, the same printers reregistered Arrowsmith's John sermons under the title *Theanthropos.* The other volumes were never printed and are likely lost; when they were first delivered we may never know.[66]

---

63. John Arrowsmith, *Theanthropos; or God-Man* [...] (London, 1660). Although the work is dated 1660, George Thomason replaced "1660" with "1659" on his copy and added "Jan. 31," thus supplying a precise date of what we would today call January 31, 1660 (in midcentury England, the year changed on March 25, and Thomason was, in his notation, correcting the printer for using the European dating of the year, a practice slowly creeping into English works).

64. NA PROB 11/289/161 fol. 179r–v.

65. *Stationers' Registers*, 2:233 (Aug. 4, 1659).

66. *Stationers' Registers*, 2:252 (Mar. 6, 1659/60). Given the number of weeks it would take to deliver the gospel of John sermons, it is possible that some of the other sermons dated to

But why should we situate this surviving lecture or sermon series to the period of Arrowsmith's ministry at St. Martin Pomeroy? After all, the epistle to the reader speaks of Arrowsmith wasting himself to the "utmost end of his last breath, to explicate the darkest places of the Sacred Scripture," implying that these sermons are examples of late-in-life preaching and allowing readers to conclude that it was another of Arrowsmith's sick-bed projects, even a deathbed project.[67] The first suggestion for placing this book during Arrowsmith's London ministry comes from the title page, for it indicates that it was printed in London and not, like his other theological publications, in Cambridge, intimating the possibility of a provenance other than the university for the original delivery of the material. Second—and significantly—the text makes occasional reference to "this city" (the marginal note identifying London) and "this City of London," placing the sermon or lecture series in London.[68] Third—and most importantly—if, as indicated, the addresses were delivered in London, St. Martin's offers the only plausible venue for the sustained project envisaged by the preacher, for Arrowsmith clearly had a long-term plan in mind when he asked his audience to pray for him "before I begin (and all the while I shall continue) to expound this Glorious Gospell."[69]

Placing the gospel of John lectures in 1640s London creates its own problems. On the one hand, the early date means that the reference in Thomas's preface to his father's arduous end-of-life labors was a general encomium and not a reference to this particular book. On the other hand—and more significantly—the London location leaves us wondering if Arrowsmith's intentions were almost too ambitious for a regular congregation. The contents of the book, though presented by the editor or printer with the marginalia typically accompanying a printed sermon, are arguably better suited for learned lectures than Sabbath sermons. For example, it is assumed throughout the study that the hearer—and later, the reader—would be familiar with (or at least impressed by) often untranslated Latin and Greek terms and phrases; there are more than a hundred places where Greek is used in the book, and surely, since the printed work is alleged to consist of largely unedited lecture material, much of this would have been uttered from the pulpit.

And yet, if these sermons date to his assembly days, as they surely do, they go a long way toward explaining why Arrowsmith so vigorously

---

Arrowsmith's earlier pastorate at St. Nicholas in King's Lynn.

67. Arrowsmith, *Theanthropos*, A2r.

68. See Arrowsmith, *Theanthropos*, pp. 122, 197, 211.

69. Arrowsmith, *Theanthropos*, p. 1.

defended in the assembly not merely a learned ministry but learned sermons.[70] The sermons contain not only foreign-language material but references to Augustine, Athanasius, Junius, Jesuits, and many others whom Arrowsmith found helpful as he engaged in a study of some of the Bible's most rewarding but also "most mysterious and obscure texts."[71] It is obvious from the start that the series was to address heavy doctrinal topics related to Christology and the atonement. The title page advertises that the book "most accurately and divinely" handles "the Divinity and Humanity of Jesus Christ; proving him to be God and man, coequall and coeternall with the Father." It does this and more, for in it, Arrowsmith also addresses the relations between triune persons, Adam and Christ, the person and natures of Christ, varieties of union with Christ, and the work of Christ conceived in terms of shepherd, soldier, and sojourner. He addresses the subjects of free will, and the Holy Spirit as the Spirit of Christ. He disputes about baptismal regeneration and the fallout between "Lutherans and Calvinists… about consubstantiation."[72] Additionally, while the title page might oversell the degree to which the book refutes "severall heresies both ancient and modern," Arrowsmith really did find the time to inveigh against Arians, Socinians, Nestorians, Eutychians, Arminians, papists, and advocates of ceremonies. Arrowsmith required much from his listeners. Most modern preachers would say *too* much.

Despite the complexity of the content, there are indications that the lectures were given to a regular audience, including the occasional artlessness of movement from one topic to another. An early sentence reads, "Ye have here the Subject, and the Predicate, which are laid down in three Propositions." This is not the kind of line that one can afford to deliver to anyone other than a committed audience, and thus the dull prose (almost unheard of in Arrowsmith's polished publications) hints that the preacher enjoyed an ongoing relationship with his auditors.[73]

The lectures were given in London to a regular audience. But were they given at St. Martin's? Could it be that they were delivered before another audience, such as the fraternity of ministers at Sion College? After all, while for obvious reasons the final production lacks the scholarly marginalia that Arrowsmith was able to give to his other publications—what his editor calls the "politeness and authority" that Arrowsmith himself added to works sent

---

70. Chad Van Dixhoorn, *God's Ambassadors: The Westminster Assembly and the Reformation of the Pulpit, 1643–1653* (Grand Rapids: Reformation Heritage Books, 2017), p. 112.

71. Arrowsmith, *Theanthropos*, sig. A3r.

72. Arrowsmith, *Theanthropos*, p. 212.

73. Arrowsmith, *Theanthropos*, p. 7.

to the press—Twigg is surely right in classing it as a serious work of theology.[74] If the lectures were delivered at Sion College, this would explain the high demands put on the listeners. Nonetheless, this cannot be the audience. He speaks to people as those who sometimes have ministers, "want ministers," and hear ministers—not the sort of relationships and activities that one assumes at a gathering of ministers.[75] Again, when Arrowsmith professes to deal with matters relating to pastoral ministry more briefly, and to unusually intricate theological matters more cursorily, he does so because of "this auditory."[76] And when directly addressing ministers, he qualifies heavily: "If any such be here, let me speak to them for encouragement."[77] No, this is a regular London congregation, of which he is the pastor.[78]

Given that these sermons date to his St. Martin's ministry and thus to Arrowsmith's time at the Westminster Assembly, they stand as an exhibit of an astonishingly focused ministry of the Word. No mention is made in *Theanthropos* of civil war, of Parliament, or of the assembly itself. As if nothing else could matter more, the entire series offers a single-minded exegetical and doctrinal exposition, along with an explication of the wonderful benefits accruing to Christians who own these truths for themselves.

It seems then that Arrowsmith's own appointment to the vacated position at St. Martin's and the opportunity to embark on a study of a challenging biblical book must have made sufficient sense to him and to others living and worshipping in the chaotic context of wartime London. There were material incentives to take the call to St. Martin's, including financial insulation at a time when the kingdom was on fire. And yet it seems only fair to acknowledge that the addition of a pastoral charge was also undertaken as a service to the leaderless congregation and as an opportunity for him to deploy his considerable gifts as a preacher and theologian on a weekly basis—not merely in the assembly of divines or in occasional sermons before Parliament or in other London churches.

There were opportunities, of course, for occasional sermons. The second such, *England's Eben-Ezer*, was preached on March 12, 1645, before a prestigious gathering at Christ Church on a day of thanksgiving for the success of Parliament's armies in the west and southwest of England. The auditors included both houses of Parliament, the leadership of the city

<hr />

74. Arrowsmith, *Theanthropos*, sig. A3v; Twigg, "John Arrowsmith."
75. Arrowsmith, *Theanthropos*, pp. 19, 100, 197.
76. Arrowsmith, *Theanthropos*, pp. 37, 193.
77. Arrowsmith, *Theanthropos*, p. 95.
78. Arrowsmith, *Theanthropos*, p. 109.

of London, and Arrowsmith's fellow assembly members. It was printed soon after.[79]

Arrowsmith was in top form for the occasion, managing to sound disarming even in his references to armed conflict. Again, there are solemn notes: the love of Christ seen in the Song of Songs is juxtaposed with the judgment of Christ in the second Psalm, and members of Parliament are warned off from becoming a "stone of offence" (1 Peter 2:8) to the cause of reform. From the perspective of assembly members, the warning must have seemed timely given the brewing conflict between the assembly and the House of Commons over the subject of church discipline that had erupted the week before—and all the more significant, at least for those in the know, as a story Arrowsmith tells is taken from Gerhard, a late-medieval "conciliarist," who had become a favorite ecclesiologist for Presbyterians.[80] But appropriately, the main message of the sermon is one of gratitude, and even the dedicatory epistle to the two houses packs in a positive-sounding progress report: real movement in reformation, growth in the numbers of people taking the Solemn League and Covenant, and improved observance of the Sabbath, due, in part, to vigorous parliamentary efforts.

The text selected by Arrowsmith, 1 Samuel 7:12, captures a triumphant moment in the history of the nation of Israel. It was an ideal choice given Parliament's own moment in its conflict with the king. Unlike the time of uncertainty early in the winter of 1643, when *The Covenant-Avenging Sword* was preached, Parliament's forces were now making clear progress. It was time to acknowledge the Lord's help, much like the Old Testament prophet Samuel did, who "took a stone, and set it between Mizpeh and Shen, and called the name of it Ebenezer, saying, hitherto has the Lord helped us."

As this post-Reformation prophet preached it, Old Testament history offered two telling lessons in one text. First, great old covenant deliverance came in multiple forms: some immediate and miraculous and others mediated through human agency. In either case, it was to be observed, no advance for God's people is possible without help from the Lord. But second, and more to the point of the occasion, help received from God ought to be commemorated by every creature, including created human beings, not least Christians, and especially eminent "professors" of the Christian faith, such as Arrowsmith's gathered audience. This is the point the preacher

---

79. John Arrowsmith, *England's Eben-Ezer or Stone of Help* (London, 1645). It was registered with the stationers by Samuel Man, Arrowsmith's preferred London printer, on March 29, 1645. See *Stationers' Registers*, 1:159.

80. Arrowsmith, *England's Eben-Ezer*, sig. A3v. For the timing of the conflict, see *MPWA*, 1:31.

developed most fully, insisting that thanks be given with the whole heart, with "parts" (or abilities), lips, lives, and estates, and unanimously, cheerfully, and with faith.

The sermon offers another view of Arrowsmith's preferred authors, including classical sources (he evidences a special appreciation for Seneca), patristic authorities (Basil, Gregory Nazianzen, and the great preacher Chrysostom), medieval writers (Hugo of St. Victor and Bernard) and Protestant divines (the ever-quotable Luther, as well as Beza, Pareus, and Willet). Lessons are learned not simply from Christian history but from Muslim and Jewish traditions.

In comparison with his first offering, the tone of this second printed sermon, while thankful, remains more cautious about the parliamentary cause than is *The Covenant-Avenging Sword*. Here we are told that the "Second Reformation" is a blessing, not least because of its lack of "outward pomp." And Parliament's (ultimately ineffective) efforts to negotiate further reforms with the king are to be lauded. But at the same time, Arrowsmith also acknowledges the "many thousands" opposed to the cause and the limits of what the assembly itself can do "towards the healing [of] the saddest of all divisions."[81]

This was a sermon for a sober thanksgiving service in a civil war with no end yet in sight. If it had been preached in April instead of March 1645, there would have been more reason for hope, for creative legislative solutions, at first resisted by the lords, ended or sidestepped the quarreling of leading parliamentary generals. And if it had been preached in the summer of 1645, there would have been cause for still greater rejoicing, for in June and July, Charles's armies were devastated in two major engagements with Parliament's forces.

Assembly Member

At the assembly of divines, where there were serious theological divisions, Arrowsmith became a contributor of outsized importance. Here again his preaching was prominent. While Parliament preferred to hear the widely acclaimed Stephen Marshall (eighteen times to Arrowsmith's three), the assembly preferred to hear Herbert Palmer, Arrowsmith, and perhaps Edward Reynolds (see table 1).[82] On the first of two occasions that Arrow-

---

81. Arrowsmith, *Covenant-Avenging Sword*, p. 12.

82. Reynolds is thanked by the assembly in session 566 for preaching (*MPWA*, 3:732), and although the Commons did not hear him preach on December 31, 1645, they awarded him one hundred pounds (*Journals of the House of Commons* [London, 1802], 4:392), suggesting that the

smith preached at the request of his colleagues (with two-hour prayers sandwiched on either side of each sermon), Arrowsmith and Palmer each preached for one hour. It was an event that Robert Baillie, a Scotsman not often inclined to praise things English, described as the "sweetest [day] that I have seen in England."[83]

Table 1. Sermons before the Assembly

Date & sess.	Ps.	Prayer	Sermon	Ps.	Prayer	Ps.	Sermon	Ps.	Prayer	Ps.	Prayer	Collect.
Oct. 16, 1643, sess. 75	Y	Burges	Whitaker	Y	Goodwin	N	Palmer	Y	Stanton	Y	Twisse	Maimed soldiers
May 17, 1644, sess. 221	Y	Marshall	Arrow-smith	Y	Vines	Y	Palmer	N	Seaman	N	—	Poor of Westmstr.
Oct. 8, 1645, sess. 514	N	Burges	Reynolds	N	Whitaker	N	Palmer	N	Ash	N	—	Widows & sick
Dec. 31, 1645	N	—	Reynolds	N	—	N	—	N	—	N	—	—
May 6, 1646, sess. 635	Y	Palmer	Cawdrey	N	Whitaker	N	Arrow-smith	N	Case	Y	—	TBD by preachers

Arrowsmith's first sermon before the assembly, arguing that the book of Revelation was being fulfilled in their own day, was on the subject of England's second reformation and the urgent need to rebuild the temple of the Lord.[84] Once again, the preacher quoted a few of his favorite authors: Cyprian, perhaps Theodoret, and regulars such as Augustine and Bernard.[85]

Such was the reception of the sermon that he was asked to preach on a second occasion, once again before the assembly only.[86] In the second assembly sermon, he argued for the uniqueness of the government of the church, a government resting on Christ's shoulders, and he pleaded for peace in the assembly. Stories rather than scholarly citations offered color in the sermon, and as he often would, Arrowsmith made constructive use of the writing of his opponents—in this case, that of a Jesuit.[87]

---

assembly held their own fast on that date, with Reynolds as preacher, and that the Commons rewarded him for his work.

83. *The Letters and Journals of Robert Baillie*, ed. D. Laing (Edinburgh: Robert Ogle, 1841), 2:184. On the request for Arrowsmith to preach, see *MPWA*, 3:80; *John Lightfoot's Journals*, p. 404 (sess. 218), p. 408 (sess. 221). The assembly also liked to be led in prayer by the persons mentioned here and especially by Jeremiah Whitaker, who was also called to pray (along with Marshall and Caryl) in session 308. See *John Lightfoot's Journals*, p. 474.

84. *MPWA*, 3:93.

85. *MPWA*, 3:89–93.

86. *MPWA*, 4:98–99, May 1, 1646 (sess. 632).

87. For the sermon, see *MPWA*, 4:106, 113–17.

If Arrowsmith was a preferred preacher among his peers, he was also one of the best Latinists and most respected scholars of the assembly. When Stephen Marshall penned a letter on behalf of the gathering intended for Reformed churches internationally, Arrowsmith was asked to translate it, along with a few extra lines inserted by the senior Scottish commissioner, Alexander Henderson.[88] Later, Arrowsmith again was asked to translate the Solemn League and Covenant into Latin on behalf of Parliament and the assembly.[89] On yet another occasion, he was asked to use his literary skills to join a fellow divine in writing a letter in English to the Church of Scotland.[90]

The assembly's most prolific letter writer and diarist, Robert Baillie, referred to Arrowsmith as a "learned divyne, on whom the Assemblie putt the wryting against the Antinomians"[91] and other errors.[92] This was a theologically demanding task, but there were other tasks too. The assembly called Arrowsmith to employ his skills as an apologist for Parliament as one of a team of members tasked to persuade Londoners to take the Solemn League and Covenant.[93] His particular assignment proved easier than planned: dozens had already signed the document before Arrowsmith even arrived at the appointed place and time, due to the work of a cooperative church warden.[94] The assembly also required Arrowsmith to use his skills as a pastor when he was asked by the body to visit the ailing prolocutor William Twisse.[95] Twisse was also on everyone's unofficial roster of great scholars, and Arrowsmith, who admired and often quoted Twisse, was a good choice by the assembly.

Arrowsmith was eventually moved off the antinomian committee and onto the "Grand Committee," an executive steering committee of sorts containing key assembly members, Scots, and members from each house of Parliament.[96] An ardent Presbyterian and clear thinker, he was asked to help "put into method the votes of the Assembly concerning government" until the assembly changed its mind about the appointment, perhaps recognizing

---

88. Baillie, *Letters and Journals*, 2:123; *John Lightfoot's Journals*, p. 226 (sess. 128).

89. *John Lightfoot's Journals*, p. 230 (sess. 130).

90. *MPWA*, 3:634.

91. Baillie, *Letters and Journals*, 2:124; see *John Lightfoot's Journals*, p. 149 (sess. 88).

92. *MPWA*, 5:224n.

93. *John Lightfoot's Journals*, p. 128 (sess. 74). For the Solemn League and Covenant, see *The Covenant: with a Narrative of the Proceedings and Solemn Manner of Taking It* (London, 1643).

94. *John Lightfoot's Journals*, p. 135 (sess. 79); *MPWA*, 2:197. Arrowsmith visited St. Benet, Paul's Wharf, London.

95. *MPWA*, 4:122–23.

96. *John Lightfoot's Journals*, p. 229 (sess. 129). For the Grand Committee, see *MPWA*, 1:24.

that he had enough on his plate.[97] The gathering also considered putting him on a committee regarding the Sabbath but again changed its mind,[98] probably in view of his continuing work on the reconstituted committee for the Confession of Faith.[99] Arrowsmith appears to have led committees working on the first nineteen heavily doctrinal chapters of the confession,[100] along with committees addressing the sacraments[101] and Christian liberty.[102] There may also have been some sympathy for Arrowsmith given his work for the university, but his ministry at St. Martin's would generate no pity. The assembly's leaders were not particularly sympathetic to the burdens of local church ministry; assembly-leader Cornelius Burges even spoke against members taking on any full-time ministry at a local church as it was an unhappy distraction from assembly work.[103]

A fuller study is needed to capture the full extent of Arrowsmith's ministry at the assembly, and any summary is bound to be untidy. It can be stated with confidence that there was no major endeavor in which he did not play a part, and while he was not a frequent speaker, he did participate in every major debate. For example, when revising the Thirty-nine Articles, Arrowsmith argued for the imputation of the active obedience of Christ[104] and offered his own formulations on faith and works.[105] While opposing antinomianism, he nonetheless spoke in favor of a "faire ministeriall way" of dealing with individual antinomians while the assembly was engaged in the process of examining their writings, and he was reluctant to determine whether antinomian writings constituted actual heresy, either according to statute or according to ecclesiastical precedent.[106] Sometimes he did not participate in a debate until it came time to discuss the best biblical support for a doctrine already voted by the gathering.[107] And even when he did support a majority position, Arrowsmith did not always concur with the majority's exegetical reasoning on behalf of the proposition voted.[108] At still

---

97. *MPWA*, 3:427.

98. *MPWA*, 3:458.

99. *MPWA*, 3:239.

100. *MPWA*, 4:300–301.

101. *MPWA*, 3:722, Dec. 15, 1645.

102. *MPWA*, 4:296–97.

103. *MPWA*, 1:50n77.

104. *MPWA*, 2:86.

105. E.g., *John Lightfoot's Journals*, p. 109 (sess. 66); *MPWA*, 2:158, 159.

106. *MPWA*, 2:148.

107. E.g., *John Lightfoot's Journals*, p. 109 (sess. 66); *MPWA*, 2:164.

108. For example, with those who denied that excommunication was a continuing ordinance for the church, Arrowsmith did not take the apostle Paul's reference to "handing over to Satan" as normative beyond the apostolic age or the particular situation in Corinth. *John*

other times, his contributions were focused on procedure, such as when he opposed the creation of a directory for preaching.[109]

On occasion, matters of pastoral practice or exegesis captured his attention, such as when he opposed a recommendation from the assembly that preachers limit the number of authors that they cite in sermons (an idea hardly in keeping with his own practice!)[110] or when he argued that the word *baptizo* comes "nearer sprinkling" than dipping.[111] Other points that he took up were academic (Was Barnabas an apostle in the usual sense?);[112] some were historical (How does Justin Martyr understand *proestos*?);[113] some theoretical (Is the distinction between pastor and doctor that of two kinds of preaching elders or two kinds of work belonging to one office?);[114] some practical (Should ministers be resident at their place of calling?).[115] While at the assembly and afterward, Arrowsmith was invested in any number of typically Presbyterian causes, such as drafting a petition for Presbyterian ordination with Edward Reynolds and Thomas Hill,[116] supporting an administration of the Lord's Supper in which church officers would vet those attending the sacrament,[117] or joining Thomas Thorowgood, another Norfolk minister and assembly member, in visiting Newgate prison in an attempt to persuade a Norfolk Royalist to subscribe to the Solemn League and Covenant.[118]

Arrowsmith may also have made other investments while at the assembly, although he could have conducted business at other points in life. In enumerating his property purchases in his last will and testament, he always specified from whom he bought the properties he acquired. When it came to his properties "neere Boston in Linconshire," Arrowsmith simply records that he purchased them from "Mr Simpson," assuming everyone would know which Simpson it was. The only obvious candidate of a close associate with this surname was Sydrach Simpson, a Boston-area native who himself

---

Lightfoot's Journals, p. 146 (sess. 86); *MPWA*, 2:257, citing Scultetus. Nonetheless, he held to the importance of excommunication (*MPWA*, 2:258).

109. *MPWA*, 3:130.
110. *MPWA*, 3:135.
111. *MPWA*, 3:213.
112. *MPWA*, 2:225.
113. *MPWA*, 2:294.
114. *John Lightfoot's Journals*, p. 181; *MPWA*, 2:371 (sess. 103).
115. *John Lightfoot's Journals*, p. 158; *MPWA*, 2:287 (sess. 91).
116. *MPWA*, 3:753.
117. *MPWA*, 4:208–9.
118. Ketton-Cremer, *Norfolk in the Civil War*, p. 280; see also Clive Wilkins-Jones, "'My Rude and Imperfect Manuscript': Sir Hamon L'Estrange's 'Observations' on Thomas Browne's Pseudodoxia Epidemica," in *Studies in Philology* 114, no. 4 (Fall 2017): p. 775.

"possessed considerable assets at the time of his death" and was contemporary with Arrowsmith as a student, assembly member, and finally as a fellow Cambridge college master.[119]

College Master

Arrowsmith ended his work at the assembly in May 1646, more than two and a half years before the great exodus of members from the assembly in 1649 as an expression of Presbyterian opposition to the execution of the king. Arrowsmith would be consulted by the remaining remnant of assembly members as late as December 1649 about an assembly-related matter,[120] but active participation in the assembly was over. Thus, in the late spring or early summer of 1646, the family was settled in Cambridge. They became members of All Saints in Cambridge, where their son Joseph was added to the family in December 1647.[121]

Arrowsmith's absence from the assembly did not halt his advocacy for its work. It is unclear how, if at all, his time was divided between St. John's College Cambridge and his London congregation, but as a college master, he still followed developments in the assembly. An instance of his continued attentiveness to assembly concerns is presented weeks after Joseph's birth. Arrowsmith was present in London to preach to the House of Commons on a fast day in late January 1647, and he chose the occasion to side with the assembly against the Commons.[122] Indeed, it is a notable measure of his persuasive charms that he was able to win the house's imprimatur for a printed version of the sermon, resulting in his third and final brief publication of the decade—notable because those present on the occasion were still recovering from the now-public struggle between the assembly and house on the subject of church discipline, and divines were still frustrated with the house's delay in approving the assembly's Confession of Faith, a work on which Arrowsmith himself had labored for many months.

A Great Wonder in Heaven

The sermon title, "A Great Wonder in Heaven," was drawn directly from Revelation 12:1–2: "And there appeared a great wonder in heaven, a woman

---

119. Tai Liu, "Sydrach Simpson," *ODNB*.

120. *MPWA*, 4:827, Dec. 6, 1649.

121. Bap. Dec. 27, 1647: England Births and Christenings, 1538–1975, accessed June 7, 2021, https://www.familysearch.org/ark:/61903/1:1:J7GG-4QT.

122. The sermon was preached January 27 and registered by Samuel Man on February 10, 1647. See *Transcript of the Registers*, p. 262.

clothed with the Sun, and the Moon under her feet, and upon her head a Crown of twelve stars."[123] The opening words of the Latin dedication introduce Arrowsmith's quiet but unmistakable advocacy of the controverted points between the assembly and the Commons. For Arrowsmith and most other Presbyterians, civil magistrates are not only "the mainstays of the Republic, followers and at the same time defenders of a vigorous piety," but also, in the remarkable mixed metaphor of Isaiah 49:23, "nursing fathers" of the church or *Ecclesiae nutritiis*.[124]

The phrase "nursing fathers" may have become Presbyterian code for a doctrine of an established church supported by civil magistrates, an arrangement that Arrowsmith and the great majority of assembly members favored, in keeping with the tradition of Calvin's Geneva. The words appear verbatim in chapter 23, paragraph 3 of the assembly's Confession of Faith—that confession not yet approved by the Commons. One reason for the delay in approval was that the work still lacked the scriptural proof texts required by Parliament. And yet it would also be delayed because a slight but vocal majority of the House of Commons favored not only the establishment of the church but an *Erastian* church directed (and not merely supported) in its government by the state, in keeping with the tradition of Zwingli's Zurich.

As the dedication to *Great Wonder* explains, the sermon shows "the bride of Christ, gleaming with the radiant beams of her husband" while "trampling down both the temptations and threats of the world," a bride "purchased by evangelical truth, yet still toiling, risking her life."[125] Arrowsmith's central point was that Revelation 12 is about the church militant, not the church triumphant. The text clarifies the relationship between Christ and his church and explains why the struggling church on earth still needs the sun—and, thus, the Son. The sermon runs a full marathon with this metaphor, with numbered lists of extended analogies structuring the sermon: there are six reasons why the church needs the Son as the earth needs the sun; four ways in which Christ imparts light as the sun does; three ways in which he imparts heat; two ways in which he imparts influence. The woman in the passage is the church, sheltered by Christ in three ways, and so on.

In *Great Wonder*, more than in his previous sermons and much like his later writings, the reader sees Arrowsmith not only as a Protestant but as

---

123. John Arrowsmith, *A Great Wonder in Heaven* (London, 1647).

124. Arrowsmith, *Great Wonder in Heaven*, sig. A2r.

125. Arrowsmith, *Great Wonder in Heaven,* sig. A2r.

an Englishman. His anti-popish salvo strikes at more than the Vatican or Rome. He targets the entire peninsula—"let Italy boast of her rich Copes, stately Altars, curious Images,"[126] etc.—and then contrasts it with England's true glory, which is its retention and proclamation of "the truth of Christ." Indeed, he writes, "I hope better things of the Kingdom and such as accompany Reformation."[127]

The sermon also displays his loyalties to the Westminster assembly: "Doubtlesse the Confession of Faith, lately presented to the Honourable Houses by the Assembly of Divines (who have therein expressed the sense of many millions besides themselves) will abundantly manifest to the world, that his crown is not wholy fallen from Englands head: yet I fear there is cause enough to acknowledge, that it doth not stand so fast on as heretofore, by reason of the many Opinionists, whose main employment is to shake it."[128] For Arrowsmith, the confidence that the Confession of Faith both expressed the faith of "many millions" and had the potential to "abundantly manifest" England's orthodoxy suggested two self-evident lines of argument in favor of approving the document. The third argument for adoption was its potential to check the rising tide of error pushed by the "opinionists"—those error-ridden writers and preachers who would increasingly occupy Arrowsmith in his later publications.[129]

It was the duty of Parliament to see the importance of the confession: "Verily whosoever bears a loyall heart to Jesus Christ, cannot but grieve to see the jewels of that crown, which he hath provided for his Churches head, pawned and sold, and embezled as they are: to see not only Arminians, Libertines, and Socinians gratified in abundance of their principles; but even Mahumetans closed with by some, in what they hold concerning the authority of Scripture, and concerning the deity of Jesus Christ, and of God the Holy Ghost."[130] Only by setting "our selves for time to come, to buy the truth" can England "within a while…be a Crown of glory in the hand of the Lord, and a royall Diadem in the hand of thy God."[131]

Arrowsmith did not forget his place. He was a master of a college, and the sermon also plugs the importance of "both our Universities" as schools of the prophets.[132] Indeed, both learning and church reform rank higher in

---

126. Arrowsmith, *Great Wonder in Heaven*, p. 30.
127. Arrowsmith, *Great Wonder in Heaven*, p. 30.
128. Arrowsmith, *Great Wonder in Heaven*, pp. 30–31.
129. Arrowsmith, *Great Wonder in Heaven*, pp. 30–31.
130. Arrowsmith, *Great Wonder in Heaven*, p. 31.
131. Arrowsmith, *Great Wonder in Heaven*, pp. 30–31.
132. Arrowsmith, *Great Wonder in Heaven*, pp. 39–40.

importance for Arrowsmith than military successes, but most important of all is an ecclesiastical reformation advanced by both magistracy and ministry working in tandem. One hand should not be cut off for the sake of the other, and "such would our condition be, if either ministers should suffer the magistracy to be cryed down; or magistrates permit the ministry to be debased."[133]

The importance of learning is on display in this sermon much more than the previous two. In addition to his customary stories and his citations of post-Reformation biblical scholars, he mentions "platonists" (perhaps because of new intellectual developments in the university in the form of the Cambridge Platonists),[134] he quotes Horace and Vergil, and he relies on church fathers, the latter including Tertullian, Basil, Augustine, and Jerome (twice). Arrowsmith also mentions the recently produced English annotations on the whole Bible, a project in which fellow assembly members participated. Other English and Scottish writers also feature more largely than in previous sermons: Joseph Mede, Thomas Brightman, and David Dickson included.

Arrowsmith could only rarely have ventured south to London once settled in Cambridge, for there was much to manage as a college master. True, student numbers were down. Young men were going off to war, fathers were reluctant to send sons far away, and prospective students risked much simply finding a safe way across the country to get to college. But there was still much to do. Cambridge was garrisoned by parliamentary troops. At St. John's they broke windows, stole money, and used the first court as a prison until the autumn of 1644. Having a master supportive of Parliament was no doubt one part of a larger plan to restore order in the college and rid it of a military presence. Under Arrowsmith's watch, the army did move out, although it was still camping just outside the city in 1647, unpaid and unhappy.[135]

There was also much college work that was more mundane. Arrowsmith's tenure inevitably included dealing with minor emergencies. Cambridge is often windy, but significant damage was done to college buildings in the 1640s by "great winds." There were perennial quarrels among fellows—in this case, tensions between the old guard that merely conformed to Parliament and Presbyterianism and the new fellows who were, by and large, enthusiastic supporters of the new order. There was trouble in dealing with

---

133. Arrowsmith, *Great Wonder in Heaven*, p. 43.

134. Arrowsmith, *Great Wonder in Heaven*, p. 8.

135. Mark Nicholls, "The Seventeenth Century," in *St John's College Cambridge: A History*, ed. Peter Linhan (Woodbridge: Boydell, 2011), pp. 137, 139, 141.

the ex-master's estate, which argued that the portraits of Charles I in the master's lodge belonged to their father and, thus, to their family. The college, under Arrowsmith's leadership, curiously insisted that the paintings stay and declared them college property.[136] And significantly, there was the problem of a lack of funds, for benefactions to the college dried up during the war, rental income from its many properties declined precipitously, and, all the while, traditional college taxation exemptions were eroded until 1646. Through all this financial instability, wine expenditures for the fellows remained stable! But only by the end of the decade did the master have the resources for real improvements: new maps for the walls of the master's lodge, improvements of the college walks, and "a major new planting of sweetbriars and honeysuckle" to improve the college grounds.[137]

Armilla Catechetica

The beaverishly busy master also exercised leadership through a heavy preaching schedule. He produced a long series of doctrinal sermons in the chapel on Sunday evenings. Notes were taken of his sermons, students were spiritually awakened, and others later remembered the long-running event fondly.[138] Thirty major topics were treated in what appears to have been an average of a half-dozen sermons per topic. The whole of the exercise, if preached in full term only, would have taken about six years to complete. By the time Robert Legard, one of the assiduous note-takers, was a student (1650–1654), Arrowsmith had reached the topic of the sacraments, further confirming that this was a long-term theological project.[139]

The St. John's College sermon series covered the full theological encyclopedia. Arrowsmith's intention, partially realized, was to turn these lectures into an approximately five-volume system of theology.[140] In the end, he was only able to prepare one volume for the printers and did not

---

136. After 1650, it would be illegal to display images of Charles I in any public building. Bernard Capp, *England's Culture Wars: Puritan Reformation and Its Enemies in the Interregnum, 1649–1650* (Oxford: Oxford University Press, 2012), p. 15.

137. Nicholls, "Seventeenth Century," pp. 127, 145; see also pp. 141–45.

138. For an awakening, see the account of John Janeway in Samuel Clarke, *The Lives of Sundry Eminent Persons* (London, 1683), p. 62; for joy in receiving the sermons, see the story of John Machin in Clarke, *Lives of Sundry Eminent persons*, p. 82.

139. Washington, DC, Folger Shakespeare Library V.a.432, Robert Legard's commonplace book. Legard was admitted Dec. 3, 1650 (see Venn). London, British Library Sloane MS 598 fols. 36, 49, 78b, 130b, notes by Foote. Cambridge, St. Johns College Library, MS 0.82 fols. [4r]–[22v], a commonplace book, contain three additional aphorisms in what appears to be Arrowsmith's own hand.

140. John Arrowsmith, *Armilla Catechetica. A Chain of Principles* [...] (Cambridge, 1659), sig. *3r–v.

live to hold it in his hands. The university's press undertook its printing, and it appeared in 1659 as *Armilla Catechetica. A Chain of Principles; Or, An Orderly Concatenation of Theological Aphorisms and Exercitations; Wherein, the Chief Heads of Christian Religion Are Asserced and Improved*. The almost five-hundred-page work contained a full scholarly apparatus and advertised Arrowsmith's comprehensive involvement in the project. No other volumes in the series appeared, which seems to have been Arrowsmith's wish when he realized he would not see the project through the press.[141] His will had put in Mary's charge any work ready for printing and even gave her very clear directions that such a work would be identified with his own initialed permission "marked by myselfe under myne owne hand in some part of the last page."[142] She in turn put the responsibility for its printing in the hands of Thomas Horton (master of Queens' College) and William Dillingham (master of Emmanuel College).[143]

Armilla Catechetica appeared in print after *Tactica Sacra*, and it even cites the earlier book. But it is important to locate it here, in the context of Arrowsmith's mid-1640s Cambridge ministry, lest its role be forgotten in terms of Arrowsmith's development as a theologian. In spite of their publication date, the St. John's College lectures were preparatory to his unexpected *magnum opus* and, in some ways, anticipate a central theme of *Tactica Sacra*.

Arrowsmith argues in *Armilla Catechetica*, from both the book of Psalms and the prophet Isaiah, that man's ultimate blessedness is found in Christ only. He develops this theme in his second aphorism, insisting that it is impossible for people to arrive at this blessedness apart from the Scriptures. Having identified this chief end for humanity, Arrowsmith turns, in aphorisms three and four, to the God revealed in nature and in the Scriptures. Here he considers God's essence, subsistence, and attributes. Still reflecting on the character of God, the fifth aphorism begins to unfold a doctrine of divine decrees, creation, and providence. The sixth and final printed aphorism addresses the problem of sin.

Those familiar with the Westminster Assembly's works will see, even in this sketch, that Arrowsmith reflects the priorities of the assembly's catechisms (a focus on the chief end of man) and the pattern of doctrinal exposition found in the first seven chapters of the Confession of Faith (Scripture, God, decrees, creation, providence, the fall, and covenant). This

---

141. Arrowsmith, *Armilla Catechetica*, sig. *3v.

142. NA PROB 11/289/161, fol. 179v.

143. Horton and Dillingham, "To the Reader," in Arrowsmith, *Armilla Catechetica*, sig. **3r.

is unsurprising as Arrowsmith was developing this line of thinking at the same time that he was helping to draft the assembly's Confession of Faith. The difference between these texts is that *Armilla Catechetica* relocates both (1) the assembly's emphasis on God's covenantal relationship with man and (2) the blessedness entailed and in view in that covenant, and then shifts them from the seventh topic (as it is in the confession) to the first topic (as it is in the catechisms). Of greater relevance to this study is the fact that *Armilla Catechetica* establishes a pattern later visible in *Tactica Sacra* (the volume presently in the reader's hands), which likewise begins by placing a theological anthropology in eschatological perspective. Eschatological blessedness is arguably the main theme in *Armilla Catechetica*. It is noteworthy that his three unpublished aphorisms, writings which have received no scholarly attention thus far, also have as their main focus man's blessedness.[144]

In *Armilla Catechetica* we also see, better than in any previous scholarly work, Arrowsmith's literary and theological influences. The apparent predilection for Seneca as a favorite pagan and for Augustine as a favorite church father is pronounced.[145] His use of medieval authors is focused on the great schoolmen and preachers: Peter Lombard, Anselm of Canterbury, Bernard of Clairvaux, Hugo of St. Victor, Bonaventure, and Thomas Aquinas, although he also employs Gerhard and figures of the southern and northern renaissance, including Marsilio Ficino and Erasmus. Understandably, the vast majority of his citations come from more than eighty Reformation- and post-Reformation-era figures, including Roman Catholic writers, fellow assembly members, and himself.

Arrowsmith was soon more than the master of St. John's. In the academic year 1647–1648, he also served as vice-chancellor of the university, and he was suitably awarded the doctor of divinity degree in January of 1648, receiving the degree at the same time as Anthony Tuckney and Benjamin Whichcote, part of an intimate circle of friends that also included Thomas Hill.[146] The vice-chancellorship involved a range of duties from

---

144. Cambridge, St. Johns College Library, MS 0.82 fols. [4r]–[22v].

145. While critical of Artistotle, Arrowsmith makes liberal use of other pagan writers including Athenaeus, Horace, Lucretius, Martial, Ovid, Petronius, Plato, Pliny, Plutarch, Pomponius, and Posidonius. With reckless disregard for chronology, the church fathers employed by Arrowsmith include Ambrose, Basil, Chrysostom, Eusebius, Fulgentius, Gregory the Great, Gregory Nazianzus, Isidore, Jerome, Justin Martyr, Prosper of Aquitaine, Socrates, Theophylact, and Tertullian.

146. Baker, *History of the College*, p. 227 (see also pp. 224ff). On Arrowsmith's friendships, see Benjamin Whichcote, *Moral and Religious Aphorisms*, ed. Samuel Salter (London: for J. Payne, 1753), p. xix.

academic administration to managing endless disputes between the town and the university and included peacemaking gestures such as sitting with the mayor of Cambridge at the town's corporate feast.[147]

More complicated than town politics were national ones. In January of 1649, King Charles I was executed, to the general opposition of Presbyterians and, of course, Episcopalians and Royalists. Both the town and the university of Cambridge were divided between those in support of the emerging republic, without king or House of Lords, and those opposed. Throughout 1649 the Rump Parliament kept an increasingly close eye on Cambridge, and both Presbyterians and Royalists feared a purge of the university by the Congregationalist-dominated Rump Parliament similar to that which took place under the Long Parliament's Presbyterian majority in the years 1644–1646.

Finally, in December 1649, news arrived that college masters and fellows would be—as civil servants, military officers, and schoolmasters were—required to subscribe the Engagement, a new oath of loyalty to the Commonwealth. This was bad news for those opposed to regicide, but the Rump's bark was worse than its bite. Arrowsmith, with almost all of the masters and the more significant fellows of colleges, were able to get away with promises not to disturb the present government, with requests for more time to consider, with personal interpretations of the meaning of the Engagement, and with other tactics of delay and avoidance so familiar to those who were part of the long Puritan tradition. John Bond, master of Trinity Hall—who also continued to serve as an official member of the Westminster Assembly—was one of only two heads of colleges to take the Engagement without qualification or equivocation.[148] The new regime left Arrowsmith in a difficult place. As master of St. John's, he had sometimes advocated the removal of Royalists but not always. Even after the regicide and against vocal opposition, where men of exceptional talent could be found, he occasionally advocated the continuance or promotion of known or suspected Royalists in the college if they were well-qualified, godly tutors.[149]

Further, 1649 was also a tumultuous year for the Cambridge Arrowsmiths personally. In May, little Mary died only days after her fourth birthday.[150] She was probably the fourth child lost to John Arrowsmith. She was possibly the first child, and certainly the first toddler, lost to his wife Mary. This can only have been a crushing grief, even as the family

---

147. Twigg, *University of Cambridge*, p. 147.

148. Twigg, *University of Cambridge*, pp. 155–56.

149. Twigg, *University of Cambridge*, p. 152.

150. Buried May 19, 1649, https://www.findmypast.com/transcript?id=R_276424040.

continued to grow. Mary was pregnant at the time of her loss, and she gave birth to Hannah in December, with Elizabeth, named after John's first wife, arriving a year and a half later.[151]

In 1651 Arrowsmith was made the university's Regius Professor of Divinity—for a theologian, an even greater privilege than the lofty administrative post he had occupied three years previously as vice-chancellor.[152] His "probationary lecture," delivered on September 1, 1651, upon his entry to his new post, was eagerly described in the correspondence of a student. The lecture opened by explaining the unique worth of Genesis 3:15 and its importance for the Christian faith. The *protoevangelium*, as the promise in Genesis 3:15 was often called, was the Old Testament equivalent of one of Paul's "faithful sayings," and as Luther explained, it contained "the doctrine of the whole Bible." In Arrowsmith's exposition of the passage, Jesuits were refuted for identifying the Virgin Mary as the "Seed" of the woman. The student's friends apparently thought highly of Arrowsmith, and while the grammar of the letter is torturous at key points, the student himself, although unsympathetic to Puritanism, appears to have been profoundly impressed with the lecture.[153]

Two years later Arrowsmith moved next door to St. John's to take up the mastership of the larger and even more prestigious Trinity College. There his health, never strong, began a slow decline.[154] J. B. Mullinger, a historian of the University of Cambridge, has argued that Arrowsmith's St. John's years were characterized by "incessant strife" but that, beginning with his 1653 move to Trinity, by contrast, Arrowsmith did his best to avoid conflicts in the college, preferring to advance the cause of orthodoxy more militantly on other fronts.[155] More recent scholarship has offered no evi-

---

151. Hannah, bap. 3 Nov. 1649, England Births and Christenings, 1538–1975, accessed June 7, 2021, https://www.familysearch.org/ark:/61903/1:1:NNYK-GVS; Elizabeth, bap. July 7, 1651, England Births and Christenings, 1538–1975, accessed June 7, 2021, https://www.familysearch.org/ark:/61903/1:1:NTG4-PRM.

152. An account of his inaugural lecture is said to survive in Oxford, Bodleian Library, 55 fol. 43.

153. George Davenport to William Sancroft, Sept. 6, 1651, in *The Letters of George Davenport, 1651*, ed. Brenda M. Pask and Margaret Harvey (Woodbridge: Boydell, 2011), pp. 31–32.

154. For his generally poor health, see T[homas] A[rrowsmith], "To the reader," in *Theanthropos*, sig. A3r. Trinity had a large fellowship that had slid to "less than forty in 1646 but recovered to sixty by 1651." Robert Neild, *The Financial History of Trinity College, Cambridge* (Cambridge: Granta Editions, 2008), p. 67n12. Arrowsmith was also likely to have been better paid (Neild, *Financial History of Trinity College*, pp. 74–75).

155. J. B. Mullinger, *The University of Cambridge*, vol. 3, *From the Election of Buckingham to the Chancellorship in 1626 to the Decline of the Platonist Movement* (Cambridge: Cambridge University Press, 1911), p. 475.

dence of a major shift in Arrowsmith's attitude to college leadership. His St. John's years were not as difficult as surviving complaints may suggest.[156] And at Trinity he did not avoid conflict at the highest levels, as is noted below with respect to the vice-master of the college. But Mullinger is correct in observing that during Arrowsmith's Trinity years, he expanded his influence by serving as a parliamentary commissioner appointed to survey the health of parish churches and to eject scandalous ministers, as well as in the service he offered as Regius Professor.[157]

There were encouragements in the midst of growing health complications, and Arrowsmith seized them as moments for gratitude. In 1656 he saw his eldest son Thomas admitted as a fellow of Trinity,[158] having previously seen him admitted as student at St. John's while Arrowsmith was master of that college.[159] And perhaps it was in these years that he rejoiced in a significant improvement of the University Library, taking special delight in the thought that the library could at last with dignity begin to be compared to the Bodleian Library in Oxford.[160]

The Anti-Weigelian Lectures

I write "perhaps it was in these years" because the celebration of these advances is found in orations that are difficult to date. Arrowsmith appended three "Anti-Weigelian" orations to his 1657 *Tactica Sacra*, here translated into English for the first time by Dr. David Noe as *Plans for Holy War*. I say that the orations are appended to *Plans for Holy War*, but it would be more accurate to say, as Arrowsmith puts it in his dedication, that *Plans for Holy War* is appended to the orations.

The title page of the book indicates that the three lectures were delivered before the university, perhaps in Great St. Mary's or, more likely, given his reference to his professorial chair (*cathedra*), from the raised rostrum of the grand old university divinity hall (*magnis Comitiis*). There, with his back to the large window overlooking the space between the old university building and Great Saint Mary's, he delivered some of his final addresses to the university as a whole.[161]

---

156. Twigg, *University of Cambridge*, 123–27; Victor Morgan, *History of the University of Cambridge*, vol. 2, *1546–1750* (Cambridge: Cambridge University Press, 2004), 480.

157. Mullinger, *University of Cambridge*, 3:475–76.

158. Twigg, "John Arrowsmith"; Arrowsmith, *Plans for Holy War*, Third Speech against Weigelianism, p. 101.

159. Venn.

160. Arrowsmith, *Plans for Holy War*, First Speech against Weigelianism, p. 79.

161. Arrowsmith, *Plans for Holy War*, p. 71.

Having made some progress with the *where* of the lectures, it is imperative to answer the questions of *who* and *when*. Valentine Weigel (1533–1588) was a German Lutheran pastor of no real distinction, and during his own lifetime, his orthodoxy was not seriously in question. Only after he died were his manuscript works discovered, admired by some, and then, two decades later, brought into print. It is because of these delays that a sixteenth-century preacher spawned a seventeenth-century sect.

Weigel held views in common with German mystics like Meister Eckhart and Tauler. He venerated Caspar Schwenkfeld and attracted interest from followers of Paraclesus (d. 1541) who sought an alternative to the "learned" medicine of the time (and who can blame them!). The publisher of his works in England was Giles Calvert, a publisher of both Quaker works and works in the German mystical tradition.[162]

Weigelianism had much in common with other forms of "enthusiasm," and once orthodox theologians caught wind of the movement, Weigelianism was promptly added to lists of modern heresies, often for dramatic effect, and rarely as a result of careful analysis. Works by Weigel first appeared in England in 1648 (*Of the Life of Christ*, stressing the "inner Christ" of Christians) and in the summer of 1649 (*Astrologie Theologized*).

Arrowsmith was one of the first English theologians to notice Weigel. George Gillespie may have been the very first in the Atlantic Isles, mentioning in 1649 the "wilde fancy of the Weigelians."[163] Edward Leigh in 1654 made passing reference to Weigel, using the same description as Gillespie but citing the major 1651 anti-Weigelian work of Reformed theologian Johannes Crocius.[164] Intriguingly, Edward Reynolds (a former assembly member) in the same year that *Plans for Holy War* came off the press, printed a sermon that railed against the Weigelians as those errorists "who tell us that there is no knowledge of Christ in any Universities; that all Schools and Academies are enemies unto Christ, and all their Learning *merae corruptelae*;[165] who shut all Learning out of the Church, and all learned men out of Heaven."[166] Richard Baxter, also in the same year,

---

162. For a modern edition of and introduction to Weigel's works, see Valentin Weigel, *Von Betrachtung des Lebens Christi. Vom Leben Christi. De Vita Christi*, ed. Horst Pfefferl (Stuttgart-Bad Cannstatt: Frommann-Holzboog, 2002).

163. George Gillespie, *A Treatise of Miscellany Questions* (Edinburgh, 1649), p. 131.

164. Edward Leigh, *A Systeme or Body of Divinity* (London, 1654), pp. 90, 361, 831, 833.

165. "Unadulterated corruption."

166. Edward Reynolds, *A Sermon touching the Use of Humane Learning* (London, 1658), p. 22.

criticized the "Paracelsians (under whom I comprehend the Weigelians and the rest of the Enthusiasts)."[167]

Everyone understood that the Weigelians attempted to undermine the academy. As Arrowsmith said in his "First Speech against Weigelianism," their "standard-bearer" declares that "there is no university in the whole world where Christ is found. In the universities, not one shred of knowledge of Christ can be found." Or, more provocatively, "Christ refused to let devils preach the gospel; therefore, he doesn't want scholars to either!"[168] What Arrowsmith calls the "churlish rudeness of certain men" who oppose "the whole liberal education that we enjoy" offers the occasion for his first oration in praise of education, and in praise of the two English universities in particular.[169]

But this is only half the problem! The first oration also raises a second issue: Weigelian-spirited *magistrates*. "The people of Transylvania," the Dutch and the Germans, were continuing to found academies, but the English, "in the course of one generation," were permitting "the strength of their *Athenaea*" to fail.[170] That this is no incidental concern to Arrowsmith is evident from the fact that here the author is at his most insistent: "Is it prudent," he asks, "that the magistrate should readily permit the schools of the Reformed churches to be torn down or weakened when all around us, the colleges of the Jesuits are on the rise through papal influence?" Again, "Is that prudent?"[171]

The Weigelian problems enumerated in the first oration included the seizure of college property and, thus, a reduction in the university's power to pursue its original purpose. As implausible as it sounds to have the master of Oxbridge's most wealthy college complain about money, Arrowsmith, imagining himself as the spokesman for the universities,[172] saw financial considerations as prime evidence of the Weigelian problem in England: "Certainly, the liberal arts are nowhere valued less than when, after their benefits have been held out to the studious through a long period of time, [college] property is unexpectedly removed." As always, authorities had some excuse for trimming academic budgets, and it may be that Trinity, the university, or some other college whose situation concerned Arrowsmith

---

167. *Richard Baxter's Account of His Present Thoughts concerning the Controversies about the Perseverance of the Saints* (London, 1657), p. 4.

168. Arrowsmith, *Plans for Holy War*, First Speech against Weigelianism, p. 88.

169. Arrowsmith, *Plans for Holy War*, First Speech against Weigelianism, p. 79.

170. Arrowsmith, *Plans for Holy War*, First Speech against Weigelianism, p. 85.

171. Arrowsmith, *Plans for Holy War*, First Speech against Weigelianism, p. 85.

172. "So the Universities conclude their address." Arrowsmith, *Plans for Holy War*, First Speech against Weigelianism, p. 88.

had been accused of mismanagement of funds. He seems to allude in the oration to an accusation of some sort when he asks if it is "really fair that those who incur some obligation through no malfeasance are deprived of their possessions as if they had wastefully squandered them?"[173]

Pressures on the salaries of worthy fellows and the stipends of capable students seem to be in view in a pair of comments about fairness and in a frank assessment of human nature. On the one hand, he asks about the poor: "Is it really fair…that charitable, deserving men should be punished through the neglect of having their gifts given to the undeserving?" Or, "Is it, finally, the pious thing to do, by taking away the subsidies designated almost exclusively for the poor to make the universities, in the end, open almost exclusively to the rich"—many of whom squander their time at university anyway?[174] And, on the other hand, he insightfully asks if people will continue to study without financial encouragements: "Who clings to learning itself once you take away the rewards? Maybe one or two men."[175]

Arrowsmith's complaints are pointed; to undermine or underfund scholarship is to "reintroduce the barbarity that paves the road to strife, slaughter, rebellion, and all manner of political discord."[176] Or, to put the problem in the form of one of Arrowsmith's own anecdotes, "The philosopher Eulogius[177] was supposed to be paid a stipend on Leo's command, but a certain Eunuchus complained. He kept repeating that the money should go to the soldiers. Leo retorted, 'May it come to pass in my lifetime that soldiers' salaries are paid out to literature professors!'"[178]

The first oration made it clear that Weigelian-type attacks were not new, and they could take both obvious and more subtle forms. They could openly rail at the universities or quietly sap their financial resources. Thus, Arrowsmith concludes, "We must admonish the university students and plead with them through the deep mercy of Christ himself to oppose, from this point on, all Weigelians to a man, both those here at home as well as those abroad."[179] Later orations make some of the same points and can be summarized with increasing brevity.

The second oration makes it clear that Arrowsmith understands the Weigelian opposition to universities to be based in part on pedagogical

173. Arrowsmith, *Plans for Holy War*, First Speech against Weigelianism, p. 85.

174. Arrowsmith, *Plans for Holy War*, First Speech against Weigelianism, p. 85.

175. Arrowsmith, *Plans for Holy War*, First Speech against Weigelianism, p. 85.

176. Arrowsmith, *Plans for Holy War*, First Speech against Weigelianism, p. 85.

177. Eulogius, 579/580–607, Chalcedonian patriarch of Alexandria.

178. Arrowsmith, *Plans for Holy War*, First Speech against Weigelianism, p. 84.

179. Arrowsmith, *Plans for Holy War*, First Speech against Weigelianism, p. 88.

style, the stale Scholasticism allegedly intrinsic to and endemic in the academic endeavor. In this second piece, Arrowsmith is willing to acknowledge the deficiencies of Scholasticism and its useless "lust for wrangling."[180]

His response is to remind his hearers, in the first place, and briefly, that Christian education predates the Scholastic form of that education: "Not only did the most eloquent orators and sophisticated debaters emerge from their schools [that is, the schools of the church fathers], but theologians did as well, consummately prepared in every respect.... I honor their hoary age as I should; I esteem their impressive learning; I embrace their positions provided they are consistent with sacred Scripture."[181]

Arrowsmith acknowledges, in the second place, that this theology was corrupted over time by Scholasticism and that "the theology of the fathers would have been a much more excellent vintage had they not diluted it with the pagan philosophy that they had first decanted from the Stoa, Lyceum, or Academy." The worst of it entered sometime after Peter Lombard, for "in the whole of Peter Lombard, we do not read the name Aristotle once.... But among Lombard's descendants—and there are as many devotees of the *Sentences* as there are of the *Summa*[182]—Aristotle fills each page, as they say. And after [they] had escorted Aristotle to the doorstep of the temple, and Thomas[183] and Albert[184] brought him to the inner sanctum, then, until the time of Luther, he held almost sole and absolute sway in theology."[185]

But that is the point! With the Reformation came a purge of Scholasticism. "At the absolute nadir of both sacred and literary fortunes, the Lord pitied his church and raised up Luther, Melanchthon, and other supporters to clean out the dregs from religion, lopping off the cancerous portions that I mentioned so the whole, healthy body would not be dragged under." This is what the Weigelians fail to see and what Arrowsmith to his own satisfaction proves, that "the vices of the old Scholastics...today are banished from our schools."

The professor's third and most important point is that the old Scholasticism, with its "barbarity of style" and "ignorance of the languages," is a thing of the past. It was once said that "if you see a Scholastic theologian, you see the seven deadly sins." But if one "sees a Reformed scholar" one beholds "not the seven deadly sins but the three theological virtues. It is evident how

---

180. Arrowsmith, *Plans for Holy War*, Second Speech against Weigelianism, p. 93.

181. Arrowsmith, *Plans for Holy War*, Second Speech against Weigelianism, p. 94.

182. *Tam sententarios quam summistas.*

183. Thomas Aquinas, ca. 1225–1274, Dominican philosopher and theologian.

184. Albertus Magnus, d. 1280, German Dominican theologian.

185. Arrowsmith, *Plans for Holy War*, Second Speech against Weigelianism, p. 95.

much these Protestant scholars have relied upon the sacred Scriptures, how little upon philosophy, contrary to the Scholastics' typical practice."[186]

Worried that he was about "to light a lamp about the subject in the clear light of day," the speaker offers this summary: "Philosophy behaved toward theology in the schools, at least of the fathers, like an *ally*; in the training schools of the Scholastics, like a *schoolmistress*; in the hallowed chairs of Reformed universities, like a *maidservant*." Considering the Reformed approach, he adds, "If anyone begrudges philosophy that post, I think such a man truly has treated theology badly, philosophy worse, and the church worst of all."[187]

Arrowsmith's third oration continues to highlight his concern with the Weigelian attack on university education, especially on literature and academic degrees. He opens by announcing that "the liberal arts curriculum was, with consummate barbarity, wrenched away from scholars and churchmen alike and scholarly degrees were devalued." Here he addresses Weigelian-like figures: Paracelsus and his assault on traditional medicine and "all the followers of Galen," "Henry Nicolis, founder of the so-called Familists," and all Remonstrants (Arminians) and Socinians. But Arrowsmith's principal concern is with the Weigelians, and he provides quotation after quotation until it "would be painful, no doubt, to go on further" in illustrating Weigelian influences. His comment elsewhere in the third oration that he "cannot by eloquence put a nice face on these developments" suggests that the problems are recent or ongoing.[188]

In this final lecture, Arrowsmith gives the impression of a man running out of steam. The lecture is less tightly ordered and is reduced to lists of quotations and the telling of stories. In the end he states that he will "conclude with a prayer, but here also strive for brevity." The prayer is simply this: "May the greatest and most almighty God grant this university such a grip on truth that, in the end, it would be easier to find a wolf in England or a toad in Ireland than a Socinian, an Arminian, or a Weigelian at Cambridge."[189]

The timing of the third oration is the one chronological detail regarding the orations about which we can be reasonably sure, for it contains Arrowsmith's proud acknowledgment of his eldest son's recently earned degree, a BA that we know was awarded in 1655 or 1656 (all other degrees earned by

186. Arrowsmith, *Plans for Holy War*, Second Speech against Weigelianism, p. 100.
187. Arrowsmith, *Plans for Holy War*, Second Speech against Weigelianism, p. 100.
188. Arrowsmith, *Plans for Holy War*, Third Speech against Weigelianism, p. 101.
189. Arrowsmith, *Plans for Holy War*, Third Speech against Weigelianism, p. 109.

Thomas Arrowsmith were awarded after his father's death).[190] A later history of the university (offering a 1655 date) suggests that the oration would have been delivered at the end of commencement "when the assemblage would probably be at its fullest."[191]

We also know that John Lightfoot took the place of Arrowsmith in chairing the 1655 disputations due to Arrowsmith's poor health. His introduction to the disputations indicates that for at least one part of the festivities Arrowsmith would be absent:

> But what is now the proper direction of my address? A sad and woeful rift must interrupt my present task. I must renew my effort not with eloquence, but tears. We weep that you are vacant, O Chair orphaned and empty. We grieve that your owner is gone, grieve his illness and that he has relinquished you. All our assemblies, most noble Arrowsmith, are sick while you are sick. And how much does it hurt that your sons are deprived of you their father, that the assemblies must do without their orator, the chair without its oracle of wisdom, and I without a brother? Your august presence, worthy of deep respect, has made you a father to us all, as has this Chair, your unsurpassed nobility, and your learning.[192]

And again, "You behold now, today, his chair vacant, orphaned, silent, when before while he was still here it was joyful, gleaming with royal grace, and triumphant in eloquence."[193]

Lightfoot's grief at the loss of an orator is palpable, but it does not indicate that his friend could not have spoken at any time during commencement or that he did not do so in 1656, the year he resigned his professorship. Lightfoot's words do suggest that Arrowsmith was rapidly declining and unable to complete all of his work. As Lightfoot would go on to say, "Arrowsmith has quite often told me this year that I should appoint some other professor to his post. He said that he could not, in view of his poor physical health, endure any longer such a heavy burden. He said that he would only serve his appointment for the present term so that his chair would not go empty. And at that point he would relinquish it."[194] This appears to have happened in 1656, but it could have been in either year that he eked out these three last orations.

---

190. Venn. Thomas became a "minor fellow" of Trinity in 1656. H. McLeod Innes, *Fellows of Trinity College Cambridge* (Cambridge: Cambridge University Press, 1941), p. 35.

191. Mullinger, *University of Cambridge*, 3:477n2.

192. *The Whole Works of Rev. John Lightfoot, D.D.*, ed. J. R. Pitman (London, 1824), 5:398.

193. Lightfoot, *Works*, 5:398–99.

194. *Works of Rev. John Lightfoot*, 5:398–99.

Clear as the approximate dating of the third lecture may be (1655 or 1656), the dating of the other two lectures is embarrassingly difficult, for it appears that in each case we have either an apparent date for an oration without an obvious justification for its main theme or an obvious justification for an oration but no certain date. Pedantic as the matter may first appear, our understanding of the dating of the orations is related to our understanding of their context and the context of *Tactica Sacra*, the companion volume to the anti-Weigelian orations.

The first oration seems to be celebrating an event that took place in the late 1640s. Arrowsmith boasts that the university is "enriched by a new library." There were only two additions to the university's collections in the 1640s and 1650s so significant that they could deserve the description of a "new library": first, a collection of Hebrew manuscripts purchased in 1647 (but only paid for much later and delivered in 1649);[195] second, ten thousand volumes seized in 1647 from the archbishop's palace in Lambeth and delivered to Cambridge in 1648 or as late as 1649. (As Arrowsmith's tenure as vice-chancellor ended in 1648, the earlier date for a celebration of the "bequest" seems sensible. This date at least makes sense in terms of what Arrowsmith expresses in his 1647 *Great Wonder*: his evident concern that the costs of militarism might swallow up a concern for scholarship—a perfectly sensible concern immediately following a war in which Parliament, strapped for cash, needed to determine whether it should direct its meager resources to disgruntled soldiers or to academics.)[196]

While the late 1640s date appears to offer a good justification for the first oration, there are still problems with it. In his first lecture, Arrowsmith complains about magistrates with Weigelian tendencies, but around 1649, Parliament actually chose to *supplement* university salaries with revenues seized from now-defunct episcopal offices and establishments.[197] This is hardly grounds for worry about Weigelianism. What is more, Parliament seemed willing to hear Arrowsmith's own concerns about maintaining orthodoxy at Cambridge. Parliamentary interventions in university life came at his own request, and he appears to have enjoyed some confidence in relating to the two houses of Parliament after 1649, even while he was opposed to the regicide. Further, the sympathetic and presbyterially inclined Earl of Manchester was "Chancellor in all but name" during the late 1640s.[198]

---

195. J. C. T. Oates, *Cambridge University Library: A History* (Cambridge: Cambridge University Press, 1986), p. 235.

196. Arrowsmith, *Great wonder in heaven*, pp. 39–40, 43.

197. Twigg, *University of Cambridge*, p. 186.

198. Twigg, *University of Cambridge*, p. 134.

Yes, there were occasional fellows with Royalist sympathies or moral lapses. Mullinger thinks that Arrowsmith was also worried about Levellers and Fifth Monarchists, especially active in 1642–1651 and 1649–1660, respectively.[199] But in general, "evidence from the later 1640s echoes [only] the age-old struggle by colleges to maintain academic standards" as well as ensuring proper worship and "better behaviour from their students."[200] Thus, the heights of concern evidenced in the first oration are hard to justify, given the realities on the ground.

If the late 1640s do not offer a political context that makes sense of the anti-Weigelian orations, what is to be done about the clear reference to the university library? The most likely answer is that the first oration offers a belated celebration of the library due to delays in setting up the library, for the books needed bookcases. The fitting of the library space, the construction of the bookcases, and the arrangement of the books would have taken some time, easily reaching into the early 1650s. Thus, an oration in the mid-1650s commencement could appropriately celebrate the library, even if almost a decade after plans for its expansion were begun.[201]

The "Second Speech against Weigelianism," in turn, makes reference to no particular event, but it does show real alarm regarding attacks against university education. Again, we are presented with a problem: What were the specific government proposals or sources of criticism that so jeopardized the work of the university? Where is proof that a Weigelian spirit was taking root, informing economic realities, or shaping policy in places of influence?

Some have pointed the finger at William Dell. As master of Caius College from 1649 to 1660, Dell was, bizarrely, critical of formal education. Mullinger believes that Arrowsmith, in speaking of the Weigelians, may have had Dell in mind, among others.[202] Perhaps. But Dell had a negligible impact on the university during the interregnum, all the more so in the 1650s as his absences grew more frequent and longer.[203]

Arguably, understanding the date of the second lecture requires a look at national events, not college politics. Significantly, the Barebones Parliament of the summer and autumn of 1653 was widely considered to be a

---

199. Mullinger, *University of Cambridge*, 3:479.

200. Twigg, *University of Cambridge*, p. 132. The appointment in 1651 of Sir Oliver St. John (ca. 1598–1673) as chancellor of the university also argues for a positive context for scholarship in the early 1650s. St. John was a friend of Cromwell, but as former solicitor general under Charles I and Parliament, he was a learned man and an advocate of learning.

201. For the transfer of Archbishop Bancroft's bequests to Cambridge, see Oates, *University Library*, pp. 247–53.

202. Mullinger, *University of Cambridge*, 3:479.

203. Roger Pooley, "William Dell," *ODNB*; Twigg, *University of Cambridge*, pp. 182–85.

politically radical parliament; in a short time, it imploded, returning power once more to Oliver Cromwell, who had defended the universities during that parliament. But during the Barebones Parliament's brief moment of power, the universities, along with the very idea of a state church, appeared to be under siege.

It is true that it was during the Barebones Parliament that Arrowsmith was appointed master of Trinity College. But as encouraging as this may have been for Arrowsmith personally, he would have been keenly aware of the committee established by the Barebones Parliament for the "advancement of learning." The committee's title was an example of Orwellian party-doublespeak if there ever was one, for one aspect of its work was to consider reallocating for other purposes moneys originally designated to fellowships and colleges. Twigg reminds us that "it was rumoured that there was a plan put forward in the Parliament to suppress universities and schools," a plan that remaining parliamentary "moderates defeated." A 1654 pamphlet alleged that a majority of 84 of 145 members of Parliament were in favor of a learned clergy and the continuance of the two universities. That majority appears solid until one considers erratic attendance at parliamentary sessions in which a well-attended minority could occasionally find itself in a majority.[204]

In fears about the precariousness of a radical parliament, we have a sufficient justification for an anti-Weigelian oration! But can the second lecture have been delivered as late as 1655 or 1656? By that point it was clear that, in general, Cromwell was a better patron of the universities than had been the Barebones Parliament. Of course, he was not perfect. The Protector had caused some trouble from the perspective of those jealous for university privilege. Cromwell had intervened in a 1654 appointment of the professor of Greek, imposing a politically connected candidate of lesser abilities; a fellow was "intruded" (or forced) on Trinity in 1656; and although certainly after the delivery of the orations, another attempt would be made by Cromwell to impose a fellow on Jesus College in 1657.[205] Nonetheless, while Cromwell interfered with the university, points of comparison were vital in assessing the risks he posed. As Arrowsmith would well know, Cromwell did so less than did his royal or parliamentary predecessors. Cromwell himself did not represent a clear Weigelian threat to Cambridge.

So how do we make sense of the persistent concern about anti-intellectualism that runs through the three lectures? Should the absence of

---

204. Twigg, *University of Cambridge*, p. 168.
205. Twigg, *University of Cambridge*, pp. 167–68, 176.

an obvious enemy lead readers to assume that Arrowsmith, like an English Don Quixote, was tilting at academic windmills? This seems unlikely. After all, as one historian reminds us, "It would seem to be a reasonable inference" that, since the lectures were printed by the university press, Arrowsmith's "allegation was no mere rhetorical invention on the part of the professor but appealed to a knowledge of actual facts among his audience."[206]

Perhaps the best answer is found in perceptions regarding the Barebones Parliament and with concerns that Cromwell, as a military man with no great reputation for higher learning, might not uphold the university's privileges and its mission to promote and protect orthodoxy. That the worst of the scare was over by the mid-1650s makes little difference. Speaking in 1655, John Lightfoot's Cambridge commencement address "expressed relief and gratitude that the universities had not been destroyed."[207] If one further considers the inverted telescope through which aging academics often view time, serious scares in the past few years could feel like fresh events, not least on public occasions that afforded room for retrospective reflection in the presence of concerned alumni. Lightfoot and Arrowsmith, born on the same day,[208] would both by this date be considered old by the standards of the time, even if Lightfoot would live many years longer than his colleague. There was sufficient political concern for historians to plausibly date the first two orations to the time of the Barebones Parliament or to the emotional aftershocks thereafter as news about the deliberations of the Parliament trickled north to Cambridge.

At the end of the day, I lean toward the second, later option, that all three lectures were given at one time in 1655 or 1656. There is sufficient evidence in those years to warrant Arrowsmith's concerns—and, of course, we must leave open the possibility that there were other significant problems known then and lost to historians now. Indeed, we know that Arrowsmith was attuned to events not always evident in print, for he and Anthony Tuckney were the university's Sherlock Holmes and Dr. Watson when it came to detecting the presence and problem of Neoplatonism at Cambridge. Perhaps there were also other undercurrents in Oxbridge or London that threatened the study of literature and languages, just as Arrowsmith thought.

Compatible with the idea that the three lectures were given at one time in 1655 or 1656 is their decreasing length, almost as though a man with weakening health were delivering three lectures over a period of a few days.

---

206. Mullinger, *University of Cambridge*, 3:479–80.
207. Twigg, *University of Cambridge*, pp. 168, 173; see also pp. 168–69, 171.
208. Twigg, "John Arrowsmith."

The first address would likely have taken little more than half an hour for Arrowsmith to deliver—already short by the standards of the day. The second lecture, briefer still, was under half an hour. The third lecture was less than twenty-five minutes in length, at most thirty minutes for a sick man speaking slowly.

Final Years

The turning point in Arrowsmith's health, and one from which he would not recover, seems to have come around 1656. In 1655 Arrowsmith was not able to be present for the annual disputation in divinity. Lightfoot gives the impression that sickness could come on Arrowsmith quickly, while also implying that he had more than once recovered, at least to a degree. He noted in 1655, "Because he [Arrowsmith] had exhausted so much effort and diligence on this post, because he came to his duty readied and intense, when that sudden illness overtook him, sometimes his sick and weakened body turned our prayers to frustration and our hope rang hollow." In 1656 "sometimes" must have become "most of the time," for Arrowsmith felt compelled to resign the Regius professorship.[209] But did he even then know that he was dying?

It was about this time that he was desperate enough to consult a doctor.[210] And yet, if readers place a stethoscope on the work that Arrowsmith was writing at the time of his decline, they will detect only a few missed beats in the otherwise strong rhythm of the book. There is an admission saying, "I had acquired [leisure] after laying aside my professorial appointment due to recently failing health."[211] This kind of understatement is not obviously reflective of a man who knows that he will never be able to return to his duties of preaching and teaching. And there is a wistful statement in his dedication to the volume that he had hoped to deliver orations (distinct from his university anti-Weigelian orations) in the college chapel "if only health had permitted." Of course, his health had not, and thus those chapel orations were replaced by the much-expanded work later published as *Plans for Holy War*.

His friends describe him suffering from what they later described as "a long and tedious sickness," and he seems to have been increasingly bound

---

209. Twigg, "John Arrowsmith."

210. I was unable to consult London, British Library Add.79 f. 105 (medical treatment of Dr. Pratt).

211. Arrowsmith, *Plans for Holy War*, 1.1.2.

to the master's lodge.[212] Recovering at home might not have been easy, for the lodge would hardly have been a quiet place to convalesce. Thomas was likely living in college rooms by this point, but the master's lodge had as many as seven children between the ages of eleven and one—another Mary (b. 1652), as well as Sarah and Judith, had joined their older siblings (although this little Mary, too, would not reach her fifth birthday).[213] And yet there must have been times of strength as well as weakness, for Arrowsmith was not completely incapacitated even in the autumn of 1657: in late September or early October 1657, his wife Mary conceived yet again, giving birth to Rebecca eight months before her husband's death.[214]

Whatever relief or medical aid may have been sought by Arrowsmith, it was to no avail. And yet even these hoped-for lectures, this work produced during sickness, reveal a man of a constructive mindset and pleasant temper, as discussed below. Posthumous assessments and recollections of Arrowsmith also indicate an unfailing generosity of spirit, even if such estimates are to be taken at a discount (people are often generous in remembering the dead, and people were more generous with the memory of the dead in previous generations than in our own). The point is that there is no lack of evidence to confirm the positive bent in Arrowsmith's character. Thomas Baker, while no friend of Puritans, reviewed the surviving evidence of Arrowsmith's Cambridge career and concluded, "Allowing for the iniquity of the times and excepting the matter of Korah [a reference to Parliament's war against the King], he was a good man."[215] John Hackett, later bishop of Lichfield and Coventry—evidently favorably disposed to Arrowsmith as a man, if not toward the full range of Arrowsmith's doctrinal and ecclesial convictions—told a correspondent that he was pleased with Arrowsmith's election to the mastership of Trinity College.[216] And even after a falling out over important doctrinal matters, Benjamin Whichcote described Arrowsmith, above all others whom he had met in his course of university life, as "my friend of choice; a companion of my special delight:

---

212. Horton and Dillingham, "To the Reader," in Arrowsmith, *Armilla Catechetica*, sig. *3v; *ODNB*.

213. Mary, bap. Feb. 24, 1653: England Births and Christenings, 1538–1975, accessed June 7, 2021, https://www.familysearch.org/ark:/61903/1:1:NTG4-PRS. The birth dates of Sarah and Judith, mentioned in Arrowsmith's will, are unknown. The death date of Mary, who is not mentioned in the 1657 will, is also unknown.

214. Rebecca, bap. July 2, 1658: England Births and Christenings, 1538–1975, accessed June 7, 2021, https://www.familysearch.org/ark:/61903/1:1:V5KT-CTQ; NA PROB 11/289/161, fol. 179v.

215. Baker, *History of the College*, p. 228.

216. London, British Library, Sloane MS 1710, fol. 192.

whom in my former years I have acquainted with all my heart, I have told him all my thoughts; and I have scarcely either spoken or thought better of a man; in respect of the sweetness of his spirit, and amiableness of his conversation."[217]

Perhaps, as is the case with a remarkable number of Christians who have suffered long with physical disabilities, the graces appreciated by others were worked in Arrowsmith through his personal trials. His particular thorn in the flesh was partial blindness. He had a glass eye, for which he was mocked, in place of an eye that had been struck by an arrow at some point in his life.[218] And he probably seized opportunities to hide that eye from view. There is, for example, one piece of evidence suggesting that in the assembly Arrowsmith sat on the tiered benches or stands to the left of the prolocutor, along with many of the older and best-educated divines. More to the point, what clues we have also suggest that he sat at the very top left corner of those stands, hinting that his missing eye was his right eye, for it is natural to assume that Arrowsmith would have presented his good eye to face the room and his fellow divines.[219]

While in declining health, as late as 1658, Arrowsmith joined other Cambridge figures in supporting a scheme to fund promising young men interested in the ministry, offering reports on interviewees to the notable Presbyterian minister Matthew Poole and to others administering the fund.[220] Reforming the ministry of the church was a lifelong goal for Arrowsmith. His first printed sermon had commended Parliament's efforts in this regard, and he had dutifully served his turn on the Westminster Assembly's examination committee.[221] Indeed, after he left its membership, the gathering still requested his assessment of a candidate.[222] He was for three years appointed by Parliament to help choose Presbyterian elders for London, and he was a member of the Presbyterian classis system in that city.[223] It appears that he saw his work at Cambridge as a continuation of this ministry to future ministers, and a letter to Richard Baxter (the two men appear to have been mutual admirers) survives in which he details his attempts to help promising students, including one "good youth" who did not follow Arrowsmith's advice, resulting in additional work for Arrowsmith as he

---

217. Whichcote, *Moral and Religious Aphorisms*, p. 7.

218. Baillie, in Laing, *Letters and Journals*, 2:123–24. For jokes about his eye, see, e.g., [John Birkenhead], *The Assembly-Man Written in the Year 1647* (London, 1681), p. 9.

219. *MPWA*, 1:209.

220. Nicholas Keene, "Matthew Poole," *ODNB*.

221. E.g., *MPWA*, 3:686, Oct. 13, 1645.

222. *MPWA*, 4:827, Dec. 6, 1649.

223. *ODNB*; Twigg, *University of Cambridge*, pp. 103–4.

resorted to more creative means to advance the young man's calling in ministry.[224] The only discordant note in this otherwise steady pattern of careful vetting of men in ministry was the fact that, curiously, "between 1650 and 1658 Trinity suspended the normal requirement that its fellows should take orders." In this, Arrowsmith continued a practice begun under the previous master, a practice that relaxed open adherence to doctrinal standards, or that refused to pressure all academics into finding a call to gospel ministry before teaching university students.[225]

The time came when Arrowsmith was able only to write and not to teach or preach.[226] After 1657, the date of his last and greatest publication, he was restricted to administration and to editing *Armilla Catechetica* for publication. He wrote his last will on December 9, 1657, but, contrary to expectations, struggled on for more than a year.[227] He died on February 15, 1659,[228] and was buried nine days later.[229] Evidently fearing a popular response that would honor him unduly, Arrowsmith formally charged that his burial was to be held "in a more private way" and not to exceed fifty pounds in expenses, lest it be characteristic of the "many notorious disorders" that he had "observed in public" funerals.[230] His funeral sermon was preached by theologian and naturalist John Ray, a senior fellow of Trinity College.[231]

What Arrowsmith left behind was a large family and a literary legacy. Mary had seven children to care for, including Rebecca (an infant) and not including Thomas (an adult). Moving house with this many children would have been no small undertaking. Thankfully for his widow and orphaned children, Arrowsmith had already at the time of the writing of his will carefully amassed sufficient personal resources for the family's ongoing care.

---

224. Arrowsmith to Baxter, in *Calendar of the Correspondence of Richard Baxter*, ed. N. H. Keeble and G. F. Nuttall (Oxford: Clarendon Press, 1991), 1:201 (letter 289). For the relationship between the two, see Keeble and Nuttall, *Calendar of the Correspondence*; and Frederick J. Powicke, *A Life of the Reverend Richard Baxter, 1615–1691* (Boston: Houghton Mifflin, 1924), p. 142, where a student seems to have been told by Baxter to sit under Arrowsmith's teaching or preaching.

225. Scott Mandelbrote, "John Ray," *ODNB*.

226. Arrowsmith, *Theanthropos*, A3r–v.

227. NA PROB 11/289/161, fols. 179r–180r.

228. Twigg, "John Arrowsmith."

229. Buried Feb. 26, 1659: Cambridgeshire Burials, accessed June 7, 2021, https://www.findmypast.com/transcript?id=GBPRS%2FD%2F403116087%2F1.

230. NA PROB 11/289/161, fol. 179r.

231. Mandelbrote, "John Ray." Perhaps it was a coincidence, but Arrowsmith also knew the siblings Robert and Anne Ray from King's Lynn, who had generously bequeathed money to Thomas. See NA PROB 11/289/161, fol. 179r.

Thomas was given all property owned by his late father in two parishes in Suffolk; Thomas's grandparents on his mother's side had previously bequeathed to him one hundred pounds, with interest accruing until he reached twenty-one. Mary Arrowsmith received from her husband all remaining properties and rents—lands in Lincolnshire, Norfolk, and Cambridgeshire, including tenements, meadows, copyholds, pastures, and other hereditaments—although it was assumed that she would have to sell some of these properties to provide for herself and to prepare gifts for children reaching adulthood. John, the father's namesake, was treated like a second firstborn son (which he was). John Arrowsmith Jr. had been given twenty pounds by friends but was nonetheless bequeathed another two hundred pounds when he turned twenty-one and was to be given another hundred at his mother's death. Joseph and his five sisters were to inherit one hundred pounds each when they reached twenty-one and a second hundred each at their mother's death.

Special care was given to the library. Mary and her daughters were first to have the pick of all works in English that might edify them. Of what remained, half were to go to Thomas, and the other half were to be divided between his two brothers if both became scholars.[232] In the end, of the two younger brothers, only Joseph attended university, and thus he inherited the other half of what remained of his father's library.

The Final Book

It was his prolonged sickness that gave Arrowsmith occasion to write his greatest work and, as this introduction has argued, his last. A ten-year silence in publication had followed his *Great Wonder in Heaven*. It was broken in 1657 by the publication of his Latin magnum opus, *Tactica Sacra*, appearing here in English for the first time in Professor David Noe's elegant and accurate translation as *Plans for Holy War*.

The existence, ambitiousness, and subject of *Plans for Holy War* are all in their own way remarkable. Anyone who has suffered from the weariness and pain attending chronic illness or the ongoing effects of serious injury will know how difficult it is to accomplish any kind of work at all, let alone the hard work of creative writing and careful thinking. Arrowsmith acknowledges that his health had recently failed, but his self-effacing words mask the challenge he faced in writing a major work of theology and the extraordinary perseverance required for and evidenced in this work.[233]

---

232. NA, PROB 11/289/161, fols. 179r–180r.
233. Arrowsmith, *Plans for Holy War*, I.i.2.

Nor was he in the final stages of writing a work, stuck with the tiring but predictable work of editing. No, Arrowsmith had managed to initiate a major new project, and of all writing projects, the most difficult kind: not a series of texts or topics discussed seriatim, as in his previous expositions of biblical books and doctrinal *loci*, but a major study of a single theme (and a theme that had only recently occurred to him as worthy of an entire book,[234] although we have seen its central argument appear in his earlier studies).

The very existence and the extreme ambition of the project are unusual for a sick man. Perhaps most surprising is the subject, for it is not directly related to his own ever-present experience of suffering. Such a project a reader could perhaps understand: a book on assurance in the face of hard providence, on perseverance in the presence of adversity, or on the resurrection of the body in months leading up to death. Instead, the book's "main purpose is to equip the Christian man for spiritual warfare as a soldier for battle, victory, and triumph."[235] *Plans for Holy War* is a lively study on Christian warfare. And strikingly, given Arrowsmith's circumstances, the Christian's main battle is not with the problem of suffering but with the problems of sin and Satan in relation to doctrine.

The story behind *Plans for Holy War* is compelling. Perhaps even more so is Arrowsmith's style. As Dr. Noe notes in his preface, the genre adopted for *Plans for Holy War*, perhaps created for the occasion, is what Arrowsmith calls "Scholastic-pastoral."[236] The professor's book is *Scholastic* in the sense that it addresses and then answers questions that academically trained Christians might ask and meets objections that have been or could be raised. But the book is *pastoral.* The whole book is written in the first person, for the book is a conversation between Arrowsmith and his readers, who are frequently addressed directly in a pastoral tone: "Whoever you are—Christian, Englishman, academic."[237] His audience is, in turns, advised to pay attention, excused for their "rising boredom," encouraged to admire good theologians, or urged to grieve the bad.[238] Throughout the book, the professor is a pastor.

The book is also both Scholastic and pastoral in the sense that it is both scholarly and accessible. Potential rough edges in the work are softened with both anecdotes and choice citations and quotations. His stories are

---

234. Arrowsmith, *Plans for Holy War*, I.i.2.
235. Arrowsmith, *Plans for Holy War*, I.i.1.
236. Arrowsmith, *Plans for Holy War*, I.i.1.
237. Arrowsmith, *Plans for Holy War*, II.iii.6.
238. E.g., Arrowsmith, *Plans for Holy War*, II.ii.5, III.iii.15, II.iii.6, II.ii.11.

almost always entertaining, even if not always plausible. His interest in telling stories seems to be more focused on adding color to his book than light.

Arrowsmith's principal audience is obviously intended to be Christian (this is a work of theology). It is equally obvious that he hoped to reach his own countrymen, and the book is characterized by a high degree of home pride. He writes about "our own countrymen,"[239] "we English,"[240] "we Englishmen,"[241] "our England,"[242] and even "our dearest mother England."[243] Passages are sometimes directed to English persons in particular, as when he tells the reader, "You are an *Englishman*. You are, therefore, very affectionate toward your country as to a common parent."[244] While he is concerned about the possibility of England's excelling all "neighboring lands in profusion of all other goods" *except* for doctrine,[245] he nonetheless singles out English theological writers for particular praise.[246]

If writing to Englishmen, why write in Latin? Arrowsmith probably wrote in Latin, in the first place, because he *thought* in Latin; it makes sense for a man as unwell as Arrowsmith to write in a mode that would be easiest for him. In the second place, he wrote in Latin to signal that this was his most important work; after all, Latin continued for some time to serve as the medium of choice for high-caliber intellectual projects. However, it is clear, in the third place, that Arrowsmith intended for his work to reach an international audience as well. A continental readership is clearly in view when Arrowsmith takes pains to introduce to "foreigners unfamiliar with the English language" ideas and works of importance that they might not be exposed to because of the language barrier,[247] when he informs his audience of works translated into English,[248] when he charts the progress or regress of doctrinal positions in England,[249] and when he signals a shared affection for select European theologians—not only, "my friend Ames,"

---

239. Arrowsmith, *Plans for Holy War*, I.iii.13, II.ix.8.

240. Arrowsmith, *Plans for Holy War*, III.iii.8.

241. Arrowsmith, *Plans for Holy War*, III.iii.17.

242. E.g., Arrowsmith, *Plans for Holy War*, I.iii.5.

243. Arrowsmith, *Plans for Holy War*, II.i.7.

244. Arrowsmith, *Plans for Holy War*, II.iii.6.

245. Arrowsmith, *Plans for Holy War*, II.iii.6.

246. E.g., Davenant in Arrowsmith, *Plans for Holy War*, I.iv.2; or Whitaker in Arrowsmith, *Plans for Holy War*, II.v.4.

247. E.g., Arrowsmith, *Plans for Holy War*, III.iii.17.

248. Arrowsmith, *Plans for Holy War*, II.ii.5.

249. Arrowsmith, *Plans for Holy War*, II.vii.5.

but also, "our friend Rivet."[250] And there are few English words in the entire work, such as "forces" quite near the end.[251]

That *Plans for Holy War* reached this secondary audience is amply demonstrated by the creation of a second Amsterdam edition in 1700 and by that publisher's preface, narrating, as it does, the high value (and high cost!) of copies of the work found in the Netherlands.[252] The English translation which readers now hold in their hands is based on the earlier Cambridge edition printed in 1657. The original Cambridge edition, despite real and imagined errors addressed in the second edition (which the translator scrupulously consulted), has the useful distinction of being shepherded through the press by the author himself, a man meticulous in his scholarly work.

What follows in the next section of the introduction is an analysis of Arrowsmith's argument as found in *Plans for Holy War*. There will be no hiding the fact that this simplified treatment only brushes lightly along the outer fringes of this magnificent book. Indeed, while a summary of the book itself is necessary and will be helpful to some readers, my analysis may also risk obscuring some of what is most interesting in the work as a whole, including its many doctrinal asides, not all of which are apparent even in the detailed table of contents provided by the author. It is expected that the indices supplied in this volume will help readers find many of these topics, but neither introduction nor table of contents nor index will help the reader see how in Arrowsmith's own mind one topic trickles into another— sometimes in a roundabout, even whimsical way, and more often directly by dint of good reasoning or thoughtful exegesis. There is no substitute for the real thing; one must pick up *Plans for Holy War* and read.

As those readers will see, there are especially painful omissions in the analysis below, and here I mention a mere handful. Academics will see that there was no space dedicated in this introduction to mining Arrowsmith's chapters and orations for all that they have to say about university life. This includes both the encouraging ("Never have the younger students crowded around with more enthusiasm to listen to sermons") as well as the amusing ("One could wish that they did not queue up to *deliver* them!").[253]

Arrowsmith's Presbyterianism, evident in the volume, is also worth highlighting as a topic that needs further consideration, not least because,

---

250. Arrowsmith, *Plans for Holy War*, III.i.7; II.v.5.

251. Arrowsmith, *Plans for Holy War*, III.iii.8

252. Arrowsmith, *Tactica Sacra* (Amsterdam, 1700), sig. *3r. For the text of the preface, see appendix B.

253. Arrowsmith, *Plans for Holy War*, First Speech against Weigelianism, p. 87 (emphasis added).

unlike other Presbyterians, he managed to make a conditional peace with Cromwell's government. That he was opposed to episcopacy is evident in these pages as much as in the Westminster Assembly—a fact glossed over by Solman, who dedicated his 1700 edition of *Plans for Holy War* to a bishop![254] Arrowsmith enjoys a little too much the honest admission of a younger Lancelot Andrews who acknowledges that under episcopacy, "the very medicine for all abuses has itself been abused. I mean ecclesiastical censure.... Christ's whip has been stripped of lashes used for punishing crimes, and Peter's keys have likewise now become rusty. Unless, of course, by your own effort, you are going to fashion new cords for the whip and a new sheen for the keys!"[255]

Matching his opposition to episcopalism is his opposition to Erastianism and Congregationalism in the 1640s and 1650s:

> It is true that the famous assembly of elders that convened at Westminster just a few years ago as ordered by the "Estates"—I mean both houses of Parliament—repeatedly attempted to reintroduce church discipline. But it happened just like with Aeneas and Creusa in the Poet:
>
> > Three times he tried to hold her tight with arms around her neck,
> > Three times in vain her image fleet escaped his reaching hands,
> > Just like the gentle winds and as a fleeting dream she sped.[256]

Which three times? We are probably not to press the poetry too hard into the mold of recent history, but it is clear that first the assembly and the Long Parliament removed episcopacy; then the Long Parliament adopted an Erastian, bowdlerized version of the assembly's Directory for Church Government (and thus a kind of Presbyterianism); and then finally the Congregationalist-informed Cromwellian parliaments refused to enforce any kind of Presbyterianism in the 1650s. For Arrowsmith, "If the common slogan is true that discipline is to religion as trunk to tree, then it is really impossible to keep faith safe when ecclesiastical censures have ceased,... [when] our sheepfold, our pens, are missing their gates, bars, and bolts."[257] It was a principle that Presbyterians had insisted upon in earlier days when the movement was suppressed under episcopacy and then emasculated under Erastianism, and it was a principle that would be repeated again in

---

254. See appendix A.

255. Arrowsmith, *Plans for Holy War*, II.ii.10. For Puritan use of early works and lectures by Andrewes, see Peter McCullough, "Making Dead Men Speak: Laudianism, Print, and the Works of Lancelot Andrewes, 1626–1642," *The Historical Journal* 41, no. 2 (June 1998): pp. 401–24.

256. Arrowsmith, *Plans for Holy War*, II.ii.10.

257. Arrowsmith, *Plans for Holy War*, II.ii.10.

the nineteenth century as parachurch ministries became a mainstream phenomenon in worldwide evangelicalism.

The one other aspect of *Plans for Holy War* that neither the translator's preface nor editor's introduction can fully capture is what the work says about the impressive extent of the author's scholarship and reading. Here we are reminded again that Arrowsmith was no amateur theologian with Olympic confidence. He was drawing on a rich life of scholarship that is inadequately summarized in terms of statistics. Nonetheless, it is at least informative that Arrowsmith, even according to conservative figures, cites around 275 distinct authors, and in many cases, he cites multiple works by an individual author. This headcount does not include the 350 or more historical and literary figures whom he mentions along the way. Of these more than 650 different characters, at least 70 were medieval theologians, exegetes, or churchmen. Arrowsmith mentions or cites almost twice as many pagan classical figures (about 130), around three dozen pagan literary figures and deities, and perhaps four dozen early Jewish and Christian exegetes, theologians, historians, and heretics, including some prominent Christian churchmen.

Understandably Arrowsmith exhibits a pronounced preference for persons who lived and wrote in the century and a half prior to the writing of *Plans for Holy War*. These were the works most easily accessible to him. The largest group of people mentioned or authors cited (about 145) were those who lived through the Protestant Reformation (generously defined from the writing of the Ninety-five Theses and the mature career of Johann von Staupitz to the death of William Perkins in 1603). One-fifth (or 125) of the total persons appearing in *Plans for Holy War* lived lives that overlapped with Arrowsmith's own half century.

Of course, Arrowsmith preferred some authors over others. Among classical authors, Vergil leads the way, followed by Seneca and Plutarch. Among Christian authors, Augustine is the undisputed leader, cited around one hundred times, with Luther as runner-up, with about seventy-five mentions—no doubt, in part, because of Luther's colorful life and constant quotability. These authors are Arrowsmith's favorites, as a survey of his earlier works would lead us to expect. William Ames features in the book a little more than half as many times as Luther, and Calvin and Beza a little less than half, but there is no real rival for either the great father or the great reformer of the church. Jerome, Chrysostom, Rivet, and Davenant enjoy more than a dozen commendations each, but scores of others do as well.

Among the errorists mentioned in the book, papists and Jesuits lead the way, but while most references to Roman Catholics are predictably negative, there are a surprising number of exceptions: Arrowsmith seemed to operate according to the maxim that one must hate the Catholicism but could love the Catholic. Arminians are the next most-mentioned problem, but while Socinians find themselves in third place, they are clearly marked out as the most dangerous heretics of Arrowsmith's day (the Cartesians are on the radar but not usually in his sights).

Mentioning Arrowsmith's opponents serves to remind us that mere citation does not equal admiration. Aristotle and Aristotelianism are mentioned often but are usually reserved for abuse in this pastoral-scholastic work. On the other hand, Davenant is cited as many times, but Arrowsmith can hardly refrain from telling his readers that "the Right Reverend Davenant" speaks "capably and splendidly" and that he is a "very great man" and "very famous"—"Davenant, a man whose memory will live happily among the orthodox forever," and whose memory Arrowsmith defends in this book as he recounts a story of a Davenant forgery.[258]

Arrowsmith supplied just over seven hundred marginal notes to *Plans for Holy War*. His ability to summon up hundreds of detailed and largely accurate citations during a time of his decline suggests that his own personal library must have been significant, that his powers of recall or his system for organizing notes and quotations were formidable, or that he still had the energy, for much of the project, to get out of the house and consult volumes in the college library. Nonetheless, this edition also supplies almost two hundred additional notes for citations not properly noted by Arrowsmith, omissions on his part that indicate time pressures, limitations to his library resources, an inability to leave the master's lodge at some points, or perhaps forgetfulness—those lines he remembered from titles he did not.

Plans for Holy War

Both the body of the book and its academic apparatus are testimony to the fact that, in the face of his own decline, it was Arrowsmith's preference to spend his final years wandering the corridors of what he calls at one point "the palace of theology."[259] The palace erected in his book has three levels.

Book I, in six chapters, argues that spiritual warfare is basic to the Christian religion. Here he walks the reader from the proto-gospel of Genesis 3:15, with its promise of Satan's defeat by the seed of Eve, all the way to the apostle Paul's discussion of the armor of God in Ephesians 6. Varieties of enmity and enemies are noted along the way, while Christ is set forth

---

258. Arrowsmith, *Plans for Holy War*, II.ix.16–17.
259. Arrowsmith, *Plans for Holy War*, II.ii.3.

as the coming captain of the Christian soldier. The book is substantially forward-looking.

For Arrowsmith, the "very close connection between Christianity and spiritual military service" is a result of the fall of humanity into sin. This connection is first articulated in the protoevangelium of Genesis 3:15: "I shall place enmity between you and the woman, between your seed and hers. It shall crush your head, and you shall crush its heel." This text, for Arrowsmith, is the prism refracting the whole spectrum of doctrinal *loci*, but it is most of all "the first statement of the gospel."[260] Thus, it is his first order of business in book I to make sure that it not be stolen from us through impoverished and erroneous treatments of the text, notably those propounded by Socinians (a leading concern to the orthodox in the 1650s). Of course, such impoverished interpretations are to be expected; after all, "it is not at all surprising that the ancient serpent, gripped as he is by the greatest concern for his own head," has attempted to mislead the world regarding his own destiny and to keep it from seeking rest in Christ.[261]

The connection between the text, Christ, and Christianity is established. But what about Christianity and military metaphors, or rather, military realities? How does Genesis 3:15, properly understood, lead readers to *Plans for Holy War*? The answer is found in the Lord's own declaration of war: his establishment of the fact that there must be enmity, must be two parties, and that this situation must continue "to the end of the age between Christ and His own on one side and the Devil on the other side with his followers."[262]

Having identified the official opposition in chapter I, the author engages in reconnaissance and review in chapter II: assessing the enemy; learning to identify the serpent, his seven leading vices, and his followers; and then surveying loyal forces—Christians and, more importantly, Christ (not the virgin Mary), who is our captain and the Seed of the woman.[263]

Each topic subsequently receives fuller treatment. In chapter III, Satan's "blazing enmity" is seen in the forces loyal to him, including a predictable battery of popes, persecutors, Arminians, demons, practitioners of magical arts, and depraved persons of all sorts, along with one unexpected group: "men of letters."[264] But then in chapter IV, we encounter the entirely unexpected, for we are told that there is a sense in which God is also an enemy

---

260. Arrowsmith, *Plans for Holy War*, I.i.2.
261. Arrowsmith, *Plans for Holy War*, I.i.3.
262. Arrowsmith, *Plans for Holy War*, I.i.5.
263. Arrowsmith, *Plans for Holy War*, I.ii.
264. Arrowsmith, *Plans for Holy War*, I.iii.

(a point heavily qualified!). Arrowsmith also insists, more straightforwardly, that our own flesh sides against us (and "the closer an enemy gets, the more dangerous he is"), that the world opposes us, and that death itself defies us.[265]

So, who is on the Lord's side? *All* Christians, as stated before. But ministers and even angels also make up the forces of our "gospel centurion." Arrowsmith explains in chapter V the duties owed to the one who says "to this one, 'Go,' and he goes." The reader is told that "Alexander's soldiers were marked with distinction; namely, 'they focused not only on their general's standard but even on his nod.' We watch for the standard of Christ in His word, His nod in the inspiration of the Spirit, and we must obey both eagerly."[266] *Plans for Holy War* is a polemical work, to be sure, but it bristles with devotion.

Arrowsmith turns his attention in chapter VI to the armor that Christians need in the fight. Here he adds "effort and elbow grease" to persuade Christians that they need the armor that God supplies, and he clarifies what this means.[267] The key to understanding the armor, as with the warfare, is Christ: each element of protection is provided by, indeed, is a metaphor for, Christ, or his works, or the benefits that attach themselves to him. Following the thought patterns of the apostle Paul in Ephesians 6 and beginning what is essentially an artful and edifying exegetical commentary on that famous chapter, Arrowsmith identifies the variety of schemes deployed by the devil and his angels against the Christian man and woman—schemes that are personal, consistent through history, and especially focused against more prominent servants of God.

By this point, the attentive reader of *Plans for Holy War* will understand that for Arrowsmith, the problem of sin takes the form of sins of understanding and not merely sins of the heart or sins of action. This emphasis on the importance of theological warfare is one of the points that makes Arrowsmith's treatment of Ephesians 6 and his explanation of the subject of spiritual warfare unique. The schemes of Satan have as much to do with the promotion of heterodoxy as they do with keeping sinners in unholy slavery or in inhibiting spiritual growth among those called to be saints. Arrowsmith's treatment of spiritual warfare does not follow the same path as William Gurnall's *The Christian in Complete Armour*, the first edition of which had been printed only two years previously, in 1655. *Plans for Holy War* is a sustained plea for Christian people, Christian ministers, and, as we

---

265. Arrowsmith, *Plans for Holy War*, I.iv.3.
266. Arrowsmith, *Plans for Holy War*, I.v.4.
267. Arrowsmith, *Plans for Holy War*, I.6.1.

will see, especially Christian magistrates and academics to take seriously the urgent need to fight for truth.

Reaching the second level of the theological palace, book II, in ten chapters, provides an ample explanation of "the Pauline panoply."[268] Here Arrowsmith details the meaning and purpose of the various pieces of armor, each of which relates in some way to Christ. Book II is focused principally on redemption as it is accomplished and applied; it considers redemptive history in the here and now, the benefits of salvation earned by Christ as exhibited in the lives of Christians. Here too Arrowsmith is intent not only on edification (although many readers will appreciate his pastoral style and approach) but on the exposure and refutation of error (the Scholastic component to the work).

Book II begins by preaching the twice-repeated Pauline injunction in Ephesians to "stand firm." Only those—and all those—who have Christ will find themselves able to stand in the fight. Arrowsmith then advances the idea that the "belt of truth" in Ephesians 6:14 represents orthodoxy both in the understanding (chapters I and II) and in the will (chapter III), insisting that the "truth of the heart is the grace of the Holy Spirit."[269]

For historians of Puritanism and the post-Reformation period, the first two chapters of book II offer material of special interest. Arrowsmith's identification of the errors of his day offers a hint of the theological turmoil of the 1650s. For why else would this Presbyterian minister worry aloud about the persistent errors of Remonstrants, pagans, Muslims, Socinians, the "papist religion," and, in England especially, Seekers, Quakers, and Thomas Hobbes?[270]

To Arrowsmith's evident sorrow, "England gives birth each year to some new monster,"[271] and chapter II is entirely dedicated to explaining why 1650s England is so convulsed with heterodoxy. Bypassing "the Scholastics who have, with great effort, brought Greek philosophy into the citadel of the church like a Trojan horse," Arrowsmith reaches back into antiquity and points the finger at "Plato and the Platonists" and Aristotle and the Aristotelians. These were the philosophers and philosophies to which promoters of Pelagianism were attracted as they boasted about their "secular knowledge."[272] Similar influences, he believed, along with a "resurgence of Skepticism," were behind the persistence of Remonstrant and Socinian

<hr>

268. Arrowsmith, *Plans for Holy War*, II.i.1.
269. Arrowsmith, *Plans for Holy War*, II.iii.4.
270. Arrowsmith, *Plans for Holy War*, II.i.3; II.i.4; II.i.5; II.i.7; II.ii.111.
271. Arrowsmith, *Plans for Holy War*, II.i.7.
272. Arrowsmith, *Plans for Holy War*, II.ii.2.

thought.[273] He adds to this a dangerous "presumption to prophesy" on the part of these errorists, but strangely, here he does not mention the recently emerging Quakers as one might expect in a chapter on the errors in England in the 1650s.[274] This is especially surprising since Arrowsmith, generally pacific during his mastership of Trinity, had accused Alexander Ackhurst, the vice-master of his own college, of Quaker-like error in 1654 and since Quakers were active in the town by 1655.[275] Instead, Arrowsmith cites as negative examples the Dutch Remonstrants, the Anabaptists, and, "from Germany,… the Weigelians."[276]

At last, the Weigelians! Twice in *Plans for Holy War*, Arrowsmith had made passing reference to Paracelsus, whom the Weigelians admired.[277] But the Weigelians themselves are a main concern, and it is here that he states his main objection to their teaching. For Arrowsmith, the Weigelians represent "bizarre progressives…who grant the civil magistrate, even though he is Christian and endowed with distinguished piety, no authority even to reform the church, much less to suppress heretics in any way at all."[278]

The old errors of the Weigelians had much in common with the newly emerging Quakers. They shared the same printer in London. They shared the same pejorative labeling as varieties of "Enthusiasm," as we have heard in the three orations. They also all relied on unmediated communications with God, opposed university education, and criticized established religion. This last Weigelian idea was, to underline the obvious, the extreme antithesis of the position held by Erastian members of Parliament in the 1640s.

Not believing in a real distinction between the government of the state and the government of the church, and subordinating the latter under the former, it had been obvious to Erastian MPs like John Selden (and also to Erastian ministers like John Lightfoot and Thomas Coleman) that a Christian magistrate must reform the church, suppress heretics, and even adjudicate cases of church discipline. This last uniquely Erastian idea the majority in the Westminster Assembly, including John Arrowsmith, vigorously opposed. Thus, in this respect, the Weigelian philosophy held a key idea in common with divines in the Westminster Assembly. So, what was the issue? The issue was that the Weigelians went too far.

---

273. Arrowsmith, *Plans for Holy War*, II.ii.2, 4.

274. Arrowsmith, *Plans for Holy War*, II.ii.5.

275. Twigg, *University of Cambridge*, pp. 191–92; see also pp. 192–95.

276. Arrowsmith, *Plans for Holy War*, II.ii.6.

277. Arrowsmith, *Plans for Holy War*, I.iii.2, I.vi.7.

278. Arrowsmith, *Plans for Holy War*, II.ii.11.

There is a clear anti-Erastianism articulated in the assembly's 1646 Confession of Faith and any number of petitions to Parliament.[279] Nonetheless, most of those same divines believed in what might be termed an establishment principle: the idea that the Christian church in a "Christian nation" should be supported by the state. That state, they argued, should not meddle, under any circumstances, with cases of discipline in the church but should suppress heresy and, if necessary, reform the church at times when it will not reform itself. Thus, for Arrowsmith, the Weigelian *unwillingness* to fight heresy with every weapon available to Christians, including the Christian magistrates' "sword," was unconscionable. Such an attitude is "against the plain meaning of sacred Scripture, the mind of Augustine, the practice of the church, and the clear dictates of reason," and he appeals to "the reform of the churches during the reigns of David, Solomon, Asa, Jehoshaphat, Hezekiah, and the other kings of Judah" to make his point.[280]

But if this was the writer's concern, why point the finger at German Weigelians, of all people? One answer might be that it seemed more prudent to do so—or, at least, more politic—than to preach against the toleration of error that characterized Oliver Cromwell's administration, for it had defaulted to defending high levels of religious liberty and, thus toleration of heterodoxy. Another reason to criticize the Weigelians, in addition to everything said thus far, is that in mid-1650s England, it may still have been unclear which movement—Weigelianism or Quakerism—would prove to be most corrosive to orthodoxy or attractive to errorists.

In registering complaints about Weigelianism, Arrowsmith further helps us understand how his anti-Weigelian orations were not merely padding for the book, an add-on feature to increase sales. The three lectures attached to the main text of *Plans for Holy War* provide essential context for the larger book and arguably offer a key to its central thesis. That thesis is that error needs to be resisted by all Christians, *including Christian magistrates*. To be sure, this thesis is not advanced to the exclusion of other concerns: Arrowsmith ends his three-chapter exposition of the belt of truth with an exhortation to all Christians—English Christians generally and academics specifically, and thus, not to magistrates exclusively. But it is clear that he wants "Christians, generally, and ministers, in particular," at a time when almost all academics were ministers, to own the theologian's task of identifying and refuting error. And it is clear that he wants the civil magistrate to back up the Word with the "sword," with such things as state-supported

279. See WCF 23.3 and *MPWA*, 5, doc. 81, 83, 84, 85, 87, 88, 93, 104.
280. Arrowsmith, *Plans for Holy War*, II.ii.12.

censorship, fines, and perhaps imprisonment or even exile.[281] Arrowsmith makes no specific recommendations, but readers would be well aware of the range of options.

As significant as the Weigelian theme is to *Plans for Holy War*, the author eventually ceases to discuss the topic overtly. This is apparent in chapters VI and VII, for example, treating "The Greaves of Evangelical Readiness" and "The Shield of Faith" mentioned in Ephesians 6:15 and 16, respectively, both of which are discussed in keeping with Arrowsmith's militaristic theme but without mention of the full range of Weigelian problems that troubled him. Indeed, the tone of each chapter is warmer, more pastoral, and less polemic than the preceding three, even if Arrowsmith does (in passing) use his greaves to defend against the kicks of a Socinian[282] and his shield of faith to deflect attacks from Arminius and Bellarmine.[283]

Actually, for Arrowsmith, the shield of faith is designed explicitly for the purpose of absorbing "the Devil's flaming shafts," as the title of chapter VIII reminds us. Thus, *Plans for Holy War* turns to another examination of our diabolical enemy and the nature of his wickedness and depravity and to an analysis of the flaming or poisoned darts that he directs toward Christians. The author concludes that darts come in the form of persecution and temptation, with both of these often assaulting the Christian's imagination.

So how does faith help? Faith "does its work either by ensuring that these shafts are not taken into the soul completely or that they do not penetrate too far." Faith helps us to apply "the blood of Christ as a medicine once the mind has been wounded."[284] Faith helps us "by distinguishing between temptations that bubble up from our own heart and the instigations implanted from without." Faith "teaches us…to form a plan, and to rest comfortably in plans well laid." Significantly, faith teaches us "to embrace Christ as our Savior, who willed to suffer diabolical instigations in the desert that He might sympathize with Christians who toil under the same cross." And faith directs us to "immediately reject these instigations," "to turn away the mind and retreat directly to other thoughts," and "if this evil stubbornly persists against all remedies," to scorn him "with holiness, not haughtiness."[285]

Given the long history of godly reflection on the matter of the believer's assurance of faith or assurance of salvation, readers familiar with Puritan

---

281. Arrowsmith, *Plans for Holy War*, II.v.6.
282. Arrowsmith, *Plans for Holy War*, II.vi.9.
283. Arrowsmith, *Plans for Holy War*, II.vii.6.
284. Arrowsmith, *Plans for Holy War*, II.viii.4.
285. Arrowsmith, *Plans for Holy War*, II.viii.6–7.

literature will not be surprised to see that in chapter IX, Arrowsmith focuses his treatment of "the helmet of salvation" in Ephesians 6:17 to the topic of "assurance of hope." Satan's attack on this head of doctrine comes from the Romanists in particular. While Arrowsmith keeps a wary eye on Lutherans and Remonstrants, his hand-to-hand combat is with the still-influential Roman Catholic apologist Robert Bellarmine (1542–1621), who argued that certainty of salvation is impossible.

Arrowsmith's own plans for holy war include shaming his opponents for saying that we cannot be assured of our standing with Christ. He prefaces his remarks with a story of the undaunted confidence of "the martyr Agatha," who, even when her persecutors were ready to cut off her breasts, defiantly announced in an astonishing display of courage, "Two breasts remain that you cannot touch: one is faith, and the other hope. These provide me, even in the midst of torment, comfort and safety. And by their nourishment, I regain the power to persevere."[286] Arrowsmith strikes again, this time undermining the strength of the Roman position by exploiting Catholic disunity. He trots out two Romanist theologians, a Carmelite and a court preacher, who disagree with the majority of other papists on the subject of assurance.[287] He hammers Rome again with improved distinctions, careful exegesis, rebuttals against charges of fanaticism, and, finally, a strong summary of the grounds of assurance.

Puritan divines themselves were often divided in what they would emphasize or even allow as grounds for assurance of salvation. Arrowsmith argues that the testimony of the Holy Spirit and "the infallibility of final perseverance" are the two main grounds for Christian confidence. Regarding the former, he sees a threefold testimony: "(1) the testimony of the Holy Spirit imparted to our spirit, (2) the testimony of our spirit that is drawn out from us by the indwelling Holy Spirit, and (3) the gifts of the Holy Spirit freely bestowed upon our spirit."[288] Regarding the latter, he sees assurance as a necessary corollary to properly framed doctrines of regeneration, election, justification, and sanctification.[289]

In chapter X, bringing book II to its conclusion, the author expounds Paul's most famous metaphor in Ephesians 6, that of the Word of God as the "sword of the Spirit." Against papists, Socinians, and select Remonstrants, all of whom attack the authority of Scripture in one way or another, Arrowsmith wields not only Augustine and an array of theologians from the

---

286. Arrowsmith, *Plans for Holy War*, II.ix.1.

287. Arrowsmith, *Plans for Holy War*, II.ix.5.

288. Arrowsmith, *Plans for Holy War*, II.ix.10; expounded more fully in II.ix.10–13.

289. Arrowsmith, *Plans for Holy War*, II.ix.14–17.

patristic, medieval, and Reformation periods of church history but also—as he must!—the testimony of Scripture itself.

Using categories that map onto the Westminster Assembly's own discussion of Scripture in the first chapter of its Confession of Faith but which had enjoyed a long history in the Christian tradition, Arrowsmith lingers over the qualities of Scripture (the majesty of its style, the heavenliness of its matter, the efficacy of its doctrine). His special emphasis, however, is on the "internal testimony of the Holy Spirit." With the Scottish theologian Robert Baron, whom Arrowsmith cites appreciatively, Arrowsmith clarifies that Protestants "by the internal testimony of the Holy Spirit…do not understand some new and extraordinary revelation of the gospel that proceeds from the Holy Spirit unmediated. Instead, they understand the effectual application of revelation previously disclosed in the Scripture itself."[290]

Arrowsmith has particular errorists in view in much of the chapter, but he ends by reminding readers that there are many (including theologians?) who "become so absorbed in other pursuits that they train themselves too carelessly in the reading of the Scriptures." We do not treat "with the honor it deserves such a consecrated trust of heaven." We "do not gaze upon it" or "store it up" in our hearts. There are "some men…that were once careful readers and listeners but who now very seldom touch their Bibles and almost never attend sermons." This is to neglect the sword of the Spirit! Thus, "We must weigh very carefully the praises the Holy Scriptures deserve so that our zeal in attending to them may grow sharper" (a pun, as ever with Arrowsmith, no doubt intended!).

It is in writing about Scripture that Arrowsmith's prose soars to sublime heights:

> The Bible is a paradise in which the two original trees grow: one is the tree of knowledge and the other the tree of life. The Scriptures are the polestar of souls, the acropolis of truth, and the treasury of piety. It is the seed that regenerates us as Christians, the milk that nourishes us as infants, the meat on which we feed when mature, the wine that revives us when weak, the medicine that heals us when sick. Yet the Pauline encomium surpasses the many other words of praise. I mean the one ready at hand, that God's word is "the sword of the Spirit." If you try to add anything to this statement, you will only diminish it.[291]

Arrowsmith adds no more by way of exhortation and defense of Scripture, choosing for the remainder of the chapter to explain how the Word

---

290. Arrowsmith, *Plans for Holy War*, II.x.6.
291. Arrowsmith, *Plans for Holy War*, II.x.7.

functions as a sword and how we might "draw that sword from its sheath and brandish it in our arguments."[292] It serves as a fitting and practical conclusion to his treatment of the Christian armory found in Christ.

Book III brings the work to its close. As Arrowsmith summarizes the whole project, "The first book of this work established what it means to be a Christian in terms of military duty. The second one dealt with the battle. Now the third book follows, in which the Christian is equipped for victory and triumph." Thus, this final book is forward-looking, ending with what Arrowsmith calls "A Modest [Outline] of the Heavenly Triumph."[293] Here, in four chapters, the author encourages his readers to steadfastness by directing them to the final victory found in Jesus Christ.

As the last chapter of book I drew us into Arrowsmith's discussion of the whole armor of God in Ephesians 6, so the first chapter of book III winds down his exposition of Ephesians 6 through a consideration of verse 18. There we hear Paul's exhortation for Christians to live "with all prayer and petition, praying at every moment in the Spirit, to this end remaining alert with all perseverance and supplication for all the saints."[294]

The chiastic structure of *Plans for Holy War* works well, literarily, and Arrowsmith's guide to prayer found in this chapter offers much material for edifying reflection. But why, for Arrowsmith, is prayer an aspect of the Christian's triumph rather than an aspect of the Christian's warfare? After all, as we are reminded in this very chapter, in which Arrowsmith borrows the words of Jerome, "It happens all the time in my praying that I either stroll through porticos, tally up some interest, am ambushed by a filthy thought, or even do things that would make me blush just to mention them. Where is my faith? Do we think that Jonah prayed like that? That the three Hebrew children prayed this way? Daniel among the lions? The criminal on the cross?"[295]

This key question (not why Jonah appears in Jerome's list, but why prayer is part of our triumph rather than our fight) Arrowsmith does not answer directly.[296] He notes that "the saints, while praying, usually recall the examples, promises, and other sayings of the sacred Scriptures, or at least refer to them." He notes the experience of notable saints like Augustine's mother, Monica, or Arrowsmith's hero, Luther. Luther prayed "with

---

292. Arrowsmith, *Plans for Holy War*, II.x.10.

293. Arrowsmith, *Plans for Holy War*, III.i.1.

294. Arrowsmith, *Plans for Holy War*, III.i.1.

295. Arrowsmith, *Plans for Holy War*, III.i.13.

296. Arrowsmith, while not unaware of his faults, also mentions Jonah as a model for prayer. See *Plans for Holy War*, III.i.3.

so much reverence that he feels like he is talking with God, with so much hope and faith as with a father and a friend." Luther "puts so much pressure on the promises derived from the Psalms, as though he were certain that everything he was asking for would come to pass."[297]

The closest Arrowsmith comes to answering this question—a very real question for Christians who find prayer itself more an experience of *struggle* than *victory*—is in a battery of quotations early in chapter I. From John Quistorp: "Paul wants us, in this our spiritual conflict—through our prayers—to flee for safety to God our Father and Christ our brother. And by these mutual prayers, we who are brothers in Christ help one another against the enemy." From Macarius: "Prayer is support to him who prays, a sacrifice to God, and a whip for the Devil." Or, "Although the demons may be powerful and no different than mountains in their strength, they are consumed by the fire of prayer like wax in the flame."[298] These serve better as strong assertions than new arguments, but of his position, Arrowsmith is confident: "Pertinax's watchword was, 'We must act like soldiers'; Severus's, 'We must work.' Ours should be 'We must pray.' The Roman supposedly conquered by hunkering down. The Christian will conquer by praying."[299]

If prayer prepares us for victory, Christ remains the author of that victory. As Paul writes in his letter to the Corinthians, "Thanks be to God who gives us the victory through our Lord Jesus Christ" (1 Cor. 15:57). Proving that victory comes through Christ is the burden of book III, chapter II. In keeping with the pattern of *Plans for Holy War*, the chapter proceeds by pointing out false authors of victory, including pagan deities, and the virgin Mary as a partner with Jesus, and by arguing against those who would undermine our confidence in this victory, here chiefly targeting the Arminian John Goodwin and his 1651 work, *Redemption Redeemed*. Where the Scriptures, and especially the book of Revelation, are properly understood, "Christ the Lord is identified as the crowned knight."[300] Thus, Arrowsmith concludes, "I salute you, soldier of Jesus, for your courage (or, rather, for the courage of the one whose soldier you call yourself). Go on boldly to the final victory, and surely the Lord Himself will praise you at the final judgment with higher acclaim."[301]

In keeping with this confidence, chapter III offers three "Apostolic Ἐπινίκια" or apostolic victory hymns from Romans 8, 1 Corinthians 15,

---

297. Arrowsmith, *Plans for Holy War*, III.i.1.

298. Arrowsmith, *Plans for Holy War*, III.i.2.

299. Arrowsmith, *Plans for Holy War*, III.i.16.

300. Arrowsmith, *Plans for Holy War*, III.ii.2.

301. Arrowsmith, *Plans for Holy War*, III.ii.14.

and 2 Timothy 4, respectively. One of the more exegetically interesting chapters in *Plans for Holy War* (and one occupied much with the topics of death and resurrection), the chapter also breathes a confidence that is Arrowsmith's own in the midst of his sickness and decline: "We are sharers in communion with Christ the Lord, not only in His offices—as it is written, 'He has made us kings and priests to His God and Father' (Rev. 1:6)—but also in His privileges. The voice from heaven proclaimed that He was the beloved Son of God in whom the Father was well pleased. The sacred Book proclaims that we are beloved and His sons."[302] Victory over death, over hades, over sin (gradually!), over the law—these are his joys, and the joy of all Christians.[303]

As elsewhere, the chapter is enriched by one doctrinal discursus after another. Eternal justification is denied: "The elect are actually justified not from eternity but in time."[304] A connection between the history and the application of redemption is asserted: "In many different instances, the sacred Scriptures make His resurrection the prototype and earnest of our own resurrection from the miseries that usually assail the church."[305] The error of "soul sleep" is refuted[306] and a new taxonomy for understanding Christ's righteousness is asserted.[307]

That taxonomy is of real interest to the history of theology. For Arrowsmith, "Christ's righteousness is threefold if considered very broadly: *personal, official,* and *collateral,*" the last category encapsulating a "total righteousness" stemming from Christ's "total obedience." As Arrowsmith sees it, "This obedience ought to be described by a single word, *activo-passiva,* rather than being divided into active and passive, as though into distinct units."[308] This leads in turn to a discussion, subtle enough to be worthy of any Scholastic theologian, of merits and rewards.[309]

Fittingly, the work ends with a "Modest [Outline] of the Heavenly Triumph." In one deeply moving line after another, the writer leaves his readers on the edge of their pews, waiting for Christ's return. He confesses for himself, "I can now see the land, or rather heaven, where my long argument must come to an end," and adds, "Christians dwell in enemy territory so long as they fulfill military service in the world.... So Christians are led

---

302. Arrowsmith, *Plans for Holy War,* III.iii.11.

303. Arrowsmith, *Plans for Holy War,* III.iii.11–14.

304. Arrowsmith, *Plans for Holy War,* III.iii.4.

305. Arrowsmith, *Plans for Holy War,* III.iii.5.

306. Arrowsmith, *Plans for Holy War,* III.iii.12.

307. Arrowsmith, *Plans for Holy War,* III.iii.19.

308. Arrowsmith, *Plans for Holy War,* III.iii.19.

309. Arrowsmith, *Plans for Holy War,* III.iii.20.

triumphant after they say goodbye to the world through death, are wreathed with their crowns, and decorated with songs of praise. They come to the 'city of the living God, the heavenly Jerusalem, ten thousands of angels.'"[310]

That this heaven contains multitudes heartens Arrowsmith, although it does not lead him down the garden path toward universal redemption.[311] Instead, what follows, still maintaining an emphasis on warfare and now victory, is a reflection on the joys of the blessed in seeing and loving God[312] and the various ways in which the blessed are described in Scripture, reflecting their exalted dignity, purity, and joy, all of which is owed "to our most blessed Mediator Jesus Christ."[313] The final note of the book is doxology, employing the words of angels who declare that "blessing and glory and wisdom and thanks and honor and authority and strength be to our God forever and ever" (Rev. 7:12).[314]

It is only here that the author declares his readiness "momentarily to draw in my sails."[315] As he does so, he urges his readers to "learn some skill in praising our Lord, a skill we must put to use through endless ages." For, "As the trophies of Miltiades once drove on Themistocles, so may the victories of those in heaven spur us on." Arrowsmith remembers here "Leonard Lessius. When he was on the very brink of bidding this world farewell, he completed a treatise, *God's Fifty Names*, and added the final touch to it four or five days before his death." He recalls a tender moment in antiquity when "Monica…for so long discussed the heavenly kingdom with her son Augustine." Finally, using George Buchanan's free paraphrase of Psalm 36, Arrowsmith recalls the prophet David, who "gasped for heaven," considering "pleasures far surpassing, purest joys strewn o'er the landscape" with "fair delights the brook of gen'rous flow delivers…its headlands in a fountain."[316] Here the subtitle's final word comes into its own, for this is a book explaining "How the Spiritual Soldier Fights, Conquers, *and* Triumphs" (emphasis added).

Conclusions

This introduction to John Arrowsmith and his most important book is no substitute for a full study of his life and thought. It necessarily highlights

310. Arrowsmith, *Plans for Holy War*, III.iv.1.
311. Arrowsmith, *Plans for Holy War*, III.iv.2.
312. Arrowsmith, *Plans for Holy War*, III.iv.3.
313. Arrowsmith, *Plans for Holy War*, III.iv.4–5.
314. Arrowsmith, *Plans for Holy War*, III.iv.9–14.
315. Arrowsmith, *Plans for Holy War*, III.iv.14.
316. Arrowsmith, *Plans for Holy War*, III.iv.15.

a polemical work by Arrowsmith at the expense of some of his more theologically constructive content and could leave readers with the impression that Arrowsmith's best energies only emerged when he had an object to assail. Arguably, historians of theology should place no greater premium on works of systematic theology than on works in defense of theology, but it is worth noting that since the purpose of this introduction is to frame a book about strategies for Christian warfare, it does not present a balanced study of Arrowsmith's whole corpus. Indeed, to the extent that *Plans for Holy War* is apologetic, it represents the exception in his oeuvre and not the rule. *Theanthropos* and *Armilla Catechetical* are principally positive works of theology with their own distinct contributions. The same may have been the case with the two exegetical volumes delivered to the printer by Thomas Arrowsmith and now lost. And yet, with that qualifier in place, it should also be noted that Arrowsmith's presentation of the protoevangelium of Genesis 3:15 in *Plans for Holy War* is more than merely stylistically creative: Arrowsmith's arguments for its usefulness as a unifying biblical theme are substantial, and his reading of Ephesians 6 as one part of that overarching theme is both helpful and striking. Other positive contributions are present in *Plans for Holy War*, as the introduction has mentioned in passing and as readers will discover for themselves.

Perhaps the most striking feature of the book itself is that Arrowsmith managed to pull off a writing style that was at once pacific and pugilistic. The fact is, his contemporaries could hardly have failed to notice that his sustained polemic rarely wanders from the winning tone characterizing the rest of his writing. His content is warlike; his demeanor, never less than earnest. But his tone remains, if not convivial, at least cordial. As such, this work is strikingly different, more confident, and calmer than much of the near-hysterical heresiography of the day, not least that produced by Thomas Edwards.

Edwards is mentioned because it seems inevitable that the sheer volume of errorists and errors Arrowsmith discusses will lead historians at some point to compare this composition to the notorious work of heresiography of the 1640s, Thomas Edwards's *Gangraena*. Both books seek to expose present errors, both call for an urgent response, and both name names, although Arrowsmith is attentive to errors on the continent to a degree that Edwards is not. And though it would be unfair to liken Arrowsmith's largely irenic work to Edwards's angry diatribe, it is Arrowsmith's work that will better help historians see why, shortly after Arrowsmith's death, even those Presbyterians not sharing Edwards's spirit would welcome a restoration of the monarchy in the hope of greater suppression of error, even with all the risks it would entail.

Arrowsmith's book and the accompanying lectures are signally helpful in reminding theological historians that books have contexts. The relevance of the anti-Weigelian lectures was not immediately apparent to the editor or translator of this volume. And in a careless moment, we considered presenting *Plans for Holy War* without them. But Arrowsmith's own deliberate pairing of the texts and our careful readings of the lectures alongside his main tome convinced us that the lectures help to explain why the book was written at all.

This is to say, in part, that there is value in tracing the multiple possible motivations for writing the work and discovering both immediate personal circumstances as well as obvious ministerial motives, such as a faithful exposition of an overarching biblical theme. There are two worlds that study Puritanism: one, it seems, looks for pure, enduring pastoral motives behind printed works; the other, questioning such idealism, looks for personal and more immediate motives for religious writing. In this case, it seems to be a bit of both. There is reason to suspect that additional study would often yield a complex of motives that all historians, including those in the same theological tradition as Arrowsmith, should expect.

Perhaps the most significant factor leading Arrowsmith to write was the problem with Alexander Ackhurst, the vice-master of Trinity about whom Arrowsmith was so exercised. Arrowsmith traveled to London to bring testimony in Parliament against Ackhurst for dishonoring both God and Holy Scripture. Imprisoned in London and examined by Parliament, the university, and then the college, Ackhurst was shuttled from one trial to another in 1654 and 1655. Arrowsmith, along with Anthony Tuckney and Lazarus Seaman (two other college masters and former Westminster Assembly members), examined Ackhurst. For the purpose of further examination in Cambridge, he was released from prison and remained free, but following an examination of his theological views by senior leaders in the university (including Arrowsmith), Ackhurst was ejected from the college, and thus from the university.[317]

Stated differently, in the case of Ackhurst, the civil magistrate failed to do what Arrowsmith thought it should have done. The fact that the Ackhurst case was punted between London and Cambridge and ultimately resulted only in ejection from a college fellowship offered the dying theologian one more data point regarding the difficulty in enforcing blasphemy

---

317. Twigg, *University of Cambridge*, pp. 191–94.

law in Cromwellian England and the inability or unwillingness of the state in his own day to take theology seriously. The weakness of the civil magistrate underlined the limits of coercion. And when sticks proved useless for correcting the increasingly chaotic environment of the 1650s, it may be that in *Plans for Holy War*, Arrowsmith decided to offer a carrot—a book on truth and heresy without much (or with much less) of the unpleasantness that often accompanied earnest polemic against error.

Reference was made above to the second Latin edition of *Plans for Holy War*, printed in 1700, and to the exorbitant cost of the work for its early modern readership. The translator and editor alike are grateful that this large work will now be given a third lease on life. It is hoped that it will reach its widest audience yet and at its lowest cost thus far, and it leaves our hands with the happy prospect of doing good work once more. *Plans for Holy War* is a true gem, and once an English audience begins to read this translation—for the first time in our own language—readers will encounter a Puritan author like few others. Arrowsmith himself is an impressive example of a generous spirit in his own day, the kind of person who made it his calling to care for colleagues, students, and the wider public. Here we have considered especially his writing, in which he extends considerable effort to voice his complaints and concerns in a winsome and attractive way. The hard work of writing well, rather than the easier task of writing much, is something that administrators need to encourage and academics need to pursue. But it is also impressive that Arrowsmith wrote the book thinking he was dying. He was wrong, for he lived a year after it was printed. But that Arrowsmith, himself an administrator in his later years, could labor with such care and in so much weakness, and with the expectation that he would never personally hear praise or thanks from those who would read his book, is a true commendation of a Christian soldier who spent his life in service of his Captain and had the faith to see that he would live another day.

Plans for Holy War,

or
How the Spiritual Soldier Fights, Conquers, and Triumphs,

in Three Books

By John Arrowsmith,
doctor and former professor of sacred theology,
master of the College of the Holy and
Undivided Trinity at Cambridge.

This also contains the same author's several
anti-Weigelian speeches and his defense on behalf of the
Reformed universities recently delivered from the
chair in the great lecture halls.

Printed at Cambridge by the most famous printer
of the university, John Field. 1657.

For sale at John Rothwell's Booksellers,
doing business in London, at the end of the street
commonly called Cheapside,
at the Sign of the Fountain in the
Goldsmiths' neighborhood.

Dedication

John Arrowsmith, gladly and because they deserve it, hereby offers, devotes, and dedicates to his most esteemed fellow soldiers, the vice-master,[1] senior fellows, and other supporters and alumni of Holy Trinity College who serve well at Cambridge under Christ's leadership, these three books of *Plans for Holy War*. These books are emissaries of evangelical piety, guardians and avengers of orthodoxy, interpreters of some of God's oracles, and protective deities in many difficulties. These *Plans* are meant to supplement whatever was missing from the *Sacred Orations*[2] that the author intended, if only health had permitted, to deliver there within the private confines of the chapel (in which he tried to temper polemic with pastoral theology, and to moderate both with philology)—together with an appendix of *Orations*[3]—to serve as witnesses of his brotherly love and reminders of common duties.

---

1. It is unclear if A. would be addressing the incoming or outgoing vice-master. William Disney, ca. 1620–1718, was vice-master from 1654 to 1655 (Venn); the Disney family was known for its associations with Lincolnshire Puritans. James Duport, 1606–1679, was vice-master from 1655 to 1665 (*ODNB*). Vice-masters identified by Jonathan Smith, archivist of Trinity College Library, Cambridge.

2. A. mentions *Sacrarum Orationum*, apparently lectures he wrote and intended to deliver. When poor health necessitated resignation of his post, the lectures were expanded, and their tittle changed to *Tactica Sacra*.

3. These are the anti-Weigelian speeches that were in fact delivered and whose translation is included in this volume.

Three Speeches against Weigelianism

An Outline of the Three Speeches

I. The speaker thanks Cambridge for his good condition. He next provides a brief review of the university's enemies and then describes the antiquity of academic institutions among Jews and Greeks alike. Praises for the English universities are set forth, and the speaker introduces the institutions themselves to plead their own case. They earn goodwill from every direction and differ in how they safeguard their revenues. The speaker recounts some notable decrees and accomplishments of Charlemagne. Finally, he evaluates the character of our countrymen.

II. The speaker claims for himself the patronage of the Scholastic theology that is now popular in Reformed schools. He shows how much one should value legitimate debate. The speaker then describes how Scholastic theology was employed among the Hebrews, among the church fathers, and finally among those theologians who are specifically styled Scholastic. He scolds most of them for their neglect of sacred Scripture, zeal for quarreling, carelessness of style, wicked habits, and abuse of philosophy. Finally, he asserts and proves that the Reformed schools and their professors are, generally speaking, free from all these faults.

III. The speaker defends the liberal arts and their use in theology and, at the same time, considers scholastic degrees. He likens errors to yeast, seeing that it is the reason why the dough grows hot, why it swells in size, and why it goes sour. The malice, arrogance, and capitulation to the wicked pleasure of men that the heterodox display correspond to these phenomena. The speaker sets out for view the outrageous conduct of certain Lutherans, the insolence of the Eunomians, Jesuits, Paracelsus, and Henry Nicolis, as well as the syncretism of different sects together with their depraved nature. He makes public Weigel's barbarous paradoxes concerning literature and academic degrees. Yet Luther, Melanchthon, and Zanchi held quite the opposite opinion on the same subjects. George Fiscellini's and Martin Martinius's deeds and the different ways they died are recorded. The author concludes with a prayer.

First Speech against Weigelianism[1]

It would be better for us—if it would please you, most distinguished scholars and treasured visitors—to head immediately to the stone quarries, hew
out stones, build an altar, collect wood, and kindle burnt offerings as a most
luminescent proof of our thanks. For if threats had any power, if oaths, if
efforts of certain shiftless men, then long, long ago our Troy[2] would have
been reduced to an empty field, our alma mater surrendered to darkness or
to our Stepmother.[3] But today, through God's singular grace and the kindness of the senatorial aristocracy, she rejoices in her broad, ancestral estates.
Enriched by a new library,[4] the envy of both the Vatican and Bodleian, she
gleams anew with the solemn renown of her great halls as well. Embracing
foreign guests in her friendly arms, these tender shoots in her motherly
bosom, she prides herself, though not too much, in this lovely offspring,
though perhaps it is not large.

How I wish that this present age and the state of society were such
that professorial orations could be brought to their conclusion with words
of praise and commendation, weighty statements, at least, and warnings,
rather than studied defenses!

Yet I feel myself pulled in another direction by the churlish rudeness
of certain men who find the whole liberal education that we enjoy and the
very word *university* not less filthy than Louis XI, king of France, found
that hated word *death* when he lay ill.[5] I will answer the worthless quibbles
of these men not through imaginative or witty words (the Spirit of God
does not lie nor snarl) but only through the clear statements of Scripture,

---

1. Followers of Valentin Weigel, 1533–1588, German Lutheran theologian, philosopher,
and mystical writer; see introduction. The speeches are translated from the 1657 edition and
compared with that of 1700.

2. I.e., Cambridge University.

3. I.e., Rome.

4. See introduction.

5. Louis XI, 1423–1483, r. 1461–1483, king of France. A. repeats this story in I.iv.7.

reason, and experience. Where else shall I begin than from that light of nature, which urges that we must take very great care of the cultivation of our minds and that nowhere is this care exercised better than in the public schools of study, where the bridle of discipline and the goads of competition are typically applied to straighten and brace up instruction?

Consequently, among all nations whom barbarism had not overwhelmed, there rose up, in addition to the elementary schools that were established to shape children, renowned schools and universities to instruct those who were older. The schools mentioned by the Sacred Annals of the Kings deserve to be listed in this group. The sons of the prophets enrolled in the school at Gilgal reportedly numbered a hundred. And fifty went out from the school of Jericho, not children but men, אֲנָשִׁים בְּנֵי־חַיִל [6] well prepared to search for Elijah's remains [2 Kings 2:16]. Palestine once had Kiriath-Sepher ("City of Literature") [Josh. 15:15], and Persia, her marketplace of learning. (Brisson wrote about this at length and with distinction.)[7] Greece had Athens, and there was Plato's[8] Academy as well as the Lyceum of Aristotle,[9] Zeno's[10] Stoa, and the Cynosarges of Antisthenes.[11] The Indians had their school of Gymnophysists;[12] the Chaldeans, one for Magi; the Egyptians, their school of Priests; the Gauls, one for Druids. The Romans provided a School for Philosophers and Orators, and the Jews, their school for Pharisees and Sadducees and the monasteries of the Essenes.[13] But the one concern that motivated God's own people more than others was that their young students not go without either adequate financial support for their studies or proper assistance in them. Before a fiery chariot took Elijah's body from their midst, a fiery zeal for the schools of the prophets had overtaken his soul. Accordingly, when he was on the very brink of saying goodbye to the world, Elijah carefully visited those schools and armed them with his final instructions, as though heaven could be gained most sweetly after he had spent the final portion of his resources on those being trained up there as the hope of the church. No matter how degenerate in other ways the descendants of the ancient Hebrews became, in this one academic aspect, however, they showed that they were entirely the heirs of their

---

6. "Sons of strength."

7. De Regno Persico lib. 2. p. 240, &c.] Barnabé Brisson, 1531–1592, French humanist and jurist, *De Regio Persarum Principatu* ([Heidelberg], 1595).

8. Plato, 427–347 BC, Greek philosopher.

9. Aristotle, 384–322 BC, Greek philosopher.

10. Zeno of Citium, 334–262 BC, Greek philosopher.

11. Antisthenes, ca. 445–ca. 365 BC, Socratic philosopher.

12. I.e., naked philosophers.

13. Essenes, members of a Jewish ascetic sect in the second century AD.

fathers. We will take the Tiberian school as an example. Two considerations make it very praiseworthy: First, the incomparable critical work of the Masoretes, which is commonly called the "fence of the Torah."[14] Second, the famous Mishnah volume that Buxtorf[15] thinks was completed in the city of Tiberias by Rabbi Yehuda.[16] Among contemporary Jews, this volume enjoys praise that is urbane, to be sure, but altogether impious. "The *Textus Biblicus* is like water, the *Mishnah* like wine, the *Talmud* like spiced wine."[17]

In the Roman world likewise, as soon as the gospel had begun to blossom, one could notice that workshops devoted to good literature had sprung up in several monasteries. But after the Cenobites[18] had run their course, and the piety and learning of the monks had been destroyed, schools were opened elsewhere to repair this ruin. It would be easy, if anyone had the desire, to gather up the writings of Middendorp[19] or Hospinian[20] and, from these authors, bluster on about the most famous universities throughout the world until the clock runs out. We are not permitted such great prolixity, and the English institutions alone— Cambridge and Oxford, Oxford and Cambridge—shall give us adequate space to say as much as is necessary. I list them this way because I am not going to waste time on the useless question of which institution is older. May God grant that each be fully restored, that when every source of strife has been pruned away, both are surpassingly ancient, both in service to each other and to all good men. Let us take them to be twins—sisters, at least—of the same mother. One should properly say of them what once was said of Leah and Rachel: "Both have built up the house of Israel" [Ruth 4:11]. They are equally designated the glory and mainstay of church and state alike, just as the two columns Jachin and Boaz were for Solomon's temple [1 Kings 7:21].

---

14. The Masorah is called the סיג לתרה (lit., "fence of the Torah") by the rabbis in Pirkei Avot 3:13, which is commonly translated into Latin as *septum legis*. This note courtesy of Dr. Kirsten Macfarlane.

15. *Buxtorf.* Tiberias cap. 5. p. 23.] Johannes Buxtorf Sr., 1564–1629, Swiss Reformed Hebraist, *Tiberias* (Basel, 1620), ch. 5. p. 23.

16. Judah ha-Nasi, 135–ca. 220, compiler of the Mishnah, a collection of Jewish oral traditions.

17. *Alsted.* Chronolog. p. 415.] Johann Heinrich Alsted, 1588–1638, Calvinist minister and academic, *Thesaurus Chronologiae* (Herborn, 1650), ch. 42, p. 432.

18. Monks or cloister-brothers.

19. Jakob Middendorp, 1537–1611, Dutch Roman Catholic theologian and historian.

20. Rodolphus Hospinianus (Hospinian), 1547–1626, Swiss Reformed theologian.

Yet both here and there, each college represents a seedbed for virtue and learning; each chair of theology, a bulwark for the truth; each lecture hall, a testing ground for virtue; each faculty office, the forge of a good mind. I have no time, therefore, for those who, with very bad grace, with no honesty, with the greatest anger, have habitually ascribed to Reformed universities those traits that famous men have laid at the feet of Jewish and papist institutions. Theodore Beza described the latter as "Satan's bellows,"[21] Luther, "thrones of pestilence" and "shining beacons of Antichrist."[22] That same author, in his dissertation *The Old and New God*, calls those same schools "synagogues of damnation" and "pits of the abyss" whose smoke darkens the sunlight of the gospel.[23] He who denounces our institutions for these faults acts like someone who concludes that all books must be burned because Christians burned spell books at Ephesus [Acts 19:19]! I have no time for them, I repeat. They should mind their own business. Their diseased eyes naturally find the two shining beacons of the English firmament[24] so repulsive that they threaten them with an eclipse no light can ever repel.

I think that I hear the universities themselves, by far the best and most qualified defenders of their own cause, speaking something like this in response to such unfair critics. "We appeal to your honesty, good men: what have we done to deserve so much hatred? No, what have we not done to deserve the love and loyalty of our people? Allow us to paraphrase the question of Christ our Lord: 'We have shown you many good works. For which of these, we ask, do you seek to stone us?' (John 10:32). Do you not yet know what the works of each of us have been and also what they are today? Consider a few examples. We have tried to place a sizable gap between the English and barbarians by educating your sons in the cultivation of their minds and proper formation of character. Learning provides virtue with the basic elements and starting points on which, when properly nourished, she grows large. And a garment dyed in the wool does not usually bleed its color. We have been careful to prevent the flood of popery and the torrent of reconstituted Pelagianism from washing over

---

21. *Beza* in Act. 6. annot. marg.] Theodore Beza (Théodore de Bèze), 1519–1605, French Reformed scholar and theologian, *Novum Testamentum Sive Foedus Graece Et Latine*, ([Basel], 1565), sub loc. Acts 6:9.

22. Martin Luther, 1483–1546, German Protestant Reformer. Reference unknown.

23. *Witemb.* An. 1522. fol. antepen. & ult.].

24. I.e., Oxford and Cambridge.

our country, by sending forth Whitakers,[25] Abbots,[26] Davenants,[27] Ameses,[28] Twisses,[29] and other heroes of that caliber who very successfully stood against the flow. We (let there be no rivalry in a statement absolutely true) have worked to make sure that there are no obstructions in the marketplace, that there are theologians in every church, lawyers in every court, doctors in every village. We have filled the government, the church, Parliament, and the army with learned men, because the more educated they become, the better prepared they are to serve the public good. Through the study of literature, men's minds are not rendered effeminate or made ill-suited to public life or incapable of military renown, as the ignorant bawl, though the history of every age shouts the opposite.

"Set before your eyes Moses, by far the most famous leader of the people of Israel. He was, nevertheless, the most carefully educated both in all the wisdom of the Hebrews and in the literature of the Egyptians. Look at Cato,[30] whose epitaph was this: 'Best orator, best general, best senator.'[31] Note Julius,[32] who—brandishing both a book and a sword—boasted that he was 'Caesar in both.'[33] Take note of Alfonso, the most wise king of Aragon.[34] When his courtiers kept complaining that he was too devoted to and buried in his studies, he said, 'I would prefer to be locked out of my kingdom than out of my office.' Finally, remember Louis,[35] Prince of Hesse, nicknamed 'the Mild' because of his exceptional gentleness. He reportedly had rejected the scepter of the Roman Empire when offered it, because he didn't think that he could govern a Christian nation properly when he had been deprived of his literature, so Sylvius tells us.[36]

"In view of all these examples, there is no reason that fair-minded observers should wonder if male and female royalty, together with other benefactors (in whose distinguished generosity God's great goodness shines

---

25. William Whitaker, ca. 1547/1548–1595, theologian and college head.

26. Probably Robert Abbot, ca. 1559/1560–1617, bishop of Salisbury.

27. John Davenant, bap. 1572, d. 1641, bishop of Salisbury.

28. William Ames, 1576–1633, theologian and university teacher.

29. William Twisse, ca. 1577/1578–1646, theologian.

30. Marcus Porcius Cato (Cato the Elder), 234–149 BC, Roman statesman and orator.

31. Pliny the Elder, 23–79, Roman statesman and scholar, *Naturalis Historia* (Leiden, 1635), vol. 1, 7.44.

32. Probably referring to Gaius Julius Caesar, ca. 100–44 BC, Roman general and statesman.

33. The reference is to Plutarch's *Life of Caesar*, 17.3.

34. Probably Alfonso V, 1396–1458, r. 1416–1458, King of Aragon.

35. Louis III, ca. 1151/1152–1190, landgrave of Thuringia.

36. Enea Sylvio (Sylvius) Piccolomini (Pope Pius II), 1405–1464, p. 1458–1464. *Commentariorum Aeneae Sylvii Piccolominei Senensis, De Concilio Basileae Celebrato Libri Duo* [Basel, ca. 1542].

forth), have supplied not only proper financial support to professors of languages and sciences but also support to heads of schools, associate faculty, and junior students. And they have so enriched us with our stipends and endowments so that we not be left without dowry, and so love of learning does not grow cold in noble minds.

"But the disaster of our present estate arises from this, that the estates, in fact, belong to us. If this had occurred without revenues, our opponents would more easily reconcile with us. It is property that produced this rigid judgment, as was the case in the Parisian slaughter,[37] when a mere coin was proof of heresy, and it was not religion but wealth that made the Huguenots. Let us take our stand here, if that is all right, and pronounce a curse on my own Muses unless they clearly grant this has been proven: it is better for the state to endow the universities than for each, when their resources have been spent, to hunt for a legacy for literature, when help has not been sought elsewhere. And let them also admit that we cannot borrow against the properties that produce revenue, which were formerly conferred upon us by multiple leases—actually, centuries ago—without, at the same time, the greatest loss and disgrace to the whole nation.

"Certainly nothing diminished Justinian's[38] reputation more—in other respects a very praiseworthy ruler—than that, while building churches, he was very concerned that funds needed for such large expenditures not run out, and so deprived teachers of the liberal arts of their agreed-upon salaries. From this it happened that, here and there, a kind of boorishness held sway in the empty schools throughout the villages. The historian comments on this in very learned words: Οὕτως τῶν ἐν ταῖς πόλεσι διδασκαλείων ἐσχολακότων ἀγροικία τῶν ἐν αὐταῖς καί ἐκράτησε.[39] From the opposite perspective, the noble statement of Emperor Leo I[40] is quite famous. The philosopher Eulogius[41] was supposed to be paid a stipend on Leo's command, but a certain Eunuchus complained. He kept repeating that the money should go to the soldiers. Leo retorted, 'May it come to pass in my lifetime that soldiers' salaries are paid out to literature professors!'[42]

---

37. St. Bartholomew's Day Massacre, August 24, 1572.

38. Flavius Justinianus (Justinian I), 483–565, r. 527–565, emperor of Byzantium.

39. *Zonar.*] Johannes Zonaras, d. 1160, Byzantine chronicler and theologian, probably from Zonaras's *Historical Epitome.* "So, rusticity held sway over the unemployed teachers in the villages."

40. Leo I, d. 474, r. 457–474, emperor of the Eastern Roman Empire.

41. Eulogius, 579/580–607, Chalcedonian patriarch of Alexandria.

42. *Lips.* monit. & exemp. politica p. ult.] Justus Lipsius, 1547–1606, Flemish Christian humanist, *Monita Et Exempla Politica* (Antwerp, 1605), ch. 18, p. 213.

"Again, we appeal to your honesty, good men. If the people of Transylvania should receive credit that the school at Alba Julia was recently founded;[43] if the Dutch, for building the noble Academy and Orange College of Breda;[44] if the Germans, for seeing to it that the University of Heidelberg was reestablished; surely the English people have not received adequate honor if, in the course of one generation, the strength of their *Athenaea*[45] is failing? Surely it is not adequate compensation when learning has been abandoned, learning that civilizes customs and makes hearts obedient and pliant to just rule, to reintroduce the barbarity that paves the road to strife, slaughter, rebellion, and all manner of political discord? Certainly, the liberal arts are nowhere valued less than when, after their benefits have been held out to the studious through a long period of time, property is unexpectedly removed. Who clings to learning itself once you take away the rewards? Maybe one or two men. Or is it really fair that those who incur some obligation through no malfeasance are deprived of their possessions as if they had wastefully squandered them? And that charitable, deserving men should be punished through the neglect of having their gifts given to the undeserving? Or is it prudent that the magistrate should readily permit the schools of the Reformed churches to be torn down or weakened when all around us, the colleges of the Jesuits are on the rise through papal influence? These typically supply our young men with abundant carnal enticements (because, as the saying goes, 'youth is gullible') to drag them by hook or by crook into their camp once they are shattered at home by passion. Is that prudent? 'The Ithacan would welcome that, and Atreus's sons pay for it dear.'[46]

"Is it, finally, the pious thing to do, by taking away the subsidies designated almost exclusively for the poor to make the universities, in the end, open almost exclusively to the rich? They, because they live entirely on their own means, are not very easily kept within the boundaries of standard instruction. Instead, they are generally also more devoted to other interests that are more profitable and less difficult, after they have graduated from one distinguished university or another. Like a dog at the Nile, they take a few licks and go away. They are not like a swan at the Thames that plunges into the water and builds a nest along its banks.

---

43. Ca. 1653.

44. 1646.

45. I.e., schools for the Muses, Oxford and Cambridge.

46. Publius Vergilius Maro (Vergil), 70–19 BC, Roman poet, *Aeneidos*, in *Opera* (Leipzig, 1616), bk. 2 (line 104). I.e., the enemy, Jesuits, would rejoice for the state to abandon Reformed schools.

"Now in order to lend my argument some strength and appeal, I would like to recount here as briefly as possible from reliable histories what Charlemagne[47] both attempted and accomplished. Claudius Clemens[48] and John Rabanus,[49] two students of the Venerable Bede,[50] crossed the channel to France. And while the brokers with whom they had sailed across set out their wares in the market, these two advertised that they had wisdom for sale. The event was reported to the emperor, and he—on the advice of our countryman Alcuin,[51] who was a product of that same school of Bede's—founded and built the famous school at Paris. He then entrusted it to the oversight of John and Claudius. After they had carefully kept watch over this responsibility for several years, the emperor, upon returning to France, wanted the young men there to appear before him and undergo an exam, in order that he might learn the character of the individual students. When this was completed, he easily determined that the young men of lower status had progressed much beyond expectation. But the nobles and the wealthier youth, immoderately engaged in maintaining their appearance, had paid only intermittent attention to the cultivation of the mind.[52] Therefore Charles—and in what follows, we are not speaking independently but quoting Aventinus—said to those who had been grouped on his right:

> 'You are to be treated as my most devoted sons for your progress in virtue, because you have nobly fulfilled my command. Your priesthoods will be very profitable and your ecclesiastical offices the most important. I will personally promote you to the court; I will select senators from among you. I will choose you for the register of government officials and for my senior cabinet.' Then to the children of the nobles whom he had placed on his left, with an expression that did not conceal his anger, he said: 'But you dandies and pretty boys, relying on the wealth and legacy of your parents, you have rejected my patronage. You have preferred vice, leisure, luxury, and sloth to liberal learning and the virtues, despising my command. This is my order, and I call the everlasting God to witness: do not expect any honor or benefit whatsoever, not even a penny, from your emperor whose commands you have scorned. I will see to it that you will

---

47. Charlemagne, ca. 742–814, r. 800–814, king of the Franks.
48. Claudius of Turin, d. ca. 828/840, Carolingian biblical exegete.
49. Rabanus Maurus, ca. 780–856, poet, teacher, and ecclesiastical administrator.
50. Bede, ca. 673–735, biblical exegete, hagiographer, and historian.
51. Alcuin, ca. 740–804, English theologian and adviser of Charlemagne.
52. Vid. *Osiandri* Centur. 8. p. 123. & *Hospinian.* de Templis, &c. p. 426.] Lucas Osiander, 1534–1604, German Lutheran pastor and hymn composer, *Epitomes Historiae Ecclesiasticae Centuriae Decimae Sextae*, [vol. 7], ([Tubigen, ca. 1602–1603?]), p. 123; Hospinian, *De Templis* (Tegernsee, 1603), bk. 4, ch. 5, p. 426.

live as a joke to all mortals, and I will make you an example unless, from
this time forward, you atone for your earlier neglect with hard work.'[53]

So wrote the famous Charlemagne, whom writers of no mean reputation
have designated by an unusual title, and one that we are unsure has ever
been attributed to another: *Father of the World*. If this makes any difference
to you, you can judge the matter for yourself.

"But now our opponents may start complaining about the character of
our countrymen, as that is so often on their tongue, almost in their very
spit! Let them seriously consider these claims: human society has never,
from the foundation of the world, been in such good shape that the majority are pleased with things that are better, much less that all are pleased with
what is best; and, one must not form an opinion about the tendency of the
majority based on the poor behavior of a minority. We willingly admit that
several times immoral young men have cropped up, loathsome and cancerous. One can perhaps say about them what Luther said about some young
men of Wittenberg, that 'so pronounced was their stubbornness that it cannot endure to admit that there are four elements.'[54] Nothing, however, is
more unjust than for the nature of these bad apples to become a yardstick
by which we measure the character of all the rest. May those who know
say what we ought to expect in Plato's *Republic*, provided they know what
they are saying. Meanwhile, we are sure that in Romulus's[55] sewer, the crop
does not grow without empty heads of grain. There is no peach without a
bitter pit, no assembly without vices, especially if it is made up of almost all
young whose veins run with blood and whose bones are filled with marrow.
From so many simmering pots there cannot help but be, not by a long shot,
some that foam and boil over. In such a large and diseased body, inevitably
at some point oozing, an ulcer, or something like that, arises.

"Therefore, against the indolent, we must counterbalance the self-
controlled, temperate, and learned. If England does not thank God for how
many of these there are, if she does not take from it some satisfaction, then
truly she must be considered the most ungrateful nation. Never among
the mature has more attention been given to prayers, lectures, and sacred
assemblies. Never have the younger students crowded around with more
enthusiasm to listen to sermons (one could wish that they did not queue
up to deliver them!). Yes, many of them can be charged with extravagance

---

53. Annal. 4°.] Johannes Aventinus, 1477–1534, Bavarian Renaissance humanist, historian,
and philologist, *Annalium Boiorum* (Frankfurt, 1627), bk. 4, p. 221.

54. Apud Contzen *Politic*. lib. 4. cap, 14, p. 245.] Adam Contzen, S.J., 1573–1635.

55. Mythical founder of Rome.

and sloth, if extreme devotion to literature is extravagance, if free time for studies is sloth! But those who typically turn pale from their pages[56] should not turn red from such accusations. Such boys think a night on the town is prison and their study carrel or classroom is paradise. And those whose life is spent in learning Christ so as to teach and in teaching Christ that they might learn have the same conviction. What of the fact that generally the extravagance that threatens us is the result of an inheritance? That the blame should not rest so much on the colleges as on the parents, who send their sons here to develop their minds but have already polluted them with the bad patterns of home? No, it is not at all surprising (though absolutely and entirely lamentable) if the vices that have invaded the entire Island have also blasted us."

So the universities conclude their address. If they had found a more eloquent spokesman, no doubt they would have stated their case much more brilliantly and to much greater effect. As for the rest, we must admonish the university students and plead with them through the deep mercy of Christ himself to oppose, from this point on, all Weigelians to a man, both those here at home as well as those abroad. Their standard-bearer, a trivial man, has shamefully dared to proclaim:

> There is no university in the whole world where Christ is found. In the universities, not one shred of knowledge of Christ can be found. Christ refused to let devils preach the gospel; therefore, he doesn't want scholars to either![57]

What a fanatic! We would need ten times as much hellebore as the Anticyrians have produced to cure him![58] If in our number there are any who hold this position, we must act (men, fathers, brothers) so that those who do not know how to yield to logic may, at last, believe their own ears and eyes, because in our sermons and life, they can hear nothing but Christ, see nothing but Christ. Livy called Greece the "salt of the nations."[59] May Cambridge and Oxford be the salt of England. So may no one be found

---

56. I.e., they do not go outside and get tanned by the sun.

57. Apud *Wendelin. in epistola dedic. quam praefixit Christian. Theologiae.*] Marcus Fridericus Wendelin, 1584–1652, German Reformed theologian, *Christianae Theologiae* (Amsterdam, 1646), sig.):(11v (*epistola dedicatoria*). The original is: "*in Academiis ne tantilla quidem Christi cognitio reperiri potest: nulla est in universe orbe Academia, in qua Christus reperiatur…noluit Christus Evangelium praedicari per diabolos.*"

58. Hellebore, a plant with medicinal powers growing plentifully near the Greek port city of Antikyra, near Corinth; medicines using hellebore could induce psychosis and could be poisonous.

59. Titus Livius (Livy), 59 BC–17 AD, Roman historian. Either a misattribution, or a summary of Livy's thought.

here a follower of the Roman Pope Paul II,[60] who (as Platina tells us) labeled as heretics, whether in earnest or jest, whoever mentioned the word *university*.[61] And he continuously urged the Romans not to allow their sons to persist in the study of literature, repeating that it was sufficient if they had learned just to read and write. That was Pope Paul, but it was not the apostle Paul. The latter, because he personally taught and argued in the school of Tyrannus, taught every one of us to have more respect for disputations and schools [Acts 19:9].

---

60. Pope Paul II, 1417–1471, r. 1464–1471, Italian pope.

61. Bartolomeo Platina, 1421–1481, Italian Renaissance humanist, *De Vitis Ac Gestis Summorum Pontificum* (1645), p. 787.

Second Speech against Weigelianism

Men, fathers, and dearest brothers in Christ:

When vices stand on the summit and errors are placed on the throne, while all things degenerate, it is difficult not to write satire, more difficult not to deserve it.[1] Among the endless Aristarchuses[2] of the great generation, two rose to prominence very recently. One of these railed at some length against Scholastic theology in his review of contemporary trends, and the other, in his review of the universities. Let us examine today, if that is acceptable, whether this beating is just or unjust. And as concern for duty requires, let us calmly consider what has been the status of institutions of learning at different times in church history and how, precisely, theology fared, paying the closest possible attention, so that, in the meantime, neither truth nor the province that we maintain suffers any loss or dishonor.

Offices for literature are believed to have existed from the remotest antiquity, rendered famous by the patriarchs and prophets that taught there. Nevertheless, after the passing of many centuries, Satan tried to corrupt some of them with his own counterfeits. He did this by setting up an oak tree at Dodona that foretold the future, on the very spot where the descendants of the *Dodonim*, from Japheth's grandsons,[3] were usually instructed about God, the Messiah, and morals. And elsewhere Satan established the oracle of Jupiter Hammon, where the offspring of Chami (otherwise known as Ham) were trained.[4]

But the schools were not yet deprived of their innocence; sacred theology did not yet suffer moral assault so long as the prophets survived. No

---

1. Here A. patterns his thought after Juvenal's *Satire* 1.30, especially *difficile est saturam non scribere*. Decimus Junius Juvenalis (Juvenal), ca. 60–ca. 140, Roman satirist.

2. Aristarchus, ca. 216–144 BC, Greek linguist and head of the Alexandrian library.

3. In Genesis 10, in the so-called table of nations, Dodanim is listed as the son of Javan (typically identified with the founder of Ionia), the son of Japheth. A.'s spelling is "Dodonim," likely to make the connection to Greek Δωδώνα appear closer.

4. Reference to the oracle of Jupiter Ammon, a Lybian (later, Egyptian) god.

heresies sprang up then (as van der Kun confirms),[5] though idolatry ran riot, until the prophets had departed from the land of the living. Their judgment was considered infallible. Then the people split into sects, and immediately the schools of the Hebrews changed into brothels of a highly speculative character. The Pharisees and Sadducees equally, like Harpies, spread their filth over everything. But even the Essenes themselves went astray, partly because they were overtaken by extreme solitude, partly by their zeal for allegory. Philo of Alexandria[6] reportedly succumbed to the first of these, and after him, Origen,[7] to the trap of the latter, which was the origin of monasticism. Nevertheless, it would seem that something wholesome remained among the Essenes from the fact that, while Christ spent time in those regions, we never read that this sect gave him any trouble nor harassed him. So, although Christ himself complained quite often about the teaching and character of the Pharisees and Sadducees, nowhere did he mention the Essenes.

Our discourse has now come down, as you realize, listeners, to a discussion of those times when not only the schools and the theology in them but also the church universal—actually, the whole world—stood in need of παλιγγενεσία.[8] As the sun of righteousness was rising, the shadows of error began to dissipate, some constellations of human perfection began to appear, and circumstances and people coming on the scene took on a new look. The blessed virgin found her far most blessed Son, already completing his twelfth year, among the teachers, ἀκούοντα αὐτῶν καὶ ἐπερωτῶντα (Luke 2:46).[9] Behold! Jesus, the undergraduate! His followers indeed pressed on in his steps. Look! In Acts, Stephen is arguing against the libertines and the sophists of different nations. See Paul against the Epicureans and Stoics, brandishing his arguments even in Athens and debating daily in the school of Tyrannus (Acts 6, 17, 19).

I think that very shrewd men such as yourselves have long before noticed how much these comments that I have made displease quarrelsome theology, even though it has become common practice among some men to launch their own speeches against our discourse with the remark from that stupid monk, who asserted that Christ was crowned with thorns in order to suffer the penalty for thorny arguments.

---

5. De Rep. Hebraeor. l. 2. c. 16.] Petrus Cunaeus, 1586–1638, Dutch theologian and Hebraist, *De Republica Hebraeorum* (Leiden, 1632), bk. 2, ch. 16, p. 193.

6. Philo of Alexandria, ca. 20 BC–ca. AD 40, Judaeo-Hellenist philosopher and exegete.

7. Origen, ca. 185–ca. 254, exegete and theologian.

8. "Regeneration."

9. "Listening to and questioning them."

I know that the lust for wrangling has always most seriously displeased the most serious students, so much so that the very famous Sir Henry Wotton,[10] when he was provost of Eton, stipulated in his will that the only epitaph to be engraved on his tomb was this: "Here lies the author of this statement: the itch to debate is the rash of the churches." And the distinguished gentleman Abraham Bucholzer, when he was thoroughly exasperated with theological quarrels, returned to the study of chronology, telling his friends, "I'd rather calculate than pontificate!"[11]

Nevertheless, it is necessary and useful to build around the church a hedge made up of these thorny arguments so that heretics do not break into the vineyard of the Lord like wild beasts and the truth does not disappear as their plunder. Certainly, the papists shudder at the disputations of our scholars and tremble at their shafts, plucked from the quiver of the Scriptures. This phrase may serve as an example, published in the year of our Lord 1532 at Geneva, when Farel[12] and Salner[13] stood clad for battle, about to contend against the faith of the Romanists from the sacred text: "If one argues with this, the whole mystery of our faith will be ruined."[14] And there is this remark from that important cardinal[15] who, after he had heard Theodore Beza's speech delivered at the Colloquy of Poissy, reportedly remarked to his companions, "I wish that either this guy were mute or we all were deaf!"[16]

Do you want me to summarize it for you? Here, in a few words, is the bulk of it. For the people, one must draw from his oratorical quiver and employ enticements. But if you must deal with educated men, then he who soldiers with the open palm of dialectic fights too gently, while he who strikes with the fist wins the palm branch of victory.

But, to return to the path from this small digression, we must descend from the apostles to the fathers. Not only did the most eloquent orators and sophisticated debaters emerge from their schools but theologians did

---

10. Henry Wotton, 1568–1639, diplomat and writer.

11. Ord. fratrum Bohem. p. 118.] Abraham Bucholzer, 1529–1584, German Lutheran theologian, [Elders and Ministers of the Bohemian Brothers], *Ratio Disciplinae Ordinisque Ecclesiastici In Unitate Fratrum Bohemorum*, ([Leszno], 1633), p. 118.

12. Guillaume Farel, 1489–1565, French Reformer in Geneva.

13. Anthony Salner, early Genevan Reformer.

14. *Abr. Sculteti* Annal. decad. 2. p. 389.] Abraham Scultetus, 1566–1625, German Reformed theologian, *Annalium Evangelii Passim*, vol. 2 (Heidelberg, 1620), [p. 389].

15. Charles de Guise, 1525–1574, French cardinal of Lorraine.

16. *Rivet.* Cathol. Orthod. part. 2. tractat. 1. quaest. 8 § 4.] André Rivet, 1572–1651, French Reformed theologian, *Catholicus Orthodoxus Oppositus Catholico Papistae* (Geneva, 1644), vol. 1, tract. 1, qu. 8, sec. 4, p. 80.

as well, consummately prepared in every respect. Is there anyone so leaden in their understanding that he is not captivated by these: the apologetic writings of Justin,[17] Tertullian,[18] Athenagoras,[19] and others; the exegetical works of Jerome,[20] Chrysostom,[21] Theodoret,[22] and other interpreters like that; the pedagogical treatises of Cyril,[23] Cyprian,[24] and Lactantius;[25] the polemic works of Optatus[26] against the Donatists,[27] Athanasius[28] against the Arians,[29] and of course, Augustine[30] against the Manichees[31] and Pelagians[32]—and I should say, not just captivated but carried off to thrilling heights? Now I am not someone who would dare to say of the fathers what Erasmus said of the church: "The fathers' authority carries such weight with me that I could agree with Arians and Pelagians if the fathers had approved what they taught."[33] Nevertheless, I honor their hoary age as I should; I esteem their impressive learning; I embrace their positions provided they are consistent with sacred Scripture. But if they depart from that standard, I respect the fathers in a way that recognizes they are mortal.

Actually, to acknowledge the real substantive point, the theology of the fathers would have been a much more excellent vintage had they not diluted it with the pagan philosophy that they had first decanted from the Stoa, Lyceum, or Academy. Why does Tertullian, with such indignation, say, "What does Athens have to do with Jerusalem? The Academy with the church? Our system of instruction is derived from the portico of Solomon. They should carefully examine what kind of Stoic, Platonic, and dialectic

---

17. Justin Martyr, ca. 100–ca. 164, Christian apologist.

18. Tertullian, ca. 160–ca. 220, theologian and apologist.

19. Athenagoras, fl. ca. 177, Christian apologist.

20. Jerome, ca. 347–419, biblical scholar.

21. John Chrysostom, 347–407, of Antioch, bishop of Constantinople, exegete, and preacher.

22. Theodoret, ca. 393–ca. 466, bishop of Cyrrhus.

23. Cyril, ca. 370/380–444, bishop of Alexandria.

24. Cyprian, d. 258, bishop of Carthage.

25. Lactantius, ca. 250–ca. 325, Christian apologist.

26. Optatus, fl. fourth century AD, bishop of Milevis.

27. Followers of Donatus, fl. ca. 310–ca. 355, desired to maintain purity of the church from *traditores*.

28. Athanasius, ca. 295–373, bishop of Alexandria.

29. Followers of Arius, ca. 260–336, who denied the consubstantiality of the Son of God.

30. Augustine, 354–430, bishop of Hippo.

31. Followers of Mani, ca. 216–76, believed in a dualistic view of good and evil in the universe.

32. Followers of Pelagius, ca. 354–post-418, who denied the Augustinian conception of sin and grace.

33. In Epistola ad *Bilibaldum*.] Desiderius Erasmus, ca. 1467–1536, Dutch humanist scholar, *Magni Des. Erasmi Roterodami Vita Accedent Epistolae Illustres* (Lyon, 1642), p. 278. This volume contains a vita of Erasmus followed by a collection of his letters.

Christianity they have produced."[34] Would he not have thundered with much more lightning in his speech, dear listeners, that man of unmatched eloquent bombast, if perhaps Nestorean years[35] had brought him to the Scholastic age, when this malignant method of teaching had grown into so tall a tree, which then was just a little shoot and a slender plant?

These successors of the fathers turned some of their insights into vice. Perhaps it will be worthwhile today to spend a little time detailing them. Neglect of the sacred Scriptures deservedly heads the list. For sure, those styled Scholastics showed more careful attention to that dung pit of the gentiles than they did to the perfumed flagons of the prophets and apostles, as if they had preferred Plato to Paul, and Aristotle by himself to all the scribes of the Holy Spirit! Indeed, in the whole of Peter Lombard,[36] we do not read the name Aristotle once (as Daneau notes).[37] But among Lombard's descendants—and there are as many devotees of the *Sentences* as there are of the *Summa*[38]—Aristotle fills each page, as they say. And after Hales[39] and William of Auxerre[40] had escorted Aristotle to the doorstep of the temple, and Thomas[41] and Albert[42] brought him to the inner sanctum, then, until the time of Luther, he held almost sole and absolute sway in theology. Then, his writings were treated as oracles. And meanwhile, the sacred oracles of God held second place, so that so great a man as Heinrich Bullinger dared to state his opinion in the following words: "Seneca,[43] by himself, has left posterity more genuine theology than all the books of almost all the Scholastics."[44]

There then comes a massive obsession with wrangling and arguing. This stirred up the great Calvin's[45] bile so much that he dubbed Scholastic

---

34. Lib. de praesciption.] Tertullian, *de Praescriptionibus Adversus Haereticos*, ch. 7 in *Opera quae hactenus reperiri*, (Cologne, 1617).

35. Old age. A reference to Nestor, a garrulous aged warrior in Homer's epics.

36. Peter Lombard, ca. 1100–1160, bishop of Paris.

37. Prolegom. ad *Lombardum* cap. 2.] Lambert Daneau, 1530–1595, French Calvinist jurist and theologian, *In Petri Lombardi* (Geneva, 1580), ch. 2, sig. **2 (*prolegomena*).

38. *Tam sententarios quam summistas.*

39. Alexander of Hales, ca. 1186–1245, English Franciscan theologian.

40. William of Auxerre (Autissiodorensis), ca. 1140/1150–1231, French Scholastic theologian, probably *Summa Aurea* ([Paris], 1514).

41. Thomas Aquinas, ca. 1225–1274, Dominican philosopher and theologian.

42. Albertus Magnus, d. 1280, German Dominican theologian and philosopher.

43. Lucius Annaeus Seneca the Younger, ca. 4 BC–AD 65, Roman Stoic philosopher.

44. In Comment. ad Rom. 1.19.] Heinrich Bullinger, 1504–1575, Swiss Reformed theologian, *In Omnes Pauli Apostoli Epistolas* (Tegernsee, 1603), sub loc. Rom. 1:20.

45. John Calvin, 1509–1564, French Reformed theologian.

theology the "art of demonic quarreling."[46] If no one forbids telling the truth while laughing, you will enjoy hearing one of our countrymen making fun of this subject in a little poem entitled *The Balm for and Rejection of the Popish Religion.*[47]

From his high oak Peter fights,[48] and John attacks from mountain.[49]
Each fierce, his hand emboldened.
Alphonsi[50] thunders, and Hugh too,[51] harsh and with more volume;
One Nick trembled, one Nick creaked.[52]
Jodocus[53] this proves, but Faber[54] then straight off disproves it,
Then Occam[55] proves again, as
Thomas[56] preps for war while Scotus[57] groans from gullet grimly.
Andrada[58] and Driedo,[59]
Throw in Catharinus[60] and Carthusian Denis,[61] mystic,
Each beats and batters hard his
Foe head on! Look Guido,[62] Capistrano,[63] and de Soto,[64]
Copo,[65] Cano,[66] dogmas old,
Each bludgeons with a dogma new, as to each is custom,
On each to waste his labor.[67]

---

46. Comment. b 1 Tim. 1.] *Diabolicam artem litigandi.* Calvin, *Commentarii*, sub loc. 1 Tim. 1:4; Calvin's Latin here is *diabolica ista ars litigandi.*

47. *Melissa Religionis Pontificiae Eiusdemque Apotrope.* See note 69.

48. Peter Lombard. The region of Lombardy is famous for oak trees. Perhaps the oak serves as an example of Aristotelian philosophy in his *Sentences'* argument on causality and necessary change. The poem pays little regard to the chronology—e.g., Thomas (d. 1274) is presented as preparing to battle with Scotus (b. ca. 1265).

49. John of Salisbury, ca. 1100–1180, scholar, ecclesiastical diplomat, and bishop of Chartres.

50. Peter Alfonsi, fl. 1106–1126, scholar and translator of scientific works.

51. Hugh of St. Victor, d. 1142, Victorine theologian and writer.

52. Nicholas of Cusa, 1401–1464, German cardinal and philosopher, and Nicholas of Lyra, ca. 1270–1349, Franciscan theologian and biblical commentator, respectively. A. skips two lines here.

53. Jodocus Trutfetter, 1460–1519, professor of philosophy at Erfurt.

54. Perhaps Johannes Faber of Bordeaux, d. 1350.

55. William of Ockham, ca. 1285–1347, English philosopher, theologian, and polemicist.

56. Thomas Aquinas.

57. John Duns Scotus, ca. 1265–1308, Franciscan friar and theologian.

58. Diogo de Payva d'Andrada (Andradius), 1528–1575, Portuguese Tridentine theologian.

59. Jan Driedo, d. 1535, Belgian Catholic divine.

60. Ambrosio Catarino Politi (Ambrosius Catharinus), 1484–1553, archbishop of Conza.

61. Dionysius the Carthusian, 1402–1471, theologian and mystic.

62. Guido Terrena, d. 1342, Catalan Carmelite and theologian.

63. Giovanni Capistrano, 1386–1456, Franciscan friar.

64. Dominic de Soto, 1494–1560, Roman Catholic imperial delegate to the Council of Trent.

65. Giacomo (Jacopo) Zabarella, 1533–1589, Italian Aristotelian philosopher and logician.

66. Melchor Cano, ca. 1509–1560, Spanish Dominican theologian.

67. A. skips ten lines here.

> So in mighty drawn-up ranks, like soldiers of fierce Cadmus,[68]
> They fall beneath each other.[69]

I can overlook the barbarity of their style. For although their "formalities, modalities, quiddities, haeceities, homogeneities," and "suppositalities"—and that class of monstrous words which almost frighten by their very sound—should be sport for refined geniuses, nevertheless, no matter how these wondry-warbling words strike the ears they can be tolerated provided they instruct the mind. And I do not think that such gross ignorance of the original languages should be blamed on these men but rather on the misfortune of the age in which they peaked. Such ignorance, the mother of many errors, definitely existed then in some form, since (according to Claude d' Espence) "knowing Greek was suspect," "knowing Hebrew almost heretical."[70] But we must not keep quiet about the wickedness of these men when it comes to their behavior. This was reportedly so great that among the Germans in the fourteenth century (according to Luther), such malfeasance became proverbial: "If you see a Scholastic theologian, you see the seven deadly sins."[71]

The shameful abuse of philosophy will close out the account. After the dogmas of faith began to be publicly enforced according to philosophy's standard, almost nothing healthy was left in the whole system of the Christian religion. If you prefer, listen to other men on this subject so no one may complain that I am carried away by sectarian zeal. "Scholastic philosophers take pleasing notions into their theological school, and from two things that are in themselves good, they have concocted something very bad; from two things that are undamaged, they have made one that is corrupt." That is Gerhard's comment.[72] "After the Scholastics rejected Plato, Aristotle was then forced into a confession of the prophets and apostles and diverted the debate on the standard of truth almost completely away from Christ himself, particularly on the doctrine περὶ τοῦ ἐνδεχομένου καὶ

---

68. Mythological founder and first king of Thebes.

69. *Georg. Goodwin.* p. 93, 94.] George Goodwin, fl. 1620, Latin poet, *Melissa Religionis Pontificiae Eiusdemque Apotrope* (London, 1620), pp. 93–94.

70. In 2 Tim. 3. digress. 17.] Claude d'Espence, 1511–1571, French Roman Catholic theologian and diplomat, *In Posteriorem D. Pauli Apostoli Ad Timotheum* (Paris, 1564), ch. 3, dig. 17, p. 116.

71. Luther. Epist. tom. 1. Epist. 129.] Luther, *Epistolarum Reverendi Patris Domini D. Martini Lutheri*, vol. 1 (Ithenae, 1556), p. 218 (*Epist.* 129); A. changes vocabulary and retains sense.

72. Loc. com. de Ecclesia §228.] Johann Gerhard, 1582–1637, Lutheran theologian, *Locorum Theologicorum Cum Pro Adstruenda Veritate*, vol. 5, (Jena, 1620), ch. 1, sec. 6, § 228, p. 1071.

αὐτεξουσίου."[73] That is Tilenus's conclusion.[74] "They entered the Lord's sanctuary with unclean feet and polluted theology with their philosophy, since they were far more devoted to the natural light of reason than was appropriate." That is Rainolds.[75] But theology has degenerated so far in some places that men have introduced and exegeted a text from Aristotle's *Ethics* for a sermon! Philip[76] tells us this happened at Tubingen.

At the absolute nadir of both sacred and literary fortunes, the Lord pitied his church and raised up Luther, Melanchthon, and other supporters to clean out the dregs from religion, lopping off the cancerous portions that I mentioned so the whole, healthy body would not be dragged under. Consequently, it came to pass that in the Reformed schools, a far different and more beautiful state of affairs then arose than what previously existed among the papist schools. And theology, which had been a serpent, according to the pattern of Moses's rod, was transformed into a shepherd's staff. More than that, within the course of only one generation, Scholastic doctors became so worthless that Chamier admitted to the Jesuit Coton[77] he "usually consulted them like someone visiting a once-impressive building. After the splendor of the halls, bedrooms, and dining areas, he does not refuse to poke his head into the bathrooms, but only for a moment because of the smell."[78] Whitaker, in his own unique way like always, comments on these same topics with deceptive modesty: "The Scholastics have more sophistry than knowledge, more knowledge than doctrine, more doctrine than usefulness, more usefulness than relevance to salvation."[79]

If anyone proves that the vices of the old Scholastics whom I have spoken about today are banished from our schools, however many there are, I do not think there will be any reason for our opponents to keep on barking. Now this important task remains, and in executing it carefully, even

---

73. "Concerning what lies within one's own power."

74. Syntag. part. 2. Disp. 16. thes. 31.] Daniel Tilenus, 1563–1633, French theologian, *Syntagma Disputationum Theologicarum* (Herborn, 1607), part 2, disput. 16, thes. 31, pp. 158–59.

75. Collat. cum *Harto* cap. 2. D. 3.] John Rainolds, 1549–1607, English Puritan and theologian, *Summa Colloquii Cum Johanne Harto* (London, 1611). An amalgamated quotation: the 1611 edition speaks of *illotis pedibus ingressi sunt Jehovae sanctuarium* on page 49 (see E1), discussing Scholastic corruption; second citation unknown.

76. I.e., Philip Melanchthon, 1497–1560, Lutheran theologian and humanist.

77. Pierre Coton, 1564–1626, French Jesuit theologian and royal confessor.

78. In Epistolis Jesuiticis.] Daniel Chamier, 1565–1621, French Reformed theologian, *Epistolae Jesuiticae* (Amberg, 1604), p. 224.

79. Ap. *Ol. Bowles* pastor. Evangelic. p. 128.] William Whitaker, quoted in Oliver Bowles, ca. 1577–1644, member pf Westminster Assembly, *De Pastore Evangelico Tractatus* (London, 1649), bk. 1, ch. 19, can. 3, p. 128.

should our strength perhaps fail, still the attempt will be worthwhile. But the attempt must be carried out in very few words so I do not bore the audience. Although today's Rome goes well beyond bold, I would scarcely believe it has reached such a point of brazen disrespect that it would dare assail the evangelical churches for barbarity of style or ignorance of the languages. Calvin's *Institutes*,[80] Jewel's *Apology*,[81] Whitaker's *Address to Campian* and *Responses to Dureau*,[82] along with the thousands of other writings of our countrymen, are so powerful due to the purity of their style that if they had been delivered from the rostrum in ancient Rome, there is absolutely no doubt that they would have won praise, perhaps applause, even if they were not understood.

Now to the question of the languages: After Constantinople was captured by the Turks, Greece fled across the Alps. Whatever Athens had once taught began to be studied in England, France, and the Netherlands. Likewise, today almost all of Palestine, together with its surrounding territories, seems to have voluntarily moved to the Reformed universities.[83]

But I will endeavor to make absolutely clear from the words, prayers, and complaints of primary sources just how much the constant quarreling has displeased both the rectors and the graduates of these institutions. When Luther had not yet appeared but was still on the horizon, Konrad Summenhart[84] taught at Tubingen. This was his complaint: "Who will free me from this divisive theology?"[85] Supposedly, Luther's own prayer was as follows (paraphrased) and was also adopted by David Pareus: "Lord, free your church from the boastful scholar, the quarrelsome pastor, and useless debates."[86] Next, Melanchthon—that man in whom true religion competed with learning, and honesty with both—when he was on the very brink of death, said, "I want to relocate from this life for two reasons: First, I want to enjoy the vision of the Son of God and of the heavenly church that I have longed for. Second, I want to be free from the dreadful and implacable

---

80. Calvin, *Institutio Christianae Religionis* (Geneva, 1559).

81. John Jewel, 1522–1572, bishop of Salisbury, *A defence of the Apologie of the Churche of Englande* (London, 1567).

82. William Whitaker, *Ad Rationes Decem Edmundi Campiani Jesuitæ* (London, 1581).

83. I.e., Hebrew and other oriental languages.

84. Konrad Summenhart, ca. 1450–1502, German theologian.

85. *M. Adam*. Vit German. Theol. p. 13.] Melchior Adam, d. 1622, German Reformed literary historian, *Vitae Germanorum Theologorum* (Heidelberg, 1620), p. 13. This echoes Romans 7, of course.

86. Vita *Parei* pag. antepen.] Johann Philip Pareus, 1576–1648, German Reformed Latinist, *Narratio Historica De Curriculo Vitae* (Frankfurt, 1633), p. 173; David Pareus, 1548–1622, professor of New Testament at the Univeristy of Heidelberg.

hatreds of the theologians."[87] Clearly, these men preferred to believe in the simplicity of the gospel than to search out inquisitive riddles. They liked salvation more than endless chatter.

Generally, piety has always been apparent in Protestant professors. So we must believe that the one who sees a Reformed scholar has beheld not the seven deadly sins but the three theological virtues. It is evident how much these Protestant scholars have relied upon the sacred Scriptures, how little upon philosophy, contrary to the Scholastics' typical practice. I wouldn't want to light a lamp about the subject in the clear light of day! So I will summarize it all in a word: philosophy behaved toward theology in the schools, at least of the fathers, like an *ally*; in the training schools of the Scholastics, like a *schoolmistress*; in the hallowed chairs of Reformed universities, like a *maidservant*. If anyone begrudges philosophy that post, I think such a man truly has treated theology badly, philosophy worse, and the church worst of all.

---

87. *M. Adam.* ibid. p. 427. in vita *Strigelii.*] Adam, *Vitae Germanorum Theologorum*, p. 427.

Third Speech against Weigelianism

The noble, venerable, learned crown for alumni and visitors alike:

As soon as the liberal arts curriculum was, with consummate barbarity, wrenched away from scholars and churchmen alike and scholarly degrees were devalued, that old complaint could have been used: "Today, the church and university alike have been saturated with poison." Although I cannot by eloquence put a nice face on these developments, still, I do not want to pass them over in silence. The task is now yours, you young men of noblest character, of brightest hope. Your favorite volumes have fallen from your grasp while the stricter Muses are considered, at any rate, not readily conversant with philology. It is worse than that, fathers and brothers. You are going to be stripped immediately of your purple insignia, and your titles will be trampled upon, unless you consent to be blasted by a savage bolt of lightning and to be styled "soldiers of Antichrist."[1]

Why would it be inappropriate to warn my own son carefully, who sits here today with us in this most distinguished lecture hall, steeped in his father's teaching, to be on guard against all strange leaven, specifically the Weigelian kind? I am presenting here just little bits and selected portions of it. The power of any kind of heterodox leaven is such that even a little bit immediately works through the whole lump, as the proverb that Paul mentions several times demonstrates [Gal. 5:9]. Error, pimped out by novelty, spreads rather quickly through the whole family, city, church, and surrounding area, as we have personally experienced a thousand times in the age we now inhabit. Luther experienced this before us, so no one should conclude that this disease perhaps roamed only through England.

There were ten years of work before we had a properly and righteously established little church. And as soon as it was in place, some fanatical

---

1. I.e., adherents or defenders of the papacy.

idiot laid hold of it. His only skill was slandering devout teachers of the Word. In one instant, he overthrew everything.

Thus Luther.[2]

I wish that young men were only drawn to the secondary properties of this leaven since they find any frantic activity pleasant, as the etymology of these words shows. Leaven makes the lump of dough "boil hot." So in Latin the word for fermentation is derived from *ferveo*, like *fervimentum*. This is just like Greek, where ζύμη comes from ζέω. Leaven also causes the dough to "swell," and thus the French and British have described it using a term derived from *levare*.[3] Finally, it makes the dough "sour"; therefore, in Hebrew, it is termed חָמֵץ from a root חָמֵץ meaning acidic.

Proponents of errors are generally very combative, somewhat more ardent in temperament, and on the whole, as they say, "on the boil." I am referring to the more inflexible Lutherans.[4] Among them, Jakob Andreae:[5] near the close of the Colloquy of Montbéliard,[6] when Beza had said, "We are grieved about this disagreement but still desire to maintain brotherly fellowship with you," Andreae offered him the right hand of human kindness but denied him that of brotherly love.[7] This is the report of Konrad Schlüsselburg,[8] who writes that he himself, according to the command of God, persecutes the Reformed as heretics with a perfect hatred.[9] Brenz[10] likewise, in his notes composed on the New Testament (if Hospinian is reliable on this), sounds the trumpet for waging ἄσπονδον[11] war with the Zwinglians.[12] And he appeals to the magistrates not to grant them any standing in the true church of Christ and no place to rest in Germany. It really breaks my heart and embarrasses Protestants how many

---

2. Tom. Oper. 4° fol. 18. A.] Probably referring to Andreas Karlstadt (Bodenstein) ca. 1480–1541, German Reformer. Luther, *Tomus Quartus Omnium Operum* (Wittenberg, 1574).

3. "To raise up."

4. Followers of the German Reformer Martin Luther and the later Lutheran tradition.

5. Jakob Andreae, 1528–1590, German Lutheran theologian.

6. 1586.

7. *Hoornbeck* summa controvers. p. 566.] Johann Hoornbeeck, 1617–1666, Dutch Reformed theologian, *Summa Controversiarum Religionis* (Utrecht, 1653), bk. 9, p. 566. The original is *se non fraternitatis, sed quidem humanitatis dexteram ei porrecturum*, while A. has *Dextram illi humanitatis quidem obtulit, sed fraternitatis negavit*.

8. Konrad Schlüsselburg, 1543–1619, Lutheran pastor and controversialist.

9. Ibid. p. 576.] Hoornbeeck, *Summa Controversiarum Religionis*, bk. 9, p. 576.

10. Johannes Brenz, 1499–1570, German Lutheran theologian and Reformer.

11. "Endless."

12. Concordia discors in praefatione.] Rudolf Hospinian, *Concordia Discors* (Tegernsee, 1607), fol. 6v (in preface). The Zwinglians are followers of Ulrich Zwingli, 1484–1531, Swiss Reformed theologian and Reformer.

times the Jesuit Adam Contzen expresses this idea: "If anyone bothers to read the Lutherans' belligerent works against Calvinists or the Calvinists' against Lutherans, he will convince himself that these are not the railing insults of men against men but the crazed ravings and roaring of demons against demons."[13]

Again, you all realize that I spoke of the swelling of a fermented lump of dough. This is a metaphor for arrogance, for the experience of every age screams that arrogance is error's completely inseparable companion. Chrysostom remarks on this in his work on the Anomoeans,[14] saying, "Paul did not plant this tree of heresy, Apollos did not water it. But arrogance planted it, jealousy watered it."[15] Bonaldus's remarkable statement will give ample proof of just how much today's Jesuits are swollen with pride. One would have difficulty saying whether it is more full of arrogance or falsehood: "You can combine together day and night, light and darkness, hot and cold, health and sickness, life and death. Only then will there be any possibility of charging any single Jesuit[16] with heresy."[17] Why should I bother mentioning Paracelsus?[18] When he had become bald in the front, he "boasted that the stupidest hair on the back of his head knew more than all the followers of Galen,[19] and his beard had more experience than all universities."[20] Why mention Henry Nicolis,[21] founder of the so-called Familists? A quite distinguished author reports that while living among the Dutch, he used to boast that "he should be preferred over Moses and Christ, in that Moses had taught hope, Christ had taught faith, while he taught that love was

---

13. Politicor. l. 2. c. 19. § 6.] Adam Contzen, b. 1573, Belgian Jesuit theologian and controversialist, *Politicorum* (Cologne, 1629), bk. 2, ch. 19, sec. 6, p. 109.

14. Followers of Eunomius of Cyzicus, d. ca. 394, Arian theologian.

15. Paraphrase of Chrysostom, *Ad populum Antiochenum Adv. Juadaeos, De Incomprehensibili Dei Natura* (Paris, 1602); *On the Incomprehensible Nature of God*, trans. P. W. Harkins, Fathers of the Church, vol. 72 (Washington, D.C.: Catholic University of America Press, 1982), p. 96.

16. Members of the Society of Jesus, founded by Ignatius Loyola in 1540.

17. *Bonaldi* Apolog. c. 3.] Francois Bonald, d. 1614, French Jesuit ascetic theologian. *Responsio Apologetica* (Lyon, 1611), ch. 3, p. 102. A. translates loosely here. The original reads, *Dies societur nocti, lux tenebris, calor frigori, sanitati morbus; tunc obtineri poterit, ut sanis opinionibus, insana haereticorum deliramenta intra Iesuitae, qua Iesuitae, cerebrum coniugari possint.* A.'s rendition reads, *Jungantur in unum dies cum nocte, lux cum tenebris, calidum cum frigido, sanitas cum morbo, vita cum morte; et erit tum spes aliqua posse in caput Jesuitae haeresin cadere.*

18. Theophrast Bombast von Hohenheim (Theophrastus Paracelsus), 1493–1541, Swiss physician and Neoplatonic theologian.

19. Mattheus van Galen, ca. 1528–1573, Dutch Roman Catholic theologian and member of the Council of Trent.

20. Apud *Hoornbeck* in commentario de *Weigelian.* pag. 6.] Hoornbeeck, *De Paradoxis et Heterodoxis Weigelianis* (Utrecht, 1646), p. 6.

21. Hendrik Niclaes, 1502–1580, German Anabaptist and mythical pantheist.

greater than both. And moreover, that Moses had stood in the foyer, Christ had entered into the holy place, but he himself had gone into the holy of holies."[22] Heretical arrogance and diabolical blasphemy, dear listeners, are separated by such a fine line!

Finally, the flavor of fermented bread mixed with acid and salt inevitably whets the appetite and ingratiates itself with the palate. Generally speaking, the cloying enticements of errors are like that. Truth breathes a kind of divinity, while heterodoxy smacks of and promotes something human. I will speak very broadly here. Socinianism was entirely engineered, or at least seems to be, to flatter the human reason, which it established as judge in matters concerning the faith; Remonstrantism,[23] to flatter human judgment, to which this error ascribed the business of salvation from stem to stern, so to speak; the papal religion, to flatter the human senses, which it gently gratifies with the most elaborate system; Libertinism, to flatter those human emotions to which it usually gave free rein.

But my oration should now return to the point where I first began. As you accurately remember, a certain man named Weigel was getting the worst of it, as if he were the keenest enemy of the liberal arts and of university ranks as well. For now, all you need to know is one or two statements of his on this topic that I have right here. There is no time to trot out the whole armada.[24] He says,

> I set before myself papists, Lutherans, Calvinists, and every other sect. I compare them to the traits of Antichrist, and from their distinctive qualities, I easily recognize how much these sects correspond to false prophets. I assert, furthermore, that the entire ecclesiastical system, together with all the schools in the New Testament, in the age of the Son, is part of a cursed tree. No good fruit grows upon it nor can ever do so.[25]

Elsewhere he says,

> True theology is simple. It does not need the arts of public speaking, grammar, dialectic, and rhetoric. It does not need the original languages—actually, has no use for them—since the apostles and prophets were just as much theologians without these.[26]

Do you want to hear more?

---

22. *Jo. Laet.* compend. historiae. Univers. pag. 583.] Johannes de Laet, 1581–1649, Dutch geographer, *Compendium Historiae Universalis* (Leiden, 1643), ch. 32, sec. 2, art. 3, p. 583.

23. Remonstrants, Dutch followers of Jacob Arminius.

24. *Camarinam*, a colony of Syracuse on the southwest coast of Sicily.

25. *Hoornbeck* Comment de *Weigel*. p. 10.] Hoornbeck, *De Paradoxis Et Heterodoxis Weigelianis*, pp. 9–10.

26. Hoornbeck, *De Paradoxis Et Heterodoxis Weigelianis*, p. 11.

No doctor, teacher, lawyer will enter heaven any more than the adulterer. No astronomer, physician, scientist, philosopher, or master of arts or languages will enter heaven.[27]

Are you not stopping up your ears, fathers and brothers? Are you not yet retching? It would be painful, no doubt, to go on further, even though there are a million other things, that

Crazed Orestes[28] would plain swear, suit a crazed man anywhere.[29]

Nevertheless, I personally am unsure whether this statement from our countrymen, not to mention Protestant theologians generally, who assert that the leading Reformers held the same opinion, is more reliable or misleading. Luther, whose reputation and influence they chatter on about more than the rest, rather vigorously attacked the papists' schools, degrees, literature, and all the rest with as much heat as he could muster, since they were disfigured by serious superstition. Still, Luther quite openly acknowledges the legitimate use of both philology and philosophy, specifically in theology. The letters that he wrote survive in two volumes published separately. In the first, he says,

> I am convinced that there is no way theology proper can survive without knowledge of literature, just as up to this point—when literature is so lamentably devastated and ruined—theology has collapsed and lies in ruins. But yet I see that never has a notable revelation of God's word occurred except when first he prepared the way, so to speak, with "Baptists as forerunners," namely, the revival and blossoming of languages and literature.[30]

In the second one, he writes, "I hold that those men are seriously mistaken and off by a mile who think philosophy and knowledge of the natural world useless for theology."[31] The same distinguished doctor—yes, more angelic even than Aquinas himself published a golden little book for training children. He dedicated it to the magistrates and nobles of the cities of Germany. In it he speaks about the study of language like this:

> Languages are like scabbards in which the sword of the Spirit, the word of God, rests at the ready. They are the boxes or treasure chests that preserve

---

27. Id. ibid. p. 24, & 25.] Hoornbeeck, *De Paradoxis Et Heterodoxis Weigelianis*, pp. 24–25.

28. Orestes, son of Agamemnon and Clytemnestra.

29. Persius, 34–62, Roman poet and satirist, *Satyrarum* (Heidelberg, 1590), 3.118.

30. Epist. tom. 2. p. 307.] Luther, *Epistolarum Reverendi Patris Domini D. Martini Lutheri*, vol. 2 (Eisleben, 1565), fol. 307v.

31. Epist. tom. 1. p. 360.] Luther, *Epistolarum*, vol. 1, fol. 360r.

this noble κειμήλιον[32] entrusted to them for storage. They are the pitchers from which we distribute the saving drink we have received, the ready storehouses from which the preacher draws out the nourishing food of the gospel. Finally, languages are the baskets in which the loaves and fishes, as well as the leftover pieces, are kept safe so they do not perish.[33]

About himself, Luther says, "I am now overcome with so much regret, because I have not read more of the poets and historians."[34] He says about ministerial candidates, "It is only right that they, more than others, be quite earnestly, or even entirely, intent upon devotion to good literature." On the topic of setting up libraries, he says, "There must be a place reserved there for the poets as well as the orators, whether they were Christian or pagan. Because," he says, "it is from them that grammar is learned." So says Luther, who, in my opinion, no one will describe as a γραμματομάστιξ[35] except as slander.

Luther's faithful Achates[36] Melanchthon immediately graced with Latin that little book on training children that I just mentioned. And in a letter, he dedicated it to all students. If I am not badly mistaken, it includes this short yet memorable statement:

> Those who here and there in their conversations dissuade inexperienced youth from the study of literature should immediately have their tongues cut out. We see how fragile true religion once became when barbarism was let in. And I am quite afraid that unless we defend tooth and nail that most beautiful gift of God, literature, we will come back to the same spot.[37]

Bravo, Philip! You have hit the nail on the head yet touched our hearts with a sure feeling of the truth.

But so my rather lengthy speech not cause you all boredom and indigestion, as I wrap up, please note what such great men really thought about our university degrees, especially the doctorate in theology and its conventions. Luther reached this rank when he was thirty years old.[38] Still, he

---

32. "Heirloom."

33. Oper. *Witeberg.* tom. 7. fol. 442.] Martin Luther, *Tomus Septimus Omnium Operum*, (Wittenberg, 1574), fol. 442r–v.

34. Ibid. fol. 444. A.] Luther, *Tomus Septimus Omnium Operum*, fol. 445r.

35. "Grammar-cop," i.e., someone who thinks rules should never be bent and is insistent on enforcing them.

36. Trusted companion of Aeneas in Vergil's *Aeneid*.

37. Perhaps in Philip Melanchthon, *Scholasticorum Academiae Witebergensis Ad Omnes Pios Cives Ecclesiarum* (Wittenberg, 1558).

38. *Mel. Adam.* in Vita *Lutheri* p. 105.] Adam, *Vitae Germanorum Theologorum*, p. 105.

modestly refused it until Staupitz,[39] to whom Luther always deferred with the greatest respect, had incessantly begged that he submit to that honor. And Staupitz had also predicted that God would have many things for him to do in the church for which Luther would find this title useful. Even though Philip[40] was content with just the title *master*, still, he viewed and spoke about the doctorate as valuable. His own words in a particular private letter make this clear:

> You notice my example. Nobody could force me to allow the honorific title *doctor* to be conferred on me. Yet I do not undervalue academic degrees. But because I hold that the state's burdens are large and inescapable, I think that such degrees should be pursued for the right reasons and then conferred.[41]

We must not ignore the example of Jerome Zanchi. Pierre Bouquin,[42] at the University of Heidelberg, conferred upon him the doctoral degree and insignia after he had completed twenty-six successful years teaching theology.[43] At that time, that institution had exactly the same customs and practices for conferring the degree that we have observed for a long time. I reach precisely the same conclusion on these topics (and I am not going to hide it) as Zanchi did, as we see from a speech he delivered there in Heidelberg.

> I hold that these ceremonies we customarily use for conferring doctorates on men are not so essential that they could not be ignored without any harm or disrepute coming on the church. On the other hand, I say that they are so deserving of respect that the despising or neglecting of them should be criticized.

That was Zanchi's position.[44]

Soon I will have to draw in my sails, provided first I have the chance to joke a bit with my son and to toss in a few stories as fathers typically do. There is a charming one Sylvius tells about a man named Giorgio Fiscellino, doctor of civil and canon law.[45] Previously, the emperor Sigismund[46] had

---

39. Johann von Staupitz, ca. 1460/1469–1525, vicar-general of German Augustinian friars.

40. I.e., Melanchthon.

41. Apud *Jo. Hoornbeck* in summa Controvers. p. 511.] Hoornbeeck, *Summa Controversiarum Religionis*, bk. 9, p. 511.

42. Pierre Bouquin, ca. 1500–1582, French Reformed theologian and exegete.

43. *Zanch.* oper. in fol. tom. 8. part. altera col. 483, 484.] Girolamo (Jerome) Zanchi (Zanchius), 1516–1590, Reformed theologian, *Orationes*, in *Omnium Operum Theologicorum*, vol. 8 (Geneva, 1619), perhaps pp. 233–34.

44. Id. Ibid. Col. 502.] Zanchi, *Orationes*, p. 233.

45. Giorgio Fiscellino, Italian jurist; in Piccolomini, *Commentariorum*.

46. Sigismund, 1368–1437, Holy Roman emperor and king of Hungary and Bohemia.

appointed him to the nobility. At that time, Hus's[47] case was being adjudicated at the Council of Constance. Sigismund himself came in accompanied by a large crowd of nobles and doctors. Each of them grouped with those of the same rank. At this point Giorgio stopped and did not see where he should go. But finally, he bypassed the doctors and sat down with the nobles. When the emperor noticed this, he broke out into a laugh and said,

> I'm really surprised that you, Fiscellino, prefer nobility to learning. Or did I not in one day grant countless simple peasants exemption from taxation and elevate them to the honor of the nobility? But do you think that throughout the whole course of my life, from all those people even one could become educated?[48]

That is how valuable this man, who stood at the very pinnacle of royal authority, considered the learning of those with doctorates. But I may as well add another anecdote, which is perhaps not quite as charming, but it is no less memorable. In the East the leading men and ambassadors have the habit of writing their titles in the places they lodge while on a journey so other people can recognize them. A Jesuit theologian named Martino Martini,[49] who recently published a book about the war he was involved in, *The Tartar War*, adopted this practice. He states that while he lived at the time in a Chinese city where the Tartars were invading, everything around him was filled with chaos and noise. Above the door of his dwelling, he wrote, "Here lives a doctor of divine law from the great West." In addition, he set out for view in his entryway some beautifully produced European books, along with some mathematical tools.[50] Clearly this plan met with the greatest success: Martini not only avoided suffering any injury from soldiers, but the leading prince of the Tartars—who commanded the troops—cordially summoned him and received him with the greatest generosity. Behold! The protective power of books! Behold! The title *doctor of theology* is a lifesaver even among actual barbarians, even while they are carrying weapons and war rages hotly!

So then, you, my son, duly armed now with your own title, use and enjoy that academic degree that you just earned.[51] I heartily congratulate

---

47. John Huss, ca. 1372–1415, Bohemian Reformer.

48. *Zachar. Theobald.* Bell. *Hussitii.* p. 38.] Zacharias Theobald, 1584–1627, German Lutheran historian and theologian (Deutsche Biographie), *Bellum Hussiticum* (Frankfurt, 1621), ch. 17, p. 38.

49. Pag. 99.] Martino Martini, 1614–1661, Jesuit missionary, *De Bello Tartarico Historia* (Amsterdam, 1655), p. 99.

50. Martini, *De Bello Tartarico Historia*, p. 127.

51. Thomas Arrowsmith earned his BA in 1655/1656. See introduction.

you for it. But the foes of the "Literary Republic"—they are blown by a different blast. Still,

Whoso envy rends in twain, rendeth he be in the main![52]

As for the rest, I shall conclude with a prayer, but here also strive for brevity. May the greatest and most almighty God grant this university such a grip on truth that, in the end, it would be easier to find a wolf in England or a toad in Ireland than a Socinian, an Arminian, or a Weigelian at Cambridge.

---

52. Marcus Valerius Martialis (Martial), ca. 40–ca. 103, Roman poet, *Epigrammata* (Amsterdam, 1650), 9.97.

PLANS FOR HOLY WAR

BOOK I

CHAPTER I

The Harmony of the Christian Religion with Spiritual Warfare

Section 1: An introduction to the title, aim, and style of the work. Section 2: An estimation of the value of Genesis 3:15; Christianity is founded on this passage, as Luther, Pareus, and Glassius affirm. Section 3: Smalcius, however, disagrees, and his first reason is refuted. Section 4: His second reason is refuted, and the interrelation of blessing and curse is shown. Section 5: The earliest origins of spiritual warfare are found in the same text. Section 6: It becomes obvious in what sense God is said to have put enmity between them.

§ 1. We have, with pleasure, assigned the title *Plans for Holy War* to this recently prepared work. Its main purpose is to equip the Christian man for spiritual warfare as a soldier for battle, victory, and triumph. We chose this title because in antiquity, as Sixtus Arcerius observes, those things that concern the science of drawing up lines of battle were called Τακτικά.[1] Now a later age employs this expression with a somewhat broader meaning, and it encompasses whatever pertains to military action. The style that I employ is not ornamental, as some say Cardinal Bembo[2] affected. He was in the habit of substituting the phrase "breeze of the western heaven" for "the Holy Spirit;" and instead of our saying, "To receive forgiveness of sins," he wrote, "To make peace with the Gods above and shades below."[3] Nor is my style at all harsh, the sort that Erasmus claims was a stumbling block to a renowned theologian. That theologian says nine years are not enough for

---

1. In Notis ad *Aeliani* Tactica non procul ab initio.] Sixtus Arcerius, 1570–1623, professor of the Greek language, *Tactica* (Leiden, 1613). Arcerius produced a Greek text and Latin translation of Claudius Aelianus (Aelian), ca. 165/170–ca. 230/235, Roman rhetorician who wrote in Greek ca. 175–325.

2. Pietro Bembo (Cardinal Bembo), 1470–1547, Italian poet, courtier, and literary theorist.

3. *Hortinger.* in Analectis. pag. 22.] Bembo in Johann Heinrich Hottinger, 1620–1667, Swiss Reformed theologian, *Analecta Historico-theologica* (Zürich, 1652), p. 22.

understanding the Scholastics' barbaric terms,[4] ones that the *Doctor Subtilis* thoroughly dealt with just in the preface to his commentary on Lombard's *Sentences*.[5] But to sum up the entire range of this point within the circuit of one term, my style is *Scholastic-pastoral*. For whenever polemic elements arise (as will happen quite often), I have not thought that I should shrink from Scholastic terms even if they sound rather rough to some people's delicate ears, since with Augustine, I am one who prefers a wooden key, provided it makes for a good fit, to one made of gold or silver that won't quite get the door open.[6] Whenever those things arise pertaining to practical theology or its handmaiden, philology, more closely, I decided to use a more elevated style, so long as it was not too meretricious but rather what befits a modest woman.[7] So much for the preface. I will now begin my multifaceted treatise with the help of our good God. May He grant that it also be multifaceted in its usefulness!

§ 2. I was thinking about Christians' military service at my leisure (which I had acquired after laying aside my professorial appointment due to recently failing health). It occurred to me first of all that there is a certain very close connection between Christianity and spiritual military service. Indeed, the foundations of both were laid in Paradise itself, and the first origins of both are found in the same Mosaic text—Genesis 3:15, of course—when Jehovah addresses the serpent as follows: "I shall place enmity between you and the woman, between your seed and hers. It shall crush your head, and you shall crush its heel."

This text, if any, is very worthy of our attention. The first item in any class, because it is the measure of what follows, deserves careful scrutiny and, on that count (provided it has merit), special approval. The πρῶτον ψεῦδος[8] in errors and the foundational principles in matters of knowledge are likewise discovered by the highest diligence. Adam deserves distinction because he was the first created man; Stephen, because he was the first martyr; and this passage, because it is the first statement of the gospel.[9]

---

4. Idem dissertat. pentad. pag. 124.] Hottinger, *Dissertationum Miscellanearum Pentas* (Tiguri, 1654), p. 124.

5. Duns Scotus on Lombard's *Sentences*.

6. De Doctrina Christian. cap. 11.] Augustine, *De Doctrina Christiana*, in *Omnium Operum*, vol. 3 (Basel, 1528), 4.11.26.

7. A. employs an elaborate metaphor here. The *ancilla* or handmaiden of theology is philosophy, or, in this instance, philology. He wants, in this instance, to use a more ornate style—*ornatu verborum aliquo*—but not that which befits, for the sake of the handmaiden, a prostitute (*meretricius*) instead of a chaste married woman (*Matronalis*).

8. "First deceit."

9. These are *protoplastus*, *protomartyr*, and *protevangelium*, respectively.

Now in fact, writers of great and distinguished reputation have spoken splendidly about this passage. "It contains whatever excellence the whole Scripture possesses." Thus Luther.[10] Pareus claims and proves that, in this passage, the whole Christian catechism is summed up concerning man's misery, restoration, and gratitude.[11] To these I add Solomon Glassius, whose words are as follows:

> From that great abyss of waters, over which the Spirit of God is said to have brooded, the whole supply of waters in the heaven and earth from the world's very start drew its origin. And even until now it still does, and will do, so all the way to its end. Just like that, whatever divine promises were made in the schools of the patriarchs both before and after the flood, among the original covenanted people of God before and after the Babylonian captivity, in the church of Christ before and after he was revealed, all these anticipate the righteousness, the remission of sins, the grace of God, and the eternal life that would be obtained because of Christ. These promises flowed forth as a pure wave of salvation and comfort from no other source than this protoevangelical oracle, as from an unsearchable abyss and an inexhaustible spring of wisdom (over which, as it were, the nourishing Spirit of Jehovah also brooded to bring men back to life). We must then certainly recognize that these are commentaries on this passage.[12]

§3. And so it is not at all surprising that the ancient serpent, gripped as he is by the greatest concern for his own head, left no stone unmoved that he might cover in shadows this text that prophesies his trampling.[13] So among those defenders of the Socinian faith, that notable man Valentinus Smalcius (wickedly enough) maintained that the words of the Lord that we are discussing here, since they first came forth from Him, "did not relate to Christ at all, nor contained within them any promise of the gospel; but it suffices for the fulfillment of the prophecy that power was given to man for conquering that serpent, which he would have regarded with hatred, regardless of how the expression is finally understood."[14] O tongue, so weak

---

10. Tom. 6. Oper *witemb.* fol. 45] Luther, *Enarratio in Genesis*, in *Omnium Operum*, vol. 6 (Wittenberg, 1561), sub loc. Gen. 3:14.

11. Tom. 1.p.126 & 130.] David Pareus, *In Genesin Mosis Commentarius* (Frankfurt, 1615), probably p. 594.

12. *Christolog.* Mosaic. p. 57.] Solomon Glass (Glassius), 1593–1656, German theologian and biblical scholar, *Christologiae Mosaicae* (Jena, 1649), pp. 56–57.

13. A. is playing on words, since *contritione*, here translated "trampling," is derived from *contero*, the same word translated above as "crush." *Contritio* also means "sorrow" or "grief," and A. captures the double meaning.

14. Refutat. Thesium *Frantzii* p. 94. & 221.] Valentin Schmalz (Valentinus Smalcius), 1572–1622, Polish Socinian theologian, *Refutatio Thesium D. Wolfgangi Frantzii* (Rakov, 1614), pp. 94, 221.

and cold (to put it very gently), so lying and dishonest (to say it with the most honesty)! Is this how, gentle Christians, we will allow him to steal our protoevangelium from us? Is this how we shall allow this great, first charter of our salvation to be torn to shreds? We must, under no circumstances, allow that!

But so we do not seem to despise our enemy rather than engage him, let us take the inquiry a bit further, to the prop on which Smalcius's claim rests. I think he has given two reasons for his opinion. "Certainly," he says, "if the origins of the gospel had begun in Paradise, it scarcely seems believable that none of the sacred writers of the New Testament would have mentioned that prophecy at least once. But yet it is plain as day that this never happened."[15] We answer: First, the writers of the New Testament did "at least" notice this passage and reproduced its sense in other words. For what else does that saying of John echo: "For this reason, the Son of God appeared, to undo the works of the Devil" (1 John 3:8)? And what about that saying of the Apostle in Hebrews: "Since the children are sharers in flesh and blood, He likewise was made a sharer in the same things, that through death He might destroy him who had the power over death, that is, the Devil" (Heb. 2:14)? What, I say, does this echo other than what this passage says: "The seed of the woman will crush the serpent's head"? Second, it is only the very words that are not repeated. Because if those things that are present here and there in Paul's writings were collected and fused into one passage, Moses's idea immediately appears as a summary of them all. "God sent forth His Son born of the woman" (Gal. 4:4). Look! There's the woman. And "He does not say to 'seeds,' as concerning many, but 'and to your seed,' as concerning one, who is Christ" (Gal. 3:16). Look! The seed! "The God of peace will crush Satan under your feet soon" (Rom. 16:20). Look! The ancient serpent, as John in the Apocalypse calls Satan (Rev. 12:9), is crushed by that seed—of course, Christ—whom Isaiah calls the Prince of Peace (Isa. 9:6). Third, even if it were granted (and there is no way we should do so) that those to whom the Holy Spirit dictated made no clear mention in the New Testament whatsoever of such an important passage, nevertheless, it will not at all follow from this either that the gospel did not originate in Paradise or that it is not contained in that clause that we have praised, as there are other arguments that establish both points.

One of these arguments will suffice for now. The most widely accepted dogma of the ancient church, both the Jewish church and the Christian one, was that Adam, while still a resident of Paradise, rested on Christ, who was revealed through the evangelical faith, and, in fact, trusted in Him

---

15. Id. ibid. p. 94. in calce.] Smalcius, *Refutatio Thesium*, pp. 94–95.

for his salvation. What the Christian church held is abundantly clear from Tertullian,[16] Epiphanius,[17] and Augustine.[18] All these condemn Tatian and mark him with the heretic's brand, since he denied Adam's salvation through faith in the seed promised to him. The opinion of the Jewish church on this topic will be evident from those words related by the author of the book entitled *The Wisdom of Solomon*, if indeed he is discoursing not only about created wisdom but also about that which is uncreated, meaning, of course, the eternal Son of God (as is evident from the comparison of chapter 9 verse 9—"With You is the wisdom that knows your works and that was present when You were fashioning the world"—with those words assigned to Christ by Solomon himself in Proverbs 8:23; to Christ, I say, however loudly the Socinians protest, as he rejoices in that very title in the same passage). The author ascribes the salvation of Adam to this very wisdom in the most learned words at the introduction to his tenth chapter, saying, Αὕτη πρωτόπλαστον πατέρα κόσμου μόνον κλισθέντα διεφύλαξεν, καὶ ἐξέτεινε—some read the text more correctly as ἐξείλατο—αὐτὸν ἐκ παραπτώματος ἰδίου ("Wisdom herself preserved the first-formed father of the world, since he alone had been created, and drew him out of his destruction"). Certainly, saving faith lays claim to no other object for itself except Christ revealed in the gospel, nor does another gospel survive in Moses in his whole history of the world's origins than this passage we are discussing. Therefore, the truth of both principles is established, provided we are allowed to draw conclusions from the silence of Scripture (why, moreover, should we not be allowed this the same as Smalcius?).

§4. So Valentinus suggests, and he follows another line of reasoning. Frantzius had said that in this passage the same words threatened the Devil with a curse and offered a promise to men.[19] Smalcius, in response to these comments, said in his usual, flippant, manner,

> Surely, something cold and hot does not proceed from God's mouth simultaneously? What does Frantzius think will become of him and his novel theology among judicious men—unless it is proved, by sure arguments or evidence, that a blessing and a curse could be contained in the same words? If Frantzius wants these very words to contain a promise, he

---

16. Praescript advers. haeret. cap. 52.] Tertullian, *De Praescriptionibus Adversus Haereticos*, in *Opera Quae Hactenus Reperiri*, vol. 3 (Cologne, 1617), ch. 52.

17. Haeret 46.] Epiphanius, ca. 315–403, bishop of Salamis (Cyprus), *Contra Octoaginta Haereses Opus* (Basel, 1578), heresy 46.

18. De haeresib. cap. 25.] Augustine, *De Haeresibus Ad Quodvultdeum*, in *Omnium Operum*, vol. 6 (Basel, 1528), bk. 1, ch. 25.

19. Wolfgang Franz (Frantzius), 1564–1628, German Lutheran theologian, perhaps *Vindiciae Disputationum Theologicarum* (Wittenberg, 1622), sec. 8, fol. 121, ch. 118, sig. Pp1r.

should have denied that they contained a curse instead of recklessly diving into such nonsense.[20]

But please, Valentinus, watch what you say! What you strongly suggest is nowhere found in the Scriptures. That blessing and curse are simultaneously included in the very same expression, provided they are taken differently, is not so unusual. Do you want an example? Look at this expression of David: "In just a little while, the wicked will be no more" (Ps. 37:10). Does this expression, while it threatens the wicked with destruction, not promise the righteous favorable things? Survey the context, and, if you can, either deny or throw doubt on this conclusion.

But to illustrate all my points more clearly, let us take them from the top. In this first and somber tragedy there were three actors who walked out into the orchestra: the serpent, Eve, and Adam. The fourth is the one who lay hidden, so to speak, behind the curtains—that is, the Devil in the serpent. The serpent was driven by the Devil and corrupted Eve. Eve, thus corrupted by the Devil, sent Adam headlong to destruction. He then effected the same for all his posterity. God, whom the Apostle calls a "God of order" [1 Cor. 14], by that same order summons them to justice, where they were brought for their sin. Then He addresses the serpent first, both as a beast and as one disguised. And that those first humans might not lose hope (they were also present then and set before the same tribunal, deeply invested in its outcome), in proportion to the mercy in which He abounds He curses the corruptor. He does this so that meanwhile He brings Adam and Eve back to life by mentioning the Redeemer, whom He promises in passing and, as it were, while accomplishing something else. You have seen on several occasions, reader, certain paintings artfully rendered, which from one angle present a beautiful appearance to the onlookers while from another, something repulsive to those who gaze at it. Such is the Lord's intention: from one perspective one sees the Devil, death; from another, He brings forth the human race, the evangelical promise set before them.

§5. Up to this point we have spoken about Christianity's origin. Now I move on to spiritual military service; it lies in this same expression, for anyone who reads, to discern the very beginnings of this service. "I shall put," the Lord says to the serpent, "enmity between you and the woman, between your seed and her seed." Behold Jehovah as He gives commands. Behold the resolute enmity, the execution of which is the basis of all military service. Behold this war's first declaration, which has been waged from the very birth of the world, is waged even now, and shall be waged to the end of the

---

20. Smalcius, *Refutatio Thesium*, p. 122.

age between Christ and His own on one side and the Devil on the other side with his followers.

These are the ideas we must discuss more fully in the following pages. Meanwhile, disregard the anxiety that here arises concerning God's providence in evil. Because it has been said very truly that "God is not the author of those things He avenges," and it is completely beyond doubt that the most exalted Deity shall most heavily avenge that hostility that the metaphorical serpent and his seed work against Christ and Christians, we are then justified in asking how He will set this enmity between them. Shall we establish God as the cause and author of such a great sin? No indeed, no indeed! Rather, let us say with Chrysostom, βέλτιον κατορυγῆναι μυριάκις, etc.,[21] than that God hear such things from us; and with Augustine, who said, "I was sinning, O Lord my God, the ordainer and creator of all things, but in no way the ordainer of sins."[22] (The famous Gomar thinks this passage commonly read as "only not the ordainer"[23] should be restored like this. "I do not doubt," he says, "but that by the abbreviation *tantummo* was written something that, by the scribes' carelessness, degenerated into *tantum non*.")[24]

So we must understand that, for the resolution of this questionable point, the active verbs, in addition to their efficacy properly stated (as it is generally expressed), signify certain other explanations and means of concurrence. Thus, they can indicate *prediction*, as in Jeremiah: "I set you over the nations for their destruction and their building" (Jer. 1:10), where the prophet is said to excel, because he predicted the future. Or sometimes *permission* is indicated, as in 2 Samuel: "He measured out two small pieces of rope, one for killing and the other for bringing back to life" (2 Sam. 8:2), where David is said to have revived those whom he allowed to live. Or sometimes *guidance* and *ordination* are meant, as in Romans 8: "He did not spare His own Son but handed Him over for us all" (Rom. 8:32). Here God is said to have handed over His Son, since by His unsearchable providence, He directed the wickedness of the Jews and the Romans, by whom Christ was handed over, that His death might bring the elect salvation.

---

21. "Better that the earth swallow you ten thousand times," &c. Homil. 23. In Acta.] Chrysostom, *In Acta Apostolorum*, in *Opera Omnia*, vol. 3 (Basel, 1539), sub loc. Acts 10 (homilia 23).

22. Confess. l 5. cap. 10.] Augustine, *Confessiones*, in *Omnium Operum*, vol. 1 (Basel, 1528), 1.5.16.

23. A. sides with Gomar, who edited Augustine's *Confessions* at this point from the suspect *tantum non ordinator* to *tantummodo ordinator*.

24. Oper. Tom. 3. pag. 171.] François Gomar (Franciscus Gomarus), 1563–1641, Dutch Reformed minister and theologian, *De Providentia Dei*, in *Opera Theologica Omnia*, vol. 3 (Amsterdam, 1644), ch. 12, p. 171.

§6. Now clearly God set forth the enmity we are discussing by all the following means. He did so not by infusing this enmity as a *physical cause* nor by provoking it through instruction and persuasion as a *moral cause*. But He did so partly by prophesying that this deadly hatred, which the degenerate creatures had recently contracted from their fall, would grow up into implacable war. Indeed, from the woman's perspective, the war was righteous and glorious; but from that of the serpent, it was equally wicked and ill-omened. God also did this partly by permission, if in fact this is true: "He does not will sin but, nevertheless, willingly permits it. This is done that, in an amazing and indescribable way," these are Augustine's words, "what happens against His will does not happen apart from His will,[25] because it would not happen were He not permitting it. But being good, He would not permit something to occur in an evil way unless, being omnipotent, He were able to act on evil in a good."[26] Finally, God does this by directing and ordaining the wickedness of Satan and the unrighteous such that they result in His glory, the advantage of His church, and the destruction of those same wicked ones at the day of the Lord. The same Augustine brilliantly says about this, "He aids the good wills of created spirits, judges the wicked ones, and ordains them all."[27]

---

25. The contrast Augustine draws is between what is *contra voluntatem* and *praeter voluntatem*.

26. Augustine, *Enchiridion Ad Laurentium*, in *Omnium Operum*, vol. 3 (Basel, 1528), ch. 100.

27. De civit, Dei. lib. 5. cap. 9.] Augustine, *De Civitate Dei*, in *Omnium Operum*, vol. 5 (Basel, 1528), 5.9.4.

CHAPTER II

The Adversaries That Are Mentioned in the *Protoevangelium*

Genesis 3:15

Section 1: The natural serpent disregarded, the metaphorical one revealed. The name "Devil" was chosen because of the disguise he wore in Paradise. Section 2: Also, because of the qualities with which he is endowed, and because of the deadly poison of both kinds of serpent. Section 3: The serpent's bite is imperceptible, and his condition is most lowly. Section 4: The seed of the serpent is twofold. The invisible seed, the spirits—that is, the powers below—why they are called the seed of the Devil. Section 5: The visible seed—that is, unrighteous men—who are marked by the same titles along with the Devil himself. Section 6: The seven vices that represent the Devil's character more than the rest. Section 7–8: We do not take the woman to mean either the church, as the Jesuit Gordon does, or the virgin Mary, as Tirinus. Each of the previous interpretations is disproven. Sections 9–10: The woman is Eve. The woman's seed means primarily Christ. The source and truth of Messiah's flesh are denoted by this title. Section 11: That the term "seed" means "Christ" is proven from Hebrew sources, as well as from Irenaeus, Leo, and Rupert. Here we also discuss Zanchi's comment. Sections 12–13: The seed of the woman in a secondary sense means Christians. The imitation of their habits suffices for the designation of "seed" and "sons." I also discuss that Eve believed upon Christ. How she can be called the mother of those who believe is shown from Spanheim, Hallus, and Ussher.

§ 1. The combatants this protoevangelical passage speaks of are the serpent and the woman, together with the seed of each. I pass over the natural serpent and the woman's natural seed, however, even if I do not completely discount them from the meaning of the passage. They belong to another venue (or, rather, wrestling ground) and do not even remotely apply to our *Plans*. It is better to proceed according to the metaphorical sense.

Anyone who has paid attention even to just the Apocalypse will have no doubt about the serpent's identity. For in that book, we find these and similar comments: "The great dragon was thrown down, that ancient serpent who is called the Devil and Satan. He seized the dragon, that ancient serpent who is the Devil," etc. (Rev. 12:9; 20:2). Now I think that there are five main reasons for assigning this title *serpent*. First, it is derived from the disguise that Satan then wore, as he was hiding under a serpent's appearance and abused that animal's physical forms to contrive his deceit. The Devil is called by the name serpent, says Hugh of Saint Victor, because he wore that creature like a garment, as if someone secretly took on a monk's clothes to commit theft more stealthily in a monastery and, when caught in stealing, was derisively called a monk because of his purloined clothing.[1] But if the Devil had not yet taken off the disguise of the serpent when the Lord was saying such things (and this indeed is quite likely, for he was caught red-handed at the same time as our first parents), then it is quite consistent with reason to include both of them[2] under the same title.

§ 2. I think that the second reason should be derived from the serpentine qualities with which the Devil is endowed. He is rightly named *serpent* and *dragon* because his character is crafty, cunning, and endowed with the highest vigilance. Thus, Moses relates concerning the serpent's artfulness, "The serpent was more cunning than all the creatures of the earth" (Gen. 3:1). In another passage, Christ Himself says, "Be as wise as serpents" (Matt. 10:16). There is reason to believe that the serpent's vigilance was the reason why dragons are sometimes thought to be the guardians of treasures, for the greatest vigilance must be employed to fulfill that task. And serpents were sacred to Asclepius[3] because a doctor ought to be as vigilant and wise as anyone. More than that, because vigilance is desirable in a military force among the Romans, the dragon was taken as the standard for certain cohorts so that they would demonstrate that quality. And as those who bore the eagle were called *Aquiliferi*, so those who carried the standard of the dragon were called *Draconarii*. This is the origin in our own speech of these expressions still in use: dragons and Dragoneers.

The extent of Satan's cunning and, likewise, vigilance is clear from John's Apocalypse, when "he is said to have stood before the woman as she was giving birth so that, when she had delivered him, Satan might devour her son" (Rev. 12:4). And he is likewise said to "lead astray the whole world" (Rev. 12:9). From Paul's letters we learn that he attributed to the Devil schemes (μεθοδείας) [Eph. 6:11] and stratagems (νοήματα) [2 Cor. 2:11]. I have no doubt at all that politicians' tricks, heretics' subterfuges, and

---

1. Tom. 1. Annot. elucid. p. 12.] Hugh of St. Victor, *Annotationes Elucidatoriae*, in *Opera Omnia*, vol. 1 (Mainz, 1617), ch. 7, p. 12.

2. I.e., the Devil and the physical snake.

3. Greek god of medicine.

atheists' deceits are almost nothing other than the, as it were, particular coils and entanglements of this ancient serpent.

The very lethal venom of each kind of serpent[4] provides the third reason. The Scriptures quite often mention this serpent's poison. "He drank the poison of asps, the tongue of the viper killed him" (Job 20:16). "They sharpened their tongues as serpents, the venom of asps was on their lips" (Ps. 140:4). This is evidently because asps instill poison in the wound they have made with their sharp-edged teeth, using venom from the very small cavities in those teeth. There they store poison for these purposes in a small sac. Thus, we have from Lucan,

> Bane in bite they hold, and bring death with fang.[5]

The Devil, likewise, spews out toxins and, by this, corrupts wretched sinners so that, in their souls, they are reduced to the same condition as the Israelites once were bodily in the desert. For when they were attacked by enflamed serpents (which the Septuagint calls τοὺς ὄφεις τοὺς θανατοῦντας),[6] as many as refused to cast their eyes upon the bronze serpent, a type of Christ, met the swiftest death. Augustine comments on this passage, "He who desires to escape the Devil's poison, let him look to the crucified Christ."[7] And elsewhere he says, "Everyone who did not look upon that bronze serpent when they were struck, died. Therefore, brothers, unless each one shall trust in the crucified Christ, he is destroyed by the Devil's poison."[8] Heed, dear reader, this ancient Christian poet:

> The time will come when by a tree the new
> Adam will for the sins of the first tree
> atone, and purify them. When on the
> tall tree hangs the golden serpent, He shall
> wash away the bite of that ancient snake,
> and all his venom, etc.[9]

§3. The serpent's imperceptible bite provides the fourth reason. Some serpents prick their victims to destroy them, but with only a very small wound, and its opening is barely evident. So it happened that Cleopatra,[10] after she

---

4. I.e., the Devil and the physical snake.

5. Lib. 9.] Marcus Annaeus Lucanus (Lucan), 39–65, Roman poet, *Bellum Civile* (Amsterdam, 1643), bk. 9.

6. "Death snakes"; cf. Numbers 21:6.

7. Augustine, *Sermo* XI.32.

8. Augustine, *Sermo* VI.5.

9. *Alcim.* Avit. lib. 2.] Avitus of Vienne, d. ca. 518, bishop of Vienne and Christian poet, *De Origine Mundi* (Basel, 1545), vol. 3, p. 337.

10. Cleopatra VII, 69–30 BC, Queen of Ptolemaic Egypt.

had decided to commit suicide, selected the bite of the asp that she might meet a milder type of death than if she had drunk the poison or fallen on a sword. The devilish toxin functions in an equivalent way. For example, Satan pricks those who are intoxicated, yet they scarcely realize that they are receiving a mortal wound. On this point we read Solomon: "Do not gaze upon wine when it reddens, when it shows the color in the cup. In the end, as a serpent, it shall bite, and as a poisonous serpent, it will sting" (Prov. 23:31–32). Hypocrites share that same fate. In point of fact, whoever has a heart that Satan has filled with deceit, as once he filled that of Ananias, is very close to death (Acts 5:3). Some poet or other says as follows about the serpent's bite:

> Nor yet do you see any wounds of the
> bite impressed.[11]

Finally, every snake's extremely deplorable and downtrodden condition supplies us with the fifth reason. It is likely that the serpent, in its primitive condition, had a more noble means of movement than that which it now employs. Of course, it would have held its body erect—not indeed the whole body, but from its navel to the head so that its chest protruded and did not scrape along the ground. Yet from the divine curse it came to pass that after Satan had abused its physical qualities to bring sin into this world, it walked not only on its belly (as before) but also on its chest. The seventy elders[12] seem to have wanted to express this idea when they render one Hebrew word using two Greek words (ἐπὶ τῷ στήθει σου καὶ τῇ κοιλίᾳ πορεύσῃ), one of which means *chest* and the other *belly*. Thus, it is commonly construed, "So you will walk upon your chest and will eat the ground" (Gen. 3:14).

Rivet supposes that these two clauses should be joined into one and that the first should be understood as the reason for the second, as if it were saying, "You shall be compelled to creep face down in the dirt, to stir up its dust by your winding movements, that the dust may fill your nostrils and mouth."[13] So the serpent's debased condition is similar to what is observed in the Devil's state. The Scripture typically portrays a very low estate through the lowering of the chest and the eating of dust, as is typical of those praying to avoid punishment or begging for their lives. So in Isaiah we read, "With their face toward the earth they shall worship you and shall lick the dust of your feet" (Isa. 49:23). In Lamentations it says, "They will

---

11. Perhaps Nicander of Colophon, fl. ca. 130 BC, Greek poet, *Theriaca*.

12. I.e., authors of the Septuagint.

13. Exercit. 35, in Genes.] Rivet, *Theologicae Et Scholasticae* (Leiden, 1633), p. 174 (exercit. 35).

set their mouth in the dust, though perhaps there is hope" (Lam. 3:29). And in the Psalms, "Our life has been cast into the dust, and our stomach clings to the earth" (Ps. 44:25). And again, "His eyes will lick the dust" (Ps. 72:9). But there is also this in Micah: "They shall lick the dust like a serpent" (Mic. 7:17)—that is, as Drusius notes, they will kiss the ground as evidence of their enslavement.[14] And even today, he says, in Asia, they are still in the habit, when they approach a king, of kissing the ground as a sign of the complete honor that they show their rulers. Now let us see how these ideas square with Satan. He was once an angel of light and a resident of heaven. After his fall, deprived of that nectar, so to speak, and ambrosia of the blessed spirits (I mean the vision and love of God), he tasted nothing except either those things that are of the earth or those infernal things that are within the earth. And that his disgrace might be complete, after the first humans were deceived, he was cast down into such a humiliation of his estate that, though he once was equal to the blessed angels, now he should be considered a mere laughingstock to men, and a weak woman will boast over him. But this happened in such a way that the praise fell not upon the woman but entirely upon her seed.

§ 4. His seed that either exposed to our view or concealed him is joined to the serpent. The invisible seed of the serpent includes in its course the entire host of demons, whatever its exact extent. For we read several times about the prince of demons and sometimes about the Devil's angels. These have sinned beyond measure, have become sworn enemies after the example of their commander, and thus heed his seed. For, to be sure, father and seed are related. The father, moreover, is very often in the sacred text called the one whom the rest imitate. In Ezekiel, the father of the Jewish people is said to be an Amorite, and their mother, a Hittite, for Israel was chasing after the practices of the Canaanites (Ezek. 16:2). And in Paul, all who are followers of Christ, although they were foreigners to the nation of the Jews, are nevertheless called the seed of Abraham, because by faith they walk in the steps of our father Abraham, a faith that was in the uncircumcision (Rom. 4:12; Gal. 3:19). Augustine's comment on this deserves commendation:

> Note the practice of the sacred Scripture. The prophet says directly to the Jews, "Your father was an Amorite and your mother a Hittite." The Amorite nation was previously not the place from which the Jews derived their descent. But because the Amorites were wicked, as well as the Hittites, the Jews imitated their wickedness and discovered them to be their

---

14. Joannes van den Driesche (Joannes Drusius), 1550–1616, Flemish orientalist and theologian, *Commentarius In Prophetas Minores* (Amsterdam, 1627), sub loc. Mic. 7:17.

parents—not as those from whom they were born but as those, by following whose practices, they were being equally condemned.

Such are Augustine's remarks.[15]

§5. For the same reason, no doubt, completely untrustworthy men can be called the serpent's visible seed, and Satan called their father. For Christ Himself approves and leads the way in this when He rebukes the Jews for attacking His teaching with their cavils: "You come from your father, the Devil, and want to fulfill your father's wishes" (John 8:44). But in another passage, Christ interprets a parable like this: "The world is a field, and the good seed are the sons of the kingdom, while the tares are the sons of the evil one" (Matt. 13:38)—that is, the Devil. The beloved disciple concurs: "The one who works sin is from the Devil; by this are the sons of God and the sons of the Devil made known" (1 John 3:8, 10).

Now a consequence of this is that, just as sons customarily take their names from their fathers, so, in the sacred text, the same names are applied to the reprobate—and especially to Antichrist (who is the visible head of the perverse church)—as to Satan himself, or, at least, names equal to them. So the one is called serpent, the others are offspring of vipers (Matt. 3:7)— indeed, even poisonous serpents for whom there is no charm (Jer. 8:17). The former is called a roaring lion, and similarly the latter. David says, concerning his enemies, "I am among wild beasts. I lie down amidst flaming coals" (Ps. 57:5), etc. Paul says of Nero,[16] "I was rescued from the lion's mouth" (2 Tim. 4:17). Satan's name is ὁ πονηρός (1 John 5:18),[17] ὁ ἄνομος of Antichrist (2 Thess. 2:8).[18] He is called, in one place, ὁ ἀπολλύων (Rev. 9:11);[19] in another, ὁ υἱὸς τῆς ἀπωλείας (2 Thess. 2:3).[20] His angels are known as τὰ πνευματικὰ τῆς πονηρίας (Eph. 6:12),[21] while he himself is known as ὁ ἄνθρωπος τῆς ἁμαρτίας (2 Thess. 2:3),[22] as though he were comprised entirely of sin and not really so much vicious as vice itself—as Martial ridiculed Zoilus.[23] Someone else, in his poem against the Roman

---

15. Tractat. 22. in Evang Johann.] Augustine, *In Evangelium Ioannis Expositio*, in *Omnium Operum*, vol. 9 (Basel, 1528), 42.10.

16. Nero Claudius Drusus Germanicus (Nero), 37–68, Roman emperor and persecutor of Christians.

17. "The evil one."

18. "The lawless man."

19. "The destroyer."

20. "The son of destruction."

21. "Spiritual creatures of evil."

22. "The man of sin."

23. Martial, *Epigrammata*, 11.93. A. alludes to a famous epigram of Martial against a wicked man named Zoilus.

Pope Alexander VI,[24] who sat on the throne of Antichrist, says that if any-one else was wicked, Alexander's depravity far excelled him:

> Let not the name of Alexander here detain you long,
> Depart, my friend! For here lies only utter crime and wrong.[25]

§ 6. But if someone should ask me, What kinds of sins especially represent Satan's character? I would say, just as it is commonly said about the works of God that His traces appear in them all, but His image is in angels and men, so, indeed, every sin shows some traces of the Devil, but some give his living image. Of this kind are the following:

First, *arrogance.* The reader should weigh carefully that passage of Paul to Timothy, where he forbids the election of a new believer to the office of elder, that he not fall εἰς κρίμα τοῦ διαβόλου (1 Tim. 3:6)[26]—that is, into arro-gance (as some say), through which the angels fell and because of which they were exiled from heaven. "Here is disclosed"—I quote Abraham Scultetus, although he himself settled on a different meaning for the passage— "that secret of the origin and reason for the Devil's fall. I am not at all sure whether this is ever discussed somewhere else in Scripture."[27] Prosper of Aquitaine, moreover, remarks shrewdly enough that "arrogance made demons out of angels, while humility makes men like the holy angels."[28]

Second, *anger.* I cite as my witness the heavenly voice: "Woe to the dwellers of land and sea. For the Devil comes down upon you filled with great, kindled wrath, for he knows that the time he has is short" (Rev. 12:12). Paul's words, again, should be weighed: "Be angry and sin not. Do not let the sun set upon your rage nor give room to the Devil" (Eph. 4:26–27). By this he means, of course, that there is no wickedness so heinous that Satan does not easily persuade men of persistent anger to undertake (this is Beza's conjecture).[29] Or perhaps it means that the one who goes to bed angry is bunking with the Devil.

Third, *jealousy.* The name "Satan" means *adversary.* "Surely he is not of God," if John has any authority with us, "whoever does not love his brother" (1 John 3:10). Why does he say this? He informs us from these words that

---

24. Rodrigo Borgia (Pope Alexander VI), 1431–1503, r. 1492–1503.

25. Pasquil. extatic. Tom. 1. p. 81.] Celio Secondo Curione, 1503–1569, Italian heterodox Reformer and writer, *Pasquillorum Tomi Duo* (Freistadt, 1544), p. 81.

26. "Into the judgment of the Devil."

27. Observat. in I^am ad Tim. p. 24.] Scultetus, *Pauli Epistolae Ad Singulares* (Frankfurt, 1624), ch. 16, p. 24.

28. Prosper of Aquitaine, ca. 390–ca. 463, Augustinian polemicist, *De Vita Contemplativa*, in *Opera* (Cologne, 1630), bk. 3, ch. 3, p. 256.

29. Beza, *Annotationes Maiores In Novum Jesu Christi Testamentum* (Geneva, 1594), sub loc. Eph. 4:27.

follow just a little after that: "Not as Cain, who rose up from his malice and slew his brother. But what was the reason that Cain murdered him? Because his own deeds were evil, while his brother's were just" (1 John 3:12). From this passage it will be clear that all those are the Devil's spawn who, because they have themselves become worthless, therefore hate others' piety. And they are, so I would say, imitating their father.

Fourth, *slander*. By this we mean especially what is employed against righteous enemies. For to speak ill of the righteous is really nothing other than to do Satan's work, since he is the first accuser of the brethren (Rev. 12:10) and, for that reason, is called the Devil.[30] But how, nevertheless, this term is held in common by slanderers of both sexes is quite obvious from the passages noted in the margin (1 Tim. 3:11; 2 Tim. 3:3; Titus 2:3). Our countryman Crakanthorp, after he had demonstrated sufficiently that the archbishop of Spalato[31] was the author of those manifold slanders against us, addressed that man like this: "See whether you have now deserved something condignly, such that in the end you might, for all your slanders, be called not Antonio de Dominis but Antonio de Demons!"[32]

Fifth, *dishonesty*. False speech is perverse speech. No, it even works using devilish perversity. For thus Christ says about the Devil, "As often as he tells a lie, he speaks in his usual way; for he is a liar and the father of lying" (John 8:44). Indeed, the tongue functions as a midwife, but the father of a lying progeny is Satan, while the mother is the wicked man's heart. For this fifth sin, the tongue of a demon (if I can say that), is an inborn and natural falsehood. For as soon as, by his fall, he crossed over from being an angel of light to being the Devil, he immediately told extravagant lies in that conversation he began with Eve.

Sixth, *leading others astray* from the path of truth to the byways of errors. Paul struck Elymas with this sort of thunderbolt, as he endeavored to turn the proconsul away from the faith: "You son of the Devil, filled with all deceit and ready for any sort of wickedness!" (Acts 13:10). In another passage Paul calls the false apostles ministers of Satan, disguising themselves as apostles of Christ (2 Cor. 11:13). Their "gospel" is the hissing of their chief shepherd. The heresy that barks against the gospel deserves to be called the

---

30. *Diabolus* is derived from the Greek verb διαβάλλω, which means "to slander."

31. Marco Antonio de Dominis, ca. 1560–1624, archbishop of Spalato.

32. Defens. Eccles. Anglic. p. 595.] Richard Crakanthorp(e), 1567–1624, Anglican theologian, *Defensio Ecclesiae Anglicanae* (London, 1625), ch. 78, p. 595. Crakanthorp wrote extensively against the transubstantiationalist views of the archbishop of Spalato.

hissing of a hellish serpent.[33] The heretic Marcion[34] once asked Polycarp,[35] "Do you recognize me?" "Oh, I know full well who you are," said Polycarp. "You are none other than the Devil's firstborn."[36]

Seventh, *the perverse passion for swearing rashly*. This relates to that comment of Christ in the Sermon on the Mount: "Let your speech be, 'Yes, yes,' 'No, no.' Anything beyond that is from the evil one" (Matt. 5:37). By speech he means social conversation (as Heins notes)[37] and implies that in casual discourse "yes" and "no" are adequate without any swearing, though at other times, this should not be considered at all forbidden. Yet, in everyday speech, the addition of an oath to an affirmation or a denial generally comes from the Devil. Even if other vices have their provoking agents—the world provokes us to greed, the flesh entices us toward licentious behavior— the habit we are now discussing is pure, unadulterated (please excuse the expression) Satanism.

§7. So far, we have steadily drawn up into their battle line our most enraged enemies, the serpent and his seed, equally invisible and visible. There stand arrayed against them the woman and her seed, both the first seed and the second. Let us proceed to talk about these.

Among the Jesuits (who are of such a combative character that they much prefer to ask questions than to trust authority, and they love to argue stubbornly rather than be satisfied with the clearest explanations) there is not yet any agreement as to who this woman is. If we should ask Jacob Gordon, he will reply, "The woman is the church, the bride of Christ, whom Eve represented."[38] If we ask Jacobus Tirinus, he will substitute for us here the blessed virgin Mary in place of the woman in these words: "By 'woman' is meant most of all the blessed virgin Mary, who, by bringing forth Christ to us, was made the truest Eve, that is, the mother of the living. Thus, she completely crushed this serpent's head and power."[39] But both interpretations really are excessively ridiculous. For although in a certain Pauline epistle, the church is compared to Eve for a more pure and conjugal love

---

33. *Euseb.* history. Eccles.] Eusebius of Caesarea, ca. 265–ca. 339/340, historian and bishop of Caesarea in Palestine, *Historiae Ecclesiasticae*, vol. 1 (Geneva, 1612).

34. Marcion of Sinope (Pontus), d. ca. 160, early Christian heretic.

35. Polycarp, ca. 69–ca. 155, bishop of Smyrna.

36. Irenaeus, fl. second century, bishop of Lyon, *Adversus Haereses*, in *Adversus Valentini* (Paris, 1639), bk. 3, ch. 3.

37. Daniel Heinsius (Heins), 1580–1655, Dutch classical scholar, *Sacrarum Exercitationum Ad Novum Testamentum* (Cambridge, 1640), p. 26.

38. Epitom. cont. Tom. 1. comment.] James Huntley Gordon (Jacob or Jakob Gordon), 1541–1620, Scottish Jesuit scholar, *Controversiarum Epitomes* (Limoges, 1612), p. 79.

39. In loc.] Jacques (Jacobus) Tirinus, 1580–1636, Dutch Jesuit exegete, *In S. Scripturam Commentarius* (Antwerp, 1645), sub loc. Gen. 3:15.

(Eph. 5:31–32), and in a certain apocalyptic vision, for the sorrows she experienced in childbirth (Rev. 12:1–2)—these are Gordon's arguments—nevertheless, nowhere that I know of in the Scriptures is Eve treated as a type of the church, either for the guilt that she caused in paradise or for the penalty for which the Lord judged her there. Nor do the sacred writings typically call Christ (who here is styled the seed of the woman) a son of the church, but either the husband or father.

§ 8. Before I rehearse Tirinus's arguments, let me beg the reader's forgiveness: no doubt these arguments will cause the reader indigestion if he has any feeling at all. Tirinus seeks to prove that Mary is meant here most of all and that to her is properly attributed the trampling of the serpent's head. He says,

> First, because Mary allowed herself no sin, not even original sin (which is the first and, as it were, head of all sins). Then, because she has in herself not even any germ of sin or depraved thought (which is the foundation or head of actual sin). Finally, because she perfectly defeated and struck down all heresies and tyrannies (which are the very heads and horns of the hellish serpent) through the power of Christ, the seed and her own son. As she herself did this, so do all Christians, who are also her seed and her sons.[40]

My first rejoinder is Seneca's famous comment: "Superstition is a raving error and debases those who cherish it."[41] Look at this noble proof! While the Jesuits, utterly blinded by superstition, offer superstitious worship to the blessed virgin and—to seem to offer it more safely—extol her as free from sins, they are full of abuse for her and openly debase the Mother of God. This, du Moulin proves as follows:

> They diminish Mary's glory and happiness while trying to increase them, and they make her inferior to other believers. For they want her to have been saved by her own merit and by her own righteousness. But the rest of the holy are saved through the righteousness of Christ that is imputed to them, which is greater than Mary's righteousness. That this righteousness, therefore, is deserving of a greater reward no person of sound mind can doubt.[42]

Allow me to add as well that it is no less absurd to attribute to Mary those qualities that Christ demonstrates than if someone should say that

---

40. Tirinus, *In S. Scripturam Commentarius*, sub loc. Gen. 3:15.

41. Seneca the Younger, *Epistolae*, in *Opera Quae Exstant Omnia*, ed. Justus Lipsius (Antwerp, 1652), *epistola* 123.

42. Enodat. graviss. quaest. p. 101.] Pierre (Peter) du Moulin, 1568–1658, Reformed minister and religious controversialist, *Enodatio Gravissimarum Quaestionum*, (Leiden, 1632), p. 101.

Alexander's mother[43] subdued the whole world by her strength and weapons, or that Monica[44] wrote against the Pelagians those tremendously learned treatises, just because this was actually done by her son Augustine. Personal qualities are not heritable, the theologians claim. They do not descend from father to son. Much less, in my opinion, do they ascend from son to mother.

§9. Why should I belabor this point? The whole lineage of the history loudly asserts that no other woman is meant here besides Eve, who alone ate the fruit when led astray by the serpent's conversation, offered it to her husband, and was arraigned by the Lord when he asked, "What is this that you have done?" [Gen. 3:13]. This does not apply at all to the church, nor at all to Mary. The demonstrative particle, which is in the original text, proves the same thing. We do not read "between you and אִשָּׁה"—that is, "a woman," indefinitely—but "between you and הָאִשָּׁה"—that is, "this woman" (as the Junio-Tremellius version has it).[45] "She is the one you[46] recently corrupted. She was first to engage in deception, and she now stands before Me trembling while I, the Lord, bring this sentence against you."

Eve was the πρωτομήτηρ, the first mother of all men. That being the case, she is also the mother of Mary, who, after she had been procreated from Eve long after, gave birth to Christ. And Eve is also the mother of Christ Himself. Since He is called the son of David and of Abraham (Matt. 1:1), both of whom died many ages before Mary was born, it actually is not at all surprising if He should be called the seed of the first woman—namely, Eve—on whom Adam bestowed that title for being the *mother of all the living* (Gen. 3:20). Let me sum this up in a word: *Christ was the only seed of Mary; He was the primary seed of Eve.* As He is God, He was οὐ πεποιημένος ἀλλὰ γεγεννημένος ἐκ τοῦ πατρός (as we read in the Athanasian Creed).[47] As He is man, He was not born from any father but was γενόμενος of the woman, not γεγεννημένος,[48] as we read in Paul (Gal. 4:4). For this reason, He is also most properly described as the "seed of the woman."

---

43. Olympias, d. 316 BC, mother of Alexander the Great and queen of Macedonia.

44. Monica, ca. 331–387, mother of Augustine of Hippo.

45. *Biblia Sacra*, translated by John Immanuel Tremellio (Tremellius), 1510–1580, Jewish convert to Christianity and Protestant Hebrew scholar; François du Jon (Francisus Junius), 1545–1602, French Reformed theologian; and Theodore Beza (Amsterdam, 1639), sub loc. Gen. 3:15, p. 2.

46. I.e., the Devil.

47. "Not made but begotten of the Father."

48. "Made, not begotten."

§ 10. We must not at all overlook the fact that from this very primitive time the truth and origin of Christ's flesh shone forth sufficiently in the title *Messiah*. About these two notions, heretics of sundry times have stirred up much confusion, really even tragedies. Even if Socinus (that supreme harasser of the churches) cared little for these matters, he was not embarrassed when he wrote as follows: "Where, when, and from what parents Jesus arose, all these and similar questions refer to the knowledge of Christ according to the flesh. The investigation of such a question is the domain of worldly-minded Jews and those like them and should be rejected. But for those who have become spiritual (as Paul testifies of himself and those like him who have the true knowledge of Christ) they no longer know Christ according to the flesh."[49]

I think these questions, however, deserve the greatest attention. Our brotherhood with Jesus Christ depends upon this point, and from it arises the comfort of believers, as the apostle teaches us: "The one who sanctifies and they who are sanctified are all of one source. Therefore, He is not ashamed to call them brothers" (Heb. 2:11). And a little later, "Because they are sons sharing in his flesh and blood, He Himself likewise also became a sharer in these same qualities" [Heb 2:14].[50] The text did not simply say, "He became a sharer in the same qualities," as Chrysostom observes.[51] And Theophylact (as usual) follows him in this.[52] But it says He became quite similar to them—that is, not according to mere appearance or conjecture (as the heretics taught) but by showing that this brotherhood really, truly existed. Here, to prevent myself from being launched onto the sea of some great controversy, I gladly accept the conclusion of Daniel Cramer:

> Whenever the Messiah is called the seed of the woman, by an infallible argument the true substance of His human nature is denoted. And lest we think that His flesh was transferred from heaven through Mary as though through a channel (as the Valentinians imagined), for this reason, by the phrase "seed of the woman," the actual fleshy and bloody mass, which the Son of God received from His mother, is expressly denoted. Consequently, no one should imagine that the substance of His generation was introduced externally. For the very kernel of all the hope and faith in the brotherhood of Christ would have been taken away from us if He had

---

49. Respons. Pro Racoviensb. ad librum Palaeologi part. 1. c. 1. p. 11.] Fausto Sozzini (Faustus Socinus), 1539–1604, Italian anti-Trinitarian, *Pro Racoviensibus Responsio* (Rakow, 1627), part 1, ch. 1, p. 11.

50. I.e., flesh and blood.

51. Chrysostom, *In Epistolam Pauli Ad Hebraeos*, in *Opera Omnia*, vol. 4 (Basel, 1539), sub loc. Heb. 2:14 (*homilia* 4).

52. Theophylact of Ohrid, b. ca. 1050/1060–d. post-1125, Byzantine exegete, *In Omnes D. Pauli Apostoli Epistolas Enarrationes* (Paris, 1548), sub loc. Heb. 2:14.

not assumed a truly human body consubstantial with ours but, rather, only an empty phantasm or if He had just set upon our eyes a heavenly idea and thus deceived us. For that which He did not assume He does not redeem.[53]

§ 11. Now the interpretation we are advancing is neither new nor one that arose yesterday, nor even the day before. But it has been acknowledged both by Jews and by Christians. As far as relates to the Jews, I cite men that are very credible and quite well versed in their writings—namely, Paul Fagius[54] and John Mercer.[55] Both of them, in handling this Mosaic passage, assert that the ancient Hebrews understood that it concerned Christ, and they cite the Targum of Jerusalem. As regards Christians, three proofs will suffice so that I don't overdo it. Irenaeus says, "The Lord rehearsed this enmity toward Him, a man made from a woman and trampling his—that is, the serpent's—head."[56] This quote follows the passage in which he recounted the portion of Genesis we are now handling. Leo the Great writes as follows:

> The all-powerful and merciful God, whose nature is goodness, whose will is powerful, whose work is mercy, just as the devilish malevolence, by the poison of its jealousy, immediately brought us death, so He prophesied the predestined remedies of His own righteousness for renewing mortals at the very beginning of the world, proclaiming to the serpent that the seed of the woman would come and, by His power, trample the raising of that deadly head. This foretold that Christ would come in the flesh as God and man, who would be born from a virgin and condemn the defiler of the human race by His uncorrupted birth.[57]

Finally, Rupert says, "Of whom are these comments made if not about one—namely, Christ? For He alone is the seed of the woman such that He is not also the seed of a man."[58]

---

53. Schol. prophetic. class. 1 p. 21.] Daniel Cramer, 1568–1637, German Lutheran theologian, *Schola Prophetica*, (Hamburg, 1606), pp. 22–23. This quotation actually begins at page 22 and continues into page 23. A. quotes Cramer almost verbatim up to the end of the first sentence above ("…is denoted."), before skipping Cramer's discussion of Hebrews 2:17 and 4:15 to continue the quotation on page 23 at "And lest we think…" A. takes some liberties with Cramer's word order in this second part of the quotation, but the sense is unaltered.

54. Paul (Paulus) Fagius, 1504–1549, German Hebraist.

55. Jean Mercier (John Mercer), ca. 1500–1562, French Hebraist.

56. Advers. haeret. l. 4. c. 78.] Irenaeus, *Adversus Haereses*, bk. 4, ch. 78. A. adds the last three words of the quotation, *serpentis scilicet, caput*.

57. De Nativit. Christi sermone 2.] Leo the Great (Leo I), ca. 400–461, r. 440–461, *In Nativitatis Domini*, in *Opera Quae Quidem Haberi* (Cologne, 1561) (*sermo* 2).

58. Lib. 3. de Trin.] Rupert of Deutz, 1075–1129, Benedictine theologian and exegete, *De Trinitate Et Operibus Eius* (Cologne, 1528), bk. 3, ch. 19, fol. 21v.

Now this observation of Rupert's reminds me of something Jerome Zanchi observed that we should not at all ignore.

> Here is seen (in Christ's incarnation, of course) a truly new manner of conceiving and giving birth, one truly conducive to a new man. Adam, the first man, was born from no other man but was immediately created by God. The second human being—that is, Eve—was formed not from a woman but from a man. The third set of human beings—that is, all the others—were from both man and woman. The fourth—that is, Christ the new man—was born from no man just like Adam. He was not born from no woman, like Eve. He was not born from man and woman, as we are. But truly in a new manner from a woman without a man, He, Himself a man, was conceived and born a male. For this fourth and final manner, which is that of Christ only, made manifest in the world's fourth and final age, was left to God's amazing wisdom, a wisdom beheld and declared in the creation of men. For the first age extended to the flood, the second to Moses, and the third to Christ, while the fourth goes from Christ Himself to the end of the world.

Thus Zanchi.[59]

§ 12. The comments above should suffice on the topic of Christ the head. The question about the members of His body is as follows: Is there any mention made of them in this same passage? Because it is a Christian army, it is made up of Christ and His followers, in keeping with this passage: "These will fight with the Lamb, and the Lamb shall overcome them (since He is the Lord of lords), along with those who are with Him, the called, elect, and faithful" (Rev. 17:14). Thus, I claim they are present here and are found under that same designation, "seed." The most accomplished theologians teach that the seed of the woman is clearly to be understood collectively, and in addition to Christ, it includes all those who are not of the serpent's seed. This, of course, is Christ's universal church, as Rivet says,[60] or, following Musculus,[61] the remaining body of the elect. So now I provide my arguments for proving that Christians truly are the secondary seed of the woman.

This word "seed" refers, in a relative manner, to the word "parent." Now, in sacred literature, not only are those from whom we are born called parents but also those whom we imitate, just as was stated above.[62] And

---

59. De Incarnat. l. 2. c. 3. quaest. 4.] Zanchi, *De Incarnatione Filii Dei*, in *Omnium Operum Theologicorum*, vol. 7 (Geneva, 1619), bk. 2, ch. 3, qu. 4, p. 67.

60. Exercitat. 37. in Genes.] Rivet, *Theologicae Et Scholasticae*, probably p. 183 (exercise 37).

61. Comment. in locum.] Wolfgang Musculus, 1497–1563, Reformed theologian, *In Mosis Genesim* (Basel, 1554), obs. 18, p. 98.

62. Hic capit. 2. §.4.] See ch. 2, sec. 4.

this is more obvious from the examples of Abraham as well as Sarah. In Paul we find that the seed is that which is from Abraham's faith, who is the father of all of us who walk in the footsteps of that faith Abraham received as a gift (Rom. 4:12, 16). And in Peter those women who imitate Sarah are called her daughters. "Sarah obeyed Abraham, calling him Lord, whose daughters you are, provided you behave well" (1 Peter 3:6). The faithful, in another passage, are also called sons, not of the handmaiden but of the freewoman—that is, not of Hagar but of Sarah (Gal. 4:30).

But now let me speak more specifically about Eve. It is sure that she was the first of all women both to have lived and to have sinned. She is also the first to have believed in the promised seed, and there are many indications that suggest she repented of her sin. Among these is that righteous hatred toward the Devil that she carried fixed deep in her heart. Hugh of Saint Victor, as he meditates on these words of the Lord—"I shall put enmity between you and the woman"—writes as follows: "Here it is indicated that when Eve returned to her senses, she repented, and this was the source of the Devil's sorrow," etc.[63] Likewise, that expression that she immediately uttered at the birth of her firstborn son was full of faith (although not free from error), if, with Fagius[64] and Forster,[65] we interpret it to mean, "I have brought forth the living Lord" (Gen. 4:1). Drusius does not entirely oppose this reading,[66] and the theologians of the Augsburg Confession vote in its favor. When I had the chance to study and consult their works, all of them, without exception, generally take the reading "A man Jehovah" in order to make the emphasis greater and thus to indicate Christ's two natures. Yet if we should construe it differently—as, "I have gotten a man from the Lord," or, "With the Lord"—it will bear the scent of piety all the same.

§ 13. Now that these preliminaries have been established, I will consider the symmetry of the reasoning. If any follow in the footsteps of those to whom the promise regarding the seed was renewed—specifically, if they are sons and seed of the aforementioned Abraham and Sarah—then by equal right they will be called the seed of those to whom the promise was originally made—that is, Adam and Eve. And perhaps they will be so by an even greater right, insofar as they who were created first were examples for Abraham and Sarah themselves and went before them on faith's narrow path.

---

63. Ap. Lippoman. in Catena ad locum.] Hugh of St. Victor, *Adnotationes Elucidatoriae*, in *Opera Omnia*, vol. 1 (Mainz, 1617), ch. 7, p. 12.

64. Fagius, *Exegesis Sive Expositio Dictionum Hebraicarum* (Isny, 1542), p. 118.

65. Johann Förster, 1495–1556, German Lutheran theologian and Hebraist, *Dictionarium Hebraicum Novum* (Basel, 1564), sub loc. יְהֹוָה, p. 190.

66. Vid. *Drusium* in comment. ad difficil. loca Pentateuch. c. 13. p. 25, 26] Drusius, *Ad Loca Difficiliora Pentateuchi* (Franeker, 1617), sub loc. Gen. 13.

To avoid the appearance of standing alone in that opinion or conjecture that I have proposed, I shall cite some well-known writers who—to put it modestly—expressed no disapproval of this same interpretation. Friedrich Spanheim writes, "Although Scripture nowhere calls Eve the mother of the faithful, nevertheless, nothing stops us from considering her such. For as she is called mother of all the living because all derive flesh from her, so because of the faith by which, as the first woman, she received the promise, Eve can, without incongruity, be called 'mother of the faithful.'"[67] But there are also those who think that the titles *mother* and *mother of the living* are attributed to her for this very reason and in the sacred text itself. I will mention two notable men from our ranks, distinguished individuals who served the Christian republic notably. The first is Dr. Joseph Hall, lately bishop of Norwich, who supported this opinion in his paraphrase of Song of Songs. There, for chapter 8, verse 5, after Christ had described His own church through her ascent from the desert, which indicates that she is called from the world, and how she reclines upon her beloved, which expresses faith, He reminds her of her former condition in these words: "I raised you up under the apple tree, where your mother who brought you forth labored over you." Hall, as I mentioned, explains these remarks in a paraphrase as follows: "You are she whom I loved long ago. I raised you to life again under the tree of delight, whose fruit was forbidden you and in which you tasted death. There your mother Eve labored over you and brought you forth, while through faith she received the gospel promise. Through this promise salvation was restored to Eve herself and to her spiritual seed."[68] The other man I will cite is James Ussher of Armagh. At the very beginning of his *Annals*, while commenting on the first human beings, he writes,

> Penalties are issued for those who have been tried and convicted, yet the promise is added that the seed of the woman will trample the serpent's head, that is, Christ will undo the Devil's works. For this reason her husband first gave her the name Eve, because she would be the mother of all the living. This not only regards natural life but also that life that comes through faith in her promised seed, Messiah. Likewise, Sarah after her is considered the mother of the faithful.[69]

---

67. Exercit. de gratia univers. p. 221.] Frederic Spanheim Sr., 1600–1648, German Reformed theologian, *Exercitationes De Gratia Universali* (Leiden, 1646), vol. 1, pp. 221–22.

68. Oper. Tom. 1. pag. mihi 266] Joseph Hall, 1574–1656, bishop of Norwich, religious writer, and satirist, *The works of Joseph Hall doctor in diuinitie, and deane of Worcester* (London, 1625), p. 266.

69. Annal. Ver. Testam. p. 2.] James Ussher, 1581–1656, Church of Ireland archbishop of Armagh and scholar, *Annales Veteris Testamenti* (London, 1650), p. 2.

CHAPTER III

A Display of the Various Types of Enmity
Also Mentioned Here

Section 1: The mutual hatred between Eve and the Devil. Section 2: The guilt of those who enter into friendship with the Devil. The guilty parties are described, including twenty-four popes and, among men of letters, Plotinus, Ermolao Barbaro, and Peter Cotton. Section 3: An example of the serpent's enmity in bruising of the heel is revealed, both as regards Christ (whose sufferings are touched upon) and Christians (1 Peter 5:8). Section 4: The wicked hate Christ comparatively, interpretively, and formally. The serpent's seed is twofold. The invisible seed, the spirits—that is, the powers below—why they are called the Devil's seed. Section 5: The different persecutions of the church, including the Church of England, Ireland, and the Piedmont. Section 6: The kernel of the proto-evangelium, Episcopius's skeptical interpretation, and two minor historical accounts. Section 7: The phraseology of the first promise is clarified, and two questions are offered on the trampling of the serpent's head. Section 8: An answer is made to the first question. Three proofs establish that Christ died in our place to satisfy divine justice for our sins. Section 9: The tricks of the Socinians and some of their arguments are evaluated, together with Peter Abelard's more reasonable position. Section 10: An answer is given to the second question. Christ abolished death and how he did it, with the observation of Paul Fagius. Section 11: Various distinctions regarding the abolition of sin. Section 12: A first conclusion on this topic—the guilt that superabounds to the person, and formal punishment according to Ames, Augustine, Chrysostom, and Aquinas. Section 13: The second conclusion is given as to when the kingdom of sin is abolished, as well as other matters. Here Castellio is critiqued, and Fox is praised. Section 14: The hatred of the pious toward demons, and the renunciation of magical arts. Section 15: The pious avoid the company of depraved people.

§ 1. Just as Jehovah Himself sounded the battle trumpet to this spiritual warfare that constitutes our discourse, so the fierce enmity between the sides began to grow hot right then and has not yet cooled off. It will be worth the effort, if I am not greatly mistaken, to set forth at least a few instances of this conflict. On careful reflection, it is clear that the mutual hatred first appeared between the woman and the metaphorical serpent. Friendships weak and poorly patched together tend toward hatred. The Shechemites entered into a very wicked treaty with Abimelech against the house of Jerub-baal (Judg. 9:24). In the end they held each other in equal contempt, until, according to Jotham's parable, fire came out of the wild briers and burnt up the cedars of Lebanon. In hell, all the reprobate shall pursue one another with a mutual hatred. There will be, moreover, the most blazing enmity between those who were brothers in wickedness while they walked the earth and lived as friends and allies in perpetrating crimes. Likewise, the woman here spoke with the Devil as a serpent in an intimate and friendly way. But after she began to realize what he had inflicted on her and her race, she immediately swelled with hatred toward the prince of devils. And after she had gotten children, no doubt, she was exceptionally diligent to keep any of them from yielding to Satan's servitude through their own hatred. The Devil, on the other hand, was very busy and was so successful that, within a few years, he had led astray Eve's firstborn Cain to the monstrous crime of fratricide (according to some interpreters, she had hoped that, in Cain, she had gotten the Messiah Himself). John testifies to this when he asserts that Cain was filled with malice and, so, murdered his brother (1 John 3:12). Hence, the very thing Rebecca long after that time feared—that she would lose both her sons in one day—happened to Eve (Gen. 27:47). In the very same day, she was robbed of Abel by death and robbed of Cain through exile and expulsion from before Jehovah's face. Let readers consider for themselves how much this event increased and sharpened the hatred we are discussing. This is precisely how that hatred was born, grew up, and grew old, yet will never die.

§ 2. Quite in keeping with the example of their mother Eve, all her offspring cherish deep down in their hearts everlasting hostility toward the Devil and his angels. No members of the human race are more degenerate or less human than those who make peace with hellish spirits or take counsel with them in any way. The first human (as we have it in Pliny) that dared to touch a lion with his hand and to render it tame was named Hanno,[1] according to the most distinguished Phoenician authors. "But he was condemned for this very reason: a man of such clever skill seemed likely to convince them of anything, and it was wrong to surrender liberty to a man to whom ferocity had yielded so much."[2] We can rightly doubt whether Hanno should have suffered for this. But there can be no doubt at all that

---

1. Hanno, fl. fifth century BC, Greek sailor.
2. Histor. nat. l. 8. c. 16.] Pliny the Elder, *Naturalis Historia* (Leiden, 1635), vol. 1, 8.16.

those who willingly subject themselves to these Stygian lions and dragons are very justly condemned. Such people willingly descend to these creatures while they try to win them over to themselves, as though to dens and caves. Nevertheless, certain of the most exalted Roman pontiffs have acted this way. Some twenty-four popes have surrendered themselves to the devilish arts![3] And some of these enslaved themselves to Satan wholesale to gain the pontificate. More than that, throughout the entire eighty-year period from Sylvester II[4] to Gregory VII,[5] no pope reigned who was not singularly notorious for wickedness. Educated men of great reputation also did this. Plotinus's[6] disciple Porphyry[7] wrote a life of his own well-beloved mentor. In it he makes very clear to his readers precisely where that famous coryphaeus of the Platonists acquired a familiar spirit—namely, in the temple of Isis[8] at Rome. He also explains that it was an Egyptian priest who procured it for him and that it habitually took the shape of a dragon.[9] In this guise it lurked beneath Plotinus's bed when he was near death and disappeared at the moment the man breathed his last. I said that it was in the shape of a dragon so no one can doubt that Plotinus's demon was from that same class that accompanied the one that John in the Apocalypse calls the dragon and ancient serpent. Beyond that, after Plotinus died, the same Porphyry introduced Apollo[10]—whom we Christians know full well was a devil—singing a hymn in praise of his master Plotinus and reflecting with a glad heart on the friendship that had once flourished between them. For so he begins:

Ἄμβροτα φορμίζειν ἀναβάλλομαι ὕμνον ἀοιδῆς
Ἀμφὲ ἀγανοῖο φίλοιο, etc.

That is,

I go forth to sound the song of an immortal hymn for my dear friend.[11]

The other notable individual is Ermolao Barbaro,[12] who, when he had gained an audience with a demon (Monlorius tells the story), asked that the

---

3. *Brightman*. in Apoc. 2.13.] Thomas Brightman, 1562–1607, Church of England clergyman and Presbyterian controversialist, *Apocalypsis D. Iohannis* (Amsterdam, 1611), sub loc. Rev. 2:13.

4. Sylvester II, ca. 940–1003, *p*. 999–1003.

5. Gregory VII, d. 1085, *p*. 1073–85.

6. Plotinus, ca. 205–270, Neoplatonist philosopher.

7. Porphyry, ca. 235–ca. 305, Neoplatonist philosopher.

8. Isis, Egyptian goddess of fertility.

9. Δράκοντος ὑπὸ τὴν κλίνην διελθόντος, "a dragon entered under his bed," &c. *Porphyrius* in vita *Plotini* non procul ab initio.] Porphyry, *Plotini Vita*, in *Opera Quae Exstant Omnia* (Basel, 1615), sig. β1v.

10. Apollo, Greek god, one of the twelve Olympians.

11. Idem ibid. non procul a fine.] Porphyrius, *Plotini Vita*, sig. γ2r.

12. Ermolao Barbaro, 1454–1493, Italian humanist, distinguished philologist, and diplomat.

creature teach him what Aristotle meant by ἐντελέχεια[13] in the definition of the human soul that he gave.[14] O you foolish man, Ermolao! You seem to have been much more concerned how to define the word "soul" than to save your own!

My third and final example (since it is not worthwhile to construct here an extended argument from Cornelius Agrippa,[15] Paracelsus, etc.) will be Peter Cotton.[16] He is the Jesuit whom Thuanus[17] says prepared a catalogue of questions to which he was waiting for an answer from a devil that was speaking through a certain young woman named Hadriana Fraxinea.[18] If anyone doubts the truth of Thuanus's history, he should consult Voetius's *The Papist Cause Abandoned*, page 180.[19]

§ 3. But let us return to the main path from this detour, so to speak. Although there will be a more expanded discussion later of the enmity that the metaphorical serpent has toward both seeds of the woman, still, nothing prevents me from making a few comments on the topic here and ὡς ἐν παρόδῳ.[20] And even less so, because in these words of the Lord to the serpent—the ones contained in the same phrase "You will bruise his heal"—the Lord presents, or, rather, offers, Himself as a very notable instance of what I am arguing. He had said above, "He will crush your head." The same term *bruising* is attested for both meanings. This always indicates a serious loss, as when in another passage, in Job, we read, "The one who will bruise me in the whirlwind and multiplies my wounds freely fills me with bitterness" (Job 9:17–18), although that same loss will in no way affect both parties— because for one the head is mentioned, while for the other, only the heel. To go after the heel is the serpent's natural habit. Thus, we have this comment of the patriarch Jacob: "Dan will be like a serpent at the roadside that bites the horse's feet and makes its rider fall backward" (Gen. 49:17). In this allegory concealing the protoevangelium, Christ is set before us as a strong man

---

13. "Full, complete reality." Liddell, Scott, and Jones, *A Greek-English Lexicon*.

14. Joh. Baptista Monlorius in libro de Entelecheia.] Juan Bautista Monllor (Johannes Baptista Monlorius), fl. 1591–1593, Italian humanist, *Perfectissima In Aristotelis Analyticorum* (Frankfurt, 1593), p. 412.

15. Heinrich Cornelius Agrippa von Nettesheim (Cornelius Agrippa), 1486–1535, German humanist and occultist.

16. Pierre Coton (Peter Cotton), 1564–1626, French Jesuit theologian.

17. Histor. sui temporis part. 5 l. 132. ad Annum 1604 p. 1135, 1136.] Jacques-Auguste de Thou (Thuanus), 1553–1617, Roman Catholic historian, *Historiarum Sui Temporis* (Frankfurt, 1621), vol. 5, bk. 132, p. 1025.

18. According to Thuanus, this was a woman born in Amiens, in northern France.

19. Gijsbert Voet (Gisbertus Voetius), 1589–1676, Dutch Reformed theologian, *Desparata Causa Papatus* (Amsterdam, 1635), bk. 2, sec. 2, ch. 10, p. 180.

20. "Along the way, as it were."

who tramples and grinds down the Devil's head beneath His feet. The Devil is like a serpent, twisting and writhing during the struggle, that, somehow, he might wound the one trampling him. Therefore, the Devil aims at His heel and deeply wounds it so Christ might not gain a bloodless victory. So in this pattern of expression, there seem to be included the various sufferings that belonged to Christ our Lord. Christ was harassed by these, as Satan stirred them up, from cradle to tomb. Actually, my statement "From cradle to tomb" is too mild. Even before Christ was born, and after he had risen from the dead, the deadly serpent did not stop assailing Him with every kind of violence, every kind of lurking device. The fullness of time had not yet arrived when the Devil was obsessed with throttling any hope in the promises of the coming Messiah. And he tried to use tyrants to destroy completely that entire nation, tribe, and family from which Christ would arise. As soon as the blessed yet inviolable virgin began to bear the womb that had conceived Christ, her blessed fetus was considered the offspring of illegitimacy and adultery. That same Satan caused this slander, since he is an amazing contriver of suspicions. After Christ's birth, that same opponent inspired Herod[21] to want to try to find the baby in order to kill him. He suggested this to Herod, I say, and, therefore, Herod's résumé for advanced savagery lacked only deicide. But he did desire to kill God.[22] Next, Christ was forced to go into exile. Afterward, when He had reached the age of the priesthood, He was led away into the desert where the prince of devils assailed Him in open war. Look at the extreme outrages that Satan's tools—Judas, the Jews, and the Romans—led him through, and to what kind of death! I think there is no need to mention the kinds of heresies the heterodox immediately used to attack His person and the teaching that arose from the resurrection itself. I am going to arm myself instead for explaining what relates to the woman's secondary seed and his heel.

Because the heel is the foundation on which the body stands, and when it is badly wounded, a man inevitably falls, so Satan is believed to strike the heel of the righteous every time he throws them down by a serious fall. Augustine favors this interpretation. He says, "The Devil watches when the heel slips, that he might throw you down. He watches your heel; you must watch his head. What is his head? It is the beginning of an evil desire. When he begins to suggest evil things, then repel him before pleasure arises and consent follows. Then you will avoid his head, and he will not catch your

---

21. Herod the Great, ca. 79–4 BC, r. 37–4 BC, king of Judaea.

22. *Causin.* Sancta curia part. 1. l. 4. p. 25.] Nicolas Caussin, 1583–1651, French Jesuit father and royal confessor, *La Cour Saincte* (Ferrand, 1544), part 1, bk. 4, p. 544.

heel."[23] Now as our Lord's food and drink while on earth was to do his Father's will, so it is Satan's dessert to divert every saint into transgressions. Even more, as there is joy in heaven for the conversion of one sinner, so there is glee in hell when a previously converted man commits some serious sin. Let us heed Peter, who says, "Your adversary the Devil is as a roaring lion, prowling about seeking whom he may devour" (1 Peter 5:8). Here he is compared to a famished lion that roars eagerly and rushes forward with insatiable hunger to destroy us. And he is described as seeking with consummate zeal not someone to bite, harm, or wound somehow. He wants someone to devour and swallow up in one gulp, so to speak (this is what καταπίνειν means). Or, as Nicholas of Lyra says, he is looking for someone to envelop in mortal guilt.[24] For as the food and drink someone devours is transformed into his substance, and we who eat by faith become sharers in the divine nature, so if Satan swallows anyone, he makes that person share in his diabolical nature. But as we consider the Devil's signature malice, the more valuable someone becomes to God, the more Satan detests him. He is a bandit that attacks the rich especially, a pirate that boards most of all those ships laden with costly merchandise. They say the panther hates humans so much that he will regularly attack a statue or even a painting of man. So because the demons cannot assail God personally, they attack His image shining forth in the saints and especially harass righteous magistrates and ministers of the Word with the most intense violence. But I will say more about this later.

§4. My next task is to show, with similar brevity, how the serpent's visible seed customarily displays its enmity against both seeds of the woman. He does this of course by feeling and action equally. As the Lord Himself testified in John, "If the world hates you, you know that it regarded Me with that hatred before you. He who hates Me also hates My Father. This is so that the word may be fulfilled that was written in their law, 'They hate me undeservedly'" (John 15:18, 23, 25)—or, as others render it, "without provocation or cause." These words provided someone with the opportunity for a very clever couplet. I thought, therefore, that I should recite it as a pious example:

> O gracious God, the world You loved without cause, hated You
> Yet without cause; You were so kind as "vengeance" on her too.[25]

---

23. In Psal. 48. com. 1.] Augustine, *Psalmi Enarratio*, in *Omnium Operum*, vol. 8 (Basel, 1528), sub loc. Ps. 48:6, 1.6.

24. Nicholas of Lyra, *Bibliorum Sacrorum*, vol. 6 (Lyon, 1545), sub loc. 1 Peter 5:8.

25. This appears to be Arroswmith's original, and mostly fluid, elegiac couplet:
   Alme Deus, te odit sine causa mundus, amabas
   Tu sine causa illum; Quam bonus ultor eras.

To illuminate a somewhat obscure subject, we say that the wicked truly hate Christ in three ways. First, they hate Him *comparatively*. The patriarch Jacob, since he loved his wife Leah less than he loved Rachel—and perhaps, less than he should have—is, thus, said comparatively to have hated her (Gen. 29:30–31). These statements of Christ in Matthew and Luke are parallel: "The one who loves his father or his mother more than Me, is not worthy of Me" (Matt. 10:37); and, "If anyone comes to Me and does not hate his father and his mother, he cannot be My disciple" (Luke 14:26). Now it is abundantly clear that the unregenerate, however many there are, love themselves and their own concerns more than Christ. And so much so that they hated Him when, in the parable, they were invited as guests to dinner. They preferred their oxen, farms, and wives to Christ, and—in the gospel history—the region of the Gadarenes preferred their pigs to Him.

Second, the wicked hate Christ *interpretively*. This is like when, in Solomon's proverbs, whoever spares the rod too much is thought to hate his own son: "The man who refrains from the rod hates his son; but he who loves him in a timely manner sees to his instruction" (Prov. 13:24). He "hates him," because neglecting someone is the same as showing him hatred. In this way, they who refuse Christ's cross or scepter undergo simultaneously the ruin and hostility of His punishment. "Many walk, as I have often told you, and now say even with tears, as enemies of the cross of Christ. Their end is destruction" (Phil. 3:18–19). So Paul wrote to the Philippians. "Lead to this place my enemies who did not want me as their king, and slit their throats in my presence" (Luke 19:27). Thus says the Lord in Luke.

And third, they hate Him *formally*. In this way, King Ahab says of the prophet Micah, "I hate him because he does not prophesy good of me, but evil" [1 Kings 22:8]. In equal manner are the wicked disposed toward Christ, not just as the God-man, Savior, and sole benefactor (for it is not possible for hatred to be maintained toward any object except due to evil). But they also inveigh against Him as lawgiver and judge. Allow me to summarize: the wicked are well pleased with the fruit of the guilt that Christ hates. When guilt and impenitence are set aside, Christ is delighted with the fruit of the punishment (so it is in Jeremiah, where God is said to administer not goodwill exclusively but also "right and justice in the earth, because in these I delight, says Jehovah" (Jer. 9:24). This justice the unrighteous hate heart and soul, and they run from it. So they hate Christ as lawgiver, who keeps them from their delights—the fruit of guilt. And they hate Him as judge, who inflicts upon them their sorrow, the fruit of the guilt by which they hatefully pursue Him.

§ 5. I must next speak about the woman's second seed—that is, the church. The visible seed of the serpent has harassed and afflicted her in a thousand ways from her first martyr Abel right down to today's confessors. The Apostle testifies about the church's legitimate sons when he writes, "They knew jeering and whips, and even chains and prison. They were stoned, cut to pieces, stretched, and cut down dead with the sword. They roved in the wild dressed in sheepskins and goatskins, wretchedly poor, afflicted, and mistreated. The world did not deserve them. They wandered in deserts and in mountains, holes and caves of the earth" (Heb. 11:36–38). The different martyrologies of sundry nations bear witness to these truths, along with these delicate verses, both in Greek and Latin, which all experience of both previous and present ages confirm. They go like this:

> αἷμα χοροῦ ἱεροῖο βάσις πέλει, εἴσοδος αἷμα
>   αἷμα πέλει πρόοδος, εἴσοδος αἷμα πέλει.

> By blood the church was founded once, and then by blood she grew.
> By blood again she was restored, and blood shall be her due.[26]

There is no need for me to mention the Jews. Paul says about them, "They even killed the Lord Jesus and their own prophets and have persecuted us. Nor do they please God, and they are at odds with all men" (1 Thess. 2:15). And what should I say about the Romans? Under their Caesars, those ten persecutions everyone talks about savagely raged. If only Christian—or, rather, "anti-Christian"—Rome had not tried to justify the old paganism! I mean especially when the Society—which they label "of Jesus"—raised its head in the world. They call it the Society of Jesus, I say, though one of its members, Jacobus Crusius—as almost everyone in Germany knows—reportedly sold out himself and his companions like this:

> It is right that the father of our Society was a soldier,[27] since, as a soldier's work is to charge the enemy with all his might and not stop until he comes away victorious, so it is ours to charge against all who resist the Roman pontiff, and to destroy and abolish them with our counsels, words, and writings, and even with civil authority. This is what the pontiff and the vows we have taken against the Lutherans desire and enjoin.[28]

There is no doubt that this bloody little battle command that spread throughout Europe in 1582 came from the same school or a similar one:

---

26. This is a famous—and anonymous—couplet that is at least as old as Erasmus and quoted by many luminaries—Turretin, etc. (A. also gives first a metrical Greek version, though it is unclear whose; it appears to be original with him.)

> *Sanguine fundata est Ecclesia, sanguine crevit*
>   *Sanguine succrevit, sanguine finis erit.*

27. That is, Ignatius of Loyola, ca. 1491–1556, founder of the Jesuits.

28. *Lucius* Hist. Jesuiticae p. 1.] Jacobus Crusius, fl. ca. 1580?, quoted in Ludwig Lucius, 1577–1642, German Reformed professor, *Historia Iesuitica De Iesuitarum* (Basel, 1627), bk. 1, ch. 1, p. 1.

Caesar, now employ your right, and snuff out Luther's sect.
Use blade, use wheel, use sea, ropes, flame, and all their hope reject.[29]

I have no desire to commemorate now the Sicilian Vespers[30] or the Parisian Massacre.[31] Indeed, more recent crimes plainly appear to have surpassed those older ones. The Marian human immolations still burn in the memories of our people. For as Sulla[32] once seemed to have found ten Mariuses[33] in one Caesar, so our England not long ago found ten Caesars in one Mary, and all of them notorious for persecution. But even Ireland, a land that writers say produces no animal worth hunting, recently produced a huge brood of vipers. This brood surpasses the degeneracy of unreasoning serpents to the same extent that it is more evil than any beast yet born. The Piedmont Massacre,[34] since it is the most recent of all the massacres, still echoes loudest in the mind. In it Roman Catholics wrought such great crimes as antiquity hardly dared imagine and posterity will never dare believe. But the groans or the tears of the pious reader, so I think, suggest I stop here. We must now go on to examine individual instances.

§ 6. The ἀποτέλεσμα[35] of all these events, the trampling of the serpent's head (among many other things I must omit to avoid the fault of long-windedness), shows our Lord Jesus Christ's enmity toward Satan. This is the only one that I will proceed to illuminate—first, by explaining the phraseology, and then, the actual content.

Now to prevent someone from complaining or from being surprised that I am giving more attention to this little clause—"The seed will bruise your head"—than to any of the rest, he should know that I consider this phrase the very center of the protoevangelical text. I take it that the promise contained in these words means comfort for the righteous and terror for the demons, no matter how the words are falsified by textual "restorers" of this age. The gloss that Smalcius, from Socinus's school, typically gave those

---

29. Anonymous couplet.

30. The Sicilian Vespers, a general massacre of the French in Sicily on March 30, 1282, the signal for which was the tolling of the bell for vespers.

31. Presumably the St. Bartholomew's Day massacre, August 23–24, 1572, a massacre of French Protestants in Paris.

32. Lucius Cornelius Sulla Felix (Sulla), ca. 138–78 BC, Roman general, consul, and dictator.

33. Gaius Marius, ca. 157–86 BC, Roman general, consul, and politician.

34. April 1655, massacre of Waldensian community; cf. the celebrated Milton sonnet, "Avenge, O Lord, thy slaughtered saints."

35. "Outcome."

words has been shown above.[36] Now here comes Episcopius, from Arminius's[37] school, who goes off-key in almost the same chord. He says,

> Even if some divine promise does not obviously appear in Genesis 3:15, and these words, "The seed of the woman will crush the serpent's head," are nowhere present in the New Testament as words containing a messianic promise, nevertheless, nothing prevents us from taking them like that, as though they referred to Satan's judgment.[38]

This is certainly a confused statement and one that tends more to deserting faith than producing it.

But so that it may be quite obvious how much comfort, as well as terror, these words contain, with the reader's permission, we will provide two short narratives. The first is featured in a dedicatory epistle that prefaces the fifth volume of Brenz's works. It concerns a certain Christopher Haas, a senator of Hall in Swabia. A certain scribe (so he was thought to be) came to Haas while he was lying in bed just a few days before the moment of his death arrived. The scribe was carrying paper, ink, and a quill, sat down at the table, and addressed the invalid with words such as these: "Christopher! List in order all the sins that you have ever committed, for God sent me to catalogue them and take them back to His tribunal, since you must give an account in His presence." Then Christopher raised himself on the couch as much as he could, and realizing now that he was dealing with Satan, with a fearless heart, replied, "The title should be written first. So please write this: 'The seed of the woman shall crush the serpent's head.' Beneath this title you can list all my sins." Satan sat there disguised, but when he heard this answer, he immediately disappeared.[39]

The theologian Johannes Willius[40] of Elbing[41] personally recounted to me the second history. He stayed with me as a guest for several months at King's Lynn in the vicinity of Norfolk. The story goes as follows: Daniel Cramer, the author of *The Prophetic School* and rector of the Stetten Academy in Germany, was once supervising some students. Among these was found one who had bound himself over to the Devil by a written agreement, inscribed in the student's own hand. The contract was brought to

---

36. Hic c. 1. §. 5.] See ch. 1, sec. 5.

37. Jacobus Arminius, 1559–1609, Dutch theologian.

38. Instit. l. 5. c. 4. p. 409.] Simon Episcopius, 1583–1634, Dutch Remonstrant leader and theologian, *Institutiones Theologicae*, in *Opera Theologica* (Amsterdam, 1650), bk. 4, sec. 5, ch. 4, p. [i] 409.

39. Brenz, *Operum Reverendi Et Clarissimi Theologi* (Tübingen, 1582), sig.):(7r (*epistola dedicatoria*).

40. Perhaps Johannes Wille, 1575–1640, but he is more often associated with Bremen.

41. Elbing, Prussia.

Cramer by another student who had obtained that autograph by chance. As Cramer sat in his study several days later, Satan came to him, beating on the door with a loud and unusual knock. And then he shouted, "Cramer, Cramer! Give me back my receipt that you have with you. Give back, I say, my receipt!" That learned and quick-witted man, as soon as he realized who it was that had accosted him, said, "Hold on a minute, Satan. Here it is! I used it as a bookmark to Genesis 3:15 in Holy Writ, where we read that 'the seed of the woman will crush the serpent's head.' Here, take it, if you dare." They say the Devil roared back at these words, and with a great commotion and stench, he left, after dashing to pieces most of the study.

§7. As regards the phraseology itself, we see that the crushing of the serpent's head means not a mild bruising but extermination. For animals that belong to that class, if they are struck in any part of the body, they, nevertheless, continue living though wounded. But if their head is shattered, they die from that blow. "It is amazing," says Franz, "if in fact it's altogether true, that serpents' tails, when cut off, grow back, and that by licking they can restore all the other parts of their bodies that have been worn away or broken off by a wound, provided the head remains sound. That's why they roll themselves into coils when they fight and carefully protect the head. For when their head is in danger, then their whole life is too."[42]

There is found in Paulus Fagius a saying of a certain rabbi in which, along with the malevolence of the Jews, this phrase's proper emphasis is obvious. This is what he said: "Among the gentiles, even the best man deserves to have his head trampled as though he were a serpent."[43] Furthermore, the head is that part of the body where the strength of certain animals resides, and so, metaphorically, it connotes their power. So in the Apocalypse, by the terms *head* and *horns* are meant those powers—both ecclesiastical and temporal—through which the Beast exercised his dominion. Truly, the power of the hellish serpent asserts itself both in death, as power over death is said to reside with the Devil, and in sins, which are deemed his works (Heb. 1:14). For indeed, John, after he had said that Christ had been made known to take away sins, at last explains himself thus: "The Son of God was made manifest for this reason, to destroy the works of the Devil" (1 John 3:5, 8).

Therefore, as regards the present topic, it seemed wise to set down two questions here and then handle them in the Scholastic manner. First, How

---

42. Animal hist. sacra part. 3. cap. 1.] Franz, *Animalium Historia Sacra* (Amsterdam, 1653), part 4, ch. 1, pp. 508–9.

43. In paraphras. Chald. ad Exod. 23. 1.] Fagius, *Paraphrasis Chaldaica Onkeli* (Strasbourg, 1546), sub loc. Exod. 23.1.

did Christ crush the serpent's head *for us*? Second, How does He crush the serpent's head *in us*? I mean, if we want to state it precisely, How did He and how does He abolish death and sin?

§ 8. This is my answer to the first question: Christ trampled the serpent's head *for us* by dying in our place, to satisfy divine justice for the sins of all His own. This is proved first by the nature of His punishments in their *genus*. According to Johannes Altenstaig,[44] punishment indicates order with respect to guilt and is received as a sort of vengeance. The evangelical prophet explains that the evils Christ endured were penal: "The chastisement of our peace is placed on Him. Jehovah makes the punishment of us all fall upon Him" (Isa. 53:5–6; this quote is from the Junio-Tremellian version).[45] Biel states clearly, "Evil punishments are not truly evil, because they emanate from the highest good—namely, God. They lead to the highest good—namely, to enjoyment of God. And these punishments," as pertains to our point, "were in the highest good—namely, Christ."[46] These penalties, therefore, did not refer to His crimes (for He was free of all sin) but to ours, as the same prophet very skillfully explains: "He was afflicted with pain for our weaknesses. He was wounded for our transgressions. Bearing the sins of many, He personally interceded for the rebels" (Isa. 53:5, 12). But these penalties, according to the Apostle, also issued forth from divine justice. "God offered Him as a propitiation by faith in His blood as a demonstration of His justice" (Rom. 3:25–26). And again, "As a demonstration of His justice" means, of course, of His avenging justice, that He "might Himself be just." For no avenging justice broke forth in the flood, in the destruction of Sodom, or at any other time more clearly than when the divine wrath due to sinners waxed hot against their surety and security. Therefore, we must believe that Christ washed away our sins because He paid their penalties,[47] and that He expiated them through the mode of satisfaction, since He Himself became a sin offering.

This is proven, second, from the particular character of those penalties that Christ paid. For it will become evident that He suffered in our place, provided it is established that His penalties were the same as regards substance as those which we ourselves would have had to pay. As the theologians agree, these penalties were partly of sensation, partly of condemnation. He suffered the penalty of sensation in his agony, when He abundantly poured

---

44. Johannes Altenstaig, ca. 1480–ca. 1525, German humanist and anti-Reformation publicist.

45. *Biblia Sacra*, Isa. 53:5–6, p. 452.

46. Gabriel Biel, ca. 1420–1495, German Scholastic philosopher.

47. A. connects here *eluisse peccata* with *luit poenas*.

fourth bloody drops of sweat from every part, "so that His whole body, which is the church," as Bernard eloquently puts it, "might be cleansed by the tears of His whole body" (Luke 22:44).[48] And He confessed that His soul in every part was filled with sorrow, even unto death. At that time He was not being persecuted by an enemy externally. Only the fire of the divine, burning anger brought forth within Him those falling drops (Matt. 26:38). He sustained the penalty of condemnation on the cross when He shouted, "My God, my God, why have you forsaken me?" (Matt. 27:46). For although Christ—since He is the beloved Son of God, who is always in the bosom of the Father (John 1:18)—could never be truly abandoned in His person proper (so I would say), nevertheless, as surety and bondsman for sinners and as one who bore their person, according to the urgency of the divine economy, He was, for a time, deserted.

Third and last, this is proved by the prepositions ὑπέρ and ἀντί,[49] which the Holy Spirit very regularly uses on this subject. He died (the apostles say) ὑπὲρ παντός and ὑπὲρ ἡμῶν,[50] therefore, in our place (Heb. 2:10). This is just as we read in the Poet: "The life of one will be given on behalf of many"[51] (1 Peter 2:21).[52] We freely acknowledge that the phrase "on behalf of" sometimes does not mean so much *in place of* as it does *for someone's good*. This explanation is the one hiding place for our opponents. But they can contrive nothing like that with regard to the particle ἀντί, especially since (as Grotius notes) in composition, it always indicates either opposition or exchange. Accordingly, when Christ is described as giving Himself ἀντίλυτρον[53] for us, where opposition is not in view, the proper meaning must be recompense and exchange, just as in Greek, those who offer themselves as sacrifices to free others from death are called ἀντίψυχοι.[54] When we read, ὀφθαλμὸν ἀντὶ ὀφθαλμοῦ, καὶ ὀδόντα ἀντὶ ὀδόντος, (Matt. 5:38)[55] no one doubts that this means an eye in place of an eye, and a tooth in place of a tooth. Why, then, should we not conclude that Christ was crucified in our place and instead of us, since He Himself said that He had

---

48. Bernard of Clairvaux, 1090–1153, abbot of Clairvaux, *Dominica Palmarum*, in *Opera Omnia*, vol. 2 (Cologne, 1641), *sermo* 3, sec. 4. A. has *sanaretur* in place of *purgaretur*.

49. "On behalf of" and "in place of."

50. "On behalf of all" and "on our behalf."

51. Vergil, *Aeneidos*, bk. 5 (lines 814–15). The "Poet," capitalized in A.'s text, is Vergil. There Aeneas's helmsman Palinurus is cast overboard in the dead of night by Morpheus, the god of sleep, and drowns. Palinurus is the sacrifice that allows all the Trojans to reach Italy.

52. First Peter 2:21 says something similar of Christ.

53. "As a ransom."

54. Vid. Grotium de satisfact. c. 9.] Hugo Grotius, 1583–1645, Dutch jurist and Christian humanist, *Defensio Fidei Catholicae* (Oxford, 1636), ch. 9, pp. 176–77. "One life for another."

55. "An eye for an eye, and a tooth for a tooth."

come to give His life as a λύτρον ἀντὶ πολλῶν (Matt. 20:29)?[56] Yet even ὑπέρ sometimes cannot help being taken in that same sense. Thus, Paul says that he chooses to be ἀνάθεμα ὑπὲρ τῶν ἀδελφῶν (Rom. 9:3)[57]—that is, in the stead of his own brothers whom he foresaw would perish unless they accepted the gospel.

§9. How do our opponents respond to these observations? They play around with words, like little boys with game pieces. They grant that Christ in fact died for us. But they say He died for our good, not in our place.[58] They admit also that He died to make atonement for sinners but not to make satisfaction. They say He died either to satisfy the divine will that desired our salvation, or for divine wisdom, which was well pleased with such a means of procuring salvation, or for the divine honor, which was restored and avenged as much (and even more) through the obedience of the second Adam as it had been damaged through the sins of the first Adam and his descendants. The satisfaction that was truly offered to divine justice they reject and denounce as unworthy of God and strenuously opposed to the sense of Scripture.

But if, however, someone should ask about the arguments that induced such men to move toward a position opposite ours, perhaps it will not be disagreeable to produce here one or two of those, so that, from those arguments, one may form a judgment about the rest. The Racovian Catechism says, "It would follow that Christ underwent an eternal death if he had satisfied God for our sins, since it is agreed that the penalty that men merited for their sins was eternal death."[59] But we must altogether deny that this follows, since the rationale at work with respect to Christ and the damned is vastly different. The latter, since they are mere men, can in no way endure the infinite anger of God at the very moment it is poured out on them. Therefore, they endure it in succession, so that the creature is not completely consumed. But Christ, true God and man in one hypostasis, according to His own infinite virtue, was able to endure the entire punishment entirely. Consequently, what He suffered in time is rendered equal to punishments that were actually eternal. But those idle babblers object further on these grounds: "The abandonment and hatred of God were the

---

56. "Ransom for many."

57. "Condemned in the place of his brothers."

58. Vid. *Crellium* in praefation. respons. ad *Grotium* p 7. & 8. Item in respons. ad c. 6. partic. 44,] Johann Crell, 1590–1633, Socinian theologian and rector of Raków school, *Ad Librum Hugonis Grotii* (Rakow, 1623), pp. 4, 342–45.

59. Cap. 8. ad quaest. 16.] Racovian Catechism (Catechismus Racoviensis), written in 1605 by Smalcius et al., a Unitarian group that broke off from Calvin's church, *Catechesis Ecclesiarum* (Raków, 1609), p. 229.

indivisible companions of the penalties we deserved. There is no way to ascribe such sins to Christ without blasphemy."[60] I answer that flaws of this kind really accompany the guilt of inherent sin but not of imputed sin. And I add, moreover, that the grace in Christ must be regarded as threefold: of union, vision, and anointing. The grace of union could not have been taken away: He was truly the Θεάνθρωπος[61] even during the three-day period of His death. The grace of vision could have been withdrawn, and it was withdrawn for a time in the abandonment He endured. The grace of anointing always remained whole and undamaged, such that it would have been impossible for abandonment or any sinful thing like that to fall upon Him.

The human reasoning evident in the other arguments yields a more than adequate harvest, as it is not afraid to contradict the Holy Spirit who very clearly asserts that "Christ suffered for sinners, the just for the unjust" (1 Peter 3:18). Such reasoning is always snarling that this cannot happen while keeping God's goodness intact. We will pass by these arguments, for the moment, and end with a prayer, seriously hoping that the change of mind and language that we read overtook Peter Abelard[62] will befall all remaining Socinians.[63] Abelard had held the same opinion that nowadays those who follow Socinus's camp latch onto with their jaws. But when he had finally reached an advanced age, Abelard wrote his *Defense* in the monastery at Cluny (where death overtook him), as an indication of his better mind and more sound judgment. In that work, as Peter of Cluny records it, we find this thesis: "I confess that the Son of God alone was incarnated to free us from our slavery to sin and from the yoke of the Devil, and by His own death, to unlock for us the entrance to life above."[64]

§ 10. The second question is this: How does the seed of the woman in us trample the serpent's head? For there is in us as well a "snake,"[65] as Macarius

---

60. This citation is not given as a quotation by A. Perhaps here he paraphrases the catechism from memory.

61. "God-man."

62. Peter Abelhard, 1079–ca. 1142/1143, philosopher and theologian.

63. *Vossius* in respons. ad *Rauensper.* c. 3.] Gerard Vossius, 1577–1649, Dutch Remonstrant classical scholar and theologian, *Responsio Ad Iudicium Hermanni Ravenspergeri* (Leiden, 1618), p. 11.

64. Ap. D. *Prideaux* Lect. 19. p. 295.] Peter the Venerable (of Cluny), ca. 1092/1094–1156, abbot of Cluny. Peter the Venerable is quoted in a work of John Prideaux, 1578–1650, bishop of Worcester, *Viginti-duae Lectiones De Totidem Religionis Capitibus* (Oxford, 1648), lec. 19, p. 295.

65. Here A. uses the term *coluber* for the first time. He has previously employed synonyms *draco*, *serpens*, and *viper*.

says, τὸν ὄφιν τὸν κατώτερον τοῦ νοῦ καὶ βαθύτερον τῶν λογισμῶν.[66] Christ tramples his head by abolishing death, whose sting is sin, then sin itself, the wages of which are death, in the manner and at the time that pleased Him. Here I will say only a few words about death, especially since I will need to deal with the topic several more times below as it occurs— unless it happens that my discourse reaches the conclusion toward which it is leading sooner than I intend.

Christ is said to have abolished death and to have brought life and immortality to the light through the gospel (1 Tim. 6:10).[67] "His life," says Bernard, "rebuilt ours; His death destroyed ours."[68] But in what sense is this so? O most honey-tongued father,[69] how does death seem to have been conquered by the head when it still rages in the members with such great license? Bernard answers sweetly (as is his practice) but also forcefully: "Death itself, actually, is not at all, as yet, forced to leave, but it is forced not to harm us."[70] I would add that Christ, by His own death, has changed the death of His people into medicine, and the penalty of sin into heaven's doorway. I will not insert anything else here except one particular observation of Paul Fagius. He says,

> The Jews claim (according to the ancient rabbis) that Satan, or the Angel of Death (as they call him), always appeared visibly to those who were just about to die. Because men were thoroughly terrified at his appearance, they claim further that the rabbis who came after the time of Christ our Savior obtained from God, through their prayers, that Satan should no longer appear visibly to those about to die as he had before. They also debate a good deal about Satan's power, that it is now diminished and weakened. Indeed, these comments—says that very distinguished man[71]—would not be made so foolishly were they not referring to the fact that those ancient Hebrews saw that Satan causes fear in those who do not know Christ the Messiah. But otherwise, he can cause no harm. For Christ Himself is He who had to trample the serpent's head in Genesis 3,

---

66. Homil. 17. circa fin.] Macarius of Egypt (Macarius the Great), ca. 300–ca. 390, Egyptian monk, *Homiliae Spirituales* (Frankfurt, 1594), p. 263 (homilia 17). "One lower than the mind and deeper than our faculties."

67. Second Tim. 1:10.

68. Serm. in transit S[ti]. Mal.] Bernard of Clairvaux, *Liber Sententiarum*, in *Opera Omnia*, vol. 5 (Cologne, 1641), sec. 22. There is a pun here in Bernard on the words of opposite meaning, *instruxit…destruxit*.

69. That is, Bernard.

70. Bernard of Clairvaux, *In Obitu S. Malachiae*, in *Opera Omnia*, vol. 2 (Cologne, 1641), sec. 4. Again, Bernard's Latin is concise, beautiful, and punning: *Mors ipsa minime quidem adhuc abesse cogitur, sed cogitur non obesse.*

71. That is, Fagius.

a fact that those ancient Hebrews perceived, as is seen from the Jerusalem Paraphrase.[72]

Actually, those who read such comments can scarcely keep from thinking of what was written by the Apostle in the letter to the Hebrews, to those endowed by their own teachers with the concepts we mentioned: "Because the children are sharers in flesh and blood, He Himself also likewise was made a sharer in the same, that through death He might abolish that one in whose presence is death's strength—namely, the Devil—and set free however many by fear of death had been condemned to slavery through their whole life" (Heb. 2:14–15).

§ 11. We must make some more comments about sin. The same Apostle asserts that "the same Christ was made manifest now once for all at the end of the ages to take away sin from our midst through the sacrifice of His own person" (Heb. 9:26)—εἰς ἀθέτησιν ἁμαρτίας.[73] The antidote the Physician of Souls brought for this serpentine poison was so powerful! There is agreement on the facts of the event, while on the manner and the extent, there is strife. So that the truth may shine forth more clearly at this crucial summit of theology—which everyone understands is of the greatest consequence—I shall bypass several distinctions and try to resolve the whole issue into one or two conclusions.

There are three things we must consider with respect to the topic of sin: its guilt, its reign, and its remnants. The guilt of sin is either simple, with respect to the demerit of the action or vicious disposition, in keeping with the penalty due it, or it extends to the person, in which case it involves not only the demerit but also the condemnation, and not only the condemnation as it has been deserved but also as it will certainly be inflicted. That sin is said to reign over the one whose soul willingly subjects its entire self to sin, not as a people to their tyrant—whose yoke they bear with the greatest difficulty but never try to shake off. No, it is as a people to their legitimate ruler, whom either they chose or embraced as succeeding to them by legal heredity. By the remnants of sin, I mean that propensity that is also sometimes called the root of vices. This attaches very resolutely even to regenerate minds and to their deepest marrow unless death plucks it out. The sacred Scriptures set before us two antidotes for removing the poison of that sin that persists—namely, remission and renewal.[74] The concept of

---

72. Chald. ad Deut. 14.] Fagius, *Paraphrasis Chaldaica Onkeli*, sub loc. Deut. 14.

73. "To put away sin."

74. A. uses alliteration: *Remissionem & Scilicet Renovationem.*

remission is, in turn, twofold. The first aspect, as we read in Grotius, is τὸ ἀφιέναι. He says,

> To this corresponds the Latin verb *remittere*, which properly means "to remove from oneself." Its extended meaning is, among other things, "not to keep a record of something," which Latin authors, by a similar phrase, express as *missum facere*. Consequently, the Greek scholiasts sometimes explain τὸ ἀφιέναι by τὸ ἀμελεῖν. Therefore, this means both to forgive sins and to dismiss debts, which, as Scripture describes elsewhere, is to cast them into the sea. This is like when the poets say that those matters that are set beyond care are committed to the winds, to be swept out to sea.[75]

Grotius then continues his discussion into the consequences of these ideas.

The second aspect of remission is from Antony Wotton's work *The Sinner's Restoration*. He writes,

> I think—and may those who make this profession listen with gentle charity—that the remission of sins denotes their mitigation. Consider this from Cicero: "Hold the reins of friendship as loosely as possible, that you may pull them in or let them out when you please."[76] So I think, therefore, that the sinner's conscience is held bound by chains on account of the guilt of his crime, and the sinner himself is obligated to pay the penalties fully, as though he was about to be whisked away at that moment to the judge's tribunal and, from there, to punishment. Thus, when mercy is obtained, they are, as it were, forgiven, or the reins that his guilt had drawn in, from a knowledge of the crimes, are relaxed. The result is that, since he has been freed from the fear of punishment and suit, he can no longer be considered guilty.[77]

Thus those men wrote, and with quite impressive learning. But the first author[78] has more regard for remission in the court of God, while the second deals with a closer consideration of that remission that is found in the court of conscience. Finally, that which I have termed renewal (for we have not yet fully woven in the thread of these distinctions) is twofold: one part is inchoate, or consists in becoming, while the other is consummate, consisting in an accomplished fact. I must soon provide a fuller discussion of both these concepts. In the meantime, now that these foundations are

---

75. De satisfact. c. 2.] Grotius, *Defensio fidei catholicae*, ch. 2, p. 66.

76. Marcus Tullius Cicero, 106–43 BC, Roman orator and statesman, *Laelius De Amicitia*, 45.

77. Part. 2. lib. 2. capite atq; etiam num. 32.] Anthony Wotton, bap. ca. 1561–1626, Church of England clergyman and controversialist, *De Reconciliatione Peccatoris* (Basel, 1624), part 2, bk. 2, ch. 32, p. 371.

78. That is, Grotius.

laid, so to speak, I shall build conclusions upon them. The first of these is as follows.

§ 12. The remission obtained by the blood of Christ removes from all those who by faith receive it all the guilt that superabounds to their persons. To be sure, God hates the sins even of the regenerate with a very great purity. But it is a simple hatred, because their persons have been reconciled to Him through Christ. He hates the sins of the unrighteous, however, with a hatred that superabounds to their persons, because they do not possess the ransom of Christ for their sins' atonement, a ransom applied to them by faith. Οὐδὲν κατάκριμα τοῖς ἐν Χριστῷ Ἰησοῦ (Rom. 8:1), the Apostle proclaims.[79] This is a universal negative proposition: "There is no condemnation for those in Christ Jesus." Contrary to this, by a particular affirmative proposition, is the statement, "There is some condemnation even for those who are in Christ, at least as regards temporal punishments." While the Romanists and others combat that first proposition, they should themselves see whether they are contradicting Paul and claiming that at least some guilt superabounds to the persons of the faithful. How much better does Augustine interpret this golden sentiment as said of Christ: "By undertaking our penalty and not our guilt, did He destroy the guilt and the penalty?"[80] I am not one who denies that materially there are afflictions for the regenerate. For very often the regenerate do not materially differ in the disasters they experience from those that befall the unrighteous. The same sword can fall upon Uriah just as it strikes the most wicked soldier. The same house can crumble upon Samson just as much as upon uncircumcised Philistines. Isaac toils with his blindness just as much as Elymas does. How minuscule a difference there is between Josiah and Ahab, if one examines the type of death they suffered, and the material of their destruction. If there had been no sin in Adam, there would have been no punishment in the world. Therefore, I should have the freedom to refer to these punishments as existing *originally*. But I deny that these are or can be deemed punishments *formally*, and I deny that, when they fall upon the regenerate, they can be classified under the category "penalty." "For just as sin itself remains in this life," says someone of our party, "even after it has been remitted, but not in the same category as before"—he means to say, I believe, that it does not remain as regnant nor as destructive—"so also some penalty for sin remains. But this also is under a different category, obviously as the means of some good, not as vengeance properly so named

---

79. "There is no condemnation for those in Christ Jesus."

80. De verb. Dom. serm. 37.] Augustine, *De Verbis Domini In Evangelio Secundum Lucam*, in *Omnium Operum*, vol. 10 (Basel, 1528), *sermo* 37.

nor as satisfaction owed God's justice."[81] Gregory explains this well: "The Father's discipline is not that of a judge's anger but the love of one giving correction."[82] Chrysostom is even better: "When the Lord takes hold of us, it is more a matter of admonition than condemnation, more of medicine than torment, of correction than punishment."[83] But of all these comments, unless I am mistaken, Augustine's is best: "Before the remission of sins, disasters are punishment for them. After remission, they are the contests and testing grounds of the just."[84] And again, "The Lord lashes us in these struggles and instructs us. The sorrow of divine punishment is medicinal; it is not penal in meaning."[85] Actually, Thomas himself is quite good here: "Temporal evils are inflicted upon the wicked as punishment, and to such an extent that, by these punishments, the wicked are not aided to attain eternal life. Upon the righteous, however, who are helped by evils of this kind, they are not punishments but more like medicines."[86] At this point we have reached our first conclusion.

§ 13. Our second conclusion follows: *renewal begun through the spirit of Christ removes the reign of sin, and when complete, it takes away any remnants of sin.* This reign is removed when someone—though, for sure, still feeling his sin but yet at no point whatsoever consenting to it—is eager to please God in all things. He hates his own παρορἀματα,[87] vigorously resists them, so that he generally overcomes them; and if ever he gives in, his whole will is not overcome but yet rises up again through repentance.

This then is the state of the regenerate for as long as they pilgrim on the journey. When, at last, we reach our fatherland, "the perfect will come, and that which exists in part shall be abolished. For then Christ will establish His church in glory; she shall have no spot or wrinkle, or anything like that" (1 Cor. 13:10; Eph. 5:27). Certainly, those who have been justified are completely cleansed, if we are considering remission of sins; not, however, perfectly—if we have regard to renewal—until they appear in glory in the

---

81. *Ames. Bellarm.* enervat. Tom. 2. p. mihi 187.] Ames, *Bellarminus Enervatus* (Amsterdam, 1630), vol. 2, bk. 5, ch. 1, thes. 1, sec. 16.2, p. 188.

82. Gregory the Great, ca. 540–604, *p.* 590–604, *Expositionis Moralis In Beatum Iob*, in *Opera*, vol. 1 (Basel, 1551), sub loc. Job 31, 21.17.

83. Homil. 28. in 1 Cor. νουθεσίας μᾶλλον ἢ καταδίκης, ἰατρείας ἢ τιμωρίας, διορθώσεως ἢ κολάσεως.] Chrysostom, *In Epistolam Pauli Ad Corinthios Priorem*, in *Opera Omnia*, vol. 4 (Basel, 1539), sub loc. 1 Cor. 11:32 (*homilia* 28).

84. De peccat. merit. & remission. c. 34.] Augustine, *De Peccatorum Meritis Et Remissione*, in *Omnium Operum*, vol. 7 (Basel, 1528), 2.34. A. replaces *quaestione* with *calamitates*.

85. In Psalm. 138] Augustine, *Psalmi Enarratio*, sub loc. Ps. 138:15.

86. 1ᵃ 2ᵃ qu. 114. Art. 10. ad 3ᵘᵐ] Thomas Aquinas, *Summa Theologiae*, in *Opera Omnia*, vol. 11, part 1 (Venice, 1593), 1-2.114.10 *ad* 3.

87. "Errors."

heavenly kingdom, or at least until they are in its suburbs, which the dying saints enter. Bede quite appositely says the following about the passage I cited: "In the kingdom of heaven, the church will exist fully and perfectly, having no spot or wrinkle or anything of that kind. For when the Apostle said not only that Christ would offer the church to Himself without spot or wrinkle but also added that she would be glorious, He showed sufficiently when she will be without spot or wrinkle. It will be, evidently, when she is in the state of glory, as it is called."[88] Augustine expresses it very brilliantly and eloquently: "No one takes away sin except Christ, who is the lamb of God that takes away the sins of the world. Moreover, He takes them away by lessening the sins that have been committed, by helping to prevent them from arising, and by leading His people to the future life where sins cannot at all exist. In this life, therefore, there is only the race path toward righteousness: in the next life there will be the prize."[89]

But a certain Sebastian Castellio raises and lifts himself with all his might against this truth, which is, so far as I understand, extremely clear. In his treatise *Offering Obedience to God*, in order to establish his own utopian perfection, Castellio distorts the protoevangelical text (among others) like this: "Is not Christ the lamb of God who takes away the sin of the world? What, moreover, does 'taking away' mean, or what does it mean to abolish the works of the Devil? Surely it does not mean to set one's hand to the task without meaning to finish it. Far from it! He deeply crushed the serpent's head and shattered its power."[90] No, Sebastian, far be it, rather, far be it from Christians to do anything but embrace, with all gratitude, this hand of Christ who renews us inchoately, to do anything but kiss it lovingly! For with Paul, Christians take it as established that "He who began a good work in us shall also complete it" (Phil. 1:6). Meanwhile, can Christ not rightly be said to have taken away our sins, when He laid low their condemnatory power, and that He trampled the head of the serpent, when He broke its condemnatory power? I will go further: He kindly bestowed upon us a perfection of the parts, such that regeneration extends through all the faculties of the soul, and the soul now renewed is oriented toward all the commands of God; the Spirit who reigns in the soul is stronger than the remnants of the flesh. That perfection by degrees, which you, Castellio, make so much noise over, must indeed be anticipated, but someplace else.

---

88. Probably Bede, *Historiae ecclesiasticae gentis Anglorum libri V* (Cambridge, 1646).

89. Lib, de perfectione Justitiae.] Augustine, *Ad Episcopos Eutropium Et Paulum, De Perfectione Iustitiae Hominis, Liber Unus*, in *Opera*, vol. 7 (Basil, 1528).

90. pag 230.] Sebastian Castellio, 1515–63, classical scholar and Protestant theologian, *Dialogi IV* (Gouda, 1613), p. 230. The verbs *erigit* and *insurgit* suggest serpentine action, in keeping with the theme.

In the meantime, let us hear these words of Cyprian: "Who will boast that he is cleansed from sins? But if no one can be without sins, whoever says that he is faultless is either arrogant or foolish."[91] Let us heed Augustine: "God, by His own grace, acts in us so that sin is destroyed and the person is set free. But when is restlessness destroyed? If it is diminished, how is it not destroyed? What is diminished in the life of those making progress is destroyed in the life of those made perfect."[92] Now, if it pleases the reader, let us heed one of our own countrymen, John Foxe, a man I consider really quite worthy and rightly count as worth more than even ten Castellios. "The life of the saints in these lands is a life not of a completed love and mortification but of one that is inchoate. For it is perceived not so much in righteousness as in justification, not so much in actual holiness but in being made holy, not in purity but in purification, and not in perfection but in progress." Thus Foxe.[93]

§ 14. There are still remaining some marks of that holy enmity that the secondary seed of the woman works against both seeds of the serpent. Concerning the serpent's invisible seed, the Thomists typically ask this: Must we, from Christian charity, love demons?[94] The sum of the answer comes back as this, that Christian charity embraces every rational creature except for demons and the damned, because all either are or, at least, from our perspective, can be sharers in holiness and blessedness. But charity abandons demons and the damned, because God has abandoned them. Thus, we cannot wish for them to possess the good of eternal life, which is charity's chief concern, because this stands in opposition to the charity that approves of God's righteousness and rests in His revealed will. The rejection of all the magic arts—a rejection that has tended to drive deep roots into their hearts—shows clearly just how much hatred those truly called Christians have toward demons. The Suda[95] testifies to the fact that the Egyptians in Alexandria had determined and decreed that astrologers should pay some sort of tribute, called the "fools' tax," because none except foolish and meddlesome men sought their advice. The servants of true piety customarily treat that class of people—not only the teachers but even their students—as guilty, and guilty not only of foolishness but of execrable impiety. I mean

---

91. Cyprian, *De Eleemosyna*, in *Opera* (Basel, 1558) (*sermo* 1).

92. Tractat. 41. in Evang Johan.] Augustine, *In Evangelium Ioannis Expositio*, 41.9.

93. De Christo gratis iustitiae. p. 162.] John Foxe, ca. 1516/1517–1587, martyrologist, *De Christo Gratis Iustificante* (London, 1583), p. 162.

94. Ad 2ᵃᵐ 2ᵃᵉ quaest. 25. artic. 11.] Aquinas, *Summa Theologiae*, in *Opera Omnia*, vol. 11, part 2 (Venice, 1593), 2-2.25.11.

95. *Souidas*, vol. 2. (Geneva, 1619). See p. 881 for discussion of taxation in general, yet the entries for *vectigal stultorum* do not appear here.

those who either seek the advice of magicians or make use of forbidden cures like ritual bindings and amulets. Such are quite wisely and properly called the Devil's sacraments, for they are visible signs that someone is seeking to obtain from demons some invisible favor or help. It will be worthwhile to note just how much Christian writers thunder against what that class of people does. Thus Augustine: "Many who find themselves beset with diseases seek help from demons. What is this if not approaching our invisible enemies, who war against our soul and seek to convince us that our salvation does not rest with God? People who do that are deaf to the voice of God, who says, 'I myself am your salvation.'"[96] Chrysostom remarks, concerning those superstitious bandages that are applied to the sick, "These are devilish tricks for covering up seduction and for offering a poisonous drug under the guise of honey."[97] Thus said Chrysostom, and he also says much more in a certain homily he delivered, in which he seeks to prove that "the Christian should rather undergo death than desire to purchase his own life or that of his friends by such cures."[98] From the Scholastics we have this statement of Estius: "Just as the law of nature dictates that there must be no fellowship between the subjects of a king and his enemies—since they do absolutely everything out of hatred for the king and to overthrow him—so also the same law of nature prevents us, who are on God's side, from all fellowship, even the smallest bit, with the Devil and his angels."[99] Aquinas made this remark: "A war has been declared between man and the demons, and so it is impermissible to employ demons' aid either through silent or explicit agreements."[100] In response to these words, Cajetan said, "Observe the root of the problem, how all fellowship with a demon is a mortal sin *sui generis*, because clearly it is fellowship with an enemy, since war between ourselves and the demons has already been declared by the king of the universe."[101] He evidently has in mind this passage of Moses. I must now add to its exegesis the finishing touch.

---

96. In Psalm. 34.] Augustine, *Enarrationes In Psalmos*, in *Omnia Opera, Octavus Tomus* (Basel, 1529), p. 168.

97. Homil. 8. in Epist. ad Coloss.] Chrysostom, *In Epistolam Pauli Colossenses*, in *Opera Omnia*, vol. 4 (Basel, 1539), sub loc. Col. 3 (*homilia* 8).

98. Chrysostom, *Epistolam Ad Colossenses, homil.* 8.

99. In lib. 2um sententiar. dist. 7. artic. 21. vid eundem in lib. 4^unt distinct. 34. artic. 6.] William Hessels van Est (Estius), 1542–1613, Dutch Roman Catholic exegete, *Sententiarum Commentaria* (Douai, 1615), bk. 2, distinct. 7, art. 21, p. 93; cf. bk. 4, distinct. 34, art. 6, p. 148. Article 6, *Maleficos utrum consulere liceat*, further discusses van Est's concerns on the topic quoted by A. above.

100. 2^a 2^ae qu. 96. art. 2. ad 3um] Thomas Aquinas, *Summa*, 2-2.96.2 *ad* 3. A. changes vocabulary but retains the sense.

101. Tommaso de Vio Cajetan, 1469–1534, cardinal and Dominican Thomist, *Secunda Secundae Summae Theologiae* (Antwerp, 1612), ques. 96, art. 2, p. 242.

§ 15. My final task here is to show, albeit briefly, that Christians profess to be in foremost opposition to villainous men also, as well as those endowed with a devilish character, such as they are. So Christians say with David, "Do I not hate, Jehovah, those who hate You? I hate them with a perfect hatred. I take them as my enemies" (Ps. 139:21–22).

If the question concerns the actual persons of the wicked—that is, whether it is right for us to hate them—the theologians answer unanimously no. John Malderus has spoken soundly and succinctly on this meaning: "The concept of a personal enemy has no equivalent among Christians."[102] But if we are talking about the faults of the wicked, then the theologians assert that we can and must hate those. Augustine makes this point especially: "Every sinner, to the extent that he is a sinner, must not be loved; and every person, to the extent that he is a person, must be loved for God's sake. Truly God is to be loved for Himself, from whom all who love Him have both their being and their love for Him."[103] The Augustine of his time, the unique glory both of our England and especially of Cambridge University, Davenant of Salisbury, marked his approval of this sentiment in words equal to Augustine's, when he wrote,

> So far as concerns men that are openly wicked, Christian charity does not even abandon such. For charity hopes all things. Accordingly, it hopes that they can be converted to God and become sharers in the communion of the saints and eternal blessedness. Thus, the righteous man hates the unrighteous, but with a perfect hatred. Perfect hatred, truly, is that which lacks neither righteousness nor knowledge. Consequently, you neither hate men because of the vices they have nor love vices because of the men that have them.[104]

An obvious example of this hatred is noted in the shunning of depraved company that Christian prudence requires of all the righteous. Among others, such escape was requisite of Augustine, whose words are very worth marking: "What an excessively hateful friendship! When someone says, 'Let's go,' 'Let's cause trouble,' that friendship is not ashamed to be shameless."[105]

And so even a famous monk should have shunned the company of the wicked, and with his memorable example, I shall set the finishing touch on this exercise of mine. At Nuremberg—so Abraham Scultetus writes in

---

102. Meditat Theologic. p. 170.] Johannes (John) Malderus, 1562–1633, bishop of Antwerp, *Meditationes Theologicae* (Antwerp, 1630), part 2, dies 12, p. 170.

103. De doctrin. Christ. c. 27.] Augustine, *De Doctrina Christiana*, 1.27.

104. In Epist. ad Coloss. p. 39.] Davenant, *Expositio Epistolae D. Pauli Ad Colossenses* (Cambridge, 1627), sub loc. Col. 1:4. A. renders *improbum* as *impium*.

105. Confes. l. 1. c. 9.] Augustine, *Confessionum*, 2.9.17.

his *Annals*—there was a certain Franciscan monk named Gallus Korn.[106] Because he had a taste for true religion and did not conceal that in his conversations, the brothers came to hate him. By chance he happened on this saying of the Apostle while opening a volume of Cyprian: "We abjure you, brothers, in the name of Jesus Christ, to remove yourselves from every brother who walks intemperately" (2 Thess. 3:6). Shocked by this statement, when he had learned its meaning from Ambrose,[107] he deserted the monastery.[108]

---

106. Gallus Korn, fl. 1521–24, German Dominican monk and preacher.

107. Ambrose of Milan, ca. 337/340–397, bishop of Milan, *In Epistolam Ad Timotheum Secundam*, in *Omnia Quae Extant Opera*, vol. 5 (Bascl, 1567), probably sub loc. 2 Tim. 3:6.

108. Annal. Decad. 1. p. 121.] Scultetus, *Annalium Evangelii Passim* (Heidelberg, 1618), p. 121.

CHAPTER IV

A Review of the Enemies
Mentioned Elsewhere

Sections 1–2: How God Himself is an enemy. Sections 3–4: In what sense our own flesh opposes us. That flesh is diffused throughout the whole person, contrary to certain Scholastics. Contrary to Castellio, rebellion against the Spirit exists also in those reborn. Jonah's affections were immoderate. Sections 5–6: The world is also an enemy. The first locus, 1 John 2:15–16, is explained, as well as 1 Timothy 6:9–10. And we see how damnable are luxury, avarice, and pride. Sections 7–8: Death is an enemy in two respects, both as it robs us and frightens us. Light is brought to bear on the words of Paul in Philippians 1:23. Death is the penalty for sin, not a natural consequence, contrary to the position of the Pelagians, de Courcelles, and Socinus.

§1. To this point we have used the protoevangelium like the thread of Ariadne[1] in a labyrinth. The very nature of the topic we are discussing forced us to enter it. But in addition to the enemies mentioned in the passage, we must not omit other enemies noted elsewhere that the Christian soldier has to deal with. God with good reason claims for Himself the chief role. In Leviticus He sets Himself against the wicked, saying, "If you shall walk in a way opposed to Me, I also shall then walk against you, and I shall strike you sevenfold for your sins" (Lev. 26:23–24). Samuel, when disguised, spoke to Saul like that: "Why do you seek my advice when Jehovah has departed from you and has become your enemy?" (1 Sam. 28:16). After Joshua and all those of his generation had died, there arose in Israel a new generation that did not know God and served idols. Therefore, "Jehovah's anger burned, and wherever they went out, the hand of Jehovah was against them for evil" (Judg. 2:8, 10, 13–15). Those highly skilled in logic hold that opposites are mutually exclusive by means of contrariety. Dissolute men seek to drive God from their mouth and, as much as possible, from

---

1. Ariadne, mythical daughter of Minos and Pasiphae on Crete who fell in love with Theseus.

their heart as well. Accordingly, when it pleases God, they are banished from their gilded happiness, as Seneca terms it,[2] and from those goods that they consider of greatest value. There is quite a well-known instance of this phenomenon in the history of Diocletian.[3] He counted nothing more worthy of his attention, prayed and strove for nothing more, than wiping out completely Christ's name and His worship. His fawning courtiers were congratulating him as though this had been happily accomplished, and they raised in Spain a memorial column to their emperor bearing this inscription: "To Diocletian Caesar Augustus, who adopted Galerius[4] in the east, wiped out the superstition of Christ everywhere, and furthered the worship of the gods."[5] But when he had kicked against the goads [Acts 26:14] a little longer, he began to perceive the steady advances of the Christian religion. The unparalleled ferocity he exercised against it was no impediment, and so he roared with all his might. And after abdicating his throne due to a mental disorder (as all the historians acknowledge), some say he began to go insane and rave.

§ 2. But really, if ever any trespass against His own children, as against Christ's most dearly beloved, the most great and powerful God habitually treats them as an enemy until they return to their duty. The book of Lamentations bears witness to this fact again and again. "The Lord bent His bow as an antagonist. He strengthened His right hand as an enemy. He has become as an antagonist" (Lam. 2:4–5). Allow me to add Isaiah to the testimony of Jeremiah. In the latter we read these words: "Surely they are My people, sons who will not act deceitfully, thus He was their Savior. But when they were rebelling and grieved the Spirit of His Holiness, He changed into their enemy. He opposed them personally" (Isa. 63:8, 10). The situation, however, was not altogether hopeless, and the people's cries were not in vain. These events did not portend their destruction but the renewal of their faith and repentance. For a little after, instead of calling on God as an enemy, they invoke him as Father. "Stretch forth Your hand from heaven, and look upon the habitation of Your holiness. For You are our Father, although Abraham had not known us, and Israel had not acknowledged us. You, Jehovah, are our Father" (Isa. 63:15–16). Therefore, Tertullian's famous statement is true: "O, is not that servant blessed whose correction the Lord threatens, whom

---

2. The citation is not given here in the margin, but is Ep. 115.9; the Latin is *e bracteata… faelicitate*.

3. Diocletian, ca. 244–ca. 313, r. 284–305, Roman emperor.

4. Caius Galerius Valerius Maximianus (Galerius), ca. 250–311, r. 293–305 (under Diocletian), Augustus 305–311, Roman emperor.

5. *Camerar.* raeditat. historic. centur. 1. c. 39 p. 180.] Philippus (Philip) Camerarius, 1537–1624, German legal scholar, *Meditationes Historicae* (Frankfurt, 1615), vol. 1, ch. 39, p. 180.

He considers worthy to show his anger?"[6] Note, dear reader, how Davenant, whom I praised above, explains this idea for you quite fully. He says, "It cannot be denied that even the sons of God, when they have relaxed the reins on their flesh, feel the anger of God lying upon them. But it does not remain on them forever, because they are not in their sins." Davenant goes on to distinguish between God's fatherly or chastising anger, and anger that is hostile and destructive. So he eventually adds these comments: "When the righteous rush into sin against their conscience, even though that bond of God's everlasting kindness—which depends on election—is not broken, nevertheless the love of friendship is temporarily broken, or at least its experience and enjoyment—which depends on faith and sanctification. And so while they fall asleep in such sins, God deals with them as enemies. Their only understanding of God is that He is dangerous and angry with them."[7]

These people are more guilty of one fault in particular: they provoke God to wage war against them, just as two apostles—James and Peter—testify in the same clear words: ὁ Θεὸς ὑπερηφάνοις ἀντιτάσσεται ("God will openly oppose the proud") (James 4:6; 1 Peter 5:5); that is, *God arranges the line of battle against them, to resist the arrogant steadfastly.* For those who stand in opposition are called οἱ ἀντιτεταγμένοι,[8] according to Budé,[9] and this ἡ ἀντίταξις[10] is the drawing up of a battle line against the enemy. Such a meaning (as a more recent writer claims) is quite suited to this passage. "For the arrogant are, as it were, trespassing on the divine glory, while they steal for themselves what belongs to God. Armed force, moreover, was typically used against trespassers and robbers."[11] Among the ancients, Ambrose endorses this understanding when he writes, "God is the one who drives back their effrontery, since He has undertaken a peculiar kind of contest against haughtiness."[12]

§3. Everyone is partial to his own flesh and blood. So the closer an enemy gets, the more dangerous he is. Likewise, divisions in the home are more grievous than those in public, and civil strife than wars between nations.

---

6. De poenitent. c. 11.] Tertullian, *De Poenitentia,* in *Opera Quae Hactenus Reperiri,* vol. 2 (Cologne, 1617), ch. 11.

7. In Colos. 3.6. p. 365.] Davenant, *Ad Colossenses,* sub loc. Col. 3:6.

8. "Enemies."

9. Guillaume Budé, 1468–1540, French Hellenist and adviser to King Francis I, perhaps from his *Commentarii Linguae Graecae* ([Paris], 1529).

10. "Opposition."

11. *Joh. Gerhardus* in 1[am] Petri p 768.] Gerhard, *Commentarius Super Posteriorem D. Petri Epistolam* (Jena, 1641), ch. 5, p. 768.

12. In Psal. 118. Octonar. 7.] Ambrose, *In Psalmum CXVIII,* in *Omnia Quae Extant Opera,* vol. 4 (Basel, 1567), sub loc. Ps. 118:51 (*sermo* 7).

The apostles vividly depict this enmity with the flesh, even using words borrowed from military science. Paul writes, "I recognize another law waging war"—that is, ἀντιστρατευόμενον—"in my members against the law of my mind" (Rom. 7:23). And James says: "What is the source of wars and conflict among you? Is it not from this, from your desires that fight"—that is, τῶν στρατευομένων—"in your members?" (James 4:1). Finally, Peter writes, "As aliens and strangers, abstain from the lusts of the flesh that war"—that is, αἵτινες στρατεύονται—"against your soul" (1 Peter 2:11).

There are some Scholastics who teach that original sin only underlies the lesser faculties of the soul, and thus, by "flesh," they understand only sensuality.[13] We leave to Bellarmine, who vigorously inveighed against this position, the task of whipping such thinkers into line. The sacred writings have taught us that the flesh is diffused through the whole man, and so in the unregenerate, it holds sole and unrivaled sway. And while, in the regenerate, it does not have complete power nor sole dominion, yet it is still present with the Spirit against whom it always fights. As we read that in Abraham's one household Isaac and Ishmael struggled, while in Rachel's one womb Jacob and Esau contended, so in the same soul, after regeneration—or rather even in the particular faculties of the same soul—flesh and Spirit are locked in combat (Gal. 5:24). In Paul's writings we find, in addition to the "passions of the flesh" (παθήματα σαρκός)—which seem to correspond to sensual desire—the "desires of the flesh" (θελήματα σαρκός) (Eph. 2:3). These latter convey the notion of rational appetite or will. Finally, there is the wisdom of the flesh (φρόνημα σαρκός), that concerns the understanding (Rom. 8:6). If anyone wants to consider each of these separately, he will readily notice how very hostile the flesh is and how much danger to the soul arises from it.

§ 4. Generally speaking, curiosity accompanies the flesh in the act of understanding, according to this statement in the letter to the Colossians: "Going on about those things that he has not seen and foolishly swollen in his own knowledge of the flesh" (Col. 1:29).[14] If only those men who prefer dangerous investigation of what is secret to sinless ignorance would just consider how deadly this curiosity is to their souls! We can safely disregard what the Holy Spirit thought it was to keep silent. Tertullian makes this point quite elegantly: "We have no need for curiosity after the coming of Christ Jesus, nor of research after the gospel. When we believe, we desire to believe

---

13. Lib. 5. de Amiss. gratiae & statu peccat. c. 15.] Robert Bellarmine, 1542–1621, theologian and controversialist, *De Amissione Gratiae*, in *Disputationes De Controversiis*, vol. 4 (Ingolstadt, 1605), bk. 5, ch.15.

14. Read, Col. 2:18.

nothing further. For we believe this first of all, that there is nothing more that we ought to believe."[15] These are not so much words as bolts of lightning that the most distinguished of the fathers hurled against this plague. Thus Chrysostom: "He who is too curious and persistent in searching out the divine profits nothing and finds nothing except severe punishment."[16] And Augustine: "Those who wish to say something about the depth of God are drowned in that depth."[17] Some of the speculations of the Cabalists,[18] as well as those of the Scholastics, and the investigations of some of our contemporaries seem to me hardly any different than brothels for libidinous thinkers. Indeed, such men boast of some special acuity. But it is really useless, if not actually harmful, like distinguishing in a leper between a certain gleam of whiteness and a shiny but contagious color. I will just state what I have found by experience: those who swear to us they have mystical sensibilities generally turn out to be freaks. Likewise, those who grasp at allegories become traitors to the texts' meaning. May they not betray their own souls too.

The flesh's inseparable companion in the will is rebellion against the Spirit, as Paul teaches: "The flesh lusts against the Spirit, and the Spirit against the flesh. These indeed are set against each other" (Gal. 5:17). Doubtless, they are joined together, as light and shadows at twilight. But they no more mix than oil and water in the same jar, or iron and clay, as in Daniel's prophetic statue. I seem to have found a living symbol of this phenomenon while reading about a recent journey. There is a river called Sava near Belgrade, the capital city of Hungary, which flows into the Danube.[19] There, for sixty miles, the waters of both rivers flow together but are not mixed. Consequently, those who travel on skiffs in the middle of the Danube can, on one side, draw up and taste water that is pure and clear, but on the other, it is muddy and sandy. Thus, the Spirit and the flesh, grace and corruption, are, so to speak, right next to each other in each faculty of the regenerate man. But they are in conflict one with another and as diametrically opposed as they can possibly be. If we trust Castellio, then the veteran soldiers of Christ have nothing to fear from this enemy, although the newly enlisted have reason to dread.[20] He holds that there are three classes of men:

---

15. De praescript. cap. 8.] Tertullian, *De Praescriptionibus Adversus Haereticos*, ch. 8.

16. Homil. 23. in Evangel. Joh.] Chrysostom, *In Ioannis Evangelium*, in *Opera Omnia*, vol. 3 (Basel, 1539), sub loc. John 3.

17. De verb. Apost. Serm. 7.] Augustine, *De Verbis Apostoli*, in *Omnium Operum*, vol. 10 (Basel, 1528), *sermo 7*.

18. Adherents to the Kabbalah, a body of esoteric rabbinic writings.

19. D. H. *Blunt*. p. 19.] Henry Blount, 1602–1682, traveler, *Voyage into the Levant* (London, 1650), p. 18.

20. De justificat. p. 86.] Castellio, *De Iustificatione*, in *Dialogi IV*, p. 86.

the unregenerate, those being reborn, and the reborn. Castellio asserts that none of the unregenerate act rightly. He acknowledges that, among those being reborn, there is a struggle between the flesh and the Spirit, between vices and virtues, but not among the reborn. He claims,

> The sacred texts nowhere say that the struggle is perpetual. Indeed, the flesh contends as long as it lives, but when dead, it does not contend: as in the proverb, "A dead man does not wage war." The flesh fought back among the Galatians who were not of sound mind, and though they had begun with the Spirit, they stopped at the flesh. Thus, Paul had to reestablish them. But to say the same about everyone is to consign both the healthy and the sick to the same definition.[21]

What a lovely theology, and one sufficiently demonstrating how little that man knows himself! Tell me, please, Castellio, how much holier and purer is this regenerate man of yours than Paul? Near the end of Romans 7, Paul quite plainly confesses that his flesh still openly wages war against him. I know what you will say: "Obviously the Apostle, in this passage, is not speaking about himself but in an assumed persona. Or he is talking of himself not as regenerate but of when he was unregenerate." And you do indeed make that very assertion elsewhere but all in vain.[22] Not to belabor the point with needless arguments, but the very passage in question conclusively demonstrates the opposite. For Paul there makes mention of the "inner man for whom the law of God was a delight" [Rom. 7:22]. But he also speaks of another "law in the members, which wages war against that law of the mind" [Rom. 7:23]. By these words, he testifies clearly that he is personally subject to that condition he describes—namely, that he perceives the internal struggle between flesh and Spirit. The man who has not been regenerated, moreover, no matter how great he might be, is still wholly flesh nor has within himself the Spirit who resists. If anyone is still not fully convinced, I ask them to consider another conclusion of that same Paul: "I pummel my body and reduce it to servitude" (1 Cor. 9:27). From this it is a simple matter to conclude that there was also something in Paul, the holiest man by far, that he had to fight against and bring into submission. So what really was this if not his flesh?

Finally, through the flesh's disordered impulses in the sensual appetite—and because of them—storms frequently arise in the soul. These come from the force of dissolute affections (Latin authors rightly call them "perturbations"). These storms have the intensity of those that spring up at sea, as perhaps you have read:

---

21. De obedient. Deo praestanda p. 248.] Castellio, *De Obedientia*, in *Dialogi IV*, p. 248.
22. De justificat. p. 67.] Castellio, *De Iustificatione*, in *Dialogi IV*, p. 67.

> East wind and north at once arise, and south
> To blot out skies with blasts of storms frequent;
> And to the shores roll up great massy waves.[23]

Set before your eyes, dear reader, the example of the prophet Jonah. I don't know whether any saint was ever more perturbed in soul than he, or more exasperated by disparate passions all around. When sent to Nineveh, he fearfully fled to Tarsus instead (Jonah 1:3). When swallowed up by a whale, with tremendous sorrow Jonah complained that he had been thrown from the Lord's sight and that his soul lay buried within him (Jonah 2:5, 8). When beyond all hope, he was revived by the shade of a mulberry tree and then filled with great joy (Jonah 4:6). But as the mulberry became scorched, Jonah was filled with wrath. This anger was so intense that when the Lord questioned him and asked, "Was it good that you burned with anger because of that mulberry?" Jonah weakly answered, "It was good that my anger burned, even to the point of my own death" (Jonah 4:9). Blessed Jonah! Why doesn't anyone heed your prophecy as a mirror not just of divine providence but also of human passions? It is obviously a monumental task to tame the remnants of the flesh—not to mention our illicit impulses—and bring them into proper order.

§5. Third place rightly goes to the world. Since it lies under the power of the wicked one (1 John 5:19), inevitably it puts forth its own wickedness against those whom Christ the Lord has called from the world and adopted to Himself as His dependents and disciples. He taught us this Himself in the gospel: "If you were of the world, the world would love what is its own. Because you are not of the world, but I have chosen you out of the world, so the world hates you" (John 15:19). Among princes who have formed alliances with each other, there tend to be common friends and enemies. Those who have entered into that lasting covenant with God, which all the regenerate earnestly appropriate, they necessarily find that the world is their enemy, just as it is God's enemy, as James attests: "You adulterous men and women! Don't you know that friendship with the world is enmity toward God? Therefore, whoever wants to be a friend of the world becomes God's enemy" (James 4:4). By "world," moreover, in this passage and elsewhere (though not in every instance), we understand, with Cajetan, not the entire sum of creation but the entire sum of what was subjected to disorder. They were not subjected by the rule of nature but by the rule of right reason.[24]

---

23. Vergil, *Aeneidos*, bk. 1 (lines 85–86). A. quotes from Vergil's description of a storm stirred up in the Mediterranean by Juno to destroy the Trojans.

24. In 1ᵃᵐ Joh. cap. 2.] Cajetan, *Epistolae Pauli Et Aliorum Apostolorum* (Paris, 1537), sub loc. 1 John 2.

That truly outstanding passage in John will illuminate this idea more clearly. It is convenient for me to cite it and explain it here: "Don't love the world nor what is in the world. If anyone loves the world, the love of the Father is not in him. Because whatever is in the world—the desires of the flesh, the lust of the eyes, and the pride of life—these are not from the Father but from the world" [1 John 2:15–16].

These are the very weapons the Devil once used to attack those first created in paradise. "The woman saw the fruit of the forbidden tree, that it was good for food" (Gen. 3:6). Look, the desire of the flesh. "It was very pleasing to the eyes." Look, the lust of the eyes. And "it was desirable for gaining understanding." Look, the pride of life. Of course, he used the same temptations against Christ in the desert, but in a somewhat different order. "Command these stones to become bread," the Devil said (Matt. 4:3). This, of course, was to satisfy the concupiscence of the flesh. The Devil showed Christ all the kingdoms of the world and their glory, to fill him with the lust of the eyes. And he said, "Throw Yourself down from the very pinnacle of the temple. The angels will save You from harm. It will amaze those who see it, and win You praise." Thus, the Devil sought to stimulate pride of life. But Christ went directly onto the opposite path, that, by His own example, He might then surpass us in boldly resisting the world, and later, by gloriously overcoming it. Oecolampadius, after he had commented on those two passages I just now quoted, said,

> Note Christ's strategies. Against the concupiscence of the flesh, which He held in absolute submission, He fasted on our behalf, He labored, was wearied, beaten, and crucified. Against the concupiscence of the eyes, He lived in absolute poverty and had no place to lay His head. Yet, humbly serving us and obeying His Father even unto death, He revealed how far He was from sinful pride.[25]

§ 6. Let us also see how great is the harm or danger present in each of these weapons individually, or attaches to them. By this our enmity with the world may be more clearly manifest. The lust of the flesh equals luxury and contains the desire for those good things that please the body (for "flesh" here has that denotation). Indeed, pleasures of the same kind—I mean the forbidden ones that go beyond the rule and limit of either Scripture or nature—kiss and then destroy us, as Joab did with Abner [2 Sam. 2:26]. They also serve us milk, as Jael to Sisera, but laced with a tent peg [Judg. 4:22]. The luxury of the body ceases along with the mind's distress; and then death bursts out laughing like this:

25. In Epist. 1ᵃᵐ Johan. Demegoria 7.] Johannes Oecolampadius, 1482–1531, Swiss Reformed theologian, *In Epistolam Ioannis Apostoli Catholicam Primam* (Basel, 1524), fol. 36r.

> As one whose jaws had glut on Sardinian
> Herbs, that icy soul he then revealed with
> Smiling mouth.[26]

Those given to luxury regard themselves as fish carried along through the clear flowing waters of the Jordan toward the Dead Sea. Someone like that is the ζῶσα τέθνηκε,[27] as Paul said of the licentious widow (1 Tim. 5:6). Day after day the reveler goes on dying more sumptuously. He is like the famous man in Luke. Dressed in purple and linen, indulging in daily magnificence, it is like he is dancing on the brink of a very deep well (Luke 16:19). And then, he unexpectedly falls into it. So we must pray, with Anselm, "Cause me to drink, O Lord, from the rushing stream of your pleasure, that I may no longer enjoy hunting after and tasting the sweetness of worldly pleasures."[28]

The sacred Scriptures teach us abundantly just how much harm arises from greed. Whoever has really considered Solomon's words I quote here will scarcely deny that "greed" means *the lust of the eyes*. Thus, "Don't wear yourself out to get rich" (Prov. 23:4); and, "Will you set your eyes on that which will not endure?" (Prov. 23:5); and, "Where there are many riches, there are many to consume them"; and, "What does it benefit the owner except that he sees his riches with his own eyes?" (Eccl. 5:11). The Preacher once complained about the works accumulated to the detriment of his Lord (Eccl. 5:13). In these and like words, James thundered into the ears of his wealthy contemporaries: "The avarice of your gold and silver clothing will testify against you and will consume your flesh like fire. You have stored up treasure for the end of days" (James 5:3). Heins thinks that this passage should be punctuated differently and thus read (not, as it commonly is, Φάγεται τὰς σάρκας ὑμῶν ὡς πῦρ) with a comma inserted after the pronoun: Ὑμῶν, ὡς πῦρ ἐθησαυρίσατε—thus, "Treasure, as you have stored up fire." "For it is no surprise," he says, "that the wicked man who provokes divine anger at the last day—the day that will decide the life and deeds of men—should be described as gathering and storing up fire for himself."[29] Indeed, Paul speaks with greater clarity and brilliance than all of them: "Those who desire to become rich fall into temptation and a snare, and into many frenzied and destructive lusts that plunge men into perdition

---

26. Vid. Adagium Rifus Sardonicus.] This is A.'s original elegiac couplet, though inspired by Vergil (*Eclogue* VII.41) and its mention of the "sardonic smile."

27. "Living dead."

28. In alloquiis coelestibus.] Anselm of Canterbury, ca. 1033–1109, archbishop of Canterbury, *Oratio XIV Ad Spiritum Sanctum*, in *Opuscula Beati Anselmi* ([Basel], 1497); or Augustine, *Meditationum*, in *Omnium Operum*, vol. 9 (Basel, 1528), 9.2.

29. Exercit. in locum.] Heins, *Sacrarum Exercitationum*, bk. 17, ch. 3, p. 563.

and destruction. Indeed, the root of all evils is the love of money. Some men, while seeking after money, have wandered from the faith and pierced themselves all around with manifold sorrows" (1 Tim. 6:9–10). Such are those who long to be rich. It is their fixed principle—rightly or wrongly, by force or fraud, by whatever means necessary—to become rich. The Apostle says that these men fall first into temptation, then into a snare. As a bird seeking food is enticed by some fowler, and immediately caught fast in a net, so for those who greedily gasp after riches, when they have been flushed out by the Devil's pipe of temptation, so to speak, he throws them headlong into every class of sin—"and into many frenzied and destructive lusts." For what is more insane than to earn for your posterity homes and estates but Gehenna for yourself, than to apply all your effort to this—that your heirs live in ease and splendor, not that you yourself are happy in death and blessed after death? These lusts are, indeed, called destructive, because (so it follows) men plunge themselves into perdition and destruction. Think of a wasp eager for honey that often perishes in a vase, or a ship that has taken on the very sea it ought to float upon and is right there swallowed up by the waters. The Apostle continues his discussion and deems love of money the root of all evil. And so Nieremberg considers this riches' greatest scandal, that they are "tools of the pleasures and the golden key of crimes. For without riches, vices are barely effective. Riches are, as it were, the hilt and handle of vices."[30] Paul adds, moreover, that certain men, desirous of money, have wandered away from the faith (1 Tim. 4:10). He cites Demas as an example. Some writers on the church at Thessalonica say that Demas, from a desire for profit, served some idol or another by officiating at sacrifices.[31] The transition from being a servant of Mammon to a priest of the Devil is really quite simple. As for the little clause that remains—"And pierced themselves all around with manifold sorrows"—this is more or less confirmed by the typical experience of the rich, and even the pagan poets affirm it.

Thus Horace:

> Anxiety follows increasing money.[32]

And Juvenal:

> That with much of evil gained,
> With fear and sorrow more is kept.

---

30. De Arte voluntatis lib. 6. c. 27. p. 495.] Juan Eusebio Nieremberg, 1595–1658, Spanish Jesuit, *De Arte Voluntatis* (Lyon, 1649), bk. 6, ch. 27, p. 495.

31. For Demas, see Col. 4:14; 2 Tim. 4:10; Phil. 24.

32. Quintus Horatius Flaccus (Horace), 65–8 BC, Roman poet of lyric, satire, and verse epistle, *Carminum*, in *Opera* (Paris, 1642), bk. 3, ode 16.

> Watchman of the massive hoard,
> Is wretched sure and all unslept.[33]

A very righteous man once said in a sermon, and I mean the most blessed martyr Hugh Latimer, "Believe me, listeners, if I considered someone my enemy and it were acceptable to wish him harm, I would choose first and foremost to have him given an abundance of riches. That way I could be sure that, though very rich indeed, he would never afterward enjoy any rest."[34]

This is the pride of life: a man habitually swollen from the extravagance of his income, from the brilliance of his children, the splendor of his estates, the style of his clothing, the size of his entourage, his reputation, the extent of his titles, honors, and accomplishments. With the wind of arrogance, he inflates the puffed-up vessels of his utterly ridiculous character until they burst. The foremost allurements of such great pride of life have been and still are the summit of imperial and papal office. Great men have found both of these positions to be very dangerous to themselves. So it happened that on the day Julian[35] was assuming the imperial purple, he kept reciting this line from Homer:[36]

> Ἔλλαβε πορφύρεος θάνατος καὶ μοῖρα κρατίη
>
> Death in purple takes me now and with her
> The strength of grim fate catches me all 'round.[37]

Indeed, he often complained afterward that "all I have gained is that I will die busier."[38] And the epitaph inscribed on the tomb of Pope Adrian VI[39] deserves mention: "Here lies Adrian VI: the worse thing he acquired in his life was that he ruled."[40]

No, indeed, if we should weigh the matter objectively, we shall easily conclude that men are disgraceful when they boast of their particular

---

33. Satyr. 14.] Juvenal, *Satyra* (Paris, 1644), 14.

34. Concion. suarum Anglic. fol. 118. B.] Hugh Latimer, ca. 1485–1555, bishop of Worcester, preacher, and Protestant martyr, *A moste faithfull sermon* (London, 1553), sig. G3v.

35. Julian the Apostate, 332–363, r. 361–363, Roman emperor.

36. Homer, fl. eighth century BC, author of *Iliad* and *Odyssey*.

37. P. *Martinii* Morentini praefat. in *Juliani* Misopogon.] Martini, *Iuliani Imperatoris Opera* (Paris, 1583), p. 18. A. quotes from the preface to the *Misopogon* of Julian. The line of Greek hexameter is from *Iliad* 20.477.

38. c. Vita Fl. Claudii Juliani, An. U. C. 1108, Christi 355, Constantii Aug. 19, Juliani aetat. 24; *Patrologia Latina*, Migne.

39. Adrian VI, 1454–1523, *p.* 1522–1523.

40. *Onuphrius*.] Perhaps generalizing from Onofrio (Onuphrius) Panvinio, 1530–1568, Italian humanist, epigrapher, and antiquarian, *Accuratae Effigies Pontificium Maximorum* (Straßurg, 1573).

honors, *embraced by a cloud instead of Juno*,[41] a mere phantasm instead of the happiness that the Holy Spirit applied in a quite similar situation (Acts 25:23).[42] For power is of very little profit. It is a great hindrance to come from a long bloodline yet, meanwhile, be distant from the blood of Christ. There is no profit in "displaying the gilt portraits of one's ancestors"[43] and not carrying God's image engraved on the heart. There is absolutely no doubt that nothing in the world is truly glorious except the soul that spurns the world's glory and strives—by oar and sail, prayer and deed—toward that glory that is heavenly. With your permission, let me again quote from John Eusebio Nieremberg: "He alone is glorious who despises both himself and glory. Let us count nothing less important than that we be counted more important. That man shall truly count who takes no account of counting for something."[44]

§7. Finally, we must consider death, since the Apostle even calls it our *last enemy* (1 Cor. 15:26). Now it is characteristic of enemies that invade their opponents that they steal their goods. Thus Christ: "When a certain armed strong man stands guard over his own house, those things inside that robbers seek are safe. But after another, stronger man comes and overpowers and binds him, then he takes away the armor the first man trusted, and then distributes the plunder" (Luke 11:21–22). So death is far and away the greatest predator. For as soon as it arrives, those who are ambitious for their own honors, dissipated in their pleasures, resplendent in wealth, intent upon their books—all of them are immediately stripped of all their outward possessions.

> Then earth and hearth and loving wife must all be left behind.
> And down to shadows grim, with groans, his life he then resigned.[45]

Next, we must consider how enemies usually inspire terror in their opponents as they approach. Once, when war threatened the king of Judah, a war the kings of Syria and Israel prepared against him, "his heart was quite disturbed, and that of his people, as when trees of the forest are stirred up from wind" (Isa. 7:2). Death, in like manner, is so frightening to the human

---

41. The villain Ixion attempts to sleep with the goddess Juno. His lust is consummated with a Juno-shaped cloud that Zeus supplies, whence are born the centaurs. Cf. Appollodorus, *Epitome* 1.20.

42. μετὰ πολλῆς φαντασίας.] "With great pomp."

43. Juvenal, *Satyra*, 8. Word order altered, sense retained. A. appears to quote from memory; his syntax is non-metrical.

44. De Arte voluntat. l. 6. c. 54 p. 533.] Nieremberg, *De Arte Voluntatis*, bk. 6, ch. 54, p. 533.

45. Horace, *Carminum*, bk. 2, ode 14 (line 21); Vergil, *Aeneidos*, bk. 12 (line 952).

race that it is rightly called the "king of terrors" (Job 18:14). Saul, when he had received news of his own death through the voice of one disguised as Samuel, suffered a complete collapse of courage (1 Sam. 28:20). In the parable told to the rich man, we hear this: "Foolish man, this very night they will demand (ἀπαιτοῦσιν) your life from you" (Luke 12:20).[46] This means, of course, from someone unwilling and resisting. For these two meanings differ (according to Casaubon):[47] αἰτεῖν means *to ask from someone who is willing*, but ἀπαιτεῖν means *to take from someone without their consent*. The wicked are not the only ones who flee and fear death—indeed, as nature leads them. Even men most famous for moral rectitude fear it. Is anyone really surprised that King Louis II of France, when he was sick, forbade, by severe edict, anyone from mentioning death within his chamber?[48] Or that the Emperor Hadrian's[49] final speech to his departing soul was, "My wandering little soul, so mild, the guest and companion of my body, you who now shall depart to a place pallid, grim, and barren, will you not, as before, join in the jests?"[50] We also have this famous saying in Euripides'[51] *Iphigenia*:

> μαίνεται δ' ὃς εὔχεται
> θανεῖν. κακῶς ζῆν κρεῖσσον ἢ θανεῖν καλῶς.[52]

This, according to Grotius's translation, means,

> That man who hastens on to death has truly lost his mind.
> For better troubled life by far than end of fairest kind.[53]

Would anyone, I say, be surprised at such things if they ever read how Hezekiah wept when his death was announced (Isa. 38:1–2)? Or how Peter himself did not want to die? For so the Lord predicted: "When you are an old man, you will stretch forth your hands, and another will bind you and will take you where you will not want to go" (John 21:18). The renowned Abraham Scultetus (who himself explained Paul's words to the

---

46. A. uses the Greek here, though he also gives a Latin gloss.

47. Ad Theophr. charact. c. 11.] Isaac Casaubon, 1559–1614, Swiss Protestant scholar at the Geneva Academy, *Theophrasti Characteres Ethici* (Lyon, 1592), p. 171.

48. *Philip. Comin.*] Read, "Louis XI," as above in Oration 1. Philippe de Commynes, ca. 1446–ca. 1511, French chronicler, *The historie of Philip de Commines Knight* (London, 1596), bk. 6, ch. 12, p. 235.

49. Publius Aelius Hadrianus (Hadrian), 76–138, r. 117–38, Roman emperor.

50. Aelius Spartianus, alleged author of six lives in the *Historia Augusta, Adrianus Imperator*, in *Historiae Augustae* (Paris, 1620). These are in verse in the original.

51. Euripides, 480–ca. 406 BC, Greek dramatist.

52. In Aulide.] Lines 1251–52.

53. Perhaps in *Tragoediarum Fragmenta Collecta* (Paris, 1626).

Philippians—ἐπιθυμίαν ἔχων εἰς τὸ ἀναλῦσαι [Phil. 1:23]—as "having a desire to depart or to return")[54] seems to fault those who consider the Apostle's words in a loose sense as "I desire to be destroyed." He was influenced by this argument most of all: it is not the separation of soul from the body that holy men in the first place desire for themselves—this is something they dread. No, it is the return of the soul to the heavenly country for which they eagerly wait. And a recent event, actually, provides us with a beautiful confirmation of this fact. Simon Sten, professor of the Greek language for many years at the University of Heidelberg, died in 1619. Before his final suffering he was asked by the minister of the divine Word "whether he desired to die and be with Christ." He then answered, almost indignantly, that this was not Paul's meaning nor the right understanding of the word ἀναλῦσαι. Instead, he said, a migration was intended. This showed clearly that he rejoiced greatly inside as he contemplated not the dissolution of body and soul but his departure to Christ.[55]

§ 8. Because some theologians cannot at all remove that enmity I have just explained, they instead try to minimize its significance. They do this to serve their own suppositions, by claiming that bodily death is a servant rather than an enemy. Or, to use their own words, it is a "consequence of nature, not a punishment for sin." This is the very expression the orthodox typically use to indicate death, while the Pelagians form up their column so as not to be compelled to acknowledge original sin. For, from this concession—that death is a punishment for sin—it follows that the death that befalls infants before they have transgressed in actuality[56] presupposes some sinful condition and, thus, that sin is part of the original endowment. The Remonstrants, on the other hand, typically employ this expression. Thereby, they follow in the Pelagians' footsteps, clearly relating the same idea, even if not all of them do so. The name Courcelle comes to mind. "Temporal death," he writes, "does not have its origin from sin but is a consequence of the feeble substance that constitutes the human being."[57] Socinus adds, "Natural death, to the extent that it is natural and common to all, is not the impost of sin but of our nature." He interprets this

---

54. Exercit. Evangelic. l. 1. cap. 62.] Scultetus, *Exercitationes Evangelicae* (Amsterdam, 1624), bk. 1, ch. 62, p. 157.

55. Simon Sten, 1540–1619, professor of Greek and ethics at the University of Heidelberg, unknown work; perhaps A. quotes from memory.

56. *Actu*, a standard Scholastic term for designating the commission of a sin as understood distinctly from its impulse or conception.

57. De Ijure Dei c. 11. non procul a fine.] Étienne de Courcelles, 1586–1659, Swiss Arminian theologian, *De Iure Dei In Creaturas* ([1644/1645]), ch. 11, p. 129.

to mean that "Adam received this nature in the very act of creation as its peculiar consequence. But the impost of sin is the necessity of dying and eternal death."[58] What a faith you have, you people who read such things! How inconsistently—or maybe I should say, clumsily—that great critic of theologians and of theology itself (if anyone prefers) blabbed on about this so-called opinion. He is right to acknowledge eternal death. If only he were sincere! For some suspect a snake lies hidden even in this grass. He is right to set death as the penalty for sin. But meanwhile, what kind of lunacy is it to consider the eternality and necessity of death a punishment and, at the same time, exclude death from the list of punishments! It is as if someone were to count among the rewards of faith the perpetuity and joy of heavenly glory and, meanwhile, vigorously deny that glory is itself a reward. If someone asks why Socinians are so tremendously averse to this assertion, this is their answer: their position is that Christ's satisfaction is penal. They categorically deny that it is offered to divine justice. They agree that Christ underwent death, because if death is considered the penalty of sin, and Christ Himself is free from sin, then it will follow that He died for our sins and, accordingly, satisfied justice.

The mind of sacred Scripture is very different from this. It states that death proceeded from sin not only incidentally and consecutively but causally and meritoriously, according to the Apostle's famous statement: "As through one man sin entered the world, so through sin came death. And thus, death reached all men" (Rom. 5:12). The position of the ancient church, so Augustine asserts, was different than that of the Socinians—and not of this or that particular church but of the church universal. He writes, "Among Christians, who truly hold the catholic faith, it is agreed that we do not suffer actual bodily death by a law of nature but as the deserved penalty for sin."[59]

Yet someone may say, "Christ removed from the righteous not only the guilt of sin but also its penalty. Therefore, death is not a penalty of sin." I answer—in addition to my comments above—not that death has been removed from the righteous but that the penalty has been removed from death. For Christ has not caused death not to exist. Rather, He has rendered it harmless. He Himself satisfied God's avenging justice by suffering for His own people and so took on Himself and removed whatever penalty, properly speaking, death contained, because He removed whatever vengeance there was in it. Bernard expresses this in his usual, very eloquent fashion:

---

58. De servatore part. 3. c. 8.] Socinus, *De Iesu Christo Servatore* ([Rakow], 1594) part 3, ch. 8, p. 294.

59. De civit. Dei lib. 13. cap. 15.] Augustine, *De Civitate Dei*, 13.15.

"There is no longer a sting but a shout of joy. Now a man dies while singing, and sings while dying. O mother of sorrow, you are exchanged for joy. You, enemy of glory, are now made a glory. You, hell's very gate, are turned into the entrance to the kingdom, and you, pit of destruction, have become the place where we find salvation."[60]

---

60. Serm. in Cantic. 26.] Bernard of Clairvaux, *In Cantica Canticorum*, in *Opera Omnia*, vol. 3 (Cologne, 1641), *sermo* 26, sec. 15.

CHAPTER V

Who the Spiritual Soldiers Are, What Are Their Duties, and Who Is Their Commander

Section 1: All who have been baptized are enlisted as spiritual soldiers. Section 2: The same designation applies to all ministers of the Word; an exegesis of 2 Corinthians 10:3–5 is given. Section 3: The title "soldier" is a mark of honor. Sections 4–5: A review of five duties of soldiers and an explanation of Paul's words in 2 Timothy 2:4. Commendation for engaging in conflict, showing obedience, and staying in the battle line. We must engage diligently in spiritual exercises and must demonstrate spiritual courage. Section 6: An exhortation for scholars. Section 7: Christ revealed Himself to Joshua at the precisely perfect moment as the captain of Jehovah's host. Section 8: It is He who provides the spiritual army with the weapons of light and justice. Section 9: The soldiers' salaries and their provisions. Section 10: Their pattern and aid. Section 11: An exhortation to Christians who serve in arms under such a marvelous general.

§ 1. Now then, the spiritual soldiers who must form up for battle against the aforementioned enemies are Christians more than other men, and ministers more than other Christians. The Romans were careful that no one engaged in war before he had sworn to do promptly everything his commander ordered and that he would never desert his post or refuse to die for the republic.[1] They memorialized this oath-taking procedure with the dignified title *sacrament*. The church adopted that very word and wished to apply it to her baptismal rite. Thus, they sought to show that each and every one of those washed in the sacred font were, by that very act, enlisted as soldiers, and so it was their duty, for as long as they lived, to bear arms under the command of the most Holy Trinity, into whose name they were baptized.[2] Consequently, not even women, helpless children, and retired

---

1. Vegetius lib. 2. cap. 5.] Vegetius, fl. ca. late fourth/early fifth century, Christian bureaucrat, author, and military theorist, *De Re Militari* (Leiden, 1607), bk. 2, ch. 5, p. 33.

2. καὶ πολιοί περ ἔοντες ἀναγκαῖοι πολεμιστάι. In the margin, "And all, even the old, were pressed into military service." *Homer* Odyss. ω.] Homer, *Odyssea*, in *Opera Omnia*, vol. 2 (Amsterdam, 1650), 24.499.

old men are exempt. "An old soldier is a disgrace," Ovid writes.[3] But in our context, it is shameful not for an old man to be a soldier but if his white hair does not sport a helmet. On the contrary, the older one is, the more gladly he serves under Christ. And thus, Mnason of Cyprus is praised in Acts because he was a very old disciple (Acts 21:16).

§ 2. Now although section 83 of the so-called Apostolic Canons declares that "no bishop, presbyter, or deacon is free to serve in the army,"[4] nevertheless, the kind of service we are discussing is what applies to them especially, indeed, more than to others. This follows, since Paul calls Archippus— whom he wanted to admonish in his letter to the Colossians to "fulfill the ministry he had received in the Lord" (Col. 4:17)—a fellow soldier in another passage: Ἀρχίππῳ τῷ συστρατιώτῃ ἡμῶν, ("To Archippus our fellow soldier") (Philemon v. 2). In 1 Timothy, he says, "I entrust you with this command, Timothy my son, that you fight the good fight" (ἵνα στρατεύῃ…τὴν καλὴν στρατείαν) (1 Tim. 1:18). In his second letter, Paul gives the same friend the following exhortation: "Endure hardships as a good soldier of Jesus Christ" (2 Tim. 2:3). Likewise, when he is explaining to the Corinthians about his ministrations in the gospel, Paul writes, ἐν σαρκὶ γὰρ περιπατοῦντες οὐ κατὰ σάρκα στρατευόμεθα (2 Cor. 10:3).[5] Now they walked in the flesh, that is, in the body just like the common lot of men that carry around bodies perhaps but somewhat less healthy than most. For their bodies are worn out with those anxieties Melanchthon describes when he says, "Three groups of people have the most demanding jobs: those who give birth, those who rule, and those who teach."[6] They had a treasure, but it was in earthen vessels adorned with no gold, although they bulged with internal riches [2 Cor. 4:7]. Yet they were not waging war according to the flesh, because they lacked political equipment, the pride of the emperor, the stratagems of war, and what is termed secular authority.

From that same passage come words that are just as pointed and appropriate to our present discussion. Τὰ γὰρ ὅπλα τῆς στρατείας ἡμῶν οὐ σαρκικὰ ἀλλὰ δυνατὰ τῷ Θεῷ (2 Cor. 10:4–5).[7] Physical weapons are as inappropriate for such conflict as are the eloquence of the theater, the colorful devices of orators, the poets' little oil jugs,[8] Scholastic subtleties, and, in general, whatever smacks of the flesh. Perhaps they have the flavor and spirit

---

3. Publius Ovidius Naso (Ovid), 43 BC–AD 17, Roman poet, *Amores*, in *Opera Omnia*, vol. 1 (Amsterdam, 1611), bk. 1, elegia 9.

4. *Corpus Iuris Canonici* (Lyon, 1624), 83, col. 2070.

5. "For though we walk in the flesh, we do not fight according to the flesh."

6. Melch. Adam.] Melchior Adam, *Vitae Germanorum Theologorum*, p. 359.

7. "For the weapons of our warfare are not carnal but powerful with God."

8. A reference to Aristophanes's *Frogs*, in which a little bottle of oil (ληκύθιον or *ampulla*)

of Cicero but not of David, the shrewdness of Scotus but not of Paul. Those things proper for a gospel pastor demand from him a far different talent and natural quality. I mean, of course, tears, exhortations, threats, careful instruction and dogmas, and discourses and writings that are filled with God and are rendered effective by God πρὸς καθαίρεσιν ὀχυρωμάτων.[9] Through Nature's fall, these strongholds and fortresses have become disfigured, though, with the Spirit's cooperation, they are toppled at the sound of the gospel, as once the walls of Jericho fell at the blowing of the trumpets [Josh. 6:20]. Now these ὀχυρώματα[10] are set partly in the human being's unregenerate intellect. Therefore, in the Apostle, there follows the phrase λογισμοὺς καθαιροῦντες.[11] Theophylact interprets this expression as indicating the syllogisms of the Greeks,[12] while Haimo believes it refers to the schemes of philosophers and demons.[13] Beza comes closer to Paul's thinking, however, when he refers the expression to the reasoning processes of a human intellect that has not yet been renewed.[14] So indeed, Calvin says quite pointedly, "For as long as we rest in our own perception and are wise in our own eyes, we are far from all perception of the doctrine of Christ."[15] Certainly, unsound reason, because it is shrewd and biting, forms a kind of hateful plot against revealed truth. This is especially so with respect to the Trinity, the hypostatic union, and the decrees of God. Thus Melanchthon: "Our understanding of predestination is sweet, when the Spirit of God has rendered foolish the judgment of wicked reason."[16]

These strongholds are partly situated in the will. Its arrogance is such—until it is regenerated through grace—as to want to struggle with God for primacy. Then the Apostle adds, καὶ πᾶν ὕψωμα ἐπαιρόμενον κατὰ τῆς γνώσεως τοῦ Θεοῦ.[17] Obviously nothing more obstructs healthy thinking than this natural haughtiness. Bernard expresses this idea beautifully when

---

becomes an object with which Aeschylus ridicules the predictable metrics of his younger contemporary Euripides.

9. "For the demolishing of strongholds." A. quotes from the Greek with no Latin gloss.

10. "Strongholds."

11. "Destroying arguments."

12. Theophylact of Ohrid, *Omnes D. Pauli*, sub loc. 2 Cor. 10:4.

13. Haimo of Auxerre, fl. ca. 840–870, Benedictine exegete, *In Divi Pauli Epistolas* ([Köln], 1531), sub loc. 2 Cor. 10:5, sig. A7r.

14. Beza, *Annotationes Maiores*, sub loc. 2 Cor. 10:5.

15. In loc.] Calvin, *Commentarii In Omnes Pauli Epistolas* (Geneva, 1557), sub loc. 2 Cor. 10:5.

16. Citat. a Thysio in praefatione ad explic. doctrinae de electione &c.] Antoine Thysius, Sr., 1565–1640, Reformed theologian and editor, *Praefatio*, in Matthew Hutton, *Brevis Et Dilucida Explicatio Verae, Certae & Consolationis Plenae Doctrinae De Electione, Praedestinatione Ac Reprobatione* (Harderwijk, 1613), sig. (b)2.

17. "And every high thing that exalts itself against the knowledge of God."

he says, "To the haughty eye, the truth is invisible, but to the eye that is pure, it is manifest."[18] Consequently, ministers of the gospel face a problem when they assail citadels and well-fortified towers that loom toward the sky using their own weapons. Yet, if the Lord grants them His power so that these weapons are δυνατὰ τῷ Θεῷ,[19] the situation will turn out as follows: wretched preachers will turn out to be the most exalted victors, αἰχμαλωτίζοντες πᾶν νόημα εἰς τὴν ὑπακοὴν τοῦ Χριστοῦ, just as Paul concludes in this passage [2 Cor. 10:5].[20] But now, since the mind has been subdued and the dominion of sin has been removed through the grace of God, those thoughts that remain surrender themselves gladly to Christ in abject service. And so they rejoice to be conquered, and the sweetness of their first freedom, if there were any, appears worthless compared to that captivity [1 Cor. 7:22].[21]

§ 3. So you see, brothers, precisely what our calling is. Every one of us is a soldier, and there is no reason we should be ashamed of or bothered by this title. The church herself is considered "encamped as an orderly battle line" (Song 6:4). The very angels are said to be the πλῆθος στρατιᾶς οὐρανίου (Luke 2:13).[22] Indeed, Jehovah himself is styled a "man of war" (Exod. 15:3). The prince of orators, who authoritatively stated that weapons were commanded to yield to the toga, in a speech he delivered entitled *Pro Murena*, nevertheless, said as follows: "All domestic affairs, every noteworthy interest, even the praise won from oratory and its careful practice, depend upon the oversight and protection of the art of war."[23] In the same way Theodosius, when it came to civil law, said that "the whole republic is most safely hemmed in by the line of soldiers."[24] Why, then, should we not say the same of the military service in which we are engaged? We should, because those who live to pursue our kind of military service defend the very idea *Christian* for the good of the whole nation or that of the city (maybe even for the world). The floodwaters waited for Methuselah to die. The downpour of fire delayed so Lot could escape. Hippo could not be destroyed before Augustine's death, as Heidelberg could not either before Pareus died. No doubt, righteous and learned preachers of the gospel, however many there

---

18. Serm. 62. in Cantic.] Bernard of Clairvaux, *In Cantica Canticorum*, sec. 8 (*sermo* 62).

19. "Powerful with God."

20. "Taking captive every thought into obedience to Christ."

21. I.e., the new condition of being enslaved to Christ.

22. "Full company of heaven."

23. Cicero, *Pro L. Murena*, in *Opera Omnia*, vol. 2 (Paris, 1565), ch. 22.

24. Novell 31.] Probably some variation of the *Novellae Constitutiones Post-Theodosianae*. Perhaps *Imperatorum Theodosii, Valentiniani, Maioriani, Anthemii Novellae Constitutiones XLII* (Paris, 1571). Theodosius II, 401–450, r. 408–450, Eastern Roman (Byzantine) emperor.

are, can, with good reason, shout their approval, as once Elijah and Elisha did, for this cry: "My father, my father, the chariot and horsemen of Israel!" [2 Kings 2:12]. This is proper for righteous and learned preachers, I say. No precocious young man, no matter how much he claims he is a soldier, is suited to such a great undertaking. The young man says he is ready, but no one will enlist him. Not even Israel was ever so foolish as to substitute boys for fathers, driverless vehicles for chariots, and those missing all their tack for real horsemen.

§ 4. I now proceed to the duties of spiritual soldiers. Foremost among these (if treated according to the standard of ordinary citizens, as they should be if we are to maintain the allegory) are as follows: to pursue their object, to obey their commander, to hold their place in the line, to cease from military exercises when not in combat, and to fight valiantly while in it.

1. *To pursue his object.* The one who is completely engaged in affairs of war considers other activities foreign to him. For such a man will not be able, for example, to prosecute happily the work of a merchant at the same time as soldiery, peddling wares and serving in the military. "No one who serves as a soldier entangles himself in the affairs of this life, so that he can please him by whom he was chosen to be a soldier" (2 Tim. 2:4). That's what the Apostle says. Among Latin writers, this way of life is typically called a "military campaign." The older writers, moreover, named it a "campaign" with good reason, because a mind bent on battles must not be distracted by other considerations. This is Cassiodorus's position in his letters.[25] Let us grant that the Christian will be busy with secular business. Nevertheless, to become entangled in them will be dangerous—in fact, I could have said lethal. The word ἐμπλέκεται[26] in Paul connotes a snare. And love of earthly things, as Augustine warns us, is "birdlime for spiritual feathers."[27] As rivers, while they flow down toward the ocean from which they arose, touch upon the banks and shoals but are not at all slowed down by them, so our souls, on their return to heaven and God, must, perhaps, touch this earth lightly but then immediately pass it by. Let the minister of the Word especially take care not to trip himself up in such worldly concerns. For the man who indulges in leisure hides his lamp under his bed, and the one who

---

25. Lib. 1. Epist. 17.] Flavius Magnus Aurelius Cassiodorus Senator (Cassiodorus), ca. 490–ca. 585, Roman politician, writer, and monk, *Variarum*, in *Opera Omnia Quae Exstant* (Geneva, 1622), bk. 1, ch. 17, p. 40.

26. "Implicated."

27. A common practice throughout antiquity was to trap birds using a sticky mixture of lime spread on branches, enabling hunters to net the entrapped birds more easily. According to à Lapide (*Commentaria In Acta Apostolorum*, vol. 1 [1627], p. 86) this comes from Augustine's *De Verbis Apost.*, sermon 33.

concerns himself with business, under a bushel. He considers his ministry as of no consequence compared to the world. Jerome once remarked wittily to Nepotian,[28] "The *business* of the priest is, so to speak, to flee a kind of disease."[29] What business does a minister have in the marketplace, especially if he is diligent, any more than a merchant should busy himself in the church? Christ should drive them both out with the whip! [Matt. 21:12].

2. *To obey his commander.* The soldier's first commendation is obedience. Whoever "prefers to rethink his commander's orders rather than follow them"[30] is considered a coward. Thus, in Livy, Aemilius Paulus[31] said that a soldier must focus on three things: (1) that his body is as strong and vigorous as possible, (2) that his weapons are well maintained, and (3) that his mind is ready for sudden orders. Everything else is left to the care of the immortal gods and his commander.[32] From our ranks, the gospel centurion said, "I say to this one, 'Go,' and he goes; to another, 'Come,' and he comes; to my slave, 'Do this,' and he does it" (Matt. 8:9). We must equally obey Christ our general. For His prerogative is giving orders, ours is obeying them. "I would rather be obedient," Luther once said, "than perform miracles."[33] This is a beautiful expression, if we understand it of the obedience owed Christ. That same peerless teacher used to call that obedience "faith incarnate." Since the invisible God was made manifest in the flesh, so the faith that lies hidden in the heart expresses itself through obedience and is made to stand in the sunlight. It was for this that, in Curtius's history, Alexander's[34] soldiers were marked with distinction; namely, "they focused not only on their general's standard but even on his nod."[35] We watch for the standard of Christ in His word, His nod in the inspiration of the Spirit, and we must obey both eagerly.

§5. 3. *To hold his place in the line.* He must hold his place, I say, for when that is lost, the world is turned to chaos, the army to a rout. "You are beautiful, my friend," says the bridegroom in the Song of Songs. "You are pleasing and lovely as Jerusalem, causing terror like the battle line of camp arrayed"

---

28. Flavius Julius Popilius Nepotianus Constantius (Nepotian), d. 350, short-lived usurper of the Roman Empire.

29. Jerome, *Hieronymi Stridoniensis Epistolae Selectae*, in *Opera Divi Hieronymi Stridoniensis*, vol. 2 (Leuven, 1596), *epistola* 12.

30. Tacit. histor. l. 2.] [Publius] Cornelius Tacitus, ca. 56–ca. 120, Roman historian, *Historiarum*, in *Opera Quae Exstant* (Antwerp, 1607), bk. 2.

31. Lucius Aemilius Paulus "Macedonius," b. ca. 229 BC/d. 160 BC, Roman general.

32. Livy, *Ab Urbe Condita* (Frankfurt, 1578), 44.34.

33. Scult. Annal. decad. 1. p.] Scultetus, *Annalium Evangelii Passim*, p. 17.

34. Alexander the Great, 356–323 BC, r. 336–323 BC, king of Macedon.

35. Lib. 3.] Quintus Curtius Rufus (Curtius), fl. first century AD, Roman rhetorician and historian, *De Rebus Gestis Alexandri Magni* (Basel, 1556), bk. 3.

(Song 6:4). Clearly, if the battle line had not been well encamped, it never would have caused terror. "A well-ordered army," says Xenophon, "is the most pleasing sight to her allies, and the greatest trouble to her enemies."[36] The need to maintain an orderly line is just as urgent for spiritual soldiers. Therefore, Paul proclaims to the Colossians that the basis of his joy is not only the πίστις of that church but also its τάξις,[37] as he remembers it together with faith (Col. 2:5). The Devil, on the other hand, who once lethally abandoned his own post, has no greater goal or desire than to overthrow the order that exists among men. In a physical body, each individual vessel is fitted to its particular humors, and if they accidentally overflow those containers, that is where disease breaks out. Thus, veins are designated for blood, and the gallbladder for yellow bile. But an abscess arises if blood leeches out of the veins. If yellow bile exceeds its vesicle, jaundice ensues. Likewise, in a political or ecclesiastical system, as often as someone ignores his particular obligations and meddles with another's, just that often churches and states become diseased and are on the very brink of death. This is the condition that the Apostle calls ἀτάκτως περιπατεῖν ("walking in a disorderly way") (2 Thess. 3:6). And this is not the only problem. There is also the issue of adopting practices well out of conformity with what the nature of one's duty requires. I will state it concisely: the worst creature to look at is a debased man, the worst man is a dishonest Christian, and the very worst Christian is a defective minister of the Word.

4. *To cease from military exercises when not in combat.* It is called an army, if we trust Varro, because it becomes better by frequent training.[38] Armies are directed toward this goal by their veterans. The Romans called these "camp leaders," while the Greeks referred to them as ὁπλοδιδάκται.[39] It was their job to discipline recruits to handle weapons, throw spears, fortify the camp, dig the ditch, establish the palisade, endure the sun and the dust, assemble quickly for the disposition of proper combat, and foresee, by preparation in the camp, whatever else could happen in the line and in battles. We also have our own daily training drills, which will be most needed and useful even when we are enjoying the most profound peace.

---

36. τεταγμένη ἡ στρατιὰ κάλλιστον μὲν ἰδεῖν τοῖς φίλοις, δυσχερέστατον δὲ τοῖς πολεμίοις. *Xenoph.* in Oecon.] Xenophon, ca. 435–354 BC, Greek historian, writer, and military leader, *Oeconomicus*, in *Quae Extant Opera* (Paris, 1625), 8.6.

37. "Faith" and "order," respectively.

38. De lin. lat. l. 4] Marcus Terentius Varro, 116–27 BC, Roman scholar and satirist, *De Lingua Latina*, in *Opera Omnia Quae Extant* (Amsterdam, 1623), [ii] 23. There is an etymological argument here too difficult to reproduce in English. A.'s *exercitus*, here translated "army," is, according to Varro, derived from the verb *exercitare*, i.e., "to train frequently."

39. *Lips.* politic. l. 5. c. 13.] A. seems to paraphrase Lipsius, *Politicorvm Sive Civilis Doctrinae Libri Sex* (Lyon, 1590), bk. 1, ch. 13.

Paul, master of ascetic self-denial, wrote, "Even in this I train myself"—ἐν τούτῳ καὶ αὐτὸς ἀσκῶ—"that, of course, at all times, I may have a clear"—ἀπρόσκοπον—"conscience before God and men" (Acts 24:16). Seneca, meanwhile, dubbed leisure "a living man's tomb."[40] I have no hesitation in calling sloth the Christian's pitfall, for it is obvious that Paul recoiled from it as though from Tartarus. We can see this from that famous summary of his duties: "By the grace of God, I am what I am, and His grace conferred on me was not in vain. No, I worked more abundantly"—that is, more—"than all the others. And yet it was not I but God's grace that worked with me" (1 Cor. 15:10). Note, he says not, "I was enriched more," but, "I worked more." Not, "I gained a richer advantage, a fatter salary, a more lavish estate." Rather, he said, "I worked more abundantly." Well done, Apostle! May God crown you more and more (if it is really right to pray for the spirits of the blessed)! But oh, if only we could all learn from your example just this one lesson: to work!

5. And last, *to fight valiantly while in combat*. When Joab was about to go to battle, he said, "Let us fight like men for our people and for the cities of our God" (1 Chron. 19:13). Likewise, Hezekiah said to his military commanders, "Take heart and be bold; do not fear or be alarmed and terrified" (2 Chron. 32:7). Paul addressed Christians with an almost equal array of words: "Be watchful, stand firm in the faith," ἀνδρίζεσθε, κραταιοῦσθε (1 Cor. 16:13). Cornificius[41] used to call his soldiers "helmeted rabbits" because they got scared so easily.[42] Moreover, as Solomon affirms, "The righteous are like a bold lion" (Prov. 28:1). To join in hand-to-hand combat with a roaring, hellish lion, one needs strength like a lion's.

In light of this, each of us must drink a bit more deeply from the apostolic exhortation: ἀγωνίζου τὸν καλὸν ἀγῶνα τῆς πίστεως (1 Tim. 6:12).[43] In their battles long ago, Etruscans used the trumpet; Arcadians, the pipe. The Spartans used the flute, and Thracians, the horn. The Egyptians employed the drum, and Arabs, the cymbal—all to arouse zeal for combat. For Christians and their ministers, may that concise but Θεόπνευστον[44] statement prove more powerful to kindle our bravery than any trumpet or drum: "Fight the good fight of faith."

§ 6. I could wish that the fighting spirit I have been trying to sketch would reside in all of us. We must, no doubt, strain every last drop of effort, as

---

40. Seneca, *Epistolae* (*epistola* 82).
41. Quintus Cornificius, d. 42 BC, Roman orator, poet, and general.
42. Jerome, *Thesaurus Temporum* (Leiden, 1606), bk. 1, p. 42.
43. "Fight the good fight of faith."
44. "God-breathed."

I have said, toward this: to acquit ourselves well as soldiers. And yet, how very few are there of such people? How very few, I say. What a pity!

Among scholars, who is there that tirelessly makes this effort? If vigorously enjoying the good life or coveting the accumulation of wealth is what it means *to pursue his object*, then yes, the scholar does that. If growing his hair long and] dressing like a courtier is *to obey his commander*, again yes. If *to hold his place in the line* is teaching before one has learned, and immediately ascending from the Sophists to the gospel authors, then fine. If *to cease from military exercises when not in combat* means holding preliminary literary exercises first within the college walls and then in the Temple of Learning[45] and then, moreover, in the public schools, the scholar does so. If *to fight valiantly while in combat* means stirring up theological controversy in the philosophers' burrows—and meanwhile, spending less time and trouble to understand the Scriptures—then yes, the scholar is a success. So, no doubt, the number of good soldiers equals the number of flies when it gets really hot!

But if, on the other hand, these activities I have recounted and others like them are characteristic of cowards and men squandering their leisure— as indeed they are—by the love of God, by the deep compassion of Christ, let us shake off, my fellow soldiers, let us shake off all our sluggishness! And may the goodness of our cause finally challenge us for once to soldier well. For our cause is by far the best and most righteous, if ever there were such. Each day with Satan's help, faults and vices assail our very souls on every side, as well as the minds of those joined with us in covenant. And so partly for our own defense, partly for others', we must, each day—I do not say merely think about, but actually—go to war. The sacred page rings out the sound of the battle trumpet! It is under your guidance, O camp leaders (I mean the prefects and tutors of the colleges), that—as Silius says—

> The tender youth soon comes of age
> in camp, as on his cheeks as yet
> untouched by feathered yellow hair
> the helmet presses down.[46]

These are the beloved tokens of their parents, the young men entrusted to your keeping for this spiritual military training in which you will form them by your instruction and examples, that their characters, which you received as marble, you may leave as silver; or if silver, you may turn them

---

45. *In Templo Academico*; perhaps a reference to the Middle Temple and the Inner Temple, two of the four Inns of Court in the heart of London's legal district.

46. Lib. 2.] Silius Italicus, ca. 26–102, Roman politican and orator, *De Secundo Bello Punico* (Amsterdam, 1628), bk. 2, p. 33.

into gold. And if any come to you already gold, you must return them set with gems. We are considering here further progress.

§ 7. Our most blessed Lord Jesus Christ, who is called in Acts the ἀρχηγὸν καὶ σωτῆρα (Acts 5:31),[47] and in the letter to the Hebrews, ἀρχηγὸν τῆς σωτηρίας (Heb. 2:10),[48] must be considered the foremost general in this militia we are describing. For that is the proper force of the word ἀρχηγός. The Lord Himself, because He customarily anticipated His incarnation and, at just the right moment, was present with His servants, revealed Himself openly to Joshua as captain through a visible revelation. This happened right when Joshua first undertook his duties. That very same Son of God earlier appeared in the bush that burned though remained undamaged. The Lord did this to show that the people of Israel—whom Moses then was appointed to steer toward safety—would survive through the flames of disaster while He stood guard. Later, Joshua saw Him stationed at the helm and moving through the center of their enemies, in appearance like a very brave man brandishing a drawn sword. And when Joshua asked the Lord, "Are you on our side or our enemies'?" He immediately answered, "I am the captain of the host of Jehovah" (Josh. 5:12–13).[49] He was fully justified in claiming this title for Himself. Hardly any title could be more majestic, since He has provided His church—and always will—what a good commander supplies his army—I mean, of course, their weapons, pay, daily meals, a good example, and help.

§ 8. First, then, let us discuss the *weapons*. People think an unarmed man is unwarlike. When it is time to join the battle, then he is called to arms. The weapons Christ supplies are denoted by a twofold character in the sacred literature. They are called "weapons of light" (Rom. 13:12), that is, most gleaming (in Romans 13). And this Paul does, if I am not mistaken, as an allusion to the practice of those same Romans. It was their established practice to dispatch soldiers to the line decked in shining armor. Thus Juvenal: "His silver shone in arms alone."[50] Suetonius, when writing about Julius Caesar, says, "He kept his soldiers so stylishly equipped that he decked them out with polished weapons of silver and gold. This was as much for their appearance as that they would grip them more resolutely in battle from fear

---

47. "Captain and Savior."
48. "Captain of salvation."
49. Josh. 5:13–14.
50. Juvenal, *Satyra*, 11.

of loss."[51] Onosander's advice also had this aim: "A general must see to it that his army gleams, equipped with shining armor. For his soldiers look more awe-inspiring when sparks, so to speak, flash off their armor."[52] But even the very lightning is cast into shadow when compared to the light of spiritual weapons—I mean the light of knowledge, true godliness, and joy. In another passage, these are called the "weapons of righteousness" (2 Cor. 6:7). Within this title we note a luminous difference between our weapons and worldly ones. For the weapons of the world are generally dedicated to unrighteousness, and "sin is granted legal standing." This was the poet's complaint.[53] We also note that famous passage of Antigonus where he mercilessly lambasts a man who provided him a commentary on the nature of justice while attacking foreign cities. Is there not also this bit about Marius, "who denied that he could hear the laws over the commotion of weapons"? Not to mention that anecdote of Pompey:[54] "Did I put on armor so that I could meditate on the laws?"[55] Horace really nailed it when he described Achilles's savagery like this:

> The laws, he claimed, were born for some but not for him to heed.
> Whate'er he had he'd gained by might, and force of manly deed.[56]

§ 9. Second, let us look at the soldiers' *pay*. Wars depend on two motivating forces: iron and gold. From the former, weapons are forged, and from the latter, salaries are paid. The mark of a good general is to see to it that, if at all possible, these are not diminished. For, the Apostle says, "Who ever served as a solider at his own expense?" (1 Cor. 9:7). So by this very argument, Paul claims that ministers of the gospel are owed a fair wage. Consequently, nothing is so unfair as when soldiers enjoy the pay owed them, while ministers of the Word are either begrudged their salaries or it is denied that these are due them. This is not the way Christ acts as commander, who "established by a particular law"—ὁ κύριος διέταξε[57]—"that those who proclaim the gospel should live from the gospel" (1 Cor. 9:14). If men regard this

---

51. Cap. 65.] Gaius Suetonius Tranquillus, b. ca. 70, Roman biographer and historian, *De XII. Caesaribus* (Leiden, 1651), bk. 1, ch. 67.

52. Strategic. c. 28.] Onosander, fl. first century AD, Greek philosopher, *Strategicus* (Heidelberg, 1600), ch. 28, p. 42.

53. *Lucan.* phars. l. 1.] Lucan, *Bellum Civile*, bk. 1. A. here cites from line 2 of the Roman poet Lucan's epic *Pharsalia*: *iusque datum sceleri*. The context is the Roman civil wars, and A. wrongly cites line 1.

54. Gnaeus Pompeius Magnus (Pompey), 106–48 BC, Roman general and statesman.

55. Vid. *Grotium* de bello & pace in proleg.] Grotius, *De Iure Belli Ac Pacis* (Amsterdam, 1642), sig. a4r (*prolegomena*).

56. Horace, *De Arte Poetica*, in *Opera* (Paris, 1642).

57. "The Lord decreed."

divine regulation I just mentioned (oh, how shameful that some consider this to be petty grasping!), the soldiers of Christ will not have to go without their pay. He will be, O man of God, whoever you are (provided you really are a man of God)—though you be treated very shamefully by the men of this world—the "Almighty will be your most precious gold, and your silver, and your strength" (Job 22:25). This is how the words of Eliphaz are rendered in the *Junio-Tremellius* version.[58]

This is the third consideration: a good general will supply *provision*. A famished army cannot maintain its discipline, as Cassiodorus remarks,[59] and commonsense proves it. Recall the famous Gaspard de Coligny,[60] butchered in that Paris slaughterhouse. He had this to say about the army: "If anyone wants to build a brilliant army, he must begin with the stomach." By this he meant that the daily ration was absolutely indispensable. This is such a keen concern to our general that He does not refuse to nourish us by His own Spirit and feed us on His word. No, He does more than that. So no one in His camp suffer hunger, He even stoops to offer us His own blood for drink and His flesh for food. Scriptural proof of this concept is very clearly given in the Evangelist: "My flesh is true food, and my blood is true drink. Whoever eats my flesh and drinks my blood remains in me, and I in him" (John 6:55–56).

§ 10. Fourth, we have the commander's *example*. The vigorous commander will go out ahead of His army not merely in words but also in actions. Thus, one of the Caesars—I am not quite sure who, but unless I am mistaken, it was Julius—when something difficult needed doing, would typically address his soldiers like this: "I do not say, 'Advance, soldiers,' but, 'Let us soldier on together.'"[61] As Lucan said of Cato,[62]

> He went ahead on foot, his spear clutched tight
> Before the faces of his host surprised,
> And showed them how to bear the task nor did
> He give command.[63]

Abimelech, in the book of Judges, said to his men: "What you have seen me do, do quickly" (Judg. 9:48). And what of Christ? Let us listen to Him directly. "I have given you an example, that as I have done for you, so you should do yourselves" (John 13:15). And let us hear what Peter says about

---

58. *Biblia Sacra*, Job 22:25, p. 356.

59. Variarum 4. c. 13.] Cassiodorus, *Variarum*, bk. 4, ch. 13.

60. Gaspard II de Coligny, 1519–1572, French Huguenot admiral.

61. Suetonius, *De XII. Caesaribus*, bk. 1, ch. 67.

62. Marcus Porcius Cato (Cato the Younger), 95–46 BC, Roman politician.

63. Lib. 9.] Lucan, *Bellum Civile*, bk. 9.587–89.

Him: "Christ suffered for us, leaving us an example, that we should follow in His steps" (1 Peter 2:21). Augustine sings in unison with both when he says, "The words of your Word are our lessons, the deeds of your Word our examples."[64] In another passage, moreover, he says, "Christ's whole life was an instruction in proper morality."[65] Likewise, Leo wrote, "In vain are we called Christians if we do not become imitators of Christ. He said that He was the way: the teacher's conversation was to be the student's pattern, and the servant would choose that humility that his master followed."[66]

Fifth, there is *help*. It is truly the commander's duty to come to the aid of even a common soldier when he is in danger. Trajan[67] reportedly dressed his soldiers' wounds with his own hand.[68] And when they ran out of bandages, Trajan did not even spare his own clothing but tore it all up for tourniquets and poultices. The sacred Scriptures teach us that Christ our Lord offered up Himself—I do not mean His clothing but His very flesh—to be torn asunder that "by his wounds we might be healed" [Isa. 53:5]. Yet He is always present through His Holy Spirit to bring needed help to Christians and ministers as they toil. For this reason, Paul wrote to the Philippians, "I can do all things through Him who strengthens me: Christ" (Phil. 4:13). He does not, of course, mean all things without exception, for he could not create a world. But when he says "All things," he means by this phrase whatever is in accord with his own calling, as Calvin notes.[69] For now, I do not want to tarry over particulars. It will be sufficient just to touch briefly, as it were, on the main points of these topics. Do we need help reading? "Christ opened the disciples' minds that they might understand the Scriptures" (Luke 24:45). We acknowledge that the Spirit of Christ is the doorkeeper to the holy books. No one may gain access to enter into these inner holy places if Christ does not admit them. Do we need to pray? Let us heed the Apostle as he writes to the Romans: "The Spirit with us bears our weaknesses. For we do not know what we should pray, but the Spirit Himself intercedes for us with inexpressible groans" (Rom. 8:26). Augustine, in his *Confessions*, remarks eloquently as follows: "There is nothing, O Lord, that You hear from me that You have not first

---

64. De vera Relig. c. 16.] Augustine, *De Vera Religione*, in *Opera*, vol. 1 (Basel, 1528). This quotation is often credited to Augustine; A.'s phrasing does not appear to be in the treatise he cites.

65. *De Vera Religione*, XXIX (29).

66. Serm. de nativitate Dei.] Leo the Great, *In Nativitatem Domini* (*sermo* 5).

67. Marcus Ulpius Traianus (Trajan), ca. 53–117, r. 98–117, Roman emperor.

68. *Dio Cassius*.] Dio Cassius, ca. 164–post-229, Roman statesman and historian who wrote in Greek, *Historiae Romanae* (Hanover, 1606), bk. 68.

69. Calvin, *Commentarii In Omnes Pauli Epistolas*, sub loc. Phil. 4:13.

spoken to me."[70] What about preaching? If there is any power in our words, it is owed to Christ. For Paul says, "The one who worked through Peter as an apostle of the circumcision also worked through me as an apostle among the gentiles" (Gal. 2:8). Finally, what about hearing? The Lord is said to have "opened Lydia's heart to heed what Paul was saying" (Acts 16:14). And concerning the Spirit of Christ, Gregory Nazianzus says, ᾧ μόνῳ Θεὸς καὶ νοεῖται καὶ ἑρμηνεύεται καὶ ἀκούεται ("Through the Spirit alone God is understood, explained, and heeded").[71]

§ 11. Since this is how things are, it really should not be at all surprising to the most careful and experienced practitioners of *Plans for Spiritual War*[72] that whenever an adult came to be baptized—after he acknowledged that he was leaving the Devil's camp by saying Ἀποτάσσομαί σοι Σατανᾷ— he would usually say at once, Συντάσσομαί σοι Χριστέ.[73] This means he must be held to a military standard: "I join myself, O Christ, to Your soldiers, and I take my place in the battle line. By Your grace, I will fight tirelessly under Your banners."

And so, my brothers, let us confidently fulfill our duties, under the auspices of such a great commander, no matter how difficult these tasks may be and how opposed to our nature. We must never give up hope, since Christ is our leader. But we also must hope for nothing when Christ is not leading. For if "a mass of soldiers without a leader is a body without a spirit,"[74] as we read in Curtius, how wretched and pitiable is the condition of those men to whom this Pauline description applies: χωρὶς Χριστοῦ, ἐλπίδα μὴ ἔχοντες καὶ ἄθεοι ἐν τῷ κόσμῳ (Eph. 2:12).[75] This passage shows that whoever is without Christ, that same person is without God and without hope. But our reason for hope will never fail so long as Christ deserves to be called (and this He does and will forever deserve) "the captain and leader of our salvation" (Heb. 2:10). The Athenians' commander Chabrias[76] used to say that an army of deer was more fearsome when led by a lion than an army of lions led by a deer.[77] The very lion of the tribe of Judah commands our army. When he approaches, even the least faithful soldier can become

---

70. Lib. 10. c. 2.] Augustine, *Confessionum*, 10.2.2.

71. In Apologet.] Gregory Nazianzus, ca. 325–389, Cappadocian father, *Apologeticus*, in *Opera*, vol. 1 (Paris, 1630) (*oratio* 1). A. gives the Greek text, together with his own Latin gloss.

72. A. here repeats the title of the work, capitalized and with a slight variation, i.e., *Spiritualium Tacticorum* instead of the *Sacrorum Tacticorum* we might expect.

73. "I reject you, Satan" and "I enlist with You, O Christ."

74. Lib. 10.] Curtius, *De Rebus Gestis Alexandri Magni*, bk. 12, p. [ii] 400.

75. "Without Christ, having no hope and godless in the world."

76. Chabrias of Athens, ca. 420–357/356 BC, professional Athenian solider.

77. A. gives no reference for this anecdote, though it is taken from Xenophon's *Hellenica*.

hardened with resolve. Once, Antigonus said to a ship's captain, who was trembling and using the mass of enemy vessels as an excuse, ἐμὲ δέ, ἔφη, αὐτὸν παρόντα πρὸς πόσας ἀντιτάττεις; ("How many boats do you think I'm worth, by comparison?").[78] Certainly, neither ten thousand men nor legions of demons, if compared to our commander's valor, are mighty enough to frighten those who value the one Christ more than all creatures.

---

78. *Plutarch*. in Apophthegm.] Plutarch of Chaeronea, b. before 50–d. post-120, Greek philosopher and biographer, *Apophthegmata*, in *Omnium Quae Exstant*, vol. 2 (Frankfurt, 1620).

CHAPTER VI

The Need for Full Armor and an Exposé of the Devil's Schemes

Section 1: The author steals a march[1] on Ephesians 6:11 and the following verses. The armor of God can be described in a threefold manner. James 1:17 is illuminated. Section 2: Why we must don the πανοπλία.*[2] The chain links of the spiritual virtues, 2 Peter 1:5–7. Our complete spiritual armor is Christ. Section 3: Logical fallacies serve the purposes of Satan as a Sophist, political deceits serve him as a prince, and schemes as a warrior. Satan's power and wickedness are connected. Section 4: Satan makes use of the fallacy of the false cause when he suggests that God is the author of sin. Both Scripture and nature suggest the opposite, and this is also exemplified by a certain historical parable. Section 5: Satan cunningly accommodates himself to the nature and position of every individual. The temptations of the Corinthian man of incest and of John Knox are opposite to one another. Section 6: The Devil typically chose for his own worship places that were previously sacred (Hosea 9:15). Hosea 4:15 illustrates this principle. The noteworthy testimony of Jerome. Section 7: Satan practices counterfeit friendship. Theurgy and white magic are very destructive. The personal testimony of Cornelius Agrippa. Section 8: The adversary is eager to strip us of the sword of the Word and the spear of prayer. The crime of certain French bishops. A careful examination of Acts 16:16–17. Section 9: The Devil is the one who sows the seeds of strife, and an evaluation of 2 Corinthians 11:3. The exceptional sayings of André Rivet and Samuel Sorbière. Section 10:* Μεθοδεία*[3] is ascribed to Satan, because he commonly goes from lesser to greater by the use of method. Alypius's example. The Devil more boldly opposes God's more famous servants. The trials of Athanasius, Bernard, and Luther. [Section 11:] Here we show that Satan in many ways merely apes God, and these ways are summarized under six headings.*

---

1. The verb which A. employs here, *aggreditur*, has martial overtones. This is a play on words.
2. "Full armor."
3. "Trickery."

§ 1. In Ephesians chapter 6, we have Paul's noteworthy admonition. I will gladly expend some effort and elbow grease to make its meaning clear (since if one looks closely, its meaning is ready at hand). "Put on the whole armor of God, that you may be able to stand against the Devil's schemes" [Eph. 6:11]. No matter how burdensome it may be for some people to carry armor, it is especially helpful for the noble soldier. Cicero says about Roman soldiers, "Our men no more consider their shield, helmet, and sword burdens than they do their shoulders, arms, and hands."[4] Pagan writers, moreover, and especially the poets, customarily dispatched leading soldiers to battle equipped with weapons given by divine powers. Thus, Vergil sends out Aeneas,[5] and Homer, Achilles.[6][7] The poets depict Perseus[8] when he was about to fight Medusa[9] as receiving weapons and gifts from three consecutive deities. From Mercury[10] he received wings; from Pluto,[11] a helmet; and from Pallas,[12] a shield along with a mirror. In a similar fashion, the Apostle says we must put on the armor of God. Or, it is called "the armor of God" because whatever is exceptional in its own category is, by a Hebraism, said to be "of God." Consequently, Abraham is named the Prince of God (Gen. 23:6), that is, most glorious. And the flame that descended from heaven to devastate Job's herds is dubbed the "fire of God" (Job 1:16) — that is, most consuming. In the Psalms, we also hear of the "mountains, streams, and cedars of God" (Pss. 36:72; 65:10; 80:11), as these all display His unique excellence. Or, it is called "the armor of God" because it includes the same weapons the Lord prepared for Himself to complete His military service in the flesh. As King Saul wanted the weapons to fit David as he went out to single combat, so also Christ dresses us in His own armor. And so those very weapons that in the Apostle are assigned to Christians the prophet here duly assigns to Christ. I call this a very learned passage: "He was dressed with justice as His breastplate, and the helmet of salvation was on His head" (Isa. 59:17). In fact, from this passage, finally, we derive that which constitutes the Holy Spirit's saving gifts of the truth, righteousness, faith, and all the rest. Indeed, all of these things, to use James's expression, are from above and descend from the Father of lights (James 1:17). Accordingly,

---

4. Tusculan. second.] Cicero, *Tusculanarum Quaestionum*, in *Opera Omnia*, vol. 4 (Paris, 1565), bk. 2.

5. Aeneas, Trojan leader in Vergil's *Aeneid*.

6. Achilles, Greek hero and protagonist of Homer's *Iliad*.

7. Cf. *Aeneid* VIII and *Iliad* XVIII, respectively.

8. Perseus, Greek hero.

9. Medusa, Greek figure, a Gorgon.

10. Mercury, Roman god of trade.

11. Pluto, Roman god of the underworld.

12. Pallas Athena, patron goddess of Athens.

these gifts are not innate within us but come from above. Nor did they fall upon us accidentally but descend according to a set order. Yet they do not at all descend in the papist sense, as Lorinus comments on this passage. He holds that all the grace communicated in this age possesses a threefold procession: it is distributed from God to Christ, from Christ to the blessed virgin, and from the virgin to us in a very orderly manner.[13] But among the orthodox, grace follows the process of distribution that Laurentius has demonstrated.[14] I mention this so one may understand that God, in the ordinary course, bestows His gifts little by little and using means.

§ 2. Meanwhile, we must remember to put on this armor of God, so that it covers us completely—not merely this part or that but the whole of it. For just as the Christian soldier is required to stand at attention both day and night, because he is never free from attack, so also, because there is never an occasion when he is not assailed by his enemies, so he must also be armed on all sides. If he is exposed at any point, then right there, through that chink, he is struck a deadly blow. The myth writers tell a tale about Achilles, whose mother, Thetis,[15] dipped him in a fountain so powerful that it made him invulnerable. But his heel, nevertheless, remained susceptible at that very spot where he was held while immersed, the part not completely dipped in the water. The story goes that Paris[16] killed him with an arrow by striking and wounding him in his heel.

Really, the man who neglects to put on this whole armor is completely defenseless. So we can say of this armor ἢ ὅλως, ἢ μὴ ὅλως.[17] This is because the theological virtues and the Spirit's saving gifts, which constitute this full armor, are so mutually interconnected that if one lacks any part, he receives no benefit from the rest. Paul, consequently, employs this word *all* five times in three short verses with a highly significant, correlated meaning. "We have not stopped praying for you that you may be filled with the knowledge of His will with *all* wisdom; that you may walk in a way that suits the Lord and may be pleasing to Him in *all* things, producing the fruit of *all* good work; that you may be mighty with *all* power, for *all* long-suffering" (Col. 1:9–11).

And so the Christian soldier must expend the greatest possible care and wear like a necklace that apostolic chain that Peter forged: "Add to your faith

---

13. Jean de Lorin (Joannes Lorinus), 1559–1634, Jesuit biblical commentator, *In Catholicas BB. Iacobi Et Iudae Apostolorum* (Mainz, 1622), sub loc. James 1:17.

14. Perhaps Paul Laurentius, 1554–1624, Lutheran theologian.

15. Thetis, sea-nymph and mother of Achilles.

16. Paris, Trojan leader in Homer's *Iliad*.

17. "You put it all on or you do not put it on at all."

virtue; and to virtue, knowledge; to knowledge, self-control; to self-control, long-suffering; to long-suffering, holiness; to holiness, brotherly love; to brotherly love, mercy" (2 Peter 1:5–7). One must, first of all, lay hold of faith, without which it is impossible to please God, and to which the other virtues must rightly yield first place. And yet, even faith itself without works is dead. So then, to avoid being ineffectual, add to your faith virtue. By this virtue we understand, with Martinus,[18] that power by which we accomplish what is proper and flee what is improper. We embrace Augustine's statement: "The ancients defined virtue as the art of living well and properly."[19] To virtue we must add knowledge, so as not to neglect the word of God. The exercise of the virtues must be conducted according to its standard, and for this reason, it is called λογικὴ λατρεία (Rom. 12:1).[20] This means, so I think, worship of the Word, as in Peter it is rendered λογικὸν . . . γάλα (1 Peter 2:2)[21]—that is, milk of the Word. To knowledge we must add self-control, which teaches us to use the good things of this present life with moderation; to self-control, patience, which means enduring the evils of this life with generosity. And yet Stoics and monks display a self-control and patience that is inadequate, since these arise from philosophical principles or those of Antichrist, not from what is spiritual and divine. Therefore, we must join to these earlier virtues godliness, which beholds God [Heb. 12:14]. To righteousness, brotherly love, that dwells with people generally but only with the good as its brothers. To brotherly love, charity, exercised toward the wicked and her enemies, as they are fellow human beings. Whoever is completely armed with these very gifts of God, that man we must describe as having put on the full armor of God. Or, to put it more briefly, he has truly put on Christ, because Christ alone is the living foundation of all graces. Therefore, after Paul said ἐνδυσώμεθα τὰ ὅπλα τοῦ φωτός, he soon adds ἐνδύσασθε τὴν Κύριον Ἰησοῦν Χριστόν (Rom. 13:12–13).[22] Perhaps he does this as a kind of exegesis, to indicate that only Christ is the full panoply.

§3. If someone asks, however, what is the purpose of putting on all this armor we have described, the Apostle answers: "To take your stand against the Devil's schemes." We can note three separate categories of schemes. The first is logical fallacies, the second is political frauds, and the third is hostile

---

18. Lexic. philolog.] Matthias Martini (Martinus), 1572–1630, German Reformed theologian, *Lexicon Philologicum* (Frankfurt, 1655).

19. De civit. Dei l. 4 cap. 21.] Augustine, *De Civitate Dei*, 4.21.

20. "Spiritual worship."

21. "Spiritual milk."

22. "Let us put on the armor of light" and "you must put on the Lord Jesus Christ."

military operations. In keeping with the three-pronged attack that the Devil usually makes, the first scheme is that of the Sophist, the second belongs to the prince, but the third, to the man of war. Now the Sophist is the most sophisticated and ancient of all these types, especially since he deceived our first parents while they were in their original state of innocence. Moreover, as Jude relates, he dared to argue with the archangel Michael. If the ancient Christian church, wounded by Augustine's arguments—not yet regenerate and still wallowing in the filth of heretics—typically prayed, "Free us, O Lord, from Augustine's logic," it will be easy to guess how much more destructive is Satan's logical sophistry.

Furthermore, he is called the prince of this world (John 12:31; 14:30; 16:11), as he stole dominion over it by the most wicked action. This is like the well-known story told of Pope Boniface VIII:[23] "He took office like a fox, reigned as a lion, died like a dog."[24] This sarcastic comment fits the Devil very well: he took office like a snake, reigned as a dragon. And this observation has good support if one consults the book of Revelation, where we read the following words: "That great dragon was thrown down, that ancient serpent who is called the Devil and Satan, who misleads the whole world" (Rev. 12:9). But again, the same prophet also shows him as a man of war. "There was," he says, "a battle in heaven. Michael and his angels battled against the dragon, and the dragon and his angels fought back" (Rev. 12:7). Likewise, "the dragon raged against the woman and went out to make war with the remnant of the woman's seed" (Rev. 12:17).

Look, reader, at your sworn opponent, how truly and terribly daunting he is! Then again, because he is powerless and ineffectual, he will just bark and not bite. Someone with no power does very little harm. Meanwhile, the church suffers very, very severe whippings. The individual cords of those whips are twisted and braided from raw power and wickedness. It is obvious from Paul's description of the same people that this is a trick of devils: "Our struggle is not against flesh and blood but against the powers, against the authorities, against the rulers of the world, that is, against the princes of shadows of this age, against spiritual forces of evil that are above" (Eph. 6:12). In that passage, the words τὰς ἀρχάς, τὰς ἐξιουσίας, τοὺς κοσμοκράτορας mean one individual power, while the words τὰ πνευματικὰ τῆς πονηρίας mean one wickedness.

---

23. Boniface VIII, ca. 1234–1303, *p.* 1294–1303.

24. Samuel de Lublino in Tractatu summularum p. 137.] Samuel z Lublina (de Lublino), ca. 1589–1642, Dominican philosopher and theologian, *Tractatus Summularum* ([Köln], 1627).

§4. The causal fallacy is one of the most important sophistic arguments that Aristotle records. The Devil commonly adopts this fallacy, as when he proclaims a gospel of division and calls true religion the source of unhappiness. But nowhere is he more dangerous than when he suggests that God is the author of sin. Homer even represents Jupiter[25] as complaining about this very issue as follows:

> …Θεοὺς βροτοὶ αἰτιόωνται
> Ἐξ ἡμέων γάρ φασι κάκ᾽ ἔμμεναι

> …It is the gods whom mortals blame,
> for from us they say all evils come.[26]

The lecherous youth Lyconides[27] in Plautus's Aulularia, for example, says along these lines, "God drove me to it. He was the one that enticed me to her."[28] What a devilish trick, to ascribe utmost evil to the utmost good and to make the Lord Himself party to human sin! To confront this very sickness, the Apostle cautions us, "No one when he is tempted should say 'I am tempted by God.' For God cannot be tempted by wickedness, and He does not tempt anyone" (James 1:13).[29] Likewise, the Lord says in the prophet, "Your destruction depends upon you, Israel; your hope rests solely upon Me" (Hos. 13:9). Why do we need to bring a prophet and apostle into the discussion when even the law of nature has dictated the same point to some of the sounder gentiles? Plato says, "We must make every serious effort that nobody in that state which we want to be well governed either say or hear, whether he is a young man or a youth, in a poem or in any story, that god is the source of the evils that happen to anyone. It is impossible to say such a thing reverently. It is not useful for the state and is incoherent."[30] Plutarch also repeats with approval this saying of Euripides: εἰ Θεοί τι δρῶσιν αἰσχρόν, οὐκ εἰσὶν Θεοί ("If God does anything shameful, he is not God").[31] As for myself, whenever I reflect upon God's providence over sin, this saying almost always comes to mind. I refer to what we read in

---

25. Jupiter, king of Latin and Roman gods.

26. Odyss. α.] Homer, *Odyssea*, 1.33.

27. Lyconides, character in Plautus's *Aulularia*.

28. Titus Maccius Plautus (Plautus), fl. late third century BC–ca. 184 BC, Roman comic dramatist, *Aulularia*, in *Opera* (Geneva, 1605).

29. Here *Apostolus* means James and not, per A.'s usual practice, Paul.

30. κακῶν δὲ αἴτιον φάναι θεόν τινι γίγνεσθαι ἀγαθὸν ὄντα, διαμαχετέον παντὶ τρόπῳ, etc.] Plato, *De Republica*, in *Opera Omnia Quae Exstant* (Frankfurt, 1602), 2.380b.

31. Libro Στωικῶν ἐναντιωμάτων.] Euripides, quoted in Plutarch, *De Stoicorum Repugnantiis*, in *Omnium Quae Exstant*, vol. 2 (Frankfurt, 1620), sec. 33. A.'s Latin translation changes the plural θεοί in both clauses to singular *Deus*.

Trebellius Pollio[32] about a certain tyrant named Marius.[33] After he had been raised in the workshop of a blacksmith and habituated to the production of knives and swords, he started to become famous among soldiers. So on day one he was made emperor, on day two he ruled, and on day three he was killed by an anonymous soldier. This soldier, as he drove the dagger into Marius's chest, indulged in the most bitter sarcasm: "You made this sword yourself."[34] Clearly, we can say the same thing about that sinner whom God's commands and warnings do not pierce but only his own sins. "You made this sword yourself. Your destruction, my man, comes from within not from without—and yet not from divine providence."

§ 5. Among political deceits, there is scarcely anything more frequent than for those who encroach upon another's power to adapt themselves to the character or condition of those whom they seek either to dominate or to use as instruments for acquiring control. So we read in Daniel that "Antiochus was compromising many by his flattery" (Dan. 11:32).[35] Likewise, in Samuel, Absalom typically said to anyone who was seeking justice, "'Your arguments are good and correct, but who will hear you, since nobody has been appointed by the king? If only he would appoint me judge in this land, so that anyone who had a lawsuit or complaint could come to me.' And so he stole away the hearts of the Israelites" (2 Sam. 15:3–4, 6). Sallust also says that Catiline[36] noted "what passion inflamed each person according to his age, and for some he bought prostitutes, but for others dogs and horses."[37] So Satan, who always prays to sail on a favorable wave, has learned to adapt to the nature and status of any kind of person. He once had ready at hand for Abimelech a kingdom [Judg. 9:1–6]; for Achan, a Babylonian garment[38] as well as shekels of silver and a golden bar. He bribed Samson with Delilah [Judg. 16], Ahab with a vineyard [1 Kings 21], Gehazi with money and clothing [2 Kings 5]. For the traitor Judas, he had thirty pieces of silver; for Diotrephes, a prelacy [3 John vv. 9–11]. As a younger man is more vulnerable to lust, so an older one becomes more prone to superstition. Satan drove Solomon, in the prime of his life, to accumulate wives and concubines beyond measure and, in old age, provoked him to the most

---

32. Trebellius Pollio, one of the authors of *The Augustan History*.

33. Probably Marcus Aurelius Marius, r. 268/269, short-lived Roman Augustus.

34. *Historia Augusta* (Leiden, 1642). Perhaps see Marius under the "Thirty Pretenders."

35. The tense in the prophet is future, but A., writing from his perspective, renders it imperfect.

36. Lucius Sergius Catilina, ca. 102–62 BC, Roman demagogue.

37. Gaius Sallustius Crispus (Sallust), 86–35 BC, Roman historian, *Bellum Catilinarium*, in *Opera Quae Extant Omnia* (Leiden, 1649).

38. In Josh. 7 it is called a garment of Shinar.

reprehensible idolatry (1 Kings 11:3–4). In times of prosperity, Satan tries to win men over by the allurement of luxury, and in times of hardship, by disinclination to suffer. He drives the very irritable to flashes of anger; the cheerful, to dissolute living. The sluggish he drives to sloth; the melancholy, to distrust.[39] The poor he pushes toward lying and theft; the rich, toward debauchery and atheism. For this reason, Agur prayed, "Do not give me poverty or riches. Nourish me with food suited to my capacity, so that, when satisfied, I am not tempted to deny you and to say, 'Who is Jehovah?' or so poverty does not push me to steal and I profane the name of my God" (Prov. 30:8–9). If Satan finds anyone weighed down by the sense of God's anger and groaning under the feeling of his own sins, he tries to push him off the edge into the pit of despair. But if he sees anyone well aware that his life is not only blameless but even fruitful, Satan tries to undermine that man's foundation with hidden tunnels of pride, since he cannot demolish the whole structure with siege engines of disbelief. I could adduce as an example of the first type[40] the notorious Corinthian man who was disgraced by the stigma of incest. The Apostle was afraid that this man, who at the time was laboring under the knowledge of his sin, would be swallowed up by sadness. Then, giving up all hope of his soul and led on by the Devil, the man would be so distraught that he would destroy himself and scandalize the church. This is why the brothers are admonished to show him mercy and comfort, "so Satan does not overwhelm us," Paul says (2 Cor. 2:7, 10–11).

I would like to explain this second type of satanic attack through a more recent but not at all obscure little story. During the time of our predecessors, John Knox[41] was a strong, conspicuous instrument for reforming Scotland. On the very doorstep of death, he spent his last night constantly groaning and sighing. When asked why, he had this to say:

> To this point in my fragile life, I have endured many conflicts and many of Satan's attacks. But now that roaring lion has assailed me very boldly and poured out all his strength at once to swallow and ruin me. He used to set my sins right in front of my eyes often, often harassed me to the point of despair, often sought to catch me in the world's deceitful snares. But because he has been shattered by the sword of the Spirit, the Word of God, he could do nothing. Yet now he attacks me by another route. That cunning serpent is bent on convincing me that I have merited heaven itself and blessed immortality because I have faithfully discharged my ambassadorship in ministry. But blessed be our God, who reminded me

---

39. *Biliosos, sanguineos, phlegmaticos,* and *melancholicos*; A. here uses the four-humors explanation of human character.

40. I.e., the man on the brink of despair.

41. John Knox, ca. 1514–1572, Scottish Reformer.

of those scriptural passages for me to throttle Satan and extinguish this flaming dart. Among such passages was this one: "What do you have that you have not received?" [1 Cor. 4:7]. And, "By the grace of God I am what I am." And, "Not I, but the grace of God in me" [1 Cor. 15:10]. And so Satan left me, thoroughly beaten. I thank God, therefore, through Jesus Christ, who wanted me to gain the victory.[42]

§ 6. We now have in this way (I mean, so very easily) winnowed out certain kinds of diabolical schemes—I am referring to those that seem less relevant to our theme and this Pauline passage (after carefully considering the context). So next we should deal more pointedly with the Devil's warlike stratagems; or, at least, we should handle some of the most important ones, those that bear his special mark.

First, we must consider how he selects physical locations to attack. Sextus Iulius Frontinus, a man of consular rank, provides us with fourteen examples of this.[43] Satan has behaved throughout almost every age as though he believed he had been assigned this duty: to pollute with idolatrous worship and other foul things those places especially that God had sanctified by His own particular, prior presence and grace. To review from the beginning, we say with that very old poet, "In a foregone age, the Greeks ate acorns before grain was discovered. They looked for oracles from the same oaks from which they took food."[44] This is how Satan deceived people, as that famous man says. The grove of Dodona in Epirus was very famous for these oracles. It is quite likely, however, that this Dodona was a rival of Delphi. We see this plainly from a little verse of Ovid: "If Delphi or Dodona herself did not tell me this."[45] It is also quite likely that the name was borrowed from Dodanim, the grandson of Japheth whom Moses mentions (Gen. 10:4). Theologians speculate that he opened a school in that very location in order to instruct his followers. Tilenus deserves to be heard on this subject:

---

42. *Melch. Adam.* in vitis Theol. exter. p. 141] Adam, *Decades Duae Continentes Vitas Theologorum* (Frankfurt, 1618), p. 141.

43. Strategemat. lib. 2. cap. 2.] Sextus Julius Frontinus, ca. 30–103, Roman governor of Britain, *Strategemata* II.2, entitled *de loco ad pugnam eligendo*. Frontinus, *Strategemata*, in *Viri Illustris Flavii Vegetii Renati Et Sex. Iulii Frontini De Re Militari Opera* (Leiden, 1644), sub loc. bk. 2, ch. 2.

44. P. *Molinae Vates* p. 165.] Du Moulin, *Vates Seu De Præcognitione Futurorum* (Leiden, 1640).

45. Ovid, *Tristium*, in *Opera Omnia*, vol. 3 (Amsterdam, 1611), bk. IV.8. A. employs this same quotation in *Armilla Catechetica*, exercitation IV.4.iv. There is a textual variation, however, between his quotation and the critical text; while A. has *non*, Wheeler's Loeb reads *hoc*.

After some time, when all the restraints on his rage were broken, Satan constructed numerous strongholds for his blasphemy, μαντεῖα and χρηστήρια,[46] just as the world's treachery deserved.[47] In these fortresses, the Devil vomited out his responses and oracles as the highest sort of insult to God and the most sure destruction of men. Accordingly, it is no surprise that the Devil transformed the very residences of the holy fathers and places where the righteous once met and assembled to listen to heavenly doctrine into such foul haunts of lies. Of course, we should not at all reject the suppositions of those learned men who think that the location of Hammon was famous for its oracle before the school of Chamus or his descendants was placed there. For it is well known all knowledge of God did not, even among those men, disappear immediately after Noah's curse. This conclusion is drawn from the events recorded in the narrative of Abraham and Isaac that deal with Pharaoh and Abimelech. And these learned men also argue that some remnant of the family and church of Dodanim remained at the κατοικητήριον[48] of the oracle of Dodona. It is entirely plausible, everyone agrees, that the Devil first commandeered and then polluted and poisoned these two very ancient oracles. He did this both because of the renown of their earlier fame and also because of their reputation in antiquity. Satan realized that, by such an appeal, he could very easily entice, trap, and persuade men.

Such are the remarks of that well-known author.[49]

We will now bring to bear on the same observation the light and faith drawn from sacred Scripture. In Hosea we read, "All of their wickedness is in Gilgal, because there I have held them in hatred" (Hos. 9:15). This was said with special emphasis because in Gilgal, in particular, they incited the Lord with their idolatry. The whole of their wicked behavior is summarized, so to speak, in this shorthand: Gilgal. Because the ark of the covenant stayed there for a while, the false prophets kept claiming that this place was more holy than others. Therefore, they tried to institute idolatry there, and therein lies an Iliad of sins. This is the position of John Tarnovius.[50]

One location was the once very famous spot of the Israelites' circumcision, those who were born in the desert. Another became famous for the celebration of the first Passover after they entered the promised land. Still another became famous for the appearance of Christ the Lord, as the

---

46. "Pagan prophecy" and "oracular responses."

47. Tilenus, as quoted by A., here uses a phrase found in Beza's *Annotationes Maiores*, sub loc. 2 Thess. 2:9. The phrase is unusual enough to believe that Tilenus borrowed it from Beza.

48. "Site."

49. Syntag. part. 1 Disput. 2. thef. 20, 21, 22] Tilenus, *Syntagma Disputationum Theologicarum*, part 1, disput. 2, thes. 17–19, pp. 12–13.

50. In Hoseam. p 309.] Johann Tarnow (Tarnovius), 1586–1629, German doctor and professor of theology, *In Prophetam Hoseam* (Rostock, 1646), sub loc. Hos. 4:15.

commander of the army of Israel, to Joshua; yet another, for the dwelling place of the tabernacle and other signs of the divine presence. And so in that location more than the rest, superstition later caused altars to be raised and placed images there. Throngs of those who had betrayed the true religion and embraced the false one gathered at these images to pray and worship. So, under the Devil's supervision, when a place was famous and considered religious, he caused the delusion of foreign worship to grow there. That was André Rivet's conclusion.[51]

In the same prophet, we find that the town of Bethaven was connected to Gilgal: "Do not enter Gilgal, and do not go up to Bethaven" (Hos. 4:15). The ancient name of this place, Bethel, was really quite a term of honor. But the Lord refused to bestow honor on this place after Jeroboam had raised his altar and golden calf there (1 Kings 12:29). Jacob said of that spot many centuries before, "This is an awe-inspiring place; this is the house of God and the doorway of heaven" (Gen. 28:17). But as Hosea prophesied, by a devilish scheme the house of God (this is what Bethel means) was turned into a house or hovel of vanity. That is what the word Bethaven connotes. Furthermore, after the Lord's ascension—and it is stunning both to describe and to hear it—with tremendous zeal Satan further defiled the very places Christ had rendered holier than all others while He walked in the flesh. Jerome can be our witness to this. He spent a lot of time in Palestine and, therefore, was familiar with these very well-known places. In his letter to Paulinus,[52] he writes as follows:

> From the time of Hadrian right down to the reign of Constantine,[53] for approximately 180 years, an image of Jupiter was worshipped at the site of the resurrection. And on the rock where the cross stood, they worshipped a marble statue of Venus.[54] The instigators of the persecution thought that they could eradicate our faith in the resurrection and the cross if they defiled these holy places with idols. At present, a sacred grove of Thammuz—that is, Adonis[55]—overshadows our precious Bethlehem, the most significant site in the world, from which the truth has gone out into the world, as the psalmist sings. And in the little grotto where Christ once cried as a baby, they now cry in anguish for Venus's lover.[56]

------

51. Commentar. super Hoseam in 4. p. 154. & 311.] Rivet, *Commentarius In Hoseam* (Leiden, 1625), pp. 154, 311.

52. Paulinus, fourth–fifth century AD, biographer.

53. Flavius Valerius Constantinus (Constantine I), ca. 272/273–337, r. 306–337, Roman emperor.

54. Venus, Roman goddess of love, beauty, and seduction.

55. Adonis, Greek divine figure and lover of Venus.

56. Jerome, *Hieronymi Stridoniensis*, vol. 2 (*epistola* 14).

§7. The second strategy is pretense of friendship. Everyone is familiar with the disgraceful behavior of Zopyrus.[57] He ingratiated himself with his King Darius[58] when the latter was besieging Babylon, unsuccessfully trying anything he could think of. To do this, Zopyrus stabbed himself in the abdomen at home and even ordered his own nose and ears cut off. Then, when he had been made privy to the king's plans, he approached the Babylonians under the pretext of being a refugee. He disguised himself as their ally and a sworn enemy of his own people based on the severe damage to his body, falsely claiming it was perpetrated by the Persians. The Babylonians, through their extreme gullibility, made the hypocrite Zopyrus commander of their entire army. He then delivered the whole army to Darius and brought the city under the Persian's control.

The Devil never brings on darker shadows than when he transforms himself into an angel of light. A pretense of holiness is usually called *doubly wicked*. But in my opinion, a pretense of friendship should be called *double hostility*. The Devil is undoubtedly more hostile when he flatters than when he rages. Leo the Great was quite right to say that "the 'kindness' of demons harms all men more than their wounds, and it is better to have earned their hatred than to have made peace with them."[59] The common belief is that demons appear filled with honesty and kindness and remain at their worshipers' beck and call for any sort of task. The Romans call them *spiritus familiares*, while the Greeks name them παρέδρεις. Theophrastus Paracelsus supposedly carried around one of these in his sword handle. Likewise, they say that Cornelius Agrippa's dog was a demon, although his student Wier denied it.[60] More reliable people say it's true, like Martin Delrio, at the end of the second book of his *Discourses on Magic*.[61] If we ask Augustine (and consult Vives[62] on him), he will teach us that the ancients separated magic into *Goetia*, which all considered off-limits, and *Theurgy*, which many considered acceptable.[63] Contemporary authors divide it into black and white magic.

---

57. Sixth century BC, Persian satrap of Babylon mentioned in Herodotus's *Histories* (see 3.153–60).

58. Darius I, ca. 550–486 BC, r. 521–486 BC, king of Persia.

59. Homil. 19. de passion. Dom.] Leo the Great, *De Passione Domini*, in *Opera Quae Quidem Haberi* (Cologne, 1561) (*sermo* 19). A. has *beneficia daemonum ait cunctis esse nocentiora vulneribus, et praestare illorum odium quam pacem meruisse*, for Leo's *beneficia daemonum omnibus sint nocentiora vulneribus, quia tutius est homini, inimicitiam diaboli meruisse, quam pacem.*

60. Johannes Weyer (Wier), 1515–1588, Dutch physician and occultist.

61. Martin Antonio del Rio, 1551–1608, Jesuit theologian, *Disquisitionum Magicarum Libri Sex* (Lyon, 1608), bk. 2, q. 27, sec. 2, p. 164.

62. Juan Luis Vives, 1492–1540, Spanish humanist and educator.

63. De civit. Dei l. 10. c. 9.] Augustine, *De Civitate Dei*, 10.9.

But if we weigh the matter fairly, I think it will be obvious that Satan uses both of them to overwhelm gullible mortals and that the very best of the whitest magic is still pitch blackness. I take as my authority for this not just any precise theologian but Cornelius Agrippa himself. Learned men, knowledgeable in these mysteries, recognize that Agrippa was a regular "Delian swimmer"[64] when it came to magic. In his work *The Pointlessness of Learning*, Agrippa says, "Many men do not at all consider theurgy off-limits, as if it were governed by good angels and the divine presence. Nevertheless, very often it is tied to demons' wicked lies while employing titles for God and the angels!" In the end, he concludes that chapter with a statement that is quite memorable (at least if we consider the writer's meaning): "The schools of theurgy are the Art of Almadel, the Art of Disclosure, the Pauline Art, the Art of Revelations, and many other similar superstitions. The more divine novices think these arts are, the more damage they do."[65]

§ 8. The third strategy is to disarm the conquered enemy. The Philistine overlords used this strategy to hold the Hebrews more completely under their control. The satirist Juvenal writes,

> Though you may take of silver and of gold all that you like,
> yet to the conquered on the field leave shield, sword, helmet, pike.[66]

But if even the weapons are confiscated, there will be very little hope left. The Hebrews found themselves, in fact, in this very lamentable condition. The sacred Scriptures say, "There was not a craftsman in all of Israel, for the Philistines had said, 'Let's be careful that the Hebrews make no sword or spear.' So then, it happened that, in time of war, not one man in the whole company of Saul and Jonathan had a sword or spear. Only Saul and his son Jonathan had them" (1 Sam. 13:19, 22). Granted, the Juvenal quote is somewhat frivolous. The sword, as Paul confirms (Eph. 6:17), is the Word of God. And what is the spear if not prayer? If this spear is hurled by faith, it strikes the enemy deeply and destroys him. The Devil's main desire and goal is to deprive the human race of these two weapons. Let us learn from a story told not so long ago about certain French bishops—and one which yet still deserves telling—how much the Devil despises the sword of the Word. These men, as the Reformed martyrologies for 1543 report, after they had finished a splendid banquet at Avignon, were passing down the

---

64. Inhabitants of the Greek island of Delos were famous for their swimming ability, and thus the proverb means anyone expert and highly skilled.

65. Cap. 46. cui titulus. est de Theurgia.] Agrippa, *De Incertitudine Et Vanitate Omnium Scientiarum* (Hague, 1653), ch. 46, pp. 156, 157–58.

66. Juvenal. Sat. 8] Juvenal, *Satura*, 8.

money changers' street. They spoke to a seller of very filthy images and were in the process of buying all of them. But they suspected that another vendor, who was selling copies of the Holy Bible, was a Lutheran. They arranged to have him sentenced to death at the stake while carrying two copies of the Scriptures hung around his neck. Thus, no one could miss the reason he was martyred. But just a little later, a law was passed declaring it a capital offense for anyone "to keep in their possession any longer any books whatsoever written in French that contained any reference to Jesus Christ."[67]

As relates to the spear of prayer, we should especially note the event Saint Luke mentions in the Acts of the Apostles. "It happened, while we were heading out to pray, that a certain slave girl who had a spirit of Apollo met us. She had earned a great deal of money for her owners by prophesying. This woman followed Paul and kept shouting at us" (Acts 16:16–17). Note the phrase Ἐγένετο δὲ πορευομένων ἡμῶν εἰς προσευχήν.[68] This word προσευχή has two meanings: both *prayer* and *place of prayer*. Earlier in this passage, in verse 13, it is used to mean *place*. Evidently, the Jews of that era, when they did not have a synagogue, used to build shrines for prayer outside the city near streams or springs. They did this following, so it is thought, Isaac's example. When he returned from a walk, he came to the well Lahai-roi in a field, where he had gone to meditate (or to pray) as evening approached (Gen. 24:62–63). So προσευχή, I repeat, means not only a place for offering prayers but also for delivering sermons. Notice what Luke says: "On the Sabbath day, we set out from the city toward the river," οὗ ἐνομίζομεν προσευχήν εἶναι.[69] This means, according to Heinsius's emendation[70] (if I'm not mistaken) of the readings of all previous scholars, "where according to received custom there was, or usually was, a place of meeting. And when we had sat down, we spoke to some women who had gathered there" [Acts 16:13]. When Paul was heading there to engage in holy service, this Pythian woman met them and got in their way. The Devil, similarly, is equally opposed to both preaching and praying. So it very frequently happens that, as in the day of war only Saul and Jonathan were found to possess sword and spear, so in all the villages whose inhabitants call themselves Christians, one hardly finds the reading of the sacred Scriptures and the offering of daily prayers in the home, not to mention both. I should hardly say *hardly*, except maybe in one or two villages.

---

67. Vid. Martyr. latin. in 8° impress. Hanoviae à pag. 273 ad 276.]
68. "It happened while we were heading out to pray."
69. "Where we thought there was a place of prayer."
70. Heins, *Sacrarum Exercitationum*, bk. 5, ch. 10, p. 286.

§9. The fourth strategy is the spreading of dissensions. The Lord of Hosts Himself used this tactic to scatter the enemies of His people when Jehoshaphat ruled, as the sacred histories relate. "Jehovah set men in place to ambush the Ammonites, the Moabites, and those who dwelt in the mountains of Seir. The Ammonites and the Moabites had taken positions against the inhabitants of Mount Seir in order to devote them to destruction and slay them. And when they had wrought judgment against the inhabitants of Seir, then they helped to destroy one another, so each man destroyed his neighbor." Or, as the ancient translation has it, "They turned upon themselves in slaughter with mutual wounds" (2 Chron. 20:22–23). Satan delights in using the same tactic against the enemies of his own kingdom, against the tender children of the catholic Church. At the same time, he sows very great and different kinds of discord all around among those who claim the title *Christian*. The Apostle's word to the Corinthians often moves me quite deeply: "I fear that, as the serpent deceived Eve through his shrewdness, so your minds, thus corrupted, may fall away from the sincerity found in Christ" (2 Cor. 11:3). I think we can gather from this that before the rise of heresies, Christian doctrine was very simple.

> At that time then a plain, brief rule to lead the better life
> Was preached to all nor only known to teachers. And no strife,
> Just common good they spread, nor yet the sage and harsh dispute
> had taken on the simple folk for others to refute.[71]

But afterward, monstrous opinions were introduced into the church through serpentine deceits. These are called the "deep things of Satan" (Rev. 2:24), and so religion degenerated into fraud. It also devolved into strident disagreements, which proceed from the same source. James called this kind of fractured wisdom "demonic" (James 3:14–15). And he said that the tongue that is destructively contentious is set on fire by Gehenna (James 3:6).

Listen, dear reader, to André Rivet explaining this subject to you in his typical, very serious manner:

> Because freedom from strife and discord is more characteristic of God
> and the heavenly virtues than anything else, all who embrace the good
> of peace and intensely hate the division and sedition opposed to it come
> near God and the heavenly mindset. Those who stand opposed to such
> practices strive to become famous for their novelty, in order to revel in
> wrangling arguments. They are of the opposite party, imitators of Satan,
> who hide beneath a dark cloud of disagreement and secretly prepare some

---

71. Samuel Petit, 1594–1643, French orientalist, *Diatribe De Iure Principum Edictis* (Amsterdam, 1649), sig. **7r (*epistola dedicatoria*). The three and one-half lines of dactylic hexameter that A. quotes here are only attested in one other source.

place to lurk. From here they can secretly shoot arrows at the body of the church. You see, the sharp-minded enemy knows the church cannot be punctured by his shafts unless she is split asunder.[72]

If there is no objection, we can add Samuel Sorbière[73] to our quote from Rivet. In the dedicatory epistle to de Saumaise,[74] which he added as a preface to the *Learned Discussion on the Law, the Decrees of Princes*, etc. of Samuel Petit, he includes the following, rather noteworthy remarks:

What has driven peace into exile? What has stirred up these flames that now burn distant nations as well as our own if not arguments over religion? Those who intend to rip apart Christ's seamless garment usually seized upon restless times. And debates described as private too often turn into open strife. Open strife then leads to wars, wars end in slaughter. I thought such contests were confined within the walls of the academy and the training grounds. Once they began to be bandied about casually from pulpits and places of authority, talked about in the hallways, and spread to the crowd, then they overwhelm entire provinces. They throw entire kingdoms into confusion and turn everything upside down. When a mere debate has turned into combat, the pen ends up being a spear dipped in gore instead of ink. The battle rages on and on. They give up pens and fight with weapons. Instead of our tongues, we use lances, and swords in place of pencils. If only examples of this behavior were not so common![75]

I sadly echo his phrase "If only." Yes, that is how things were, and that is how they are, since nobody can call into question these days the truth of that prophecy Paul declared many hundreds of years ago: "I know that after me, fierce wolves, not sparing the flock, will come in among you. And even from your very midst there shall arise those who speak perversity, to pull away disciples after them" (Acts 20:29–30). That Lion of Tartarus[76] undoubtedly ties these wolves together by their tails, just like Sampson once did with his foxes, although their heads were on opposite ends [Judg. 15:4]. And with torches strapped on here and there, he tries to fill the Lord's grain field with a bright blazing inferno, even though these territories are obviously Christian. I would rather describe such things with weeping than round them off with eloquence.

---

72. In oratione habita Lugd. Batavorum Ann. 1620.] Rivet, *Oratio De Bono Pacis* (Leiden, 1620), pp. 24–25. A. skips over a Greek sentence from the original but otherwise quotes verbatim.

73. Probably Samuel Sorbière, 1615–1670, French translator and Roman Catholic convert.

74. Claude de Saumaise, 1588–1653, French classical scholar and theologian.

75. Petit, *Diatribe De Iure*, sig. **6r–v (*epistola dedicatoria*).

76. I.e., the Devil.

§ 10. The fifth tactic is approaching those who commit lesser crimes. The story goes that Pompey, while traveling with his army through loosely allied territories, sought leniency from the stewards of a certain city. He wanted them to receive inside their own walls a few of his soldiers, those who were in poor health and weak, in order to recover. But the Romans, when the watch guard had been slaughtered during the night, unlocked the gates of the city to let in the entire army. So the Devil generally attempts to commit lesser crimes in order to open an easier route to more serious ones. Perhaps this is why the Apostle classifies all Satan's schemes as τὰς μεθοδείας,[77] to intimate that he methodically, according to a particular fixed order, proceeds from a lesser to a clearly greater crime. Heresies and other serious problems usually begin as minor indiscretions. As is generally the case, one reaches the summit of wickedness little by little, and nobody became utterly depraved in an instant.[78]

Now, dear reader, take a close look at Alypius.[79] This is what his friend Augustine, very tightly bound to him by the closest intimacy, said about him:

> He was strongly opposed to gladiatorial games. But some of his class-mates, with a friendly kind of compulsion, dragged him toward the amphitheater, even though he steadfastly refused and even fought back. Alypius said to them, "Even if you drag my body to that spot and make me stand there, can you force my mind and eyes to pay attention to those sights? So even though I am there, I shall be absent, and so I will defeat you and those games." When they arrived at the games, everything was ablaze with most riotous pleasures. Alypius held the entrance to his eyes closed and commanded his mind not to indulge in such great wickedness. If only he had blocked off his ears as well! For at a certain blow of combat, when the crowd's loud noise struck him sharply, he was overcome with curiosity. Even though he was somehow prepared, no matter what happened, to despise and rise above even a glimpse of the action, he opened his eyes, and his soul received a heavier blow than the body of the combatant whom he wanted to see. And Alypius's fall was worse than that of the man whose fall made the crowd roar. As soon as he saw that blood, he immediately drank in its immense cruelty. He could not turn away but gazed rapt on the spectacle and, forgetting who he was, absorbed all the vengeful scenes. He deeply enjoyed the wickedness of the competition and became drunk on violent pleasure. He was not the same man now who had entered the amphitheater but became just one of the crowd he

---

77. "Methods."

78. Juvenal, *Satyra*, 2.

79. Alypius of Thagaste, fl. late fourth/early fifth century AD, bishop and friend of Augustine.

had joined. He truly became a companion of those who had dragged him there. What else could I say? He stared, he cheered, he burned. He left there with a madness that would drive him to return, not only with the friends who had first led him stray, but even ahead of them and bringing others along too.[80]

The sixth tactic is assaulting those who are more prominent. Tarquin the Proud[81]—when his son lived among the Gabii and through messengers was asking his father what he wanted to happen—struck with a rod the heads of some poppies that were taller than the rest. He intended to communicate that the aristocrats should be assassinated.[82] Ovid says in his Fasti,

> Time did not wait for chiefs who fell in ancient Gabine town.
> The walls when stripped of leaders fair then quickly tumbled down.[83]

Likewise, when Periander[84] asked Thrasybulus,[85] the Milesian tyrant, for advice in the presence of his messenger, the latter cut off heads of the highest stalks of grain. He then commanded the messenger to report to Periander what he had seen. The Devil considers it his most urgent task to attack the servants of Christ and the more solid columns that support the church by whatever means possible. This could be siege engines, tunnels dug underneath, or missiles. "Satan rose up against Israel and incited David to take a census" (1 Chron. 21:1). "He stood at the right hand of Jehovah's high priest in order to oppose him" (Zech. 3:1). He struck the apostle Paul with blows (2 Cor. 12:7). In Athanasius we read Anthony's statement: "All demons have bitter hatred toward men, more serious hatred for Christians, and reserve their most ferocious antagonism for monks."[86] The story goes that Bernard was tickled with a small amount of vainglory that a demon had introduced while he was preaching. When that very godly man realized what was happening, he interrupted the sermon he had prepared, turned to Satan, and said: "I did not undertake this work for your sake, and neither will it end for your sake or end with you."

---

80. *August.* Confess. lib. 6. cap. 8.] Augustine, *Confessionum*, 6.8.13. A. omits some phrases from this long quotation.

81. Tarquin the Proud, r. 534–510 BC, traditionally last king of Rome.

82. *Florus*, l. 1. c 7.] Lucius Annaeus Florus, fl. second century AD, Roman poet and historian, *Epitome De T. Livio Bellorum Omnium Annorum Duo Libri Duo*, bk. 1, ch. 7. The quotation is not verbatim and, thus, seems to be from memory. The *Epitome* was frequently published in the early modern period. For one published in England, see Florus, *Rerum a Romanis Gestarum Libri IV* (Oxford, 1631).

83. Ovid, *Fastorum*, in *Opera Omnia*, vol. 3 (Amsterdam, 1611), bk. 2, p. 34.

84. Periander, ca. 627–587 BC, tyrant of Corinth.

85. Thrasybulus, d. 688 BC, tyrant of Miletus.

86. Probably Athanasius, *Vita S. Antonii Eremitae* (Augsburg, 1611). Anthony the Great (Anthony the Anchorite), d. 356, monastic father.

What about Luther? "I think that Satan, from my boyhood, anticipated in me some of the things that he is now suffering. He, therefore, angrily rose up to destroy and hinder me by unbelievable devices. Consequently, I often wondered whether I was the only mortal Satan was attacking."[87]

§ 11. We will take as the seventh and, at the same time, last tactic (so the reader not become sick of all this) imitation of the enemies' habits. Two rather notable examples, among others, survive in Frontinus. The first was when the Arcadians were besieging the stronghold of the Messenians.[88] They had made some of their own weapons resemble those of the enemy, and when they had learned that reinforcements were approaching, they put on the garments of those for whom they waited. By this trick they were admitted as allies and so gained possession of the place and slaughtered the enemy.

The second example is when Antiochus[89] intercepted some pack animals that had gone out from the fortress Suenda in Cappadocia to forage. Antiochus was then besieging that fortress. After killing the animals' handlers, he sent his own soldiers back into the city, dressed in the garb of the slaughtered and carrying the foraged grain. When the guards were tricked by this ruse, the men in disguise entered the fortress and let in the rest of Antiochus's troops.[90] It is quite clear that, from the very earliest beginnings of the world right down to this day, Satan has aped God and Christ and, by this device, greatly harmed the church. I will touch upon just the most conspicuous examples of this behavior, briefly and observing no particular order.

1. God entered into a free covenant with His elect, in which He promises that He will be their God, and He imposes upon them this stipulation: they are to be His people and walk uprightly. Similarly, the Devil stoops down to make a covenant with his servants, witches, and magicians. He promises to give them whatever they want, provided, in turn, they pledge to obey him. And just as God wanted the children and seed of the righteous included in His covenant as well, such that the parents are bound to instruct them in the knowledge and worship of Jehovah, so the Devil drives those who profess his hellish arts to bind their own offspring to him, their daughters most of all, and stain them with the same magic arts. And it is nothing new that even mothers have led their daughters into this life with

---

87. In Epist. ad Patrem suum praefixa libro de votis monasticis.] Luther, *De Votis Monasticis*, in *Omnium Operum*, vol. 2 (Jena, 1557). The quotation is precise and unaltered.

88. Strategem. l. 2. c. 2. exemp. 4. & 9.] A. cites *Strategemata* II.2, examples 4 and 9, but the very slightly altered quotation is from book III. Frontinus, *Strategemata*, sub loc. bk. 3, ch. 2, ex. 4.

89. Antiochus I Soter, ca. 324–261 BC, king of the Seleucid empire.

90. Frontinus, *Strategemata*, sub loc. bk. 3, ch. 2, ex. 9.

whips—or to have attempted it.[91] In reality, as the Lord requires faith from His worshippers and has established the new covenant on this condition, so Satan instructs his own to believe in him. They say that wizards and witches also demand this from their clients.

2. Christ thought it good to attach two seals, as it were, to the document of His covenant of grace: baptism and the Supper. The Devil has scrupulously imitated both of these rites. The priests of the mystery cults had both their ritual washings and their drink offerings. Augustine says of the first, "In many blasphemous, idolatrous rites, men are brought forward to be baptized."[92] And Tertullian writes, "Nations far removed from all understanding of spiritual powers serve their own idols with the same efficiency, but they deceive themselves with their destitute waters. For through ceremonial washing they are initiated into the sacred rites of someone like Isis or Mithras."[93] Lipsius adds a remark on drink offerings to what Cornelius Tacitus says of Seneca's death: "At the end he entered into a pool of warm water, sprinkling those of his servants who were nearest and adding the remark that he was sprinkling that water for Jupiter the Deliverer."[94] Lipsius comments, "This is what Thraseas said on the brink of death: 'Let's pour a libation to Jupiter the Deliverer.' The reason great men joked like this at the end of their life was that they were following Greek habits, who just before leaving a banquet habitually poured a libation to Zeus Soter. Roman men departed life this way, pouring something for Jupiter the Deliverer."[95]

Grotius says the following in his commentary on the expression of the Evangelist, "Drink of this, all of you": "In ritual settings, blood was typically poured into platters, as is attested in the fourth book of Statius's[96] *Thebaid* and elsewhere. But because it was savage to drink blood, the practice was established among the more civilized nations to drink wine in place of blood, as it is called the 'blood of the grape,'" etc.[97] Why is it a surprise that the Devil usually imprinted some hidden symbol on the bodies of

<hr>

91. *Zepper.* explanat Legum Mosaic. forens. l. 4. c. 5. ibid. p. 298.] Wilhelm Zepper, 1550–1607, German Reformed theologian, *Legum Mosaicarum Forensium Explanatio* (Herborn, 1604), bk. 4, ch. 5, p. 293.

92. De Baptism. contra Donatistas.] Augustine, *De Baptismo Contra Donatistas*, in *Omnium Operum*, vol. 7 (Basel, 1528), 6.25.47.

93. Libro de Baptismo.] Tertullian, *De Baptismo Adversus Quintillam*, in *Opera Quae Hactenus Reperiri*, vol. 3 (Cologne, 1617), ch. 5. Isis, Egyptian goddess of fertility. Mithras, Indo-Iranian god worshipped throughout the Roman empire.

94. Annal. l. 15. non procul a fine.] Tacitus, *Annales*, in *Opera Quae Exstant*, ed. J. Lipsius (Antwerp, 1607), bk. 15.

95. Tacitus, *Annales*, sub loc. bk. 15, note 140, p. 287.

96. Publius Papinius Statius (Statius), ca. 50–ca. 96, Roman poet and author of the epic *Thebaid*.

97. Ad Matth. 26, 27.] Grotius, *Annotationes In Libros Evangeliorum* (Amsterdam, 1641),

wizards and witches, just as once God willed that those covenanted to Him would carry the mark of that covenant on their body through circumcision?

3. When Satan, the teacher of the heathens, invented their Pallas—that is, wisdom, as born from Jupiter's brain—he attempted through this fairy tale a kind of painted imitation. And through this painting, he meant to remove the eternal generation of the Son from the eternal Father. Indeed, he also tries to corrupt faith in the incarnation by frequenting human bodies, occupying and possessing them, as they call it. But because Christ the Θεάνθρωπος[98] is the only mediator between God and men, pagans under the Devil's control imagined that certain demons or lesser spirits and demigods existed. The pagans relied upon the intercession of these creatures with the more powerful gods. Our countryman Mede, in his golden little book, *Apostasy of the End Times*, proves this with numerous examples.[99]

4. Abraham, as Moses records, makes a compact with Jehovah through dismembered livestock. A burning lamp passed between the portions of these animals that lay cut on both sides (Gen. 15:9–10, 17). This lamp stands for, so I think, God Himself. Satan taught the gentiles to use the same ceremonies or ones similar to these to ratify their own covenants. Livy tells us, "The front part of a dog is cut off, and one portion is set along with the entrails on the right of road, the other on the left. Between this sundered victim are led armed troops."[100] The Lord required Abraham to sacrifice his own son. From that time forward, the Devil began to require human sacrifices, which is the very pinnacle of inhuman behavior. When the Greek fleet was detained at Aulis by opposing winds, Calchas[101]—the Devil's priest—advised them to calm the winds by the sacrifice of Agamemnon's[102] daughter Iphigenia.[103] Tiresias[104] promised victory to the Thebans if they slaughtered the daughter of King Creon[105] as a sacrifice. In Vergil, Sinon[106] says that the Greeks received this oracle:

---

vol. 1, sub loc. Matt. 26:25, p. 453. There appears to be a printing error, so that verse numbers 26 and 27 are not present and the quotation appears to be under verse 25 instead.

98. "God-man."

99. pag. 9 & seq.] Joseph Mede, 1586–1638, Hebraist and biblical scholar, *The apostasy of the latter times* (London, 1641), pp. 9–14.

100. Lib. 39.] Livy, *Ab Urbe Condita*, 40.6.

101. Calchas, diviner in Homer's *Iliad*.

102. Agamemnon, king of Mycenae.

103. Iphigenia, daughter of Agamemnon.

104. Tiresias, blind prophet of Apollo.

105. Creon, successor to Oedipus and king of Thebes.

106. Sinon, Greek solider who deceived the Trojans.

By blood you once appeased the winds, with slaughtered maiden fair.
With blood now seek the way back home through Argive life unspared.[107]

But even the sacred writings very plainly show that the Israelites once became so insane that they offered their own children in sacrifice to demons and compelled them to pass through fire (2 Kings 17:17; Jer. 32:35; Ps. 106:35). Now the particular demon (I note this merely in passing) to whom such reprehensible rites were offered is named Moloch in the numerous passages of Scripture that deal with his worship. Moloch,[108] moreover, was also known as Sol[109] and Baal,[110] because of the lordship he exercised, taking the place of a king among the stars. Now the sun is understood as the universal cause that fundamentally promotes life (from this comes the philosophers' famous statement, "Sun and man produce man"). Therefore, sun worshipers used to drag their sons through fire, since they thought they had been born by the sun's power. By this ritual, they were professing, and sort of saying, "From you are all things, and we give you what came from you."[111]

5. Christ has illuminated the whole world with His gospel. The Devil also poured forth his oracles and, by these, tried to drive the world to madness. Actually, because the oracle of God was once located within the recesses of the tabernacle, covered on all sides by curtains, as Moses records in Exodus, similarly the Devil imitated God. He typically released his oracles from behind curtains within temples' innermost places. So we read in the poet:[112] "The tripod rumbled when the innermost places were laid open." And, "Phoebus's tripod has not deceived you."[113]

6. Finally, Christ sustained His gospel teaching through miracles. And Satan also had his wonderworkers who turned the eyes of the people toward him and away from Christ. "The man of sin and son of perdition is coming" (2 Thess. 2:3). Paul says of this man that he operates "in the effective power of Satan, together with all might, signs, and deceptive wonders" (2 Thess. 2:9). Philostratus[114] wrote eight books about Apollonius

---

107. Vergil, *Aeneidos*, bk. 2 (lines 116, 118–19). A. omits line 117.

108. Moloch, Canaanite god.

109. Sol, Roman sun god.

110. Baal, Canaanite fertility god.

111. *Muis* in Psalmos pag. 637.] Simèon de Muis, 1587–1644, French Hebraist and archdeacon of Soissons, *In Omnes Psalmos* (Paris, 1630), sub loc. Ps. 105:37.

112. As Paul is called *Apostolus*, so Vergil is *Poeta*.

113. Aeneid. l. 3. carm. 92. & l. 6. carm. 347.] Vergil, *Aeneidos*, bk. 3 (line 92); *Aeneidos*, bk. 6 (line 347). The word that Vergil uses and A. repeats is *cortina*, which can mean both "prophetic tripod," as it does here, and "curtain." A. through some sleight of hand finds a connection between the Exodus passage and these pagan instances of oracular consultation based on a double entendre.

114. Lucius Flavius Philostratus (Philostratus), ca. 170–ca. 250, Greek Sophist.

Tyaneus.[115] Hierocles[116] was so motivated by the scope and excellence of these accomplishments that in the book he wrote entitled *Truthlover*—compiled from Philostratus's writings—he not only compared this Apollonius to Christ the Savior but even preferred him. This insult so embittered Lactantius that he attacked Hierocles, though concealing his name, like this:

> Although he sought to undermine Christ's miraculous deeds, still he did not deny them. And he wanted to show that Apollonius had done things that were equal or even greater. It is surprising that he omitted Apuleius, whose many amazing accomplishments are usually remembered. Why then, you insane oaf, does no one worship Apollonius as a god except maybe you alone? Clearly, you deserve Apollonius as your god. The true God will punish you both for all eternity.[117]

End of the first book.

---

115. Apollonius of Tyana, d. ca. 98, neo-Pythagorean philosopher and anti-Christian writer.

116. Sossianus Hierocles, fl. early fourth century AD, Roman administrator.

117. Institut. l. 5. cap. 3.] Lactantius, *Divinarum Institutionum*, in *Opera Quae Extant Omnia* (Leiden, 1652), 5.3, pp. 308–9.

PLANS FOR HOLY WAR

BOOK II

CHAPTER I

The Belt of Truth in the Understanding, That Is, of Orthodoxy

Section 1: The soldier's orders. Section 2: An explanation of the words of the apostolic text, Ephesians 6:14. The Christian must stand firm. How this is possible when Christ is present. What it means to fasten on the belt of truth. The belt of truth has two parts: orthodoxy and sincerity. Section 3: A noteworthy saying of Mirandola; the degeneracy of paganism, Judaism, and Islam. Section 4: Judgment passed on Socinianism. Grotius's former opinion on that topic. Section 5: The evil spirit of the papacy; Christianity's supreme beauty. Section 6: The twofold analogy of the belt of truth. Section 7: Presentation of a complaint concerning contemporary errors.

§ 1. The topics I thoroughly discussed and debated in the previous book are very general—that is, "Take up your weapons, men, take them up. Set your face against the iron, soldier."[1] "Hannibal[2] is at the gates,"[3] "Caesar in the forum,"[4] "Catiline in the senate!"[5] "Now we need courage, now a stout heart."[6] So grant me a little leniency, dear reader, if I, struck by the extent of the dangers, immediately retreat to military κελεύσματα.[7] Now *Satan* stands for Hannibal, *the world* for Caesar, and *Catiline* for the flesh. All these rise up and attack us both from a distance and at close quarters. Therefore, those who were not warlike, especially the unarmed, were, as the saying goes, set on the very razor's edge. So my concern in the book just now begun will be to explain the Pauline panoply fully. My explanation will not be as grand as the subject requires but just what my slight strength can offer.

---

1. Vergil, *Aeneidos*, bk. 2 (line 668). A. has quoted the first portion of Vergil and finished the line with his own composition.

2. Hannibal, b. 249/247 BC, Carthaginian general.

3. Cicero, *Philippica*, in *Opera Omnia*, vol. 2 (Paris, 1565), bk. 1.

4. Cicero, *Epistola Ad Atticum*, in *Opera Omnia*, vol. 3 (Paris, 1565), 14.10.

5. Cicero, *Orator*, in *Opera Omnia*, vol. 1 (Paris, 1566), 37.

6. Vergil, *Aeneidos*, bk. 6 (line 261).

7. "Commands."

§ 2. The belt of truth that we must put on is found first in these words: στῆτε οὖν περιζωσάμενοι τὴν ὀσφὺν ὑμῶν ἐν ἀληθείᾳ ("Stand firm then, and surround your waist with truth")[8] [Eph. 6:14]. Not once but twice in this section—which is a particular locus of my subject, that is, the middle of Ephesians 6—the Apostle admonishes the Christian soldier to stand fast. This notion is also further suggested by the fact that, in all the armor displayed, there is no element attached to the soldier's back. And thus, we must not retreat nor think of fleeing from the spiritual war we wage. Vespasian[9] once said, "A commander must stand fast in the face of death."[10] But the statement suits the rank-and-file soldier too. And those who have on their side Emmanuel, God with us, have all the reason they need to stand firm. The saints in Antioch learned this as soon as the majestic name Christian was bestowed upon those who profess our faith. In AD 52 there was a raging earthquake there. Many buildings collapsed, and 4,870 people perished beneath the ruins. A certain righteous man was warned, the story goes, by a holy vision. He commanded the citizens, as they fled the city and kept shouting with constant screams of terror, to write on the upper posts of their buildings, Κύριε ἐλέησον, ("Lord have mercy").[11] Στῆτε, he said, Χριστὸς μεθ' ἡμῶν ("Stand firm, Christ is with us"). When this was done, God's anger subsided.[12]

Stand properly secured, says the Apostle. Among the ancients, it was considered shameful for this area of the body to be loosely attired. So Persius says

> Isn't it disgraceful to live like the disheveled Natta?[13]

It is a nasty business to go about with your clothes improperly secured. On this point we have that remark of Sulla, who repeatedly warned the aristocrats about Caesar, saying, "Beware of that boy with the poor-fitting toga."[14]

Bind up your loins with truth. Peter references the same parts and also adds the word *mind*: "Bind up the loins of your mind" (1 Peter 1:13). The mind is, in a sense, the most important part of the person and encompasses his most noble abilities, such as understanding and will. The truth that

---

8. A. uses the Greek here and then provides his own Latin gloss.

9. Titus Flavius Vespasianus (Vespasian), 9–79, r. 69–79, Roman emperor.

10. Suetonius, *De XII. Caesaribus*, bk. 8, ch. 24. A. has altered the grammar to fit his syntax.

11. A. uses the Greek here and then provides his own Latin gloss.

12. Vide *Euagrium*, l. 4. cap. 5.] Evagrius Scholasticus, ca. 536–600, church historian, *Historiae Ecclesiasticae*. A. is making general reference to the Antioch earthquake story as described in bk. 4, ch. 5. See a collected English volume of several patristic historians including Evagrius Scholasticus, *The Ancient Ecclesiasticall Histories* (London, 1650), pp. 472–73.

13. Persius, *Satyrarum*, 3.31.

14. *Sueton.*] Suetonius, *De XII. Caesaribus*, bk. 1, ch. 45.

binds up the understanding and stands against error is orthodoxy. The will is bound by the truth that is blamelessness of heart. Theologians call this genuineness, and it is contrasted with hypocrisy.

§ 3. Now then, we must begin with orthodoxy, so that we can proceed on the basis of clearer distinctions, no matter how idle people these days utterly reject the substance of orthodoxy and even hiss at the word. Among such are the Dutch Remonstrants. They strut around like pompous fools[15] at the mere mention of attaching the adjective *orthodox* to the church.[16] "Adjectives like this are foolish luck charms hung around the neck of a controversy like a witch's necklace."[17] Mirandola famously said that "philosophers search for truth, theologians find it, believers possess it."[18] Of course, the truth that forms the content of our discourse is found only among Christians of a true profession. If we compare the initiates of other religions to these true Christians, we see just how monstrously far they wander away from what is true, if not utterly hate it. I myself have experienced this more often than it would be right to admit voluntarily. Whenever I pause to consider the various types and images of religion that have existed for so long (some kind of religion has existed pretty much everywhere), then my whole heart is caught up in rapturous admiration for the authentic beauty of Christianity each time. In comparison to it, all the items other faiths peddle, however numerous they are, offer those who think about it carefully things more misshapen than any kind of Thersites.[19]

In paganism I think we see Adam's degenerate offspring shamefully worshipping creatures set far beneath them, until the divinities of one nation become a source of ridicule to other pagan groups. The Roman satirists held the Egyptians' gods in derision, especially Juvenal at the start of Satire 15.[20] In Judaism I see the detestable spite of prejudice. Therein lies the reason why this nation, placing their faith in the dogma of the permanence of the Mosaic law, their unique adoption as sons, the great success of the Messiah according to the flesh, and other traditions that they received from

---

15. Plautus, *Pseudolus*, in *Opera* (Geneva, 1605), 2.4.17, p. 659.

16. Nicolaus Vedel, 1596–1642, German-Dutch Reformed theologian.

17. *Vedel.* Rhapsod. pag. 124.] Simon Episcopius, *Vedelius Rhapsodus* (Harderwijk, 1633), bk. 2, ch. 6, p. 124. Vedelius Rhapsodus is a pseudonym for the Dutch Remonstrant Simon Episcopius, a student of Jacob Arminius. Nicholaus Vedel in 1632 wrote *Arcana Arminianismi* (Secrets of the Arminians) in which he critized Episcopius's views. The latter responded in 1633 with *Vedelius Rhapsodus Sive Vindiciae Doctrinae Remonstrantium, A Criminationibus & Calumniis Nicolai Vedelii.*

18. Giovanni Pico della Mirandola, 1463–1494, Italian scholar and Platonist philosopher.

19. Thersites, a character from Homer's *Iliad*, book 2, notorious for his physical and moral deformity.

20. Juvenal, *Satyra*, 15.

the fathers, right down to this very day so strongly recoil from the person of Jesus Christ and His church.

In Islam we behold the remarkable power and force of deception. For there is hardly anything more shocking than that one imposter, when he had gotten a gentile man as father (as the saying goes), a Jewish woman as mother, and a certain apostate monk as his ally, should afterword stitch together from some shreds of Pagansm, Judaism, and Christianity a religion very similar to its origin. And then he made it fit the particular character of individual elements in the Qur'an, and so plunged into absurdity one fifth of the known world (if Breerwood's calculations are correct)![21] How shocking that he markets himself to the world as God's choice prophet, surpassing all the rest, and so gains credibility.

§4. In Socinianism—a veritable chasm—a real abyss of impiety opens its jaws at us. This faith is, not without justification, called a more refined version of Islam. The leaders of this atrocious sect do in fact extol the personhood and eternality of God the Father. Nevertheless, they philosophize in a very weak and skeptical manner on His simplicity, omnipresence, foreknowledge, and various other attributes. At the same time, they violently deny the deity, eternality, and satisfaction of the Son, though acknowledging His person. Likewise, they also deny the personhood and deity of the Holy Spirit, however much they seem not to doubt His eternality. Most blessed Christ! How is it that You tolerate such great disrespect from those for whom You suffered so much? Most Holy Spirit! How does anyone reject You by means of You, and preach that he has been personally taught by the Holy Spirit to deny His deity? O eternal Father of our Lord Jesus Christ, please forgive them. For they do not know (so we hope) what they are saying and are driven by some kind of spirit.

Meanwhile, there are some who argue fiercely that the Socinians should be erased from the roll of Christians. Note this, reader, from Grotius himself before he had gone over to that sect. Writing in 1611 to Antonius Walaeus,[22] Grotius makes these remarks about the Socinians: "Not only do I consider them unworthy of the title *Christian*. They do not even deserve to be called heretics. Although they hold onto Christianity in name, so far as I understand it, because their own teachings are entirely at odds with the universal faith of all times and peoples they demolish Christianity's

---

21. Scrutin. Religion. cap. 14. p. mihi 118.] Edward Brerewood (Breerwood), ca. 1565–1613, antiquarian and mathematician, *Enquiries Touching the Diversity of Languages, and Religions, Through the Chiefe Parts of the World* (London, 1635), p. 118.

22. Antonius Walaeus (Walaeus), 1588–1639, Dutch Reformed theologian.

substance. Consequently, I consider them only a little bit removed from followers of Mohammed, who actually do not even revile Jesus."[23]

§5. In the papist religion—whose lackeys conduct Antichrist's business under Christ's name—one can see a mangled mess along with a mirror of shamelessness. I mean that in the Romanists' pontiff there are jumbled together both a prelate and an absolute ruler, in the canon, Scripture and tradition; in the mass, sacrament, and sacrifice; in their teaching on conversion, will, and grace; in justification, both faith and works; in salvation, both mercy and merit. They jumble these together so that no room remains for the simplicity of the gospel. Moreover, the Roman church has shamelessly dared—displaying that whorish effrontery that she considers pure and undefiled—to arrogate to herself that infallibility that by right belongs only to the sacred Book. Thus Campion: "Whatever the church orders me to believe, I believe just as much as that I am alive."[24] The papist religion worships saints and angels in addition to God and recognizes other advocates in addition to Christ. And after making one distinction after another (such as that there is a twofold mediator—of redemption and of intercession—and that worship has three parts—λατρεία, δουλεία, ὑπερδουλεία),[25] along with the prostitute in Solomon "she wiped her own mouth" (Prov. 30:20). Although she committed adultery, she boldly claims she has done nothing wrong.

But when I gaze deeply upon you, great increase of Jehovah, you real, authentic Christianity that Reformed Protestants profess and practice, as resplendent in your own domain as the Holy Book describes you, I can scarcely restrain myself. I must shout, "Hail, queen of religions! If the feet of those who proclaim you are lovely, oh how beautiful is the face of Him who first revealed you! Christ is the radiance of the Father, and you are the radiance of Christ. We know that man is the perfection of the visible world; the perfection of man is understanding; of understanding, knowledge; of knowledge, religion; and of religion, Christianity. You lay open to poor little wretches God in Christ, Christ in the flesh, and salvation in both. Adam's descendants cannot find this salvation anywhere else."

§6. Let us now see how particularly this truth can be likened to the belt of truth. The belt claims for itself not the least important place among

---

23. *Wallaei* oper. in fol. pag. 399.] Grotius, *Opera omnia* (Leiden, 1643), vol. 2, ch. 6, sec. 4, p. 399.

24. *Campian.* opuscul. orat. 5. p. 317.] Edmund Campion, 1540–1581, English Jesuit and martyr, *Decem Rationes Propositae* (Antwerp, 1631), p. 317 (*orat.* 5).

25. "Worship, servitude, veneration."

soldiers' equipment. They are usually decorated with seals of silver or gold and sometimes jewels as well. So Vergil says of Pallas,

> High on his shoulder one could spy a belt with buckles graced
> And bright these flashed in well-known light, etc.[26]

There is also this from Claudian:

> Does Parthia boast such buckles bold with all these different gems?
> To circle 'round a royal chest, etc.[27]

Thus, orthodoxy renders both churches and individuals beautifully adorned and pleasing in the sight of the righteous. John says to the elect lady, "I rejoiced greatly because I found your children walk in the truth" (2 John v. 4). He says also to Gaius, "I have no greater joy than to find my children walking in the truth" (3 John v. 4). Reformed writers have showered Leiden University with countless words of praise, and rightly so. But in my opinion, there is hardly any comment more worthy of regard than the one that William Rivet, brother of André, stamped upon it, when he calls it the Sanctuary of Orthodoxy.[28]

But a belt usually is not used only for decoration. It also is good for practicality and convenience. Men used to put coins in their belts and carry them there. This is the origin of that statement in the military laws that Aurelian[29] once passed: "The soldier should deposit his salary in his belt not in a tavern."[30] The proverbial saying is that the penniless have lost their belt, as we find in Horace:

> He who has lost his belt will go wherever you would like.[31]

Equally so, those who hold orthodoxy exceedingly dear become exceedingly rich. "I know," says the Lord to the angel of Smyrna, "your poverty, but you are rich" (Rev. 2:9). How could that be? Because of very fierce devotion to the truth? Who in the world, so long as he is shrewd, would not prefer the riches of those they called "the poor of Lyon" to the wealth of the merchants, however numerous, of "mystic Babylon" [Rev. 17.5]? The wealthy

---

26. Aeneid. ult.] Vergil, *Aeneidos*, bk. 12 (lines 941–42).

27. De raptu *Proserpinae* lib. 2.] Claudius Claudianus (Claudian), ca. 370–ca. 404, Roman poet, *De Raptu Proserpinae*, in *Quae exstant*, ed. Kaspar von Barth (Frankfurt, 1650), bk. 2 (94–95).

28. Epist. Apolog. ad *Thom. Russel.* pag. 202.] William Rivet, 1580–1651, French Reformed theologian, *Epistolae Apologeticae Ad Theophilum Rossellum* (Český Brod, 1648), p. 202. *Orthodoxiae Sacrarium*: Rivet has ὀρθοδοξίας sacrarium. The marginal citation by A. reads "Thom.," but it is Theophilus to whom William wrote the letter of defense.

29. Lucius Domitius Aurelianus (Aurelian), ca. 215–275, r. 270–275, Roman emperor.

30. *Historia Augusta.* See "Deified Aurelian."

31. Horace, *Epistolarum*, in *Opera* (Paris, 1642), bk. 2 (*epistola* 2).

are to be valued very highly who value truth more than wealth. Speaking of which, among my several possessions I particularly appreciate, before other books by papist authors (I will not deny it), Cornelius Jansen, the bishop of Ypres. We have this story about him and some of his writings: "Once when he was asked by one of his associates which of God's attributes should most be worshipped, he answered, 'Truth.' And quite often, while walking in his own garden in solitary contemplation, one could hear and see him with eyes raised toward heaven burst forth in this expression: 'O truth.'"[32]

§7. But finally, to unfasten the restraint of warranted grief, there is good reason to mourn for our dearest mother England, and especially in these most recent years. For a long time, the belt of orthodoxy was held in high repute among us, together with its buckle. But the buckle, it seems, became completely rotten when Jeremiah, at God's command (after he had removed it from his loins), hid it in the cleft of a rock (Jer. 13). Therefore, if it is possible for the truth to rub shoulders with poor miserable wretches, then "O Theology, you poor wretch. How unhappy we are as we are initiated into your rites!" Now truly those times Hilary described to Constantius[33] have returned: "People's faith was based on the times instead of the Gospels. And while men became anathema to one another, almost no one now belongs to Christ."[34] Optatus said to the Donatists about this, "You say, 'It is permitted.' We say, 'It is not.' Between your permission and our denial the hearts of the people are jerked back and forth."[35] Look around, reader, and tell me, if you can, what fine point of faith controversy has not polluted? What limb is there in the whole body of Christian religion not permeated by some leprous heresy? But if only this pestilence were not spreading out farther into territories across the sea! But just as once with Africa,[36] so now—how painful!—England gives birth each year to some new monster. One man cries "Gospel" so that he can drive out truth. Another man snobbishly sneers[37] that "even a thief is predestined to be so" and meanwhile schemes to steal and pillage the Pauline doctrine of predestination. A third man, while

---

32. In Synopsi vitae *Jansinii* praefixa ipsius *Augustino*.] Cornelius Otto Jansen (Jansenius), 1585–1638, Roman Catholic bishop of Ypres, *Augustinus* (Leuven, 1640), vol. 1, sig: a4v (*vitae auctoris*).

33. Constantius II, 317–361, r. 324/337–361, Roman emperor.

34. Lib. 2.] Hilary of Poitiers, ca. 315–367/268, bishop of Poitiers, *Ad Constantium Augustum*, in *Quotquot Extant Opera* (Paris, 1631).

35. De schismate Donatist. pag. mihi 65.] Optatus, *De Schismate Donatistarum Adversus Parmenianum, Libri VII* (Leiden, 1613).

36. Africa in Greek mythology was the source of many monstrous creatures killed by heroes.

37. The colorful metaphor A. employs is *adunco, quod aiunt, naso suspendens*, i.e., looking down an aristocratic nose. It is proverbial and from Horace, *Satyra*, in *Opera* (Paris, 1642), bk. 6.

he argues that the assembly recently held at Westminster was wrong as all heaven, himself is wrong as all hell. A fourth man "tried to redeem redemption," but at what cost? Obviously, at the cost of reprobating election itself and reducing grace to something that is not grace. A fifth man—but I must restrain myself. For it is better to hold my tongue about our countryman Biddle's errors and hideous blasphemies than to say even a few words.[38] But if I wanted to pursue in this essay the Borborites[39] and Gnostics of this era, as well as the Seekers,[40] Quakers,[41] and other fanatics, my complaint would not only drag out the clock but end time itself![42]

---

38. John Biddle, 1615/1616–1662, schoolmaster and religious controversialist.

39. Borborites, second-century Gnostic sect.

40. Seekers, English nonconformist anti-Trinitarians.

41. Quakers, followers of George Fox, pacifists.

42. The clepsydra was a water device for keeping time. A. says were he to continue, he would fill up that as well as a large barrel (amphora).

CHAPTER II

The Origin and Particular Causes
of the Heterodoxy Raging in England

Section 1: Fascination with ancient philosophy is the first specific cause for the current errors. A historical parable. Section 2: Well-known Scholastics and Pelagians, together with certain fathers. Augustine's critique of Platonism and Jansen's of Aristotelianism. Section 3: Philosophy in an assisting and dominating role. Melanchthon and Luther seemed quite incensed with philosophy's domination, while Castellio favored it. Section 4: The second specific cause is the resurgence of Skepticism. Its assailants: Seneca, Cicero, Augustine, Luther, and Alting. Its defenders: the Remonstrants and Descartes. Section 5: The third specific cause is the presumption to prophesy. An evaluation of Jeremiah 21:21–32 based on Calvin and Luther. The complaints of Jerome, Bernard, and Peter of Blois. Section 6: Episcopius and Theophilus Nicolaides attack "mediated commission." An explanation and defense of Romans 10:13–15. The position of New England Presbyterians regarding the presumption to prophesy. Section 7: Four orthodox theses regarding freedom in preaching. Section 8: The fourth specific cause is the reckless appropriation of the Holy Spirit. Some ancient heretics are noted; Reformed authors are praised. Section 9: The fifth specific cause is utter disregard for catechetical instruction. The φλυαρία[1] of de Valencia, the mind of Luther and Pareus. Section 10: The sixth specific cause is the failure to apply church discipline. The vigor of discipline in the early church, its corruption under the papacy, imperfection after Reformation came, both in Germany and in England under the bishops' rule. The state of discipline when episcopal rule was ending. Buchholzer's prayer and complaint. [Section 11:] The seventh specific cause is the improper settling of the question of the power the Christian magistrate has in sacred matters. Thomas Hobbes's opinion, mistaken in its excess, is explained and rejected. [Section 12:] Refutation of others' position who err through some lack.

---

1. "Nonsense."

§ 1. Now as I was considering the source of the enormous evils among us, in addition to the typical causes of error (which I here omit)—like divine permission, devilish deception, and the depravity of human nature—seven other reasons immediately appeared before me. I think that these, by a peculiar influx, have contributed greatly to the increase in that flood of errors I complained about.

First: *excessive fascination with ancient philosophy.* There is a historical account in Philip Camerarius[2] given as an aside. If this is turned into a parable, it will depict in vivid colors the very portrait, as it were, of our circumstances. There were two kings, one in England and the other in France. When each had drawn up his troops in battle line and were on the verge of imminent conflict, they decided to try a diplomatic parley. The kings separated themselves from their armed men and met at an ancient shrine that stood in plain view of both armies. Meanwhile, they brought with them only their servants, an equal number agreed upon for each and armed, to stand guard at the entrance to the shrine. The peace talks were held in an amicable fashion. Both kings are planning to return to their supporters. Suddenly and unexpectedly a serpent emerges from its lair and attacks the kings with a terrible hissing. They quickly draw their swords better to defend themselves against the viper, and burst through the doors. The guards, thinking that the old hatred has broken out afresh, also ready their weapons for the conflict. When each army, standing not far off in battle array, sees this, they rejoin the battle as though on cue. The kings are helpless to stop them, and hand-to-hand combat rages so fiercely that, in short order, thousands of men die.

Just like this, in different parts of the world as well as here among our own people, pious colloquies have been held several times. And very often these colloquies offered good men some hope for peace in the conduct of religion. But the ancient serpent has never failed to provide an occasion to renew the fighting. What is his preferred route for invading the ancient shrine if not the moral philosophy of the ancients? Paul appropriately warned the Colossians about this, saying, "Be careful that no one plunders you through philosophy" [Col. 2:8]. By these ancient philosophers I mean men who are woefully ignorant of the original fall and everywhere blather on about αὐτεξούσιος, τὰ ἐφ᾽ ἡμῖν,[3] the power of nature, of reason, of the will, and all that sort of thing. I mean everything opposed to the judgment

---

2. *Camerar.* meditate. history. cent. 1 cap. 69. p. 309.] Camerarius, *Meditationes Historicae,* vol. 1, ch. 69, p. 309.

3. "Self-government" and "within our power," respectively. These terms are staples of Stoic thought.

of revealed truth. As Scaliger can verify, some theologians of our religion[4] are convinced that they can measure vast territories with a ten-foot rod made from these ideas.[5] Lorenzo Valla elegantly says of such men, "I think that no one who admires philosophy too ardently can please God."[6] Truly, Gassendi[7] seemed to die of love for Epicurus,[8] Ficino[9] for Plato, Lipsius for Seneca, and Ermolao Barbaro for Aristotle. I have written of him above.

§ 2. I bypass the Scholastics who have, with great effort, brought Greek philosophy into the citadel of the church like a Trojan horse. From this, the city's destruction followed. If only every last one of the fathers had been immune to that itching desire. But there are also some of them who attribute more than is proper to nature's power because, as children, they were imbued with philosophy in the schools of the pagans. Even the papists acknowledge this, like Sixtus of Siena[10] and Francisco de Toledo,[11] among others. Let's listen, if you don't mind, to Juan Maldonado commenting on John 6. "Let the reader be careful if he reads Chrysostom on this passage that he not fall into the Pelagian heresy."[12] But if he does not know what value there is in these heretics, Bradwardine will teach him in these words: "The ancient Pelagians were puffed up by the windy reputation of secular knowledge. They despised the council room of theology and kept demanding philosophy."[13] This is how modern theologians spoke who dwelt in our England. Augustine long before detected what Bradwardine observed. On almost the very first page of his *Retractions*, Augustine took back from the philosophers the praises he had previously given them. "I now, with good justification, disapprove of that commendation by which I raised Plato and the Platonists higher than was appropriate, even for unbelievers, especially that I approved of those philosophers against whose errors Christian

---

4. I.e., the Reformed.

5. De subtilit. exercit. 365. § 3.] Julius Caesar Scaliger, 1484–1558, Italian scholar and physician, *Exotericarum Exercitationum Liber XV De Subtilitate* (Frankfurt, 1582), exerc. 365, sec. 3, p. 1120. A. alters the quotation slightly by inserting *se* between *metiri* and *posse*.

6. In tractatu quodam suo de libero arbitrio.] Lorenzo Valla, ca. 1406–1457, Italian humanist, *De Libero Arbitrio* (Basel, 1518), fol. 12v.

7. Pierre Gassendi, 1592–1655, French philosopher and mathematician.

8. Epicurus, ca. 341–270 BC, Greek philosopher.

9. Marsilio Ficino, 1433–1499, Italian humanist and philosopher.

10. Sisto di Siena (Sixtus of Siena), 1520–1569, Italian Franciscan theologian and convert from Judaism.

11. Francisco de Toledo, 1532–1596, Spanish Jesuit theologian.

12. Apud *Lucium* in Histor. Jesuitica p. 216.] Juan de Maldonado (Maldonatus), 1531–1583, Spanish Jesuit and biblical exegete, quoted in Lucius, *Historia Iesuitica De Iesuitarum*, bk. 2, ch. 4, p. 216.

13. De causa Dei in praefatione.] Thomas Bradwardine, ca. 1300–1349, theologian and archbishop of Canterbury, *De Causa Dei* (London, 1618), sig. b1r (*praefatio*).

doctrine must be defended."[14] With equal if not greater force, Jansen of Ypres inveighs against Aristotle:

> Aristotelianism should stop its bawling. It was condemned in that case where Pelagius and Julian kept prattling on about it in full throat. And yet the Pelagian heresy on grace and freewill is simply thoroughgoing Aristotelian philosophy. But what has Aristotle or any other pagan philosopher ever heard, or could ever even conjecture, about grace operating on the will? What could these men grasp about the weakness of the will, about those terrible afflictions that by themselves necessitate the grace of Christ?

And finally, he concludes, "We should consider nothing on this topic more suspect than the philosophy of Aristotle. When they defended the freedom of the human will, Julian and Pelagius were armed only with the weapons of Aristotelian philosophy."[15]

§ 3. These are their statements, dear reader, and I do not disagree with them. Nor certainly have I quoted them in order to detract in any way from sound philosophy. Far be it from me to begrudge someone the praise he deserves. Indeed, so far as I am concerned, sound philosophy should take first place, no, even glory in its own proper domain. I mean in the natural and civil realm. "Let it strut in its own realm."[16] But it must not invade the palace of theology. This Reuben must be content with his own bedroom and not climb into the embrace that belongs to his father, so as not to despoil its excellence [Gen. 35:22].[17] Clement of Alexandria, in a remarkable passage, says, "Philosophy must submit to theology just as Hagar to Sarah. She must submit to teaching and correction. But if she does not obey, 'expel the slave woman.'"[18] I gladly embrace the slave woman just as much as anyone, but I hate philosophy when it wants to dominate. The early standard-bearers of our Reformed faith also hated it. Philip Melanchthon (if Bellarmine has any credibility as a source) once said,

> Philosophy crept gradually into Christianity. The term *free will*, radically foreign to the Holy Scriptures and to the Spirit's disposition and

---

14. Retractat. l. 1. cap. 1.] Augustine, *Retractationum*, in *Omnium Operum*, vol. 1 (Basel, 1528), 1.1.4.

15. In praefat. ad librum sextum *Augustin.* sui, qui est de gratia Christi Salvat. p. mihi 255.] Jansen, *Augustinus, Seu Doctrina Sancti Augustini*, vol. 1 (Paris, 1641), ch. 6, p. 256.

16. Vergil, *Aeneidos*, bk. 1 (line 140).

17. The reference is to Jacob's son, who slept with his father's concubine Bilhah.

18. Stromt. lib. 1.] Clement of Alexandria, ca. 150–ca. 215, Greek Christian theologian and apologist, *Stromatum*, in *Opera Graeca Et Latina Quae Extant* (Paris, 1629), bk. 1, p. 285. This is a Latin gloss of the Greek original and corresponds exactly, including in most details of punctuation, to Francis Turretin's *Locus I: Quaestio 13.5*, thus making it likely that A. and Turretin employed the same source for this quotation. Cf. Gen. 21:10.

judgment, was adopted. The equally destructive word *reason* was tossed in from Plato. These days we have embraced Aristotle instead of Christ. So, immediately after the church's promising beginnings, Christian doctrine began to crumble due to Platonic philosophy.[19]

Luther, Melanchthon's σύγχρονος,[20] states emphatically,

> Men renowned for their intelligence demand that God act in accordance with human judgment and that He do what seems correct to them, or cease to be God. The hidden aspects of His majesty count for nothing, but He must explain why He is God or why He wills something, or what He does appears to lack justice. The flesh does not consider God worthy of enough glory to believe that what God says or does is just and good if it exceeds or surpasses a definition from the Justinian Codex or book 5 of Aristotle's *Ethics*.[21]

The very torchbearer of the gospel restored says these things. But as for what the Socinians, what the Remonstrants, set in the position of greatest importance, we know this well enough that it needs no description. Castellio by himself can speak for the rest. He wrote, "On the topic of predestination and free will, the common mob has a better and more healthy position than those who read books. For the illiterate follow the judgment of reason and their own senses."[22] O yes, they make such brilliant judges, such superb standards against which to measure the Christian religion!

§ 4. Second: *the resurgence of Skepticism*. Pyrrho[23] was quite influential among the philosophers.[24] He held that there is a certain ἀκαταληψία and ἐποχή[25] among all objects and individual instances (according to Diogenes Laertius). Seneca makes the following comments about Pyrrho's adherents, comparing them with others who taught irrelevancies: "Those who teach what is unnecessary impart knowledge that provides no benefit. But Skeptics remove the hope of knowledge altogether. It is preferable to know things that are useless than to know nothing at all. One group

---

19. *Bellarm.* in praefat. ad lib. de gratia & libero arbitrio.] Melanchthon, quoted in Bellarmine, *De Gratia Et Libero Arbitrio*, in *Disputationes De Controversiis*, vol. 4 (Ingolstadt, 1605), p. 670 (*praefatio*).

20. "Contemporary."

21. De servo arbitrio c. 173. edit. *Kimedontianae*.] Luther, *De Servo Arbitrio* (Neustadt, 1591), ch. 173.

22. *Castellio*, praefat. in suos Dialog.] Castellio, *Dialogi IV*, sig. **2r (*praefatio*).

23. Pyrrho, ca. 360–270 BC, Greek founder of Skepticism.

24. In vita *Pyrrhonis*.] Diogenes Laertius, fl. ca. AD 200, Greek biographer of philosophers, *Peri biōn dogmatōn kai apophthegmatōn tōn en philosophia* (Rome, 1594), ch. 9.

25. These are "inability of direct apprehension" and a corresponding "suspension of judgment," respectively.

does not advance understanding, the other gouges out my eyes. I would be hard-pressed to say whether I am more bothered by those who want us to know nothing or by those who have not even left us this: that there is anything to know."[26] I myself believed that this Skepticism or Pyrrhonism (even those philosophers known as Academics embrace it) would long ago have lain dead and been buried in the tomb—namely, when Cicero's volumes appeared and then, secondly, when Augustine published *Against the Academics*. But among theologians, the Dutch Remonstrants seem recently to have brought it back to life. These are their words: "The very soul of theology is snuffed out and shattered when there are particular positions to which one must consistently and firmly adhere."[27] Among the philosophers, the Cartesians have revived Skepticism. Their leader, René Descartes, in the first principles of his philosophical system, immediately states that it is most useful that "we at once be intent on doubting in life everything in which we will find even the slightest hint of uncertainty. But even for those items that we doubt, it will be helpful to consider them false so that we can discover far more clearly what, in fact, is most certain and most readily known."[28] Do not these quotations (even though they are not entirely coherent) seem to derive from the spirit of ancient Skepticism? I mean of the sort whose worshippers—while they hold that they know nothing or take nothing as true but confine themselves within the boundaries of probability—always flit about in the dark mist of doubt, like blind gladiators in the shadows? Such σκέψις[29] is diametrically opposed to the articles of faith and paves the way to outlandish opinions. Erasmus wrote at the opening of his *Diatribe* on free will that he was "not pleased by assertions that [he] would easily withdraw to the opinion of the Skeptics wherever the unquestioned authority of the divine Scriptures and the decrees of the church permitted it."[30] How did Luther respond? He used to say, "I was so certain about that doctrine that I published that I will not submit it to the judgment of angels, because through it I will, along with other men, judge even the angels."[31]

---

26. *Senec.* epist. 88. circa finem.] Sencea, *Epistolaes* (*epistola* 88).

27. Apolog. suae fol. 7 in examine censurae praefationis Leidensium.] Episcopius, *Apologia Pro Confessione* ([Leiden], 1629), fol. 7r.

28. René Descartes, 1596–1650, French philosopher and mathematician, *Principia Philosophiae* (Amsterdam, 1656), part. 1, sec. 1–2, p. 1. A. substitutes *dubitavimus*, perfect tense, for the original future *dubitabimus*.

29. "Skepticism."

30. Erasmus, *De Libero Arbitrio Diatribe Sive Collatio* (Basil, 1524), pp. 2–3. Johannes Beb. (Froben?). This and the following quotation A. likely took from Luther's response to Erasmus.

31. *Joh Laeti* compend. univers. history. p. 545.] De Laet, *Compendium Historiae Universalis*, ch. 31, sec. 2, art. 1, p. 545. A.'s quotation is considerably different from the original, but the 1653 edition is the only one he could have consulted. De Laet wrote: *de doctrina sua nempe divina tam certum ut iudicio Angelorum eam nollet submittere, quando per eam cum hominibus*

In his reply to Erasmus, he said, "Skeptics and Academics should stay away from us Christians. But those who are even more stubborn than the Stoics in advancing categorical statements are welcome. Take those away and one has taken away the Christian faith."[32] That's what he said. I am certainly quite fearful of Henry Alting's prediction: "Theological skepticism, in the end, leads to atheism."[33] Meanwhile, I am sure that it has driven the deepest roots into very many people.

§5. Third: *the presumption to prophesy.* Of course, we can expect an abundant harvest of errors wherever the right to plant seed is granted to anyone. The Lord says in Jeremiah, "I did not send forth prophets, and yet they ran. I did not speak to them, and yet they prophesy" (Jer. 23:21). Calvin comments on this passage, "Wherever the church is established properly, there no one should force himself into the office of prophet or pastor, not even if he equals all the angels in holiness."[34]

Please pay attention, reader, to the words that follow in the prophet just a little later: "'Because I myself have not sent them nor instructed them, they do not help this people,' says the Lord" (Jer. 23:32). These words so affected Luther that he wrote something about them in his commentary on Galatians (not on the page that survives in his works but in another collection of his works that he authorized, published at Wittenberg in 1535; this was later translated into English). Right near the beginning he wrote:

> Calling is mediated through men and yet is divine. And this refers to the general calling in the world after the apostles. Nor should it be changed but should be considered of great importance because of the radicals of our time who despise it and push forward another kind of calling. They claim that, by this calling, the Spirit compels them to teach. But they are lying frauds. Yes, they are driven by a spirit, but not a good one: it is a wicked one.

And a little later, he writes, "It isn't enough to have the Word and sound doctrine. One must also have a definitive call. Without this, whoever enters office comes to kill and destroy. God never profits the work of those who have not been called. And although they produce some wholesome things,

---

etiam Angelos esset iudicaturus. A. has: *de illa quam vulgavit doctrina, certum adeo fuisse ut eam iudicio a Angelorum nollet submittere, quoniam etc.* A. appears to paraphrase from memory.

32. De servo arbitrio cap 4.] Luther, *De Servo Arbitrio*, ch. 4.

33. Problem. Theolog. part: 1. p. 17.] Heinrich Alting, 1583–1644, Flemish Reformed theologian, *Scriptorum Theologicorum Heidelbergensium*, vol. 2 (Amsterdam, 1646), part 1, p. 17.

34. Calvin, *Praelectiones: In Librum Prophetiarum Ieremiæ* (Geneva, 1563), sub loc. Jer. 23:21. There are some changes to the quotation, but the sense is retained.

yet they do not at all edify."[35] That is what Luther said, and perhaps with more than enough heat.

If only this evil had been confronted when the time was right, or that, in our beloved Britain, it would be as soon as possible! Now, here is an opportunity to resurrect Jerome's well-known complaint:

> Yesterday they were catechumens, today they are bishops. Yesterday philosophers, today—when they have barely fallen from Aristotle's pocket—they are elevated to the dignity of a bishopric. They teach the Scriptures that they do not understand. They are more teachers of the inexperienced than students of the learned.[36]

Bernard likewise complains,

> If you are wise, you will present yourself as a little reservoir and not a large sluice. The second one receives and releases water at almost the same time. But the first waits until it is filled and, if there is anything left over, shares it without harming itself at all. Now we have many sluices today in the church but precious few reservoirs. These are so filled with grace that they want to pour out before they are filled, more ready to speak than to listen, and eager to teach what they have not learned.[37]

And finally, we have this from Peter of Blois: "Today unhappy men strive by right and wrong means toward the pastor's seat of authority. They do not notice that, for them, this throne is a plague, while, for both themselves and others, it is an opportunity for destruction."[38]

§6. In the meantime, the Dutch Remonstrants seem to have scratched the itch our countrymen have for public harangues. One of them, Episcopius, holds that "it is legitimate for a Christian person to teach the divine Word any time he wants, if he is suited to teaching and if those who want to be taught demand his instruction resolutely and insistently."[39] And the Anabaptists do this as well, who (as Zanchius confirms) defend the principle that "anyone may place himself in ministerial office and assume ecclesiastical

---

35. Luther, *In Epistolam S. Pauli Ad Galatas Commentarius* (Wittenberg, 1535), sub loc. Gal. 1:1.

36. A. appears to combine two quotations in one. For the second part of the quotation, see Jerome, *Hieronymi Stridoniensis*, vol. 2 (*epistola* 8).

37. Serm. 18. in Cantic.] Bernard of Clairvaux, *In Cantica Canticorum*, sec. 3 (*sermo* 18).

38. Epist. 12.] Peter of Blois, 1125/1130–1212, archdeacon of Bath, *Opera Petri Blesensis* (Mainz, 1600), p. 48 (*epistola* 13). A.'s quotation is substantially the same as the source, save he substitutes *occasio* for *causa*.

39. Thes. privat. Disput. 26. thel. 5.] Episcopius, *Collegium Disputationum Theologicarum* (Dordrecht, 1618), disp. 26, thes. 5, p. 77. A. quotes the thesis unaltered but abridges it.

duties provided he feels called by the Spirit, as they say." [40] From Germany, as we read in Crocius, the Weigelians maintain with numerous but very worthless arguments that those who have a mediated call cannot preach divinity and Christ crucified.[41] From Poland we have the Socinians. One of their number, Theophilus Nicolaides, formulated the question like this: "May one teach without being sent, that is, without any preceding human calling, and may others grant someone permission (they call this 'mediated commission') to teach others the gospel of Christ when that person is suited [2 Tim. 2:24] for teaching and leads a blameless life?" Nicolaides replies: "We must note this first of all: there is no commission that proceeds from men, even if it is conveyed through mediation. Furthermore, commission is not necessary for the establishment of a minister."[42] Such are the views of those men. But the Apostle opposes them. His words to the Romans are quite clear and written, so to speak, with the sun's rays: "Whoever calls on the name of the Lord shall be saved. How will they call upon Him in whom they have not believed? How will they believe in Him about whom they have not heard? How will they hear without someone preaching? And how will they preach unless they have been sent?" (Rom. 10:13–15). This passage establishes the calling of God as necessary for salvation, faith for the calling of God, the hearing of the Word for faith, preaching for the hearing of the Word, and commission for preaching, and it does so, obviously, in an orderly fashion. For sometimes it can happen in an extraordinary way that one not sent preaches fruitfully. Just as sometimes, by a unique providence, a deaf man believes without hearing.

The Socinians, in keeping with their keen insight—which is nowhere more sophisticated than when mocking the Scriptures—and the Remonstrants, who plow with their heifer [Judg. 14:18], usually answer as follows. They say, "Yes, commission was necessary for the apostles whom Paul is talking about, because they had to preach a new and previously unheard doctrine. But those ministers—whose duty it is not to announce something

---

40. In quartum praecept. column. mihi 768.] Probably a reference to A.'s edition of Zanchi's *Orationes*, as above.

41. *Anti-Weigel.* part. altera c. 2. quaest. 1ª.] Johannes Crocius, 1590–1659, German Reformed theologian, *Anti-Weigelius*, vol. 2 (Kassel, 1651), ch. 2, ques. 1, sec. 1.4, p. 34.

42. In refutat act. de Ecclesia & ministror. p. 97. & p. 105.] This is a pseudonym for the Polish Socinian Valentinus Smalcius. Smalcius, *Brevis Refutatio Tractatus De Ecclesia et Missione Ministrorum R.D. Alberti Borkowski: Quo Socinum Cum Theophilo Impugnare & Miedzibozium Defendere Conatur* (Raków, 1614), pp. 97 and 105. A.'s quotation from page 105 omits from within the quotation the phrase *nec manuum impositionem*, "the laying on of hands." A.'s text differs here from the original. He uses the third plural *appellant*, while Smalcius the third singular *appellat*, presumably referring to Borcovius. Cf. Henk van den Belt, Riemer Faber, Andreas Beck, and William den Boer, *Synopsis Purioris Theologiae, Synopsis of a Purer Theology: Latin Text and English Translation* (Leiden: Brill, 2016), p. 623n4.

new but only those teachings that the apostles had passed down—need not wait for commission."[43] I have no problem allowing such a response so long as it concerns *unmediated commission*. There is no argument about that. But if it is used to invalidate mediated commission, then, in order to make clear the vanity and φλυαρία[44] of this subterfuge, I say, first, from the premises granted, commission is necessary for the Socinian doctors and the Arminians, at least, but also for almost all who nowadays enter into the pastoral seat of authority and hold the speakers' lectern though they are not called. For they are preaching a generally new doctrine and one that even the apostles themselves did not hear. Namely, they preach a doctrine of Christ ψιλῷ ἀνθρώπῳ,[45] forgiveness of sins without satisfaction offered to God, middle knowledge, and the final apostasy of the saints, together with a thousand other monstrosities.

I say, second, that ambassadors and heralds (from whose service Paul, in this passage, borrows his metaphor, and these were called κήρυκες)—even the ones who do not proclaim new treaties but simply revive ancient ones previously proposed by others—must have official sanction. If they should dare to venture on ambassadorial responsibilities before they are commissioned, then they are guilty of *lèse-majesté*. Third, it is very easy for readers to measure accurately the proofs of the Reformed churches that support the necessity of external commission from their existing confessions. They can measure them not just by one or two scoops, as the saying goes, but by the whole load. Nevertheless, at present, I want to provide nothing except the vote of the militant churches in New England. This I do, in fact, all the more willingly because perhaps there are those who believe that our brothers there, who are certainly most dear to us, strongly favor the opposite position. Nine years ago, John Norton, a minister of the New England church of Ipswich, wrote his *Response to Apollonius*. He did this at the urging of his fellow presbyters who also commended his book by their vote. In that volume we read these very words:

> We have not yet learned from the Scriptures, and by no means do we believe, that there is any command of Christ ordaining a private brother, enjoying no ecclesiastical office, to hold an ordinary and fixed right to

---

43. Catechism. Raccoviens. in cap. de regimine Eccles. *Theoph. Nicolaid.* passim. *Episcop.* thes. privat. disp. 26. thes. 2, & 3.] *Catechesis Ecclesiarum* (Racovian Catechism) (Raków, 1609), p. 298ff; Smalcius, *passim*; Episcopius, *Collegium Disputationum Theologicarum In Academia Leydensi Privatim Institutarum* (Dordrecht, 1618), sub loc. disp. 26, thes. 2 and 3.

44. "Nonsense."

45. "As a mere man."

preach on set occasions (though he may do so from time to time) before the whole assembly and in a church that has an adequate minister.[46]

§ 7. But I do not want to abandon the freedom to edify, even while I attack presumption in prophesying and clarify the proper position on this very important theological point. As the issue now stands at a troubled crossroads, I would like to set down the actual state of the controversy. Then, through several theses, I will draw into the open what I, at least, think; and if men of sound judgment disapprove, then I will leave it there for their consideration. This is the heart of the question: Is it proper for men who are not ordained to expound and apply the Scriptures publicly and as a matter of course? By the way, by those who are *not ordained*, we mean all they who have not yet been solemnly set apart to the ministry of Word and sacraments by a preceding exam and are, thus, separated from those who have an interest in these ordinances.

Let this be the first thesis: *those who are not ordained may publicly expound and apply the Scriptures at present, provided they are going to be ordained at some future point.* But they may not do so ordinarily, nor with equal right as they who are ordained. This means that as "sons of the prophets," who grow in hope and usefulness to the church, as ministerial candidates, whose every study and effort is directed to this end, they can hold public discourses on different occasions for the discovery and trial of their gifts, in keeping with acquiring the office of a gospel pastor. For the "expectant," as they are called somewhere, even though they are not really and actually ministers, nevertheless, are so potentially, in terms of their attitude, and—as the saying goes—*in proxima potentia.*[47] Yet even these warm-up exercises, so to speak, make the candidates more suitable for ecclesiastical service and render those who will eventually ordain them less likely (as Paul forbids) to "lay hands on anyone carelessly" [1 Tim. 5:22].

But I leave it to others to decide whether this should be a normal, ordinary circumstance in an established assembly. Granted, they may, as has been stated, preach at different times (and I would add, if I may, many times). Yet it will in no way follow from this that they can definitely preside over a church for a two-, three-, or even four-year period (as I recently learned some have done). And they may not receive from that church the "double honor" that is due presbyters who labor in the Word and teaching, because they are themselves not yet presbyters. What I stated concerning the inequality of right will become obvious soon enough. We can rightly

---

46. Pag. 124.] John Norton, 1606–1663, minister in America, *Responsio Ad Totam Quaestionum Syllogen* (London, 1648), ch. 11, p. 124.

47. I.e., very close to being able to do so.

discern a fourfold division between a brother who is still in a private capacity (no matter how loaded he is with exceptional gifts) and one who has been properly constituted a minister of the gospel. The unordained man teaches from the obligation of a common charity and brotherly love. The ordained man does so from the obligation of a particular office and with a father's authority. The former preaches so as to *profit* his hearers but not so as to *have authority* over them.[48] The latter preaches and profits and presides at the same time, in keeping with the command to the Thessalonians: "We ask, brothers, that you acknowledge those who labor among you and exercise oversight over you in the Lord and admonish you" (2 Thess. 5:12). There is also this comment in the letter to the Hebrews: "Obey your leaders"—or ones placed over you (τοῖς ἡγουμένοις ὑμῖν)—"and submit to them; for they keep watch over your souls as those who must give an account" (Heb. 13:17). The unordained man may preach the word at any time, but he may not administer baptism or the Supper. This is a point the majority of our adversaries freely grant. These two responsibilities are only allowed the one who is ordained.

Finally, some general promises pertain to the unordained man. These are the kind of promises that generally move Christians to works of mutual charity. But Christ made this specific promise to the ordained man: "Behold, I am with you all your days unto the end of the age" (Matt. 28:20). It was not limited to the apostles, I say, because they were not granted to survive until the end of the age. But in keeping with their responsibility, it was also given to the apostles' successors in pastoral office.

The second thesis follows: *those who are not ordained, nor going to be ordained in the future, although they may ordinarily expound and apply the Scriptures, may not do so publicly.* Although I say "ordinarily," there is the proviso that it be done privately, and according to these commandments: "These will be the words that I command you today"—that is, all of Israel—"in your heart. And you will impress them carefully upon your sons, and you will speak of them when you sit in your home, and when you walk along the path, when you lie down and when you rise up" (Deut. 6:6–7). Similarly, "Admonish one another, and build one another up, just as you are already doing" (1 Thess. 5:11). One's own talent has been entrusted to each, within the sphere of his own calling [Matt. 25:14–30]. He must invest it diligently, to profit in faith and good character those who belong to him. This man, whoever he is, must be a bishop in his own house but not ἀλλοτριοεπίσκοπος[49] among outsiders [1 Peter 4:15]. If the same man, in the pastoral seat of authority, undertakes, without legitimate commission,

---

48. A. employs a pun, contrasting *prosit* and *praesit.*
49. "A troublesome meddler."

something permitted within the bounds of his own home, it would be just like bursting into an aristocrat's home without the master's leave, seizing the keys, instructing everyone in their duty, and, in the guise of the steward, managing household property at his own discretion. Or, it is like doing so against the will of the father of the household.

The third thesis follows: *in a church that is either not yet established or so disorganized or weak that it lacks pastors and there is no system of lawful ordination present, then it is permissible, for a time, for private brothers to whom God has given generous gifts to exposit the Scriptures publicly and ordinarily, as well as apply them. This is done with the understanding not that ordination has taken place but that it has not been neglected.* This is my reasoning: divine law grants to moral law a conventional rite when necessity requires it. "Necessity," as the commendable saying goes, "defends those whom she compels." Our countryman, the right famous Fulke, calls this the "calling of providence."[50] I believe that the situation Aedisimus[51] and Frumentius[52] found themselves in among the Indians is common knowledge. They had previously not held any ecclesiastical office in India.[53] Yet they convened public assemblies and performed the divine mysteries. Likewise, it is common knowledge what the captive woman did. She reportedly led the Iberians to an adequate knowledge of the Christian religion.[54]

Now finally, here is the fourth thesis: *in a church properly constituted and quite healthy, unordained men may not ordinarily expound and apply the Scriptures publicly.* They are not permitted, because they do not have either type of commission. They lack the unmediated commission that they dared not claim for themselves since they lack gifts of miracles and tongues. They also lack the mediated commission, which required two elements: δύναμις and ἐξουσία.[55] Sometimes these are separated, of course, because women can have *the law of God on their lips* (Prov. 31:26). Nevertheless, *they are not permitted to teach in the church* (1 Tim. 2:12; 1 Cor. 14:34). The endowment of gifts supplies the first requirement. Ordination alone will confer the latter prerequisite, complete in all respects. Both of these constitute a commission.

---

50. Advers. Rhemenses in Roman. 10.14.] William Fulke, 1538–1589, theologian and college head, perhaps *Contra Testamentum Rhemense* (*Confutation of the Rhemish Testament*) [c. 1589].

51. Edesius, fl. fourth century AD, missionary to India and Abyssinia (Ethiopia).

52. Frumentius, ca. 300–ca. 380, bishop of Axum.

53. Vide Theod. lib 1. cap. 23.] Theodoret, *Ecclesiasticae Historiae*, in *Opera Omnia*, vol. 3 (Paris, 1642), bk. 1, ch. 22, pp. 570–71. In spite of A.'s comments, Edesius and Frumentius are traditionally credited with introducing Christianity to Abyssinia (Ethiopia).

54. Sozomen, ca. 400–post-445, church historian, *Historiae Ecclesiasticae*, vol. 2 (Geneva, 1612), bk. 2, ch. 6, p. 234.

55. "Power" and "authority."

I will conclude this portion with an oath. I wish that Cyprian's words concerning the Novatians[56] could never be rightly applied to those who today force themselves into the seat of pastoral authority. Rigault deserves credit for this comparison:

> There are men who, with no divine appointment, place themselves voluntarily over assemblies of reckless men. They put themselves in positions of authority, with no rite of ordination. They sit in the seat of pestilence; they are destruction and disease for the faith and deceive with the serpent's mouth. They are workmen who corrupt the truth, spewing out lethal poisons with their disease-ridden tongues. Their speech crawls forward like a cancer.[57]

§ 8. Fourth: *reckless misappropriation of the Holy Spirit*. God's promise to send Christ was prominent under the Old Testament. Under the New Testament, they waited for Christ's promise to send forth the Holy Spirit more abundantly in these last days. For this reason, the Devil entered and possessed the bodies of mortals (as is clear from the gospel writers), particularly in that age when the Son of God assumed flesh. He did so to diminish the astounding mystery and miracle of the incarnation. Likewise, when the Lord and supreme teacher promised His disciples the Spirit of truth, who would guide them into all truth (John 16:13), false teachers also began to boast about their guidance from the Holy Spirit. Nowadays, their boasting is much more common than before.

The ancient writers who catalogued heresies relate that Montanus[58] called his followers "spiritual," but all the rest he labeled "carnal" and "ψυχιχούς."[59] The ancient writer Harmenopolos, in his book that deals with schismatics, makes these remarks about the Massalians and Euchites:[60] Ἐνθυσιασμὸν τὰς τῆς ὀνείρων φαντασίας καλοῦσι ("They call the fantasies of their own dreams 'outpourings of the Holy Spirit'").[61] Reformed theologians also, each in his own day, have complained about this practice. Luther writes, "Today, those who are fanatical spirits want whatever they

---

56. Novatians, followers of Novatian, d. 257/258, who rejected the reinstatement of lapsed clergy.

57. Observat. ad *Cyprianum* pag. 165. *Cyprian.* de unitate Eccles. Edit. Paris. A. 1648. p. 210.] Cyprian, *De Unitate Ecclesiae*, in *Sancti Caecilii Cypriani Opera Nicolai Rigalti Observationibus Ad Veterum Exemplarium Fidem Recognita Et Illustrata* (Paris, 1648), p. 210. Nicolas Rigault, 1577–1654, French Roman Catholic humanist and philologist.

58. Montanus, fl. ca. 170, early heretic who believed he was the Paraclete.

59. "Natural men." Cf. 1 Cor. 2:14.

60. Massalians (Messalians) or Euchites, members of a Christian sect from Mesopotamia that spread to Asia Minor and Thrace.

61. Likely a reference to the Hexavivlos, a codification of Byzantine law, by Constantine Harmenopolos, fourteenth century, Thessalonian judge and curator of legal texts.

dream up to be the Holy Spirit. But Basil pointedly said οὐ πᾶν ἐνύπνιον εὐθὺς προφητεία.”[62] Calvin wrote a notable treatise against the fanatical and raging sect of the Libertines.[63] They label themselves "spiritual." This is the title of that admirable book, in whose second chapter Calvin says, "All they talk about is the Spirit, but they speak in a foreign idiom," etc.[64] Bucer said, "Heretics, no less than the orthodox—if not more so—claim for themselves the Spirit of truth."[65] Our countryman Davenant identifies three unique characteristics of frauds, the last of which is, "They not only love and promulgate teachings that arise from their own carnal thinking, but they also become so swollen with them that they take their own dreams as the actual revelations of the Holy Spirit. They think they have been filled with the Spirit when, in fact, they are just stretched out and swollen with an empty wind."[66] Davenant cites as an example the papists. Among all the ways they bully Christians without any biblical authority, they are not ashamed to steal for themselves the apostles' saying: "It seemed good to us and to the Holy Spirit" [Acts 15:28].

When it comes to my own situation, I am very prepared (at least, I ought to be and try to be) to increase in the Paraclete, without whose in-pouring we are and can do nothing. I very readily embrace that statement of Elihu found in Job: "The Spirit is with men, and the breath of the Almighty renders them understanding" (Job 32:8). There is also this quote of Augustine: "Don't think that any man learns something from another man, that is, anything good. We can exhort through the sound of our voice. But if the one who teaches is not within, then the sound we make is worthless. The inner teacher teaches, Christ teaches, inspiration teaches."[67] Nevertheless, such are the times, such the men with whom we live, that I should not be at all surprised if each person falls into the trap of error and becomes so foolish that the mere mention of "Holy Spirit" is more than enough for accepting that man. Calvin very plainly illustrates this in the following comments on John:

---

62. Tom. 4. fol. 511.] Luther, *Enarratio In Psalmos Graduum*, in *Omnium Operum*, vol. 4 (Jena, 1558), sub loc. Ps. 132:12. "Not every hallucination is *ipso facto* prophecy." From Basil of Caesarea, ca. 330–379, Cappadocian father.

63. Calvin, *Contre la secte phantastique et furieuse des Libertins qui se nomment Spirituelz* [c. 1545].

64. Operum tom. 7. p. 433.] Most likely Calvin, *Opera Omnia Theologica: In Septem Tomos Digesta* (Geneva, 1617).

65. In Epist. ad Ephes. praefat. p. 13.] Martin Bucer, 1491–1551, German Reformed theologian, *Praelectiones Doctiss., In Epistolam D. P. Ad Ephesios* (Basel, 1562), p. 13 (*praefatio*). *Spiritum scilicet veritatis* is not present in the original.

66. In epist. ad Coloss. c. 2. v. 18. pag. mihi 304.] Davenant, *Ad Colossenses*, sub loc. Col. 2:18.

67. Tractat. 3. in epist. Joannis.] Augustine, *Expositio In Epistolam Beati Ioannis*, in *Omnium Operum*, vol. 9 (Basel, 1528), 3.13.

"Beloved, do not trust every spirit, but test the spirits to see if they are from God. Because many false prophets have gone out into the world." The apostle could have said that we should not trust any men at all. But because false teachers deceptively take the title of the Spirit, he leaves that title to them and at the same time warns that it is ridiculous and worthless unless they truly evince what they profess. He means that they are fools who, thunderstruck at the mere sound of this honorific title, do not dare to ask questions about the content.[68]

§ 9. Fifth: *utter disregard for catechetical instruction.* Gregory de Valencia recounts, with approval, the plan of a certain merchant of Piacenza, who reasoned as follows:

I have decided I want to embrace the papal rather than Lutheran religion. My main reason is that there I can learn the truth by a short cut—that is, if I say what the pope says and deny what the pope denies. But in the other system, if I wanted to become Lutheran, I would have to learn catechism and search the Scripture. This, in fact, I cannot do, because I have to keep an eye on Italian shipping and research the transportation of international goods.[69]

De Valencia then adds, "God would have no complaint at all against this man on that frightful day of judgment."[70] A Jesuit says this? Would we really say that implicit faith equally suits street salesmen and charcoal vendors? Has your merchant committed no sin by substituting the pope in place of Christ? Is it not at all a problem that he considers catechism, much less the sacred Scriptures, less important than Italian shipping and commerce? Forgive us dunderheads across the Alps if we feel more reverence for the Scriptures, more respectful of catechisms.

I grant that there are also in our ranks some people (those who profess a "free theology," as they say), who find lists, summaries, systems, confessions, and other things of that class a pretty worthless business and who generally hold that religion is something low and common that can be gotten from three-penny catechisms. But Martin Luther thought about it much differently. In a certain letter to Wolfgang Fabricius Capito[71] in 1539,[72] he wrote, "I am somewhat indifferent and hesitant about the arrangement of

---

68. 1 Epist. 4. 1.] John Calvin, *In Omnes Pauli Apostoli Epistolas* (Geneva, 1556), sub loc. 1 John 4:1.

69. Analys. de Eccles. p. 205.] Gregory de Valencia, 1549–1603, Spanish Jesuit theologian, *Analysis Fidei Catholicae* (Ingolstadt, 1585), pp. 205–7.

70. Ibid. p. 207.] Valencia, *Analysis Fidei Catholicae*, p. 207. A. alters word order and substitutes the synonym *iudicio* for de Valencia's *tribunali.*

71. Wolfgang Fabricius Capito, ca. 1478–1541, German Reformer and theologian.

72. Other sources say July 9, 1537.

my volumes. All the more because, driven by hunger like Saturn's, I prefer that they had all been swallowed up. I recognize no book as really my own except perhaps *Bondage of the Will* and the catechism."[73]

There are similar statements attributed to David Pareus. After he had put the final touch on that system of orthodox doctrine he had received from his teacher Ursinus,[74] deeply moved, with joy in his heart, he said, "Now, O Lord, let your servant depart in peace, because I have accomplished what I desired."[75] And yet, when giving his son Philip his papers seven months before his death, that dignified old man said of himself, "Truly, I assure you that other than the sacred Bible there is hardly any other book I have handled more frequently than this catechetical treasure. Compared to it, I count all my other long nights of work as worth hardly a nutshell."[76] Catechetical instruction is a kind of ballast to the mind, if I may use such an expression. And so those who do not want "to be tossed about and carried to and fro by every wind of doctrine according to the vicissitudes of men through their scheming shrewdness with its hollow deception" (Eph. 4:14) must drink from it sincerely and deeply. This is how Beza translates Paul's words to the Ephesians, with adequate care, no doubt, but also adequate emphasis.[77]

I would be remiss if I ignored the words of praise great men have ascribed to Luther's shorter German catechism. Selnecker said it contains as much good content as it does words, as many useful helps as letter-points.[78] Anton Probus,[79] superintendent of Weimar, adorned the catechism with these short verses:

> Those living words by God's own finger etched in Luther's heart,
> The catechism holds them fast, nor e'er be rent apart.
> Of Scripture all the juice here lies, sweet honey, marrow's bone,
> More than six thousand worlds in worth, this one small gem alone.[80]

§ 10. Sixth: *the failure to apply church discipline.* The apostle Paul memorably says, "I praise you, brothers, because you have remembered all my concerns, have retained the traditions just as I entrusted them to you"

---

73. Teste *Zanchio* in lib. 3. miscellan. & *Wendelin.* in.] Zanchi, *De Praedestinatione,* in *Omnium Operum Theologicorum,* vol. 7 (Geneva, 1619), p. 289. The mythical character Saturn devoured all his children to prevent his own replacement by an heir.

74. Zacharias Ursinus, 1534–1583, Reformed theologian.

75. Teste Phillip. Pareo in vita patris sui.] Pareus, *Narratio Historica,* p. 137.

76. Pareus, *Narratio Historica,* p. 138.

77. *Biblia Sacra,* sub loc. Eph. 4:14.

78. Nicholaus Selnecker, 1530–1592, German Lutheran theologian.

79. Anton Probus, 1537–1613, German Lutheran theologian.

80. Ap. *David Mayerum* in Jubilaeo Evangelico. pag. 92.] David Meyer, 1572–1640, Lutheran theologian, *Omnium Sanctorum Iubilaeus Evangelicus* (Frankfurt, 1617), sec. 11, p. 92.

(1 Cor. 11:2). From this expression, one can easily deduce how vigorously church discipline was practiced among the very first Christians. Because the Apostle undoubtedly taught frequently on this topic, especially as regards false teachers, we have remarks like this: "I pray, brothers, that you keep a careful eye on those who instigate divisions and minor obstacles contrary to the teaching you have learned, and that you keep away from them. Reject a heretical man after a first and second warning" (Rom. 16:17; Titus 3:10). And there are many other such warnings. But church discipline became miserably polluted under the papacy, and devolved into a money-making scheme, as Marco Antonio de Dominis, the archbishop of Spalato, admits. "We have exchanged the keys of the kingdom of heaven for the keys of coffers and vaults."[81] There is a letter by Zacharias Ursinus, the pinnacle of theologians, written to Andreas Stephanus, the antistes[82] of the Bohemian Brethren.[83] Dated 1574, it provides evidence for just how far the German Reformation has departed from its disciplinary purity.

> It is true that our prayers and devotion, for some time now, are aimed at seeing better order among us. Nevertheless, the term *church discipline* has become quite distasteful, since some men promote and conduct it rather foolishly and without regard for the occasion. Others reject it with much bitterness and flat out. So a majority shun church discipline and want to eliminate it. At this point, we have barely held on to the word *discipline* at all, or just a mere shadow.[84]

Truth and the evidence of his own circumstances wrung quite a complaint from Lancelot Andrews, the leading man of his order. This complaint shows clearly just how healthy English discipline was under the episcopacy. In 1593, during a speech addressed to the clergy, he said this to the prelates and elders who had gathered in a provincial synod:

> The very medicine for all abuses has itself been abused. I mean ecclesiastical censure. I ask you please to note this, and to apply medicine to your own medicine. For the tools we have been given to overthrow wickedness, the whip of Christ and the keys of Peter, now strike only the moneybag. And yet Christ's whip has been stripped of lashes used for punishing crimes, and Peter's keys have likewise now become rusty.

---

81. De Repub. Eccles. lib. 5. c. 7. parag. 86.] Marco Antonio de Dominis, ca. 1560–1624, archbishop of Spalato, *De Republica Ecclesiastica*, vol. 2 (London, 1620), bk. 5, ch. 7, para. 86, p. 331.

82. In early modern times, the antistes was the highest church office in Swiss and other European Reformed churches; he served as a moderator or president of a synod or church council.

83. Later known as "Moravian Brethren" and *Unitas Fratrum*.

84. Zacharias Ursinus to Andreas Stephanus, 1574.

Unless, of course, by your own effort, you are going to fashion new cords for the whip and a new sheen for the keys![85]

After the bishops' prelacy was discarded, our church discipline has become like Creusa[86] to her husband Aeneas long ago:

She left him weeping, longing still to parley more at length,
Departed on the slender breeze, a mist, a sigh, a wraith.[87]

It is true that the famous assembly of elders that convened at Westminster just a few years ago as ordered by the "Estates"—I mean both houses of Parliament—repeatedly attempted to reintroduce church discipline. But it happened just like with Aeneas and Creusa in the Poet:

Three times he tried to hold her tight with arms around her neck,
Three times in vain her image fleet escaped his reaching hands,
Just like the gentle winds and as a fleeting dream she sped.[88]

But if the common slogan is true that discipline is to religion as trunk to tree, then it is really impossible to keep faith safe when ecclesiastical censures have ceased, or that wolves do not enter when the sheepfolds are in the condition Bucholz[89] sorrowfully ascribed to the German churches. "I wish," he said, "that our churches possessed the holy rigor of ecclesiastical discipline. Our sheepfold, our pens, are missing their gates, bars, and bolts."[90]

§ 11. Seventh: *the disagreement over the power that belongs to the Christian magistrate in church affairs was poorly resolved.* Now there are two positions on this question at opposite ends of the spectrum. The first is excessive, while the second is defective. Both sides commit a perverse error: one group wants to surrender to the magistrate almost every aspect of conducting religion, and the other ascribes to him almost nothing. Moreover, these errors are the sort that come from the womb with many siblings. Thomas Hobbes of Malmesbury is the main source of the first position, which errs by its excess. In his *Philosophical Elements of a True Citizen*, Hobbes states, "Citizens can confer upon the magistrate or those who hold executive authority

---

85. Opuscul. posthum. pag. 41.] Lancelot Andrewes, bishop of Winchester, *Opuscula Quaedam Posthuma* (London, 1629), p. 41.

86. Creusa, daughter of Priam and Hecuba, and first wife of Aeneas.

87. Vergil, *Aeneidos*, bk. 2 (lines 790–91).

88. Vergil, *Aeneidos*, bk. 6 (lines 792–94). A. includes here an asterisk and this comment in the margin: "I will plainly state that discipline, which for a long time was counted as nothing, has recently vanished."

89. Abraham Buchholtzer.

90. In epistola ad F. R. quae habetur in libro cui titulus, Ratio disciplinae fratrum Bohemorum, p. 120.] *Ratio Disciplinae Ordinisque Ecclesiastici In Unitate Fratrum Bohemorum* ([Leszno], 1633), p. 119.

in the state the power of deciding how God is to be worshipped, or rather, they must."[91] But in his book entitled *Leviathan*, Hobbes asked, "What if the king, or the senate, or any other supreme authority should forbid us to believe in Christ?" He then answered, "Such a prohibition is entirely invalid because neither faith nor disbelief ever follow men's dictates." Again, he asks whether "one must obey the command of a lawful ruler who orders a Christian to profess with his mouth, at least, that he does not believe in Christ." He responds that "such obedience is permissible when the profession of the mouth is only an outward reality, provided inwardly, in his heart, the Christian retains his private faith in Christ." But look: "How will one give an answer to the Savior's clear word, 'If anyone denies Me before men, I will deny him before my Father who is in heaven'?" In reply, Hobbes says, "Whatever one is compelled to do under duress, in order to accommodate the practice of his ruler, provided he does not act sincerely but only to be in conformity to his country's law, this is not, in the final analysis, his own action but his ruler's. Nor is he the one who, in such a circumstance, is denying Christ, but his king and the law of the land are."[92] And yet, with one prophet, I should shout, "Be shocked, O heavens, over this, and may His gates be utterly abandoned" (Jer. 2:12). And I should proclaim with another, "Jehovah with His very hard, long, and strong sword will notice Leviathan, that twisted serpent, and will kill it" (Isa. 27:1). Tell me please, reader, if you will, has any book ever been found that more forcefully opened the door to every kind of disbelief? Indeed, I believe no such book exists, if we are talking about titles that bear the name of Christ.

Now the main advocates for the second position were once the papists. They held that political officers ought to be free from every concern for church affairs. The sole exception was care for the bishops' decrees and the sanctions entrusted to magistrates for execution. Becan, in his refutation of the Advisory Preface of King James,[93] holds this position: "What will kings do about church and religion? I will say it in a word. They must guard and defend the former, not as masters but as ministers, not as judges but as prosecutors."[94] "Yes, what noble praise and ample plunder you have taken,"[95] O lords of the nations! Teachers like this are happy for you to become public servants, or, if you prefer, butchers, of your lord the pope. Other bizarre progressives have recently formed alliances, at least partly,

---

91. Pag. 279.] Thomas Hobbes, 1588–1679, English philosopher, *Elementa Philosophica De Cive* (Amsterdam, 1657), ch. 15, p. 279.

92. pag. 271.] Hobbes, *Leviathan* (London, 1651), part 3, ch. 42, p. 271.

93. King James I, 1566–1625, king of Scotland, England, and Ireland.

94. Tom. 2. p. 496.] Martin Becan, fl. 1550–1624, French Jesuit theologian, *Iacobi Angliae Regis Apologiae* (Mainz, 1609), part 1, ch. 8, sec. 4, p. 128.

95. Vergil, *Aeneidos*, bk. 4 (line 93).

with the papists. I mean primarily those from the Weigelian party who grant the civil magistrate, even though he is Christian and endowed with distinguished piety, no authority even to reform the church, much less to suppress heretics in any way at all.

§ 12. They also assert this (I wish I could say this without their objection) against the plain meaning of sacred Scripture, the mind of Augustine, the practice of the church, and the clear dictates of reason. The Scripture rather pointedly desires Christians to pray for kings and for whoever is placed in a position of authority (1 Tim. 2:2), because we are indebted to their guardianship. And this not only for a life upright and holy, suited to a citizen, but also for a life that is righteous and devout. The events that took place in terms of the reform of the churches during the reigns of David, Solomon, Asa, Jehoshaphat, Hezekiah, and the other kings of Judah are sufficiently familiar and celebrated in the sacred histories. But it is also worth noting, if I am not mistaken, that, in the book of Judges, a verdict was rendered again and again in the same words not only for the unpunished commission of adultery and murder but also for idolatrous worship performed with impunity. These are, "Because in those days there was no king in Israel, but each man did what seemed right in his own eyes" (Judg. 17:1; 18:2; 19:1). So then, it is a simple thing to conclude that citizens should have been restrained by the ruler's sword from idolatrous worship just as from adultery and murder, if only there had been an active sword then. This is because these ethically disgraceful acts (they are equally consequential under both covenants) are not here described as invalidated because of the lack of a priest but the lack of a political ruler.

We will get Augustine's vote from two absolutely undisputable proofs. The first is addressed to Boniface.[96] "Kings serve the Lord when they do those things to serve Him that they cannot do except as kings—I mean, forbidding and punishing, with a holy rigor, things that arise contrary to the Lord's commands."[97] The second passage is from his work *Against Cresconius*. "This is how kings serve God, as they are divinely commanded, to the extent that they are kings: if they command, in their own kingdom, good deeds and forbid wicked ones. Not only deeds that deal with human society, but also those that affect divine religion."[98]

As for what the practice of the church was, this will be quite clear from the documents of that era when the Emperor Constantine was allowed

---

96. Boniface I, d. 422, r. 418–422.

97. Epist. 50.] Augustine, *Omnium Operum*, vol. 2 (Basel, 1528), 5.19 (*epistola* 50).

98. Lib. 3. cap. 51.] Augustine, *Contra Cresconium Grammaticum*, in *Omnium Operum*, vol. 7 (Basel, 1528), 3.51.56.

to enroll under the name of Christ. He claimed for himself (as Eusebius reports) a bishopric τῶν ἐκτός.[99] But he called ministers bishops τῶν ἔσω τῆς Ἐκκλησίας—that is, of sacred responsibilities conducted in public addresses—since those actions that are commanded must be rather carefully distinguished from those that are elicited.[100] Magistrates function decretally for those matters that deal with God's worship *immediately*. These activities are handled evocatively, however, by ministers only. That being the case, the authority of a political governor is objectively ecclesiastical. The same Constantine, in his letter to the churches, written after the Council of Nicaea, said, "I have determined that I must strive for this above: that, in the church, most blessed peoples, one faith, a pure charity, and a worship nowhere diverging from God the author of all things is respected."[101] We also have the heroic statement of the Emperor Justinian, well worth remembering: "I have no less concern for the circumstances that benefit the most holy churches than for my own soul."[102] I can add Leo as well, who says, "Human society cannot possibly be safe unless both royal and priestly authority defends anything dealing with the divine confession."[103] The fathers of the Council of Chalcedon thanked the emperor lavishly like this: "You have corrected the church; you have restored the orthodox faith."[104] Finally, we read of Julius Firmicus writing to the two Augustuses, Constantius and Constans:[105] "Necessity orders you, most hallowed emperors, to take vengeance on and punish idolatry. And you receive this command from the law of God Most High."[106]

Now as for reason, after it has learned from the sacred Book that magistrates have been appointed "to be the cause of fear for evildoers" (Rom. 13:3) and that heresies are counted "among the works of the flesh" (Gal. 5:19–20), then it immediately concludes that the magistrate is obligated, according to his duty, to strike fear into heretics. This is so that the failure

---

99. "Of the outsiders."

100. In vita *Constantini* lib. 4. c. 24.] Eusebius, *De Vita Constantini*, in *Historiae Ecclesiasticae*, vol. 1 (Geneva, 1612), bk. 4, ch. 24. A. gives the Greek for "of things outside" and "of things inside the church" with no gloss.

101. Ibid. l. 3.] Eusebius, *De Vita Constantini*, bk. 3, ch. 16.

102. Novell. 3.] Novellae Constitutiones, 3.

103. Epist. 29. ad *Pulcheriam Augustam*.] Leo the Great, *Ad Pulcheriam Augustam*, in *Opera Quae Quidem Haberi* (Cologne, 1561), *Epistola* 31.

104. Davenant, *Determinationes Quaestionum Quarundam Theologicarum* (Cambridge, 1634), p. 57.

105. Constans I, ca. 323–350, r. 333/337–350, youngest son of Constantine I and Roman emperor.

106. Julius Firmicus Maternus, d. post-360, Roman writer, astrologer, and Christian apologist, *De Errore Profanarum Religionum* (Basel, 1603), pp. 102–3. A. has *idololatriam* in place of *malum*.

to punish sin does not incite heretics to sin. Nevertheless, I would not want this concept to extend to capital punishment (so long as heretics are exposed as such) when gentler remedies are available, like forbidding them to teach, financial penalty, imprisonment, exile, etc. I will not deny that Luther's moderation on this topic—Luther, who seldom lacked zeal—seems very commendable. To the question of whether magistrates may execute false prophets, he replied,

> I am reluctant for a verdict of blood, even when it is abundantly merited. The consequence of such a precedent that we see among papists and antichrists, and among Jews, frightens me. Once the decision was reached to execute false prophets and Jews, eventually only holy and innocent prophets were executed. Wicked magistrates—relying on that statute's authority—turned into false prophets and heretics whomever they pleased. I fear that the same thing will happen among us if, by a single example, men take for granted that deceivers must be executed. After all, we still witness that papists abuse this arrangement to spill innocent rather than guilty blood. Therefore, I cannot at all consent to the execution of false teachers. Banishing them is sufficient. If our descendants want to abuse that punishment, their sin will be less severe, and they will harm only themselves.[107]

---

107. Tom. 2. epist. pag. 381.] Luther, *Epistolarum*, vol. 2, fol. 381v.

CHAPTER III

The Belt of Truth or Integrity in the Will

Section 1: The first quality of truth is conformity to a paradigm; the paradigm of integrity, the ἀρχέτυπον,[1] is the simple[2] nature of God; the ἔκτυπον[3] is God's mind in the Word. The τόπος διδαχῆς[4] found in Romans 6:17. Section 2: The second quality of truth is a longing for illumination. John 3:20–21 is a passage illustrating this. The etymology of εἰλικρίνεια.[5] Section 3: The third quality of truth is sustained self-consistency. Integrity means being always the same. The fourth quality of truth is assurance of victory. What a comparison between Isaiah and Matthew teaches us. Section 4: A threefold correspondence between integrity and the belt. Paul and Hezekiah were equipped with integrity. The trickery of a certain Persian ambassador. A saying of Epiphanius on Constantinople. Section 5: The soldiers' great need for a belt, and the Christian soldiers' even greater need for a belt of truth. A comparison of Abraham and Balaam. Section 6: An exhortation to put on the belt of truth, aimed at Christians, Englishmen, and especially academics.

§ 1. A second salutary application of the truth follows, and we identify this as integrity. The psalmist says of this, "Behold, You have desired truth in the inmost parts" (Ps. 51:6). Joshua says, "Fear the Lord, and serve Him with a perfect and completely upright heart" (Josh. 24:14). And Paul, "Let us keep the feast not with leavened loaves, but with those of εἰλικρίνεια καὶ ἀλήθεια" (1 Cor. 5:8).[6] There are, moreover, four characteristic qualities of the truth, each of which corresponds to integrity.

The first is conformity to a paradigm, as the formal reason of any category of truth consists in a certain kind of conformity. The truth of that

---

1. "Archetype."
2. "Uncompounded."
3. "Ectype."
4. "Standard of teaching."
5. "Integrity."
6. "Integrity and truth."

subject is conformity to its form in the divine mind. We act with truth when our deeds conform to what we say and promise. We speak with truth when our speech lines up with our thoughts. We think properly when subjects are apprehended by us as they truly are in themselves and no differently.

The paradigm of integrity is twofold: the ἀρχέτυπος and the ἔκτυπος. The first is God's very nature, because it is most simple and entirely free from composition (John of Damascus brilliantly says of this, "Composition is the foundation of conflict, conflict of separation, separation of dissolution, and dissolution is as incompatible with God as anything can be").[7] This is the archetype of Christian integrity that does not know deceit. We can properly conclude this from Christ's very famous statement about Nathaniel: "Behold, a true Israelite in whom there is no dishonesty" (John 1:48). Second, the mind of God revealed in the Word and containing within itself a living image of the divine nature can be called the paradigm or ectype, as the sacred text does not deny. In Romans the regenerate are described as "given over to the pattern of teaching": "You have sincerely listened to that pattern of instruction"—εἰς τόπον διδαχῆς—"to which you have been committed" (Rom. 6:17). When a molten image is being shaped, the metal that is supplied to the mold will be formed according to the mold's own pattern, such that, if there are any lines engraved more deeply than the template, they stand out in greater relief on the image. Similarly, those precepts of God that are impressed more deeply in the sacred Book and are more urgent than others—like believing in Jesus Christ, showing repentance for our sins, loving God and our neighbors, together with other instances of first importance, as they say—drive their roots deeper into a believing heart. Among hypocrites, however, the situation is quite different. This is why our Savior says, "Woe to you, hypocrites, scribes and Pharisees. You tithe mint and dill and cumin, yet you neglect the weightier things of the law: justice, mercy, and honesty" (Matt. 23:23).

§2. The second characteristic quality of the truth is a desire for illumination. Tertullian expresses this beautifully when he says, "The truth is ashamed of nothing except being hidden."[8] The Lord makes this point in John and illustrates it by its opposite. These are His words: "Whoever does things that are evil hates the light, nor does he come into the light, so that

---

7. Orthodox. fid. l. 1. cap. 4 Σύνθεσις ἀρχὴ μάχης, μάχη δὲ διαστάσεως, διάστασις δὲ λύσεως, λύσις δὲ ἀλλότριον θεοῦ παντελῶς.] John of Damascus, ca. 660–ca. 750, Greek theologian and doctor of the church, *Ekdosis Tes Orthodoxou Pisteos* (Bern, 1531), bk. 1, ch. 4, fol. 4r.

8. Tertullian, *Adversus Valentinianos*, in *Opera Quae Hactenus Reperiri*, vol. 3 (Cologne, 1617), ch. 3. A. has *praeterquam* in place of *nisi solummodo*.

his deeds are not exposed" (John 3:20). Those who plot theft hate the light, and because their eyes are sickened with disease, they cannot bear the rays of the sun. Τὰ κρυπτὰ τῆς αἰσχύνης (2 Cor. 4:2),[9] to use the apostolic expression; things that the night alone knows, these find the light hateful, as something that betrays and even corrects them. Augustine hits the nail on the head when he discusses those who are not regenerate: "Because they do not want to be deceived, they are unwilling to be convicted of falsehood. They love the truth when it illuminates, hate it when it exposes them."[10] Somewhere, Lactantius quite aptly writes, "They who please themselves with vices will not believe us, even if we should take the sun into our own hands."[11] So too, this is how it was with Herod and others who heard John the Baptist: "He was a burning and shining lamp, and the Jews wanted" (John 5:35), as Christ attests, "to bask in his light momentarily. But Herod himself feared John, because Herod knew that he was a just and holy man. And he kept watching him, and he did many things when he heard him, and he listened to him with pleasure," as we have in Mark (Mark 6:20). But as soon as this blazing lamp had begun to shoot flames into Herod's conscience and to scrape it with a biting truth, that hypocrite immediately glowed hot, arrested and shackled John, and threw him into prison because of Herodias, the wife of his brother Philip. For John had told him, "It is not lawful for you to have her," as Matthew records (Matt. 14:3–4). The Lord, in the passage we commended above, continues and soon adds, "But he who is intent upon the truth comes into the light, so that his deeds become evident, because they were done before God" (John 3:21). Accordingly, a man of integrity among the Greeks was called εἰλικρινής, παρὰ τὸ τῇ εἴλῃ κρίνεσθαι (sincere, according to his unmixed judgment). This means that he was known and judged by the gleam of the sun. We could liken this to the eagle that is said to test its young and to know and care for, as its own, only those chicks that can look with undaunted gaze at the sun's rays. Or we could allude to merchandise one receives. The buyers' habit is to push into the sunlight and carefully scrutinize the wares they have purchased. The upright in heart make it their habit to seek earnestly for as much light as is necessary and to pray with the psalmist, "Send forth your light and truth, that they may guide me" (Ps. 43:3). Even more, though the light may convict them, they nevertheless love it and gladly receive it. Abigail fulfilled for David the role of one who brings conviction. But the light that she brought to him was not so unwelcome that it kept him from saying, "Blessed is Jehovah who sent you, blessed be your counsel, and may

---

9. "The hidden things of shame."

10. Confess. l. 10. c. 23.] Augustine, *Confessionum*, 10.23.

11. Lactantius, *Divinarum Institutionum*, 7.1, p. 448.

you yourself be blessed who has restrained me" (1 Sam. 25:32–33). Let this noble expression found at the end of Stobaeus serve as our conclusion: "No one by praiseworthy actions conceals the darkness because he fears that the light may expose them. No, instead he hopes that the whole world is like the sun upon the deeds he openly commits."[12]

§3. Let us take continual self-consistency as the third characteristic quality of the truth. The two words *always* and *same* can be rightly ascribed to the truth as a marker. For highly skilled logicians agree that although sometimes a true conclusion can be derived from false premises, nevertheless, nothing except the truth can ever be concluded from true premises, taken properly. They sometimes articulate that point like this:

> From false comes false, yet sometimes true will follow plain and straight,
> From true can follow naught but true as logic will dictate.

And so integrity is always self-consistent. The Christian who is rich in sincerity looks to God and holds concourse with Him no matter where He is. Not only does the sincere Christian do so publicly or in the church but also at home in his private chambers. The same psalmist who said in a certain song of ascent, "I rejoice that they say to me, 'Let us go up to the house of Jehovah'" (Ps. 122:1), will proclaim elsewhere, "I shall unceasingly walk in uprightness of my heart within my own home" (Ps. 101:2). Lactantius wisely wrote, "If it is left behind in the temple, it is not true religion."[13] Martial once said, "He is not truly sad who is sad without a witness."[14] But I would like to change this a little bit and say, "He does not truly worship who worships without a witness." With others, righteousness generally may be, as the philosophers say about the colors of the rainbow, οὐ κατ' ἀλήθειαν ἀλλὰ κατ' ἔμφασιν.[15]

The fourth characteristic quality of the truth is assurance of victory. The truth is sometimes concealed but never conquered. I will use Tertullian's words: "Because it is not God, the truth can be darkened. It cannot be snuffed out because it is in God."[16] Although this statement occurs only in the Apocrypha, nevertheless, the idea that it conveys is sufficiently in

---

12. Serm. 6. n. 38. ὅλον ἅμα τὸν κόσμον ἥλιον γενέσθαι πρὸς ἃ κατορθοῖ βούλοιτ' ἄν.] John Stobaeus, fifth century, Greek compiler, *Keras amalthaias* (Zürich, 1559), p. 81 (*sermo* 8).

13. Lactantius, *Divinarum Institutionum*, 5.19, p. 353.

14. Martial, *Epigrammata*, 1.33, p. 26.

15. "Not aimed at truth but at appearance."

16. Tertullian, *De Anima Adversus Haereticos Et Philosophos*, in *Opera Quae Hactenus Reperiri*, vol. 3 (Cologne, 1617), ch. 91.

line with the canon: "The truth is great and will win the day."[17] That truth endowed with the name *integrity*, even though it may perhaps be over-whelmed in this or that battle, at last fully prevails in war. Also, when the flame of hypocrisy is extinguished through rebirth, there are often trouble-some embers remaining; but these are not deadly. Though King Asa was, at first, somewhat irked at the prophet who threatened him with catastrophe, and he so opposed the light (something totally wrong for a man of integrity to do) that he did not remove the high places from Israel, nevertheless, the Holy Spirit testified of him that "he was a man upright in heart and remained so all his days" (2 Chron. 16:10; 15:17). The words of the prophet, "In truth he will bring judgment" (Isa. 42:3), are translated in the Evan-gelist as "until he brings judgment to victory" (Matt. 12:20). Perhaps we should conclude from this revision that the truth of grace—that is, integ-rity (according to Fisher's translation)[18]—always ends in victory.

§4. Our argument must now extend to the question of why this truth is likened to a soldier's belt. Here is how I explain it. The belt functions not only as decoration, as mentioned before, and for profit. It is also useful as a defensive device by encircling that part of the body between the seams of the breastplate and the midriff. This part is very easily wounded. Because the ribs terminate there, the body has no natural defense. It is commonly thought that King Ahab died when an arrow struck him a lethal blow there (1 Kings 22:34). In a similar way, Paul's blamelessness of heart kept him safe from the shafts of the false apostles who attacked him on all sides with slander (one could have used Bernard's famous statement, "Words fly light but wound heavy").[19] The Corinthians, especially, shot at Paul. But the truth that Paul knew guarded him and made him quite bold. And so, in his letter to those very Corinthians, he declares, "This is my boast, the testimony of my con-science, that we have conducted ourselves in the world with God's sincerity and purity; not with fleshly wisdom, but with God's grace" (2 Cor. 1:12).

The force of immediate death overwhelmed Hezekiah. No missile could be more razor sharp than that! Nevertheless, when he remembered that integrity he had shown before in the course of his life, this became his comfort and protection. So he prayed, "Please, Lord, remember how I have walked before You in truth and an upright heart and the good I have done in your eyes" (Isa. 38:3).

---

17. First Esdras 4:41.

18. Johannes Piscator (Fischer), 1546–1625, Reformed exegete.

19. Bernard of Clairvaux, perhaps *Sermones [de tempore et de sanctis et de diversis]* (Mainz, 1475), *sermo* XVII.

The belt serves as a strong support over the other individual elements of armor. In particular, it holds the breastplate secure and supports the sword. For this reason, integrity must be considered absolutely essential for the healthy performance of all the duties of religion (1 Tim. 1:5). Our faith must be ἀνυπόκριτος [Rom. 12:9].[20] Μὴ ἀγαπῶμεν λόγῳ μηδὲ τῇ γλώσσῃ ἀλλὰ ἐν ἔργῳ καὶ ἀληθείᾳ (1 John 3:18).[21] Preaching is ὡς ἐξ εἰλικρινείας (2 Cor. 2:17);[22] prayer must not come from lying lips (Ps. 17:1).

Let me make a few comments about this. The truth of the heart is the grace of the Holy Spirit. This grace brings with it the rest of the gifts of salvation. Without grace, love itself would not be loved, faith itself would not be trusted, and no one would place hope in hope itself. What is more, wickedness is doubled wherever righteousness verges into craft and when the religion that glories in sincerity becomes a pretense. Let us take the famous Persian ambassador as an example. While he lived among Christians, he kept that very timeworn doxology, *Soli Deo Gloria*, on the tip of his tongue, almost in his spit, so that others would believe he shared their conviction concerning the Most High God. In the meantime, he would say to himself, at every turn, that he acknowledged and worshipped the sun as God. The story goes that when Epiphanius was about to leave Constantinople—where he had dragged out his stay too long—he said, "I leave behind me three great things: a massive city, a massive palace, and massive hypocrisy."[23] O city badly belted and bereft of holiness since it lacks truth!

§5. Finally, it was once the regular practice in national armies to wear a belt. In Homer, one's entire armor is denoted by ζώνη, and ζώννυσθαι means ὁπλίζεσθαι, as Eustathius[24] and the Suda attest. The Greeks also routinely say εὔζωνος[25] to indicate someone who is ready and set for a journey, a battle, or some other task. Even in the sacred literature, we find that this circumlocution *girdled with a belt* means *armed*, and to *put on a belt* means *to take up weapons*, while to *take off a belt* means *to have them stripped* (2 Kings 3:21). In Ahab's warning, we read, "The one who has put on armor must not boast like he who has taken it off" (2 Kings 3:21).[26]

---

20. "Without dissembling." A. gives the Greek with no Latin gloss.

21. "Beloved, let us not love with word nor tongue, but with deed and truth."

22. "From sincerity."

23. Perhaps Socrates, *Historia Ecclesiastica*, VI.

24. Perhaps Eustathius of Thessalonica, d. ca. 1193, archbishop of Thessalonica, *Eustathiou Archiepiskopou Thessalonikes Parekbolai Eis Ten Homerou Iliada Kai Odysseia* (Basil, 1560).

25. "To be equipped with a belt," "to be armed," and "well-belted," respectively.

26. First Kings 20:11.

In the Christian army, undoubtedly, the need for truth is far greater. For when the secular soldier is disarmed, he can still be, nevertheless, some kind of soldier at least. But no one who lacks integrity should truly be considered a Christian, even if he is very superior in the gifts of nature and in the gifts of grace, in addition, common to the elect and reprobate. Consequently, Paul's comment in this very famous passage is ὁσιότης τῆς ἀληθείας:[27] "If that is how you have been instructed, as the truth is in Jesus, to put on the new man that has been established according to God in righteousness and the holiness of truth" (Eph. 4:21, 24). This seems to more than hint at the notion that whenever truth is missing, holiness is entirely absent. If one pulls truth out of the center, then it is possible for the hypocrite to surpass true Christians by completing the same, external works of religion as they. And so far as appearance goes, they may do so with greater zeal. A veteran actor, after all, will sometimes seem more truly happy or sad than those who deeply, truly feel such emotions. Abraham, the father of the faithful, routinely made satisfaction for himself with a sacrifice on one altar and with one victim. But look at the hypocrite Balaam. In one go he built seven altars, and, upon these, he placed, one at a time, two flocks of different kind, offering to the Lord as a burnt offering a bullock and a ram (Num. 23:1–2). No, I will not fear to go even further. The Devil himself can pass himself off as a Christian and win praise among the careless. He feigns faith and reverence toward God. "The demons believe," the Apostle says, "and they tremble" (James 2:19). We will take it from the very best of witnesses that there was a spirit in the Pythian priestess who shouted, "These men are servants of the Most High God. They proclaim to you the way of salvation" (Acts 16:17). Look how this demon talks so persuasively. By his testimony, Paul and Silas are identified as servants of God, God Himself is identified as the Most High God, and the gospel is identified as the way of salvation. If anyone still wants more proof, see, in the Evangelist, the Devil bending his knee and praying with superb eloquence: "Jesus, Son of the most high God, I beg You not to torment me" (Luke 8:28).

§6. But there is no reason why we should wonder that the gorgeous face of truth is sought in vain among hell's denizens, no matter what disguises they take on. For here among the world's sojourners—I almost said the church's—it is exceedingly rare. "The truth stumbles in the streets," the prophet once said (Isa. 59:14). We also complain that it has fallen both in our homes and in our churches. In the state of human affairs, nothing ever happens without some idol and a vain image. The parhelion imitates

---

27. "True holiness."

the sun, falling stars imitate real ones, and counterfeit stones mimic pearls. Sophistry wears the mask of true doctrine, just as the hypocrisy that wanders all over wears a mask of righteousness. They say that Pachomius,[28] the most famous ancient abbot, presided over thirteen hundred monks.[29] He divided them into twenty-four groups according to the number of letters in the Greek alphabet. Then they who were in the individual groups were named by that same letter to designate their character as much as possible. So the more simple minded ones were named Iota, since that is the simplest possible letter, as it consists of one straight little line. But subtle monks, whose minds were complicated and, thus, not easily discerned or examined, were known as Zetas or Xis. These letters, you see, are twisted and contain numerous sharp curves that suitably express these men's character. If we should follow the same practice in making divisions among those who profess the Christian religion, then there is much reason to fear that very many of us well deserve a spot in these bent letters. Accordingly, dear reader, whoever you are—Christian, Englishman, academic—wake up! May these very titles stir you to pursue and practice the truth.

You are a *Christian*. You are bound by that title to pursue, with utmost diligence, whatever is most pleasing to God. Truth is foremost among these. We know this from David's expression: "I know, my God, that You test the heart and You love integrity" (1 Chron. 29:17). We know it as well from Christ's own testimony: "The time is coming and is now here when true worshipers shall worship the Father in spirit and in truth. For the Father seeks those who will worship Him" [John 4:23]. The heart of righteousness is integrity. If this is missing, then men's works are dead bodies, and God considers them dead, no matter how truly beautiful they seem to men. The Lord's comments to the Pharisees are pertinent here. He himself often branded them with this mark of hypocrisy: "You justify yourselves in men's sight. But God knows your hearts. That which men hold in high esteem is an abomination in the sight of God" (Luke 16:15).

You are an *Englishman*. You are, therefore, very affectionate toward your country as to a common parent. But if you want to give her good advice, the most advantageous path to travel is through training in the truth. For if any are hypocritical, "the nations are hypocrites." "They are a people of wrath and of burning fury."[30] The words of Jehovah in Isaiah concerning the king of Assyria are full of warning: "I will send him to a dishonest and hypocritical people, and against the people of my anger I will commit him. I will command him to take away spoil and to rob them of plunder; I will

---

28. Pachomius, ca. 290–346, early monastic and founder of coenobitic monasticism.
29. *Zozomen. l. 3. cap. 13.*] Sozomen, *Historiae Ecclesiasticae*, bk. 3, ch. 13, p. 279.
30. Perhaps an echo of Jer. 7:20.

place him there to trample them underfoot like the dust of the streets" (Isa. 10:6). Not so long ago, Louis XI, king of France, complained that his court, "although stuffed with all manner of good things, still lacked one—that is, the truth that no one was ready to declare to him."[31] Woe to our England (may God the Greatest and Best prevent this) if she ever becomes bereft of that truth that is my essay's subject—no matter how she excels neighboring lands in profusion of all other goods.

You are an *academic*. You have been educated in a place where everyone claims to be a devoted seeker of the truth. The Platonists regarded this as so valuable that very often they would say that from this conjunction—God's desire for the body-soul composite—there was absolutely no doubt that he took light as the body and truth as the soul. Now if all truth is precious, as indeed it is, then this also includes the truth that renders men dilettantes and regurgitators of the truth. Surely we should hold that that which makes men saved and blessed is judged of greatest value. The peerless statement of Mirandola that I mentioned above is worth repeating here: "Philosophers search for truth, theologians find it, believers possess it."[32] I do not care to ask too pointedly whom, precisely, he meant by "believers." I would gladly understand that he means those who share in authentic integrity, and from this, I would conclude that we are led by philosophy to search and hunt for truth, nothing more. We owe the acquisition of truth to theology that is drawn from the Word of God, but we cannot attain to possession of truth that conveys us to heaven except after the completion of a life lived sincerely in pursuit of true religion. The entrance to everlasting blessedness shall be revealed to Christians who possess this nature and quality and to them alone. Jerome translates a passage of the prophet Isaiah regarding this blessedness as though the words were Christ's to the angels and described unlocking heaven: "Open the gates, and let the righteous nation, guarding the truth, enter in" (Isa. 26:2).

---

31. *Richteri* Axiomat. politica p. 243. & *Camerer*. medit. histor. centur. 1. cap. 90.] Gregor Richter, 1560–1624, German Lutheran theologian, *Axiomata Historica Eaque Politica* (Goerlitz, 1599); Camerarius, *Meditationes Historicae*, vol. 1 ch. 90, p. 420. A. paraphrases.

32. See above, II.i.3.

CHAPTER IV

The Breastplate of Dispositional
and Actual Righteousness

Section 1: Righteousness is a kind of garment. This means not imputed but personal righteousness, as Matthew 5 also demonstrates, according to Scultetus. Section 2: Scriptural teaching on original righteousness, which dispositional righteousness replaces in the regenerate, as well as the positions of the Socinians, papists, and Remonstrants. Section 3: A refutation of the papists' slander that falsely states Luther and Calvin vacillated as to whether righteousness should be considered inherent and actual. Grotius is identified as guilty of the same slander. Section 4: The definition of actual righteousness. A defense of the Decalogue against Antinomians, as the rule of morality that also obliges the regenerate. Section 5: A reply to 1 Timothy 1:9, that the law has not been imposed upon the righteous man. Section 6: The gospel does not exempt one from pursuit of the holy living prescribed in the law but in many ways advances it. Section 7: The analogy of the breastplate to righteousness. Section 8: The imperfection of personal righteousness as well as its total inability, for that reason, to justify and save.

§ 1. Καὶ ἐνδυσάμενοι τὸν θώρακα τῆς δικαιοσύνης (Eph. 6:14).[1] These are the Apostle's next words and the ones to which we must now give our attention. People dress in everyday garments out of necessity. Military cloaks and robes of magistrates indicate office and rank, and weapons serve to protect the body. Righteousness is likened to all of these: "My soul exalts in my God, because He has clothed me in garments of salvation and has surrounded me with the vestment of righteousness. I have been clothed in righteousness, and I have wrapped myself in my judgment as with a cloak and diadem" (Isa. 61:10; Job 29:14). In another passage, Paul reminds us that "weapons of righteousness are on the right and left" (2 Cor. 6:7). Here he extols the breastplate of righteousness.

But whose righteousness? Is it personal? Imputed? Although one can distinguish between such terms until more suitable ones can be found, I

---

1. "And when you have put on the breastplate of righteousness."

will give my own answer to this question after describing Abraham Scultetus's erudite and helpful opinion on a related subject:

> I have often and with some strong irritation heard our preachers explain our Lord's words "Unless your righteousness surpasses that of the scribes and Pharisees, there is no way you will enter the kingdom of heaven." They then run off to an exposition of the righteousness of faith, as though our Savior here condemned legal righteousness and praised that of faith. But the whole thrust of this chapter's explanation of righteousness strongly opposes such an interpretation. Christ, at the very beginning of His discourse, urges His disciples to a life of gleaming purity. In the middle of His sermon, He does not invite us to faith but to faith's genuine works and to things commanded in the law. Therefore, a very abundant righteousness is not set against the righteousness of faith but against the righteousness of the law. And the righteousness of the law is set against the hypocrisy of the Pharisees. I pray that I escape that particular fault.[2]

Although I am the kind of man, if anyone is, who considers imputed righteousness very important as the sole refuge against the weightiest guilt that arises from our sins, nevertheless—if I am not mistaken—I take it that Paul is here dealing with personal righteousness. Because elsewhere he calls the breastplate of righteousness that he just mentioned the "breastplate of faith and love" (1 Thess. 5:8). The Scholastics label the whole of personal righteousness with these two terms, dispositional and inherent, meaning actual righteousness and righteousness of works, respectively, as a brief summary.

§2. Now, in my opinion, the nature of dispositional righteousness will shine forth more clearly if we briefly touch on a few points of righteousness. The sacred Scriptures plainly teach that God made man upright (Eccl. 7:19). Our theologians take this uprightness to mean not only removal of unrighteousness but also the ingrafting of righteousness and inward justice. For the Hebrew word יָשָׁר means not only *upright in every way* but also *righteous*, *good*, and *pure*. Accordingly, the translators of the Septuagint sometimes render it εὐθύς, sometimes δίκαιος, καλός, or καθαρός. Moreover, this word, in the Psalms, is even used to denote God's righteousness (Ps. 92:16), and in the Pentateuch, it refers to saints whom God has regenerated (Num. 29:10). Therefore, when the word is attached to Adam, it no doubt includes those virtues that flashed forth in our first parent as he was created in God's image, and in those that are described as being restored in the regenerate through a new creation. We ascribe this original righteousness to Adam, and we defend the notion that it was natural to him. By

---

2. Exerc. Evang. lib. 2. c. 19, p. 59.] Scultetus, *Exercitationes Evangelicae*, bk. 2, ch. 19, pp. 59–60. Scultetus does not provide the Bible verse but says only *versus vigesimi capitis 5. Matthaei.*

original righteousness, we understand not any particular virtue but a unified combination of all of them that made the appetite comply with the will, the will with right reason, and right reason with God in a most pleasing harmony. The Socinians, however, do not even acknowledge original righteousness. Schmaltz,[3] in his refutation of Franz's theses, says, "This wisdom and holiness that Franz as well as others attribute to Adam is a mere notion born in their brains. In the sacred Scriptures, there is not even one syllable about this."[4] That same author, while refuting a book by Smiglecki[5] entitled *New Monsters of Arminianism*, says, "It is an old and putrid fable that the first human being was adorned with holiness and supernatural gifts from the moment he was created."[6] They are not at all reluctant to grant Adam negative holiness, but they deny him a positive one. They hold that Adam was formed innocent and in no way wicked. Nevertheless, on their account, he was not made good and endowed with righteousness. The papists acknowledge the very same holiness, but they deny that it was natural in the first man. Rather, they say it was "superadded" to nature like a golden bridle (Bellarmine uses this metaphor) to restrain the rebellion of our affections. They give this "bridle" a place even in the upright original man and woman.

The Remonstrants consider our dispute with the Socinians highly inconsequential compared to the one we have with the followers of Rome, as they themselves acknowledge in their *Defense*. They say, "Remonstrants hold this whole line of inquiry to be ill-conceived and pointless."[7] And a bit later in that passsage, "They can keep purchasing such a worthless controversy for a really paltry sum." Now I would prefer to have their permission in this, but if not, I will say it, even though they are unwilling: this matter has been adjudicated far better by the leading theologian of the Augsburg Confession, Balthasar Meisner. In his discussion of this very topic, he said, "Unless this one point is decided properly, the foremost articles of our religion are most certainly vitiated. For this question is, so to speak, a two-way theological path, on which the gate of truth and falsehood lies open."[8]

Now that these preliminary concerns have been dispensed with, I claim that the original righteousness belonging to Adam and to all his posterity perished through the fall. But in the regenerate, through the grace of Christ, that same image according to which our first parents were formed

---

3. I.e., Smalcius.

4. Disp. 2. p. 44.] Smalcius, *Refutatio Thesium*, 2, pp. 44–45.

5. Marcin Smiglecki, 1562–1618, Polish Jesuit philosopher and theologian.

6. Pag. 215.] Smalcius, *Responsio Ad Librum Martini Smiglecii* (Rakow, 1613), ch. 24, p. 215.

7. Cap. 5. fol. 60.] Episcopius, *Apologia Pro Confessione* (1630), ch. 5, fol. 60v.

8. Sobriae philosophiae part. 2. sect. 1. quaest. 24.] Balthasar Meisner, 1587–1626, German Lutheran theologian, *Philosophia Sobria* ([Frankfurt], 1626), part 2, sec. 1, ch. 1, qu. 24, p. 194.

is restored. And so dispositional righteousness was substituted for original righteousness. Unless I am mistaken, this is why the great Davenant defines dispositional righteousness like this: "By inherent righteousness, we understand the supernatural gift of sanctifying grace that is opposed to original sin and that repairs and renews in the individual faculties of the soul that image of God that was polluted and demolished through original sin."[9]

§3. Even if our theologians embrace this meaning of dispositional righteousness wholeheartedly and acknowledge, with one voice, that justifying faith accompanies it in all that are mature, our opponents still accuse us of completely removing it from the faithful, as though we would remove the sun from the world! Let Christ—to whom hearts lie open—judge between us. Let His church pass judgment on the few points that seem to be here subjoined. Bellarmine himself does not scruple to gin up a tired old controversy with these words: "Calvin and the Lutherans grant that there is in us no inherent righteousness."[10] A certain freshly minted Jesuit followed suit: Silvester Petra Sancta.[11] When writing against Molina,[12] he said, with excessive confidence, that "Luther and Calvin have erased good works from the record book of eternal life, while they taught that faith alone suffices for salvation."[13] What Luther, gentlemen, what Calvin do you have in mind? Certainly, those whose writings we have exhausted held quite a different position. Let's listen to them, if you don't mind. "The proper place of both faith and works should be diligently taught and expounded. For if works alone are taught, as happens in the papacy, faith is lost. If only faith is taught, carnal men immediately begin to dream that works are unnecessary."[14] That's what Luther said. In another passage, he writes, "Through faith in Christ we are not set free from works but from our opinions about works, that is, from the foolish presumption of a righteousness attained through works."[15]

Now what about Calvin? "Man is justified by faith alone, and yet objective holiness is not separated from the gratuitous imputation of

---

9. Davenant, *De Iustitia Habituali*, in *Praelectiones De Duobus* (Cambridge, 1631), ch. 3, p. 212.

10. De justificat. l. 2. cap. 1.] Bellarmine, *De Iustificatione*, in *Disputationes De Controversiis*, vol. 4 (Ingolstadt, 1605), bk. 2, ch. 1. Vocabulary changed, sense retained.

11. Silvestro Pietrasanta (Silvester Petra Sancta), 1590–1647, Italian Jesuit priest and heraldist.

12. I.e., du Moulin.

13. Apud *Riveium* in Jesuit. vapulant. p. 186.] Rivet, *Iesuita Vapulans* (Leiden, 1635), p. 186.

14. In cap. 5. ad Galata.] Luther, *Commentarius In Epistolam Pauli Ad Galatas*, in *Omnium Operum*, vol. 4 (Jena, 1558), sub loc. Gal. 5:15.

15. Oper. Latin. tom. 1. fol. 472] Luther, *De Libertate Christiana*, in *Omnium Operum*, vol. 1 (Jena, 1556).

righteousness."[16] He says again, with great learning, "We are never reconciled to God without, at the same time, receiving the gift of inherent righteousness."[17] What reliable readers you are! Are these the words of men who openly deny inherent righteousness or rather of those who affirm it in the most absolute terms? Are they the words of those who erase or establish good works? Yes, our side does exclude good works from the act of justification itself. In this vein, Luther said, "Beware of sins, but be much more on your guard against good works."[18] Evidently, he said this because there is no danger that someone would base his justification on sins. But we should be quite afraid that someone, blinded perhaps by Pharisaical arrogance, would look for righteousness in his good works. But as regards salvation, our side recognizes that good works are necessary in the very sense that Zacharias Ursinus explained: "Good works are necessary for salvation not as cause to effect or merit to reward but as antecedent and consequent, or as the medium without which one does not reach the end."[19] Given that this is the case, I am really very surprised at Grotius's effrontery—a man abundantly familiar with the writings of our side—in ascribing to them a quite bizarre position. The mind truly reels to recall it. (Yes, no excrement stinks more than what flows from the pens of the learned.)

> You state that in all who are truly justified, repentance always follows. What is this repentance? Living as one pleases, and then saying to the minister, when death is imminent, "I renounce what I have done, and I believe that Christ's righteousness is imputed to me and that it is true because I believe it." With this farewell message, he immediately floats off to heaven. And to entertain doubt about this is the mark of hellish lack of belief.[20]

How I could wish that you had not said, or rather made up, such things, Hugo, you rare genius, since nothing is further from our practice and our thinking.

---

16. Instit. l. 3. c. 3.] Calvin, *Institutio Christianae Religionis* (Geneva, 1561), 3.3.1.

17. Lib. de vera religione reformand. Ecclesiae.] Calvin, *Tractatus Theologici Omnes* (Geneva, 1612).

18. The quotation attributed to Luther likely comes from an early fragment or edition of Luther's *Table Talk*, a translation of which the Westminster divines reviewed for publication but then declined to print. See Chad Van Dixhoorn, ed., *The Minutes and Papers of the Westminster Assembly* (Oxford: Oxford University Press, 2012), vol. 4, pp. 508–9, 512–15; vol. 5, p. 321 (doc. 120).

19. Catech. part. 3. qu. 91. artic. 3.] Ursinus, *Explicationum Catecheticarum* (Geneva, 1603), part 3, qu. 91, sec. 5, p. 577.

20. *Grotius* in voto pacis, pag. 115.] Grotius, *VotumPpro Pace Ecclesiastica* (1642), p. 115.

§4. We have somewhat unexpectedly fallen into pleading a defense—as you see, reader—not only of dispositional but also of actual righteousness. It rests for sure upon a well-established proposition. This proposition is consistent with the effort to assign to each person what belongs to them, first to God himself, then to everyone that is one's neighbor, according to the rule of that divine law we believe and profess binds even the regenerate. There are some people who think differently, and these are called Antinomians. We have two arguments that will suffice to refute them.

The first is taken from the nature of the law originally given to Adam, the root of the human race. This was given to him as a rational creature, then it was repeated through Moses and handed down to the Israelites under the same understanding. This is the difference between the three Mosaic laws.[21] The judicial law was given to the Hebrews as a body politic, the ceremonial law to them as the church, and the moral law to them as human beings. Therefore, the same law was delivered to all men and, therefore, to the regenerate just the same as to everyone else. They do not cease to be creatures when they become Christians. And so they are bound by the Decalogue, which contains a comprehensive repository of eternal and natural law just the same as others. Or rather, they are equally bound to it so far as it is a duty, although not so far as it is a punishment. The supervenient grace of Christ has abolished its terror for those who believe. So then, it still retains its authority to give them commands but not to condemn them. As a consequence, when John Hus said goodbye (as he himself remarks in a certain letter to the Bohemians) to hosts who had received him warmly, he would typically commend the Decalogue to them in place of his final farewell.[22]

The second argument is derived from a certain comment of the Apostle that is quite germane to this debate. Paul's letter to the Ephesians was written not to the unregenerate but to those who had been born again, as is clear in the introduction. "To the saints who are in Ephesus, and the faithful in Christ Jesus" (Eph. 1:1). Moreover, he addresses them like this: "Children, obey your parents in the Lord, for this is right. Honor your father and your mother (which is the first commandment with a promise), that it may go well with you and that you may live long in the land" (Eph. 6:1–3). Can the Antinomians explain why Paul uses these words? Why does the Apostle press upon the Ephesians the very words of the Decalogue to shape their morals if the moral law does not oblige as a rule even those who are reborn?

§5. But they counter that in another passage, the Apostle treats the law differently, saying that "the law is not imposed upon the righteous man"

---

21. A. does not say "types" but *inter tres leges Mosaicas*.

22. *Theobald. belli Hussitii.* p. 20.] Theobald, *Bellum Hussiticum*, ch. 11, p. 20.

(1 Tim. 1:9), δικαίῳ νόμος οὐ κεῖται.[23] In order to grace this prize-winning passage with a more complete answer, we must carefully weigh two points: the force of the negative particle and the significance of the word κεῖται. In the Scriptures, the word *not* sometimes negates absolutely and means *in no way whatsoever*, as in the command, "You shall not steal." Sometimes it has a restrictive force, or a type of limitation, and thus means *not with respect to this or that*. An example is when the Scripture says, "The one who is born of God does not sin" (1 John 3:9). This is not at all taken in an absolute sense, for otherwise, it would not be a true proposition, because the law was given to Adam in his original state when he was righteous—no, completely righteous. But it should be understood restrictively to indicate something in respect of which the law has not been put in place—that is, condemnation. Therefore, the meaning is that the law has not been placed over the righteous man in such a way that it condemns him, as he has been justified by faith in Christ and, through His Spirit, reborn to holiness of life.

This point is rendered more clear by the verb κεῖται, in which we can discern the weight of the curse that rests upon those who transgress the law. This is the meaning of the word, as when we read that "the axe lies at"— κεῖσθαι—"the root of the tree," obviously to cut it down (Matt. 3:10). Augustine somewhere remarks that "the law has not been imposed upon the righteous as a burden that crushes him with dread of punishment." This shows that the word κεῖται has a legal connotation and that κεῖσθαι refers to a case pending in a court against someone. And so Paul, here in this passage, plainly seems to intend the same meaning as in a passage in Galatians: κατὰ τῶν τοιούτων οὐκ ἔστιν νόμος[24] (Gal. 5:23). But this does not at all preclude the imposition of the law as a standard and rule for godliness.

§6. But if the Antimonians say that the obligation of the moral law— whatever, in the end, they take that to mean—has been removed from believers through the gospel, this releases them from the pursuit of that godliness, at least, that the law commands. In so doing, they will certainly argue in a way that not only prejudices actual righteousness but also disparages the gospel itself, even though there is no other more effective spur to moral holiness than the gospel! "Behave yourselves," the Apostle says, "in a manner that befits the gospel of Christ" (Phil. 1:27). He means, as much as possible, blamelessly. I am calling the very words of the gospel as my witness, and this comment especially: "Truth" is defined as "what is in accordance with righteous living" (Titus 1:1). I am citing examples, most of all our Lord Jesus Christ, "who did not sin, nor was any deceit found in His

---

23. "The law does not obligate the righteous man."
24. "Against such there is no law."

mouth" (1 Peter 2:21). And furthermore, some of the commands of Christ and the apostles (as one can note in the Lord's Sermon on the Mount and the Pauline epistles) are obviously the same as those that occur in the law. Finally, this applies to the promises as well. Of these, Paul says, "Because we have these promises, beloved, let us purify ourselves from all iniquity of flesh and spirit, persevering to the end with holiness in the fear of God" (2 Cor. 7:1). "If anyone teaches differently, consider him anathema" [Gal. 1:8]. Meanwhile, the good will guard themselves against those opinions that loosen the lock on extravagant living, or rather, throw open the gate to the worst kind of wickedness. I do not mean the opinions that arise from men who abuse the most important evangelical teachings, pulling them toward their own destruction, but the opinions that come from men who squander their own natural talent and perversely pamper themselves with a false rebirth and faith. So long as they preach against the Redeemer's benefits in a way quite different from what is proper, they completely throw off the Creator's yoke. Here is a good place for me to adduce Pico della Mirandola's celebrated warning in his second letter to his nephew:

> It is unquestionably a great disgrace to disbelieve the gospel, since the blood of the martyrs loudly proclaims its truth. The voices of the apostles echo with it, signs and wonders prove it, reason confirms it, the world testifies to it, the first principles of nature speak of it, the demons confess it. It is a far greater fault—if one does not doubt the truth of the gospel— nevertheless to *live* as if one did not doubt its falsehood.

A little later in the same passage, he says,

> But you, my son, strive to enter through the narrow door, and do not pay attention to what the majority does. You must do what the law of nature, reason, and God show you. For you will enjoy no less glory if you are happy with only a few people. And your punishment will be no lighter if you are miserable with the multitude.[25]

I will also add another example to make it a little more clear that morals become pure where the gospel is taken deep down into one's bones. They say that monstrous lust ruled over Geneva under the papacy and that, before the flag of the gospel was raised there, the children were often born with skin disease.[26] The proof of this is those isolated little hovels, which today we see in the common cemetery. People afflicted with leprosy from that era were cordoned off in these hovels. But from 1535, when that city embraced the purity of the gospel, it seems that only one man was afflicted

---

25. Pico della Mirandola, *Opera Quae Extant Omnia*, vol. 1 (Basel, 1601), p. 233 (*epistola* 1).
26. I.e., from sexually transmitted diseases.

with leprosy.[27] My source for this is what Matthieu Cottière wrote in his *Commentary on Revelation*, published at Sedan in 1625.[28]

§7. The next topic is the comparison between the breastplate and righteousness. A cuirass covers and protects the heart. This is why the Greeks called it καρδιοφύλαξ, though it actually reinforces the whole chest. Within its circumference are contained the remaining organs near the heart, which doctors call "vital." Likewise, God watches over His saints by His own righteousness, so that they are never slain by a lethal wound. This breastplate protects them most of all against the endless temptations that lead others to death. How few men would not succumb to sin if an aristocratic woman accosted them with the same solicitation Potiphar's wife used on Joseph long ago. And yet such a strong resolve, such a constant effort to render unto God that which was Potiphar's, protected him, so that after rejecting the shameless woman, he righteously declared to her, "Behold, my lord has entrusted to me everything that he owns and has not held back anything except you who are his wife. How could I commit this evil deed, a very great crime, and sin so against God?" (Gen. 39:8–9). Second, the breastplate of righteousness protects the saints against slanders and criticisms of other people, even though they bite very deeply. Job was treated in the worst possible way by his friends and was listed with hypocrites. He resisted their reviling with the breastplate of his own righteousness. "Far be it from me," he said, "to justify you. Until I die, I will not renounce my innocence. I cling to my righteousness. I will not abandon it. My soul will never reject it" [Job 27:5–6]. The derogatory remarks of men are powerless to inspire fear in those who know that God has accepted them and that they are counted as righteous. When Luther was condemned at Nuremberg by the leading men of the Roman Empire, he said, "This business was resolved one way in Nuremberg but another way in heaven."[29] Augustine, likewise, once said of Cyprian, after the proconsul had passed the sentence of death against him, "There was one throne on earth, but a second tribunal resided in the heavens. Cyprian received his sentence from the lower court, his crown from the higher one."[30]

Finally, the breastplate of righteousness protects the saints against the many little terrors of death itself, those that usually make others faint. I call Solomon in Proverbs as my witness: "The treasure houses of wickedness profit nothing, but righteousness will free you from death. The wicked man

---

27. This argument apparently means by *lepra* venereal disease.

28. Matthieu Cottière, 1619–1646, French Reformed pastor and writer, *Apocalypseos, Domini Nostri* (Saumur, 1615), ch. 11, p. 278. The 1625 date A. gives is an error: the Latin appeared in 1615 and the French in 1642.

29. *Melch. Adam.* in vita *Luth.*] Adam, *Vitae Germanorum Theologorum*, p. 123.

30. In Psalm. 36. conc. 3.] Augustine, *Psalmi Enarratio*, sub loc. Ps. 36:33 (3.13).

will be ruined in his own hatred, but the righteous finds hope even in his death" (Prov. 10:2; 14:32).

§ 8. These topics, however, require far less discussion than if the wisest king[31] had stated that personal righteousness is the cuirass against the guilt of sin and God's wrath, or if one could escape eternal death through the merit of personal righteousness, as the Jesuit Vasquez seems to have believed. When writing about inherent righteousness, he stated, "It of course makes one's soul righteous and holy and, thereby, a daughter of God. This is how one renders the soul an heir and deserving of eternal glory." He goes even further, saying, "God Himself cannot make a man righteous who does not deserve eternal happiness, even though He can, by His absolute power, cause him not to be blessed."[32]

Solomon somewhere comments on the imperfection of personal righteousness: "There is no righteous man on earth who does good and does not sin" (Eccl. 7:20). The apostle John tells us, "If we say we do not have sin, we deceive ourselves, and the truth is not in us" (1 John 1:8). Among the fathers, we also have Jerome: "This is the true wisdom of a man, to know that he is imperfect and, as I would say, that the perfection of all those in the flesh who are righteous is imperfect."[33] The imperfection of personal righteousness in pilgrims makes it so that there is no possible way anyone can be justified through it, not even Paul. This is his frank admission: "I am not aware of any guilt in myself, but this is not how I am made righteous" (1 Cor. 4:4). He also makes this prayer: "May I be found to be in Christ, not having a righteousness from the law" (Phil. 3:9). I will contrast with the novice Jesuit Vazquez, whose truly horrific words I have now quoted, the words of that veteran abbot, Bernard of Clairvaux. With far greater eloquence and much more soundness, he said of this, "If we have any righteousness, it is lowly. It is perhaps proper, but it is not pure. For how could our righteousness be pure when it cannot yet even be free from guilt?"[34]

I am now ready, as I put the finishing touch on this portion, to consider the connection between the belt of truth and the breastplate of righteousness—which occurs in the same sentence. I hope that as I deal with this linkage, it will offer my mind a sufficiently clear argument—and likewise, as I write. And I hope the reader will find the effort not entirely useless.

---

31. I.e., Solomon.

32. *Vasquez.* in 1ᵃᵐ 2ᵃᵉ Disp. 204. cap. 4.] Gabriel Vázquez, 1549–1604, Spanish Jesuit theologian, *Commentariorum Ac Disputationum* (Ingolstadt, 1609), bk. 2, p. 564ff.

33. Advers. *Pelagium* lib. 1. c. 5.] Jerome, *In Dialogos Adversus Pelagianos*, in *Opera Divi Hieronymi Stridoniensis*, vol. 2 (Antwerp, 1579), bk. 1, ch. 5.

34. De verbis Isa. Serm. 5.] Bernard of Clairvaux, *De Verbis Esaiae Prophetae*, in *Opera Omnia*, vol. 2 (Cologne, 1641), sec. 9 (*sermo* 5).

CHAPTER V

The Connection between Truth and Righteousness

Section 1: The complementary character of truth and righteousness. The transition from vices to errors and from errors to vices. Section 2: A comparison between the Remonstrants and their opponents regarding righteous living. Sections 3–5: Praises for Augustine, Gottschalk, Calvin, Whitaker, Perkins, Ames, and Rivet. Section 6: The flawed dogmas of the Remonstrants concerning unrighteousness toward God. The sayings of Augustine and Prosper are contrasted with the assertions of Grevinckhoven, Plaifere, and John Goodwin. Section 7: In everything we must render glory to God and yield to His absolute dominion. Theodore Cornhert's retraction.

§ 1. There is no need to describe how strong a connection exists between personal righteousness and the truth used for integrity, because truth is the very core of personal righteousness. Now that we have dispensed with that, we will consider only the connection between orthodoxy and righteousness. Righteousness and truth are equal as regards their nobility, and from their union issues forth a blessed road. Following this road, we eventually gain our homeland through vision, the pinnacle of truth, and through delight, the marrow of righteousness. Now truth is the likeness of light; righteousness, that of a heavenly ardor. The ornament of truth is righteousness, and the reward of righteousness is truth. Truth is constructed through righteousness; righteousness is instructed through truth.[1] When righteousness collapses, truth is further jeopardized. When truth is wounded, righteousness is generally damaged. They are like the stomach and the brain in the human body. The brain's sickness flows down into the stomach, while, from a healthy stomach, steam rises into the brain. So when righteousness is not satisfied, the transition to unsound dogmas is simple. One can see this in the Gnostics, who, after they had defiled themselves with shameful embraces, taught that their own sexual practice, which was actually quite

---

1. *Astruitur* and *instruitur*, respectively.

disgusting, was a μυστικὴν κοινωνίαν (mystical communion), as Clement of Alexandria explains.[2] What an awful thing to teach! But when one starts peddling dogmas that are just a little compromised, a very easy path to the most heinous morals is immediately opened. John Islebius,[3] the father of the Antinomians, in his advanced old age, reportedly became more like an Epicurean, according to Osiander, than a pious theologian.[4]

§ 2. Discounting the most prominent sects for the moment, I will test the Remonstrants and their dogmas against this Lydian stone, so to speak. And I will do this all the more gladly because, among the other paradoxes swarming in that arm's-length volume, this claim really irked me and—I won't deny it—provoked my anger. I am referring to the volume in which a learned and eloquent man[5]—but one of inferior judgment—embroidered and decorated a garment[6] of cheap and worthless fabric. He wrote,

> In the writings of those who constitute the Counterremonstrants, in that five-article controversy that has recently set all the Netherlands on fire and which now spreads through England, I deeply miss the spirit and heat of the vibrant piety one usually sensed in others' books. I mean they who side with indefinite election, universal redemption, a will that is free to spiritual good, moral suasion, and the final apostasy of the saints.[7]

So sweet things become bitter to a palate once poisoned, and those struggling with a little girl's sickness find nothing more tasty than chalk or coal. I am intending to stitch together a kind of defense that, although late, is nevertheless genuine. I don't want others to think that those who have, with clear vigor and holiness, defended God's particular grace, each man in his own generation, have no defender. For whoever has judiciously compared Pelagius with Augustine, Hincmar[8] with Gottschalk,[9] Castellio with Calvin, Baron[10] with Whitaker, Arminius with Perkins,[11] Grevinckhoven[12]

---

2. Stromat. l. 2. 100.] Clement of Alexandria, *Stromatum*, bk. 3, p. 416.

3. Johann Agricola (John Islebius), ca. 1492/1494–1566, German Lutheran theologian.

4. Centur. 16. p. 802.] Probably Lucas Osiander, *Epitomes Historiae Ecclesiasticae Centuriae Decimae Sextae.*

5. John Goodwin, ca. 1594–1665, Independent minister.

6. I.e., Theophylact of Nicomedia, d. 845, Byzantine bishop and writer, who wrote a work entitled ἀπολύτρωσις, a title similar to John Goodwin's 1651 work Ἀπολύτρωσις ἀπολυτρώσεως (*Redemption Redeemed*), which A. is quoting.

7. I. G. Ἀπολύτρωσις. cap. 9. § 24.] Goodwin, *Redemption Redeemed* (London, 1651), ch. 9 sect. 24.

8. Hincmar, ca. 806–882, archbishop of Reims.

9. Gottschalk, ca. 804–ca. 869, German monk and theologian.

10. Petrus Baro (Peter Baron), 1534–1599, Reformed minister and religious controversialist.

11. William Perkins, 1558–1602, theologian and Church of England clergyman.

12. Nicolaas Grevinckoven, 1568–1632, Dutch Remonstrant theologian.

with Ames, and—so that I, perhaps, don't go on too long—Grotius with Rivet—yes—if, after this, he has the same opinion as that upstart writer whom I praised,[13] I think that man was either indulging his feelings, mislead by party spirit, or starstruck ἀμετρίᾳ τῆς ἀνθολκῆς.[14] Now I do not want to censure those who have taken the opposite position, so as not to seem to rage against dead men's ashes. Still, nobody would bat an eye if I, called forth from our ranks, plead my case with a little more excellence but also, perhaps, at greater length.

§3. Let us begin with Augustine. While reviewing the errors of his life in the *Confessions* and confessing errors of judgment in his *Revisions*, he disarms man in both works. He speaks about grace like one who had felt its power; of sin, like one who hated it; of heresies, like one who had learned to despise them utterly. This golden—or, I should say, jewel-encrusted—sentence shows just how much he valued God and how little he valued the world: "Whether the world is happy or the world is ruined, I will bless the Lord who made the world."[15] In some books, he fills the role of the pastor; in others, that of a learned teacher. In some, he is an orator; in others, a combatant. In his letters, we see all these on display. Whoever reads through one famous volume and passes over all the rest (although nothing of all he wrote deserves to be ignored) will observe there the whole Augustine: a theologian and, at the same time, a Christian through and through. Let Gottschalk stand in for Augustine, both as a servant marked by that saint's name and, in fact, a servant of God. Gottschalk was a vehement advocate of the same dogmas. As a consequence, when Hincmar presided as the archbishop of Reims, Gottschalk underwent three punishments.[16] The first was deposition from office. This was a precaution to make sure that Gottschalk was heard only privately in his priestly office and not more broadly by the people. The second punishment was whipping. The man's body was torn by forty lashes until he relented and threw into the fire with his own hands, when he was almost dead, statements he had gathered from the Scriptures and from the fathers as the basis for his case. And the third punishment was imprisonment. The most distinguished authorities say he endured this for the rest of his life, more than twenty years, at the determination of

---

13. Said ironically of Goodwin.

14. "By boundless obstinacy."

15. Augustine, *Sermons on the New-Testament Lessons*, in NPNF 1, ed. Philip Schaff, vol. 6 (1888; rev. ed., Peabody, Mass.: Hendrickson, 1999), p. 433 (sermon 55).

16. *Mauguin.* historicae & Chronicae Dissert. c. 9.] Gilbert Mauguin, d. 1674, *Vindiciarum Praedestinationis Et Gratiae, Tomus Posterior, Continens Historicam & Chronicam Synopsim*, vol. 2 (Paris, 1650), ch. 9, [ii] pp. 82–86.

the French king's[17] counselors. These authorities, James of Armagh[18] and Gilbert Mauguin, worked very hard to piece together Gottschalk's history.

Now, let the Dutch Remonstrants also trout out their supporters' exiles and incarcerations to defend their crumbling cause. Is there anyone of their followers of whom they will immediately say—when compared with Gottschalk—"We call him mini-Atlas"?[19] Meanwhile, that man's amazing faith, humility, and steadfastness shone forth under the cross. One can clearly see all of these in his two *Confessions,* which were just recently published. Before that cross of suffering, Gottschalk's goodness was just as evident. That is why Walafrid Strabo greeted him on his return from Italy with a kind of celebratory poem. In it he testified that the man's life was more upright than the law of Lycurgus. Only one thing was lacking: because he was so buried in his studies, he did not grow as close to his friends as he should have. Thus Strabo:

> There is one thing I must lament with somewhat greater grief:
> That though the life you live is better spent than Spartan law
> Commands, yet still you sit on all your mortal gold stacked up
> there all alone.[20]

§ 4. Right next to Gottschalk is Calvin, a truly amazing man, and one (as his epitaph states) "from whom virtue herself could virtue learn." Salmasius[21] said that he would prefer "to be the author of just one book of *The Institutes of the Christian Religion* that Calvin published than to have written everything Grotius ever released."[22] This is, for sure, an adequate expression of praise. But Calvin's *Instruction in the Christian Life*[23] has certainly yielded him far greater honor both with the church as well as with God. While the Romanists bark at this work and have changed the name *Calvinus* into *Lucianus*[24] by a most spiteful anagram, still they unwittingly make our case.

---

17. Lothar II, ca. 835–869, r. 855–869.

18. I.e., James Ussher.

19. Id. ibid. c. 1. p. 47. & *Armachan.* history. *Gotteschal.* p. 39.] Mauguin, *Vindiciarum Praedestinationis*, vol. 2, ch. 1, p. 47; Ussher, *Gotteschalci, Et Praedestinatianae Controversiae Ab Eo Motae, Historia* (Dublin, 1631), ch. 4, pp. 38–40.

20. Walafrid Strabo, ca. 808–849, German poet and biblical exegete. A. is probably quoting this work from either Mauguin, *Vindiciarum Praedestinationis*, or Ussher, *Gotteschalci, Et Praedestinatianae Controversiae.*

21. Claude Saumaise (Claudius Salmasius), 1588–1653, French classical scholar and theologian.

22. *Alex. Morus* in Oratione cui titulus est *Calvinus.* p. 11.] Alexander More (Morus), 1616–1670, Reformed church minister and writer, *Alexandri Mori Calvinus* (Geneva, 1648), p. 14.

23. Calvin, *Institutio Christianae Religionis*, 3.7–10. This portion is often called the "Golden Booklet of the Christian Life."

24. Lucian of Samosata (Lucian), ca. 120–ca. 180, Greek satirist.

For this distinguished man of God, and he alone, shared this in common with Lucian, that both were wounded by dogs, though in different ways. If only Calvin had as many imitators as he has detractors! Where in the world shall we find someone that deserves to be compared with Calvin, even if we only consider his most casual writings? "Everyone knows how very much he wrote. Each year he preached 286 sermons and delivered 186 public lectures, and this was in addition to his other countless duties."[25]

These are William Whitaker's words, himself a very valuable man and lauded with countless praises! In fact, even Bellarmine thought it just for us to be bothered at least a little. Because, when he thought of Whitaker, he several times said, "I am jealous of England for having Whitaker. Yes, he is my opponent, but he is knowledgeable and humble."[26] I could say more, that he was downright brilliant in the face of envy and lived as a holy example. May you enjoy your rewards, O blessed spirit, and gladly drink the glory you once merely tasted. Meanwhile, we here in Cambridge will be gripped again and again by our longing for your dear presence and will commit to our distant posterity the memory of your great name.

§5. And what of Perkins? The Reverend Montagu supposedly burst out in these words while delivering the funeral sermon held at Perkins's grave-side: "Here lies the man who taught the English to worship God."[27] Just as Socrates drew philosophy from the clouds down to earth, so, in our day, Perkins was almost the first to have brought theology, which very many men had enveloped in the mists of their speculations, back to praxis. It was once said of Petronius's *Satyricon*, "Take away the naughty parts and you take away all of it." But I am not afraid to state unequivocally about Perkins's books, "Take away the sacred portions and you take away all of it." Really all of them, however many there are, have almost the exact same taste as the very marrow of piety.

Ames should come next after Perkins as a student and acolyte. His strengths were so evident to all good men, even those with significant experience, that Maccovius[28] himself reportedly announced before his listeners during lecture and debate that "if [his] opinion stands with that of the most reverend Ames" then it is with a most pious judge or opponent. Maccovius had nursed some grudge against Ames, while he lived, because of their

---

25. *Whitak.* Controvers. 2. q. 5. quae est de notis Ecclesiae cap 15. p. mihi 536.] Whitaker, *In Quibus Tractatur Controversia De Ecclesia*, in *Opera Theologica*, vol. 1 (Geneva, 1610), cont. 2, qu. 5, ch. 15, p. 536.

26. Bellarmine reportedly hung a picture of Whitaker above his desk. C. S. Knighton, "William Whitaker, 1547/8–1595," *ODNB*.

27. James Montagu, (1568–1618), bishop of Winchester.

28. Jan Makowski (Johannes Maccovius), 1588–1644, Polish Reformed theologian.

differences of opinion on several key points of theology. Nevertheless, after Ames died, Maccovius made that statement quite often.

André Rivet should now close off the column. In a letter he wrote to his brother William, in 1650, on the topic of good old age, when he himself was 79, he quoted the psalmist's prayer. "God, You have taught me from my childhood, and I have pointed to Your wondrous deeds down to this day. Now then, since I am also so old and gray, do not abandon me, God, until I reveal Your arm to this generation and Your strength to every generation yet to come" (Ps. 71:17–18). Rivet then adds,

> I myself, dear brother, for many years now repeat this prayer each and every day, and often hour by hour. I feel that these same things apply to me, for God has taught me from my childhood. By preaching the Word of God to the generation in which I have lived, I have shown forth God's arm. I have also tried, by my writings—and by God's grace, that was not completely in vain—to declare to the coming generation His truth and might.[29]

The *Death-bed Proverbs* of this man (disregarding other writings) give abundant proof of how completely steeped he was in the aroma of holy living and the full assurance of faith. As men typically say that the sunlight is more pleasant at the very moment that it sets, so our friend Rivet sent forth the sweetest rays when he drew closest to death. He said,

> You press me round, O my God, but my soul dwells in a wide space. Blessed be the Lord, who already has caused me to enjoy gladness and peace. It has been two days since I lived any longer a living life, but now I am living the life of the blessed and of those who dwell above. I am longing for the hour when He will say to me, "Come, good and faithful servant; enter into the glory of your Lord." God dwells in me and I in Him. I wait, I believe, I endure, I cannot be moved. The Spirit of God testifies to my spirit that I am one of His sons. O inexpressible love![30]

These are the kind of statements that Arminian scholars think are impenetrable mysteries, if not monstrosities.[31]

§6. I now proceed to their dogmas. When these have been reduced to a brief summary, you will find they reflect very poorly on a God who grants righteousness its due. Because there are two, so to speak, hinges on which all theology turns—God's glory and His grace—it is a very

---

29. Rivet, *Epistola Ad Reverendum Virum* (Breda, 1650), p. 22.

30. Rivet, *Operum theologicorum… Tomus Tertius* (Rotterdam, 1660), under *Oratio Funebris Iohannis Henrici Dauberi*, fol. 11v.

31. I.e., because they question or deny the perseverance of the saints.

serious business that the Arminians make God's grace dependent on human judgment so that they can openly profane His glory. These words of Nicolaas Grevinckhoven are well known everywhere, but not—sad to say—everywhere discredited: "I set myself apart, and for that, why am I not allowed to boast about myself? That I accomplished this is due to God's showing me mercy; but what I willed rests on my own authority."[32] Molina replied to these words quite clearly: "The mark of a truly generous man is not to want to owe God too much nor to wish to be buried under His kindnesses."[33] Among our countrymen, a fellow named John Plaifere was seized with the same insanity in an English book, released after his death, entitled *I Appeal to the Gospel*:[34]

> As pertains to the question, When two men are equally called, of whom one is converted and the other not, who is it that decides, God or man? I answer that man makes a decision, not God. But Augustine made this statement hateful to pious ears by twisting the Apostle's well-known passage, "Who chose you?" (1 Cor. 4:7). But in another passage, faith, love, and things of that sort are mediated gifts that proceed from God's grace but also from human will. And insofar as they proceed from the will, they leave to man himself some authority to choose and also some (though very little) grounds for boasting.

These are Plaifere's comments.[35]

A more contemporary writer, whom I mentioned in the second paragraph of this chapter, spoke with more restraint while aiming at the same target: "A man thinks it well done if he holds that 999 out of 1,000 parts of the business of conversion and perseverance must be credited to grace, while only one remains to grant to free will."[36]

But how much better is Augustine. "We live more securely if we give the whole to God, not entrusting ourselves to Him only partly."[37] How much more wisely and truly did Prosper say, "It is not true devotion to surrender

---

32. Nicolaas Grevinckhoven, 1568–1632, Dutch Remonstrant theologian, *Dissertatio Theologica* (Rotterdam, 1615), p. 253.

33. Enodat. quaest. p. 185.] Du Moulin, *De Libero Arbitrio*, in *Enodatio* (Leiden, 1632), tract. 6, ch. 1, p. 185.

34. *Appello Evangelium*.

35. John Plaifere, d. 1608/1632?, English Arminian theologian, *Appello Evangelium* (London, 1651), pp. 258–59.

36. *I G.* in praefat. ad Ἀπολύτρωσις.] Goodwin, *Apolytrosis apolytroseos* (London, 1651), sig. c2v (preface).

37. Augustine, *De Praedestinatione Sanctorum*, in *Omnium Operum*, vol. 7 (Basel, 1528), 2.6.12.

almost everything to God. No, it is theft to keep back even a little." And again, "The whole grace of God is rejected unless it is wholly received."[38]

What about our friend Paul? "I have worked," he said, "more than all of them. Yet not I, but God's grace that is with me" (1 Cor. 15:10). This is a vehement advocate for grace; he never fails to rebuff arrogance. "What do you have that you did not receive?" (1 Cor. 4:7). Be on your guard against pride, no matter who you are. Be on your guard not to sacrifice to your own net.[39] That is not how Peter acted. After he caught that great multitude of fish, although they were caught from his own boat, in his own fishing net, through his own labor, he claims nothing for himself but falls at Christ's feet to worship [Luke 5]. Pay attention, dear reader, to this short parable. A crown that had rested on the head of a certain king by chance fell from the boat into the river. One of the rowers jumped into the deep and got hold of the tiara. But he could not easily carry it in his hands while swimming, so he placed it on his own head. The king gave him a gold coin for recovering the item. But he also sentenced him to execution, because he had worn the crown. The glory for a deed done well is God's own crown, but sometimes, because of a man's carelessness,

> Although it fell not off, to fall indeed it might have seemed.[40]

Christians, generally, and ministers, in particular, must take pains to keep God's glory safe at all times. But if we are not afraid to place upon our own heads this recovered glory, perhaps we will meet with temporary rewards and yet pay an eternal penalty.

§7. I will now quickly wrap up the rest of this particular point. I am not at all hesitant to prosecute the Remonstrants as guilty of unrighteousness and plunder. This is why: they do not want to acknowledge the absolute dominion and αὐτοκρατορική[41] authority of God either to elect or pass over His creatures at His own will (which is the chief privilege of divinity). May God impart to them a more sound understanding, as supposedly was given to Theodore Cornhert of Amsterdam.[42] He had written, with gross calumny, against the doctrine of Calvin, Beza, and Daneau on God's secret predestination. But when he was near death, the Holy Spirit taught him better, they say, and he shouted out to the Lord, "I possess my soul from

---

38. In epistola ad *Demetriadem*.] For the first quotation, Prosper of Aquitaine, *De Gratia Dei*, in *Opera* (Cologne, 1630), ch. 44, p. 412.

39. I.e., worship something that is merely a tool.

40. Ovid, *Metamorphoseon*, in *Opera Omnia*, vol. 2 (Amsterdam, 1611), bk. 2, p. 27.

41. "Imperial."

42. Dirck Volckertszoon Coornhert (Theodore Cornhert), 1522–1590, Dutch Protestant theologian.

You! It is God's choice, according to His good pleasure, whether He wishes to save or to reprobate it. I have nothing to complain about."[43] They say that moles finally open the eyes, blind until then, just one time before they die. I would not begrudge the Remonstrants eagle-eyed vision! Maybe then they could very quickly, with greatest accuracy, discern what are the particular conditions that make for ecclesiastical peace! I pray, with all my heart, that they might have the moles' special gift, at least, that death may find the Remonstrants are Counterremonstrants.

---

43. Hoornbeck summa controvers. p. 435.] Hoornbeeck, *Summa Controversiarum Religionis*, bk. 6, p. 435. A. adds *vellet*.

CHAPTER VI

The Greaves of Evangelical Readiness

Section 1: The use of military greaves. Greaves are compared to acting and suffering, which make their ἑτοιμασία[1] twofold. Section 2: What Christian acting is and how it is fitting. An argument against the εὐτραπελία[2] that Paul disapproves of, though it is still practiced in the academies. Section 3: The usefulness of "abounding in the work of the Lord" [1 Cor. 15:58]. Melanchthon's prayer, Latimer's story. Sections 4–5: How Christians, especially ministers, must suffer. Section 6: The gospel's influence in creating patience. The examples of Luther, Elzear, and Bernard. Section 7: Some ψευδώνυμα[3] gospels. Why the gospel is called a "gospel of peace." Section 8: An exhortation to harmony. The συζυγία[4] of peace and truth. Section 9: Six adages on the issue of whether Christians who profess the gospel may wage war.

§1. Passing over to the third element of armor, we must note especially the way greaves were used by ancient soldiers. Goliath reportedly wore iron leggings above his feet (1 Sam. 17:6). In Homer, the Greeks are called ἐϋκνήμιδες and the χαλκοκνήμιδες Ἀχαιοί.[5] Vegetius reminds us that infantry wear iron greaves.[6] The Romans reportedly used military footwear called *caligae*, from which one of the Roman emperors took his name, Caligula.[7] This is because he was raised in the army and so wore his shoes army-style instead of how it was done in the city. The Suda translates *caligas* as στρατιωτικὰ ὑποδήματα.[8] There is no doubt this is the equipment to

---

1. "Preparedness."
2. "Coarse joking."
3. "Falsely named."
4. "Yoking."
5. "Lovely legged" and "bronze-greaved Achaeans."
6. Lib. 1. c. 20.] Vegetius, *De Re Militari*, bk. 1, ch. 20, pp. 24–25.
7. *Dio.*] Dio Cassius, *Historiae Romanae*, bk. 57.5.6. Gaius Julius Caligula (affectionately known as "little boots" when he was a boy), 12–41, r. 37–41, Roman emperor.
8. "Military sandals." A. gives the Greek with no Latin gloss.

which the Apostle refers in the next verse that I must now address: Καὶ ὑποδησάμενοι τοὺς πόδας ἐν ἑτοιμασίᾳ τοῦ εὐαγγελίου τῆς εἰρήνης (Eph. 6:15).[9]

When we compare Christian virtues to military greaves, the two common elements we find are *acting* and *suffering*. The second one prepares men's hearts for enduring evils, while the first makes them ready to perform all manner of good. He who has carefully weighed another saying in Holy Writ will easily believe that both of these virtues are described by the word ἑτοιμασία[10]—namely, πρὸς πᾶν ἔργον ἀγαθὸν ἑτοίμους εἶναι (Titus 3:1).[11] There is also Peter's statement in Luke, "Lord, I am prepared to go"—ἕτοιμός εἰμι—"with You even to prison and death" (Luke 22:33). And Paul's in Acts: "I am ready"—ἑτοίμως ἔχω—"not only to be chained but also to die in Jerusalem for the name of the Lord Jesus" (Acts 21:13). So both of these deserve to be called *gospel readiness*, since through the gospel, Christians are stirred up deep in the heart to the exercise of both. May I succeed, with Christ leading me, in making all these ideas shine more brilliantly in the little essay that follows.

§2. Men whose feet are equipped with good shoes usually tread where the barefooted dare not venture. I mean along rough and uneven roads, through stones and thornbushes, amid places bristling with sharp spines and wild briar. So each day those who partake of *Christian activity* embark on the κατορθώματα[12] that the lazy cannot even touch. Plautus mentions the "shod teeth" of some parasite that made it easier for him to eat.[13] Paul ascribes to Christians "shod minds," indicating that they are most prepared for all manner of good works. Yes, there is nothing for Christians more appropriate or more useful.

We serve a God who is pure act. It is, consequently, fitting that we likewise work up a sweat with pure action. We worship Christ, and with utmost accuracy I borrow this saying of the poet to describe Him: "Many things he endured and many he accomplished,"[14] to become our example not only of enduring much but also of accomplishing much. Christians should be active and, so far as possible, earnestly so. But to make foolish jokes is quite unbecoming, especially for ministers and academics. It is hard to know how this may frighten others' minds, but to me, Bernard's comment to Eugene[15]

---

9. "And with your feet shod in the readiness of the gospel of peace."
10. "Readiness."
11. "Command them to be ready for every good work."
12. "Straight paths."
13. *Plaut.* in captivis.] Plautus, *Captivi*, in *Opera* (Geneva, 1605), p. 169 (1.187).
14. Horace, *De Arte Poetica*, 1.413.
15. Eugenius III, d. 1153, *p.* 1145–1153.

is like thunder: "Jokes among those without holy orders are just jokes. But in the mouth of a priest, they are blasphemy. You have consecrated your mouth to the gospel. You are forbidden now to open it for such purposes, and it is sacrilegious to make it a habit. It is a disgrace when you are provoked to laughter and more disgraceful when you cause it."[16]

Chrysostom's comment is similar: φοβήθητι μή σου γελῶντος ὁ Δεσπότης ὀργίζηται, ὁ τοὺς μὲν κλαίοντας μακαρίσας, τοὺς δὲ γελῶντας ταλανίσας, "Be careful that while you laugh, the Lord does not become angry."[17] I myself am quite wary that, as we have fallen in love with the Aristotelian notion of wit, we may founder against the Pauline definition (I mean the kind of wit Paul forbids). In so doing, we might surrender to the heathen the most illustrious academies (whenever laughter is indulged beyond what is appropriate) as objects of ridicule. The Athenians firmly decreed that "no one was allowed to laugh freely in the Academy, because they tried to protect that place against harm and keep it free from and impervious to degeneracy of the mind." So says Aelian.[18] He who censures sarcasm must be free of it himself. Pineda wisely said of those eager to write without self-control that it was "itching-pen disease more than writing."[19] Likewise, among our men, this wit (I will say it plainly) is more lust for them than charm for us. Or if it is delightful, it should be counted among the comments that Claudian makes, that "from the center of the fountain of delights, something bitter arises."[20] And indeed, that bitterness will rise up if ever (heaven forbid) disrespect goes so far that nobody is thought to have acted like a "son of the soil"[21] unless he shows that he is "a son of hell," and when only the wickedest biped is considered the noblest oracular tripod!

§ 3. One can deduce from a certain Pauline exhortation precisely how this *activity* that we preach will be helpful. "Be steadfast, unmovable, always abounding in the work of the Lord, knowing that your labor will not be in vain in the Lord" (1 Cor. 15:58). Very many men want to abound—but

---

16. De Consider. lib. 2. prope finem.] Bernard of Clairvaux, *De Consideratione*, in *Opera Omnia*, vol. 4 (Cologne, 1641), bk. 2, ch. 13.

17. Tom. oper. 6. serm 66. cui titulus] ὅτι οὐ χρὴ εὐτραπελίζειν τὸν ἀσκήτην] Chrysostom: "That the ascetic must not tell jokes."

18. Ἐν Ἀκαδεμίᾳ μηδὲ γελάσαι ἐξεουσίαν εἶναι, &c. *Aelian.* Variar. lib. 3. cap. 35.] Aelian, *Variae Historiae Libri XIIII* (Paris, 1583).

19. Probably Juan Pérez de Pineda, ca. 1500–1568, Spanish Protestant Reformer; perhaps Alonso de Pineda, fl. ca. 1560–1564, Spanish Jesuit and philosopher.

20. Titus Lucretius Carus (Lucretius), ca. 95–52 BC, Roman poet, quoted in Claudian, *Animadversiones In Epigrammata*, in *Quae Exstant*, ed. Kaspar von Barth (Frankfurt, 1650), p. 983. The line quoted is from Lucretius's *De Rerum Natura*, 4.1133–34.

21. *Terrae filium*, the official university jester.

more in leisure than work. So we should say that they are more filling time than living life and that they want to exist for a long time, not really to live.[22] They must understand, no matter how many of them there are, that in our religion, Christian sloth is a monstrosity. I also want them to remember that Satan finds work for those he finds unemployed. Instead, I should say that although the Devil tempts other men, he himself is tempted by the lazy. But really there are countless people who want to abound in wealth, few who want to abound in well doing.[23] This makes Melanchthon's prayer all the more heroic. Chytraeus relates that he had been greatly delighted by a certain expression of Achilles, which is found in Philostratus. It goes like this: Ἐμὸν ἔσω τὸ πλεῖον τῶν ἔργων, χρήμασι δὲ πλεονεκτείτω ὁ βουλόμενος, "Give me the work, and whoever wants to can have the credit."[24]

It is not sufficient, however, to abound in just any kind of work, since acting wickedly profits nothing. This is why the Apostle admonishes us to "abound in the work of the Lord," that is, we are to do good and do it well. A monk whom Latimer describes for us found this idea very disagreeable. It will be no trouble to insert a short account here that Latimer once told during a sermon delivered before King Edward:[25] "There was once at Cambridge, in the same college as mine"—this was either Catherine's or Pembroke, as Latimer was an alumnus of both—"a certain charming and witty monk. This fellow was eating and telling stories when one of his friends had recited, by chance, this line: 'There's nothing better than to be happy and behave well.' Suddenly, the monk interrupted with these words: 'Get rid of that word *well*. It should be banished overseas. If the line had been missing that word *well*, it would have been quite good. For I can *be happy*, and I can *behave*, but there is no way I can *behave well*.'"[26] For men of this kind, lazy and senseless, fire and sulfur will be their portion. "But glory and honor and peace belong to whoever does good in the right way" [Rom. 2:10]. Their effort, no doubt, can be fruitless in the world, but their labor in the Lord will not be in vain. This is because God Himself will reward His own worship, just as He promised to Abraham, the father of the faithful: "I

---

22. Seneca, *De Brevitate Vitae*, in *Opera Quae Exstant Omnia* (Antwerp, 1652), bk. 1, ch. 1. This is a reversal of a very familiar Senecan quotation, *non ille diu vixit, sed diu fuit*, "such a man has not lived for a long time, he has merely existed for a long time."

23. The Latin pun *opibus…operibus* is difficult to capture, though I have tried "wealth… well-doing."

24. *Chytraeus* in viatico itineris extremi pag. 380.] Nathan Chytraeus, 1543–1598, German humanist and scholar, *Viaticum Itineris Extremi* (Herborn, 1608), p. 380. A. gives the Greek and his Latin gloss.

25. Edward VI, 1537–1553, r. 1547–1553, king of England and Ireland.

26. *Hugo Latimerus* Concion. Anglican. fol. 52. p. B.] Latimer, *The seconde [seventh] sermon of Maister Hughe Latimer* (London, 1549), sig. k4v.

am your guardian and your very great reward" [Gen. 15:1]. Consequently, Augustine decided to pray in his heart, "May You who shall be my reward be my joy."[27]

§4. The ancients were accustomed, moreover, to put sharpened stakes and iron spikes on the road the enemy was going to pass along, both to slow down his army and to wound it. There is a passage in Judith relating to this topic, where the Israelites are said "to have got ready for war by scattering things in the field for their foes to stumble against" (Judith 5:1). Military greaves are a protection against these and similar obstacles. Patience, similarly, is a kind of stronghold against all manner of punitive evils that surround us in the church militant, as they call it. For this reason, Paul writes to Timothy, "Endure evils"—κακοπάθησον—"as a good soldier of Jesus Christ" (2 Tim. 2:3).[28] Politicians counsel not to levy soldiers from cities where life is a little bit easier, but from the countryside. There the common people have learned how to suffer winter and summer equally, how to sleep on the ground, and how to endure sweat and dust, since they have been fed on hard work. "A sturdier soldier hails from a tough region, while the city man and house slave is more slack," as Seneca explains.[29] Obviously, the man accustomed to easy living will turn out quite ill prepared to handle weapons, for the soldiers' lot is generally very difficult. Christians should expect an Iliad of evils, and this is why Luther designates them *Crossbearers*. Tertullian, in his short work *To the Martyrs*, writes, "The most important festival that the Spartans used to celebrate was called the Διαμαστίγωσις.[30] In this rite, each aristocratic young man was scourged with whips before the altar, while his parents stood by and urged him to endure it."[31]

Look! This is like the pattern of discipline the heavenly Father uses on us: "Whom God loves He chastises, and He whips"—μαστιγοῖ—"whomever He acknowledges as a son" (Heb. 12:6). Notice also that encouragement is mixed in with the whippings in the preceding verse: "Have you forgotten the encouragement which speaks to you as sons? My son, do not make light of the Lord's chastisement nor be broken when He reproves you" [Heb. 12:5]. We readily acknowledge that different people suffer fewer and easier

27. Augustine, *Manuale*, in *Omnium Operum*, vol. 9 (Basel, 1528), ch. 3.

28. A. uses the Greek κακοπάθησον in the middle of his Latin gloss, though other mss. have συγκακοπάθησον.

29. *Lips.* civil. doct. in. lib. 5. cap. 12.] Lipsius, *Politicorum Sive Civilis Doctrinae Libri Sex* (Antwerp, 1623), p. 164; see Seneca, *Epistolae* (*epistola* 51).

30. "Scourging."

31. Tertullian, *Ad Martyras*, in *Opera Quae Hactenus Reperiri*, vol. 2 (Cologne, 1617), ch. 4. The sense of the quotation is retained.

hardships, just like soldiers stationed at their posts are protected against the mass of dangers that fall on their brothers in the line. But some predicament tests, has tested, or will test every last one of them. "You are quite effeminate," Jerome says somewhere, "if you want to enjoy this world and then reign with Christ afterward."[32] That was not Augustine's attitude, whose encouragement applies here: "O Lord, burn here, cut here, so long as You spare me for eternity."[33] Nor Fulgentius's: "O Lord, grant me patience now, leniency later."[34]

§ 5. The supreme judge over all leads his "Timothies"[35] through rocky, steep places to heaven, ahead of other Christians. Paul, again in the same letter, writes, "Be alert in all circumstances," κακοπάθησον, ἔργον ποίησον εὐαγγελιστοῦ (2 Tim. 4:5).[36] He says this as though the evangelist's work consisted in whatever is generally strenuous or miserable. So the Scripture calls ministers workmen of the Word—that is, in the harvest. And it calls them fishermen—that is, at sea—stars that are constantly moving, clouds that burst forth when heavy with water. It calls them lamps that go out while still giving off light, salt used up as it seasons. And finally, it calls them farmers who toil in an endless cycle.[37] Truly, we see that Christ offered His disciples, with one hand, the office of Apostle and, with the other, the cross. Preaching and persecution are basically twins. The preacher must overturn every stone, even the one with a scorpion sleeping under it. God curses him if he does not preach the gospel, but men will curse him if he does. As Peter went off to feed the sheep, his ears still rang with the Lord's question, repeated three times: "Do you love? Do you love? Do you love me?" [John 21:15–17]. Wherever the faithful pastor of souls turns, he always meets some hardship that he can only escape through love. And love does not know the meaning of the word *difficulty*.

In the Roman military, when the supreme commander was leading his soldiers from camp, he asked them three times, through the herald, whether they were prepared for war. The soldiers also would answer three

---

32. Jerome, *Epistolae Selectae*, vol. 2 (*epistola* 6).

33. Augustine, quoted in Jeremias Drexel, 1581–1638, German Jesuit scholar and spiritual writer, *De Aeternitate*, in *Opera Omnia*, vol. 1 (Lyon, 1647), cons. 5, sec. 3, p. 15. A.'s quotation is identical to Drexel's, and the same Fulgentius quotation immediately follows; this seems to be a paraphrase of Augustine, since no verbatim quotation of his exists. Perhaps from *Psalmi Enarratio*, sub loc. Ps. 33 (*sermo* 2): *Ideo videtur non exaudire, ut sanet et parcat in sempiternum.*

34. Fulgentius, fl. ca. 480–550, bishop of Ruspe, *Opera Quae Extant Omnia* (Basel, 1587), sig. α8r (*vita*).

35. *Timotheos*, those honored of God.

36. "Suffer hardship, do the work of an evangelist."

37. Vergil, *Georgicorum*, in *Opera* (Leipzig, 1616), bk. 2 (line 401).

times—cheering with a kind of bestial war cry and lifting their right hands toward the sky—that they were ready.[38] And what about you, minister of the gospel, whoever you are, or candidate for such an important office? Christ is watching you just like that, asking as He once did the sons of Zebedee, "Can you drink the cup that I drank? Can you take up the cross while you preach the cross?" [Matt. 20:22]. The man who cannot is missing at least one of the greaves of evangelical readiness.

§6. But why are they called greaves of *evangelical* readiness? Evidently, because the gospel is not only something by which we are prepared for action (as I have shown above) but also something that makes us ready to suffer. This I will soon show, as God allows me. Minds armed with patience tolerate easily things that are difficult for others. Peter compares patience to weapons: "Since, therefore, Christ suffered for our sake in the flesh, arm"—ὁπλίσασθε—"yourselves also with the same understanding" (1 Peter 4:1). Why do I say they "tolerate"? They easily conquer, but what is still more is that they ὑπερνικῶσι,[39] provided they have learned from the gospel to fix their gaze upon the suffering Christ and to comport themselves according to His example. Luther puts this very nicely when writing to Spalatin:[40] "Whenever I gaze upon Christ's passion, I am incredibly annoyed that this temptation of mine seems to so many high-ranking people so hard to bear, when really it is nothing."[41] Justus Lipsius pretty much got it right also. When he was in his final death throes, he was advised by a certain friend standing close by—a man very familiar with the writings of the Stoics. This man suggested arguments to him to strengthen his soul in perseverance, though in vain. Lipsius supposedly turned toward Christ, saying, "Give me, Lord Jesus, Christian patience."[42] What Seneca wrote of himself in a certain book of Q. Sextius[43] applies to the Christian who has been inspired by the Holy Spirit and the gospel books. He said, "No matter my state of mind when I read this"—he meant Sextius, but you should have in mind the gospel—"I want to confront all dangers, I want to shout, 'Why are you stopping, Lady Luck? Bring it on; you see I'm ready.' I want to

---

38. *Joseph.* de bello Judaico, l. 3. c. 3.] Flavius Josephus, ca. 37–ca. 100, Jewish historian, *De Bello Iudaico*, in *Opera Quae Exstant Nempe* (Geneva, 1611), bk. 3, ch. 3.

39. "More than conquer," a reference to Rom. 8:37, where it is in first person plural.

40. Georg Spalatin, 1484–1545, German Lutheran theologian.

41. *Scultet.* Annal. Decad. 1. p. 55.] Scultetus, *Annalium Evangelii Passim*, p. 55.

42. *Melch. Adam.* in vita *J. Lipsu.*] Adam, *Vitae Germanorum Theologorum* (Frankfurt, 1618), 20, 53.

43. Quintus Sextius, fl. ca. 50 BC, Roman philosopher.

have something to conquer, something to test my endurance."[44] There is in Surius a remarkable example of this principle:

> Count Elzear evidenced no patience because he had such a large household and was so often overwhelmed by numerous responsibilities. So he reportedly said to his devoted wife, "You know I sometimes feel irritated in my heart toward those who annoy me. But then I set my mind to thinking about the wrongs inflicted on Christ, and I say to myself—because I want to imitate Him—'Even if your servants pluck out your beard and pummel you with blows, all this would be nothing compared to many worse things your Lord endured.' You certainly should know, my wife, that I will never stop remembering the wrongs inflicted on my Savior until my own soul is completely at peace."[45]

I think that this tremendously eloquent and holy statement of Bernard's will stamp all these ideas on our minds:

> You are, Lord Jesus, both the mirror of my suffering and my prize for doing so. You both strongly challenge me and set me all ablaze. You train my hands for battle by the example of Your courage. You crown my head after Your victory with the presence of Your majesty, whether I gaze upon You as You fight or wait upon You as the one who not only gives the crown but also is the crown itself.[46]

§ 7. Meanwhile, as you read these things, you must remember that the gospel that trains us for all these tasks is not that apocryphal document that the Valentinians[47] call the *Gospel of Truth*.[48] Nor is it the one that the Nazarites labeled the *Fifth Gospel*,[49] nor the *Gospel of Perfection*.[50] And it is not the gospel that John of Parma,[51] the Italian monk, published under the borrowed name *The Everlasting Gospel*, nor the one published under the title *The Gospel Kingdom*. No, it is what is contained in the sacred books of the Old and New Testaments and identified by Paul as the *gospel of peace*. This is undoubtedly the correct name, because this gospel reveals the most sure,

---

44. *Senec.* epist. 64.] Seneca, *Epistolae* (*epistola* 64).

45. Tom. 5. in vita *Alzearii* c. 23.] Laurentius Surius, 1522–1578, German Roman Catholic hagiographer, *Vita S. Elzearii Comitis*, in *De Probatis Sanctorum Historiis*, vol. 5 (Cologne, 1580), ch. 23, p. 422.

46. Serm. 47. in Cantic.] Bernard of Clairvaux, *In Cantica Canticorum*, sec. 6 (*sermo* 47).

47. Valentinians, followers of Valentinus, second-century Gnostic theologian.

48. A purported gospel that may have been written in Greek between 140 and 180 by Valentinian Gnostics.

49. Perhaps the "Gospel of the Nazarenes" cited by Paschasius Radbertus, ca. 790–ca. 860, Carolingian theologian.

50. The "Gospel of Perfection" (*Evangelium Perfectionis*) is a lost text from the New Testament apocrypha, mentioned once by Epiphanius and once in an infancy gospel.

51. John of Parma, 1209–1289, Italian Franciscan preacher.

reliable path to make peace with God and to maintain that same peace within our own ranks. At the same time, this gospel promotes both peace of conscience and of harmony. I gladly offer, as an example of peace of conscience, Martin Luther. He confessed,

> I was a man whose conscience was very disturbed and trembled at the mention of God's righteousness until, by the Spirit's leading, I had understood the meaning of that passage in Paul, "I am not ashamed of the gospel of Christ." For the righteousness of God is revealed through it from faith to faith, just as it was written, "The righteous man will live by faith." At that point, I realized I had been completely reborn and had entered through open doors into paradise itself. From that point on, the whole Scripture looked quite different to me. As much as I had previously hated the phrase "God's righteousness," now, with an equally great love, I praised it as the sweetest word I could hear. That passage of Paul was, for me, the very gate of paradise.[52]

Christians in the earliest days of the church provide ample evidence of the second kind of peace: mutual harmony. All of them, after they had drunk deeply of their Lord's new commandment to love one another (John 13:34), just as He Himself had said, they were "of one heart and one mind" (Acts 4:32). But then their inferior descendants abandoned this royal highway of peace and, far and wide, right down to this very day, offered sacrifice to discord. And this has happened in England more than almost anywhere else. It has gone on for a long time, since Robert Grosseteste,[53] the bishop of Lincoln, was rejected and complained before the papal consistory, "Money, money, how powerful you are, especially in the Roman court!" Gregory IX,[54] pope at the time, restored him and said, "You Englishmen, most wretched of all people. Each and every one of you gnaws at the rest and is bent on impoverishing him!"[55] This said, the pontiff seemed to prophesy like Caiaphas, if one considers what has now happened in the century that just concluded.

§ 8. But come, brothers, please, by the love of God, by the tender mercies of Jesus, let us behave in such a way that the common expression "All praise peace but few practice it" no longer finds a home among us. Because

---

52. In praefation. Tom. 1. operum Latinorum Jenensium.] Luther, *Opera* (Iena, 1556), bk. 1, on the penultimate page of the preface.

53. Robert Grosseteste, ca. 1170–1253, scientist, theologian, and bishop of Lincoln.

54. Gregory IX, ca. 1148–1241, *p.* 1227–1241.

55. *Matth. Paris.* in *Henr.* 3. ad Ann. 1250.] Matthew of Paris, ca. 1200–1259, English Benedictine medieval chronicler, *Historia Maior* (Paris, 1644), sub loc. 1250, p. 517. A. refers to Grosseteste's dispute with Henry III, 1207–1272, r. 1216–1272. A. seems to have the wrong pope in mind, since it was Innocent IV, d. 1254, *p.* 1243–1254, who in 1250 acquiesced to Grosseteste's demands for reform in England, though the quotation is authentically Gregory's.

Jehovah is our God of peace, our mediator is the Prince of Peace, our brothers are sons of peace, our Scripture is the gospel of peace, let us, therefore, cultivate peace with one another; let us strive to cultivate it, at least, as far as lies with us [Rom. 12:18]. If not, we must immediately discard the glorious and dazzling titles of Christians and evangelicals. We should now, at last, imitate Bernard, who said to the brothers who had offended him, "I will cling to you even if you don't want me to; I will cling to you even if I don't want to. When you cause trouble, I will make peace; I will step aside from anger lest I step toward the Devil."[56] Let us imitate Gregory Nazianzus. When an argument at the synod broke out over his bishopric, they say that he made this speech to the fathers then assembled together:

> Gentlemen, fellow pastors of the sacred flock, it is disgraceful and completely inappropriate that we, who teach peace, wage war against each other. I beg you, by the very Trinity, that you conduct all things peaceably. But if I am the cause of division, if I am that Jonah, throw me into the sea if you want, that the storm may subside. Take away my bishop's chair, drive me from the city. Do in the end whatever seems good to you so long as you seek peace and love it together with truth, as the prophet Zechariah counsels.[57]

What a truly gospel spirit! For peace and truth exist in the church as veins and arteries in the physical body. Truth supplies it with energy and blood; peace, with life-giving humors. The veins must be opened to care for the church's salvation. But be careful, whoever you are, surgeon of souls, that while you are wisely opening a vein, you do not foolishly split an artery. Be on your guard not to outrage peace while you are nurturing truth. As for me, I embrace, with both arms, as they say, the axioms of two very famous men. Although these ideas seem to butt heads with one another, nevertheless, they enjoy a friendly enough agreement. The first is from Erasmus: "I hate discord so much that I even dislike factious truth."[58] The other is Musculus: "A curse upon that harmony that cannot be established except by discrediting and condemning the truth and Christ's kingdom."[59]

§9. There is one verdict left to render here when it comes to dealing with the title *gospel*. It is against those who conclude that Christians may not,

---

56. Epist. 253.] Bernard of Clairvaux, *Epistolae*, in *Opera Omnia*, vol. 1 (Cologne, 1641), sec. 10 (*epistola* 252).

57. Gregory Nazianzus, *Opera*, vol. 1 (Paris, 1630), sig. u4r (*vita*).

58. In epistola ad *Barbirium*. Anno 1521.] Probably in Erasmus, *Epistolae D. Erasmi Roterodami Ad Diversos* (Basil, 1521).

59. Ap. *Hoornbeck* in sum. controvers. p. 588.] Hoornbeeck, *Summa Controversiarum Religionis*, bk. 9, p. 586.

inasmuch as they profess the gospel of peace, wage war under any circumstances. Erasmus concludes, "Military office has no part in gospel purity, and many necessary evils are allowed in human society that are tolerated because they prevent greater evils; I do not endorse such a part of evangelical doctrine."[60]

Erasmus puts war in that category. The Socinians, after scratching their heads carefully, speak far more boldly and eloquently. Says Schmaltz, "We deny that Christians may wage wars, and we argue that it is incompatible with Christian holiness. Ostorodius[61] states that he is constrained by conscience and, because of obedience to the commandments of Christ as well as his eternal salvation, disapproves of wars."[62] As though salvation hinged on this very dogma! So I thought it proper to frame and summarize this subject in the following maxims.

First, no one, much less a Christian man, may consider war pleasurable, for finding pleasure in something wicked is diabolical. In the prophet, war is described as an ἀντονομαστικῶς[63] for evil: "I am the Lord, and there is no other, fashioning the light and creating shadows, making peace and creating evil" (Isa. 45:7).[64] In this passage, as shadows are contrasted with light, so evil is with peace. Striving for the particular evil of war is referred to as a vice numerous times in the Psalms: "Scatter the people who delight in war" (Ps. 68); "my soul has dwelt for a long time with those who hate peace" (Ps. 120).

Second, no one, whether or not he is a Christian, may undertake an unjust war. Cajetan expresses this with adequate intensity:

> Men who run toward the sound of money at the very word *war*, not caring whether it is just, have passed beyond the careful examination of conscience. It is obvious that, until they come to their senses in the state of eternal damnation, they are like those who run toward destruction and plunder with no concern for whether the war is just or unjust.[65]

---

60. Annotat. ad Lucae cap. 3. p. 213.] Erasmus, *In Novum Testamentum Annotationes* (Basel, 1555), sub loc. Luke 22, p. 227.

61. Cristoph Ostorodus, d. 1611, German Socinian theologian.

62. Instit. Germanic. p. 177. apud *Calovium* in Socinismo profligatio, p. 1004.] These are distinct quotations from two different pages in Abraham Calov (Calovius), 1612–1686, Lutheran theologian, *Socinismus Profligatus* (Wittenberg, 1652), art. 5 ("On the Political Magistrate"), contr. 3, pp. 993 & 1004, respectively. According to Calov, the quotation by Smalcius comes from one "Frantz, p. 393," while the Ostorodus quotation (as A. notes) comes from the "Germanic Institutes."

63. "Stand in."

64. Cited as v. 7, but the quotation includes part of v. 6.

65. Summula peccatorum in voce Bellum, § 5.] Cajetan, *De Peccatis Summula* (Paris, 1530), sub loc. Bellum, sec. 2, fol. 18v.

Third, the faithful were permitted to wage just war before the law was given as well as under the Mosaic economy. I take as my witness Abraham. God expressly approved of Abraham's action through his priest after Abraham had won an armed victory against the kings who plundered Sodom. Melchizedek said, "Praise be to God Most High, who has surrendered your enemies into your hand" [Gen. 14:20]. I cite also Moses and Joshua, who, with Hebrew weapons, drove back the attacking Amalekites. I cite Jephthah as well, who fought against the Ammonites to protect his borders. David also attacked them in war, because they had mistreated his ambassadors. What about the Apostle's assertion that Gideon, Barak, Sampson, and others waged wars, prevailed in war, drove the armies of their assailants to flight (Heb. 11)? And he says that they did this "by faith," which, without any doubt, entails a sure persuasion that he believed that they pleased God by what they did.

Fourth, the law of Christ does not abolish the right to wage war. It is likely that the Lord possessed the same understanding that belonged to His precursor, the Baptist, and to His followers, the apostles. And they approved of war as something permitted. To the soldiers who asked, "What then shall we do?" the Baptist answered, "Be content with your pay" (Luke 3:14). From this passage, Augustine infers, "He argues that they must find their pay sufficient; he in no sense prohibited them from military service."[66] But if we must adopt a different interpretation, then John would have ordered them to do something absurd and inequitable. It would be as if he had said, "Be content with your pay and accept it on the grounds of your military service. But do so only on this qualification, namely, that if your commander orders you to fight, you are not to obey him, because warfare must clearly be rejected by those who serve the cause of salvation." But as for the apostles, after Paul said of the magistrate, "He does not bear the sword in vain, but is vengeance on the wrongdoer," he immediately adds, "For these reasons, you pay tribute, because they are ministers of God laboring at this very task" (Rom. 13). So then, we must pay the magistrate tribute so that from it, soldiers might be paid their salaries. For this was the particular purpose of taxes at that time, as Tacitus states: "Without weapons, nations cannot have peace, and without taxes, soldiers don't get paid."[67] Therefore, Paul accepts military service as much as tribute from subjects and the duty of the magistrate. The apostle John numerous times in his Apocalypse teaches that Christian princes must war against Antichrist using soldiers of that same Christian faith. And he predicts that it will come to pass that Gog and Magog die in a defensive war waged by Christians.

---

66. Epist. 5. ad *Marcellinum*.] Augustine (*epistola* 5). A. uses *asserit* in place of *praecepit*.
67. Histor. l. 4.] Tacitus, *Historiarum*, bk. 4.74.

Fifth, ancient Christians never dreamed that the gospel prevented them from waging war. Tertullian said, "We sail, and we serve in the military together, and we spend time in the country, and we conduct business, buy, and sell."[68] Augustine writes, "It is not wrong to serve in the military but sinful to do so for the sake of plunder."[69] Bernard:

> Christian soldiers with confidence fight the Lord's own battles, not at all afraid to sin by slaughtering their enemies or afraid of danger from dying. This is because we must either bear death for Christ or inflict it. It contains no reproach and deserves much glory. The soldier of Christ takes life without concern and dies even more confidently. He profits himself when he dies, profits Christ when he takes a life. The death he inflicts is Christ's gain; the death he suffers is his own gain.[70]

Sixth, one chapter of Acts is more than adequate to support the orthodox position on this issue and overturn all the tricks, shall we say, of its detractors. It is the tenth chapter, where, in the first and second verses, we find this statement: "The centurion of the Italian cohort was a devout and God-fearing man" [Acts 10:1–2]. Ergo, one may be both a soldier and a Christian. The Lord decided this man deserved to have an angel sent to him, as we see in verse 3. Therefore, the military estate can be consistent with the reception of God's grace. This centurion, in verse 7, sent to Peter a "devout soldier from among those who accompanied him." Soldiering, therefore, is no barrier to a life of devotion. In verse 22, Peter admonished the centurion according to God's command, but there was not even one syllable about demitting military office. Therefore, fulfilling one's military duty is allowed. Finally, in verses 44 and 45, the Spirit fell upon the military men who were baptized in the name of Christ. Therefore, Christ and His Spirit do not recoil from waging war.

---

68. Apolog. c. 42.] Tertullian, *Apologeticus Adversus Gentes Pro Christianis*, in *Opera quae hactenus reperiri*, vol. 1 (Cologne, 1617), ch. 42.

69. Serm. 19. de de verb. Dom.] Augustine, *De Verbis Domini In Evangelio Secundum Matthaeum*, in *Omnium Operum*, vol. 10 (Basel, 1528), *sermo* 19.

70. Serm. ad milites Templi, cap. 3.] Bernard of Clairvaux, *Exhortatio Ad Milites Templi*, in *Opera Omnia*, vol. 4 (Cologne, 1641), ch. 3.

CHAPTER VII

The Shield of Faith That We Must Take Up over All the Other Armor

Sections 1–2: An examination of the nature of faith. A defense of the division of faith into dogmatic faith, faith of miracles, and saving faith. Section 3: Christians never have complete assurance when they forsake the faith, and rarely in the state of spiritual infancy. Sections 4–6: A critique of the position that many contemporary Protestants suppose is true and some of the Reformers held, namely, that faith consists in a kind of complete assurance by which faith works justification. But these people are excused, and we demonstrate how it happened that their position was abandoned. Sections 7–8: This thesis that the person of Christ the Mediator is the proper and formal object of justifying faith is explained and proven. The critical observation of Wotton and Gataker. Sections 9–10: An explanation of the analogy of faith to a shield from etymologies and historical notices. Sections 11–12: Why we must place faith over all the rest. The Devil attacks faith more than others. Faith surpasses the other virtues, even love. A demonstration of Paul's internal consistency. A full explanation of the end of I Corinthians 13. Section 13: The praises due to faith.

§1. The world trains men in mere stage-play, but the church, in military service. The banner of the cross is raised aloft and the Prince of Peace Himself summons Christians to arms. They won't be set free with the gift of the wooden sword[1] before they have exchanged life for death. When the holy Apostle remembered this duty, like a veteran general he encouraged his own dear Ephesians—raw recruits—and simultaneously armed them. He shows them the divine panoply (πανοπλία), and among the various weapons, he wants them to know the shield of faith is by far the most valuable: ἐν πᾶσιν ἀναλαβόντες τὸν θυρεὸν τῆς πίστεως [Eph. 6:16].[2]

---

1. The *rudis* was a wooden sword given to gladiators when they had earned their freedom or retired from military service. This is a brilliant combination of metaphors for the warfare of the Christian life.

2. "Over all of them taking up the shield of faith."

By "faith" here we understand not the content of faith. For unless I am mistaken, that applies to the sword of the Spirit, the Word of God, discussed in the following verse. Instead, it refers to that by which we believe. Now among theologians of our school, faith is typically discussed in three ways. These include, first, faith in fundamental principles or dogmas. This faith entails knowledge of very many dogmatic propositions of the Christian religion, together with the assent that is attached to them. John asserts that this faith existed in many of the Jewish leaders. These men, although they were not brave enough to profess Christ because of the Pharisees (to avoid ejection from the synagogue), still they are described as having believed in Christ (John 12:42). Second, there is the faith of miracles. Paul says of this, "If I have all faith to move mountains but I do not have love, I am nothing" (1 Cor. 13:2). In this passage, we cannot take "all faith" as meaning every different kind of faith, since Paul intimates that there is another kind that never lacks love. But he means the highest degree of faith of one category, of the kind that concerns the miracles of the first class. We must count moving mountains among these. Third and finally is saving faith. Paul describes this when he says, "By grace you have been saved through faith" (Eph. 2:8). And Peter says, "Receiving the reward of your faith, the salvation of your souls" (1 Peter 1:9). In this passage of Ephesians we are dealing with, the Apostle does not desire for himself a faith in principles. For that kind of faith does not extinguish the Devil's shafts. No, more often those shafts extinguish faith, as illustrated by the Savior's parable about the πρόσκαιροι.[3] Nor should we seek after and strive above all for the faith of miracles, which the elect and reprobate share. But we ought to desire the faith productive of salvation and peculiar to the elect. This faith, although it is unique as regards species, claims two degrees: a reliance and a full assurance. We must, meanwhile, defend this ancient distinction, because nowadays innovators busily try to collapse it.

§2. The learned words of Chrysostom adequately demonstrate that this distinction was once well-known and considered entirely unobjectionable. He says, πίστιν οὐ ταύτην λέγω τὴν τῶν δογμάτων, ἀλλὰ τὴν τῶν σημείων.[4] But to confer upon this idea a greater light of understanding and perhaps authority, I want to persuade the reader to pay quite close attention to the three corollaries that follow.

---

3. An allusion to the parable of the sower with a variation on the words from Mark 4:17, "Those who believe temporarily."

4. Chrysostom, homily 29, on 1 Corinthians 12. "I am describing a faith not of dogmas but of signs."

First, faith in fundamental principles or dogmas applies to everyone who is truly regenerate but not to them alone. Because, in this new creation, as in the original one, God says, "Let there be light," and he calls all of his followers "sons of light." Nevertheless, other men also possess these principles. Why should I bother to mention men? Even the demons possess a historical faith, for "they believe and tremble" (James 2:19).

Second, faith of miracles does not apply to everyone nor the regenerate only. It does not apply to everyone, for John the Baptist—as we read in John's gospel—"worked no miracle" (John 10:41). It does not apply to the regenerate only. For they who will publish miracles nevertheless will hear, "Certainly I never knew you" (Matt. 7:23).

The third corollary is twofold, and its division is as follows. There is saving faith (some call this justifying faith, others call it the faith of the elect), as it corresponds to a degree of resting faith in everyone truly regenerate. It also applies to them alone and at all times—that is, in every condition after Christ's grace has been received. Insofar as it corresponds to the degree of full assurance, it is in all of them, perhaps, and only them, but not always. Those passages of Scripture that describe Christians as living by faith constitute the faith of the third corollary's first portion. And the "new creation" and "faith working through love" are, in turn, equivalent to one another. This is clear in Galatians if we compare chapter 5 verse 6 with chapter 6 verse 15. But now let us move on to the second part of the third corollary.

I am not one of those who strenuously denies that full assurance of faith (provided that it is present among the mature) applies more slowly or quickly, in the end and in its own time, to everyone who is regenerate—even when he is a sojourner here below. And I would not at all doubt that full assurance belongs only to the regenerate (for no matter how the unregenerate boast and sleep soundly, there is more distance between their false confidence and true certainty of faith than between heaven and hell). Nevertheless, I assert, with the greatest confidence, that it does not attach to them always.

§ 3. Now there are two conditions pertaining to the person who has been grafted into Christ. In one of these, the assurance I have mentioned is never found completely, while in the other, it is found quite rarely. The first condition is that of desertion, and it is actually diametrically opposed to full assurance. For if God has deserted a person as regards the interior feeling of the soul, how can he be certain about grace? If he is certain, how did he abandon it? Truly, if the faith by which one is justified is a sure persuasion of the grace of God toward ourselves, it follows that the man who—after he has been converted—has been abandoned by God for even a small amount of time has fallen away from his own justifying faith for that time at least. This is a position that Thomson,[5] writer of the *Diatribe*, was willing to purchase at great cost, along with those who like him defend the intercision of grace.[6] The latter status is that of the spiritual infant. So long as Christians are underage, the heavenly Father does not bestow upon them that great a supply of joy. But—to borrow Paul's phrase—He leads them little by little to εἰς πάντα πλοῦτον τῆς πληροφορίας (Col. 2:2).[7] Those who have not yet submitted, in the school of Christ, to the hand of the rod seldom become sharers in the gifts granted the leaders. Far be it from us to set limits on any state of Israel. It can happen, and sometimes even does, that certitude, partly intuitive, partly discursive, springs up at the very beginning of new life. But generally speaking, it is positioned between a resting faith and a full assurance, between reasoning and learning. Reasoning is the foundation of learning, and therefore, animals are incapable of this. Resting faith, in like manner, is the basis of full assurance. Those who do not lean on Christ, because of the deficiency of their faith, but instead upon themselves and their own gifts, whatever they are, are strangers to this full assurance. Learning bestows honor upon the reason that has been trained and, so I would say, elevated by study. In a similar fashion, full assurance usually crowns resting faith that has been strengthened by frequent exercise of that faith. Learning can be lost through neglect or by sickness even though reason itself survives. Assurance can also be lost while a resting faith still persists. Finally, just like every human being is rational, but not every one is learned, so also all true believers rest upon their faith, but not all of them have full assurance.[8]

§4. Meanwhile, I confess, for it is more obvious than is right to deny, that some of the principal Reformers taught something a little bit different, as did some others of the most distinguished men in the church of God. They did this typically when they discussed sure persuasion and full assurance in their own definitions of faith. Luther, for example, writes, "A mere historical faith does not rest upon nor trust in the word, but says, 'I hear that Christ suffered and died.' True faith has this perception: 'I believe that Christ suffered and died for me. I do not doubt this and assent to this faith and trust in that word against death and sin.'"[9] Calvin in this followed

---

5. Richard Thomson, d. 1613, philologist and Church of England clergyman, *Diatriba De Amissione Et Intercisione Gratiæ Et Iustificationis* (Leiden, 1618).

6. I.e., the notion that grace can be fully given and then cut off temporarily.

7. "All the riches of full assurance." A. gives the Greek with no Latin gloss.

8. *Certiorantur*. A. quotes Perkins's *infra* using a cognate of this word, thus indicating his likely source for the concept.

9. In cap. 48. Genes.] Luther, *Enarratio In Genesim*, sub loc. Gen. 48:21.

Luther: "We will possess a proper definition of faith if we say that it is a sure knowledge of divine kindness toward us, founded through the Holy Spirit on the truth of the free promise in Christ both revealed to our minds and sealed upon our hearts."[10] Others have followed these trailblazing heroes. Beza says, "We call faith a kind of sure knowledge that the Holy Spirit, by His singular grace and goodness, more and more engraves upon the hearts of the elect. By this knowledge, it comes to pass that each of them, more sure in his own heart of his own election, applies to himself the promise of salvation in Jesus Christ."[11] Jerome Zanchi: "Faith is nothing other than a sure persuasion conceived by God's word that we have been freely elected in Christ, saved through Christ, and are going to be glorified with the church of Christ."[12] Finally, Perkins: "True faith is an infallible and specific grant of certainty regarding forgiven sins and eternal life."[13]

There will be no need, I think, for more proof. It is plain enough that on this particular dogma, this is the received position. So there is no doubt that whoever thinks differently about it would fall under suspicion of heterodoxy. Therefore, our predecessors would scarcely dare entrust to writing an opposing position without an exculpatory preface. John Foxe and the Scot Robert Baron are my sources for this. Foxe writes as follows in his book *The Christ Who Freely Justifies*:

> If freedom be granted me in a free church to confess what I believe, then my thinking leads me to this position: I hold that this confident trust in the mercy and certainty of promised salvation is something that must be very tightly joined to faith and which each person should necessarily appropriate for himself. But although it be most truly appropriated, nevertheless, it is not something that alone, by itself, properly and absolutely alleviates us of our sins and justifies us before God. But I hold that there is something else proposed in the gospel, which by nature must precede this certainty in some way and justify us before God. For faith in the person of the Son necessarily precedes, and this first reconciles us to God. Then confident trust in this very sure mercy etc. follows that faith.[14]

Baron, in his work *Philosophy Serving Theology*—after he had taught that the act of faith that precedes justification as its instrumental cause differs

---

10. Institut. lib. 3. cap. 2. § 7.] Calvin, *Institutio Christianae Religionis*, 3.2.7.

11. Confess. c. 4. artic. 5.] Beza, *Confessio Christianae Fidei* (Geneva, 1587), ch. 4, art. 5, p. 19.

12. Oper. in fol. Tom. 7. part: 1. col. mihi 227.] Zanchi, *De Praedestinatione*, p. 227.

13. Reform. Catholic. cap de salutis certitudine.] Perkins, *Catholicus Reformatus* (Hanau, 1601), contr. 3, ch. 4, pp. 56–57. A. has *vera fides est infallibilis et particularis certioratio de peccatis remissis et vita aeterna*, rather than *Fides vera est certa, infallibilis ac specialis fiducia de remissione peccatorum suorum, ac vitae aeternae adeptione.*

14. Pag. 246.] Foxe, *De Christo Gratis Iustificante* (London, 1583), pp. 46–47.

from a trusting action by which we are persuaded that we have obtained remission of sins, the condition that he considered subsequent—supplied this coda at the end:

> I embraced this position when I first began to work at theology but considered it suspect because of its novelty. And so I had condemned it to everlasting darkness. But this very year, when I was reading the remarkably erudite *Observations and Censures* of David Pareus against Bellarmine's fourth book,[15] I found the same opinion plainly stated there. Therefore, relying on and fortified by the testimony of such a great man, I have not been afraid to publish it.[16]

§ 5. If one asks about this position (very much in retreat nowadays among the English preachers and writers alike), it is helpful to present it not in my own words but in those of that most notable Davenant. He says,

> The word *fiducia* denotes two things. First, the act itself of resting upon and clinging to Jesus Christ, by which we embrace Christ with both arms, as it were, and through that act, we try to obtain from God the Father pardon, grace, and glory. And we hold that this is that act that justification always attends—that is, full remission of sins and acceptance into grace and divine favor—whether or not the sinner, at that very first moment, lays hold of πληροφορία[17] of the pardon he has obtained. *Fiducia* sometimes also may denote the resulting effect of justifying faith, namely, a full persuasion and, as it were, vigorous realization of the forgiveness that has been wrought, as well as of the divine favor that has been obtained.[18]

But far be it from me to darken with black coal, as the saying goes, those very learned and holy men whom I praised above as somehow disagreeing with Paul. They rather should be held in honor by the orthodox, using this kind of reverent defense, which I now undertake. Although there are two principal acts of saving faith, namely *innitentia* and *certioratio*[19] (I will use theological terms even though they are not at all Ciceronian), certain Reformed scholars are less concerned about the former than would be appropriate. They make mention of only the second act in their definitions of faith. This seems to have been the case especially with those who were seeking to teach their readers and listeners not to stop at the lowest

---

15. Pareus, *Roberti Bellarmini De Amissione Gratiae & Statu Peccati* (Heidelberg, 1613).

16. Exercit. 3. artic. 20.] Robert Baron, ca. 1596–1639, Church of Scotland minister and writer on theology, *Philosophia Theologiae Ancillans* (Oxford, 1641), exercit. 3, art. 20, sec. 6, p. 247.

17. "Full assurance."

18. Determinat. quaest. 37. p. 167.] Davenant, *Determinationes Quaestionum Quarundam* (Cambridge, 1634), qu. 37, pp. 167–68.

19. "Resting upon" and "gaining certainty," respectively.

points but to rise up to the very pinnacle of utmost virtue. And so, unless I am mistaken, they were led to this conclusion partly from excessive zeal to refute the Roman bishops. For they think it satisfactory for the churches to choke down some vague general assent in place of an intact faith. They were also partly led by excessive regard for the experience of their own people. Because the joy of Jehovah is strength (as Nehemiah once said to the Israelites who were exhausted with grief, Neh. 8:11), so it is very likely that God, the most great and powerful, bestowed upon them[20] unique certainty. He did this in order to strengthen those heroes, whose work He deigned to employ in purging His church, to undertake such great responsibility and such exhausting tasks. Therefore, it came about that they described not so much ὀλιγοπιστία (which they discussed elsewhere) as πληροφορία.[21] "They who hold another position," Ames says in his *Anti-Synodalia Scripta*, "misconstrue what is said well."[22] I add, moreover, that justification is twofold. One type is in the court of heaven, the other in the court of conscience. We hold, and most accurately, that the faith that is the instrument of the first kind is a resting and striving faith. But they whose case we are now defending, while they have special regard for the second kind—that is, justification that occurs in the court of conscience—have not improperly established that its instrument is full assurance of faith.

§6. It will not be a tangent, meanwhile, to show briefly what means the Lord used to drag the truth even from those who are unwilling. The most merciful Father has kindly led His church back to the straight path. He did this so that error would not last any longer, and error would not produce some prejudice in the souls of devout believers who were nevertheless devoid of this kind of assurance. God accomplished this by the following means in particular. He supplied the enemies of truth and all that class with weapons that the orthodox could in no way strip away until they were compelled to acknowledge this simple truth: assurance of grace does not belong to the essence of faith by which God justifies.

May I be allowed to introduce two arguments as an example. One of these belongs to Arminius, the other to Bellarmine. Let us start with Bellarmine, as he is more like someone boasting than arguing. This is how he peddles himself to his readers:

The sectarians of our day teach that all men are justified by a particular faith alone. By this, each person believes with certainty that he is righteous before God because of Christ. This can be likened to any paradox

---

20. I.e., the first generation of Reformers mentioned above.

21. "Meager faith" and "full assurance," respectively. A. gives the Greek with no Latin gloss.

22. Pag. mihi 202.] Ames, *Anti-Synodalia Scripta* (Amsterdam, 1633), ch. 5, pp. 202–3.

you want. For this is not something above or beyond all reason but clearly contrary to it. This is my conundrum: when I begin to believe that I am righteous, either I am righteous or unrighteous. If I am righteous, therefore, I am made righteous through that faith that comes after my righteousness. If I am unrighteous, that faith is false. Therefore, it is not a divine faith that justifies, unless we claim that men are justified by a lie.

Those are Bellarmine's comments.[23] Now let those who belong to the position that we discreetly attack note how each horn of this dilemma can be avoided. We should not fear this dilemma at all, since we say that the formal act of justifying faith is not the certitude of an acquired remission but a resting faith or act of *trust*. By this we rest upon Christ or lean upon the mercy of God through Him, who by nature proceeds that act by which we believe that our sins have already been remitted.

One can see that the Arminians are arguing for their own concept of general redemption in the following manner: "That which each and every person is bound to believe is doubtless true. Each and every person is bound to believe that Christ died for himself. Therefore, this is by far the truest statement." They then struggle to prove the minor premise: "Faith in Christ—according to the explicit confession of the Counterremonstrants— is a kind of certain persuasion and full assurance by which he who embraces the Savior by this *fiducia* believes that Christ was crucified and died not only for the sins of others but also for his own."[24]

Such is the very madness of that shaft that the Remonstrants fiercely brandish in their own *Synodical Acts*. Theologians of our school answer in a variety of ways. But they do not in any way prove the case (and I say this while desiring to preserve the honor of the others), except those who separate the certitude of special grace from the essential concept of justifying faith by which one is justified. This latter group easily resolves the problem, partly by distinguishing between two things: first, believing in Christ— which precedes justification and echoes the bare resting upon His person as most equipped to fulfill exactly the exalted office of mediator; second, believing that Christ died for oneself—which (if properly accomplished) connotes full assurance and is not found except in the one who has already been justified. They also resolve it, in part, by asserting that the first act is required of everyone, at least those living within the confines of the church. But the second is required only of those to whom by grace it has been granted to have exercised the first.

---

23. De Ecclesia l. 4. cap. 11.] Bellarmine, *De Conciliis Et Ecclesia*, in *Disputationes Ee Controversiis*, vol. 2 (Ingolstadt, 1605), bk. 4, ch. 11.

24. Pag. 337.] Perhaps paraphrased from *Acta Et Scripta Synodalia Dordracena Ministrorum Remonstrantium In Foederato Belgio*, vol. 1 (Harderwijk, 1618/1620), p. 337.

§7. To prevent any latent obscurity in such an important subject, I have appended here a brief and Scholastic proof of this thesis: *The person of Christ the Mediator is the proper and formal object of justifying faith.* The person of Christ the Mediator can be considered either simply—that is, by abstracting it from the merits that arise from His works as the God-man—or it can be considered with respect to how it is clothed in merits and with the Mediator's righteousness requisite to acquire salvation for the faithful. Justifying faith, moreover, admits of a threefold concept. We understand it either *with respect to species*, as when it establishes the species of faith as distinct from the faith of fundamental principles and of miracles, by which it corresponds to the title *faith* but not with justifying efficacy. The second concept is faith taken in a *reduplicative* sense. This denotes faith not only *per se* but that by which one is justified. Finally, the third concept is faith taken *comprehensively*. This entails both degrees of faith, namely, the reliance through which we are justified in the divine court, and the full assurance through which we are justified in the court of conscience. Now that I have explained these preliminaries, I posit the following three arguments.

First: justifying faith, understood with respect to species, claims for itself the person of Christ the Mediator as its principal object but not as its singular object. This faith gravitates toward all that God was pleased to reveal but primarily toward Christ, according to that πολυθρύλλητον[25] aphorism: "The circumference of faith is the word of God, the center of faith is the Word, God."

Second: that same faith, when taken in a reduplicative sense, as that by which one is justified, takes Christ's person as its formal object. For it is constituted and designated justifying faith based on its consideration of Christ, likewise, with respect to its singular object. For these two terms, *to constitute* and *to designate*, signify formal causation, because it regards the person of Christ alone by which faith justifies. The wounded Israelite looked upon the bronze serpent for salvation with the same eye that he beheld fountains, rivers, mountains, trees, and other things of that type. But he looked with saving gaze, as such, upon the serpent alone. This faith looks upon Christ's person, I repeat, and it alone, but not considered simply. Rather, it looks upon Him as He is clothed with the merits and righteousness that accrue from His active and passive obedience. Therefore, every time faith listens to Christ it is at the same time a faith in the Savior's righteousness. Peter expressed this pointedly at the very outset of his second letter: πίστις ἐν δικαιοσύνῃ τοῦ Θεοῦ ἡμῶν καὶ σωτῆρος Ἰησοῦ Χριστοῦ (2 Peter 1:1).[26]

---

25. "Very well-known." A. gives a rare Greek word here with no Latin gloss.
26. "Faith in the righteousness of our God and Savior Jesus Christ."

Third: The object of justifying faith, with respect to its degree of full assurance, is complex (it contains axioms of this sort: Christ died for me, I am a son of God, my sins have been forgiven). But it is not complex as regards the person of Christ, what that is and its qualities, under the aspect of Mediator. The resting faith through which we are justified refers to and terminates in this person. Ames sets out the whole issue quite succinctly, yet with clarity and lucidity:

> Faith justifies only on this ground: to the extent that it apprehends that righteousness for which we are justified. Such righteousness, moreover, does not rest in any axiomatic truth to which we grant assent but in Christ alone, who was made sin for us, that we might become righteousness in Him. Therefore, expressions that show that we must seek righteousness in the person of Christ alone are repeated frequently in the New Testament.[27]

§ 8. Our next task will be to weigh carefully some insights from several different passages. Paul, in speaking about Christ, says, ἐν τούτῳ πᾶς ὁ πιστεύων δικαιοῦται (Acts 13:39).[28] And elsewhere he writes, καὶ ἡμεῖς εἰς Χριστὸν Ἰησοῦν ἐπιστεύσαμεν, ἵνα δικαιωθῶμεν ἐκ πίστεως Χριστοῦ (Gal. 2:16).[29] John also says in his gospel, "He who does not believe has already been condemned, because he has not believed on the name of the only begotten Son of God" (ὅτι μὴ πεπίστευκεν εἰς τὸ ὄνομα; John 3:18). And in his first epistle, he says, "This is His commandment, that we believe on the name of His Son Jesus Christ" (ἵνα πιστεύσωμεν τῷ ὀνόματι τοῦ υἱοῦ αὐτοῦ Ἰησοῦ Χριστοῦ; 1 John 3:23). There are countless other passages that either directly establish the person of Christ (for this is what "the name" means) as justifying faith's formal object or point to Christ Himself by that expression.

We really should listen to our two countrymen Anthony Wotton and Thomas Gataker on this subject. Wotton writes, in his *Treatise on the Sinner's Reconciliation,*

> What does it mean to believe in Christ? Is it only to believe that the things that Christ says are true? But why then was it necessary for the Holy Spirit to make use of such a novel and unusual word, especially one that was esoteric and fairly unfamiliar? There is no doubt that this expression εἰς Χριστὸν πιστεύειν[30] is entirely from the Holy Spirit and peculiar to

---

27. Medullae l. 1. cap 27. thes. 17, 18.] Ames, *Medulla S.S. Theologiæ* (London, 1629), bk. 1, ch. 27, thes. 17–18, pp. 140–41.

28. "In Him, everyone who believes is justified."

29. "And we have believed in Jesus Christ that we may be justified by faith in Christ."

30. "To believe in Christ."

Him. He did not borrow it from any Greek source, not even from the authors of the *Septuagint*, who rendered the Hebrew Scriptures in Greek. Therefore, it seems extremely likely that the Holy Spirit—because He used a novel form of expression that clearly means *fiducia*—intended to introduce something other than this word's usual meaning.[31]

Obviously (as Wotton explains just a bit later),[32] the meaning is that *fiducia* is justifying faith. By this we trust Christ, to obtain pardon through His merits and satisfaction.

Gataker confirms Wotton's conclusion and says, in his *Treatise on the Style of the New Testament against Pfochen*,

The phrase πιστεύειν εἴς τινα is found thiry-six times in the gospel of John—that is, to believe εἰς τὸν Κύριον, εἰς Χριστὸν, εἰς τὸ ὄνομα,[33] and similar expressions. Precisely where could one find phrases like this among the ancient Greeks in the works they wrote? No doubt, those who have with the greatest possible diligence thoroughly examined all of them, even the various fragments, have, as yet, unearthed for us nothing like that.[34]

§9. So far we have been equally occupied with outlining and constructing the nature of justifying faith. In order to draw out the similarity between this faith and the shield, we will draw help partly from etymology, partly from history. The Hebrew word מָגֵן, meaning *shield*, is derived from the root גָּנַן, *has protected*. Etymologists derive the Latin word *clypeus* from Greek ἀπὸ τοῦ καλύπτειν, because it conceals and so also watches over. The prince of poets says, "Under sweep of shield they shelter safe."[35] And from another passage, "Their bodies protected by long shields."[36] The helmet protects the head exclusively; the breastplate, only the chest. But the shield, as a versatile weapon, offers protection to the whole body.

No matter how many times enemies attack, faith provides protection for the whole soul. The world roars. It threatens poverty, prison, swords, torture racks, and even the cross. Whoever is fitly ensconced behind the shield of faith will be very well prepared to answer, with Basil, "You should frighten children with these little hobgoblins! They can strip me of my life;

---

31. Part 1. lib. 2. cap. 14. § 3.] Wotton, *De Reconciliatione Peccatoris* (Basel, 1624), part 1, bk. 2, ch. 14, sec. 3, pp. 82–83.

32. Ibid. § 6.] Wotton, *De Reconciliatione Peccatoris*, part 1, bk. 2, ch. 14, sec. 6, p. 85.

33. "To believe in someone," "in the Lord," "in Christ," and "in His name," respectively.

34. Cap. 8.] Thomas Gataker, 1574–1654, Church of England clergyman and scholar, *De Novi Instrumenti Stylo Dissertatio* (London, 1648), ch. 8, pp. 88–89.

35. Vergil, *Aeneidos*, bk. 2 (line 227).

36. Vergil, *Aeneidos*, bk. 8 (line 662).

they can't take away truth."[37] Yet to face a homegrown enemy, our own flesh, is bad enough. It tries to allure us with the rattle of coins, honors, and petty pleasures. The man who gazes by faith upon Christ will consider these enticements set before him worth no more than a straw. "May your money perish with you"—so Galeazzo Caracciolo heroically said—"if any of you think all worldly wealth deserves comparison with the splendors of my Jesus that I enjoy even for one short day."[38] A certain bishop said about Luther, when he—should I say bravely or faithfully?—scorned the Romanists' whoremongering enticements, "Damn! This German animal cares nothing for money."[39] That hellish lion can keep roaring till his heart's content!

But the next chapter will be a more suitable place to deal with the Devil and how to extinguish his flaming arrows. Here I want to add only Augustine's famous comment: "One conquers a visible enemy by striking him, an invisible one by having faith."[40] Certain other scholars—and among these, the name Pliny is prominent—thought that *clypeus* was derived from ἀπὸ τοῦ γλύπτειν, *to sculpt.*[41] Men who had not yet accomplished anything difficult used a shield that had no decorative badges. This is why Vergil says, "Unrenowned with barren shield."[42] Nevertheless, the shields belonging to higher-ranked soldiers were usually painted or covered with pictures. This is the origin, as Lipsius shows,[43] of family crests. But among Christians, there was also a custom of decorating their shields with both pictures and inscriptions. One man had his silver shield inscribed with the whole of the Apostles' Creed as a kind of summary of the evangelical faith.[44] Another skillfully carved on his shield the story of Christ's birth.[45] This epigram helps us grasp the intent:

---

37. *Theodor.* hist. eccles. l. 4. c. 17.] Theodoret, *Ecclesiasticae Historiae*, probably bk. 4, ch. 16, pp. 682–84. A. provides only his Latin gloss.

38. Galeazzo Caraccolio (Galaecius Caraccolius), 1517–1586, Italian Calvinist, perhaps quoted in Niccolò Balbani, 1522–1587, preacher in Italian Calvinist congregation in Geneva, *Galeacii Caraccioli Vici Marchionis vita* ([Geneva], 1596).

39. *Mel. Adam.* in vita *Lutheri* p. 158.] Adam, *Vitae Germanorum Theologorum*, p. 158.

40. De verb. Domin. Serm. 8.] Augustine, *De Verbis Domini in Matthaeo* (*sermo* 8).

41. Natural. hist. lib. 35. c. 3.] Pliny the Elder, *Naturalis Historia*, vol. 3, bk. 35, ch. 3.

42. Vergil, *Aeneidos*, bk. 9 (line 548).

43. Analecta ad militiam. lib. 3. dialog. 2.] Lipsius, *De Militia Romana* (Antwerp, 1602), bk. 3 dia. 2, probably p. 108.

44. *Aloysii Novarini* Schediasmata. l. 4. num. 100.] Luigi Novarini, 1594–1656, Italian Roman Catholic theologian, *Schediasmata Sacro-prophana* (Lyon, 1635), bk. 4, ch. 22, num. 100, p. 124.

45. Idem Electorum sacrorum l. 2. num. 491.] Novarini, *Electa Sacra*, bk. 2, perhaps ch. 21, num. 491, p. 260.

Ὦ πόσον εὐήθης ὁ ζωγράφος ὅτι χαράσσει
  Κοίρανον εἰρήνης ἀσπίδι τικτόμενον.[46]

That poet at least, whoever he was, did not find it at all inappropriate to display upon a shield, an instrument of war, the Prince of Peace. I am completely convinced that Christ's history and person are most suited to the shield of faith, as is evident from my comments in the preceding paragraphs.

§ 10. We now transition to history. Plutarch tells us that the Athenians customarily rejoiced if any soldier brought back his shield safe from the battle, even if he had lost his sword. They immediately crowned him by placing upon his head, like a tiara, a shield. Some scholars maintain that David himself references this very old custom in the final verse of Psalm 5: "O Lord, You crown us with the shield of your good favor."[47] It is certain that those men stand fast who have preserved their surpassingly noble crown, the shield of faith. "I have kept the faith," Paul says. "What remains is the crown of righteousness stored up for me" (2 Tim. 4:7–8). Furthermore, the ancient authors extol Myrtilus's[48] shield. He was a soldier of massive courage. When he had sailed on a seafaring expedition, his boat accidentally sank. Relying upon the same shield that he had used to fight, he swam safely to harbor. This is the source of that epigram:

> Escape from dangers twin I made in one small buckler round,
> Once when pressed hard upon the soil, and once when on the sound.[49]

Look now at this distinguished badge of faith. There is nothing really on sea or land, nothing in good times or bad, more useful to the man in danger, nothing more productive of his salvation. When the allurements of royalty led Moses into extreme danger, "by faith he refused to be called the son of Pharaoh's daughter." When a tyrant filled with anger threatened him, "by faith he left Egypt, unafraid of the king's blazing wrath" (Heb. 11:24, 27). Finally, many times soldiers have been forced, from most severe hunger, to gnaw the hide torn from their shields after they had softened it with warm

---

46. "How tenderhearted was that man who with his chisel skilled
      Engraved the Prince of Peace, His lowly birth, upon a shield."

A. gives the Greek with no Latin gloss. The couplet is anonymous and comes from a Greek anthology (see Loeb, vol. 9). We know A. used *Anthologia Graeca Florilegium Diversorum Epigrammatum In Septem Libros Distinctum* (Venice, 1550), see p. 396n3 in this edition.

47. *Jac. Coreni* clypeus patientiae, p. 61.] Jakob Coren, 1570–1631, *Clypeus Patientiae* (Lyon, 1622), bk. 1, ch. 1, p. 6.

48. Myrtilus, charioteer of King Oenomaus.

49. *Alciat.* Emblem. p. 572. 573.] Andrea Alciati, 1492–1550, Italian jurist and humanist, *Emblemata* (Leiden, 1594), pp. 572, 573 (*emblema* 161).

water.[50] Livy says that something like this happened at Casalinum,[51] and Silius Italicus reports of Saguntum,

> Their naked shields, of hide stripped bare, they chewed to make a meal.[52]

Hegesippus relates that when Vespasian was besieging the Jews in the sacred city and they could find no relief from starvation, some of them tore the skins from their shields "to make food for themselves from what had failed to defend them."[53] So then, the promises of the gospel are the straps of leather from which the shield of faith is constructed. If we can ἰδιοποιεῖσθαι[54] these, they will supply food to the famished, even in most extreme scarcity. Jerome once said, "Faith has no fear of famine."[55] And this is really no wonder, because faith itself becomes Christians' nourishment.

§ 11. Now it remains for me to show why the spiritual soldier must take up this shield over all the other equipment. That one must do this is obvious from the fact that the Devil attacks this weapon first because of its strength, and more than all the other items. The Devil, personally and quite pointedly, desires and attempts to do this, both on his own and by dispatching subordinates. After the Emperor Julian had surrendered himself to Satan's captivity, he began to rage wildly against the faith. Then his famous mocking comment became known: "You Christians have nothing else to say, nothing in your heart except 'Believe,' 'Believe'!" (οὐδὲν ὑπὲρ τὸ πίστευσον τῆς ἡμετέρας ἐστί σοφίας).[56] What a fitting statement for the chief of apostates! We will find him less infuriating, however, if we call to mind not so much the words as the irreverent jokes certain pontiffs made against the virtue of faith. Whenever they label us "Only-Faithers" and "Faith-Aloners"[57] they mock us pretty much like Julian did with his taunt.

---

50. Ap. *Lipsium* de militia Romana lib. 3. Dialog. 2.] Lipsius, *De Militia Romana*, bk. 3, dia. 2, p. 111. Lipsius quotes the same line of Italicus.

51. Livy, *Ab Urbe Condita*, 23.19.13.

52. Italicus, *De Secundo Bello Punico*, bk. 2, p. 35.

53. Hegesippus [Pseudo-Hegesippus], second century church historian largely preserved through Eusebius, *De Bello Iudaico* (Cologne, 1575), bk. 5, ch. 39, p. 611.

54. "Repurpose."

55. Jerome, *Epistola XIV Ad Heliodorum Monachum*, sec. 10, in *The Principal Works of Jerome*, ed. Philip Schaff, NPNF II, vol. 6 (1893; rev. ed., Peabody, Mass.: Hendrickson, 1999), p. 17. Jerome: *fides famem non timet*; A.: *Fides non metuit famem*.

56. *Nazianz.* Orat. 1. contra *Julianum*.] Gregory Nazianzus, *Adversus Iulianum Imperatorem Prior Invectiva*, in *Opera*, vol. 1 (Paris, 1630), p. 97 (*oratio 3*). A. gives the Greek with his own quite free Latin gloss.

57. *Solifidianos* and *Fidesolarios*, respectively. These could also be translated "Solifidians" and "Fidesoliasts."

But come now, reader, let us examine more distinguished sources. Bellarmine calls that specific[58] faith that we profess "Luther's figment."[59] Andradius terms it a "most mindless insanity."[60] But Panigarola beats them all. He reportedly said, "If anyone should say, 'I believe that I shall be saved through the blood of Christ,' he makes this claim from his foolishness and is, in fact, committing a grave sin."[61]

Second, it is evident that what we have called the shield must be put on first and foremost because faith rightly holds first rank among the other virtues. For in that list of spiritual gifts that the Apostle published, faith is—so I would put it—the first link of the chain: "Add to your faith virtue, to virtue knowledge, to knowledge self-control, to self-control patience, to patience holiness, to holiness brotherly love, to brotherly love charity" (2 Peter 1:5–7). This chain-link of faith, suspended from Christ like a magnet, pulls toward itself all the other rings—since what has begun in faith forms a chain—and terminates in charity. "The house of God is founded by faith, built up by hope, completed by love," says Augustine.[62] Ἀρχὴ ζωῆς πίστις, τέλος δὲ Ἀγάπη.[63] So wrote Ignatius in his letter to the Ephesians.

§ 12. I would not casually compare these most distinguished virtues without good reason. For charity's natural tendency would rather yield its own position to another than quarrel about it. But because the same Apostle ascribes as much to faith here in Ephesians[64] as he elsewhere does to charity in Colossians—"Over all, put on charity" (Col. 3:14)—the reader will grant Paul the courtesy of thinking him consistent, provided that can be done satisfactorily. And it can be done satisfactorily if we state that charity really does rule over all the virtues that pertain to a proximate end and are entailed in the second table of the law. But faith, we say, also rules over charity itself. Now since the proper acts of all these virtues are produced from love *by command* (as the Scholastics say) and not *by elicitation*,[65] so acts of love itself depend upon faith's command. This is why Paul says to

---

58. *Fidem specialem*; this refers to faith with respect to species, as explained in the first distinction of the thesis in section 7.

59. De poenit. l. 1. c. 6.] Bellarmine, *De Sacramento Poenitentiae*, in *Disputationes De Controversiis*, vol. 3 (Ingolstadt, 1605), bk. 1, ch. 6.

60. Orthodox. explicat. l. 6. p. 477.] Andradius, *Orthodoxarum Explicationum* (Cologne, 1564), bk. 6, p. 477.

61. Apud *Andream Rivetum* in 13 Disp. p. 237.] Francesco Panigarola, 1548–1594, Italian Franciscan preacher, quoted in Rivet, *Catholicus Orthodoxus*, vol. 1, tract. 4, qu. 16, p. 299.

62. Augustine, *De Verbis Apostoli*, 20.1.

63. Ignatius, ca. 50–ca. 130, bishop of Antioch, *Ad Ephesios*, in *Epistolae* (Paris, 1608), p. 250 (*epistola* 11). "The beginning of life is faith; its end, love."

64. I.e., Eph. 6.

65. *Imperative* and *elicitive*, respectively.

the Galatians, "Faith working through charity," as a mistress through her maidservant (Gal. 5:6). And likewise, to Timothy, "The end goal of the command is charity proceeding from an entirely genuine faith" (1 Tim. 1:5). In this passage of Ephesians, moreover, it says, ἐπὶ πᾶσιν ἀναλαβόντες,[66] meaning "above all things" without exception. But in the Colossians passage, it says, ἐπὶ πᾶσιν δὲ τούτοις τὴν ἀγάπην, meaning "above all things" with a certain limitation.[67] The word τούτοις[68] restricts the supremacy of charity to virtues that concern a proximate goal, such as mercy, kindness, and things of that sort that Paul had mentioned earlier in the passage.

But here the last verse of 1 Corinthians 13 sticks out and slows us down as we rush along. There Paul even raises charity above faith itself in a most eloquent fashion: νυνὶ δὲ μένει πίστις, ἐλπίς, ἀγάπη, τὰ τρία ταῦτα· μείζων δὲ τούτων ἡ ἀγάπη.[69] I will say only briefly that in this passage, the Apostle is comparing the three virtues, called theological, as concerns their duration. He is looking not at the duration of their essence (which is equal for all three in the country of the blessed) so much as of their principal duty. And here there will be room for some inequality. The act of hope is peculiar to the longing for future blessedness. As soon as we obtain this complete and absolute blessedness, the act of hope will immediately cease. Then all that will remain is the expectation of everlasting happiness. Similarly also, because faith's principal duty is to rest upon Christ the Mediator that we may acquire remission of sins, we must discharge this obligation as soon as we say goodbye to sin, though some sin may remain in other respects. But charity, so far as concerns its highest duty (which is always one and the same in both states, that of grace as well as of glory) will never fail [1 Cor. 13:8]. Why do I say "fail"? It will never totter or grow tired, and as it grows rich by fresh additions in heaven, in this celestial, or rather royal, land, it will hold almost total sway. Let love reign supreme even now, as she certainly will in the future among those who behold God face-to-face. Only let what is rightly owed to faith, love's parent, remain untouched among those who are still pilgrims.

§ 13. How can I extol you, Faith, most noble of the virtues? You are the hinge upon which the gate of heaven turns, the channel through which the water of life is drawn up, that little wedding band by which the mind is betrothed to God. You are the holding vessel for Christ's blood, the sole condition of the new covenant, and the most important part of the new

---

66. "When you have taken up over everything."
67. "In addition to all these things, love."
68. "To these things."
69. "But now these three remain: faith, hope, love. The greater of these is love."

creation. They who find rest through you are safe, and they who receive certainty of their salvation are happy. You are the eye of our souls, the hand, the mouth, and all things. You could, with justification, claim for yourself what that maiden, the very one who gave birth to God, once said about herself: "My spirit exalts in God my Savior, because He has seen the lowly estate of His maidservant. Therefore, all generations hereafter shall call me blessed" [Luke 1:46–48]. But why, brothers, should we not incessantly preach faith as that most blessed of graces? Does not the Holy Spirit, in Hebrews 11, seem to lavish wild praises on it? There is truly no more pleasant sight than to see a bride, as with Solomon in *Song of Songs*, "leaning upon her beloved" (Song 8:5). Bernard describes this "leaning" so beautifully: "The bride leans upon him in vain if he is not leaned upon. But if he is leaned upon, then all things are possible for she who leans upon the one who is in every way capable."[70] Nothing is sweeter to the taste than this assurance of faith. Peter says, "Be eager to make your calling and election sure. For if you will do these things, you will never fall. In this way you will receive a broad entrance into the kingdom of our Lord and Savior Jesus Christ" (2 Peter 1:10–11). Those who have not been completely assured do, in fact, enter, provided they rest upon Him. But in the meantime, like a small boat with its oars pulled in, its hull gaping open, or split maybe, its rudder lost, it barely limps into port. For those who rejoice in full assurance, πλουσίως ἐπιχορηγηθήσεται ἡ εἴσοδος [2 Peter 1].[71] They are like a ship that is very well-equipped and loaded with foreign merchandise. While sailors applaud, trumpets blast, sails and banners are unfurled, a favorable wind carries it from the furthest Indies to the fatherland of her merchants.

---

70. Serm. 6. in Cantic.] Bernard of Clairvaux, *In Cantica Canticorum*, *sermo* 85, sec. 5. Bernard does not have *sin autem innitatur*.

71. "A path shall richly open up." A. gives a portion of the Greek with no Latin gloss.

CHAPTER VIII

The Devil's Flaming Shafts
That Faith Extinguishes

Section 1: The Devil is called ὁ πονηρός[1] because he is formally, entirely, definitively, and efficiently evil.[2] Sections 2–3: His flaming shafts are persecutions, temptations, and satanic instigations.[3] An interpretation of 2 Corinthians 12:7 and a hypothesis. Section 4: The twofold concept of extinguishing. Faith extinguishes persecutions. Section 5: The extinguishing likewise of temptations. Some statements of Luther and Gesner that are full of fiducia. Section 6: Faith supplies six antidotes for satanic instigations. A distinction between temptations of the flesh. A useful story from Johannes Climacus. Section 7: Satan's titles and Christ's are diametrically opposed. Why satanic instigations, when repulsed, do no damage. Section 8: Steady praise for Jean Gerson. Satan assails us in so many different ways because he knows he will suffer such numerous punishments. The theory of Martin Antoine Delrio.

§1. Pausanias tells us the story that the following expression was once engraved on Agamemnon's shield: οὗτος μὲν φόβος ἐστὶ βρωτῶν.[4] Paul suggests, in the same verse in Ephesians, the first part of which we covered in the previous chapter, that this could legitimately be engraved on the shield of faith: ἐν ᾧ δυνήσεσθε πάντα τὰ βέλη τοῦ πονηροῦ τὰ πεπυρωμένα σβέσαι [Eph. 6:16].[5] In order to give these words a more luminous interpretation, I must fully explain three things: who precisely ὁ πονηρός is,[6] what exactly are his flaming shafts, and finally, what kind of skill believers need to extinguish all of them.

---

1. "The evil one." The word is found in Matt. 6:13 and 1 Cor. 5:13.

2. A. uses adverbs here to express something like the fourfold Aristotelian causality.

3. Tertullian, *De Pudicitia*, in *Opera Quae Hactenus reperiri*, vol. 5 (Cologne, 1617), ch. 13. This word *iniectiones* to describe the action of Satan in particular is from Tertullian.

4. Pausanias, *Pausanii Commentarii Graeciam Describentes*, ed. Marcus Masurus (Venice, 1516), p. 130.

5. "With this you shall be able to extinguish all the flaming arrows of the evil one."

6. "The evil one."

There is no doubt that the Devil, branded with the same burning mark so many times, is wicked. Theologians search as carefully for that first act of devilish wickedness as geographers do for the Nile's source. The currents of both, nevertheless, are evident to all. And there is no one, so I hold, who will deny that the Devil is utterly wicked.

First, he is utterly wicked *formally*. We take this as given with regard to the Holy Spirit: in one respect, subjects and persons that are extraordinary are honored with the title *angel* (examples include calling manna *angelic bread*, calling David wise *like an angel of God*, Paul speaking in the *tongues of angels*, and Christ writing His apocalyptic letters *to the angels of the churches*). Likewise, from the opposite perspective, those that are especially objectionable are named after the Devil. The Lord says to Peter, Ὕπαγε ὀπίσω μου Σατανᾶ,[7] when Peter stunk of worldliness (Matt. 16:23). And he said of Judas, "One of you is a devil" (John 6:70). James says of worldly wisdom that it is "earthly, bestial, and demonic" (James 3:15).

Second, the Devil is depraved *entirely*. There are certain remnants of the moral virtues even in apostates. But in Satan, these are completely missing. Even if sometimes he makes an effort, at least, at the appearance of truth, meanwhile he is nurturing some abomination, readying it so that he may smooth out a path to deception. This is why demons are called τὰ πνευματικὰ τῆς πονηρίας (Eph. 6:12), that is, according to Beza, "spiritually depraved."[8] For they are doubtless spirits in whom wickedness reigns unrivaled.

Third, he is depraved *definitively*.[9] This is the origin of the famous statement "To err is human, but to persist in error is diabolical." The Lord says of Israel, "Will not the one who has turned away return?" (Jer. 8:4). There is no need for the good angels to return, because they never turned away. Similarly, the Devils turned away such that they cannot return. But to true Israelites, however much they were rejected for their sin, the returning grace shall be given.

Fourth, he is utterly wicked *efficiently*. The sacred page makes abundantly obvious how much effort Satan has used in generating every kind of wickedness, from the very beginnings of the world all the way down to the present day. Who was it that drove our first parents[10] to taste of the Tree of Knowledge, accompanied by the loss of the Tree of Life? And who drove that fratricide Cain to slaughter, with one blow, almost one quarter

---

7. "Get behind me, Satan."

8. "Spirits of wickedness," A. gives the Greek and Beza's Latin gloss, *Spirituales Improbitates*. Perhaps sub loc. Eph. 6:12 in *Annotationes*.

9. *Finaliter*, without possibility of change and with respect to purposes and destiny.

10. *Protoplastos*.

of the world?[11] The Devil. Who stood at the right hand of the priest Joshua as he was performing sacrifices in order to thwart him [Zech. 3:1]? Who attacked Christ personally in the desert? The Devil. Who pushed Judas to betray Jesus, David to take a census of the people, Ananias to embezzle from the church? The Devil. Who tested Job with cancerous sores, Paul with blows, and has ensnared the whole world with atheism, sexual immorality, idols, and bloodshed? The Devil. No mortal exists, even were his eloquence astounding, who can portray the Devil more darkly wicked than he deserves to be depicted. As we frequently read of Christ and of heaven, so also of Satan's malice: truly it surpasses all exaggeration.

§ 2. So far as concerns his flaming darts, τὰ βέλη τὰ πεπυρωμένα [Eph. 6:16], Eustathius's remark is helpful: βέλος ἐστὶ πᾶν πόρρωθεν βαλλόμενον.[12] The word βέλος has quite a broad application, for it includes in its range every projectile thrown to attack a distant enemy. These include javelins, torches, lances, spears, spits, arrows, torsion darts, and everything of that sort. Lipsius gives a very full list in his *War Engines*. These are designated πεπυρωμένα by a metaphor borrowed from military usage.[13] This means *from torches*, that is, from small burning shafts commonly thrown against the enemy. Statius says of these,

> And javelins that fell, with missile streaming strands ablaze.[14]

Or the image was adopted from poison-tipped arrows. As soon as they open a wound, they catch fire as the heat of the toxin spreads from there throughout the whole body. Now Satan's flaming darts specifically (as I tried to define them within fixed limits) seem like they can be restricted to persecutions, temptations, and satanic suggestions.

Christ allows us no further doubt as to whether Satan's persecution is necessary. In His letter to the church of Smyrna, He said, "It shall come to pass that the Devil will cast some of you into prison to test you" (Rev. 2:10). And Jacob allows us no doubt whether Satan is the dart. As he was about to die, Jacob prophesied as follows concerning Joseph: "Although they shot at him, although archers pursued him with deep-seated hatred, still the strength of his bow endured" (Gen. 49:23–24). And Peter leaves no

---

11. I.e., four people were alive at that time, and by murdering Abel, one quarter of the population was destroyed.

12. "A dart is anything hurled from a distance." Probably Eustathius of Thessalonica, *Parekbolai Eis Ten Homerou Iliada Kai Odysseia*.

13. Lib. 4. Diolog. 4. & 6.] Lipsius, *Poliorcetica* (Antwerp, 1596), bk. 4, dia. 4, p. 207; dia. 6, p. 218ff. "Flaming."

14. Statius, *Thebaid*, in *Opera Quae Extant* (Cologne, 1612), 5.387, p. 161.

doubt that the dart should be described as "flaming," for he himself calls it πύρωσιν, μὴ ξενίζεσθε τῇ ἐν ὑμῖν πυρώσει (1 Peter 4:12).[15]

Now it is entirely appropriate for us to assign temptations to the one who has the name ὁ πειράζων [1 Thess. 3:5].[16] The shafts, to take an example, are what stir up lust. Solomon says of the youth ensnared by the prostitute's charms, "He immediately follows her like an ox to the slaughter until an arrow pierces his liver" [Prov. 7:22–23]. And temptation involves fire as well. Everyone is familiar with the Apostle's saying: κρεῖσσόν ἐστι γαμῆσαι ἢ πυροῦσθαι [1 Cor 7:9].[17] Students of philology know what Horace said on this topic:

> Go off now quick to where the pleas of cloying youth entice,
> That is, if you would like to roast your liver over twice.[18]

We also have Vergil's statement about Dido:[19]

> She feeds the wound from her own blood, ensnared by blinding fire.[20]

And also Catullus's comment about another woman:

> Up leapt the flame throughout her breast and deep within her heart.
> It raged through bones, all set alight, in marrow's lowest part.[21]

And last, there is this comment from Musaeus, in his poem on Cupid's arrows. Again and again, with a phrase that could not be more specifically suited to the topic at hand, he calls Cupid's shafts πυριπνείοντας ὀιστούς, "fire-breathing projectiles."[22]

§3. Instigations are completely and utterly diabolical. Satan persecutes us through the world, tempts us through our flesh, but personally and on his own initiative attacks us. His shafts are very pointed, for they penetrate and permeate the imagination. The imagination is compelled while suffering convulsion to receive, whether it wants to or not, "frightening things about

---

15. "Fiery," "do not be surprised at the fiery trial among you."

16. "The tempter."

17. "It is better to marry than to burn."

18. Carmin. Lib. 4. Ode 1.] Horace, *Carminum*, bk. 4, ode 1 [lines 10, 12]. A. has somewhat awkwardly combined part of two lines from Horace's *Odes*.

19. Dido, legendary queen of Carthage.

20. Vergil, *Aeneidos*, bk. 4 (line 2).

21. Gaius Valerius Catullus, ca. 84–ca. 54 BC, Roman poet, in *Catullus Tibullus Propertius* (Amsterdam, 1630), 64.92–93.

22. Probably Musaeus Grammatiucs, fifth century, late antique author, *On the Loves of Hero and Leander* (London, 1647). A Greek-Latin version exists as *Mousaiou Poiemation Ta Kath Hero Kai Leandron* ([Venice, 1517]).

the faith," as Bernard says, "and horrifying things about the Godhead."[23] But his shafts are described as flaming, if anything ever deserved the title, because they burn and torment the mind beyond what one can describe with much precision. In Gerson these instigations are termed "hellish flies, constantly biting and filthy."[24] William of Paris writes, "The spirit of blasphemy is a swarm of thoughts so distressing and troubling that, generally speaking, such a trial is like martyrdom."[25]

There is a very difficult passage in 2 Corinthians 12. If it is proper to interpret it a little bit differently than most people usually do, then there will be every reason to hold that faith is not removed from people who suffer such things. ἐδόθη μοι σκόλοψ τῇ σαρκί, ἄγγελος Σατανᾶ, ἵνα με κολαφίζῃ (2 Cor. 12:7).[26] Moulin,[27] Cameron,[28] and Gualter,[29] very famous scholars, after disproving beyond a reasonable doubt the common interpretations that Paul is referring to some especially obnoxious opponent—burning lust or the gadfly of arrogance—thought they would propose their own explanations. But these are mutually incompatible. The first holds that Paul is hinting at a disease that the Devil has incited to recur periodically. The second scholar takes a more literal approach: that there is a wicked angel harassing the Apostle's body with actual whips. The third, however, thinks Paul is referring to his own conscience, because Satan is reminding him of what he had done to the church when he was a young man and an adult. I am not interested right now in revising their opinions, although I do want to bring to light an interpretation that differs from all the rest and leave it to men of sound judgment to decide.

Because the word σκόλοψ means a sharpened stake, in the phrase ἐδόθη μοι σκόλοψ τῇ σαρκί,[30] there is a reference to those stakes and splinters that, during Paul's era, punctured Christians' bodies [2 Cor. 12:7].

23. Bernard of Clairvaux, *De Conscientia Tractatus*, in *Opera Omnia*, vol. 5 (Cologne, 1641), ch. 6, *Divinitate*.

24. Tractat. contra tentation. blasphem.] Jean le Charlier de Gerson (Jean Gerson), 1363–1429, French theologian and spiritual writer, *Tractatus Foedae Tentationis*, in *Opera*, vol. 4 (Paris, 1606), col. 975. A. has *immundae* rather than *immundas*.

25. Lib. de tentation. & resistentiis.] William of Auvergne (William of Paris), ca. 1180–1249, French Scholastic philosopher and theologian, *De Tentationibus*, in *Opera Omnia* (Vannes, 1591), ch. 1, p. 283.

26. "There was given me a thorn in the flesh, a messenger of Satan to buffet me."

27. Vates l. 2. c. 12.] Du Moulin, *Vates* (Leiden, 1640), bk. 2, ch. 12, p. 115.

28. Myrothee. p. 237.] John Cameron, ca. 1579/1580–1625, Reformed minister and theologian, *Myrothecium Evangelicum* (Geneva, 1632).

29. Comment. in locum.] Rudolf Gwalther (Gualter or Gualther), 1519–1586, German Reformed theologian, *In Posteriorem D. Pauli Apostoli Ad Corinthios Epistolam Homiliae* (Zürich, 1572), ch. 12, fol. 124r (homily 55).

30. "I was given a thorn in the flesh."

I am referring to the bodies that the attendants of Nero's cruelty sometimes used as evening torchlight. If this is accurate, then, no doubt, whatever kind of torture this metaphor points to will be a hotly blazing dart. Juvenal περιφράζει[31] such a death like this:

> …You'll glow just like that brand
> of men who burn and smoke while with their chokered necks they stand.[32]

Seneca recounts the same sort of punishment, mentioning and condemning this prayer of Maecenas:[33] "While life lasts, all is well. Uphold me in this life, even if I should rest on a sharpened cross."[34] Lipsius comments on this, "They sit on a sharpened cross who have been pierced with a sharpened spike extending from their rear and emerging through the mouth."[35] When Paul says, "Messenger of Satan," in the nominative case, what else could he mean if not the very prince of devils? Is it not plausible that it was he who tested Adam in paradise, Christ in the desert, and Paul in this dread-heavy struggle?

We should understand the blows with which the Devil strikes as what theologians call "instigations." In a fight, these blows usually come thick and fast, and even in a very short space of time they are repeated ten, one hundred, or even one thousand times. And this is not a novel interpretation, since Jean Gerson, chancellor of Paris, held it. He lived almost three hundred years ago, and in his treatise *Against the Temptation to Blasphemy*, he writes the following about these chilling ruminations: "Sometimes they occur by a mere suggestion of some hostile, disturbing figment, saying, 'Deny God,' or, 'Curse God.'" And a little later, he says, "This kind of goad was given the Apostle, as many learned doctors hold."[36] I think this is adequate to dispel criticism for novelty.

§4. Now let us examine just how effective faith is in extinguishing these darts. The wisdom of the flesh, because it is itself from the Devil, customarily sends back the opponent's lit shafts with extra fuel added. The other gifts[37] of the Holy Spirit can relieve some of these, while a general grace resists the opposing corruption. But it is only faith that extinguishes them all.

---

31. "Glosses."

32. Juvenal, *Satyra*, 1.

33. Gaius Maecenas, d. 8 BC, Roman equestrian famous for his love of luxury and poor poetry.

34. Epist. 101.] Seneca, *Epistolae* (*epistola* 101). The original is in verse.

35. Seneca, *Epistolae*, ed. J. Lipsius (*epistola* 101).

36. In calce tomi 4. edit. Paris. colum. 973.] Gerson, *Tractatus Foedae Tentationis*, col. 973. A. skips several lines in these quotations.

37. *Charismata*.

And this is particularly of two types, one of which is προφυλακτικός.[38] It does its work either by ensuring that these shafts are not taken into the soul completely or that they do not penetrate too far. This is similar to the way that leaden balls launched from siege machines reportedly are extinguished when they strike an earthen wall. The other kind is θεραπνευτικός,[39] by applying the blood of Christ as a medicine once the mind has been wounded. This is likened to the life-giving salves that extinguish the fear that poison-tipped arrows kindle.

Let us begin then with persecutions. Hebrews 12 makes abundantly clear faith's tremendous power both to ward off blows of persecution and to heal them when they land. The martyrologies confirm this, along with ecclesiastical literature of every genre. Says Cyprian, "Antichrist threatens, but Christ defends. Death bears down, but immortality follows. The world is torn away from us, but paradise lies open. Earthly life is snuffed out, but eternal life awaits."[40] Tertullian: "Crucify us, torture us, condemn us, grind us down. Your wickedness proves our innocence. We grow in size every time you measure us. The blood of Christians is seed. We thank you for your verdicts. When you condemn us, God acquits us."[41] Gordius,[42] according to Basil, declared, "Do not begrudge me my blessed hope. The more torments you add, the more rewards I shall receive."[43] There is also this from Prudentius:

> Torture and prison, hooks and molten plates, and death
> Itself the final blow, for Christians is mere sport.[44]

Finally, lest I belabor the point and the subject's charm cause me to drag out my discourse, I finish off with this from Martin to his friend Philip.[45] "So far as concerns the success of our cause in public, I am almost a casual onlooker, and I don't give a snap for those threatening and savage papists. If we fall to ruin, we will fall with Christ, he who rules the world. I would rather fall with Christ than stand with Caesar."[46]

---

38. "Defensive."

39. "Restorative."

40. De exhortat. martyr. c. 12.] Cyprian, *De Exhortatione Martyrum*, in *Opera* (Basel, 1558), ch. 12, p. 178.

41. Apologet. cap. ult.] Tertullian, *Apologeticus*, ch. 50.

42. Gordius, d. 362, Roman judge, Christian convert, and martyr.

43. Basil, *In Gordium Martyrem*, in *Opera Omnia*, vol. 1 (Paris, 1618), p. 522 (*homilia* 19).

44. Hymno in laudem *Vincentii*.] Aurelius Prudentius Clemens (Prudentius), 348–ca. 410, Roman Christian poet, *Vincentio Mariyri*, in *Prudentii Poetae Opera* (1610), fol. 94v (hymn 5).

45. I.e., Luther to Melanchthon.

46. *Melch. Adam.* in vita *Lutheri* p. 138.] Adam, *Vitae Germanorum Theologorum*, p. 138.

§ 5. More troubling shafts now call for my attention, I mean flaming temptations. And yet faith has also learned how to snuff out these. Although the fiery serpent (whom we understand as the tempter) may wound us, there is no way he can inflict death upon us, provided we never stop gazing upon the bronze serpent, Christ our Lord. For the Savior was prefigured through manna from heaven in almost the oldest of legal types. This is because His flesh is true food. And He was also prefigured through the water from the rock, because His blood is true drink [John 6:55]. So also He was prefigured through the serpent who brought salvation in the desert, because His grace is true medicine. Faith caused Joseph to close up his ears against the enticements of the woman who ruled his house and made Peter deaf to the clinking gold Simon Magus offered. Satan managed both of these temptations. Every day, faith makes Christians flee the Devil when he approaches at one time or another, pulling them back from those delicacies of vice that were perhaps going to give them opportunity to sin. This is in keeping with Augustine's very healthy warning: "Try to escape the forceful onset of lust if you want to win a victory."[47] Once in a while, Christians will flee him at his first approach by opposing him bravely. This is James's counsel—"Resist the Devil and he will flee from you" (James 4:7)—as well as Peter's. He writes, "Your adversary prowls around like a roaring lion seeking someone to swallow up. Resist him firmly by faith" (1 Peter 5:8–9).

Set Luther here before your eyes as a man who fought with all his strength. After he fortified himself with faith, Luther spoke to the Devil more like somebody winning than struggling. He said: "Mr. Satan, your threats and terrors have absolutely no effect on me. There is someone named Jesus Christ in whom I believe. He has set aside the law, condemned sin, abolished death, destroyed hell and is, O Accuser, your accuser!"[48] What we read from the theologian Gesner[49] is almost identical to Luther's comments: "Granted, the Devil will come and test me, a wretched sinner, with his strength. I will hold before him the Son of God hanging from the cross, and I will say to him, 'Against Him have I sinned, not against you. I believe I belong entirely to Him. If you defeat Him, you will also defeat me.'"[50]

---

47. Lib. de honestat. mulierum.] Augustine, *De Honestate Mulierum*, in *Omnium Operum*, vol. 9 (Basel, 1528), 1.1.

48. *Luther.* tom. 4. fol. 55. A.] Martin Luther, *Commentarius In Epistolam Pauli Ad Galatas*, sub. loc. Gal. 2:19. *O Satan, Satan tuus.*

49. Solomon Gesner, 1559–1605, German Lutheran theologian.

50. *Melch. Adam.* in vit *Theol. Germ.* p. 746.] Adam, *Vitae Germanorum Theologorum*, p. 746.

§6. The most burning shafts of all still remain: diabolical instigations. My attention now tarries over this topic. Faith also teaches us how to extinguish these flaming darts.

First, by distinguishing between temptations that bubble up from our own heart and the instigations implanted from without. The former generally prompt us toward things that are rather pleasing to nature and more consistent with the direction of a reason vitiated by the fall. In other words, this happens so peacefully and gradually that the mind remains in control of itself even at the moment of greatest heat. But the latter kind rush in with more than human force like lightning and more quickly than premeditated passions typically do. They fill the mind with such dread that they almost seem to expel the very heart from the chest. At the same time, the mind perceives and sorrows that those things are beginning subtly to take hold—feelings at whose presence even the most depraved nature starts to tremble.

If we stopped at those suggestions that we do not ourselves give birth to but only suffer, and which, accordingly, contain more distress than disgrace, they would be no different than the painful slag that flies off the Devil's anvil. The guilt then will belong to the Devil. We are no less impervious to blasphemy than Benjamin was to theft, when a silver goblet was found in his grain sack though he himself had no knowledge of it [Gen. 44]. But as was once and truly said, with abundant theological acumen, though with little poetic charm, "Temptation does no harm except when the tempted obeys." But Bernard expresses this same sentiment both beautifully and thoroughly when he writes, "Satan bites when he drags us toward consent. When he only suggests something, he is barking. And then he does not wound us but offers a crown, because although he may exhaust the one who resists, he does not bring under his sway the one who does not consent."[51]

Faith teaches us, second, to form a plan, and to rest comfortably in plans well laid. Because the flesh depends on the secret things of Satan, it willingly conceals his hidden actions with a veil of silence. And so,

The wicked shame of foolish men conceals all wounds uncured.[52]

But when faith has gained a harbor in which it can safely spread out, then it should reduce all things to this one point—namely, how it may more often and more happily experience a healing hand. Let us take as our example the very zealous monk described in Johannes Climacus. "This man," he says,

---

51. De interiori domo cap. 47.] Bernard of Clairvaux, *De Interiore Domo*, in *Opera Omnia*, vol. 5 (Cologne, 1641), ch. 26.

52. Horace, *Epistolarum*, bk. 1 (*epistola* 16).

reported to me later what he experienced. For twenty years, he was harassed by a spirit of blasphemy. After he had tormented his flesh in vain with fasting and long nights of prayer, he carried to a certain very holy old man—whom he feared to look at directly—the temptation written on a piece of paper and lay face down before him. After the old man investigated the matter more deeply and determined that the monk was suffering a feeling of blasphemy but without consent, he smiled. Lifting the prostrate brother from the ground he said, "Please place your hand, son, on my head." When the monk had done that, the veteran soldier of Christ reportedly said, "May this sin, brother, that has attacked you for so many years be upon me, or let it attack me from here on out."[53]

At these words, the monk began to recover. And his illness, both chronic and acute, right then and there began, by God's grace, to cease raging.

§7. Faith teaches us, third, to embrace Christ as our Savior, who willed to suffer diabolical instigations in the desert that He might sympathize with Christians who toil under the same cross. Therefore, the sacred text affirms that "He was made manifest to destroy the works of Satan" (1 John 3:8). And for this reason, the sacred Scriptures have assigned specific titles that are precisely opposite to those by which the Devil is identified. Satan is called "the dragon"; Christ, "the Lamb of God." The Devil is the "adversary"; Christ, our "surety" and "friend." Satan is the "roaring lion"; Christ, the "good shepherd of the sheep." Satan is ὁ πονηρὸς; Christ, ὁ δίκαιος.[54] The Devil, "master of shadows"; Jesus, "Father of lights." Satan is known as the "steward of death", but Christ, the "author of salvation." The former is the "accuser"; the latter, our "defender." Finally, Satan is known as the destroyer, ὁ ἀπολλύων [Rev. 9:11]. But He is known as Jesus, which means Savior.

Fourth, faith teaches us to immediately reject these instigations. A significant part of piety is to guard against our thoughts that they not accidentally become blasphemous and ill-tempered. A garden is not polluted by nettles that the indignant gardener removes as soon as he sees them sown from the bypaths. No, the harmful grasses that germinate and sprout from within, these pollute the garden. Likewise, the soul is contaminated by internal lusts and not by things that Satan introduces, so long as we ceaselessly and earnestly reject and eradicate these instigations. The reason is that, at the very earliest stage, it is within one's power to temper his own lustful desires. But he can never prevent the Devil from attacking his imagination.

---

53. Scala paradisa gradu 23.] Johannes (John) Climacus, ca. 570–ca. 649, Christian ascetic and writer, *Scala Paradisi* (Cologne, 1583), sub loc. Gradus XIII, p. 203.

54. "The evil one," "the righteous."

§ 8. Fifth, faith teaches us to turn away the mind and retreat directly to other thoughts. It is not safe to engage in a give and take argument, as the saying goes, with the Devil. He is far and away the most experienced and desperate Sophist of all. "We overcome a shameful temptation better fleeing than fighting. For the more someone tries to put out this kind of flame by blowing on it, the more he fans it to life." Thus, the chancellor of Paris.[55] He also thought that they were really wise who paused while diabolical instigations washed over them internally. And if someone feared that he was going to be devastated by their blasts, to try to catch the north wind in his cloak. In so doing, he did not lessen the wind's blast but felt its full force.

Sixth and finally, faith teaches us that if this evil stubbornly persists against all remedies, then we must scorn the Devil with holiness, not haughtiness (heaven forbid), and despise his harmless darts. If you don't mind, dear reader, please note the instruction, example, and parables of Gerson. He says, "It is helpful for the Christian, relying upon divine aid, to laugh at and disregard a wicked spirit, saying, 'Unclean spirit, if you could do anything more to me, you would be doing it. I could not care less about you, because I call upon the Lord my God as my helper, that I may never give in to you at all."[56] In that same passage, he states that he knows a certain man who quickly recovered by using that medicine, because "a very arrogant spirit does not allow itself to be spurned for long."[57]

In another passage, he likens those who hold Satan in low esteem to "full-grown children; those who dress up as scary ghosts typically do not so much frighten such children but just seem absurd. And they are like travelers arduously training in preparation for a journey. The harmless barking of dogs and honking of geese bothers them so little that they don't even notice."[58]

But if anyone finds it unusual that Satan—who is so incredibly knowledgeable—could be unaware that the more evil he does the saints, the more he is going to suffer, yet he still injures the saints in numerous ways and makes no end of evildoing, I would like such a person to consider this: Satan's knowledge is so constrained by evil hatred that his spite appears to exceed his intelligence. Delrio brilliantly and forthrightly states, at the very threshold of the preface to his *Discourses on Magic*,

> There are no truces, there is no peace where hatred and envy have no
> limit or end. The Devil loves to reap thistles for himself, while he brings
> upon us thorns. He enjoys enlarging his own punishment and increasing

---

55. *Gerson.* Tom. 4. colum. 976.] Gerson, *Tractatus Foedae Tentationis*, col. 975–76.

56. Idem operum part. 3. col. 442. C.] Gerson, *Pro Devotis Simplicibus*, in *Opera*, vol. 3 (Paris, 1606), col. 442.

57. Gerson, *Tractatus Eiusdem*, col. 442.

58. Idem part. 4. col. 974. A.] Gerson, *Tractatus Foedae Tentationis*, col. 974.

his peculiar torments, provided he implicates as many men as possible in eternal suffering. Meanwhile, he mocks humanity as the divine image, discolors what Christ's precious blood has made white, and delivers over to its former slavery that image which was claimed for freedom. With a victory plainly Cadmean,[59] Satan destroys by being destroyed, and driving the sword through his enemy's side, he sends it into his own vital organs.

Thus del Rio.[60]

---

59. I.e., a victory "involving one's own ruin."

60. Delrio, *Disquisitionum Magicarum* (Mainz, 1624), sig.):( ):( ):(2r (*proloquium*).

CHAPTER IX

The Helmet of Salvation,
or the Assurance of Hope

Sections 1–2: Full assurance is compared to a helmet. How assurance of hope relates to certainty of knowledge and faith. This is twofold, both intuitive and discursive. Sections 3–4: An investigation of whether this certainty is both complete and perpetual. Section 5: Assurance is founded on the certainty of present grace and the infallibility of final perseverance. Some Romanists, but not all, try to undermine both of these. Marinario and Eisengrein are commended. Section 6: A refutation of Bellarmine's first conclusion on the impossibility of certainty. An exegesis of Romans 8:38–39. Censure of Tirinus. Sections 7–8: A review of conclusions 2ª and 3ª. The Romanists' σκέψις[1] and Protestants' πληροφορία[2] are demonstrated with various examples. Section 9: A careful examination of Bellarmine's conclusion 4ª, "No certainty without a special revelation." What we should grant Bellarmine, and what we should deny. A distinction is drawn concerning revelation. Sections 10–11: The testimony of the Holy Spirit is posited as cause 1ª of full assurance. Two passages are carefully explained—2 Corinthians 1:21–22 and 2 Corinthians 5:56. Our teaching on this subject frees us from fanaticism. Section 12: The testimony of our own spirit as drawn out by the Holy Spirit is posited as cause 2ª of full assurance. Five claims are made on this topic. Section 13: It is proven in various ways from 1 John that the saving gifts of the Spirit are cause 3ª. Section 14: The current status of the question as to whether they who have been born again can fall from grace. Section 15: Three theses are presented on this topic: 1ª The grace of election cannot be annulled. An explanation in defense of 2 Timothy 2:19. Section 16: 2ª The grace of justification is not interrupted. A response to arguments from Adam's fall and more serious sins of the faithful. Section 17: 3ª The grace of sanctification does not die away. The extent of saints' falls. Section 18: An epilogue, together with incisive quotations from Davenant.

---

1. "Skepticism."
2. "Full assurance."

§ 1. The largest part of wisdom for a snake consists in taking care of its head. Therefore, so as not to neglect defense of the body's chief part, the Apostle adds these words: καὶ τὴν περικεφαλαίαν τοῦ σωτηρίου δέξασθε ("And take up the helmet of salvation" [Eph. 6:17]). In another passage, he expresses it like this: "Equipped with the breastplate of faith and righteousness, and with the hope of salvation as your helmet" (1 Thess. 5:8). A comparison of these passages shows sufficiently that we must understand the helmet of salvation as the certainty of the hope of laying ahold of eternal salvation. As the helmet protects the head and guards it, so it cannot be harmed by deadly blows from various directions, so also the certainty of salvation preserves the mind of the Christian soldier unharmed against injurious battery of two types of evil.

If the evil of punishment strikes, the helmet makes the head not yield, and—more than that—sometimes even makes it rejoice. This is the reason for the Apostle's statement: "You suffered with joy the plundering of those things that belong to you, like those who know that you have more permanent property in the heavens and something that remains" (Heb. 10:34). There is also this from Cyprian: "The strength of immovable hope thrives among you and durability of faith. And amidst the ruins of a degenerate age, your mind stands erect. Patience never exists without joy, and the heart is always confident in its God."[3]

The comments that the martyr Agatha[4] reportedly made, according to those who labored diligently in detailing the saints' lives, are evidently of the same nature. She said to the persecutor Quintian,[5] who had ordered her breasts cut off,

> Are you not ashamed, tyrant, to cut from my body the part from which you suckled on your own mother? But go ahead, rage as much as you can. Still, two breasts remain that you cannot touch: one is faith, and the other hope. These provide me, even in the midst of torment, comfort and safety. And by their nourishment, I regain the power to persevere.[6]

But if a temptation to the second kind of evil arises—namely, guilt—the one most sure of his salvation can guard against it best. We must not let that putrid poppycock, which our adversaries keep foisting on us over and over, deceive us. I am referring to their claim that such assurance is strongly opposed to true religion and loosens the restraints on license. In reality, we

---

3. Serm. de patientia ad *Demetrianum.*] Cyprian, *Contra Demetrianum*, in *Opera* (Basel, 1558), p. 103 (*tractatus* 1).

4. Agatha, d. before ca. 460, Christian martyr.

5. Quintian, by tradition, a Roman proconsul infatuated with Agatha.

6. *Beyerlinck* Apophthegm. Christian. p. 58. ex *Surio.*] Laurentius Beyerlinck, 1578–1627, Flemish Jesuit theologian, *Apophthegmata Christianorum* (Antwerp, 1631), p. 58.

must understand their argument is utterly worthless. Bernard, to be sure, clearly opposed their position when he wrote as follows in one of his very prudent letters: "He who has been loved without deserving it does not love undeservedly. The man who knows he has been loved without a beginning loves without end."[7]

Or we could take John instead, who is an infallible witness: "Whoever has this hope in himself"—in the Lord—"keeps himself pure, just as the Lord is also pure" (1 John 3:3). Such a man does not defile himself (as those men snarl) but purifies himself. Notice that this purification is not at all connected to the world's standard but to Christ's example: "He purifies himself just as the Lord is pure" [1 John 3:3]. But I also cite as evidence the experience of believers. Do they not feel that the obedience and observance of full assurance rests within them, in their very bosom? Therefore, we must call upon the prince of our salvation, with the greatest possible earnestness, that He may choose to arm each and every one of us with this sacred helmet of hope, so long as we dwell among the living, and until such time as we exchange this life for death. Jerome wrote his *Helmeted Prologue*.[8] May God, in His infinite goodness, grant that we have our sort of "helmeted epilogue"—that is, at least in this very recent struggle, may we possess the most sure hope of eternal salvation.

§2. Now assurance's nature and quality will shine forth much more clearly if, after setting out various distinctions, we next respond to three points of inquiry. Those who read Paul's writings encounter a threefold assurance. The first is full assurance of understanding, πληροφορία τῆς συνέσεως, as mentioned in Colossians 2 [Col. 2:2]. The second is that of faith, πληροφορία πίστεως, as explained in Hebrews 10 [Heb. 10:22]. The third is full assurance of hope, πληροφορία τῆς ἐλπίδος, as in chapter 6 of the same letter [Heb. 6:11]. The true meaning of the individual citations will appear more obvious when formed into a practical syllogism as follows. There is no doubt that he who is adopted as a son of God shall be an heir of heavenly glory. I have been adopted as a son by the grace of God. Therefore, I shall also be an heir of heavenly glory. The Christian immediately lays hold of the major premise of this syllogism of mature grace, by assurance of knowledge, as the gospel truth. And he grants it the most firm and complete assent as much as he can. He grasps the minor premise by assurance of faith, as it relies, of course, upon the testimony that the Spirit of adoption applies to our spirit. Finally, he embraces the conclusion that follows from these premises by means of assurance of hope, as the Apostle teaches: "We

---

7. Epist. 107.] Bernard of Clairvaux, *Epistolae, epistola* 107, sec. 7.

8. Jerome's introduction to the Book of Kings in the Vulgate.

have been brought by faith into this grace by which we now stand, and we glory in the hope of God's glory" (Rom. 5:2).

Next, although certainty of faith can be distinguished from certainty of hope, it cannot, nevertheless, be separated. For this reason, the poet, in one of his very well-known verses, calls hope *trusting*:

> Hope trusts, and favors life to last as part of her design,
> And says that always shall the day that follows be more fine.[9]

In the sacred writings as well, the same Hebrew word בָּטַח is sometimes construed as *he believed* but sometimes as *he hoped*. But even the Apostle measures hope according to the measure of faith when he says, "May the God of hope fill you with all joy and peace by believing, that you may overflow with hope through the power of the Holy Spirit" (Rom. 15:13).

But both of these are twofold, either *intuitive* or *discursive*. Intuitive faith is that which arises from the Holy Spirit's unmediated testimony; it places salvation right before our eyes and has within it the firstfruits of the beatific vision. The other is discursive, which is assembled from the feeling and spiritual experience of the holy dispositions with which God's grace endows us. It is also made up of the works that our consciences testify internally are done according to God, ἐν Θεῷ εἰργασμένα, as the Lord says in John (John 3:21).

§ 3. After these appetizers, we must ask first whether this full assurance we are discussing is *absolutely* complete in the present condition, excluding all wavering. I answer no; it is not. For the kindling of sin remains in our hearts, in the remnants of our concupiscence—when sanctifying grace does not oppose it. No, it is there even with the Spirit's own most resplendent sealing. This, again and again, is the source of new and erupting doubts. Nevertheless, full assurance can be described *respectively*, because an intuitive certitude—for as long as it lasts, even though it does not completely root out the seed of sin—generally removes the feeling of doubt. This is Chrysostom's view, who wrote, ὅταν τὸ πνεῦμα μαρτυρῇ, ποία λοιπὸν ἀμφιβολία.[10] His comments that follow this quote are very emphatic. Full assurance can also be described as *discursive*. Although it does not remove either the seed of doubt or its feeling, yet it overcomes wavering and prevents

---

9. Albius Tibullus, d. 19/18 BC, Roman poet, *Tibullus Cum Commentario* (Vannes, 1567), p. 192 (*elegia* 7) [2.6.20].

10. Homil. 14. in cap. 8. ad Roman.] "Whenever the Spirit bears witness, a sort of doubt remains," Chrysostom, homily I.14 on Romans 8. Greek edition of Chrysostom's works: *Tou En Hagiois Patros Hēmōn Iōannou Archiepiskopou Kōnstantinoupoleōs Tou Chrysostomou*, vol. 3 (Eton, 1611).

it from becoming lethal. And so, although in battle this assurance perhaps yields, it finally emerges from the war victorious.

If I am not mistaken, much light is shed on this topic if we establish the symmetry that exists between certainty and doubt, on the one hand, and holiness and sin, on the other. Where sin reigns, as it does in all the unregenerate, there can be hypocrisy and a certain kind of counterfeit but not even one particle of holiness. Likewise, where doubt reigns, as it does among the sorry wretches whose hope has been corrupted, then a kind of empty confidence or presumption can possibly arise at bright moments. But there is not, properly speaking, even a shred of assurance. Deep within the hearts of the regenerate, sin dwells along with holiness, but a few degrees down and from sources quite opposed to one another—namely, the Spirit and the flesh. Doubt dwells there in the same way, together with certainty. This doubt, on Isidore's definition, is a fear indifferent toward each side of the contradiction—that is, an acceptance of both conditions, together with dread and a firm resolve toward neither. And yet full assurance is *respectively* called holiness even in the pilgrim estate, in keeping with Paul's statement: "I am fully persuaded, in your case, brothers, that you are filled with goodness" (Rom. 15:14). Why should we not, likewise, understand this certainty, because it blocks out sin's dominion, as πληροφορία,[11] a word that means *fullness?* Because, finally, by the Spirit's leading, under whose banner the soldier fights, it utterly and finally routs the compact ranks of doubt that come rushing in from all sides.

§4. The second question is whether this assurance is permanent. I answer with a distinction—namely, that it is permanent as regards its foundation. The Apostle testifies to this when he says, "The one who believes in the Son of God has this testimony within himself" [1 John 5:10]. But it is not so as regards its application. For the Spirit blows where and when He chooses, and He does not always, by His activity, testify with our spirit that we are sons of God [Rom. 8:16]. Instead, He sometimes withdraws and removes Himself. This is the origin of Bernard's frequent sighs: "The hour of His presence is rare; brief is His visit. If only it had lasted!"[12] But the grace that clings to us many times languishes so that we are barely strong enough to draw out any certain comfort. If someone demands an explanation for this gloomy condition that sometimes darkens discursive certainty even in the consciences of those who at other times regularly walk in the light of the divine countenance, I would hardly consider giving any other answer than

---

11. "Full assurance."

12. Serm. in Dominis. infra octav. *Epiphan.* & Serm. 23. in Cant.] Bernard of Clairvaux, *In Cantica Canticorum, sermo* 23, sec. 17.

that it is discursive. Since indeed, as the logic wizards teach us, we more readily agree to those propositions apprehended by way of first principles than by inference, the conclusion also always follows the weaker premise. But because certitude results from a discourse like this—everyone who truly believes will partake of eternal life, I truly believe, therefore I will partake of eternal life—so the mind grasps the major premise far more firmly than the minor one. The major premise is the foundation most plainly revealed in the Scriptures. The latter is inferred from experience and is sometimes more, sometimes less vigorous, based on whether we find the truth of our own faith more clear or more obscure. Therefore, it is a simple matter to conclude that the weaker portion of the syllogism is that which is assumed and thence the conclusion—which follows of necessity—is grasped quite weakly. Consequently, it entails very little certainty, no matter when the fruits of faith appear, whether just barely or insufficiently.

§5. The third point of inquiry is whether this assurance has been established with adequate completeness. I answer that it has. There are, in fact, two particular foundations of the full assurance we are discussing: certainty of present grace and infallibility of final perseverance. Because grace is the first glimmer of glory, glory is also the noonday of grace. Because the embryo of glory is grace, then also mature grace passes into glory. Whoever, under the present circumstances, is sure that he has been established in grace and has learned from the sacred Scriptures that the regenerate never fall from grace, there is no way such a man can easily or for a long time doubt whether he himself must be glorified [Rom. 8:30]. The path of salvation and the path that leads to our fatherland are related to one another by such a fixed law that no one promises himself anything from the latter that he has not already in part received from the former. But it is impossible for the man sufficiently established on the path of salvation and persevering in it to doubt about the path that leads home.

The Roman doctors attempt to undermine the foundation of both of these and so to deprive soldiers of Christ of the helmet of salvation through a kind of theft. For this reason alone, even if there were no others, Luther states one must abandon the papacy: "Had there been no other sin in the doctrine of the Romanists than teaching we must doubt and waver, hesitating and unsure about the forgiveness of our sins, grace, and our salvation, still we have legitimate reasons to separate ourselves from an unfaithful church."[13]

---

13. In cap. 41. Genes.] Luther, *Enarratio In Genesim*, sub loc. Gen. 41:38. *De remissione peccatorum, gratia…justas tamen habemus causas cur ab ecclesia infideli nos sejungeremus* does not appear to be in the original source.

I do not want to pin this charge on all of them, and I am aware with what candor and, at the same time, orthodoxy the Carmelite Antonio Marinario[14] spoke in the speech he made before the fathers at the Council of Trent. He said,

> This is the characteristic quality of true faith—namely, to raise us up to God as sons to a father, to make Christ ours and, in turn, us Christ's, so that we may, with Him, become one body, and in the same body, we may live, reign, rejoice, and glory in the Spirit. Consequently, those who have, through Christ, received righteousness do not wander in a maze of doubt. But with surety of mind, peace of conscience, and joyful heart, taught by that Spirit who produces within them the testimony that they are the sons of God, they dare to cry "Abba Father."

He continues and adds near the end of this comment, "If the heavens fall, if the earth disappears, if the whole world crumbles, I shall stand upright in God's sight. If an angel from heaven tries to persuade me of something else, I will say to him, 'Anathema.'"[15]

Yet I know what Martin Eisengrein, formerly court preacher of His Imperial Majesty,[16] boldly said about this subject once, and, indeed, many times in his *Apologeticus* on the certainty of grace. I will only quote two passages. The first is from the second chapter.

> No Christian, as long as he lives in this world, can advance by God's grace to the point that he can establish with certainty that his sins have been forgiven and that God is propitious to him. But the Council [i.e., Trent][17] has never taught that he must, devoid of all comfort, shake with doubt and fear in everlasting uncertainty. No catholic and approved scholar has ever been the author of this position.[18]

The second passage is from chapter 6 and is expressed with a still greater confidence. He says:

> Here I take my stand and, with strong voice and unmistakable words, proclaim that no catholic and acknowledged doctor has ever opposed the position our adversaries charge us with; namely, that when it comes to remission of sins and God's grace, one must be constantly trembling and in doubt, without any comfort and peace of conscience. I make this

---

14. Antonio Marianario, 1500–1574, Italian Tridentine theologian.

15. Perhaps taken from Paolo Sarpi, 1552–1623, Venetian jurist and theologian, *Historiae Concilii Tridentini* (Frankfurt, 1621). A. will later reference this work when discussing the minutes of Trent.

16. Maximilian II, 1527–1576, r. 1564–1576, Holy Roman emperor.

17. A.'s editorial addition.

18. Pag. 48, 49.] Martin Eisengrein, 1535–1578, German Roman Catholic theologian, *De Certitudine Gratiae* (Cologne, 1569), ch. 2, pp. 48–49.

statement without hesitation and without dissembling. And may God cause my voice to echo throughout the whole Christian world.[19]

May this testimony of Eisengrein be given the greatest possible weight. If it is correct in all respects, it truly holds very great sway with us. But if this good man were now to return from the dead and read the Jesuits' writings, he would not dare to make this assertion about his descendants, even though he stated it with considerable boldness about their ancestors. I will now, bypassing the others, engage in close combat with just Bellarmine. In just one chapter, with four assertions, he worked vigorously to undermine the foundation of this certainty using his earlier contrivances.[20] I will next try to dispense seriatim with all the assertions he lists.

§ 6. This is his first assertion: it is not possible to have certainty of *faith* concerning one's own righteousness. It is a solemn duty for Romanist authors to attack, with all their might, the certainty of a faith beneath which nothing false can subsist. But meanwhile, so that they don't appear to throw their own people headlong into an abyss of despair, they acknowledge that there is certainty of *hope*. Nevertheless, this is done in such a way that they actually substitute for a full assurance of infused and theological hope (which, as Paul attests, does not produce disorder and, as Durand[21] states, cannot fail to support what is already present) a bizarre sort of moral credulity and persuasion supported by empty and deceptive conjectures. What fine certainty this is! How valuable they consider it among the affairs of this age, counting it hardly worth a wooden nickel! But my comments above in the second paragraph of this chapter demonstrate sufficiently that the Romanists must either deny the certainty of hope that they seem to assert or, together with us, assert that certainty of faith they so stubbornly deny. That is, provided it is their intention to derive their theology not from the swamps of the Scholastics but from the fountains of Israel.

I now will discuss, in particular, the foundations on which Bellarmine builds his argument. There is a passage where he commends the love by which we cherish God as the pinnacle of inherent righteousness.[22] But elsewhere, on the topic of charity, he supports a different understanding of a much-heralded passage found at the end of Romans 8.[23] There Paul, in his own name, as well as others', forcefully attaches to faith a certainty concerning love and, thus, concerning his own righteousness. The words

19. Pag. 177.] Eisengrein, *De Certitudine Gratiae*, ch. 6, p. 177.
20. De iustificat. l. 3. cap. 8.] Bellarmine, *De Iustificatione*, bk. 3, ch. 8.
21. Samuel Durant (Durand), 1574–1630, French Reformed theologian.
22. De grat. & libero arbitr. l. 1. c. 6.] Bellarmine, *De Gratia Et Libero Arbitrio*, bk. 4, ch. 6.
23. De Iustificat. l. 3. cap. 15. D.] Bellarmine, *De Iustificatione*, bk. 3, ch. 15.

are, πέπεισμαι γὰρ ὅτι οὔτε θάνατος οὔτε ζωὴ, etc.—that is, "I am persuaded," or *I am sure*, "that neither death, nor life, nor angels, nor principalities, nor powers, nor any other created thing can separate us from the love of God that is in Christ Jesus our Lord" (Rom. 8:38–39).[24] Cajetan says of this passage, "It is not about the certainty of the evidence but the certainty of the persuasion. And this, of course, is the certainty of faith."[25]

Bellarmine is really just focusing on trivialities, while he limits his observations to those who have been predestined as a class.[26] For here the Apostle descends to the hypothesis that applies both to himself—"I have been persuaded"—and also to other believers—"can separate us." And Bellarmine does not win the debate so long as he argues that the verb πέπεισμαι does not indicate any certainty of faith but rather some sort of hypothetical confidence. For although τὸ πείθεσθαι sometimes does mean *likely persuasion*, surely it very often treats of faith, salvation, or some other unrelated cause, as in the numerous passages Bellarmine cited. David Pareus noted this. He criticized this interpretation in a candid and reasonable way, as would someone with both his exacting judgment and unimpeachable morality.[27] Nevertheless, as often as Scripture attributes our πεποίθησιν [Eph. 3:12][28] of salvation to either faith or a proprietary cause, then it means πληροφορία,[29] an infallible and full assurance of faith. This is true here in Romans and in the passage in Timothy where Paul says, "I know in whom I have believed"—καὶ πέπεισμαι—"and am persuaded that He is able to keep safe what I have entrusted to Him against the day" (2 Tim. 1:14). The newly minted Jesuit Tirinus found it safer to retreat to another κρησφύγετον[30] after he realized his allies had been driven from these and similar defenses. He handles this passage in his commentary like this:

> I am sure that nothing will be able to separate us contrary to our will or by compulsion. But we ourselves alone can, by our own depraved will, remove ourselves from God. Therefore, the expression "I am sure" does not mean a comprehensive and absolute certainty but merely one that depends partly on God and His divine providence and partly on us. It

---

24. "For I am persuaded that neither death, nor life."

25. Cajetan, *Epistolae Pauli*, sub loc. Rom. 8.

26. De Justificat. l. 3. c. 9. in respons. ad sept. testimon.] Bellarmine, *De Iustificatione*, bk. 3, ch. 9.

27. *Bellarm.* Castigat. lect. 275. pag. 726.] Appears to be related to David Pareus, *Roberti Bellarmini Politiani Societatis Iesu Theologi Cardinalis De Amissione Gratiae & Statu Peccati* (Heidelberg, 1613), but this work only reaches lect. 106.

28. "Bold confidence."

29. "Most certain."

30. "Rabbit hole."

means nothing except a conditional certainty: if we are willing to work together with God and are unwilling to separate from Him.[31]

What remarkable shrewdness these Jesuits have! But far be it from us to allow the marrow and quintessential property of faith—as a distinguished member of our party calls full assurance—to be ripped away.[32] I want to know, if I may, Jacobus Tirinus, whether you think that our will to which your men grant so much is a god or a creature? If you say a god, then you are the sort of man who deserves to have Christians bury him with stones. If you say a creature, then there is absolutely no doubt that it is included within the apostolic expression οὔτε τις ἑτέρα δυνήσεται ἡμᾶς χωρίσαι [Rom. 8:39].[33] Augustine very fittingly said that "the saints, by God's gift, invincibly will that which is good and invincibly do not will to abandon it."[34]

§ 7. This is Bellarmine's second assertion: "Even if it is perhaps possible for someone to possess this certainty, no one is obligated to do so." Really? I had believed that it was one of the duties of Christians whom Paul urges ἀκριβῶς περιπατεῖν (Eph. 5:15),[35] εἰς τὰ ἄκρα βαίνειν,[36] not to settle in the depths but to struggle vigorously to reach the very peaks of all virtues. But I also believe that we all must strive to gain that assurance that Christ our Lord promised to His disciples when He said, "On that day, you will know that I am in my Father, and you are in Me, and I am in you" (John 14:20). Bellarmine somehow grows cold and allows an indescribable frost to spread across his interpretation of this very sweet expression:

> If anyone strives, in this life, to lay hold of what the Lord says, this will be the immediate answer: to know that we are in the Son and that the Son is in us is not to know that we are justified but to know that Christ is the head of the whole church. For this is how Christ is in us, that is, He is in the church, and the church is in Christ, because He Himself is the head and the church is His body.[37]

---

31. Tirinus, *Commentarius in Vetus et Novum Testamentum* (Antwerp, 1632), sub loc. Rom. 8:38–39.

32. *Esteius* in oration.] George Estye, 1560/1561–1601, Church of England clergyman and author, *Oratio De Certitudine Salutis Et Perseverantia Sanctorum Non Interrupta* in *Brevis Et Dilucida Explicatio*, p. 64.

33. "Nor any created thing shall be able to separate us."

34. De Corrept. & gratia cap. 12.] Augustine, *De Correptione Et Gratia*, in *Omnium Operum*, vol. 7 (Basel, 1528), 1.12.38.

35. "Walk circumspectly."

36. "To climb up to the high places."

37. De Justificat. l. 3. cap 9. in respons. ad quartum.] Bellarmine, *De Iustificatione*, bk. 3, ch. 9.

Good grief! What weak exegesis! What comfort would you possibly have, no matter who you are, to know that Christ is in the church unless at the same time you could know that you are a living member of that same church, so that Christ is also in you? This is the origin of that well-worn expression, "Of what use to me is a distant God? Woe to the man who does not have God as his own." But in fact, we can press these clear principles even further. The Apostle says in Hebrews, Προσερχώμεθα μετὰ ἀληθινῆς καρδίας πληροφορίᾳ πίστεως (Heb. 10:22).[38] In this passage, certainty of faith seems just as obligatory as a sincere heart or drawing near to God. There is also Peter's statement: "See to it that you make your calling and election sure" (2 Peter 1:10). The text reads βεβαίαν ποιεῖσθαι. Hesychius says "this means Πληροφορία βεβαιότης."[39] There is no reason why we should not understand this to mean a βεβαιότητα πληροφορία.[40] But it is impossible for anyone's calling to be secure who has not yet been convinced of his own faith and repentance.

§ 8. Bellarmine's third assertion now follows, presented like this: "It is not a valuable exercise for people ordinarily to have certainty that they possess grace." I have demonstrated above in the first paragraph of this chapter how valuable certainty is for promoting piety. Soon I will show just how valuable the true theory and practice of full assurance is for distinguishing between the true church and her counterfeits.

Now this is the truth of the circumstance: most of the Romanists neither can nor want to have assurance about grace and their own salvation, because they think it is safer to dwell in uncertainty. "It is safe and very humble," says Peter a Soto,[41] "to doubt God's grace toward me and His presence."[42] The Remonstrants, perhaps, want certainty, but they cannot have it without violating their own hypotheses concerning the faith common to the reprobate and the elect, as well as the apostasy of the saints. As Seneca beautifully said, "The distraught mind is anxious for the future and miserable before suffering any miseries. It is worried that the things that it enjoys may not last to the end. It will never be at rest but, by waiting for the future, will lose the present things that it could have enjoyed. It is equally poised between losing something and being afraid of losing it."[43]

---

38. "Let us draw near with a true heart in full assurance of faith."

39. Perhaps Hesychius of Alexandria, fifth century, Greek lexicographer, *Hesychii Alexandrini Lexicon* (1521). "Full assurance of steadfastness."

40. "Full assurance made secure."

41. Pedro de Soto (Peter a Soto), 1495–1563, Spanish Tridentine theologian.

42. Apud *Meisnerum* Anthropol. decad. 3. p. mihi 477.] Meisner, *Anthrōpologia Sacra* (Strasbourg, 1625), vol. 3, disput. 9, thes. 1, quaes. 1, sec. 12, p. 477.

43. Epist. 98.] Seneca, *Epistolae* (*epistola* 98).

Only the orthodox have been granted, in keeping with their doctrinal positions, the desire and ability to possess assurance at the same time. Not only is the full assurance we preach (and which many, by God's grace, greatly enjoy) the chief ornament of our religion, it is also the down payment. Among the Romanists, this assurance is vanishingly rare. But no one—if he has ever examined the logic of the dogmas they customarily defend— should be surprised that these men always take a turn for the worse and that the closer they are to death, the more lavishly they doubt. Pius V[44] supposedly said (as Cornelius a Lapide, among others, reports), "When I was religious, I had good hope for my soul's salvation. When I was made a cardinal, I was afraid. But when I was elected pope, I nearly despaired."[45] What did Bellarmine have to say, that great beacon in the papist firmament, the one who is my present concern and who probably outshone every last Jesuit in learning and holiness? Silvester Petra Sancta, who translated his Latin biography of Bellarmine into Italian, mentioned on the frontispiece of the work a certain manuscript Bellarmine had personally written about his own life at his friends' urging. But Bellarmine wrote it in the third person, and it ends with these words: "He wrote this in the year 1613 AD, saying nothing about his own virtues, because he does not know whether he truly has any. He kept silent about his vices, because they are unworthy to be committed to writing. When judgment day arrives, may they be found to have been expunged from God's book. Amen."[46]

At that point, the "Papist Hercules" was rounding off the seventy-first year of his life (of course, he was born in 1542) when he so frankly admitted that he had no certainty that he had received grace. But if Marcellinus Cervinus[47] should be asked whether someone at death's door could possess certainty about his salvation, he would give this response (we know from his nephew Bellarmine, who also carefully recorded Cervinus's biography). Bellarmine says, "As death approached, Cervinus cast himself down to the depths of humility and seemed terribly afraid of divine judgment. When some began to beg him to pray for them in heaven, he told them, 'That is too great a task. It is not such an easy road that leads to life. I will conclude that God is extraordinarily kind to me if I reach purgatory after many years.'"

---

44. Pius V, 1504–1572, *p.* 1566–1572.

45. In num. 11. vers. 11.] Cornelius a Lapide (Cornelissen van den Steen), 1567–1637, Flemish biblical exegete, *Commentaria In Pentateuchum Mosis* (Antwerp, 1630), sub loc. Num. 11:11.

46. Probably Petra Sancta, *Vita R. Bellarmini Cardinalis Italice Primum Scripta, Latine Reddita, Et Aucta A S. Petra Sancta* (Antwerp, 1631).

47. Marcello Cervini (Marcellus II), 1501–1555, pope from April 9, 1555, until May 1, 1555. His sister Cinzia Cervini was Robert Bellarmine's mother.

This is not at all what the orthodox experience, thank God. And it is not at all the general experience of those who have been quickened to life, or rather, those who have died.[48] I have already described above the full assurance André Rivet possessed on his deathbed.[49] Luther, as he drew his final breath, said, "I thank you, heavenly Father, that you have revealed to me Christ whom I have believed, loved, and honored. Although now I must lay aside this body, I know for sure that I shall remain with You forever and that nothing can pluck me from Your hands."[50] When Caspar Olevianus[51] had drawn near to death and his strength was spent, someone stood next to him and said, "My brother, are you sure of your salvation in Christ Jesus without any doubt, just as you taught others?" In a low voice, Olevianus answered, "Absolutely."[52] Robert Rollock,[53] getting ready to exchange death for life, prayed like this: "Come Lord Jesus, that I may come to You. What a sweet, welcome, and happy departure from this life. Come, O Lord, my sweetness. Set free this my soul, that she may enjoy You, her husband." So also, he professed, "My mind is at peace in a sickened body. I am gripped by no fear of death, sin, or Satan. They have no power over me."[54]

Now, so as not to pass over in deep silence our own countrymen, it seems good to add one or two Englishmen to the men I just mentioned. "Because the Lord has mercy, this heart of mine, how exceedingly great is the rejoicing that fills it all! I feel nothing within except Christ. My desire to be with Him burns with an indescribable heat." These are the words of Robert Bolton of Oxford.[55] "My soul is filled with joy. I believe that, in a short time, I shall see the light of the Lord in the land of the living. I know whom I have professed, whom I have preached, whom I have believed. And now I see the heaven I have gained, into which I must soon be received. No anxiety for anything else holds me, except for the faithful flock I am about to leave." So said Samuel Hieron, a former pupil of our Cambridge.[56]

§9. We now have arrived at Bellarmine's fourth and final assertion: "No one really possesses this certainty except those to whom God has specially

---

48. A play on words, *animati* and *exanimati*, i.e., those who have died in Christ.

49. Hujusce libri cap. 5. § 5.] See book 2, chapter 5, section 5 of the present work.

50. *Melch. Adam.* in ejus vita p. 154.] Adam, *Vitae Germanorum Theologorum*, pp. 154–55.

51. Caspar Olevian (Olevianus), 1536–1587, Reformed theologian.

52. Idem vit. theolog. Germ. p. 602.] Adam, *Vitae Germanorum Theologorum*, p. 602.

53. Robert Rollock, 1555–1599, Church of Scotland minister and university principal.

54. Idem in vitis Theol. exter. p. 188.] Adam, *Decades Duae Continentes*, p. 188.

55. *E. Bagshaw* in vita *R. Boltani*.] Robert Bolton, 1572–1631, Church of England clergyman; Edward Bagshaw, 1629/1630–1671, Independent minister and religious controversialist, *Mr. Boltons last and learned worke of the foure last things* (London, 1632), sec. 17, sig. C6v.

56. *R. I.* Medicus in sua de mor. *S. H.* narrat. quae habetur part. 1. oper. M^{ri} *Hieron* post pag. 763.] Samuel Hieron, d. 1617, Church of England clergyman and devotional writer.

revealed their own justification." The Romanists are far too ready to resort to this excuse, like deer to the caves of Dicte,[57] to dislodge the shafts that are deadly to their position. They try to hide in special and extraordinary revelation. They ascribe to it almost exclusively whatever full assurance sojourners are granted. I shall deal with them generously. I will gladly grant that no one attains full certainty of grace and salvation apart from some revelation. Bernard made this concession before me: "Who is the righteous man if not he who repays with love the God who loves him? This does not happen except when the Spirit by faith reveals to this man God's eternal plan for his future salvation."[58] Bernard also says in another passage: "Who has known the thought of the Lord? Here faith must assist us, so that what lies hidden about us in the heart of the Father is revealed through His Spirit."[59] I would go further and say that special revelation is necessary for someone to become assured of grace. Of course, I do not mean this in the way in which the Romanists take it. They set special revelation against the ordinary kind. No, I mean it in a sense altogether reasonable, if we designate that revelation as special that has been given to each individual person as an individual and is not revealed to others. Thus, we have the well-known quote from the Apocalypse: "I will give him a white stone, and on that stone is written a new name, which nobody knows except the one who receives it" (Rev. 2:17). But if the papists should argue that no one is granted assurance except by a kind of revelation that is completely unambiguous—that is, extraordinary—and is bestowed upon only a very few Christians of the first rank (which was Bellarmine's interpretation), then we must deny that.

To gain greater clarity on this topic, let us divide revelation into the categories *diabolic* and *divine*. I posit that divine revelation is twofold: *extraordinary* and *ordinary*. Extraordinary revelation is that in which the prophets once rejoiced. In our day, this either does not exist at all or is exceedingly uncommon. Ordinary revelation contains two species. We may call one of these *doctrinal*, inasmuch as it illuminates the eyes of our mind for the comprehension of the sacred Scriptures. Thomas says of this, "No one who possesses grace lacks the gift of understanding. But just as the Holy Spirit, through the gift of charity, disposes the human will so that it is properly guided toward some supernatural good, so also, through the gift of

---

57. This is a fairly obscure mythological reference to Mount Dicte in Crete, known for its caves that hid wildlife.

58. Epist. 107.] Bernard of Clairvaux, *Epistolae*, *epistola* 107, sec. 9.

59. Serm. 5. de dedicat. Ecclesiae.] Bernard of Clairvaux, *In Dedicatione Ecclesiae*, in *Opera Omnia*, vol. 2 (Cologne, 1641), *sermo* 5, sec. 7.

understanding, He illuminates the human mind to understand truth. The upright will must be directed toward this truth."[60]

But the second species of ordinary revelation is *personal*, as it makes clear to all manner of people what state they are in with respect to God, whether a state of nature—which is revealed as a spirit of servitude—or the state of grace to which the Spirit of adoption testifies [Rom. 8:15]. Bernard expresses this beautifully in the letter that I just praised. Perhaps I may collate into one quotation the comments he scatters here and there: "The initial mystery of righteousness alone," he means in effectual calling,

> hidden before the ages for those who had been predestined and set apart for blessing, in some way began to emerge from the abyss of eternity. Then it came out into the light for the consolation of the wretched soul, that great plan that had lain concealed from eternity. You, a human being, have as a witness of this hidden truth the Spirit who justifies and testifies by this very Spirit, to your spirit, that you are also, personally, a son of God.[61]

§ 10. No one can fail to see just how appropriate these comments are for illustrating the present subject. Nevertheless, it will become more obvious if I give some proof to Christians of mature faith that they regularly and consistently rejoice in that certainty we defend. I will take as my foundation this rule that all the logicians sufficiently ratify: an effect is established by both immediate and proximate causes that have themselves been established. There are, moreover, three immediate and proximate causes of πληροφορία:[62] (1) the testimony of the Holy Spirit imparted to our spirit, (2) the testimony of our spirit that is drawn out from us by the indwelling Holy Spirit, and (3) the gifts of the Holy Spirit freely bestowed upon our spirit. If I can demonstrate that all of these are causes of assurance and that they are normally established in the regenerate, I have won the debate.

If our opponents deny that the Holy Spirit's testimony (here is where we should begin) is the cause of full assurance, then they have the Apostle as an opponent. He sets this Spirit of adoption against the spirit of bondage to show that it is the source not of anxious dread but of a righteous security in the Lord (Rom. 8:15). He also then clearly states that the influx of this confidence is from the guarantee received from the Spirit. "This is the God who has established us for this very purpose, who has also given us the guarantee of the Spirit. Therefore, we are always confident in heart" (Θαρροῦντες οὖν πάντοτε) (2 Cor. 5:5–6). The fathers cast their votes with us. Augustine writes, "Let the soul declare, let the soul declare with

---

60. Aquin. 2ᵃ 2ᵃᵉ qu. 8. art. 4.] Thomas Aquinas, *Summa*, 2-2.8.4.
61. Bernard of Clairvaux, *Epistolae*, sec. 5, 7 (*epistola* 107).
62. "Full assurance."

assurance, 'You are my God,' because God has said to our soul, 'I am your salvation.'"[63] Macarius de Sanctis, while he was still speaking to those who dwell on earth, said, "Even though they have not yet, in this age, entered into the full inheritance prepared for them, nevertheless, they are very confident because of the guarantee that they have already received, just as if they had already received the crown and become sharers in the kingdom."[64]

Do you, readers, want something still more clear than that? Let us go back now to Paul. "God is the one who strengthens us with you in Christ and who anoints us. He it is who also sealed us and imparted to our hearts the Spirit's guarantee" [2 Cor. 1:21–22]. There are almost as many pledges of assurance here as there are words: βεβαιῶν,[65] χρίσας,[66] σφραγισάμενος,[67] ἀρραβῶνα.[68] God *strengthens* us: if this does not seem like enough, he has *anointed* us. Priests, kings, and prophets were certified for the office that they fulfilled by this very ceremony. If this does not render believers sufficiently assured, *he has sealed* them. Is there anyone in whom such signed documents do not produce faith, after this seal is set upon them? No, there is something still more significant: *he has given a guarantee*. No surer sign among men is possible, for the one who accepts it, because it will be grafted onto the possession of what is promised or of what is acquired.

§ 11. Our opponents say that it is not typical for all the regenerate indiscriminately, so they claim, to receive such a proof by the law of providence "sooner or later" (these are the two adverbs that I must hammer on repeatedly). But instead, it is, by a unique privilege, granted only to a select few, singled out from the general mass of the faithful. If this is their claim, then the blessed Apostle again contradicts them. Paul, in his letter to the Galatians, treats that same Spirit—who he says to the Romans "testifies with our spirit that we are sons of God, and if sons, then also heirs who are going to be glorified with Christ" (Rom. 8:16–17)—as common to all the regenerate. He writes, "Because you are sons, God has sent forth the Spirit of His Son into your hearts, crying, 'Abba, Father'" [Gal. 4:6]. Notice that he says "because" you are, or "whereas" you are, or "to the extent" that you are.[69] Those who have an adequate knowledge of dialectic or have even waved at

---

63. In Psal. 132.] Augustine, *Psalmi Enarratio*, sub loc. Ps. 148:12 (2.17).

64. Ἀσφαλεῖς εἰσιν ἀπὸ τοῦ Ἀρραξῶνος, οὐ ἐδέξαντο νῷ, ὡς ἤδη ἐστεφανωμένοι καὶ βασιλεύοντες. *Macar.* Homil. 17. pag. mihi. 248.] Macarius of Egypt, *Homiliae Spirituales*, p. 248 (*homilia* 17).

65. "Establishing."

66. "Anointed us."

67. "He has sealed."

68. "He has given a guarantee."

69. Three Latin explicative conjunctions: *quoniam*, *quia*, and *quatenus*.

it from the doorstep know just how strong is the consequence that follows from the expression "To the extent."

Because they did not dare to disparage the credibility of such a great authority, they went down a different path and put their emphasis here: "Nobody can be certain that the Holy Spirit is the author of that testimony from which he derives comfort. Anyone, without distinction, can fear whether—deceived by an evil spirit and grown secure to his own destruction—he thinks that he is in grace when he is actually outside it." Those are the comments of Gregory de Valencia.[70] "From our perspective, this testimony cannot be sure, because we cannot be altogether sure that it is from the Holy Spirit and not from the Devil." That is the position of Cornelius a Lapide.[71] This is quite a soul-torturing theology! Who could believe that the Holy Spirit would betray and inform on Himself? That when the sun rises, with its rays it not only reveals but also distinguishes itself from everything else it illumines? John seems to agree when he says explicitly, "The Spirit is the one who testifies that the Spirit is truth" (1 John 5:6). Let the Jesuits continue to make themselves hateful to God and His servants by their blasphemies. We prefer to confess with Ambrosius Catharinus that the Holy Spirit never speaks to us without at the same time informing us that He Himself is the one speaking. At the Council of Trent, he did more than just give lip service to this principle.[72] I am well aware that men of depraved judgment seize upon this opportunity to slander our theologians. (They hold that all the arguments that claim the Spirit testifies to us are as valuable as an old wives' tale.) As though our men were trying to inject into the church hollow doctrines of private inspiration! But that is no reason why we should be afraid of any such μορμολύκειον[73] expression, as long as we are not cognizant of even the least folly in our principles. But in fact, even this word itself *inspiration* was originally sound: Ἐνθουσιασμός ἐστιν ὅτε ἡ ψυχὴ ὅλη ἐλλάμπηται ὑπὸ τοῦ Θεοῦ (thus both the Suda and Hesychius).[74] When we take inspiration in this sense, I wish that we were all Enthusiasts! According to Gregory Nazianzus, heavenly blessedness is quite simply τῆς βασιλικῆς θεωρία Τριάδος ἐλλαμπούσης καὶ ὅλης ὅλῳ νοῖ μιγνομένης.[75] But "when the heretical offspring grew up just a

70. Tom. 2. Disp. 8. qu. 4. punct. 4. pag. 1284.] De Valencia, *Commentariorum Theologicorum* (Ingolstadt, 1592), p. 1276.

71. Comment. in Rom. 8:16. p. 107.] A Lapide, *Commentaria In Omnes Divi Pauli* (Antwerp, 1627), sub loc. Rom. 8:16.

72. Hist. Concil. Trident. Latin. pag. 162.] Sarpi, *Historiae Concilii Tridentini*, pp. 161–62.

73. "Hobgoblin."

74. "Inspiration occurs when the entire soul is illuminated by God." Hesychius of Alexandria, *Hesychii Alexandrini Lexicon* (1521).

75. *Nazian.* Orat. de Grandine.] Gregory Nazianzus, *In Plagam Grandinis Oratio*, in *Opera*,

little bit, such people afterward came to be called fanatics and Enthusiasts, imagining that they were governed by a divine light. When they had laid aside divine Scripture, then they rushed ahead to their own invented revelations or demonic urgings." This is how Matthias Martinius describes them.[76] But the extent of our contempt for such madness is so well known, I think, that I don't need to bother with a tedious proof. For we embrace no revelation except that which is consistent with the Word down to the finest point, since the revelation we designate *doctrinal* is the expounder of the Holy Scripture. The revelation that we have said is *personal* proclaims to us precisely what is valid and logically derived from that same source.

§ 12. The second cause of assurance is properly constituted as our own spirit's testimony concerning ourselves, drawn out by the Holy Spirit who dwells within. So John writes, "If our heart does not condemn us, $\pi\alpha\rho\rho\eta\sigma\iota\alpha\nu$ $\check{\epsilon}\chi o\mu\epsilon\nu$ $\pi\rho\grave{o}\varsigma$ $\tau\grave{o}\nu$ $\Theta\epsilon\acute{o}\nu$" (1 John 3:21).[77] What would be the point in the Apostle saying that God's Spirit "$\sigma\upsilon\mu\mu\alpha\rho\tau\upsilon\rho\epsilon\hat{\imath}\nu$[78] with our spirit that we are sons of God" if the same testimony were not reflected back by the individual's spirit (Rom. 8:16)? But the man who calls into question its latitude should heed Solomon's comment: "The spirit of man is the lamp of Jehovah" (Prov. 20:17). There is also this from Paul: "What man knows the things that belong to man except the spirit of man who is in him?" (1 Cor. 2:11). From this we can conclude that faith and love, no matter where they blossom in the soul, spread out very broadly. Augustine very clearly says, "We see faith itself, when it is in us, in ourselves."[79] And Davenant: "The revelation of faith within us is inevitable, for faith is the image of the light that makes itself as visible as other things."[80] From this source the regenerate derive testimonies about themselves. "Remember, O Lord, that I have walked before You in truth and with a perfect heart" (Isa. 38:3). These are the words of Hezekiah. Paul says, "This is our boast, this the testimony of our conscience, that we have conducted ourselves in the world with God's honesty and integrity" (2 Cor. 1:12). "I call upon you, Lord, with a faith

---

vol. 1 (Paris, 1630), p. 230 (*oratio* 15). "Contemplation of the royal Trinity that illuminates and permeates by its whole mind all that is."

76. Probably Martinus, *Lexicon Philologicum.*

77. "We have boldness before God."

78. "Testifies."

79. De Trin. lib. 13. cap. 1.] Augustine, *De Trinitate*, in *Omnium Operum*, vol. 3 (Basel, 1528), 13.1.3.

80. Determ. p. 16.] Davenant, *Determinationes*, qu. 3, p. 16.

that, though weak and helpless, is still faith."[81] So wrote Caspar Creuziger.[82] Now this testimony of our spirit, such as it is, is drawn out by God's Spirit. I think we must pay careful attention to this testimony and, thus, learn (as we must) not only to distinguish full assurance from empty faith but also to discern between the Holy Spirit's workings and testimonies.

Please allow me here, by the reader's good grace, to set before your eyes five very important—and yes, quite uncommon—claims. Allow me freely to submit them to the reader's judgment, if perhaps his faculties are trained in such mysteries. I claim first that the Spirit's threefold operation generally arises before testimony to Himself appears. Thus, that testimony is never displayed before any of its operations and is rarely displayed before all of those operations become evident. The first operation is the *infusion of sanctifying grace*, which is mentioned several times in John 3 in connection with rebirth from the Spirit. The second operation is the *illumination of infused grace* to make possible true discerning of that same grace. Paul talks about this in his letter to the Corinthians: "We have received the Spirit who is from God, so we know the things that God has given to us" (1 Cor. 2:12). The third is the *effectual representation of that grace radiating in our spirit* as the foundation of consoling testimony. The Apostle appears to do more than merely hint at this when he writes in Romans, "I speak the truth in Christ, I am not lying, συμμαρτυρούσης μοι τῆς συνειδήσεώς μου ἐν πνεύματι ἁγίῳ" (Rom. 9:1).[83]

I claim second that the first of these operations renders us holy, the second renders us aware of our own holiness, and the third makes us certain, by a discursive assurance, that our consciences are not mistaken in this conviction. Consequently, the first operation is not sufficient for knowledge unless the second is also present, nor is the second sufficient for πληροφορία[84] if the third operation is missing. For just as, among the unregenerate, this applies to the spirit of servitude, so among the regenerate, it relates to the Spirit of adoption. Very many of the unregenerate have some internal awareness of how serious their faults are and that these deserve the lake of fire. Nevertheless, not one of them confronts himself with this conviction and says, "Eternal death hangs over my head," before that verdict, elicited by the spirit of servitude, is awakened. Likewise, many of the regenerate perceive within a living righteousness and faith that becomes effectual through love. Yet each of them is not able, in their own case, to draw the

---

81. *M. Adam.* in vit. Theol. Germ. p. 197.] Adam, *Vitae Germanorum Theologorum*, p. 197.

82. Either Caspar Creuziger (often Cruciger), 1504–1584, or his son Caspar Creuziger (often Kaspar Creutziger), 1525–1597, both German Lutheran theologians.

83. "And my conscience bears witness to me from the Holy Spirit."

84. "Full assurance."

following conclusion: "I myself, one of the faithful, will truly, somehow, obtain salvation." This will not happen until, by the Spirit of adoption, he is stirred up to produce testimonies of that kind.

Third, whenever the Holy Spirit sees fit (in order to strengthen this certainty of faith) to add His own testimony to such a pronouncement of our spirit, the question is placed, at least while that peace of mind endures, beyond every contingency of doubt. Because then there arises a general coalescence of all witnesses, both those in heaven and those which are on earth (I will say more about these later). Without this convergence of testimonies, some room for doubt will always remain. Fourth, there is absolutely no doubt that all those people, no matter how many there are, who boast in the testimony of the Spirit but do not feel the grace of the Spirit at work within, in the heart, are allowing themselves to be deceived, either by their own φιλαυτία[85] or by the Devil masquerading as an angel of light. Because, although the Holy Spirit is at work in those to whom He has not yet condescended to testify, nevertheless, He never testifies to anyone regarding their salvation in whom He has not already efficaciously worked.

Fifth, it is true that the measure of one's certainty generally corresponds to the degrees of indwelling grace. This is why Bernard says, "One increases in confidence to the extent that he grows in grace."[86] Nevertheless, sometimes the one who is less sanctified can actually enjoy more assurance. The explanation for this is that the Holy Spirit, on whose sole "nod" and control all πληροφορία[87] depends, communicates Himself to any individual He wills. But sometimes He desires, according to His own judgment, to supply less illumination, to elicit less testimony, and to testify less in that place where He has granted more indwelling grace. This is so that it may be obvious how freely He shares all things. In such a circumstance, it inevitably happens that even he who experiences less grace enjoys considerable assurance. Similarly, lowercase letters appear clearer at midday than uppercase markings at twilight.

§ 13. We have identified as the third cause the gifts of the Spirit freely bestowed upon our spirit. These are, of course, the infused dispositions of grace, and from them proceed the practice of faith and love. He who denies that all the regenerate experience the saving gifts of the Spirit thereby explicitly denies that they are regenerate. Nor should someone find faith and love missing in any of the regenerate, since these qualities fill up both sides of the page of religion. This now is my only remaining task, to prove

---

85. "Self-love."

86. Serm. 3 in Cant.] Bernard of Clairvaux, *In Cantica Canticorum*, sec. 5 (*sermo* 3).

87. "Full assurance."

that the gifts of this same Spirit are the cause of assurance. John makes this claim so often and so clearly in his first letter that I personally would dare to pit him against all the defenders of Trent and the other opponents of our position. The holy apostle, in that one passage, either answers very clearly all those wagonloads of arguments that they trundle out in their polemical works or supplies the basis for a response. Lest anyone think that this is a flippant statement, I would like to sum up the main points in a few words.

The papists grant us that a probable conviction concerning grace should arise from surmises. But they deny that an assurance of faith that can be void of falsehood may thus arise. Yet John insists upon this quite often— "From this we recognize," "By this we will know," etc. Even more, he very eloquently says, ἐν τούτῳ…πείσομεν τὴν καρδίαν ἡμῶν, "By this we make our hearts sure" (1 John 3:19). In fact, he says with absolute clarity, γινώσκομεν ὅτι ἐγνώκαμεν, "We know that we have known" (1 John 2:3), as if he were saying, "We are certain that we are certain." And so this occurs by a genuine certitude. There are those who impart certainty generously from present grace. The Lutherans and the Remonstrants should be included in this list. But they hardly acknowledge that there is any full assurance with respect to the future state. John asserts both kinds of assurance: "Beloved, we are now sons of God" (1 John 3:2). Yes, he says "now." But what will happen in the future? "We know what we will be, because when He Himself shall be made manifest, we will be like Him because we will see Him as He is" [1 John 3:2]. Our opponents insist, however, that only a few reach this point, and these individuals, by a particular privilege, are placed far beyond the common lot of the faithful. But John says, "We write these things to you that your joy may be full" (1 John 1:4). How can it be full? Obviously by knowing that you have eternal life (1 John 5:13). Now please tell me to whom, blessed apostle, you wrote these things for this purpose? "I wrote to you," he says, "fathers. I am writing to you, young men. I am writing to you, little children" (1 John 3:19).[88] This means that he is writing to the regenerate of whatever rank, whether the first, second, or third. But because the human heart is so deceptive, how is it possible— they say—that the faithful can enjoy infallible certainty? This is my answer: because Christ has instilled within them a new heart and has given this new heart new light. For this is how John writes: "We know that the Son of God has come and has given us the mind to know that He is true. And we are in the truth, that is, in His Son Jesus Christ" (1 John 5:20). They throw back at us again that it is sufficiently obvious that there are some who believed they were ingrafted in Christ and yet have fallen from the faith. From this,

---

88. 1 John 2:13–14.

they conclude that it is possible that the same fate is common also to others who truly believe. But John holds the opposite: "They went out from us, but they were not from us. For if they had been from us, they would have certainly remained with us. But they went out from us to make it clear that not all of them were from us" (1 John 2:19).

Finally, I want to make it clear that I am not using the term *faith* here trivially on such an important topic, because they may think I am dealing with insufficiently compelling testimony. In reality, our champion John, in his final chapter, cites six witnesses to testify, in unison, to render eternal life fixed in and of itself and also certain for us. "There are three," he says, "who testify in heaven: the Father, the Word, and the Holy Spirit" (1 John 5:7). Those things that have transpired in heaven among the three persons of the undivided Trinity have made eternal life, in itself, assured from eternity. "There are three who testify on earth: the Spirit, the water, and the blood" [1 John 5:8]. From these, moreover, the same life becomes certain for us.

Now look, reader, at all the causes of full assurance evident in this one very brief sentence, causes that we have been discussing so far. The Holy Spirit is a witness in both places. This is because He has not only acted on our behalf in heaven with the Father and the Son but also because He has worked with us here on earth. Through His unique testimony—which I discussed previously—He is the procreating cause of intuitive certainty. Now why should we not understand here, as is often the case elsewhere, that by water is meant sanctifying grace? Obviously, these are the gifts of the Spirit that bring salvation, that display the material cause of discursive certitude. As pertains to the blood, either I am mistaken or this testimony nicely coincides with what our own spirit provides and with what we have taught is just the efficient cause of the same certainty but less prominent. This notion, of course, is present in Hebrews, where we read that the "sprinkling of blood speaks a better word than the blood of Abel" (Heb. 12:24). This is because it does not shout of slaughter and hell, as the blood in the story of Cain cried out to him. But instead, it soothes the hearts of the regenerate with a very gentle, peaceful message. Consequently, in the same passage we are commanded "to press on by a faith made certain, by the sprinkling of our hearts that are cleansed from a wicked conscience" (Heb. 10:22). Now because this blood removes the bite of conscience, it is described as testifying, as though the Holy Spirit were shouting, while the blood renders us capable of crying, "Abba, Father."

§ 14. Next we must discuss the other foundation of the full assurance that we have thus far treated. I mean, of course, the infallibility of final perseverance. Our theologians very often make this assertion: "The regenerate cannot fall from grace." By "regenerate," they mean those and those alone who—having received Jesus Christ by faith, in whom also they are busy walking just as they have received Him—become living members of Him in His mystical body, new creations, and sharers in His divine nature. By "grace," we mean partly God's favor and love, or *active* grace. We also partly mean inherent righteousness, which is summarily comprehended in justifying faith and genuine love, and which is called *passive*.

Now *going out from among them* sounds a somewhat more somber note than simply to *withdraw* or *reverse course*. Whoever withdraws from grace or wanders away from the path of righteousness sins. The one who, through frequent omissions and lapses in good works and through the doing of evil works, reverses course has weakened the patterns of his own virtues, even if he has not lost or wasted them altogether. But he who has *gone out*, whose faith is not only perverted but also subverted, whose love is not only shaken but also scattered, this man eventually falls into complete and absolute apostasy. When the people in this passage are described as *unable* to go out, it is not so much the possibility of losing passive or inherent grace that is denied with respect to the actual subject. If we consider each individual as a fallible creature, each would surely fall if the Lord did not uphold His elect with one hand while He tests them with the other. No, it is more a matter of the denial of the ability to lose active grace—I mean divine influence and favor—with respect to God. Our most long-suffering Father has never thought good to remove this favor completely, in light of the goodness and faithfulness toward His own in which He abounds. We see, therefore, that final perseverance is due not to the rootedness of faith (as some so loudly croak) but, above all, to God's sustaining hand. The topic under discussion as currently framed will be sufficiently proven, so I think, if light and faith are reconciled in the three theses that follow.

§ 15. The first thesis is this: electing grace is never revoked. There is a noteworthy passage of Paul writing to Timothy on this topic: "The foundation of God stands firm, and it possesses this seal, that the Lord knows who are His own" (2 Tim. 2:19). Almost every one of these words breathes out a kind of solidity and permanence. Election is designated as the foundation, and nothing in a building can be more stable than this. To remove all possibility of doubt, Paul calls the foundation "firm" and describes it as standing. Actually, the foundation is described as "to have stood," ἕστηκεν, in light of the fact that it stands fast from eternity to eternity. For the foundation is not man's (whose character is generally unreliable) but God's own, with whom there is not even the slightest shadow of change. In addition a seal is fixed upon this foundation. Who does not know that men consider things built with seals certain and genuine? Far more certain and genuine are those things that God has sealed in His own eternal counsel. Moreover, to this foundation, there has been attached as a seal this phrase: "The Lord knows who are His own" [2 Tim. 2:19]. We are not deceived on those subjects that we know, although we may repeatedly be mistaken in subjects where we only make conjectures. Without doubt, God's knowledge is much more infallible. Augustine notably writes, "If even one of the elect perishes, God is deceived. But none of them perishes, because God is not deceived. If any of the elect perishes, then God is defeated by human wickedness. But none of them perishes, because nothing defeats God."[89]

This particular passage of Timothy really inflames the Remonstrants, since they hold that there is no such thing as assurance of election for individual people. In their workshop, they hammer out a mutable, fluctuating, and migratory decree. Therefore, they do not move a single stone so as to waste their strength on it. We will carefully consider only those elements that the author of a recent work has adequately—really, more than adequately—brought to light on the subject of redemption. That brilliant and studious man (far be it from me to begrudge someone the praise he is due just because he holds a different opinion) makes two claims. "It is obvious that the nature of the metaphor and also its context prevent this passage from being understood in terms of individual election."[90] And his second point is that "the Apostle is not speaking about a particular divine decree but about the gospel compact and covenant." As pertains to the first point, he notes, from Samuel Petit, that "the word θεμέλιος here must not be construed as *foundation* but as *compact* or *contract*. And the metaphor is derived not from buildings but from the registers of a legal agreement, which, among the Jews, were not considered binding unless seals had been affixed to them." The argument, moreover, that he tries to use to establish his interpretation of his associate Petit, one that only Petit demonstrates, goes as follows: "It is not foundations that, properly speaking, are fortified by a seal but writings. For who has ever heard of a seal placed on the foundations of buildings, or what could be the reason for affixing one there?"[91] This is our response: First, this learned man adduces no argument to prevent the term θεμέλιος, in the text that we are discussing, from being construed as *foundation*. This is because it was not as unusual as it seems to

---

89. De Corrept. & gratia c. 7.] Augustine, *De Correptione Et Gratia*, 7.14.

90. I. G. ἀπολίτρωσ. cap. 14. § 14. pag. 359, 360.] Goodwin, *Apolytrōsis Apolytrōseōs*, ch. 14, sec. 14, p. 360. Goodwin has "However, that by the Foundation of God (in the place in Hand) should be meant, the Election of some particular Persons by God, hath neither the good-will of the Metaphor or Phrase, nor yet of the Context, for it."

91. *S. Petit*. Varir. lection. l. 1. c. 10.] For the first quotation, Petit, *Variarum Lectionum* (Paris, 1633), bk. 1, ch. 10, see pp. 34–41; perhaps paraphrasing from pp. 34–35.

Petit to place seals on foundations during the building process. If he wants to, he can learn this from Grotius. The latter writes, "Particular sayings used to be inscribed on foundation stones as a good omen.[92] Σφράγις here refers to what is inscribed on a stone, just as elsewhere it means something engraved on a ring."[93] Allow me to use a simple example. This recherché author whom I am now critiquing was not so long ago a fellow of the Royal College of Cambridge University.[94] I am referring to the college whose first stone was placed on April 5, 1448. The following inscription was added to that stone: "The Lord shall be a refuge for our Lady Queen Margaret, and this stone shall serve as proof."[95]

Second, the metaphor of a foundation is entirely consistent with election. For election is that upon which our salvation rests and on which are constructed all those benefits that guide us through to salvation. This is why the Apostle says, "God has blessed us with every spiritual blessing in Christ, just as He chose us in Him" [Eph. 1:3]. Let's listen to Grotius again, since nobody will accuse him of being too sympathetic to the Counterremonstrants: "In the same way that those who are building a grand structure typically first set beneath it solid foundations, likewise God, while constructing His eternal city, laid out particular decrees, like foundations that remain unshaken. This is the particular quality of the foundation."[96]

Third, although the reading that I am defending is accurate and θεμέλιος does mean a *compact*, nevertheless, the passage can be understood as dealing with election, because when the Father gave to Christ, from before all eternity, those whom He had chosen, this was when the covenant between the Father and Son for the elect began. Paul says of this, "For the hope of the eternal life that God, who does not know how to lie, had promised before all time" (Titus 1:2). So far as the second point goes—that is, the context—it flows very well if by θεμέλιος we understand *foundation*, and by *foundation* we understand *election*. The apostasy of Hymenaeus and Philetus comes right before this section. So that this not strike fear in the saints, as if the same fate were also threatening them, the Apostle immediately adds, "But the foundation of the Lord stands firm" [2 Tim. 2:19]. It's as though he were saying, "Apostasy has laid hold of those who were προσκαίρους,[97] who had faith but not the faith of the elect. A much

---

92. "Seal."

93. *Grotius* Annot. in 2 Tim. 2. 19.] Grotius, *Annotationes In Novum Testamentum* (Paris, 1646), sub loc. 2 Tim. 2:19.

94. Queens' College, Cambridge, founded in 1448 by Queen Margaret of Anjou.

95. *Joan. Caius* Histor. Cantabr. Academ. lib. 1. pag. 70.] Johannes (John) Caius, 1510–1573, scholar and physician, *Historiae Cantabrigiensis Academiae* (London, 1575), bk. 1, p. 70.

96. Ibid.] Grotius, *Annotationes In Novum Testamentum*, sub. loc. 2 Tim. 2:19.

97. "Temporary believers."

firmer foundation is set beneath you, and one that will not suffer a deadly fall. 'The Lord knows those who are His'—that is, He chooses His elect particularly, preserves those whom He has chosen, and finally glorifies those whom He has preserved, no matter what the case may be for the non-elect."

§ 16. This is the second thesis: justifying grace is never lost. We will take this well-known statement of the Apostle as our summary of multiple arguments: "Whom He justified He has also glorified" (Rom. 8:29). But God glorifies no one that is situated outside the estate of grace. Therefore, no one who has been justified falls from grace. At this point, our opponents wear themselves out by insisting unsuccessfully (usually shouting themselves hoarse) upon the fall of Adam, who fell completely from his first, original righteousness.[98] Unsuccessfully, I say, because it is completely ἀπροσδιόνυσος.[99] We indeed acknowledge that Adam fell, but not from the justifying grace that presupposes sin. Adam was *just* in his original state, but he was not *justified*. Because there was no preceding sin, there was no crime for him to be absolved of. What about the fact that his righteousness was a legal righteousness and a condition of the covenant of works, while ours—the subject of this inquiry—is a gospel righteousness and a benefit of the covenant of grace? Even if then his estate before the fall was purer, nevertheless, ours (provided we are truly regenerated and justified) is surer, supported as it is by a better covenant and not at all relying upon our fallible will but on the help of our mediator, Jesus Christ. This help is more efficacious than what was long ago given to Adam, before there was a need for the Mediator's reconciliation. Augustine, in passing, makes a very serious remark on this point.

> The aid of perseverance was granted to the first man, who—in that good in which he had been made upright—had received the ability not to sin, the ability not to die, and the ability not to abandon the good itself. This was not a gift to guarantee his perseverance but one without which he could not, through free will, persevere. But now, to those who are saints, predestined to the kingdom of God by the grace of God, not only is such support in perseverance granted but the kind that bestows upon them actual perseverance. Consequently, not only are they not able to persevere without such a gift, but in fact, by this gift, persevering is precisely what they do.[100]

A little bit further on, he writes,

---

98. *Iustitia sua primaeval.*

99. "Beside the point." A. uses here a fairly rare Greek word, which he no doubt read in Cicero's correspondence.

100. De Corrept. & gratia c. 12.] Augustine, *De Correptione Et Gratia*, 12.34.

God not only gave to His saints the kind of help He gave to the first man—namely, that without which they could not persevere if they so desired—but even works in them also to will. So, because they will not persevere unless they both are able and will, the possibility of persevering is granted to them, and the will of divine grace is generously bestowed. In fact, their will is so kindled by the Holy Spirit that they are thus able because they will. Likewise, they will thus because God works to make them willing.[101]

But he makes this comment, as I said, merely in passing.

They also unsuccessfully raise against us the objection that the sins of the faithful are more serious—as if these annulled the covenant of grace and those people who were previously justified could fall into mortal hatred of God and, thus, be dislodged from the estate of justification. We readily acknowledge that those who sin in this way deserve to be renounced and snuffed out, if we consider the nature of their offense, as well as the fact that God hates their sins so much that His hatred includes displeasure along with the will to inflict upon sinners some harm and trouble. Nevertheless, we deny first that the covenant of grace from God's perspective is broken by transgressions of that same kind, even though from man's, it is very seriously and, yes, very shamefully violated. In marriage the conjugal bond is not dissolved by the act of adultery, when the injured party, through legal means, rejects the one causing the offense. Likewise, the covenant of grace is not rescinded by any trespass of demerits, no matter how great, but by the act of God—whom those sins offend—driving away from participation in His grace the one who has abandoned it. The merciful Father (as an expression of His goodness and στοργή[102] toward His elect) openly declares that He will by no means do that, provided they repent, as always happens by the Spirit's administration. This passage from the prophet speaks to that point: "The proverb goes as follows: if a man divorces his wife, and she leaves him and marries another man, she will never be restored to him later, will she? But you have lived promiscuously with many lovers but still return to Me, says the Lord, and I will take you back" (Jer. 3:1). This is why the covenant of grace is called an eternal covenant, διαθήκη αἰώνιος (Heb. 13:20), precisely because it is never broken by God. Instead, from eternity to eternity, He embraces in His most loving arms all those who have been joined to His covenant.

We deny second that the deadly hatred that opposes the love that belongs to eternal life comes upon those who have once been justified. Davenant explains this both capably and splendidly.

---

101. Augustine, *De Correptione Et Gratia*, 12.38.
102. "Affection."

God's love toward the regenerate is not founded on their perfection or on any kind of purity but on Christ the Mediator. He has transferred their sins to Himself and so has set them free from God's anger and hatred. He does hate their sins, but not the people themselves to whom those sins cling, because they have been atoned for by the blood of Christ.[103]

§ 17. This is the third thesis: sanctifying grace never perishes. I would like to begin this paragraph with a statement from Augustine that the Reverend Abbot[104] uses to conclude his rebuttal: "Temptation in the heart of the elect often hides the light of righteousness but does not destroy it. And it pulls that light toward the wan shadow of fear, as it were, but does not snuff it out altogether."[105] Consequently, one apostle describes us as being reborn from a seed not corruptible, but incorruptible (1 Peter 1:23). And another says that the seed of God remains in the regenerate (1 John 3:9). Marco Antonio de Dominis had written, in his *Plan of Return*,[106] that he was held in the Church of England because the grace of the righteous cannot be lost. Crakanthorp answers,

> We do not claim that grace *per se* cannot be lost, nor do we even think it. Both the fall of very holy men and the daily experience among all God's servants shows plainly that God's grace not only can be lost *ex parte* but that it frequently is. There is in everything—like in the ocean, for example—a certain back and forth of divine grace, a constant flow. There is also sometimes a flowing back. This is unlike the moon: not always consistent and scarcely ever at its full. But it is like aspects of light. Similarly, the righteous suffer both an increase and decrease of heavenly grace.[107]

But the Savior Himself instructs us that divine grace is not completely or definitively lost. Just where does He do that? If anyone asks, very many passages from the gospel of John can be produced to demonstrate this. Among these are the following. "My sheep hear My voice, and they follow me. I give them eternal life. They will not perish eternally, and no one will snatch them from My hand. Whoever drinks from this water that I shall give will not ever thirst again. But the water that I shall give him will become within him a fountain of water that springs up to eternal life" (John 10:27–28; 4:14). Theophylact remarks on these words that whenever the

---

103. De Justitia habituali cap. 5. p. 226.] Davenant, *De Iustitia Habituali*, ch. 5, p. 226.

104. I.e., Robert Abbot.

105. Gregory the Great, *Expositionis Moralis In Beatum Iob*, sub loc. Job 7, 8.6, col. 251. A., and perhaps Abbot, believes he is citing Augustine rather than Gregory.

106. De Dominis, *Sui Reditus Ex Anglia Consilium* (Paris, 1623).

107. Defens. Eccles. Anglic. p. 593.] Crakanthorp(e), *Defensio Ecclesiae Anglicanae*, ch. 78, p. 593.

heavenly water is drawn up, it not only persists but also multiplies and creates a fountain of life that keeps flowing continuously.[108]

Allow me to illustrate the whole of this discussion with a three-part example. Mephibosheth fell, and throughout the remainder of his life, he was saddled with lameness. Still, he lived and had some strength [2 Sam. 9]. Eutychus fell from the dining room onto the street below and seemed very close to death. Nevertheless, life remained in him, and so he immediately recovered [Acts 20]. Eli fell and died from a broken neck [1 Sam. 4:18]. Truly the saints can fall like Mephibosheth, and they can receive a wound that renders them lame. More than that, they can fall to their death like Eutychus and, for a time, suffer an eclipse of the soul. Yet they cannot fall dead like Eli and so be completely stripped of all spiritual life.

The foregoing analysis would be adequate to compel assent from honest papists even, like Eisengrein, Catharinus, and Marinario were. But you won't persuade the money-grubbing monks, even if you can persuade them that the righteous have a duty to strive with every effort to gain more certainty in grace. They actually care about selling indulgences and masses and that the cleric should enjoy an entirely obedient laity. They are interested in teaching the art of doubting and in cursing full assurance as "blasphemy." So they have learned (I will here quote from Pierre du Moulin) that "the people's fear is the priest's profit," and "it is easier to fleece the silver off a terrified man."[109] But the one stained with corruption is even more so. If, Christians, you will listen to me—why do I say "me"?—if you will heed the Holy Scripture, if you will heed learned men reformed according to that Scripture, then may it be your concern and heart's desire, all of you that care about your salvation, to put on this helmet of salvation!

§ 18. In the meantime, no one should be fooled or judge prematurely the remarks at the end of Mr. Davenant's *The Death of Christ*. They don't belong to that very great man but are actually a forgery. While readers are studying predestination and reprobation there, they come across a tacked-on document that bears this title: "*The Position of the English Church on Predestination as well as Supporting Points by the Same Author*," so it claims, "*Written at the Command of His Most Serene Majesty*." These are that document's startling words:

> Certainly, this position that is generating so much controversy—that is, the sure perseverance of all those who have once believed and been

---

108. Theophylact of Ohrid, *Commentarii In Quatuor Evangelia* (Paris, 1635), sub loc. John 4:14.

109. Du Moulin, *De Certitudine Perseverantiae*, in *Thesaurus Disputationum Theologicarum* (Geneva, 1661), p. 726.

regenerated—was never affirmed by any of the fathers of the ancient church. Instead, all of antiquity rejected it, and the uninterrupted experience of all ages has absolutely refuted it. And only in this age was it known and, from the strife that arose between Zwingli and his followers and Luther, it was introduced into the church.[110]

The book I'm talking about came from the printshop of Roger Daniel in 1650.[111] As for me, as soon as I encountered these remarks, "I was dumbfounded, and my hair stood on end."[112] I, who had, of course, so many times drunk deeply from the *Preliminary Lectures* and *Conclusions* of the Right Reverend Davenant, who had devoured his exegetical works, polemics, and synodical writings and tried to direct almost all of his doctrinal writings into my own strength and life's blood, could I really believe that such a monstrosity had ever fallen from this man's pen? I was thinking something suspicious was behind this, but there was no way I could sniff it out. And so I was deeply grieved that such a great blow had befallen such a good man and befallen truth itself. Meanwhile, Providence never slept, and after a few months went by, the prison was shattered and, in 1651, erupted in light: "The thief was predestined—and there was some value in his crime."[113] So then, from the attendants of that scoundrel,[114] there appeared the very work I had previously complained about, but now ascribed to a different author and with a different title. It was called *The Position of the Church of England on Predestination and Its Consequences as Expounded by Dr. Overall, Prof. of Theology at Cambridge.*[115] Oh what a good stroke! Everything is now well, nor will anyone hereafter be allowed to abuse the name and prestige of the very famous Davenant to prop up their apostasy! Davenant, a man whose memory will live happily among the orthodox forever.

---

110. Davenant, *Sententia Ecclesiae Anglicanae De Praedestinatione*, in *Dissertationes Duae* (Cambridge, 1650), ch. 5, sig. Kk2r.

111. Roger Daniel, 1590–1667, printer. Daniel offended the House of Commons in 1642 and perhaps in 1644. An event in 1650 (perhaps the event here described by A.) led to the loss of Daniel's patent as printer to the University of Cambridge; he continued printing in London until the mid-1660s.

112. Vergil, *Aeneidos*, bk. 2 (line 774).

113. Ovid, *Metamorphoseon*, bk. 2 (line 332).

114. Probably Roger Daniel.

115. John Overall, bap. 1561, d. 1619, bishop of Norwich.

CHAPTER X

The Sword[1] of the Spirit, the Word of God

Sections 1–3: Two historical narratives are presented. The first conclusion with respect to the faith by which one comes to believe that the Scripture is God's Word. What Augustine long ago thought about the church's testimony, what today's Protestants think, and what position, by contrast, papists hold. Section 4: The second conclusion. The Holy Scripture's innate qualities, the majesty of the style, the heavenliness of the matter, the efficacy of the doctrine that is verified by different kinds of examples. Sections 5–6: The third conclusion. The position of our theologians on the testimony of the Holy Spirit. Disagreement of the Socinians and the bishops. Our men wrongly charged with "Enthusiasm." Section 7: Reproof of contempt for the sacred Scripture. The advancement of its praises. Section 8: Christian soldiers are defended by the Word of God as by a sword. Our enemies are routed by that same weapon, namely, the heresies, vices, and sorrows. This statement is supported by, respectively, Bugenhagen, Augustine, Lactantius, Thomas à Kempis, and Baptista Mantuano. Sections 9–10: Why the Word of God is called sword of the Holy Spirit. An exegesis of 2 Peter 1:20–21. A concluding exhortation.

§ 1. Eusebius, in his *History*, tells us about Marinus.[2] This man's military valor got him elected to the office of centurion. But as soon as it became clear he was a Christian, within three hours he was ordered to decide whether he would give up his office or his faith. Theotectus,[3] the bishop of Caesarea, meanwhile, holding up the sword as the symbol of military office together with a copy of the Bible, obviously because it was the storehouse of the faith, said, "Take whichever of these you prefer. You cannot enjoy both." Marinus immediately took the Bible and so was crowned a martyr.

---

1. *Machaera*, a Latinized Greek word referring to a short, thrusting sword.

2. Lib. 7. cap. 14.] Eusebius, *Historiae Ecclesiasticae*, vol. 1 (Geneva, 1612), bk. 7, ch. 14, p. 194; Marinus of Caesarea, d. ca. 260, Christian martyr.

3. Theotectus, late third century AD, bishop of Caesarea.

At that moment, the Bible and the sword were separated. But in the following description of military equipment found in Paul, they are very closely joined. For next in the Apostolic passage, we find, "καὶ τὴν μάχαιραν τοῦ πνεύματος ὅ ἐστιν ῥῆμα Θεοῦ," "And the sword of the Spirit, which is the Word of God" [Eph. 6:17]. Wolf comments on this passage when, in his memoirs, he relates that, on the day Edward VI was crowned king of England, he was offered three swords. These represented his sovereignty over three kingdoms: England, Scotland, and Ireland. The king reportedly said, "One sword is still missing." When asked which one that was, he replied, "A copy of the Holy Bible. For it is the sword of the Spirit, and I must cherish it far more than all others."[4]

Both groups, the papists and our side, believe that the sacred Book is the Word of God rather than of man. But there is the greatest disagreement as to what precisely, in the end, determines the faith. That is, what establishes our belief such that, when we arrive at that point, there is no need for further examination? Now, in order to restrict within more narrow limits the range of this particular controversy, I would like first to set forward a particular distinction and then to tease out, in three conclusions, the particular elements of greatest importance, if not all of them. We can posit a threefold origin for that faith that we owe to the divine authority of the sacred Scripture. The first is *introductive*, the second is *argumentative*, and the third is *productive*. Based on this preceding condition, there now follow several conclusions.

§ 2. The first conclusion: it can happen and often does that the *introductive* origin of the faith is the testimony of the church. This means that some believe Scripture to be the very word of God *through* the church as a first witness. Yet this is not *because* the church is the successful argument for assent but because of the Word of God itself. It is like this: a mother may point her fingers to the sky and say to her little boy, who was previously unaware, "My child, that is the sun." If he afterward believes with sufficiently firm resolve that it is the sun, it is not because his mother has taught him but because he has begun to perceive clearly for himself, each day, the sun's warmth and light. Calvin writes, "We acknowledge that those who have not yet been illuminated by the Spirit of God are led toward teachability by respect for the church. Thus, they are able to learn from the gospel the faith of Christ. And so, in this way, we admit that the church's authority

---

4. Lection. memorab. centur. 16. p. 601.] Johann Wolf, 1537–1600, German Reformed theologian, *Lectiones Memorabiles Et Reconditae* (Lauingen, 1608).

is an introduction[5] that prepares us for faith in the gospel."[6] It seems that Augustine had the same thing in mind when he wrote that very contentious statement, "I would not have believed the gospel had the authority of the catholic church not compelled me."[7] Rivet's comment is very effective in explaining Augustine's meaning:

> It was typical for African writers to use the imperfect in place of the pluperfect. For example, Augustine had written somewhere, "It is up to us what we believe." He then makes this retraction: "This, indeed, I would not say if I already knew that faith lies within God's gifts."[8] Here he uses the imperfect "I would say" in place of "I would have said," and "I would know" in place of "I had known." For the meaning here is, "I would not have wanted to speak like that then if I had known what I now know," namely, that the situation is different. Thus, in the saying that is now commended, "I would believe" is taken for "I had believed." Consequently, the meaning of the passage is, "When I was a Manichee, I would not have believed the gospel, and I would not have been drawn to the faith, unless I had been compelled by the church's authority." And so he does not want those who now believe to rely upon the church's authority but those who do not yet believe simply to begin from it.[9]

But the Romanists are not at all satisfied with these concessions, because they grant the church hardly anything beyond the ministerial proof of a herald instead of the judgment of a magistrate. They fight bitterly for the authority and magisterium of the church over Scripture.[10] Their efforts lead them by a kind of amazing, actually absurd, method to make their analysis of the catholic church correspond to the Roman church, and of the Roman church to correspond to a legitimately established general council, and of that council, to the pope as its presider. And they argue that he presides not as a man (for they admit as a man he is liable to error) but as a pontiff. And they treat him not like just any pontiff but as one who decides *ex cathedra* not on something generally controversial but on Christian law and faith. They never stop blathering about the catholic church, an ecumenical council, and other impressive words of that sort. But really these

---

5. *Isagogen.*

6. Institut. l. 1. cap. 7. § 3.] Calvin, *Institutio Christianae Religionis*, 1.7.3.

7. Lib. contra Epist. Fund. c. 3.] Augustine, *Contra Epistolam Manichaei*, in *Omnium Operum*, vol. 6 (Basel, 1528), 5.6.

8. Retract. l. 1. cap. 23.] Augustine, *Retractationum*, 1.23.60.

9. Isagog. ad S. Script. in 4°, cap. 3. § 22.] Rivet, *Isagoge, Sive Introductio Generalis* (Leiden, 1627), ch. 3, sec. 22, pp. 27–28.

10. Vid. *Gerhard.* Disp. Theol. part. 2. p. 1598. & sequent.] Gerhard, *Disputationum Theologicarum, In Academia Ienensi Conscriptarum & Publice Habitarum, Partes Tres* (Jena, 1645).

phrases are nothing more than "gewgaws for the people."[11] When it comes to the question itself, and the main point of the controversy is addressed, then the Roman pontiff is the one and only individual to whom they grant supreme jurisdiction to decide dogmas of faith and rule on the αὐθεντία[12] of Scripture. Gregory de Valencia wrote eight lengthy books analyzing the Catholic faith. In the last volume, he sets out and then strives to prove this very thesis:

> However often the Roman pontiff uses that authority with which he has been endowed to defend questions of the faith, the position that he determines as the position of the faith all the faithful must receive as divine precept. And we must conclude that he uses this very authority as often as he makes either pronouncement—whether by himself or together with the council of bishops—in such a way that he wants it to be binding on the church universal.[13]

§3. I guess this Gregory likes to make big jokes out of a big problem! I could quicker believe that the king of Spain enjoys the right of infallibility because it says in Proverbs, "Prophecy is on the lips of the king, and in judgment his mouth will make no mistake" (Prov. 16:10)! That's easier to accept than that the whole Christian faith must be contained in the chamber of the pope's heart (I am referring to what is very often a cesspool of vices and errors), just because the Lord says to Peter, "I have prayed for you that your faith may not fail. Upon this rock I shall build my church. Feed my sheep" [Luke 22:32; Matt. 16:18; John 21:17]. There are several other statements that this whole Jesuit trick relies on.

So far as concerns the theory on the divinity of the biblical texts, it is as Tertullian once wrote of the Romans in his *Defense*. It had been their custom to grant or deny apotheosis (ἀποθέωσις) to their own gods by senatorial vote. He wrote, "With you, divinity is measured by human will. If God does not please a man, He will not be God. So now man will have to be more gracious than God."[14] This is precisely how Romanists today behave toward the Scriptures. For unless the church (i.e., in effect, the pope) makes a decision, they will rank the written Word of God almost no higher than Mohammad's Qur'an, the historian Livy, or Aesop's fables. Stapleton says, "We trust the Scripture because of the church's authority only."[15] Bellarm-

---

11. Juvenal, *Satyra*, 3.

12. "Actual authority."

13. De Valencia, *Analysis Fidei Catholicae*, part 8, p. 430.

14. Tertullian, *Apologeticus*, ch. 6.

15. Triplicat. advers. *Whitak.*] Thomas Stapleton, 1535–1598, Roman Catholic theologian, *Triplicatio Inchoata Adversus Guglielmi Whitakeri* (Antwerp, 1596), probably p. 52. Stapleton makes similar statements throughout the work.

ine writes, "Catholics believe what they believe because God has revealed it, but they believe God has revealed it because they hear the church speaking and declaring that."[16] Eck: "The Scripture is not authentic." Hosius: "The Scripture carries with us a very small amount of weight." And finally, Andradius states that "there is nothing in the Scripture that compels us to believe unless the church's authority grants the Scripture that quality."[17] Against all these authors, I set this one argument.

Divine faith is that through which we receive the dogmas and principles of the Christian religion, because they are transmitted in the sacred writings, and we believe that the sacred writings proceeded from God. So it is impossible for this divine faith, in the end, to rely upon human testimony. This would be very much like a chimera, as though "a woman with a lovely torso terminated in a deformed fish."[18] But if the final resolution of the faith were counted as resting on the authority of the church, it would follow that the divine faith, in the end, relied upon human testimony. There is nothing more ridiculous than this. My thesis is demonstrated by this: the testimony of the church, whatever we finally take it to be, is the testimony of men. Every one of these men individually is fallible. The recognized leaders among Romanist theologians have not dared to maintain the contrary of this position with confidence. Bellarmine himself says, "The word of the church—that is, of its council or of the pontiff when he is teaching *ex cathedra*—is not, in its entirety, the word of a man. It is not something subject to error but is, in some way, the word of God."[19] What a sheepish and bashful claim! Becan, on the other hand, unequivocally states, "Assent that depends on the authority of the church is not the assent of theological faith but of another, inferior type."[20] What then is the upshot of this? Is it not that they who ultimately ground their faith on the authority of the church alone plainly acknowledge that they believe all the things they believe not by theological faith but by human faith? Meanwhile, God's servants do not have the right to grant dominion over their own souls—that have been redeemed by the blood of Christ, sealed by His Spirit, instructed

---

16. Lib. 6. de liber. arbitr. cap. 3. § At Catholici.] Bellarmine, *De Gratia Et Libero Arbitrio*, bk. 6, ch. 3.

17. Ap. *Chamier*. Paustrat. tom. 1. l. 6. c. 15. § 7.] Johannes Eck, 1486–1543, German Catholic theologian; Stanislaus Hosius, 1505–1579, Polish Roman Catholic theologian; and Andradius, quoted in Daniel Chamier, *Panstratiae Catholicae*, vol. 1 (Geneva, 1626), bk. 6, ch. 15, sec. 7, p. 174. The entire Eck quotation is, *Scriptura non est authentica, absque auctoritate Ecclesiae*.

18. Horace, *De Arte Poetica* (1.3–4).

19. De verbo Dei l. 3. cap. 10.] Bellarmine, *De Verbo Dei*, in *Disputationes De Controversiis*, vol. 1 (Ingolstadt, 1605), bk. 3, ch. 10.

20. Tract. de fide l. 8. qu. 8. § 8.] Becan, *Theologiae Scholasticae* (Mainz, 1620), ch. 8, qu. 8, sec. 8, p. 144.

in His Word—to any man or community, such that they owe the beginning (γένεσις) or the resolution (ἀνάλυσις) of their faith (both of which manifest God) to any man's authority, or confess that they do.

§4. The second conclusion: the argumentative foundation of this faith is the character and nature of the Scripture itself or, as they are called, innate criteria (κριτήρια). The sacred Scriptures are designated a light to our feet (Ps. 119:105). It is the characteristic of light to make visible not only other things but also itself. The Holy Scripture has, to this point, shone forth in the midst of so many divergent parties and flashed upon them, by its rays, as the first foundation of all theological truth. And it has no need for a priori demonstration in order to believe in it, any more than the light of the sun needs illumination by some other light for it actually to be seen. Salviani writes, "Human statements need proofs and evidence. But the Word of God witnesses to itself by these very means."[21] Athanasius: ἀφ ἑαυτοῦ ἔχει τὸ γνώριμον.[22] The Word reveals itself by its own marks and indicators. Proofs lie planted within the deepest organs, so to speak, of the sacred Book, and it uses these to make others believe in its divinity. The following three arguments claim for themselves a prominent position.

First, *majesty of style.* In this there is always something wondrous joined with the greatest simplicity, as the words themselves are generally quite unremarkable. This sense of magnificence forces itself upon the reader's mind. As when an angel presents himself to be gazed upon under the guise of a human being, no doubt one can recognize a human face, and the outline is shaped like parts of the human body. Nevertheless, there is always something foreign, as I would put it, that overwhelms one's mind and quietly warns that this is not really a human being but an apparition. Likewise, the style of Scripture contains something (as a famous and worthy man said)[23] that I can hardly express and yet is plainly sensed by those who read it. By this quality, one can easily distinguish it from human productions, just as pretty much anyone can discern the flavors in all kinds of foods, although it is difficult to explain why they taste different.

Second, *heavenliness of the matter.* There is no denying that the Holy Scriptures contain mysteries beyond the grasp of human reason: a Trinity of persons in the same essence, the hypostatic union of two natures in the

---

21. De provid. lib. 3.] Salvian, ca. 400–post-ca. 468, priest and author in Gaul, *D. Salvani Massyliensis Episcopi, De Vero Iudicio Et Providentia Dei* (Basel, 1530), lib. 3, fol. 12r.

22. Lib. contra Gentes.] Athanasius, *Oratio Contra Gentes*, in *Opera Quae Reperiuntur Omnia*, vol. 1 (Heidelberg, 1600). "God's word derives its intelligibility from within itself."

23. *Jo. Camero* Operum in 4°, Tom. 3. p. 135.] Cameron, *Praelectionum In Selectiora Quaedam Novi Testamenti Loca* (Saumur, 1628), tome 3, p. 135.

same person, resurrection of the same bodies, and things like that. They also contain dogmas that are unwelcome to the human will, such as those on original sin, mortification of the flesh, absolute necessity of grace, bondage of the free will, and the ἀδυναμία[24] of the natural faculties in spiritual matters. Finally, the sacred Scripture speaks prophetically of events that extend beyond the sphere of human foreknowledge. This human foreknowledge is typically hazy—no, actually blind—to future contingencies. But the Scripture predicts the outcome with no less certainty than if it were an eyewitness.

Third, *efficacy of doctrine*. Augustine once praised this efficacy as follows: "Fishermen's words are read, orators submissively bow their heads."[25] Savonarola:

> God is my witness that I have often noticed a certain impatience and mild inattention of the hearers as I preach to the people. While I wander through the lively doctrine of philosophers and through words of human wisdom to display the depth of sacred eloquence to the dilettantes and bloated minds of this age, I see that not only uneducated ears are less engaged but so are those of the learned. But whenever I turn to the majesty of the sacred page, I note everyone's rapt attention and that all faces are fixed on me like marble statues.[26]

But in fact, very many others have also experienced this phenomenon in their own consciences. Luther said of Romans 1:17, "This passage of Paul was really my gateway to paradise."[27] Franciscus Junius makes the following comment about the beginning of John's gospel: "I read part of the chapter, and I am so affected that suddenly I realized that the divinity of the argument, the majesty of the writing, and its authority surpass by a very great distance all the streams of human eloquence."[28] The martyr Thomas Bilney[29] describes his experience of 1 Timothy 1:15 like this:

> When I bought Erasmus's edition of the New Testament, I was drawn more by the beauty of the Latin than by God's Word. The first passage I hit upon, so I remember, was this one. Oh what a remarkably gorgeous idea Paul expresses! It was a sure passage, and one worthy of all of us embracing, that "Jesus Christ came into the world to make sinners

---

24. "Helplessness."

25. De Verb. Dom. Serm. 59.] Augustine, *De Verbis Domini In Evangelio Secundum Ioannem*, in *Omnium Operum*, vol. 10 (Basel, 1528), 59.12.

26. Triumph. crucis lib 2. c. 2. prope finem.] Girolamo Savonarola, 1452–1498, Italian Dominican preacher, *Triumphus Crucis* (Antwerp, 1633), bk. 2, ch. 8, p. 100.

27. Luther, *Omnium Operum*, vol. 1 (Jena, 1556), *praefatio*.

28. In ipsius vita.] Adam, *Decades Duae Continentes*, p. 195.

29. Thomas Bilney, ca. 1495–1531, evangelical Reformer and martyr.

whole." This one phrase, by God's internal instruction within my heart, thrilled my soul so much! My heart was wounded and nearly desperate from knowledge of my prior sins. This passage so cheered my heart that soon I seemed to feel inside a peace of inestimable extent.[30]

Finally, not to go on too long, Johann Isaac Levi made these comments on Isaiah 53: "I plainly confess that this chapter led me to the Christian faith. I read that chapter more than a thousand times."[31] And the comments that follow in the same passage are well worth reading. Five rabbis denied that Jesus was Messiah, and Levi refuted them from the same passage, at the Frankfurt market. This is a good time to add the story that de Andrade relates about some African Jews that he knew. By reading only that same chapter, they were led to abandon home, fatherland, parents, and vast wealth in order to dedicate themselves to Christ Jesus (so de Andrade says) with burning zeal.[32]

§5. The third conclusion: the Holy Spirit's work, and it alone, is the productive origin of that same faith. Let the church testify as much as she can, let the Scripture shine forth with her inborn light as much as she usually does. If, however, the operation of the Holy Spirit is absent, that Spirit who touches the heart with His breath to reveal the divinity that shines in that sacred Book, then divine faith will be absent. Without the Spirit, the church's testimony will produce nothing more than human faith, and the genius of the sacred Scripture nothing more than theological conjecture. This is the very point that our theologians make. Calvin says, "Just as God alone is the proper witness to Himself in His Word, so that word in the hearts of men will not find faith before it is sealed by the inward testimony of the Spirit."[33] Chamier writes, "Far be it from us to deny that a man can be compelled by many arguments who yet rises up against the authority of the sacred Book and denies that it is divine. But we assert that someone may be so convinced that he is persuaded it is the rule of faith, yet that cannot happen completely apart from the Spirit's inner movement."[34] And Whitaker

---

30. In Epistola Latina ad Tonstallum, quae habetur in Actis & monument. *Jo. Foxii*, volum. 2. edit. ult. p. 266.] Foxe, *The Ecclesiasticall historie: containing the Acts and monuments of martyrs*, vol. 2 (London, 1641), p. 266. This edition contains Latin text followed by an English translation.

31. Defens. veritat. Hebricae adversus *Lindanum*, lib. 2. p. 82, 83.] Johannes Isaac (Levi), 1515–1577, German Hebraist and Jewish convert to Christianity, *Defensio Veritatis Hebraicae* (Cologne, 1559), bk. 2, p. 82.

32. Defens. Tridentinae fidei lib. 4. fol. 352.] Andradius, *Defensio Tridentinae Fidei Catholicae* (Ingolstadt, 1580), bk. 4, fol. 352r.

33. Instit l. 1. c. 7. parag. 4.] Calvin, *Institutio Christianae Religionis*, 1.7.4.

34. Lib. 6. de canone cap. 1. parag. 7.] Chamier, *Panstratiae Catholicae*, vol. 1, bk. 6, ch. 1, par. 7, p. 147.

says, "Although when we are conquered by external testimonies, we cannot for shame deny that the sacred literature is God's Word, nevertheless, we attain a sure and saving πληροφορία[35] when that same Spirit who wrote and published those books has convinced our minds of the Scriptures' reliability. He who lacks the Spirit, no matter how many thousands of times he hears the church, still will always remain, in himself, uncertain and doubting."[36] Robert Baron of Aberdeen says,

> We must carefully distinguish between the principal effective cause of assent to the faith and its principal objective cause. The Holy Spirit, through His internal illumination of the understanding and effectual moving of the human will, is the principal effective cause of assent to the faith. But the Word of God itself, by its own internal light, power, and majesty, showing forth to us its divinity, is the principal objective cause, or rather principal foundation, of assent to the faith.[37]

But in addition to the papists, the Socinians also generally disagree with this position, as do some of the Remonstrants. The author of a brief inquiry, an insignificant Socinian, makes these comments at the very outset of his third book: "They make a second error with regard to the Judge, and one that is more apt to lead astray the unwary as it has the appearance of greater holiness and piety. I mean when they take the Holy Spirit as judge of the faith. Simply put, without Him, they are unwilling to grant any judgment to anyone in matters of divinity." This is how Episcopius, the Remonstrants' main standard-bearer, talks: "Obviously they are fools who say that, in addition to or beyond the testimony of the church, the internal testimony of the Holy Spirit is required for us to understand that these books are divine and have divine authority."[38] Could there be anything more clear or ridiculous than these statements? Certainly they must believe that the Apostle had a far different understanding when he wrote to the Thessalonians, "Our gospel has found credence among you not only by the Word but also by power, the Holy Spirit, and much assurance"—καὶ ἐν Πνεύματι ἁγίῳ, καὶ πληροφορίᾳ πολλῇ (1 Thess. 1:5).[39] Is it not abundantly evident from this passage that no one can receive the Word of God in power, with certainty of conviction, unless through the Holy Spirit, who works that certainty

---

35. "Full assurance."

36. Oper. in fo. Tom. 1. p. 10. vid. ibid. p. 78.] Whitaker, *Ad Decem Rationes*, in *Opera Theologica*, vol. 1 (Geneva, 1610), p. 10; Whitaker, *De Sacris Literis*, in *Opera Theologica*, vol. 1 (Geneva, 1610), bk. 1, p. 78.

37. Disp. de formali objecto fidei, p. 27.] Baron, *Disputatio Theologica, De Formali Objecto Fidei* (Aberdeen, 1627), qu. 3, sec. 4, p. 27.

38. Institut. Theologic. lib. 4. c. 5. p. 235.] Episcopius, *Institutiones Theologicae*, bk. 4, ch. 5, p. 235.

39. A. combines here Latin and Greek.

internally in the heart? This is all the more reason why Tertullian's comment in his book *Prescribing Heretics* should tend to the same point. There we read, "They who do not accept Scripture cannot acknowledge the Holy Spirit who is sent to those who are learning."[40] And to take a passage from a little bit before that, "Christ, as He sits at God's right hand, has sent the delegated power of the Holy Spirit to guide those who believe."[41]

§ 6. But at this point, they begin to shout again and again that we actually support the Enthusiasts and that we allow revelations apart from the Word. But their claim is specious and quite stubborn. Our representatives should at least be heard, so that they are not condemned without a trial. The man Baron, whom I just commended, says,

> Two revelations correspond to *Enthusiasm* properly designated. The first pertains to the revelation of the object, and a characteristic of this kind is to disclose things that are completely unknown. The second is a revelation pertaining to ability, which opens the eyes of the mind to understand those things that are disclosed. Revelations of each kind were given among the scribes of God, who, of course, were inspired in a fashion beyond the normal means. But those who receive illumination in our day have only one kind of revelation, the kind sufficient for understanding and believing what was originally revealed in the Scriptures. This is, of course, that second kind of revelation granted as an aspect of ability, and so it is inaccurate to apply the term *enthusiasm* to such people.

In another passage, Baron writes, "By the internal testimony of the Holy Spirit, they do not understand some new and extraordinary revelation of the gospel that proceeds from the Holy Spirit unmediated. Instead, they understand the effectual application of revelation previously disclosed in the Scripture itself."[42] Johannes Cloppenburg, in his posthumous work, stated, "The internal testimony of the Holy Spirit is not an ἄγραφον word that one should trust in addition to the sacred Scripture. But it is the living word of Scripture ἀπόγραφον upon our hearts.[43] Consequently (if one has regard to the vivid depiction of doctrine), the written word is the same as that which is read publicly."[44] We read this in Johannes Maccovius: "The

---

40. Tertullian, *De Praescriptionibus Adversus Haereticos*, ch. 22.

41. Tertullian, *De Praescriptionibus Adversus Haereticos*, ch. 13.

42. Apolog. pro Disp. de formal. object. fidei, p. 736. 763. & 769.] Baron, *Disputatio Theologica, De Formali Objecto Fidei* (Aberdeen, 1631), pp. 736, 763, 769.

43. Because A. uses ἄγραφον ("unwritten") and ἀπόγραφον ("imprinted"), there is a pleasing play on words.

44. Exercit. super *L. C.* in Disp. de method fidei thes. 4.] Johannes Cloppenburg, 1592–1654, Dutch Reformed theologian, *Exercitationes Super Locos Communes* (Franeker, 1653), disp. 2, thes. 1, sec. 4, sig. B3r.

testimony of the Holy Spirit is as a light that so floods the mind that it gently illuminates it. Thus, it shows the mind the reasons implanted in the very subject set before it as an object of belief, though such reasons were previously hidden."[45] Finally, we have William Whitaker. No one has defended the cause of Scripture against the Romanist doctors with more eloquence or boldness than he. Whitaker provides us with this golden statement, in his own name and that of all our supporters: "We honor the church's ministry. We guard against internal promptings separated from the external Word as Satan's foolish schemes. From the Scriptures, we are wise; with the Scriptures, we form our perceptions; because of the Scriptures, we believe."[46]

§7. In the meantime, as this proposition has been set forth and proven—namely, that sacred Scripture is the very Word of God (and we are confident that this has been done adequately)—Christian men must show absolutely no tolerance for those who deprecate the sacred books in any way. Those French bishops whom I just mentioned have shown themselves markedly guilty of this crime, or rather, disgraceful outrage.[47]

And yet there is another fault quite similar to this—namely, when men become so absorbed in other pursuits that they train themselves too carelessly in the reading of the Scriptures. Illyricus counts Robert the Gaul,[48] who lived around 1290, in his *Catalogue of Witnesses to the Truth*. "He suitably compared Sophists and Scholastics of those times that labored carelessly over the sacred books—strongly devoted, meanwhile, to speculative and useless inquiries—to a man carrying a vessel of fine wine at his side and, likewise, the finest bread. But leaving both of these untouched, he eagerly and vainly gnawed at the stone carried in his hand."[49] It is altogether proper and necessary for other books, however many there are in the whole world, to immediately submit before the gaze of the sacred text, just as the other patriarchs' bundles bowed worshipfully before Joseph's sheaf.

Now, of course, all those must blush with shame who have forgotten these and similar commandments: "Look for it from the book of Jehovah and read" (Isa. 34:16); "Pay close attention to the reading" (1 Tim. 4:13); "Search the Scriptures" (John 5:39). They do not treat with the honor it deserves such a consecrated trust of heaven. They say that when Alexander had been offered a small storage case of countless worth along with the

---

45. *L. Com.* p. m. 28.] Maccovius, *Loci Communes Theologici* (Franeker, 1650), p. 28.

46. Oper. in folio Tom. 2. p. 121.] Whitaker, *Sacrae Scripturae*, in *Opera Theologica*, vol. 2 (Geneva, 1610), bk. 1, ch. 10, p. 121.

47. Lib. 1. c. 6. § 8.] See bk. 1, ch. 6, sec. 8 of the present work.

48. Perhaps Gallus Robertus (or Robertus Gallus), fl. ca. 1290 or fl. 1341 (CERL).

49. Matthias Flavius Illyricus, 1520–1575, Croatian Lutheran theologian, *Catalogus Testium Veritatis* (Basel, 1556), pp. 840–43.

spoils of Darius, he thought Homer's poems were the most valuable thing he could store in it. This was even though the material the case was made of surpassed all the rest of the plunder, and the workmanship surpassed even the material! Likewise, the authors of the *Historia Augusta* tell us that the Emperor Aelius Verus[50] loved Ovid's *Ars Amatoria* so much that he read it quite often right before going to bed and, before falling asleep, would set it on his bed cushion.[51] You should be ashamed, Christian, you should be ashamed that you do not have the Word of God ready at hand, that you do not gaze upon it, that you do not store it up in your heart, when such important men have held Homer's word, even Ovid's, in such high esteem!

Yet if some men are found (and this age is quite rich in them, if any age ever was) that were once careful readers and listeners but who now very seldom touch their Bibles and almost never attend sermons, I think that it is far more appropriate to count such men among the dead than it was when Pythagoras[52] once reckoned as dead those who deserted his school. Supposedly, Pythagoras put κενοτάφια[53] in the places where these deserters usually sat to show that they were dead in the moral sense.[54] We must weigh very carefully the praises the Holy Scriptures deserve so that our zeal in attending to them may grow sharper. The Bible is a paradise in which the two original trees grow: one is the tree of knowledge and the other the tree of life. The Scriptures are the polestar of souls, the acropolis of truth, and the treasury of piety. It is the seed that regenerates us as Christians, the milk that nourishes us as infants, the meat on which we feed when mature, the wine that revives us when weak, the medicine that heals us when sick. Yet the Pauline encomium surpasses the many other words of praise. I mean the one ready at hand, that God's word is "the sword of the Spirit." If you try to add anything to this statement, you will only diminish it.

§ 8. But why is it called a "sword"? I will very briefly give one argument and then a second. With the sword, soldiers defend themselves in the midst of battle. Likewise, Christians defend themselves with Scripture. Christ is the prince of our army, who went before us as an example. When He met the tempter in a duel in the desert, the only weapon He used was this sword. "It is written," He said; and a second time, "It is written," and even a third, "It is written" [Luke 4:4, 8, 12]. Using only this weapon, He protected Himself

---

50. Lucius Aelius Verus, 130–169, r. 161–169, Roman emperor. Not to be confused with his father, Lucius Aelius Caesar, heir of Hadrian, who died before Hadrian and thus never succeeded to the throne.

51. *Historia Augusta* (Cologne, 1527), p. 157.

52. Pythagoras, ca. 580–ca. 500 BC, Greek mathematician and philosopher.

53. "Grave markers."

54. *Porphyr.* in vita *Pythag.*] Porphyry, *Liber De Vita Pythagorae* (Rome, 1630).

against the Devil. That ancient enemy trembled not, as the Romanists would have it, at a picture of Christ but at the Scripture. He feared not the sign of the cross but the word of the cross.

Beyond that, our opponents are also put to flight by a sword. In this way, God's Word puts to flight *heresies*, *vices*, and *sorrows*. First, allow me to illustrate this notion of heresies by two examples. The first will be from John Bugenhagen.[55] Luther, as all know, after he had abolished the silly tales of the Antichrist and the fables of the Scholastics, drank deeply and almost exclusively from God's Word. Among other things, he wrote a book called *The Babylonian Captivity*. As Bugenhagen was reading through it during a meal, he abruptly blurted out as follows: "Many heretics, opposed to Christ, the suffering Savior, have infiltrated and sorely harassed the church. But there was never any heretic more poisonous than the author of this book!" Several days later, as he read and reread the book more carefully and weighed more precisely its individual claims, he returned to his companions at the college where he lived and recanted. He said, "Why should I belabor it? The entire world is blind and plunged in Cimmerian shadows. This one man, and he alone, sees the truth."[56] The second example is that of Paolo Vergerio,[57] bishop of Justinopolis.[58] Sleidan says of him,

> He began to write a book, which he entitled *Against the Apostates of Germany*. But while carefully ransacking Protestant literature in order to refute them and closely pondering their arguments, he felt himself caught and beaten. And so when he had abandoned hope of becoming a cardinal, an office the pope had promised him, he went off to visit his brother, the bishop of Pula. Vergerio relates to his brother what happened. At first, his frightened brother bemoans Vergerio's circumstance, but influenced by his prayers, when he had devoted himself to the thorough reading of Scripture and had weighed especially the chief doctrinal point, justification, he relented. And so Vergerio's brother also decided that the Romanist teaching was false. Therefore, congratulating one another, they began to instruct the people throughout Italy.[59]

---

55. Johann (John) Bugenhagen, 1485–1558, German Lutheran preacher.

56. *M. Ad.* vit. Theol. German. p. 313.] Adam, *Vitae Germanorum Theologorum*, p. 313.

57. Pietro Paolo Vergerio, 1498–1565, Italian bishop, jurist, and late Protestant convert (after 1549).

58. Koper, Slovenia.

59. *Sleidan Comment.* Relig. lib. 21.] Johannes Sleidanus (John Sleidan), 1506–1556, German humanist and historographer, *De Statu Religionis Et Reipublicae* ([Geneva], 1559), bk. 21, fol. 361. A. uses *Protestantium* in place of *adversariorum*, *Vergerii* instead of *illius*, adds the phrases *qui ei a Pontifice designatus erat* and *quid ipsi factum sit commemorat* while omitting a number of words and phrases.

The second opponent that God's Word puts to flight is *vices*. While still a young man, Augustine had been ensnared by the traps of sexual dissipation. After some time, he was driven by a voice saying "Take, read; take, read." He picked up the apostolic volume and read Romans 13, where he had first cast his eyes. Eventually, Augustine fell upon these words: "Not in gluttony and drunkenness, not in promiscuity and sexual immorality, not in fighting and strife, but put on the Lord Jesus Christ and make no provision for the flesh in concupiscence." "I did not want to read any further," he said, "and I didn't need to. As soon as I reached the end of that sentence, as if the light of assurance had flooded my heart, every shadow of doubt fled."[60] But what came next, good man? "How suddenly and sweetly it happened," he says, "that my heart was free from vain trifles! Those worthless affections I had been afraid to lose it was now joy to expel. You drive them out of me, You the true and highest sweetness"—that is, Jesus Christ. "You drove them out and entered Yourself in their place, sweeter than all pleasure," etc.[61]

This flat-out brilliant passage of exhortation from Firmianus Lactantius shows clearly enough just how powerful the sacred literature was in rooting out vices:

> Give me a man who is overcome with anger, cursing, and unrestrained. With just very few of God's words, I will make him as gentle as a sheep. Give me someone filled with lust, greedy, stubborn, and I will soon give him back to you set free. Give me someone afraid of pain and death, and before long he will look with contempt upon the cross, fire, and bull of Phalaris.[62] Give me an adulterer swimming with desire, a glutton; now you will see him sober, chaste, and self-controlled. Give me someone cruel and bent on blood, and soon that rage will be transformed into true gentleness. Give me the unrighteous man, the foolish, the sinner. In short order he will become just, wise, and innocent.[63]

The third opponent is *sorrows*. The wisest of kings once said, "Grief in a man's heart crushes him, but he will rejoice in a good word" (Prov. 12:25). There is no word better than God's Word, nor anything that gives birth to greater joy. This is why Paul said, "What was written before was written for our instruction, that through endurance and the comfort of the Scriptures we might have hope" (Rom. 15:4). Thomas à Kempis[64] reportedly wrote this motto in his books, unless I am remembering incorrectly: "I have looked

---

60. Confess. l. 8. cap. ult.] Augustine, *Confessiones*, 8.12.29.

61. Indul. Confess. l. 9. c. 1.] Augustine, *Confessiones*, 9.1.1.

62. An ancient torture device.

63. De falsa sapientia, lib. 3. cap. 26.] Lactantius, *Divinarum Institutionum*, 3.25, p. 212.

64. Thomas à Kempis, ca. 1380–1471, mystical theologian.

for rest in all places, but I have found it nowhere except in a corner with a book."[65] Truly, the Scripture is just such a volume that it alone, or more than all the rest, will give our souls rest. Let Battista of Mantovano add his proof with the following quotation. These are his words:

> The reading of sacred Scripture will afford you a great and inspiring cure for the pains of the body and sadness of the soul. I have very often put this to the test. Whenever I was surrounded by the countless cares that make mortals' life so turbulent and savage, I always fled to the sacred books as to a most fortified citadel and to the immediate medicine for my struggling soul. In them I have found the solace I sought. My hope and my longing were not deceived.[66]

§9. Thus far the explanation for why it is called a sword. Let us go on to state why it is called "the sword of the Spirit." This is, of course, because the Word of God, originally dictated by the Holy Spirit, is distinguished from human writings by the Spirit of God speaking in the heart. And from the same Spirit speaking in the Scriptures, one receives a sure and infallible interpretation. These remarks, so I believe, are sufficiently clear from the comments I made earlier in this very chapter. The third point becomes clear from that passage of Peter where we learn "no prophecy of Scripture is a matter of ἰδίας ἐπιλύσεως," that is, *private interpretation*. "For prophecy was not provided by the will of man, but holy men of God spoke as they were driven by the Holy Spirit" (2 Peter 1:20–21).[67] The Apostle seems to argue in the following manner. He holds that the explanation of Scripture ought to proceed from the one who inspired it. This means the Spirit of God. Thus, each man is the proper and best interpreter of his own words. The Scriptures are the very words of the Holy Spirit. Therefore, they must not be interpreted according to the private judgment of just any individual, or according to the understanding and private spirit of just any man. No doubt by the expression ἰδίας ἐπιλύσεως we are to understand most readily either a private interpretation or exegesis. For just as, in Latin authors, the word *explicari* is derived from the unrolling of layers, so among the Greeks, the word ἐπίλυσις is derived from the breaking of chains, since exegesis is, as it were, untying some knot. Bernard says quite forcefully, "As the Scriptures were produced by the Spirit, so they long to be read by the Spirit.

---

65. *S. Torshell* exercit. in Malach.] Samuel Torshell, 1605–1650, Church of England clergyman, *Commentary upon the whole prophesie of Malachy* (London, 1641), sub loc. Mal. 4:4, p. 87.

66. De patientia l. 3. cap. 32.] Giovanni Battista Spagnoli (Baptista Mantuanus), 1448–1516, Italian Carmelite and neo-Latin poet, *De Patientia* (Strasbourg, 1510), bk. 3, ch. 32, fol. 97v–98r.

67. A. provides the Greek expression from Peter as well as his Latin gloss.

So also they must be interpreted by that very Spirit."[68] Now the private spirit of a Christian man is one that understands and believes that either this meaning or that one is the authentic meaning of any given passage. But it is a spirit illuminated by God's public Spirit to grasp, understand, and believe. Therefore, we hold that this understanding and faith, with respect to the execution, proceed from a private spirit. But with respect to origin, they are derived from that public Spirit who speaks in the Scriptures.[69] When one appeals to councils, the fathers, and the confessions of Churches, one goes before fallible judges. But only what the Holy Spirit says in the Scriptures, as they are mutually referenced, should be considered proven. Consequently, that famous council in Acts 15, because it had rendered its decision in keeping with the standard of evidence Peter and James had produced from sacred literature, stated, "It seemed good to the Holy Spirit and to us" (Acts 15:28). Obviously, they meant, "Good to the Spirit who spoke in that evidence, and therefore good to us, because good to the Spirit who spoke thus."

§ 10. Now then, men and brothers, let us draw that sword from its sheath and brandish it in our arguments. But we must especially brandish it above all in our assemblies. Whoever is a minister of the word, may he be another Apollos, "an eloquent man, powerful in the Scriptures" (Acts 18:24). Although he may be eloquent, so far as I'm concerned, it must be with an eloquence not drawn from the theater but instead theological, manly, and moving—that is, biblical eloquence. Just as Moses once said, "If only the whole people were prophets of Jehovah" (Num. 11:29), so I am prepared to hope that "all prophets of Jehovah are orators." Let him be astonishingly eloquent, provided he is at the same time very fluent, not in poets and historians, not in philosophers and the study of words, not in the Scholastics and the fathers, much less in the traditions and lives of the saints, but in the Scriptures. Fine, let him read all books, so long as he is most acquainted with the Holy Spirit's library. The story goes that at Oxford, King James said, "If I were ever captured, and the choice of prisons were set before me, I would choose the Bodleian Library before all other places."[70] But look, someone greater than Bodley is here. The sacred Book is the library of the Holy Spirit, and it is such a collection that it can hardly

---

68. Serm. ad Fratres de monte Dei.] Bernard of Clairvaux, *Tractatus De Vita Solitaria*, in *Opera Omnia*, vol. 5 (Cologne, 1641), ch. 10, sec. 31.

69. The Scholastic phrases, attested in Scotus *inter alia*, are *quoad actum* and *quoad ortum*, respectively.

70. An anecdote also circulated as, "If I were not a king, I would be a university man; and if it were so that I must be a prisoner, if I might have my wish, I would desire to have no other prison than that library [the Bodleian]."

be turned into a prison. No, not even hardly, because it confers freedom on its inhabitants as our Savior said: "If you abide in My Word, you will truly be My disciples. And you shall know the truth, and the truth shall set you free" (John 8:31–32).

They who have once learned from God this skill, as I would call it, of the swordsman (I say "from God" because all authentic preachers of the gospel are Θεοδίδακτοι)[71] must be doggedly on guard not to hide the sword of the Word. For there is really nothing like it, as David said of Goliath's sword, when the Hebrews hid it behind the ephod [1 Sam. 21:9]. Instead, preachers must draw out that sword in the people's presence with frequent sermons. May they bring to mind Aaron, I pray, who found the pomegranate inadequate without its bell [Exod. 28:34]. May they be mindful of Pentecost when the Spirit was descending: He did not come down in the form of *hands*, as though the world must be subdued by force and weapons. And He did not come down in the form of *feet*, as though one must run away when he threatens. Not in the form of *ears* or *eyes*, the instruments of learning. He descended, instead, in the form of *tongues*, the organs of teaching. With these we must pray to God on behalf of the people, must address the people concerning God. But scholars and everyone everywhere who possesses genuine talent and zeal for good literature must work hard at the original languages, as they are called, at least for this reason: because they are the sheath in which is stored what I have dealt with to this point— namely, the sword of the Spirit.

End of the second book.

---

71. "God-taught."

PLANS FOR HOLY WAR

BOOK III

CHAPTER I

The Preparation for Victory
through Holy Exhortations

Section 1: Ephesians 6:18 is discussed throughout the whole chapter. The first part of the sentence and its connection with the verses that precede it. The use of Scripture in prayer. Section 2: The second part of the verse. Prayers are compared to auxiliary troops. Pagan senators, poets, orators, and soldiers also began their projects with prayer. Section 3: Prayer must be directed to God alone. Individual prayers are commended in three related ways: public, private, and secret. Section 4: We must not in any way petition God for things not promised in His Word, much less for things that His Word prohibits. Sections 5–6: We must pray for spiritual goods like the forgiveness of sins, the rooting out of vices, and increase of virtues. An argument against the philosophers and Pelagians who teach something different. Section 7: Why and how we must ask for temporal goods. Section 8: Mortals approach God in three related ways, namely, by creation, redemption, and adoption. The exegesis of Galatians 4:6. Section 9: Those who have been reborn can and must speak to God, as must the unregenerate. This is explained in four theses. Section 10: When we are to pray. The meaning of Διαπαντός. The canonical hours of the Romanists. Sections 11–12: What "praying in the Spirit" means, if we understand it as coming from ourselves; what it means, if we understand it as coming from the Holy Spirit. An explanation of Romans 8:26 and James 5:16 (where the phrase δέησις ἐνεργουμένη[1] is found). Section 13: What it means to be alert in our prayers, bodily and mental alertness. Section 14: The meaning of προσκαρτέρησις.[2] The analogies of Luis de Granada. Section 15: Prayers of imprecation, and what we should think about the curses found in sacred Scriptures. Section 16: An exhortatory conclusion. Section 17: Prayer according to the standard of the Lord's Prayer.

---

1. "Effectual prayer."
2. "Perseverance."

§ 1. The first book of this work established what it means to be a Christian in terms of military duty. The second one dealt with the battle. Now the third book follows, in which the Christian is equipped for victory and triumph. After the full armor is described completely, there follows an apostolic command in these words: διὰ πάσης προσευχῆς καὶ δεήσεως προσευχόμενοι ἐν παντὶ καιρῷ ἐν πνεύματι, καὶ εἰς αὐτὸ ἀγρυπνοῦντες ἐν πάσῃ προσκαρτερήσει καὶ δεήσει περὶ πάντων τῶν ἁγίων ("With all prayer and petition, praying at every moment in the Spirit, to this end remaining alert with all perseverance and supplication for all the saints") [Eph. 6:18]. I think it is quite timely for me to discuss at the beginning of this little book the connection of this verse with what has gone before, along with its meaning.

This commandment perhaps has a connection with the words that immediately precede—namely, "Take up the sword of the Spirit, which is the word of God" [Eph. 6:17]. They imply that, in all our speaking to God, we must look to the Scriptures. In fact, all sacred exhortation is like a building that requires lumber and stones for its construction. The sacred Scripture is the forest where the lumber is felled, the quarry where the stones needed for the building's structure are unearthed. This is why the saints, while praying, usually recall the examples, promises, and other sayings of the sacred Scriptures, or at least refer to them. Augustine said of his mother Monica, "She kept insisting, O Lord, on bringing your sureties before you"—that is, the promises God had used to put Himself, so to speak, into debt.[3] Veit Dietrich[4] comments to Melanchthon, when writing about Luther's prayers, "Good God, how much spirit, how much faith is present in his very words! He asks for something with so much reverence that he feels like he is talking with God, with so much hope and faith as with a father and a friend." A little bit later, he writes, "Luther, while praying, puts so much pressure on the promises derived from the Psalms, as though he were certain that everything he was asking for would come to pass."[5] The apostles based their own prayers on the prophetic statements given in Psalm 2 (Acts 4:25–26). But what we notice in Mary's song from Luke 1 surpasses them all. Chemnitz's discussion of this passage begins with these words: "I hold that the most direct explanation of this song requires observing and studying the passages of Scripture that Mary, by the impulse of Him whom she carried in her womb, picked and wove together as the little blossoms

---

3. Augustine, *Confessiones*, 5.9.17.
4. Veit Dietrich, 1506–1549, German Lutheran theologian.
5. *M. Adam.* vit. Theol. Germ. p. 142.] Adam, *Vitae Germanorum Theologorum*, p. 142.

of her celebratory song."[6] This is the very thing that Chemnitz, a most exquisite writer, attempts to demonstrate in each of his arguments. We will be satisfied with just a few examples, because his work is—or deserves to be—in everyone's hands. "My soul is exalted in God my Savior," Mary said [Luke 1:47]. Almost the same words are found in the next to last verse of Habakkuk 3: ἐγὼ δὲ ἐν τῷ κυρίῳ ἀγαλλιάσομαι, χαρήσομαι ἐπὶ τῷ Θεῷ τῷ σωτῆρί μου [Hab. 3:18].[7] Then she continues, "Because He has regarded the low estate of His maidservant" [Luke 1:48]. Almost precisely the same words are found in I Samuel 1:11, where Hannah says in her prayer, ἐὰν ἐπιβλέπων ἐπιβλέψῃς ἐπὶ τὴν ταπείνωσιν τῆς δούλης σου.[8] Next, "This is why all generations will call me blessed," Mary says [Luke 1:48]. These words are taken from Leah's statement in Genesis 30:13: Μακαρία ἐγώ, ὅτι μακαρίζουσίν με αἱ γυναῖκες.[9] Mary next quotes from a psalm: "His mercy is from generation to generation of those who fear Him" [Luke 1:50]. This is almost an exact quotation of Psalm 103:17: τὸ δὲ ἔλεος τοῦ κυρίου ἀπὸ τοῦ αἰῶνος καὶ ἕως τοῦ αἰῶνος ἐπὶ τοὺς φοβουμένους αὐτόν.[10] Next come these words: "He has demonstrated strength by His arm; He has taken Israel for His Son. So He remembered His mercy" [Luke 1:51, 54]. These words are very similar to the ones found in the seventy translators[11] of Psalm 98:2–3: ἔσωθεν αὐτὸν ἡ δεξιὰ αὐτοῦ καὶ ὁ βραχίων ὁ ἅγιος αὐτοῦ, ἐμνήσθη τοῦ ἐλέους αὐτοῦ τῷ Ἰακωβ καὶ τῆς ἀληθείας αὐτοῦ τῷ Ἰσραήλ.[12] This is especially true if we add the following words from Isaiah 41:8–9: Σὺ δέ, Ἰσραηλ, παῖς μου.[13] And right after that, οὗ ἀντελαβόμην.[14] For this is what Mary said: Ἀντελάβετο Ἰσραὴλ παιδὸς αὐτοῦ, μνησθῆναι ἐλέους [Luke 1:54].[15] Almost all the rest of the words come (though not literally) from Hannah's song in 1 Samuel 1:2, as well as Psalm 113:7.

§2. Some theologians connect this commandment not so much to this or that particular point as to the whole apostolic discourse on Christians'

---

6. *Chemnit.* harmon. evang. c.] Martin Chemnitz, 1522–1586, German Lutheran theologian, *Harmoniae Evangelicae* (Geneva, 1628), bk. 1, ch. 5, col. 47.

7. "I will rejoice in the Lord, I will be glad in God my Savior."

8. "If looking upon me you have regard for the low estate of your maidservant."

9. "Blessed am I, because the women bless me."

10. "The mercy of the Lord is from generation to generation upon those who fear Him."

11. Here A. uses another expression for the Septuagint.

12. "His right hand and His holy arm have wrought salvation; He remembered His pity for and His faithfulness to Israel."

13. "You, Israel, are My son."

14. "Whom I have taken."

15. "He received Israel His son, He remembered His mercy."

weapons and armament. They do so as follows: John Quistorp, professor at Rostock, writes,

> In time of war, those beset by foreign enemies seek help from their close allies through written messages. And these allies, in turn, do not deny their brethren. Similarly, in the last verse of the passage, Paul wants us, in this our spiritual conflict—through our prayers—to flee for safety to God our Father and Christ our brother. And by these mutual prayers, we who are brothers in Christ help one another against the enemy.[16]

Certainly, auxiliary forces often deserve credit for victory in war. Likewise, in our spiritual conflict, we must credit the holy exhortations that call upon God to be present with those who struggle. In that vein, we have this quote from Macarius: "Prayer is support to him who prays, a sacrifice to God, and a whip for the Devil." And this gem is his also: "Although the demons may be powerful and no different than mountains in their strength, they are consumed by the fire of prayer like wax in the flame."[17]

Actually, this very idea—that we must pour out our prayers before God so that the duty we undertake succeeds, no matter what, in the end, comes to pass—is not only familiar to Christians and Jews. Indeed, among the Jews, it has become quite proverbial: "Whoever finishes his work before praying is like the man who builds only the roof."[18] This idea was also well understood by the pagans, and so it happened that the leading men in the state—senators, poets, orators, soldiers—each typically prefaced all their important tasks with prayer. One of Xenophon's political principles was this: πειρᾶσθαι σὺν τοῖς θεοῖς ἄρχεσθαι παντὸς ἔργου, ὡς τῶν θεῶν κυρίων ὄντων οὐδὲν ἧττον τῶν εἰρηνικῶν ἢ τῶν πολεμικῶν ἔργων ("Try to venture upon every task with the help of the gods, because the gods oversee and control matters of war precisely as they do domestic affairs").[19] And from Plutarch we learn that Scipio went to the Capitoline Hill to pray before going to the senate to govern the republic.[20] Beyond that, the poets themselves were also touched with the same sense of reverence. This is

---

16. *Quistorp.* Comment. in loc. p. 199.] Johann (John) Quistorp, 1584–1648, German Lutheran theologian, *In Divinam S. Apostoli Pauli Ad Ephesios* (Rostock, 1636), p. 199.

17. ὑπὸ τῆς εὐχῆς καίονται, καθάπερ ὁ κηρὸς ὑπὸ πυρός. *Macar.* homil. 43.] Macarius of Egypt (the Great), *Homiliae Spirituales*, p. 475 (*homilia* 43).

18. *Buxtorf.* florileg. Hebraic. p. 282.] Johannes Buxtorf, Jr., 1599–1664, Swiss Reformed Hebraist, *Florilegium Hebraicum* (Basel, 1648), p. 281.

19. Xenophon, *Oeconomicus*, 6.1.

20. Plutarch's *Lives* discuss this event in the life of the Roman General Publius Cornelius Scipio Africanus (Scipio the Elder), 236–184/183 BC; but it is Livy, in his account of "The Trial of Scipio" (*Ab Urbe Condita* 38.51), who records the detail A. mentions here.

the source of the famous slogan "The Muses got their start from Jupiter."[21] At the conclusion of his preface, Valerius Maximus says, "The first public speakers began with Jupiter. The very best poets drew their starting point from some divinity."[22] Not even Ovid neglected this solemn duty. At the beginning of his work the *Metamorphoses*, this is how he prays: "O gods, inspire my beginnings."[23] The same applies to orators, as is clear from an equal number of proofs and examples. Pliny the Younger, at the threshold of his *Panegyric*, says, "Gentlemen of the senate, our forefathers set a wise and careful precedent by beginning their political deliberations as well as their public speaking with prayers." Pliny himself immediately lends credence to this notion by his own example, breaking forth in the following words: "It is then all the more proper and pious for us to beseech you, Jupiter Optimus Maximus, once the founder and now the preserver of our empire, that my speech correspond to the dignity of a consul, the dignity of the senate, and the dignity of the emperor."[24] Demosthenes began like this in the speech he delivered against Aeschines, saying, πρῶτον μὲν, ὦ ἄνδρες Ἀθηναῖοι, τοῖς θεοῖς εὔχομαι πᾶσι καὶ πάσαις.[25] If anyone desires more proof, I ask him to consult Diogenes Laertius in his life of Protagoras.[26] That man reportedly counted prayer among the elements of proper oratory.[27] He should also take a look at the comments Aelian makes concerning Pericles[28] in book 4 chapter 10 of his *Historical Miscellany*.[29] He can also consult what Servius[30] writes as a commentary to Vergil's words:

> When on the gods he thus had called
> the king from lofty throne commenced…[31]

But it is more relevant for us to find out what soldiers did. They also typically pray when girding themselves for battle. Plutarch says of Marius that

---

21. Vergil, *Ecloga* 3, in *Opera* (Leipzig, 1616) (line 60).

22. Valerius Maximus, fl. ca. 27–31, Roman historian, *Factorum Et Dictorum Memorabilium* (Leiden, 1651), p. 2 (*prologus*).

23. Ovid, *Metamorphoseon*, bk. 1, p. 3.

24. Pliny the Younger, ca. 61–ca. 112, Roman statesman and author, *Epistolarum et Panegyricus* (Leiden, 1640), pp. 326–27.

25. Demosthenes, 384–322 BC, Greek orator and statesman. See, ΤΜΗΜΑ ΔΕΥΤΕΡΟΝ / *Demosthenis Orationum Pars Secunda* (Venice, 1554), fol. 6r. "I pray first of all, gentlemen of Athens, to all the gods and all the goddesses." Oration 18, *De Corona*.

26. Protagoras, ca. 490–420 BC, Greek philosopher.

27. Diogenes Laertius, *Peri Biōn Dogmatōn Kai Apophthegmatōn*, bk. 9, ch. 8.

28. Pericles, ca. 495–429 BC, Greek statesman.

29. Probably Aelian, *Variae Historiae Libri XIIII*.

30. Servius, ca. 380–before-ca. 430, compiler of commentaries on Vergil.

31. Vid. *Turneb.* Adversar. l. 25. cap. ult.] Vergil, *Aeneidos*, bk. 11 (line 301).

πρὸς τὸν οὐρανὸν ἀνασχὼν ηὔξατο τοῖς θεοῖς.[32] And Vergil writes of Turnus[33] that

> Then from the gods he much implored
> and with his prayers assailed the sky.[34]

This is what we see demonstrated among the pagans at nature's dictate in a citizens' militia. The Apostle in this passage urges Christians to engage in this activity much more and with much greater success. We ourselves, following the syntax and flow of the actual words as they are positioned in the original text, will show precisely how much meaning each contains.

§ 3. διὰ πάσης προσευχῆς (i.e. "With all prayer"). προσευχή is πρὸς τὸν Θεὸν εὐχή.[35] The preposition πρὸς indicates the object of prayer and the end at which it aims—that is, God alone. Consequently, he who does not direct this worship toward God is profane, and he is an idolater who directs it to anything other than God. Augustine supports this idea: "He alone deserves worship who, as the one worshipping enjoys Him, makes that worshiper blessed. And if there is some mind that does not enjoy Him alone, it is miserable, no matter what other object it fully enjoys."[36] Hilary of Poitiers casts his vote with us also: "You cannot escape the fact that, even under the curse, creation possesses religion."[37] Also, Alexander of Hales: "True religion consists in service of the one true God." And in another passage, he says, "All divine worship offered to a creature is idolatry."[38] Really, all the noteworthy fathers who assert true deity on the basis of its praiseworthiness agree with us. Epiphanius says of Christ that οὐ κτιστὸς τοίνυν ὁ ἅγιος Λόγος ὅτι προσκυνητός ("The Holy Word of God, because it must be worshipped, cannot be created").[39] Gregory Nazianzus, in writing on the Holy Spirit, says, εἰ δὲ προσκυνητὸν πῶς οὐ σεπτόν, εἰ δε σεπτόν, πῶς

---

32. "Looking up to heaven he prayed to the gods." Plutarch, *Tou Sophōtatou Ploutarchou Parallelōn Bioi* (Florence, 1517). (See Loeb, *Plutarch's Lives*, "Caius Marius," ch. 26.2.) The 1517 edition contains the full *Bioi*, whereas the Frankfurt *Omnia* of 1620 did not have the full life.

33. Turnus, Rutulian hero of the Aeneid.

34. Vergil, *Aeneidos*, bk. 9 (line 24).

35. "Prayer directed toward God."

36. Contra *Faustum* lib. 2. c. 5.] Augustine, *Contra Faustum Manichaeum*, in *Omnium Operum*, vol. 6 (Basel, 1528), 20.5.

37. De Trinit. 1.8.] Hilary of Poitiers, *De Trinitate*, in *Quotquot Extant Opera* (Paris, 1631), bk. 8.

38. Summ. part. 3. q. 30 § 1. & part. 2. qu. 106. memb. I.] Alexander of Hales, *Universae Theologiae Summa* (Venice, 1575), vol. 3, fol. 113r. The second quotation appears to be a paraphrase of a line in vol. 2, q. 158, memb. I, *On Idolatry*, fol. 388v.

39. Ancorat. n. 50.] 50.5. Epiphanius, *Liber Ancoratus, Omnem De Fide Christiana Doctrinam Complectens* (Basil, [1544]). This is a Greek edition with a Latin gloss on the title page.

οὐ Θεός; ("If he is deserving of worship, how is he not holy? If he is holy, how is he not God?").[40]

The adjective πάσης that Paul adds here seems to imply prayer of all kinds—not merely public but also private and even secret. We must pray publicly when Christians are gathered in their places of worship. So then the ancients called these kinds of prayers *oratoria*. Those who fight together must pray together. "All of us are God's beggars when we pray. We stand together before the door of the great Father of our family—no, we even lie there on our faces and groan with supplications. We want to receive something from Him, and this something is God Himself."[41] So Augustine writes. Now just as everyday some rich man supplies the mob of beggars at the doors of his house with alms and thus proves his generosity, likewise, the mob of our prayers accomplishes much for God's glory. Tertullian writes about the Christians of his time, saying, "We travel together to the assembly and the congregation, like a hastily formed crowd with its demands, to canvass God by our prayers. This sort of violence is pleasing to God."[42] Among the Jews, there is a famous quote of Maimonides that carries this meaning: "Whoever lives in a city where there is a synagogue and does not pray there with the public assembly, this is a person who deserves to be called a wicked neighbor."[43] This is well said, especially since such a person takes away from the needy in his neighborhood the help that he owes them.

Now I steadfastly disagree with a certain theologian of Salamanca in this statement:

> I think that one must affirm that the prayers that take place in the church are more effectual than those offered elsewhere. This is not due solely to the effort of the one performing the work[44]—since the elegance of the sanctuary, its decoration, and other aspects stir us up more to pray with greater fervency, and as a consequence, what they gain by petition is more effective. But they are also innately[45] more effective. And so, all things being equal as concerns those who pray, prayers delivered in church are more pleasing to God and more effective for obtaining what is sought because of their consecration, etc.[46]

---

40. Orat. 37.] Gregory Nazianzus, *Oratio De Spiritu Sancto*, in *Opera*, vol. 1 (Paris, 1630), p. 609 (*oratio 37*).

41. Serm. de Tempore 15.] Augustine, *De Verbis Domini In Matthaeum*, *sermo* 15.

42. Apolog. 1.39.] Tertullian, *Apologeticus*, ch. 39.

43. Lib. de oration cap. 8.] Moses Maimonides, 1138–1204, Jewish philosopher, *Mishneh Torah, Sefer Ahavah, Tefilah and Birkat Kohanim*, 8.1. A common Hebrew edition of the *Mishneh Torah* with Maimonides's words is the Venice edition of 1574.

44. *Ex opere operantis.*

45. *Ex opere operato.*

46. *Raphael de la Torre* in 2ᵃ 2ᵃᵉ q. 83. artic. 3. p. 301.] Rafael de la Torre, ca. sixteenth or sev-

Nevertheless, I admit that public prayers have more efficacy, so that the advantage attached to them is real. But reverence does not depend upon the place chosen for the assembly. We must credit whatever efficacy exists not to the place but to the communion of saints, whose power is stronger when united.

Every individual head of household,[47] in addition, must also offer prayer privately in his own home. For this reason, Paul addresses servants' masters, as such, as follows: "Masters, demonstrate justice and impartiality to your servants since you know that you also have a Master in heaven. Persevere in prayer, staying watchful in prayer with thanksgiving" (Col. 4:1–2). We can establish the practice of daily household prayer on the basis of this passage, or at least it seems possible to do so, especially when the sense of the context is taken into account. The whole passage is directed to equipping the Christian household. Managers of households can hardly stand it if someone denies that they deserve an almost royal authority within the confines of their property. I want you to understand, whoever you are, you who are called a king in your own household, that your Lord in heaven expects you to act like a priest in that same setting, offering up, day after day, in the presence of those who belong to you, the sacrifices of prayer and praise.

Our Savior also admonishes us with respect to secret prayers, as they are called, and He is our sole instructor. "When you pray, go into your own closet, and with the door closed, pray to your Father in secret. And the Father who sees you in secret will repay you openly" (Matt. 6:6). So then, every place will be adequate for prayer, so long as there is opportunity and something to pray about. Consider, Jeremiah devoted himself to sacred prayers in a pit, Daniel in the den of lions, Job while sitting in a pile of dung, Hezekiah while he lay on his bed, the three children in the furnace, Jonah in the belly of a whale, Christ in a garden, Peter on a balcony, and Paul while in prison. Thus, what follows are the words of the fathers. Chrysostom: "Wherever you are, pray. You yourself are the temple, don't look for some place to pray."[48] Augustine: "If you wish to pray in the temple, pray within yourself. And always act such that you yourself are God's temple. For God listens in the same place He dwells."[49] Bernard: "No matter where you are, you do not need to seek a place to pray, because you yourself are that

---

enteenth century, preacher at Salamanca, *Summa Theologica* (Cologne, 1630), quaest. 84, art. 3, disput. 3, p. 301.

47. *Paterfamilias.*

48. Ad popul. Antioch. homil. 79. Sententia 333.] Chrysostom, *De Oratione*, in *Opera Omnia*, vol. 6 (Paris, 1636), *homilia 2.*

49. This appears to be A.'s paraphrase of Augustine, *In Evangelium Ioannis Exposito*, in *Omnium Operum*, vol. 9 (Basel, 1528), tract. 15, p. 95. Here Augustine discusses John 4 and Ps. 137 in relationship to how and where we must worship.

place."[50] But another golden expression of that same author now comes to mind, something that would be almost criminal to overlook for someone discussing this topic. "O righteous soul, be alone. Flee the public, flee the members of your own house. Or, don't you know that you have a modest husband, and one who is entirely unwilling to bestow His presence upon you in the presence of others?"[51]

§4. καὶ δεήσεως ("And with petition"). Δέομαι, in Greek, means *I need*, and so δέησις denotes a request for the things we perceive we need. πᾶσα δέησις means a petition to acquire all those goods, whether spiritual or temporal, provided they are promised in the Word, either directly or indirectly. But if not promised, then we must not seek them even if they seem very good and very useful. For example, it is hardly possible to imagine something better or more advantageous than a manifest vision of the divine essence and of the Holy Trinity while we are pilgrims. But we must not ask for that, because pilgrims are nowhere promised such. But the Jesuits, obviously God's dear offspring (as I note in passing), boast about attaining that vision and teach that it can be obtained and must be sought. Among others, I cite Juan Eusebio Nieremberg, in whose works we encounter the following remarks:

> Our holy patriarch Ignatius, when he was quite afflicted and exhausted with penance, received a more full and more clear manifestation than words can express [God standing in his presence as a light]. The most zealous father Didacus Martinius almost always saw himself bathed in a certain most glorious Trinitarian light, or of one of the three persons.[52] And it was revealed to the holy man, father John Ferdinand,[53] that a particular monk of our society was being held in purgatory for a long time because he had not earnestly desired to behold the Most Holy Trinity.[54]

This is what he says. But really, what a marvelous society that must be whose initiates are so often granted what God denied Moses himself, even though He used to speak with Moses like a friend! But really, how cheating and dishonest you are, Juan Eusebio, that you either fabricated such

---

50. In meditationibus alicubi.] Bernard of Clairvaux, *Meditationes Piissimae*, in *Opera Omnia*, vol. 5 (Cologne, 1641), ch. 6, sec. 18.

51. Serm. 40. in Cantic.] Bernard of Clairvaux, *In Cantica Canticorum*, sec. 5 (*sermo* 40).

52. Didacus Martinius, Jesuit; story from Juan Eusebio Nieremberg, 1595–1658, *De Adoratione In Spiritu Et Veritate* (Antwerp, 1631), p. 447.

53. Perhaps Juan Fernández, ca. 1526–1567, Spanish Jesuit and missionary to Japan.

54. De Adorat. in Spiritu & veritate, p. 446, 447.] Nieremberg, *De Adoratione In Spiritu Et Veritate* (Antwerp, 1642), bk. 4, ch. 16, p. 447. The phrase *Lumen scilicet Deum coram ipso sistens* is A.'s parenthetical comment.

things or gullibly swallowed, through inordinate charity toward your fellows, things they made up!

So, just as we must not ask for what is not promised in the Word, much less can we seek what that same Word forbids. It was both pointless and wicked for the followers of Baal to pray from morning until noon for the success of their idolatry. As Chrysologus notes, "We must be careful to demand from God only what is worthy. For he who demands wicked things from God judges that God is the author of evil and so perceives Him. And the man who prays for things petty and unworthy is as a corrupted petitioner who disregards the giver."[55] Suarez, moreover, writes, "He who demands of God something evil is not seeking it from God as God. But he conceives of God as though He were some man or a demon that could advance his wicked guilt."[56] The particular depravity of pagan theology (to give this warning also, in passing) is evident in this kind of thinking. They make the gods the supporters of their crimes and so boldly asked them to favor their sins, like the thief in Horace:

> O Fair Laverne, let me deceive yet just and righteous seem.
> Pour ink upon my sins, and o'er my tricks a clouded dream.[57]

We also recall the merchant in Ovid's *Fasti* book 5:

> Give profit to me, profit please, with joy that is my "due"
> And that I fool the buyer with my lies—throw that in too![58]

It is no wonder that such ideas displeased the wiser pagans—Seneca, to name one. "How much madness," he said, "do men possess? They whisper to God such incredibly shameful prayers. If any god hears them, he won't reply. And they describe to God what they want no man to know."[59] In another passage, he writes, "How many prayers there are that are shameful to admit! How few that we can pray while someone's watching!"[60] Therefore, he offered Lucilius this advice: "Live among men as if God watched. Speak with God as if men listened."[61]

---

55. Serm. 132.] Peter Chrysologus, ca. 400–450, bishop of Ravenna, *Sermones In Evangelia* (Mainz, 1613), *sermo* 132.

56. De Religione tom. 2. p. 5.] Francisco Suárez, 1548–1617, Spanish Jesuit philosopher and theologian, *Opus De Religione*, vol. 2 (Lyon, 1630), tract. 4, bk. 1, ch. 2, sec. 4, p. 6.

57. Horace, *Epistolarum*, bk. 1 (*epistola* 16, lines 60–62).

58. Ovid, *Fastorum*, 5.689–90.

59. Epist. 10.] Seneca, *Epistolae* (*epistola* 10).

60. De Beneficiis l. 6. cap. 38.] Seneca, *De Beneficiis*, in *Opera Quae Exstant Omnia* (Antwerp, 1652), bk. 6, ch. 38.

61. Seneca, *Epistolae* (*epistola* 10).

§5. Now, in our addresses to God, we must earnestly seek, above all, the attainment of spiritual goods. Things of first importance deserve our utmost attention. That of the highest value requires our highest concern. Savonarola piously remarks, "He who asks God for small things does Him great injury. Temporal blessings, moreover, are small matters, but spiritual ones are great, especially Christ."[62] Examples of this class (to get down to specifics) are forgiveness of sins, uprooting of vices, and increase of virtues. Prayer is very effective for acquiring all of these.

The psalmist said of the first one, "I will confess to Jehovah against myself my own deceits, and You have forgiven my iniquity; because of this, every saint will pray to You at the right time" (Ps. 32:5–6). "Because of this" means, as Simone de Muis interpreted, "immediately, no matter how often one falls into any sin, I will pray and confess, stirred up by the example of forgiveness that You have given me."[63] Bernard should testify to what he learned: "How often has prayer, when it took up in near despair, made me jubilant and confident of God's forgiveness!"[64]

The Lord said of the second one, "Pray that you not enter into temptation" [Matt. 26:41; Mark 14:38]. One learns by experience that there is an antipathy between vices and prayers. Necessarily then, one of these eventually happens: vices will wreak slaughter and destruction on our prayers to God, or our prayers to God will do the same to our vices.

Regarding the third one, the virtues called *theological* are faith, hope, and love. Prayer feeds and fosters all of these. Augustine beautifully said of faith, "Let us believe so that we pray. And let us pray that the very faith by which we pray not fail. Faith pours out prayer, and prayer, when it has been poured out, gains a firm faith."[65] But the frequent exercise of prayer increases and perfects our hope, because it so often elevates us to hope. This statement about hope is very true, that "the life of mortal life is the hope of life immortal."[66] No one earnestly asks for what he does not expect at some time or another to gain. Even infused dispositions increase the more they are practiced. Consequently, the psalmist rightly joins hope and prayers: "Hope in Him, all you congregation of the people. Pour out your hearts before Him. God is our help forever" (Ps. 62:9). When it comes to love toward God—who is perfectly good and, what is more, perfectly desirable—this is at the same time kindled and enhanced by our addresses in prayer. Just as the frequency of their conversation among men is the

---

62. In Psal. 51.] Savonarola, *Meditationes In Psalmos Miserere* (Leiden, 1633), p. 37.

63. De Muis, *In Omnes Psalmos*, sub loc. Ps. 32:6.

64. Serm. 32. in Cant.] Bernard of Clairvaux, *In Cantica Canticorum*, sec. 3 (*sermo* 32).

65. Serm. 36. de verb. Dom. c. 2.] Augustine, *De Verbis Domini In Lucam* (*sermo* 36).

66. Attributed to or said of martyrologist John Foxe.

firewood of friendship, so neglect indicates either hatred or disinterest. Treachery and betrayal sever friendship with a single blow. But there are agents that weaken and dissolve it gradually, and Aristotle lists interrupted conversation as one of these in his review: πολλὰς δὴ φιλίας ἀπροσηγορία διέλυσεν.[67] The relationship between God and men is similar. Thus, Jude in his letter connects love and prayer: "But you, beloved, praying in the Holy Spirit, keep yourselves in God's love" (Jude vv. 20–21). So here I must cite the man I recently blamed, Nieremberg. This is his argument: "Angry men would rather perish than seek from a deadly enemy the cure for their need, so that they do not have to talk to him. They are just as insolent toward You, You who are easiest to talk to yet essentially inexpressible." This is how Nieremberg describes God. "They often go without, they are afflicted, often perish, because they do not ask You for help nor talk to You. This is a greater instance of hatred than two people living in the same house, and one refusing to talk to the other. That man is a liar if he says he loves God and never talks to the one who resides within him. Silent friendship is indistinguishable from hatred."[68]

§ 6. Is there anyone who believes that any of these conclusions could be called into question? Nevertheless, there have been some (I could wish there weren't any such today!) who resolutely denied that prayer was useful for the purposes I just described. And some have denied that it was useful at all, much less necessary. I'm talking about the philosophers and Pelagians. Sirach once said of the antediluvian giants, "The ancient giants did not pray for forgiveness for their sins; they perished while trusting in their own strength" (Sir. 16:8).[69] Such were the followers of Nimrod. Josephus tells us that he taught his men to ask for nothing from God but to attribute everything to their own strength.[70] It would appear that the gentile philosophers have drunk from the same spirit. They, in keeping with the αὐταρκεία[71] and hubris in which they boasted, believed and taught that prayers were unnecessary, at least when it came to acquiring virtue. We have it on Augustine's authority that they believed happiness had to be bought with effort not received through asking.[72] But let the gentiles give their own account,

---

67. Ethic. l. 8. c. 5.] Aristotle, *Ethicorum* (Frankfurt, 1577), 8.5. "Lack of conversation has destroyed many friendships."

68. De Adorat. in Spir. & verit. lib. 2. c. 1.] Nieremberg, *De adoratione*, bk. 2, ch. 1, p. 108. *O affabilissima ineffabilitas.*

69. Sir. 16:7.

70. Josephus, *Antiquitatum Iudaicarum*, in *Opera Quae Exstant Nempe* (Geneva, 1611), bk. 1, ch. 5.

71. "Self-reliance."

72. Epist. 52.] Augustine, *Liber Epistolarum*, in *Omnia Opera*, vol. 2, sub loc. Epist. LII (p. 150).

let them produce evidence from their own books: "Who ever thanked the gods that he was a good man? But of course, he could thank him for being rich, distinguished, and healthy. These are the reasons men invoke Jupiter, 'Best and Greatest.' It is not because he makes us righteous, self-controlled, and wise. No, it is because he makes us healthy, free from sickness, affluent, and full of possessions."[73] These are Cicero's words. In Horace, a devotee of Stoic philosophy,[74] we read,

> It is enough to beg from Jove what he does give and take
> (He should give life, provide us wealth).
> But that my mind's at peace is up to me, make no mistake.[75]

But Seneca was the leading authority of that same school of thought. He says, "It is disgraceful, at this stage, to harass the gods with prayers. Why do you need to pray? Make yourself happy!"[76] And in another passage, he says, "It's foolish to ask someone else for a good conscience when you can get it from yourself."[77]

The Pelagians seem to have followed in the footsteps of these same men. They ascribed to human nature and free will so much ability to acquire what is necessary for salvation that they denied the necessity of prayer. Says Augustine: "They destroy the prayers that the church offers, whether for unbelievers and those who resist God's teaching that they turn to God or for believers, that their faith might increase and that they persist in it. They argue that men acquire such things not from God but from themselves!"[78] These men have gone so far in their insanity that, in keeping with the spirit of their dogmas, they have endeavored to remove two petitions from the center of the Lord's Prayer: the one, a request for forgiveness of sins, and the second, for victory over temptations. They removed the second petition because they taught that it is our responsibility to overcome temptations to sin by our own strength and without divine assistance.[79] Furthermore, they taught that the intention of the petition consists solely in this, that we not suffer any evil over which we have no control. Examples include falling from a horse, breaking a foot, or being murdered by a bandit. They deleted

---

73. De Natur. Deorum lib. 3.] Cicero, *De Natura Deorum*, in *Opera Omnia*, vol. 4 (Paris, 1565), bk. 3.

74. This is an unusual identification, since Horace is uniformly described as Epicurean rather than Stoic.

75. Horace, *Epistolarum*, bk. 1 (*epistola* 18).

76. Epist. 31.] Seneca, *Epistolae* (*epistola* 31).

77. Epist. 41.] Seneca, *Epistolae* (*epistola* 41).

78. Lib. de haeres. cap. 88.] Augustine, *De Haeresibus Ad Quoduultdeum*, ch. 88.

79. Vid. hac de re tota *Jansenium* de haeresi Pelagiana. l. 4. c. 15.] Jansen, *Augustinus*, vol. 1, bk. 4, ch. 15, col. 215.

the first petition because they kept blabbing that the state of perfection and inability to sin also existed in this life, and so it was redundant to say, "Forgive us our debts."

In addition, they used three dodges to defend themselves and their followers from the sharp implication of their own words. First, they said that the Lord's Prayer had been prescribed to the apostles when they were still weak but that it did not apply to the perfect. Secondly, if it were granted that the apostles prayed like this after attaining maturity, then they did not say "Forgive us our debts" so much for themselves as for those who were still immature sinners, those with whom they were joined in the body of the visible church. Third, if one were to concede that the apostles did pray for themselves like this, then they argued that the saints used this petition to demonstrate their humility and did not pray it sincerely. As I was carefully weighing such arguments, I remembered a certain memorable saying that is the only fitting response to round off this passage: "A lie is a very slender thing, which you can easily see through if you look closely."[80]

§ 7. Now I am going to move on from spiritual goods to the temporal ones for which we can also safely ask. Godliness, which is useful in all circumstances, holds promise for the present life as well as the life to come (1 Tim. 4:8). Accordingly, Christ taught us when praying to say, "Give us today our daily bread" [Matt. 6:11; Luke 11:3]. The experience of the saints under both covenants bears this out. Jacob asked God for food and clothing (Gen. 28:20). Ezra and his companions along the way sought by their prayers a straight path both for themselves and for their little children (Ezra 8:21). Agur prayed for food along the journey: "Nourish me with the food that is my portion" (Prov. 30:8). Christ Himself prayed for the passing of the cup (Luke 22:42). And Paul prayed for a εὐοδία (Rom. 1:10).[81] Thomas, with tremendous learning, writes: "We may desire temporal goods but not desire them foremost such that we set them before us as our end. Instead, we must desire them as supports to help us strive toward blessedness, to the extent, of course, that they maintain the life of the body, and to the extent that they serve us instrumentally for acts of the virtues."[82]

Now in point of fact, our prayers must be carefully proportioned according to the differing nature of their content and according to the measure of the promise. We must also prioritize the things for which we ask. The Lord Himself asked in one way for the blessedness of His people: "Father, I desire that those whom You have given Me also should be with Me, that

---

80. Seneca, *Epistolae* (epistola 79).

81. "Prosperous journey." A. uses the Greek with no Latin gloss.

82. 2ᵃ 2ᵃᵉ qu. 83. art. 6.] Thomas Aquinas, *Summa*, 2-2.83.6.

they may behold the glory that You have given Me" (John 17:24). Yet on another occasion, He prayed for His own release from suffering: "Father, if it be Your will, remove this cup from Me" (Luke 22:42). I acknowledge that I have sought guidance on this topic from many Scholastics as well as from the Reformed theologians. But I think that my friend Ames has hit the mark more than all the others. I will not refrain from quoting his words at length, because they really capture the whole issue from stern to bow:

> We must petition the Lord for everything in precisely the same way it was promised. We must pray for, without qualification, spiritual goods, therefore, insofar as they are necessary for salvation, because they have been unqualifiedly promised to believers and those who seek such goods. But if the things we ask for belong to the class of those things that admit of degree, they cannot be sought without qualification in every degree. Because these things themselves, not their degrees, are without qualification necessary and have been promised by God without qualification. Nevertheless, we must ask for the measure of God's grace without qualification, as we need it to avoid reproaches and scandals and to hold onto a good conscience. On the question of temporal goods, insofar as we can hope that these will prove useful to us for our salvation and bring glory to God, to that extent we may ask for them. This kind of petition is not, in a formal sense, conditional either in its words or meaning, because a conditional assertion definitely makes no assertion or posits it according to an antecedent. Thus, a conditional petition actually is no petition at all. Thus, the kind we are dealing with is an unqualified petition, but it entails a subject that is either expressly or implicitly joined to it according to God's most wise ordination.[83]

Either I am quite badly mistaken or this very precise man has with these words (that are by no means too many) said much more than Suarez himself managed to say in the four or five very long chapters he dedicated to the treatment of this subject.[84]

In addition, let's listen to Augustine most of all, who sums up many ideas in just a few phrases:

> When God is angry, He grants what you ask, and when propitious, God denies what you ask. When you ask for temporal goods, ask moderately, ask with trepidation. Leave it to Him to grant whether things turn out well. If He knows that they will not be good for you, may He not grant

---

83. *Ames*. Cas. Conscien. lib. 4. cap. 20.] Ames, *De Conscientia Et Eius Iure* (Amsterdam, 1631), 4.20.1–8, p. 147.

84. De Relig. Tom. 2. lib. 1. c. 17. & seq.] Suarez, *Opus De Religione*, vol. 2, tract. 4, bk. 1, ch. 17, p. 43.

them. It is the doctor, not the sick man, who knows what will harm and what will help.[85]

But it seems even the pagans were not completely unfamiliar with this little bit of our theology. The satiric poet says,

> To gods divine you must permit to weigh what suits us most.
> And what is useful for our needs, leave to the heav'nly host.
> For they will give what suits the most instead of pleasures fair,
> Since man to them, than to himself, occasions greater care.[86]

§ 8. Προσευχόμενοι (i.e., *praying* or *making supplication*). This word refers to those people who bear the duty of praying. We can, at this point, rightly ask two questions about these people. The first is, *By what right do mere men approach God?* And second, *Who ought to approach God through their prayers?* On the first question, we speak to God by threefold right.

First, *by right of creation.* "It is the peculiar right of a rational creature to pray." So says Thomas.[87] Suarez, taking "peculiar right" in the strict sense, adds, "What belongs to each member of a class and only that member."[88] This obviously does not apply to God, because He does not have a superior to call upon. Nor does it apply to brute creatures, because prayer is an act of reason. But the light of nature orders human beings to approach God through prayer. In Homer, Nestor[89] says of Telemachus,[90]

> …καὶ τοῦτον ὀίομαι ἀθανάτοισιν
> εὔχεσθαι: πάντες δὲ θεῶν χατέους᾽ ἄνθρωποι

> …That man, I think, the deathless ones beseeches through his prayers.
> Yes, all who walk below have need of gods amid their cares.[91]

The following words of the Latin poets are just as good: "An angry god is softened by a praying voice."[92] "Incense and prayers soothe the gods."[93] We also have this famous saying from Cicero: "That worship of the gods is the very best and, likewise, most righteous and holy, most filled with godliness,

---

85. De verb. Dom. Serm. 53.] Augustine, *De Verbis Domini In Ioannem, sermo* 53.

86. *Juvenal.* Satyr. 10.] Juvenal, *Satyra*, 10.

87. 2ᵃ 2ᵃᵉ qu. 83. art. 10.] Aquinas, *Summa*, 2-2.83.10.

88. De Relig. tom. 2. p. 33.] Suarez, *Opus De Religione*, vol. 2, tract. 4, bk. 1, ch. 12, sec. 7, p. 36.

89. Nestor, aged king of Pylos.

90. Telemachus, son of Odysseus and Penelope.

91. Homer, *Odyssea*, 3.47–48.

92. Ovid, *De Arte Amandi*, in *Opera Omnia*, vol. 1 (Amsterdam, 1611), bk. 1.

93. *Placant thura, precesque Deos.* Identification of this source is nearly impossible. A. seems to be referencing Martial, *Epigrammata*, 405.4, and perhaps also referencing Julius Caesar Scaliger's poem on Paris, 1574.

if we revere them always with a sincere, complete, and uncorrupted heart and voice."[94]

Second, *by right of redemption*. The psalmist several times makes mention of this while praying. "May the words of my mouth and the meditation of my heart be acceptable to You, Jehovah, my rock and my redeemer" (Ps. 19:14). And in another passage, he says, "Into Your hand I commit my spirit; You have redeemed me, Jehovah" (Ps. 31:6).[95] And so we owe all confidence in prayer to our redemption through Christ, as the Apostle teaches: "In whom we speak boldly and approach with confidence through faith in Him" (Eph. 3:12). Admetus, king of the Molossians (as we read in Thucydides)[96] forgave his enemy Themistocles[97] while gazing upon his own little son, as Themistocles held the child in both hands and offered him back to his father. If that is how a tyrant behaves, what will our most gentle God do? Will He not stoop down to us with inexpressible forgiveness, receive with inexpressible grace those who hold forth Jesus Christ as their delight, embracing Him with the arms of a living faith, and praying to Him? Look at these very sweet promises that flow from the Redeemer's own mouth: "If you ask for anything in My name, I will do it" (John 14:14). "Truly, truly I say to you, whatever you ask from the Father in My name, He will give you" (John 16:23).

There was once an established practice in Christian churches, and there even is today, to stamp prayers with these or similar words: "Through Jesus Christ our Lord." But even many centuries ago, before the Messiah came in the flesh, we cannot doubt that the people of God looked to Him in their prayers. This is the origin of that practice, no matter where they were when praying, to say, "Looking toward the temple of Jerusalem." John 2 makes it clear that this "looking toward the temple" was a type of the Christ who would be incarnated. Likewise, this is the source of the constant mention of the covenant entered into with the fathers—that is, the covenant of Christ who would be sent. Sometimes, the quite lofty moniker "anointed" for "Adonai" is used. "Look to our shield, O Lord, and gaze upon the face of Your anointed" (Ps. 84:10).[98] So the psalmist writes, and Junius explains this passage as referring to Christ.[99] "Cause Your face to shine upon Your sanctuary, which has been laid waste because of the Lord, Adonai"

---

94. De Nat. Deor. l. 2.] Cicero, *De Natura Deorum*, bk. 2.

95. Here A. numbers according to the Hebrew text; read, Ps. 31:5.

96. Lib. 1.] Thucydides, ca. 455–ca. 400 BC, Athenian historian, *Histories* (Frankfurt, 1594), p. 89, sec. A–B, (1.136 in Loeb citation).

97. Themistocles, ca. 528–459 BC, Athenian statesman.

98. Here A. numbers according to the Hebrew text; read, Ps. 84:9.

99. *Biblica Sacra*, sub loc. Ps. 84:10.

(Dan. 9:17). This means, according to the same interpreter, "because of Christ the mediator who was made heir and Lord of all." Buxtorf made some valuable observations about the name Adonai, relying on a certain ancient rabbi. For example, no one can be identified with the name Jehovah except by the name Adonai, this is the palace in which Jehovah dwells, and many other similar points. He then added something of his own: "These skillful comments about the name Adonai represent to us our Lord Jesus Christ. For no one comes to the Father except through Him. Therefore, Daniel, in his prayer in chapter 9, used this name in particular: 'Make Your face to shine because of Adonai.'"[100]

Third, *by right of adoption*. The Apostle spoke about this as follows: "Because you are sons, God sent the Spirit of His Son into your hearts, crying, 'Abba, Father'" (Gal. 4:6). By nature's dictate, sons have the right as sons to approach their parents to gain by petition the things they need. In civil law we have the saying, "The obligations of the one received into adoption are transferred to the adoptive parent."[101] So it is no surprise if God—to support those whom He has stooped to adopt into the number of His sons—should send not only into their mouths but also into their hearts that Spirit who is called the Spirit of the Son. This is not only because He proceeds from the Father as from the Son but also because He works in His adoptive sons as in His natural Son. The Spirit, almost without interruption, roused the natural Son in the days of His flesh to constant conversation with His Father and to pouring out prayers of the utmost intensity. The Son, then, is said to have offered His supplications with loud groaning (Heb. 5:7). His Spirit is described as crying, "Abba, Father." This word connotes great forcefulness in crying out. The others indicate assurance and urgency. I am omitting numerous comments the reader can locate that relate to the emphasis of this phrase, especially as found in Beza,[102] van den Driesche,[103] Daniel Heins,[104] Grotius,[105] and, in particular, Louis de

---

100. De Nominibus Dei Hebraic. dissertat. thes. 54.] Buxtorf, Jr., *De Nominibus Dei Hebraicis* (Basel, 1645), thes. 54, sig. Fr, Fv.

101. D. de Adopt. L. 45.] *Corpus Iuris Civilis*, vol. 1 (Lyon, 1583), bk. 1, tit. 7, sec. 45, p. 145.

102. Notis in Marc. 14.36. Rom. 8.15. Gal. 4.6.] Beza, *Annotationes Maiores*, sub loc. Mark 14:36; Rom. 8:15; Gal. 4:6.

103. For a discussion of "Abba pater" with reference to all three verses cited, see Drusius, *Ad Voces Ebraicas Novi Testamenti* (Franeker, 1616), pp. 3–5; Drusius, *Annotationes In Totum Iesu Christi Testamentum*, sub loc. Gal. 4:6.

104. Heins, *Sacrarum Exercitationum*, sub loc. Rom. 8:15.

105. Grotius, *Annotationes In Libros Evangeliorum*, sub loc. Mark 14:36; Grotius, *Annotationes In Novum Testamentum*, sub loc. Gal. 4:6.

Dieu.[106] I will only concentrate on those that seem to me more germane to the topic, but without prejudice to anyone else.

If the word *Abba* or *Father* were used just once, it would denote reliance. Primarily, it would denote that reliance that sons use when they become suppliants. It is a far greater reliance on their fathers than on those distant. Repeated expressions, quite beyond the emotion they seem to suggest, also indicate urgency. It is not sufficient for a son in need of his father's help just to say once, "My father, bring help!" Instead, he again and again repeats what he said: "My Father, Abba, Father, Father, Father." So we read that Christ, on the cross, repeated Himself like this, in His expression "My God, My God." The psalmist, in his eightieth hymn, very often repeated the same form of address, to make clear the church's urgency in her petitions. But he did not use exactly the same words and instead employs some variety, by introducing several different words. Consequently, he says in verse 4, "O God, restore us." In verse 7, "O God of Hosts, restore us." And in the last verse, "Jehovah, God of Hosts, restore us."

§ 9. Now for the second question: Who should approach God through their prayers? My response is that everyone must pray, whether or not they have been born of the Spirit. As regards the regenerate, heaven forbid that there be any doubt. For prayer is more essential for Christians than breathing is to the proper function of living creatures. All who live by faith breathe through prayer. As soon as Saul was described as endowed with saving faith, the Lord said to Ananias, "Look, he prays" (Acts 9:11). This idea is echoed in Paul, that "all who call upon the name of our Lord Jesus Christ in every place" (1 Cor. 1:2) are the same as all who are truly Christian. The Apostle, in this passage, seems to describe such people by prayer as by a well-known characteristic. It is beyond all doubt that the regenerate are carried along voluntarily toward this most holy interaction. It is as natural for air to be warm or for the sun to shine as for the regenerate to speak to God. Of course, this is why he has been made a new creation: to have the ability and desire to interact closely with his God.

But with respect to the unregenerate, some were unsure whether they should approach and call upon God, because the Spirit states, "How will they call upon the one in whom they have not believed?" (Rom. 10:14). I have four things to say to remove this difficulty. First, it is the correct conclusion to draw from the statement that they cannot call upon Him as they should. But it does not at all follow that they should not because they cannot. It is clearly invalid to argue from the negation of ability to negation of

---

106. Louis de Dieu, 1590–1642, Dutch Reformed minister and orientalist, *Animadversiones In D. Pauli Apostoli Epistolam Ad Romanos* (Leiden, 1646), sub loc. Rom. 8:15.

the corresponding obligation. A creditor does not lose his right just because the debtor becomes insolvent. Second, it is true that the unregenerate cannot, by their prayers, in that condition, please God acceptably unto eternal salvation except in a very weak sense. (This seems to be the meaning of the passage if we take into account the context. All the more so because, after the words "Whoever calls upon the name of the Lord shall be saved," this immediately follows: "How will they call upon Him"—that is, so as to be saved for eternity—"in whom they have not believed?") Nevertheless, they can call upon Him acceptably for temporal profit. The examples of Ahab and the Ninevites prove this.

Third, the reason for the prayers of the regenerate is definitely quite different from the unregenerate's reason for offering prayers. This concerns (1) their right to do so. The regenerate man acts by right of sonship, but the unregenerate, by right of creation. (I just spoke about these topics.) It also concerns (2) their foundation for doing so. For the regenerate man prays on the basis of saving faith. Thus, εὐχὴ τῆς πίστεως is heard (James 5:15).[107] This is the prayer of faith that proceeds from the regenerate. Here it means either from the mere natural desire of the self-concerned creature or from dogmatic faith that believes God exists and provides for the wretched.

Fourth, although the account given just now is accurate as stands, still the unregenerate are held to speak to God in proportion to the measure of the grace they possess. There is a passage in Acts that I believe our adversaries cannot forcibly twist to make us change our conclusion. In that passage, Simon Peter admonishes Simon Magus like this: "Your heart is not right in the sight of God. Repent of your wickedness and beg God to forgive your heart's connivance. For I see that you are gripped by the bitterest envy and are at the crossroads of unrighteousness" (Acts 8:21–23). I am not someone who would dare dissuade the unregenerate from prayers, such as they are, when I see the apostle urging this Simon Magus, someone entirely vile, to pour out prayers. We have a supporting reason as well that dictates that we must choose the least evil outcome. For a lesser evil, by comparison with a greater, derives some semblance of good. Now we must hold that the unregenerate man is less displeasing to God when he prays according to his practice than if he were to abandon completely all manner of prayer. This is because that which is good in itself is superior—with respect to the substance of the act—even though it is sinful with respect to the manner in which it is done. What about the fact that grace sometimes springs from this, and such prayer, even though it is not a substantive change, sometimes proves to be a change toward something substantial, if the Lord has

---

107. "The prayer of faith."

mercy? While God administers more effectual aid (yet from grace, not from obligation) toward the one who is both doing what is in his power[108] and worshipping as he is able, that man is made more capable of worshipping as he should, since he is now endowed with faith and regeneration.

§ 10. The Apostle continues: ἐν παντὶ καιρῷ ("In every season," or rather, "On every occasion"). He does not say χρόνῳ[109] but καιρῷ.[110] In other passages, he uses the adverbs ἀδιαλείπτως (1 Thess. 5:17)[111] and διὰ παντός ("at all times"; Heb. 13:15). If someone teaches, as the Euchites[112] did (the ancient church customarily identified them as heretics), that nothing else was incumbent upon the Christian other than the duty to pray and that the whole course of our life should be devoted to sacred prayers, he ought to bark up another tree.[113] For this fruit cannot be gained from this source. Because the passages just cited imply exclusively that we must offer to God regular prayers at specific times as our perpetual sacrifice, so, when it is appropriate, we must offer extraordinary prayers. As Mephibosheth was ordered to eat at David's table always (2 Sam. 9:7; the Septuagint has διὰ παντός),[114] it did not mean he was supposed to load up on food and drink all day and all night. Rather, at fixed times for lunch and supper he should come to the table. Drusius expresses this well: "Praying without ceasing is most properly taken to mean that not a day goes by without fixed times for prayer."[115] Thus, we have the proverbial expression "Prayer is the key of the day and lock of the night." Truly, the Christian faith bids us morning and evening, everyday, to pray to God as a solemn custom, and this is in addition to the frequent, spontaneous prayers that a particular moment draws from godly hearts. "The whole of religion," says Lactantius, "is to imitate the one you worship."[116] Our Lord Christ led the way for us in this. We read about him πρωῒ ἔννυχον λίαν ἀναστάς (Mark 1:35)[117]—that is, as Franciscus Lucas Brugensis argues that it should be translated, "when He had arisen in the morning, at dawn, He went out to a solitary place, and

---

108. *Facienti quod in se*, a famous Scholastic idea the Reformers generally opposed.

109. "Time."

110. "Season."

111. "Unceasingly."

112. Euchites, from the Greek εὐχῆται, "those who pray." The Euchites were also known as "Messalians."

113. *Aliam quercum excutiat oportet*, "shake another oak" (i.e., keep asking without effect), a Latin translation of a Greek adage recorded by Erasmus.

114. "On every occasion."

115. Epist. 58. ex *August*. de haeres. c. 57.] Augustine, quoted in Drusius, *De Quaesitis Per Epistolam* (Franeker, 1595), pp. 113–14 (*epistola* 58).

116. Augustine, *De Civitate Dei*, 8.17.2. This seems rather to be Augustine's quotation.

117. "Rising very early in the morning."

there He prayed."[118] And in another passage, "When He had sent away the crowd, He went up the mountain by Himself to pray. And He was alone there in the evening" (Matt. 14:23). Now in point of fact, we find some traces of this godly practice even among the pagans. These words found in Hesiod to some extent relate to this point. The poet gave this advice:

> Καδ᾽ δύναμιν δ᾽ ἔρδειν ἱερ᾽ ἀθανάτοισοι θεοῖσι,
> As within you lies, to th'immortal gods make sacrifice.

Immediately after, he added,

> Ἤ μὲν ὅ τ᾽ εὐνάζῃ, καὶ ὅταν φάος ἱερὸν ἔλθῃ
> Both when you sleep and when the sacred light of dawn comes on.[119]

The Romanist writers usually suggest for these fixed times matins, primes, terces, sexts, nones, vespers, and a whole ad nauseam host of quite insubstantial, not to say ridiculous, divisions. Among other men, there is one (from their perspective) not at all ignoble—namely, the Jesuit Emmanuel Sa. He published a book called *Confessor's Aphorisms*.[120] The book is fairly small, yet he labored at it for almost forty years (as he admits in the dedicatory letter). Am I wrong about this? If anyone reads the comments found there about the canonical hours, wouldn't he say, with Martial,

> What a shame to consider trifles so hard
> And stupid to labor long over fools' thoughts.[121]

I will not, therefore, take the time to refute them so I don't seem to have misallocated precious hours. I would rather go on ahead with Paul.

§ 11. Ἐν Πνεύματι ("In the Spirit"). This short phrase, if it applies to our spirit, means that we must pray:

First, *from the heart*. Prayer is not a work of the lips alone but of the whole heart. This is why John of Damascus defined it as ἀνάβασις τοῦ νοῦ πρὸς τὸν Θεόν.[122] The Jesuit Massutius glossed these words as follows:

> There are three things that contribute the most to grasping the superior quality of any operation—namely, that an action is of the most complete form in its class, that it proceeds from and is set in motion from

---

118. Franciscus Lucas, ca. 1549–1619, Dutch Catholic exegete and textual critic, *In Sacrosancta Quatuor Iesu Christi Evangelia* (Antwerp, 1606), vol. 2, p. 582 (sub loc. Mark 1).

119. Ἐργ. καὶ ἡμέρ. lib. 1. prope finem.] Hesiod, fl. ca. 700 BC, early Greek poet, *Opera et Dies*, in *Hesiodus Graecolatinus Cum Schematismis* (Basel, 1580), lines 336, 339.

120. Manuel (Emmanuel) de Sá, 1530–1596, Portuguese Jesuit theologian, *Aphorismus Casuum Conscientiae*, 1595.

121. Martial, *Epigrammata*, 2.86. The lines are in hendecasyllables.

122. Orthodox. fid. lib. 1. cap. 14.] John of Damascus, *Ekdosis Tes Orthodoxou Pisteos*, fol. 20r. "The mind's ascent to God."

the most noble origin, and that it is aimed at a very lofty object or end. John of Damascus summed up all these ideas in these words: "The mind's ascent to God." The first is expressed by the word *ascent*. The second, as it is predicated of a person's loftier part, is expressed by *mind*. The third, because it refers to God, is simply expressed by that word.[123]

I add that we should not at all dismiss Medina's formula: "A voiced prayer is the sign of a mental prayer. Therefore, that it not be a false sign, the one who prays with his voice must pray with his mind. For otherwise, a voiced prayer remains a false sign and, thus, vicious."[124]

Second, we must pray *fervently*, as concerns the zeal of the affections and a sufficiently intense exertion of the whole person. There are those who think that it is of no consequence whether they pray privately or publicly. But I'm very pleased with the view of a particular theologian, albeit a Romanist: "There are four tasks I hold to be the most difficult of all. These are (1) giving birth, (2) teaching in a school, (3) commanding in a war, and (4) praying in church."[125] What does Holy Scripture say? "προσευχὴ ἐκτενής (fervent prayer)," it says, "was offered by the church for Peter when he was in prison" (Acts 12:5). This word is used elsewhere as well: "Holding ἀγάπη ἐκτενής (fervent love) toward one another" (1 Peter 4:8). The text says of Elijah, προσευχῇ προσηύξατο (James 5:17)—that is, very intensely—and he prayed with every effort of his strength.[126] For in Hebrew, when cognates are added to the verb, it indicates intensity, as Grotius explains.[127]

What does our Savior say? "Ask, and it will be given you; seek, and you shall find; knock, and the door will be opened to you" [Matt. 7:7]. It is as if he said, "Ask for what you need. Is what you are asking for not granted? Seek. Is what you seek denied? Knock. God wants to be compelled." Jacob wrestled with an angel to enjoy His blessing. The one who coldly asks is plainly instructing God to say no.

Third, we must pray *knowledgeably*. Otherwise, what our Savior said as a reproach to the sons of Zebedee—"You do not know what you are asking" (Matt. 20:22)—will rightly apply to us. Under the Mosaic law, the

---

123. De Coelest. conversat. l. 1. c. 3. p. 14.] Tommaso Massucci (Thomas Massutius), fl. ca. 1633, Jesuit theologian, *De Caelesti Conuersatione Per Internam Orationem* (Rome, 1622), bk. 1, ch. 3, p. 14.

124. Codic. de Oratione Tractat. 6 p. 176.] Juan de Medina, 1490–1546, Spanish Catholic theologian and ambassador to Rome, *De Poenitentia, Restitutione, Et Contractibus* (Brixen, 1606), tract. 6, quaes. 14, p. 436.

125. Apud *Drexell.* Rhetor. coelest. lib. 2. c. 2. in limine.] Drexel, *Rhetorica Caelestis*, in *Opera Omnia*, vol. 3 (Lyon, 1647), bk. 2, ch. 2, p. 106.

126. "He prayed prayerfully."

127. Grotius, *Annotationes In Novum Testamentum*, sub loc. James 5:17.

priest was warned not to burn incense on the altar in the morning when tending the lamps (Exod. 30:7). The aroma signifies prayers and the lamps, knowledge. Prayer must never be offered except when the lamp of the understanding is aflame. But prior meditation is requisite for lighting this lamp, which, in Gerson, is called the "sister of reading, nurse of prayer, governess of work, and, of all things alike, both the perfecter and finisher."[128]

§ 12. But if we instead refer the preceding words of the Apostle directly to God's Spirit (as they do at least partly, even if not completely), then they reveal how necessary the Holy Spirit's efficacious aid is for shaping prayers that will please the Most Exalted Presence. And they show how fittingly the Spirit, in Zechariah, is named "the spirit of grace and supplication" (Zech. 12:10). There is no way we can here overlook this outstanding passage: "Τὸ πνεῦμα συναντιλαμβάνεται ταῖς ἀσθενείαις ἡμῶν ("The Spirit bears with our weaknesses"). For we do not know what we ought to pray for. But the Spirit himself intercedes for us with inexpressible groans" (Rom. 8:26). Ἀντιλαμβάνεσθαι means *to hold, with outstretched hands, those who are about to fall.* Pareus argues that this is a metaphor from guiding children, or from the ill who sway back and forth.[129] Both must be supported by a cane so as not to fall. The Holy Spirit offers us this help. But συναντιλαμβάνεται emphasizes the preposition greatly. Louis de Dieu applies it to the Father and Son, since the Holy Spirit was sent by both of them and, dwelling with them in the elect, is always active.[130] Other interpreters, and Beza sides with these,[131] prefer to take the preposition as referring to us as we work, as though the Spirit Himself were said, as it were, partly to carry with us the burden of praying, that we not grow weary beneath it. Συναντιλαμβάνεσθαι means *to undertake a task along with someone else as though directly.* This is Fischer's understanding.[132] The Spirit bears our weaknesses with us—as in other tasks we perform, so uniquely in praying. Our weaknesses are more manifest here than anywhere else, and we do not ourselves know what we should pray for. Often we ask for things that would hurt us, often those that will not benefit us without the Spirit's presence. For this reason, Augustine says, "Without the spirit of faith, no

---

128. Perhaps Gerson, *De Meditatione Cordis* [1496].

129. Pareus, *In Divinam S. Pauli Apostoli Ad Romanos* ([Geneva], 1609), sub loc. Rom. 8:26.

130. De Dieu, *Animadversiones In D. Pauli Apostoli Epistolam Ad Romanos*, sub loc. Rom. 8:26.

131. Beza, *Annotationes Maiores*, sub loc. Rom. 8:26.

132. Piscator, *Analysis Logica Epistolae Pauli Ad Romanos* (Herborn, 1608), sub loc. Rom. 8:26.

one will exercise proper belief. Likewise, without the spirit of prayer, no one will pray in a healthy way."[133]

For the same reason, Johannes Climacus also states, "Prayer has God as teacher, who teaches man knowledge and who, as man prays, suggests to him what to say."[134] But Paul himself surpasses all the rest and very eloquently writes, αὐτὸ τὸ πνεῦμα ὑπερεντυγχάνει ὑπὲρ ἡμῶν ("The Spirit himself intercedes for us" [Rom. 8:26]). But He intercedes not as mediator *ex officio*, by the strength of His own merit. Intercession is Christ's prerogative alone. No, He intercedes as advocate, counseling His client as to what he should say in his own case. Therefore, τὸ ὑπερεντυγχάνειν[135] is the responsibility of advocates, who dictate for their clients the things they lack (this is Grotius's observation,[136] who was, by far, the most experienced in civil law, both its terminology and content). The Spirit dictates prayers to the regenerate and, thus, intercedes because He causes us to intercede, and He groans by causing us to groan. This meaning is clearly derived by comparing the passage in Galatians (Gal. 4:6), where the Spirit is described as "crying, Abba, Father," with the one from Romans (Rom. 8:15). In the latter passage, we are described as having received the "Spirit of adoption by whom we cry, 'Abba, Father.'" Prosper puts it very well: "What good can we have without Him, since it is also because of Him that we pray correctly?" And shortly after, he says, "The Holy Spirit fills His own instrument, and the finger of God, as it were, plucks the strings of the cords, the hearts of the saints."[137]

The meaning of the last words—στεναγμοῖς ἀλαλήτοις[138] [Rom. 8:26]—and their precise implication are not yet clear. I will make a few remarks here. The philosophers teach that an entity of very large substance, such as God, is absolutely impossible to define. The same is true for an entity of very small substance, such as prime matter. Permit me to apply the same argument to the sighs and groans of the godly. Sometimes they are inexpressible due to their great size—to wit, when the oil of the Holy Spirit is lavishly poured into their hearts as from a full cordial. This is the meaning Paul expresses in another passage when he says, ῥήματα ἄρρητα [2 Cor. 12:4].[139] These are ideas that must be expressed in silence but not in speech. But sometimes this oil is only distilled drop by drop. This was how it came

133. Epist. 105.] Augustine, 105.17 (*epistola* 105).

134. *Climac.* gradu 29.] Climacus, *Scala Paradisi*, perhaps an edition of 1601 or 1624.

135. "Intercession."

136. Grotius, *Annotationes In Novum Testamentum*, sub loc. Rom. 8:26.

137. Epist. ad Demetriad.] Prosper of Aquitaine, *Ad Demetriadem*, in *Opera* (Cologne, 1630), pp. 876, 877.

138. "Unspeakable groans."

139. "Unspeakable words."

upon Isaiah, when he complained, "I was chirping like a stork or a swallow. I was cooing like a dove" (Isa. 38:14). In this example, the thoughts cannot be expressed due to their fineness. We should heed Luther on this topic:

> Our faith gasps for Christ very weakly in temptation, proportionate to our feeling. But the one who searches hearts hears that distant groan as a very loud shout. Compared to this unutterable groan, the massive and frightening roaring of the law, sin, death, the Devil, and hell are absolutely nothing and inaudible. And, after a few other remarks, Paul says the Spirit intercedes for us in temptation not with a long speech but only a groan, though it is unutterable. "Ah, Father!" This word is truly very short but all-embracing. The little word "Father" has been formally expressed in the heart with an eloquence that Demosthenes, Cicero, and every most exalted orator who has ever lived in this world cannot equal. This notion is not expressed with words but with the groans that all the orators' countless words cannot express. The feelings are unutterable.

Luther made these remarks in his *Commentary on Galatians*.[140] The *Commentary* was gathered from his lectures and published separately (with his consent) at Wittenberg in 1535. Then later it was translated into English. I thought I should recommend this volume again, because many truly exceptional points are found there that one would search for in vain in the commentaries on this epistle among Luther's folio works.

There are also other passages in which the aid—and more than aid—that the Holy Spirit provides us during prayer is detailed with adequate clarity. "The Spirit and the bride say, 'Come'" (Rev. 22:17)—that is, the Spirit through the bride, or the Spirit speaking in the bride. "Praying by the Holy Spirit" (Jude v. 20). Among other passages, there is Πολὺ ἰσχύει δέησις δικαίου ἐνεργουμένη (James 5:16).[141] The central difficulty for translators is the word ἐνεργουμένη, which the Vulgate renders as "attentive." Beza renders it "effectual,"[142] and this, for sure, is far better. Yet if we translate it that way, either the words πολὺ ἰσχύει will seem redundant or the participle ἐνεργουμένη will. Because what "accomplishes much" is "effectual," and what is "effectual" "accomplishes much." Actually, because something "accomplishes much," it is therefore deemed "effectual." And because it is "effectual," it "accomplishes much." So, let us see whether we can offer an exegesis that not only fits our own purposes better but also

---

140. Praelect. in Galat. 4.6.] Luther, *Commentarius In Epistolam Pauli Ad Galatas*, sub loc. Gal. 4:6.

141. "The prayer of a righteous man accomplishes much."

142. In 1 Cor. 12:6. Προφῆτις ἐνεργουμένη πονηρῷ πνεύματι. *Aretas* in Apoc. 6.] Beza, *Annotationes majores*, sub loc. 1 Cor. 12:6; probably Arethas of Caesarea, d. 932/944, bishop and exegete, *In Ioannis Apocalypsim* (Basel, [1554]).

fits the Apostle's meaning. Hilary sometimes construes ἐνεργουμένη as "commanding." Beza calls this a "novel" interpretation. But he says it is neither awkward nor displeasing. And why should a δέησις ἐνεργουμένη be anything other than a prayer the Spirit worked within us? Men who have been taken over by a demon and compelled by an evil spirit are specifically described as ἐνεργούμενοι. Perhaps here also in James that prayer is called ἐνεργουμένη that God's Holy Spirit working within us has dictated and formed in our hearts. The learned may judge this interpretation for themselves. We must now hurry on to the rest of this chapter.

§ 13. καὶ εἰς αὐτὸ τοῦτο ἀγρυπνοῦντες ("And being alert for this very purpose" [Eph. 6:18]). Because prayer is a significant portion of the worship that must be offered in public, believers of old used to display a painted or sculpted lion on the doors of churches to teach us that one must stay alert. The lion, they say, sleeps with its eyes open, as if to keep watch. Hence this bon mot:

> They set the lion at the doors of churches on the watch,
> Because he sleeps with eyes unclosed alert with high regard.[143]

These two concepts are quite often linked in the holy text: "Watch and pray" (Matt. 16:41). "Be on guard, praying on every occasion" (Mark 13:33). "Strive boldly in prayer, staying watchful in it" (Luke 21:36). "Be sober-minded and alert in your praying" (Col. 4:2; 1 Peter 4:7). Of course, in the early church, both kinds of vigilance were necessary. The nature of the times demanded a bodily vigilance. The circumstances, with raging persecution, forced those who professed the name Christian to assemble at night. The sequence of the story makes it clear that the church offered prayers for Peter at night (Acts 12:5, 12). Tertullian, in his *Defense* for the believers of his generation, said, "So they are content, remembering that they must worship God at night."[144] The same author, in book 2 of his work *To His Wife*, showed that Christian women should not marry pagan husbands, and he used an argument taken from these nighttime vigils: "What pagan will gladly allow his wife to leave his side to attend nocturnal gatherings? Which will calmly tolerate her joining the solemn, nighttime Paschal rites?"[145] There was never a time that did not require mental vigilance. It is required today, too, and will be so long as the church militant endures. The

---

143. *Camerar.* meditate. histor. Centur. 1. pag. 117.] Camerarius, *Meditationes Historicae*, vol. 1, ch. 22, p. 117.

144. Tertullian, *Apologeticus*, ch. 39.

145. Tertullian, *Ad Uxorem*, in *Opera Quae Hactenus Reperiri*, vol. 2 (Cologne, 1617), bk. 2, ch. 5.

rule of the theologians applies here: "In the business of religion, the heart does not become what it does not do." But once vigilance fails, the heart either will be absent during prayer or will be most shamefully distracted. So, numerous men, even very holy ones, complained that their hearts had deserted to the world's camp. Jerome writes, "It happens all the time in my praying that I either stroll through porticos, tally up some interest, am ambushed by a filthy thought, or even do things that would make me blush just to mention them. Where is my faith? Do we think that Jonah prayed like that? That the three Hebrew children prayed this way? Daniel among the lions? The criminal on the cross?"[146]

Bernard writes:

Hear my confession, most righteous God, and have regard for Your righteousness. Hear how often the pressing jumble of my thoughts drove You from my memory. These thoughts, like a crowd at some spectacle, routinely press into my heart. They call it back to worldly cares, they ply it with pleasures, and at the very moment when I am preparing to lift my mind to You, I am routinely pulled down toward earthly concerns.[147]

Bernard also says in another passage, "Though physically I am in the chorus, in my heart, I am engaged in some other task. I sing one thing and think another. I utter words but pay no heed to their meaning. Woe is me, that I sin in the very place where I ought to be correcting my sins."[148]

§ 14. ἐν πάσῃ προσκαρτερήσει ("With all perseverance"). The Greek word κράτος means *strength*, and κρατερός and καρτερός are synonyms. Προσκαρτερεῖν means *to apply all one's strength resolutely to some task*. So the word is used of magistrates and of the apostles, whose work, if any, demanded the highest fortitude and resiliency of mind (Rom. 13:6; Acts 6:4). So here προσκαρτερεῖν partly means *exerting all one's effort in prayer* as athletes do while wrestling. An example is the patriarch Jacob, whose struggle Hosea seems to recount with prayers and tears (Hos. 12:4). But the more strength there is, the longer those who pursue the work according to their own strength persist in it. Therefore, the word προσκαρτέρησις is also used for training and perseverance. The value of perseverance in prayer is quite significant. Christ our Lord told a parable relating to this subject, that we "must always pray and μὴ ἐγκακεῖν (not grow weary)" (Luke 18:1). The old translation has "not fail."[149] Fischer uses "non elanguescere" (i.e.,

---

146. Dialog. adversus Luciferianos.] Jerome, *Hieronymi Orthodoxi Et Luciferiani Dialogus*, in *Opera Divi Hieronymi Stridoniensis*, vol. 2, ch. 6.

147. De interior domo, cap. 29.] Bernard of Clairvaux, *De Interiori Domo*, ch. 16.

148. Ibid. cap 33.] Bernard of Clairvaux, *De Interiore Domo*, ch. 19.

149. *Non deficere*, in the Vulgate.

"not grow weary in praying, but press on continually until we are heard").[150] Chrysostom brilliantly says, "Don't retreat until you have received what you want. Then stop when you have received it. Actually, don't stop then but instead persist, giving thanks for what you received, so that what you have received may stay with you."[151] The godly writer Louis Granada develops a number of different comparisons that are quite well suited to the task of prayer. He says, "It is like seeds thrown on the ground. The more they lie hidden in the earth's depths, pressed down by the cold, then the more vigorously and richly they sprout, because they have driven their roots more deeply in. In the same way, prayers multiplied over a longer period of time receive greater gifts from God." And again: "Just as the hen will never hatch her chicks if she abandons them right when she begins to nest on them, so he who quickly gives up on prayer due to lack of spiritual thirst or sluggishness will not harvest its fruit." But there is also a third comparison: "The man who wants to start a fire by striking flint is not satisfied to strike just once but strikes again and again until finally he produces a spark. Likewise, whoever prays to the Lord, even if he is not heard at the moment he prays, must, nevertheless, persevere. Because if he perseveres in knocking on the door, he will at last gain his desire."[152]

There is something that the lazy use as an excuse. They say that prayers are not always heard, not even the prayers of those who persevere. And this is the source of their flagging. I reply first that we must distinguish between the time of our waiting and the time of divine generosity. God, in His own time, hears prayer, although not in our time, when we believe that we have prayed long enough. Chrysostom, with much godliness and eloquence, writes, "If God has the power to grant something, it is also in His power to grant it when He wishes. He Himself best knows the time. Therefore, let us persevere in our supplications."[153] Augustine does not disagree, saying, "When God grants something after a fairly long wait, He is proving, not denying, the worth of His gifts. When things desired for a long time are obtained, it is sweeter, while things given quickly are

---

150. Piscator, *Analysis Logica Evangelii Secundum Lucam* (Herborn, 1603), sub loc. Luke 18:1.

151. Tom. 2. de variis locis in Matthaeum homil. 17.] Chrysostom, *Ex Variis in Matthaeum Locis*, in *Opera Omnia*, vol. 2 (Basel, 1539) (*homilia* 16).

152. Luis de Granada, 1504–1588, Spanish Dominican spiritual writer. For the first and second quotations, see his *Conciones De Tempore* (Vannes, 1578), fol. 279r., fols. 179v–180r.

153. Εἰ γὰρ τοῦ δοῦναι Κύριος, καὶ τοῦ ποτε δοῦναι Κύριός ἐστι, &c. *Chrysost.* in Psal. 129.] "If He is Lord of might, He is also Lord of exercising that might when He chooses" — a comment resembling Chrysostom, *Commentary on the Psalms*, trans. R. C. Hill (Brookline, Mass.: Holy Cross Orthodox Press, 1998), vol. 2, pp. 188–90 (Ps. 129).

cheap."[154] Though, I would add that they who are heard more slowly generally receive a greater accumulation of blessings. Abraham waited for offspring from Sarah continually, until he was one hundred. Isaac, the son of promise, was finally born, and in his seed, all nations would be blessed. Although Isaac received the promise, he beseeched God long and fervently for his sterile wife Rebecca. She eventually bore twins and produced, as it were, two nations from one birth. Samuel's mother, Hannah, sterile for a long time, gained her son by her prayers—and he was a prophet. Elizabeth, the wife of Zechariah, after persevering in prayer for a long time, finally gave birth to John the Baptist. Among those born of women, there was never anyone greater.

Second, we must distinguish between God hearing us as regards our will, wish, or good pleasure and His hearing us for usefulness, salvation, and advantage. God always hears His children in the latter way as is fitting for those who pray and persevere. But He does not, necessarily, in the former way. We find that some men are not heard as regards their will, but they are heard for salvation. "Israelites were heard according to their will, and when the food was still in their mouths, you know what they went after. Therefore, don't think being heard according to your will is something good." These are Augustine's words.[155] So then we must say that the Lord hears us as regards salvation, although not according to our wish, though what He grants is even better than what we ask. God did not grant Paul release from the goad in his flesh, though he asked for that, but gave him something better for him—an increase in grace. Thus, Calvin says, "There is no doubt that Paul was heard in terms of the goal of his prayer, even though he was formally rejected."[156] God seems to hold his ears completely closed against those who seek what will harm them (as very many do). Prosper, in his hymns, talks about this in a way most eloquent and lucid:

> God grants us much for He denies what sure would cause us harm.
> The errant He forbids to sin by prayer that they have made.
> He would be angry to allow what He prevents in love.
> Man's prayer denied, yet happy let the humble heart learn joy.
> And from his soul begin to drive what once he did desire.[157]

---

154. De verb. Domin. Serm. 1.] Augustine, *Sermo* 1.

155. In Epist. Joann. Tract. 6. & de verb. Dom. Serm. 53.] Augustine, *De Verbis Domini in Ioannem*, in *Omnia Opera*, vol. 10 53.7; *Expositio In Epistolam Beati Ioannis*, in *Omnia Opera*, vol. 9, tract. 6. The quotation in tract. 6 is truncated.

156. *Calvin.* in 2 Cor. c. 12.] Calvin, *Commentarii*, sub loc. 2 Cor. 12:8.

157. Prosper of Aquitaine, *Epigrammaton* 96, in *Opera* (Cologne, 1630), p. 512.

§ 15. We have now, at last, reached the final words of this little verse: καὶ δεήσει περὶ πάντων τῶν ἁγίων ("And with supplication for all the saints"). This saying of Chrysostom's is well known: "It is natural to pray for oneself; it belongs to grace to pray for others. Necessity bids us pray for ourselves; love urges us to pray for others."[158] Yes, for all others, however much they are strangers, and particularly for the saints, as they are our fellow soldiers and share in the same battles. The communion of the saints requires this. Luther considered this communion so important that he wrote, in his consolatory *Tesseradecas*, "Others carry my burden; my virtue is actually theirs. The faith of the church comes to the aid of my fear. Their fasting is my benefit. The prayer of another man was offered for my sake," etc.[159]

But another idea arises here from what the Apostle says belongs to the saints alone. This does not concern the saints and so is a question: Must we also pray for the wicked, or should we instead pray against them? But if imprecation is impermissible, what should we think about those dreadful, cursing prayers found here and there in the sacred text? In order to abbreviate my discussion, I assert the following.

First, some imprecatory prayers are indeed forbidden. I mean whichever ones proceed from either impatience or vindictiveness or arise from any kind of wicked emotion whatsoever. An example of this is the curse Micah's mother pronounced on the thief who stole from her 1,100 shekels of silver. She called down a thousand diseases on his head, debt, death, and hell (Judg. 17:2).[160] Regrettably, there are such horrible things everywhere! The following complaint applies just as much to our times as to Salvian's: "The first shafts of anger are always cursing, and we angrily hope for things that in our weakness we cannot bear. We use wicked prayers instead of weapons."[161]

Second, many of the imprecatory prayers that were permitted applied not so much to the sinners themselves but to their cause, their efforts, and their plans. So David prayed, "Please, Lord, thwart Ahithophel's plan" (2 Sam. 15:31). The disciples prayed, "Now, O Lord, look at their threats" (Acts 4:29). And Paul said, "May those who disturb you be cut off" (Gal. 5:12).

Third, the imprecatory prayers attacking persons are generally not very specific. They do not apply to this or that person individually but are

---

158. Paraphrase of Pseudo-Chrysostom, in Thomas Aquinas, *Catena Aurea*, sub loc. Matt. 6:9.

159. Oper. *Witteberg.* tom. 2. f. 22.] Luther, *Tomus Secundus Omnium Operum Reverendi Domini Martini Lutheri* (Wittenberg, 1546).

160. The nature of her curse does not seem to be recorded in this text.

161. *Salvian.* l. 3.] Salvian, *De Gubernatione Dei* (Oxford, 1633), bk. 3, sec. 8.

indefinite, prayed against one class of persons or another. An example is this apostolic thundering: "If anyone does not love the Lord Jesus Christ, let him be anathema. Come, Lord Jesus" (1 Cor. 16:22).

Fourth, those imprecatory prayers brandished against specific persons individually are generally not so much categorical as hypothetical. And they are aimed at the destruction and ruin of the wicked in a qualified sense. It is on the condition that they cannot be healed and that the vindication of divine glory and the church's salvation demands their destruction. Paul certainly singles out Alexander by a unique distinction as apostate and as someone whose hope is already abandoned. He separates Alexander from other deserters who have sinned merely from weakness and were not yet incurable. Paul seems to pray against him very pointedly. "Alexander the silversmith did me a great deal of harm. May the Lord repay him according to his deeds" (2 Tim. 4:14). But in the case of other men, he is far more mild and, indeed, strikes a very different tone. "All those," he says, "who deserted me, μὴ αὐτοῖς λογισθείη" (2 Tim. 4:16).[162]

Fifth, many of the categorical imprecatory prayers seek only temporal loss and so have as their end that sinners repent and are corrected, not destroyed. An imprecation of this kind (as our countryman Ames notes) has the force of intercession. It looks to avert a greater evil through that evil that it seeks.[163] David prayed this way: "Fill their face with shame, and let them seek Your name" (Ps. 83:17). And so there is no doubt that this does not at all conflict with Christian charity, because we can also seek this for ourselves, that God would afflict and correct us rather than permit us to fall into sin, or that He would call us back to Himself by these means when we have already fallen into sin.

Sixth, all prayers that seek destruction or seem to threaten it are prophetic rather than true prayerful addresses. An example is when the psalmist prayed, "Set a punishment against the punishment of their iniquity, and do not allow them to come before Your righteousness. Remove them from the book of the living and may they not be enrolled with the righteous" (Ps. 69:28–29). And these are words not so much of prayer as of preaching; they are not so much vows as they are prophecies. Augustine says, "A prophet sang of what would take place, not by the will of longing but by the spirit of foresight."[164] And in another passage, he writes, "When curses are spoken according to prophecy, they do not come from an evil wish but

---

162. "May it not be counted against them."

163. Medull. lib. 2. cap. 9. thes. 77.] Ames, *Medulla*, 2.9.77, p. 310.

164. De Serm. Domin. in monte l. 1. sub finem.] Augustine, *De Sermone Domini In Monte Secundum Matthaeum*, in *Omnium Operum*, vol. 4 (Basel, 1528), 1.21.72.

from the Spirit of knowledge of the one bringing the denunciation."[165] In a similar vein, Theophylact also spoke of Paul's dreadful predictions against Alexander. He said, "It is a prophecy rather than a curse."[166] There is also the author of the questions and answers in the works of Justin Martyr: "These words are neither κατάρα (cursing) nor λοιδορία (reviling). Instead, Πρόρρησις πρέπουσαι ἀνδρὶ Ἀποστόλῳ, μὴ ἐκδικοῦντι ἑαυτὸν ἀλλὰ διδόντι τόπον τῇ ὀργῇ ("They are the prophecy suited to a man who is an apostle. Not of a man who is avenging himself but of one yielding to his anger").[167]

Seventh, Christians are forbidden to pursue, with dreadful prayer, their own private enemies who have harmed them. The Savior said, "Love your enemies, bless those who curse you, do good to those who hate you, and pray for those who oppose and persecute you" (Matt. 5:44). The Lord's practice was consistent with this commandment. As He hung on the cross, He did not curse His persecutors but prayed for them, saying, "Father, forgive them" (Luke 23:34). The first martyr, Stephen, did this as well: "O Lord, do not charge them with this sin" (Acts 7:60). Following him, we have the example of John Hus. While his opponents read in his presence the council's sentence of condemnation, he knelt and raised his eyes toward heaven. They say he prayed as follows:

> I beseech You, Lord God, from the bottom of my heart, by Your immense majesty, forgive my enemies for this. You know well that I have been falsely accused and overwhelmed by false witnesses and fictitious errors and that I have been unfairly condemned. Therefore, by Your mercy, which no one will ever fully embrace in speech, I beg You, do not punish them for this.[168]

This really is the mark of Christians. Among them, as Pererius notes,[169] there are three degrees of love. The lowest is deeply loving someone who loves you. Higher than that is loving someone who does not love you. And the highest is loving even the one who hatefully persecutes you. Among the

---

165. Contra *Faustum* Manich. l. 16. c. 22.] Augustine, *Contra Faustum Manichaeum*, in *Omnium Operum*, vol. 6 (Basel, 1528), 16.22.

166. Theophylact of Ohrid, *Omnes D. Pauli*, sub loc. 2 Tim. 4:14.

167. Justin Martyr, *Apokriseis*, in *Tou Hagiou Ioustinou Philosophou Kai Martyros* (Paris, 1551), p. 288.

168. *Zechar. Theobaldi* Bellum *Hussiticum* pag. 49.] Theobald, *Bellum Hussiticum*, ch. 20, p. 49.

169. Disp. 43. in cap. 13. Joan.] Benito Pereyra (Benedictus Pererius), 1536–1610, Spanish Jesuit philosopher and exegete, *Selectarum Disputationum In Sacram Scripturam* (Lyon, 1610), vol. 5, disput. 43, sub loc. John 13, p. 279.

Jews of old, the most righteous men were the Hasidics[170] or Essenes.[171] It was their stated policy, so they say, to pray to God like this: "Forgive and spare all who harass us."

Eighth, it is safest to refrain completely from imprecatory prayers. This is because moderation in prayer is proper, and it is difficult not to mix in our personal feelings, but also because few men these days, perhaps not a one, have been given the spirit of discretion and prophecy. It was that spirit that once motivated David, Paul, and several others as they prayed. If any of us were governed by that same spirit and in the same measure as the holy prophets and apostles were, he could perhaps thunder out, as they did, the same dreadful prayers against the public and intractable enemies of God and His church. But because we are very far removed from the purity of feeling reflected in such great servants of God—and we are, moreover, ignorant without the revelations such men possessed as to whom we should consider truly intractable—we will safely follow the standard rule that Paul gave us. "Bless those who curse you," he said, "bless, and do not curse" (Rom. 12:14).

§ 16. This, my brothers, is what remains: let us pray. And what I am telling you now I would like to say to all Christ's soldiers: let us pray. Pertinax's watchword was "We must act like soldiers";[172] Severus's, "We must work."[173] Ours should be "We must pray." The Roman supposedly conquered by hunkering down. The Christian will conquer by praying. And so, may you all remember (if you have forgotten) the calloused knees of Saint James.[174] Remember that Luther spent a minimum of three hours each day in prayer, the very hours most suited to his studies.[175] Remember how our countryman Bradford knelt even while he was buried in his books.[176] In Jerome's account of Paul the Hermit, his corpse was found in a posture of prayer, his knees dutifully bent, his hands raised to heaven. Immeasurably blessed

---

170. Hasidics, adherents of Hasidism, a mystical Judaism known for its strict adherence to rabbinical traditions.

171. *Grotius* in Matth. cap. 5. vers. 44.] Grotius, *Annotationes In Libros Evangeliorum*, sub loc. Matt. 5:44.

172. Publius Helvius Pertinax, 126–193, r. January–March 193, Roman general and short-lived emperor.

173. Lucius Septimius Severus, 145–211, r. 193–211, Roman general and emperor.

174. Eusebius, *Historiae Ecclesiasticae*, bk. 2, ch. 23. According to Eusebius, the story comes from bk. 5 of Hegesippus.

175. Adam Melchior, *Vitae Germanorum Theologorum* (Heidelberg, 1620), p 142. A. tells a more elaborate version of the same story in his *Armilla Catechetica* (Cambridge, 1659), p. 192.

176. John Bradford, ca. 1510–1555, evangelical preacher and martyr. For his habit of studying while on his knees, see John Foxe's *Actes and Monuments* (London, 1583), bk. 11, p. 1628.

was his soul without a body, whose body, even without a soul, assumed so reverent a posture![177]

We will next discuss the famous εὐφημία[178] of the Spartans that is preserved in the ancient histories. "The oracle of Jupiter Ammon replied to the Athenian ambassador, who was trying to learn why the gods at the time gave victory to the Spartans rather than to the Athenians. The oracle replied with a memorable phrase: they liked the Spartans' εὐφημία (as Socrates takes it in Plato's *Alcibiades II*) more than the sacrifices of all the Greeks."[179]

In the meantime, we must know that just as Christians are trained by prayer for victory, so they are trained for prayer by exercising humility. The father of the faithful, Abraham himself, is our model: "Behold, I have begun to speak to the Lord, I who am but dust and ash" (Gen. 18:27). Rivet remarks on these words, "The richest source of our humility is to compare ourselves with divine majesty."[180] Others have drawn the same conclusion, among whom was Bernard. He abased himself in prayer, saying,

> I stand here among the sons of God like some monster. I take up space as a fruitless tree, and like a worthless ox I eat more than I produce. I am a disgrace among men, more vile than a beast, worth less than a corpse. A filthy dog has a more tolerable stench among men than the sin-sick soul does with God. Thus, I am disgusted to be alive. I'm ashamed to be alive because I make so little progress. I am afraid to die because I am not prepared.[181]

The former English bishop and martyr Hooper was much the same. When he was very near death, he addressed Christ and said: "O Lord, I am the abyss below. But You are heaven. I am a slough and sewer of sin. You, most gentle Redeemer, please be propitious to me, a most wretched sinner, in view of Your great and inexpressible righteousness. You who have passed through all the heavens, draw me to Yourself, I who have sunk so low."[182]

§ 17. I am now pleased to attach here the prayer that not so long ago I prepared according to the standard of the Lord's Prayer, to bring an end to this perhaps excessively long chapter. *Our Father, who art in heaven.* To You, as our Father, we owe the greatest reverence, the greatest love. To You

---

177. Jerome, "The Life of Paulus the First Hermit" (*Vita Sancti Pauli*), in *The Principal Works of Jerome*, ed. Philip Schaff, NPNF II, vol. 6, p. 300 (sect. 15).

178. "Prayer song."

179. Plato, *Alcibiades II*, in *Opera Omnia Quae Exstant* (Frankfurt, 1602), 148e–149b. This appears to be a paraphrase with some comments by A. rather than a quotation.

180. Exercit. in Gen. 93.] Rivet, *Theologicae*, p. 456 (exercise 93).

181. De interior. domo, c. 35.] Bernard of Clairvaux, *De Interiore Domo*, ch. 20.

182. John Hooper, 1500–1555, bishop of Gloucester and Worcester. Final words of John Hooper, probably in Foxe, *Actes and Monuments*.

who dwell in heaven, we owe the greatest worship. We have no reason to doubt Your tender mercies toward us. Though we are wretched little sinners, yet we are Your sons since You are the Father of our Lord Jesus Christ and, in Him, our Father. Likewise, we have no reason to doubt Your power either, because You *art in heaven*. You who are alone able, pour out upon us, please, the Spirit of adoption in our hearts, through whom we may cry, "Abba, Father," so that we can, with proper feeling, revere Your heavenly majesty. As the Spirit guides and directs us, *hallowed be Thy name*. May Your glory endure intact forever, and may whatever glory redounds to You from our characteristics or practices be common currency with us. Root out, O Lord, and destroy Islam, Judaism, papacy, atheism, and anything else everywhere that dishonors the most holy names of Jehovah and Jesus. To this end, *Thy kingdom come*. May all Israel, at long last, be brought back, the full complement of the gentiles be brought in, the heterodox exposed, the unregenerate converted, and the increase of grace multiplied upon the regenerate. May the gospel of Your kingdom run forth and receive glory in the whole world and especially on these British and Irish shores. Fill the civil magistrates with wisdom, Your ministers with zeal, and all the people with righteousness. Do not refuse to nourish, in Your bosom, both universities and especially our Cambridge. Let the goal always be, that *as Thy will is done in heaven, may it also be done on earth*. It must not become our habit (as it has been thus far) simply to humor the world, Satan, and the flesh. Please guarantee that, as we learn and keep Your will accurately—even as we are on earth—like the angels who have been granted the enjoyment of the beatific vision, we may be very ready then to rest in Your providence. And may we obey all Your commands individually with respect and consistency and with the utmost zeal and trust, just as the angels do (though we cannot equal them).

But also, *give us this day our daily bread*. Bread, O Lord, not delicacies. We are not at all concerned for those things that bring luxury. We reverently seek life's necessities. Please grant Your servants that measure of tranquility, health, and prosperity adequate for our journey. Meanwhile, plant within our hearts a sound mind so that, while we *use* this present life, we only *enjoy* You, the true God, and Jesus Christ, whom You sent. Through and because of His merit, *forgive us our debts, just as we forgive our debtors*. In addition to that first fall that infected our whole nature and the whole mass of our works, through the sins that day by day ensnare us, we have daily become debtors to Your justice (so that even our very prayers need leniency, our tears need cleansing). And yet none of us can satisfy Your justice in even the smallest way. Yet because Your Christ, our Jesus, has made satisfaction for us on the cross, we flee to You, Father of all mercies, as suppliants begging forgiveness, averting punishment, waiting on Your grace. This full certainty of grace and pardon we will experience the more we quite freely forgive those with whom we have some quarrel.

Yes, O Lord, You who are our sun and shield, because we live in this world full of snares, because we bear deceptive hearts and we have to deal with an enemy extensively equipped with tricks and deceits of every kind, *lead us not into temptation, but deliver us from evil.* Grant us to stay constantly vigilant and to pray, so we do not fall into Satan's snares. But if Your providence decides to test us with temptations, do not make them fatal. Trample the serpent's head in our hearts, by Your blessed seed, so that, although now we are drowned beneath innumerable floods, we, at last, by your grace, may rise above them and be welcomed safely and happily into the heavenly harbor. I make all these requests of You with greater confidence because *Thine is the kingdom, and the power, and the glory.* Yes, it offers us a great source of comfort that we believe and profess that the kingdom that all things serve belongs to You, Father, Son, and Holy Spirit, triune God; that the power by which all things come to be is Yours; and finally, that the glory toward which all things point their sails is Yours as well, forever and ever. Amen.

CHAPTER II

The Author of Spiritual Victory
and His Supports and Rewards

Sections 1–2: The pagans credit their divinities for all the victories they win; Christians credit God and Christ. Section 3: We reject the error of the Romanists, who make the blessed Mary an equal partner with Christ the Lord in trampling Satan. Section 4: Some light is shed on these passages, 1 Peter 5:8; 1 Corinthians 9:25; and Hosea 4:11. A demonstration that moderation undergirds spiritual victories. Section 5: This same idea is confirmed with respect to vigilance from multiple quotations of the fathers and others. Section 6: A similar demonstration is given for faith, with supporting elucidation from Revelation 12:22 and 1 John 5:4. Section 7: An exposition of the prize promised to the victor in Revelation 2:7. Section 8: Likewise, an explanation of the prize mentioned in verse 17 of the same chapter. An explanation of the "hidden manna," "the white stone," and the "new name inscribed on it." Sections 9–13: A discussion of additional prizes, Revelation 3:5. The physical book, the ecclesiastical book, and the Lamb's Book of Life. A lengthy discussion of the question whether someone can be erased from the Lamb's Book of Life, against the author of Redemption Redeemed.[1] *An explanation of Moses's and Paul's oaths, along with the status of the traitor Judas. Section 14: The famous victors' ἐξομολόγησις[2] that Christ shall make, what it includes, and how we should value it.*

§ 1. There are very many arguments that demonstrate that those devoted to pagan theology credited all the victories they earned to their divinities. Among these are that they assigned to Victory a place among the goddesses whom they zealously worshipped as divine. On one occasion in Rome, when a statue of victory was struck by lightning and only its wings fell off, Pompey concluded this meant that the Roman legions would finally stop losing. This oft repeated couplet demonstrates the idea nicely:

---

1. John Goodwin, 1651.
2. "Confession."

'Ρώμη παμβασίλεια, τὸ σὸν κλέος οὔποτ' ὀλεῖται:
νίκη γάρ σε φυγεῖν ἄπτερος οὐ δύναται

Rome a mighty queen you are, great shall your glory be.
Victory unwinged from you can never, ever flee.[3]

They believed that their tutelary gods would desert their city and people and move elsewhere before it would be possible for the people or city that they guarded to fall under the enemy's power. This is why, in Vergil, Aeneas says about Troy, after it was captured following ten years of battle,

Then all departed, all the gods, with shrines and altars left.
Though by their power this had stood...[4]

This is the origin of that practice Macrobius discusses, that the Romans typically called out foreign divinities with special songs. You can read in Macrobius about its use and, at the same time, its effect.[5] This is the practice it is believed Balak used against God's people. And he hired Balaam for that purpose until experience taught them that "sorcery had no effect against Jacob nor divination against Israel" (Num. 23:23). Similarly, the pagans developed the practice after winning victories of storing plunder in their gods' temples, and lavished praises and acts of thanksgiving upon these gods. After the Philistines captured the ark of God, "they led it into the temple of Dagon" (1 Sam. 5:1–2). And after capturing Samson, "they assembled to celebrate a great sacrifice to their god Dagon and for festivities. They said, 'Our god has given our enemy Samson into our hands'" (Judg. 16:23). We also know that when the supreme Roman general conquered his enemies, after celebrating a triumph, he placed a triumphal crown in the lap of Capitoline Jupiter to acknowledge him as the giver of victory.

§ 2. Christians, on the other hand, seeing that they enjoy far better teachers, acknowledge and celebrate God in Christ as the sole author of all their victories. This is true whether they win victories over external enemies or spiritual ones. In the book of Revelation, Christ the Lord is identified as the crowned knight who "goes forth conquering and to conquer" (Rev. 6:2). The destruction of Jerusalem is preeminent among this great Victor's first deeds, after He returned to heaven, together with the slaughter of the Jews. He predicted this slaughter in a parable in Luke: "But My enemies who did not want Me to rule them, bring them here and slay them in My presence"

---

3. *Anthol.* Gr. Epig. l. 4. c. 21.] *Anthologia Graeca Florilegium Diversorum Epigrammatum In Septem Libros Distinctum* (Venice, 1550), bk. 4, ch. 21, fol. 209v.

4. Aeneid. l. 2.] Vergil, *Aeneidos*, bk. 2 (lines 351–52).

5. Saturnal. l. 3. cap. 9.] Ambrosius Theodosius Macrobius (Macrobius), fl. ca. AD 400, Latin grammarian and Neoplatonist philosopher, *Saturnaliorum* (Paris, 1585), bk. 3, ch. 9.

(Luke 19:27). His agent Titus, even though he was completely unfamiliar with the Christian rites, dared not ascribe this slaughter to anyone but God. In fact, after the city was captured and destroyed, Titus allegedly shouted, when he viewed the remaining fortifications, "Clearly, we have fought with God's help, and it was God who separated the Jews from their fortifications. What human hand or war machine could beat these towers?"[6] Moreover, Titus did not take the eponym *Judaicus*, according to the custom of other generals who adopted a title from their conquered provinces.[7] What is more, as the Suda states, when all of Syria, Egypt, and all the neighboring nations sent him crowns and called him victor, Titus refused them and said, "I did not do it. My hands were God's tools, as He revealed His anger."[8] These events are not so surprising if you remember the noble saying of the Christian Emperor Charles V.[9] When he had routed an extremely large number of Saxons and others with a small band of soldiers, he wrote to the Roman pontiff about the outcome and said, "I came, I saw, but Christ conquered."[10]

But if our discourse is about spiritual victories, then the Apostle testifies that God shows their origin, increase, and end rest in Christ. He says, "Thanks be to God who gives us the victory through our Lord Jesus Christ" (1 Cor. 15:57). And in another passage: "In all these things, we are more than conquerors through Him who loved us" (Rom. 8:37, 39). And Paul shows who this man is in the very last verse of that same chapter when he reminds us of the love of God in Christ Jesus our Lord. Although when Paul guides us here, we do not really need the fathers' testimony, nevertheless, I think it will be pleasant and useful to show in a few words what they thought. They say that when Cyprian was a pagan and a wizard,[11] he fell desperately in love with a certain Christian virgin named Christina. The Devil promised to give him carnal access to her. When the Devil was unable to do so but instead affirmed, against his will, that Christina's God was stronger, Cyprian took this opportunity to embrace the Christian religion and rejected his Devil worship.[12] As for what Augustine discovered, he describes it himself with exceptional eloquence:

---

6. *Joseph.* de Bello Judaico. l. 7. c. 16. p. 667.] Josephus, *De Bello Iudaico*, bk. 7, ch. 16, p. 967.

7. *Xiphilin.* p. 217.] Joannes Xiphilinus, eleventh century, Byzantine monk and epitomator of Dio Cassius, Ἐκ τῶν Δίωνος Ἐκλογαὶ Ἰωάννου τοῦ Ξιφιλίνου. *E Dione Excerptae Historiae Ab Joanne Xiphilino* ([Paris], 1592). Greek/Latin edition.

8. *Suidas*, vol. 2 (Geneva, 1619), p. 919.

9. Charles V, 1500–1558, r. 1519–1555/1556, Holy Roman emperor.

10. *Surius* in Commentar. rerum toto orbe gestar.] Surius, *Commentarius Brevis Rerum In Orbe Gestarum* (Cologne, 1567), sub loc. anno 1547, p. 553.

11. This is Cyprian of Antioch, not the more well-known bishop of Carthage.

12. *Zepper.* Legum forens. l. 4. c. 5.] Zepper, *Legum Mosaicarum*, 4.5 p. 303.

There was no tempter present, and You, God, made him leave. The opportunity and time for temptation were gone, and You caused that. Then the tempter appeared, and the opportunity and time as well. But You held me fast, so I did not give in. The shadowy tempter came as he is, and You strengthened me to reject him. The armed tempter came, and he was strong, but You restrained him so he did not conquer me, and You strengthened me. The tempter came, when he had transformed himself into an angel of light, and You shouted at me so he would not deceive me. You filled me with the light so I could recognize him.[13]

Bradwardine was very near the generation of the fathers. In him we find these words that I now happily quote:

O the marvelous condescension of divine grace toward us wretched and ungrateful men. It preserves us safe and unharmed, untempted by such a numerous and mighty storm of temptations. When we are tempted, divine grace preserves us unconquered amid such numerous and powerful tempting impulses. And divine grace, by itself, not through us, heaps up numerous and abundant rewards for those who conquer.[14]

§3. Contemporary Romanists, therefore, who make the blessed virgin share in the special prerogative of Christ—as the author of spiritual victory and one who personally triumphs over the Devil—deserve to be roundly rejected. This results from their corrupted reading and even worse understanding of the protoevangelical text. For when the verse began to be read as "She herself will bruise your head," this error turned to madness, and the Mariolaters devised a way to grant Mary the honor of "Redemptrix." In various parts of Germany (my source is Gerhard),[15] there is a painting at the very bottom of which stands a sinner with his face turned toward the blessed virgin. He is pleading with her using this prayer: "Holy virgin, I beseech you: Mary, defend me now." On one side, the virgin Mary, with bared breasts, speaks to Christ her Son, pointing at the sinner with her finger: "Because at these you have suckled, Son, I beseech You to forgive him." On the other side, we see Christ, showing His wounds to the heavenly Father with these words: "See My wounds, Father; grant what My mother asks." The heavenly Father, from His position above, answers, "I will grant whatever You seek, Son, and deny You nothing." Coster wrote a *Handbook of Controversies*, and on its cover, one can see a painted image of the blessed Mary trampling the serpent. It includes this caption: "She shall crush your

---

13. Soliloq. c 16.] Augustine, *Soliloquiorum Animae Ad Deum,* in *Omnium Operum,* vol. 9 (Basel, 1528), ch. 16.

14. De causa Dei lib. 2. cap. 7.] Bradwardine, *De Causa Dei,* bk. 2, ch. 7, p. 491.

15. Lec. comm. in 4°, vol. 8. p. 719.] Gerhard, *Loci Theologici,* vol. 8, sec. 387.

head."[16] The Jesuit Angelinus Gazaeus appended some elegies to his *Pia Hilaria*, and among them is a poem entitled "Placed in the Middle I Know Not Where to Turn." The whole piece is a competition between superstition and eloquence. At the very beginning, the reader will find these words, and if he is orthodox, will find them offensive:

> I waver here and meditate between the milk and gore,
>   Between delights of breast and side thus set.
> Be nursed by milky breast or fed on blood—which pleases more—
>   To take Your joys, O Christ, or Mary yours?
> To mingle mother's milk and blood of Son, this I long for,
>   Then better medicine I could not take. [17]

But because we make some concession, as is the pagan practice, to painters and poets, let us see whether the Romanist theologians express the same thought. "You, man, have sure access to God when the mother is standing before the Son, and the Son before the Father. The mother shows her Son her chest and breasts; the Son shows His Father His side and wounds." Thus Antoninus.[18] We also have the following:

> In these words, "She shall crush your head," the virgin's victory over the Devil is revealed in four ways. First, because of who is trampling. It says "she" because it was not a man, but a woman. Second, because of the manner of trampling, because she did not strike nor wound but trample. Third, because of the part that she trampled: she did not trample his tail but his head. Fourth, because of the person whom she trampled. It was not one of the lesser demons but the very prince himself.

Those are Barradius's words.[19]

> The mother of mercy helps the Father of mercies in the work of our salvation. So then, why does the Lord say in Isaiah, "I alone trampled out the winepress, and no man from among the nations was with me"? It is true, O Lord, that there was not a man with You, but one woman was with You, the one who took in her heart all the wounds that You had received in Your body.

---

16. Francis Coster, 1532–1619, Flemish Jesuit theologian and writer, title page of *Enchiridion Controversiarum* (Cologne, 1589).

17. Pag. 298.] Angelin Gazet, 1568–1653, French Jesuit scholar, *Pia Hilaria* (Antwerp, 1629), p. 298.

18. Part. 3. Summae titulo 3.] Bernard of Clairvaux, quoted in Antoninus of Florence, 1389–1459, Dominican moral theologian, *Summae Sacrae Theologiae*, vol. 3 (Vannes, 1582), ch. 4, tit. 31, fol. 510v. *Filius Patri latus et vulnera* does not appear to be in the original.

19. Harmon. Evang. l. 3 c 7.] Probably Sebastian Barradas, 1543–1615, Portuguese Jesuit theologian and exegete, *Commentaria In Concordiam Et Historiam Evangelicam* (Antwerp, 1621).

So says the author of a certain *Marialia* published at Strasbourg in 1493.[20] And to prevent someone from saying that these are just comments originating from ignorant monks, I would like the reader to note another statement of the more learned Jesuits (they want others to recognize and celebrate them as the most learned!). Their distinguished champion Alfonso Salmerón baldly stated, "Mary, of course, stood under the cross as coredemptrix, just as Eve, alongside Adam, introduced evil into the world."[21]

§ 4. I think that the supports for spiritual victory Peter lists in the following words are especially significant: "Be sober minded and watchful, for your enemy the Devil prowls around like a roaring lion, seeking someone to devour. Resist him firmly by faith" (1 Peter 5:8–9). The first point is sobriety. Paul speaks of this when discussing Christians' athleticism: πᾶς ὁ ἀγωνιζόμενος πάντα ἐγκρατεύεται.[22] "They do so to receive a perishing crown, but we to get one that does not perish" (1 Cor. 9:25). Tertullian once commented on this passage that "athletes are set apart for a more rigorous training to have time to build strength. They refrain from luxury, from delicacies, from strong drink, and so forth. The more they work at their training, the more hope they have for victory."[23] But as for what the Apostle means by ἐγκρατεύεται, hardly anyone could express it more clearly than the poet from Venusia:

> The man who longs to reach the mark and strives to gain his goal,
> Endured and struggled much, dear boy, through cold and sweaty toil.
> He stayed away from sex and wine.[24]

The poet has very aptly joined together sex and wine, since "a stomach swelled with wine," says Jerome pointedly, "quickly spills over into lust."[25] The inspired prophet also joined them together: "Fornication, wine, and new vintage steal away the heart" (Hos. 4:11). The senseless rarely become champions. Instead, their heart is swept away by these two temptations. So not only is victory thwarted but the soldiers surrender their hearts altogether to the enemy.

---

20. Lib. 1. cap. 5.] Richard of Saint-Laurent, d. ca. 1250, French canon and theologian, *De Laudibus Beatae Mariae Virginis* (Strasbourg, 1493), fol. 13v.

21. Oper. tom. 10. Tractat. 41. p. 339.] Alfonso Salmerón, 1515–1585, Spanish Jesuit and biblical scholar, *Commentarii In Evangelicam Historiam, et in Acta Apostolorum*, vol. 10 (Köln, 1613).

22. "Whoever competes practices self-control in everything."

23. Exhort. ad martyres.] Tertullian, *Ad Martyras*, ch. 3.

24. *Horat.* de Arte poetica.] Horace, *De Arte Poetica*.

25. Jerome, "To Amandus," in *The Principal Works of Jerome*, ed. Philip Schaff, NPNF II, vol. 6, p. 110 (letter 55, sect. 2).

Augustine, with great brilliance, says, "Drunkenness is a smooth demon. He who possesses that spirit does not possess himself. The one who acts under its influence does not commit sin, but the whole of him is sin."[26] Wilhelm Schickard tells a very memorable story about eleven rabbis upon whom the pagan King Pirgandicus[27] had forced three choices: eat pork, drink pagan wine, or lie with prostitutes. They preferred wine to the other options, although they committed these acts too. For when they were well drunk, the table was secretly turned around and, without their knowledge, they were served unclean meats. In a drunken stupor, they were joined to wanton women.[28]

Illicit sex generally opens the path to other vices as well and, typically speaking, to the most shameful idolatry. So Balaam easily enticed the Israelites to Moabite idolatry through trafficking with Moabite women (Rev. 2:14). Foreign women were the enticement that led Solomon's heart toward other gods (1 Kings 11:4). But André Rivet records the clever quip of a certain well-known man in our lifetime. This man saw a great prince leaving his home where his concubine lived, and that home was right next to a church. As the church was the first place he stepped into in order to participate in the Roman superstition, he said to those standing nearby, "It is only one step from a brothel to a Mass."[29]

§5. Vigilance holds the second place of importance. If it is present, everything is in very good shape. If it is missing, all is lost. Marcus Cato besieged a city, as the authors of Roman history recount, that the citizens were very vigilantly and stoutly defending. Nevertheless, they say, he captured it with the following strategy. He feigned retreat, as though the siege were broken, but did not go very far away. Now the city had spent its fourth day without its attacker, and so began to neglect the watch, let down its guard, and forget the enemy. But Cato returned by unknown and secret paths. He assailed the city with surprising force and, on the fifth day, overwhelmed it.[30] By a similar stratagem, Satan ambushes our souls. For this reason, we must keep unbroken vigil, and the Christian must be like Argus[31] if he is to remain unconquered. The poet describes him like this:

---

26. Ad sacras Virgines.] According to A., Augustine, *De Sancta Virginitate*.

27. Pirgandicus, fl. ca. 74 BC, by Talmudic tradition, a Jewish king in Africa.

28. Jus Regium Hebraeorum, cap. 5. p. 149.] Wilhelm Schickard, 1592–1635, German Lutheran professor of Hebrew and astronomy, *Ius Regium Hebraeorum* (Strasburg, 1625), ch. 5, p. 149.

29. Comment. in Hoseae 4. 11.] Rivet, *Commentarius*, p. 142.

30. This is most likely Cato the Elder, serving under Quintus Fabius Maximus at the siege of Capua, a city that had abandoned Rome for Hannibal in 211 BC.

31. Argus, Greek monster with one hundred eyes.

One hundred eyes encircled round the head of Argus grim,
So in their turn by twos they slept while others watched o'er him
And kept him safe. The rest from their position did not stir.[32]

The bride was on her guard not to fall asleep completely. She said, "I slept, but with my mind I stayed awake" (Song 5:1). There are four creatures that John describes in Revelation as filled with eyes in front and behind (Rev. 4:6, 8): ἔσωθεν γέμοντα ὀφθαλμῶν.[33] Macarius makes the same assertion about every soul that is truly Christian. He says that it carries God with it, or rather, is carried by God, because "the whole soul, of course, becomes an eye."[34]

The vigilance of godly men is very great, or at least, it ought to be. In point of fact, the more godly they become the greater need they have of diligence, because they are liable to greater harm. Among the Romans, the better equipped guards used to be stationed in the part of the besieged city most exposed to enemy guile.[35] And the men who held the most responsibility in government were considered most deserving of honor. It was very important for them not to yield to pleasures. Instead, in order to remain mindful of the sizable danger that awaited them, they had to be intent on the city's safety more than the rest. Now, lest any seasoned soldier think he has won victory so many times that he can sleep "on both ears,"[36] I want him to know that his vigilance must continue throughout his life. There is no situation on earth that places the Christian soldier beyond the reach of the missiles' strike. Let us listen to Bernard: "Nowhere is safe, neither in heaven, nor in paradise, much less here on earth. For in heaven, the angel fell away from the divine presence; Adam, in paradise, fell from his position of pleasure; Judas, on earth, from the Savior's school."[37] Therefore, my fellow soldier, whoever you are, be watchful that you come out victorious. Don't ever promise yourself safety, lest you become to your adversaries a joke and plunder alike. Be careful not to say, "There's not a single enemy in sight." For you carry with yourself an enemy—namely, your own very person. Let Jerome teach you, who said, "It is a sign of very great character to fight with oneself every day and to watch over the enemy within using

---

32. Ovid, *Metamorphoseon*, bk. 1.

33. "And yet they also were filled with eyes on the inside."

34. Ἡ ψυχὴ ἡ βαστάζουσα τὸν Θεὸν μᾶλλον ἢ βασταζομένη ὑπὸ τοῦ Θεοῦ γίνεται ὅλη ὀφθαλμός. *Marcarius* homil. 33. pag. 428.] Macarius of Egypt ("the Great"), *Homiliae Spirituales*, p. 428 (*homilia* 33). A. has ἢ βασταζομένη rather than δὲ βασταζομένη.

35. *Joann. a Chokier* in suis ad *Onosandri* Strategicum notis pag. 30.] Jean de Chokier, 1571–1656, jurist and theologian, *Thesaurus Politicorum Aphorismorum* (Mainz, 1613), p. [ii] 30.

36. I.e., completely heedless of his surroundings.

37. De diversis 30.] Bernard of Clairvaux, *De Diversis*, in *Opera Omnia*, vol. 2 (Cologne, 1641), sec. 1 (*sermo* 30).

Argus' one hundred eyes."[38] And you should not be ashamed to learn from Epictetus, who concludes his sketch of the progressing philosopher like this: Ὡς ἐχθρὸν ἑαυτὸν παραφυλάσσει καὶ ἐπίβουλον ("He carefully watches himself as his own lurking, sneaky enemy").[39] Although, perhaps, you are old, still you must be carefully on guard against what the Apostle calls "youthful passions" (2 Tim. 2:22). What Jerome experienced even as a holy old man should strike us with terror and actually sharpen our vigilance. He complains in a letter to Eustochius[40] about keeping safe his virginity:

> How many times have I myself, here in the desert—in a vast solitude scorched by the sun's heat, which offers monks a wretched place to live— kept thinking I was among Roman delights. Often I imagined myself in a group of young women. My face was pale with fasting, and my mind, hot-swollen with desires in a stone-cold body. And right before a man whose flesh was almost dead, the pure fires of lust kept bubbling to the surface.[41]

Maybe you are sick of the mob and ready to talk with the man Thomas à Kempis praised? "Whenever I spent time among men, I returned less a man."[42] But be careful that solitude doesn't make you complacent. Pay attention, please, to what the famous abbot of Clairvaux said to a certain pious woman who aspired to desert life. "Even the desert holds much opportunity for the one who wants to behave wickedly, and the wood provides cover; solitude gives silence. Of course, the evil that nobody sees nobody confronts. And when there is no fear of being rebuked, the tempter approaches confidently. Sin is committed more freely."[43] Augustine can finish off this section nicely. After he reminds us of the fall of Samson, David, and Solomon, he goes on to say, "Therefore, stay alert, brothers, and do not give up, because you are aware that you are not more holy than David, more brave than Samson, or more wise than Solomon."[44]

§6. The third support is faith. Constantine the Great ordered a coin to be struck that showed the image of a cross with this inscription: "In this sign you will conquer." As a consequence, much superstition crept into the church, so that now many people consider the message of the cross

---

38. Epist. 8.] Jerome, *Epistolae Selectae*, vol. 2, *epistola* 19.

39. *Epictet.* Enchirid cap. 72.] Epictetus, ca. 55–ca. 135, Stoic philosopher and teacher, *Enchiridion* (Cologne, 1596), ch. 72, p. 36.

40. Julia Eustochium, 370–ca. 419, early monastic under the influence of Jerome.

41. Epist. 22.] Jerome, *Opera Divi Hieronymi Stridoniensis*, vol. 1 (*epistola* 22).

42. De Imitat. Christi lib. 1. cap. 20.] À Kempis, *De Imitatione Christi* (Cologne, 1626), bk. 1, ch. 20, sec. 2, p. 28.

43. *Bernard.* epist. 116.] Bernard of Clairvaux, *Epistolae*, sec. 1 (*epistola* 115).

44. Ad fratres in eremo serm. 16.] Augustine, *Sermones Ad Fratres Suos In Eremo*, in *Omnium Operum*, vol. 10 (Basel, 1528), *sermo* 17.

less important than the mere sign. Revelation guides us more reliably with these words: "Then the accuser of our brethren was cast down, he who accused them in the sight of our God day and night. But they themselves conquered him through the blood of the Lamb and through the word of their testimony" (Rev. 12:10–11). Behold, please, dear reader, the blood and word of Christ, the twofold object of saving faith. So then it is evident that faith greatly undergirds the victory that we win over Satan. But we gave this a sufficiently extended explanation above when we discussed the Devil's shafts that are extinguished by the shield of faith.

Nevertheless, it will be worth the effort to add in here an explanation of a particular passage from John concerning the world. He said, "This is the victory that overcomes the world—our faith" (1 John 5:4). The Apostle, in his letter to the Hebrews, clarified John's expression by a really fine example. Moses overcame by faith the good things of the world, but especially the bad. Among the good things of the world, men value honor, pleasure, and wealth the most. The common slogan for these is "These three the world considers its trinity."[45] The text tells us that Moses won a very sure victory over all these individual gods. With respect to honors, we read, "By faith Moses refused the advantage of being called the son of Pharaoh's daughter." When it came to pleasures, "he chose rather to suffer the same hardships with God's people than to hold on to the temporary joy of sin." As for wealth, "he considered the reproach placed on Christ greater riches than the Egyptians' storehouses" (Heb. 11:24–26). The king's anger is very properly listed among the particular evils of this world. Solomon says of this, "The king's resentment is like the roaring of a young lion" (Prov. 19:12). Moses, from that same passage, counted this anger as nothing: "By faith he left Egypt, unafraid of the king's burning wrath" (Heb. 11:27). With Moses, let me join Luther, whose courageous statement is famous: "I care nothing for Rome's wrath or her approval."

§7. The prizes of spiritual victory found in Revelation are remarkably diverse and extraordinary. Rewards are mentioned at the end of each letter to the seven churches in Asia. These are not simply rewards for those who fight. After all, many have given their names to Christ by an external profession who have never trusted their souls to him by faith at all. And many have enlisted as soldiers who are not listed among the victors. No, these rewards are only for those who fought bravely in the spiritual conflict all the way to victory. I have selected three of these prizes, and from them, one can estimate the rest.

---

45. Anonymous.

I will begin with Christ's very lovely statement to the church of Ephesus: "I will allow the victor to eat from the tree of life in the midst of paradise" (Rev. 2:7). There is an earthly paradise that the Lord planted in the beginning and then entrusted to our first parents for them to care for and cultivate. This, with good reason, is taken as a type of the heaven of the blessed, and all the more so because Paul uses paradise and the third heaven as synonyms (2 Cor. 12:2–4). There is no reason for anyone to be surprised that this palace of the blessed spirits—a place more happy than anything that ever existed on earth—is called paradise, when the hell of Gehenna is named after the Valley of Hinnom, the most miserable and horrible of all locations.

The Tree of Life is placed in the middle of this paradise that I have described, as a symbol of that blessed immortality to which Adam, at the right moment, would have been translated, apart from death's interposition, had he just remained sinless. And it is also a type for Christ who, Paul tells us, both "caused death to disappear" and "brought life and incorruptibility to light through the gospel" (2 Tim. 1:10). Solomon applied this apt word of praise to the tree in his celebration of uncreated wisdom (found in chapter 3 as well as chapter 8 of Proverbs as will be obvious when the passages are compared). He said, "It is a tree of life for those who embrace it, and blessed is anyone who possesses it" (Prov. 3:18). And so it is likely that, by the eating of the Tree of Life, participation in our Lord Jesus Christ is thereby promised to all Christian victors. This is the participation that would lead all of them to that eternal life from which our first parents had fallen and, thus, were shut out from dwelling in Paradise and eating the Tree of Life. John Cluver supports this interpretation. These are his words:

> When man was led astray and conquered by that tempter the Devil, he passed over into his power, was driven out of Paradise, and forbidden to eat from the Tree of Life. But he returned to the possession of that original blessedness that he had lost through the Devil's deceit and envy. He is promised that he will eat from the Tree of Life in the midst of God's paradise. This eating signifies restoration of the joy, freedom, and eternal life lost through the fall [Rev. 2:7]. Those who are on pilgrimage and serving as soldiers in this age do not experience this completely. For we are not yet in paradise, although Christ has restored to us the right to enter it.[46]

§ 8. I now go on to that most glorious promise that the Lord attaches to the letter He sent to the church of Pergamum. "I will allow him who conquers to eat from the secret manna. And I will give him a white stone, and on that

---

46. Dilucul. Apocalypt. tom. 2. p. 80. 81, 82.] Johannes Clüver, 1593–1633, German Lutheran theologian and pastor, *Diluculi Apocalyptici Seu Commentarius Posthumus*, vol. 2 (Lübeck, 1646), ch. 2, pp. 80–82.

stone is written a new name that nobody knows except the one who receives it" (Rev. 2:17). Manna had an amazing sweetness, and its taste, says an ancient interpreter, was like the finest flour mixed with honey. Or, as Junius says, it had the flavor like a wafer made of honey (Exod. 16:32).[47] I believe this is why it is placed here, to represent the sweetness of joy that Christ supplies. And it is called the "hidden manna" because the remains of that heavenly bread were hidden in the ark, as the whole of Christians' comfort is stored in the Lord Himself. Thus, Paul says, "If then there is any comfort in Christ" (Phil. 2:1). Or it is called that because its sweetness is concealed from the unregenerate. Then, Christ drenches the victor's soul after a job well done in this sweetness. Therefore, Solomon says, "My soul knows its own bitterness, and a stranger shall not partake of its joy" (Prov. 14:10). Yet the fountain of this comfort is the individual feeling of unmerited justification and adoption. It seems that the first of these can be identified as the "white stone," and the second, by the "new name." I mean that the feeling is so designated, not the accomplished action, since here the focus is on the prize that follows victory rather than the act of justification or adoption that precedes it.

It is a simple matter to believe that the white stone represents remission of guilt. Anyone who has studied Ovid's poetry knows these lines:

> The ancients practiced law with pebbles black and snowy white,
> By one the guilty they condemned, by others cleared the right.[48]

I should also mention Alcibiades's[49] statement. As Plutarch records, he answered a certain man who was trying to convince him to surrender to his country to stand trial: "I would not even surrender to my mother μή πως ἀγνοήσασα τὴν μέλαιναν βάλῃ ψῆφον ἀντὶ τῆς λευκῆς."[50]

In the passage I am discussing, there is a "new name" inscribed on the stone, the name of the sons of God. This is because adoption is always very closely attached to justification. The supreme awarder of prizes mentions this as a reward in another passage. His words are, "The victor shall, by right of inheritance, gain all things. And I will be his God, and he will be My son" (Rev. 21:7). The word *new* is used, perhaps, for this reason, because when something unexpected adds a certain excellence and allure to objects, very often the word *new* is used to mean *exceptional* and *important*. One can see this displayed among the sacred writers in the well-known phrase

---

47. *Biblia Sacra*, sub loc. Exod. 16:32.

48. Metamorph. l. 15.] Ovid, *Metamorphoseon*, bk. 15.41–42.

49. Alcibiades, ca. 450–404 BC, Athenian general and statesman.

50. "Lest through ignorance she should perhaps cast the black pebble instead of the white one when she votes." Plutarch, *Apophthegmata*.

of the psalmist, "Sing a new song" [Ps. 96:1], and also when the Savior said, "A new commandment I give you" [John 13:34]. But we also find the idea in Servius, who interprets the word *new* in some passages of Vergil as exceptional or important. An example is found in the third eclogue: "Pollio himself composes new songs."[51] We also have this one from book 2 of the *Aeneid*: "Then a new terror passed through all his quaking limbs."[52] And one from book 4 as well: "What new guest here has approached our home?"[53] Finally, from book 9: "With brilliant, new strength."[54] The Apostle clearly testifies that this is the very great name of the Son of God, when he says, "Behold what manner of love the Father has given to us, that we should be called the sons of God" (1 John 3:1). But why is no one described as knowing the name except the one who receives it? "Because," says Matthieu Cottière, in his comment on this passage, "those who are not sons of God mock the privilege of the sons of God as though it were a fairytale."[55]

Although these notions do not seem to us at all inconsistent, nevertheless, others remain entirely unpersuaded, the more so because the victor does not here receive the stone and the name inscribed on it. The pebble, moreover, was not usually retained by the accused when votes were cast. It was thrown into an urn. So they decided to follow another path of interpretation and find the source of the metaphors not from the courtroom but from athletic competition. The foremost advocate of this position is Samuel Petit, whose words it is easy to quote:

> When the Lord says that victors are admitted to the feast of manna, what follows depends upon that comment and so references prizes won in the games. Champions at the games enjoyed feasting at public expense and dining at public board. They were not admitted to the table freely unless they proved, by a token, that they belonged to τῶν ἱερῶν συσσίτων.[56] In the same way, the Lord acknowledges that He will receive at the public feast of manna τοὺς νικῶντας[57] and promises that He will give them a white stone etc. for their admission. This stone is a symbol and a token and a warning to everyone not to forge His name. The Lord proclaims that He will personally engrave upon it a new name that no one knows except the one who receives it.[58]

Petit partly justifies his interpretation of this passage from *codex Theodosianus*

---

51. Vergil, *Ecloga*, 3 (line 86).

52. Vergil, *Aeneidos*, bk. 2 (lines 228–29).

53. Vergil, *Aeneidos*, bk. 4 (line 10).

54. Vergil, *Aeneidos*, bk. 9 (line 641).

55. Cottière, *Apocalypseos*, sub loc. Rev. 2:17.

56. "These sacred meals."

57. "Those who have conquered."

58. Variar. lect. lib. 1. cap. 8.] Petit, *Variarum Lectionum*, bk. 1, ch. 8, p. 32.

and partly from the commentary of Arethas on this passage of Revelation. Those who enjoy fishing through the speculations of learned men should consult these volumes.

§9. Some additional points need to be made by way of commentary on what was written to the church at Sardis. "He who conquers will be clothed in white garments. I will never blot out his name from the book of life, but I will acknowledge him in My Father's sight and in the sight of His angels" (Rev. 3:5). I do not touch on the white garment here because below, in the final chapter of this book, we will have an opportunity to talk about it at greater length. But the charm of the content as well as its difficulty induce me to deal a little more fully with the Book of Life.

It long ago became customary, and even today is normal, to write down, in books, as a memorial of some accomplishment, the names of those elected to some dignity or office. This is why Roman senators were popularly called *Patres Conscripti*,[59] and soldiers are described as "enrolled." Therefore, in the Holy Scriptures, a book is ἀνθρωποπαθῶς[60] ascribed to God Himself. The names of His elect are said to be in this book. Thus, Paul mentions Clement together with his other helpers "whose names," he says, "are in the book of life" (Phil. 4:3). It is called the Book of Life, moreover, because this is the purpose for which men are elected—that is, to enjoy eternal life in heaven. But in another passage, it is named "the Lamb's book of life" (Rev. 13:8; 21:27), because Christ is the head of the elect, although He is not the head of election. And the elect are not brought to life except through His blood, that of a lamb blameless and spotless (1 Peter 1:19). Heaven is the library for this book, and therefore, we have the apostolic expression "To the general assembly and the gathering of the firstborn who are ἐν οὐρανοῖς ἀπογεγραμμένων" (Heb. 12:23).[61] However many are added to the rolls through the eternal decree of election are described as "written down in heaven."

Now in order to deal more precisely with the matter at hand, there are two things that the Spirit of Christ tells the elect about this book. The one is that their names are written in it, and the second is that, from it, they shall never be erased. Now I am not someone who thinks that any one of the elect, simply because he is regenerated and endowed with faith, is assured immediately of his election and its immutability. Nevertheless, I believe that, after several trials of one's integrity and frequent contests against spiritual

---

59. Enrolled fathers, i.e., men elected as senators whose names were then written in the register.

60. "Anthropomorphically."

61. "Written down in heaven."

enemies—undertaken and completed successfully—victors seldom attain a πληροφορία,[62] yet they definitely get that certainty that I have explained. The Lord discusses the first of these with the seventy disciples in the gospel of Luke: "Do not rejoice about this, that spirits submit to you. But rather rejoice that your names are written in heaven" (10:20). For if this had not been the case, after the demons had been cast out, the seventy would have themselves been cast among the demons, according to this statement: "Whoever was not found written in the book of life was cast into the lake of fire" (Rev. 20:15). The second one is treated here in the Lord's letter to the members of the church at Sardis. Here it is more than hinted that the eternal decree of election can never be revoked, and that the Book of Life is entirely unable to suffer erasure, much less that its roll could be purged. Augustine, in his commentary on a passage of the psalmist, says, "I grant that names can be blotted out of the book of the living. Brothers, we must not accept the idea that God would erase whomever He has enrolled in the Book of Life. If a man said, 'What I have written stands,' does God write down anyone's name and then erase it?"[63]

§ 10. But the recent author of *Redemption Redeemed* approved of none of these conclusions. So then, if you don't mind, I will subject one or two paragraphs of his work to an examination.[64] This is from a passage where he produces different kinds of exceptions and then argues for them. But if I understand the argument at all, his exceptions are decidedly invalid. First, he struggles to prove that it is not an unworthy act for God to erase someone whom He had inscribed in the book. This is because, when Moses says, "Erase me from the book You have written," the Lord replies, "I will erase him who has sinned" (Exod. 32:32–33). I reply that no matter this argument's meaning, it has no bearing on the case. For the book that Moses mentions here is very different from what we are presently discussing. Allow me to illustrate. Because life is taken in three ways—*naturally, spiritually,* and *eternally*—it will accord with the sacred text to assign a threefold meaning to the Book of Life as well: what is physical, what is ecclesiastical, and what belongs to the Lamb. The physical book is the one that contains a list of those who enjoy temporal life. Those who are destroyed by a violent or premature death are erased from it. The ecclesiastical book contains a record of those who are members of the visible church, inasmuch as they are leading a spiritual life, whether they do so truly or merely in appearance.

---

62. "Full assurance."

63. In Psalm. 68.] Augustine, *Psalmi Enarratio*, sub loc. Ps. 68:29 (2.13).

64. *I. G.* Ἀπολύτρωσ. cap. 13. § 31.] Goodwin, *Apolytrōsis Apolytrōseōs*, ch. 13, sec. 31, pp. 332–33.

The Lamb's Book is the one I have described above. I think that the psalmist mentioned the first book when he said, in Fischer's version, "My bones were not hidden from You when I was made in the secret place. I was knit together very skillfully in the earth's deepest places. Your eyes beheld me as an embryo, and in Your book were written all these things, when none of them yet existed" (Ps. 139:15–16).[65] The prophets discuss the second book. Isaiah: "And it shall come to pass that whoever is left in Zion and as Jerusalem's remainder shall be called holy" (Isa. 4:3). Ezekiel: "My hand will be against all the prophets who make allowance for vanity and who divine lies. They shall not participate in the assembly of My people and shall not be enrolled in the register of the house of Israel" (Ezek. 13:9). Or, as another translator takes it: "They shall not be written in the scripture of Israel." David writes, "Let them be blotted out of the book of the living and not enrolled with the righteous" [Ps. 69:29]. Zanchi comments:

> The list of those who profess Christ is called the Book of Life and of the Living. Those called and elected to eternal life are counted in the church's number. "Let them be deleted from the book etc.," means, "O God, blot out their hypocrisy and cause them to be known for what they are. Erase them from the list of saints who are in the church."

These are his remarks.[66] The passages of Revelation I cited just a moment ago mention the third book.

Now I maintain that we must understand erasure from the book as referring to the physical or ecclesiastical book, but never the Lamb's Book, whenever anyone is described as erased from the Book of Life. Judas, Arius, and Julian[67] were erased, and so were others, from each of the first two books. But no mortal was ever erased, or could be, from the last book. Clearly Moses's vow was not aimed at the idea that he should be deprived of eternal life in exchange for the salvation of his countrymen. Instead, its point was that he would rather undergo a temporal death, even a very bitter one, rather than all of them perishing.

§ 11. But one can use the context to support this position. The Israelite people, while Aaron assisted as midwife, gave birth to the most heinous idolatry. God avenged this idolatry the day before Moses took this oath: he unsheathed a sword to slay three thousand men in one day (Exod. 32:28). To prevent the erasure of the whole nation by a similar disaster, their leader

---

65. Piscator, *Psalmorum Versio Nova*, in *In Librum Psalmorum Commentarius* (Herborn, 1611), sub loc. Ps. 139:15–16, p. 913.

66. De Natur. Dei, l. 5. c. 3. col. 583.] Zanchi, *De Natura Dei*, in *Omnium operum Theologicorum*, vol. 2 (Geneva, 1619), bk. 5, ch. 3, p. 583.

67. I.e., Julian the Apostate, r. AD 361–363, Roman emperor.

prayed and offered himself to die instead. He surrenders to any kind of disgraceful death when he says, "Blot me out of Your book You have written" (Exod. 32:32). He means, of course, the physical book. But the Lord said no. "I will blot out of My book those who have sinned," but not you who have shown that you are innocent of the guilt of idolatry (Exod. 32:33).

Next, one can argue from the absurd conclusion that burdens the opposite position. Truth Himself once said, "No greater love has anyone than this, that he lay down his own life for his friends" (John 15:13). Clearly this has reference to undergoing temporal death in their place. But if Moses were permitted to submit to eternal destruction to gain salvation for the Jews, it would follow that, in this, a greater love than the greatest had been found. Finally, we have an example from Paul's corresponding vow, which is as follows: "I should hope that I myself were anathema to Christ for my brothers, my kinsmen according to the flesh" (Rom. 9:3). If Paul, as he made this vow, restrained himself within the confines of temporal evils, we cannot believe that Moses surpassed them. For love under the gospel was more intense than under the law. Of the ancient commentators, Jerome says,

> If we consider that Moses's speech petitioned God on behalf of the Jewish people, saying, "If You forgive them their sin, forgive it. But if You are unwilling to do so, blot me out of the book You have written," then we will notice that Moses and Paul had the same feeling toward the flock that was entrusted to them. For the good shepherd lays down his life for his sheep. This means, "I prefer to be cut off from Christ, and blot me out of the book You have written." Paul desires not to perish eternally but only for the moment. The Apostle wants to die in the flesh that they might be saved in the spirit, to pour out his own blood that the souls of many might be saved. We can prove, from many Old Testament citations, that *anathema* sometimes indicates physical death.

Those are his comments.[68]

But let us individually review some other, more recent writers on Paul. Among foreign authors there is John Michael Dilherr. After teaching at length that sacred objects and especially holy men—who oftentimes were signs of impending divine wrath—were termed *anathema* to lessen and avert that wrath (whether offering themselves voluntarily as victims or put to this purpose by the people as a whole), Dilherr brings in Paul as an example, as follows:

> When he wants to express to the Romans the extent of his love and the fervor of his affection toward the Jews, he uses this word *anathema* of

---

68. Epist. ad *Algusiam* quaest 9] Jerome, *Opera Divi Hieronymi Stridoniensis*, vol. 3, qu. 9 (*epistola* 151).

himself as though it were some ritual unfamiliar to them. He was implying, according to some, that he burned with so much love for the Jews
that he regarded the sum of his vow as this: for their salvation, he would
become a man set apart, or *anathema*—that is, he would purchase their
security and salvation by his own death.[69]

Among our countrymen, the very learned Hammond, in his commentaries, interpreted the phrase ἀνάθεμα εἶναι ἀπὸ τοῦ Χριστοῦ as "to be
excommunicated from the body of Christ" (which is the church) [Rom.
9:3].[70] This is how Grotius took it[71] (whom Hammond followed). He said
that ἀπὸ τοῦ Χριστοῦ means *from the church of Christ*, which is called
Christ in 1 Corinthians 12:12 and Galatians 3:27. It was a custom among
the Hebrews for wives to be called by their husbands' names (Isa. 4:1).
Hammond also argued that, in the earliest stages of the Christian church,
the close attendant of excommunication was "handing over to Satan," and
its companion, ὄλεθρον σαρκός[72]—that is, extraordinarily severe bodily
sufferings [1 Cor. 5:5]. After this, Hammond strengthened his interpretation of the Pauline passage by comparing it with a certain statement of the
martyr Ignatius in his letter to the Romans: Κόλασις του διαβόλου ἐπ᾽
ἐμέ ἐρχέσθω, μόνον ἵνα Ἰησοῦ Χριστοῦ ἐπιτύχω.[73] "Here," says Hammond, "the phrase κόλασιν τοῦ διαβόλου must not be taken in any sense
to mean *penalties of hell*, especially since they are totally incompatible. They
mean *whatever temporal punishments are inflicted by the demons leading up to
death*."[74] Examine, if you please, dear reader, the other comments he makes
about Moses and the Book of Life in the same passage. They are well worth
reading and entirely consistent with what I have written in these pages.

§ 12. The next passage quoted here is from a very well-known author.[75]
My current project here has motivated me to read him, and I have carefully examined his interpretation up to Revelation 3. The Lord, he says,
promises the church at Sardis that He was not willing to erase from the
Book of Life *him who conquers*. Therefore, this author concludes that such

---

69. Disput. Academic. Tom. 1. p. 436.] Johann (John) Michael Dilherr, 1604–1669, German Lutheran theologian and philologist, *Disputationum Academicarum* (Nuremberg, 1652),
sit. 7, p. 436.

70. Henry Hammond, 1605–1660, Church of England clergyman and theologian, perhaps *Deuterai Phrontides* (London, 1656), sub loc. Rom. 9:3.

71. Grotius, *Annotationes In Novum Testamentum*, sub loc. Rom. 9:3.

72. "Destruction of the flesh."

73. "Let the Devil's punishment come upon me, provided I can enjoy Jesus Christ."

74. H. Hammond, *Of the power of the keyes* (London, 1651), paraphrasing pp. 107–8.

75. I.e., John Goodwin.

erasure was a routine practice—or, at least, that it is possible.[76] I respond that this passage proves our point, because in it, Christ asserts that He is unwilling to erase one whom He had enrolled. Grotius appropriately notes that the phrase οὐ μὴ ἐξαλείψω τὸ ὄνομα αὐτοῦ ἐκ τῆς βίβλου τῆς ζωῆς [Rev. 3:5][77] means "He will have a right to eternal life and will perceive that within him."[78] A little bit later, moreover, there is an instance of litotes (λιτότης). Οὐ μὴ ἐξαλείψω means *I will diligently preserve.* "But," the learned Goodwin says, "it would be vain for Christ to promise what cannot happen."[79] But it is not at all in vain, because promises of this type are designed to make believers more sure of the infallibility of perseverance and to fill them with greater thankfulness for it.

Goodwin finds a third reason to disagree, claiming that our theologians

> are deceived about the concept of the Book of Life. It is nothing more than God's general intention for those who are going to be saved, not as regards their actual names, but their characteristics. And so, because they believe, for as long as they believe, they can be described as enrolled in the Book of Life and to be erased from it if ever they fall from their faith.[80]

But this, *pace* Goodwin, is not exegeting Scripture but doing away with it altogether. For the enrolling of the names very clearly indicates election of persons—I mean, of individual persons, and *qua* persons at that—not merely as someone endowed with a particular characteristic. Surely ὀνόματα (Num. 1:2)[81] in the sacred literature very often is taken for persons: κατ᾽ ἀριθμὸν ὀνομάτων (Acts 1:15; Rev. 3:4; 11:13)[82]—that is, of persons. And it is taken like this many times elsewhere.

Goodwin finds a fourth exception to the whole argument our theologians routinely advance from the Book of Life. With some confidence he asserts that "this is more a matter of the exterior than of the heart."[83] My retort to his witty remark should make him suffer a bit: clearly it is the mark of unique giftedness to laugh at what you cannot solve.

---

76. Grotius, *Annotationes In Novum Testamentum*, sub loc. Rev. 3:5.

77. "I will not erase his name from the book of life."

78. Annot. posthum. ad Apocal. 3.5.] Grotius, *Annotationes In Novum Testamentum*, sub loc. Rev. 3:5.

79. Goodwin, *Apolytrōsis Apolytrōseōs*, ch. 13, sec. 31, p. 332. This seems to be from Goodwin: "He clearly supposeth, that there were, or at least, might be, some, whose Names he would blot out of this Book: otherwise it would be no matter of honor, or specialty of priviledge, which He promiseth herein."

80. Goodwin, *Apolytrōsis Apolytrōseōs*, ch. 13, sec. 31, pp. 332–33.

81. "Names."

82. "According to the number of the names."

83. Goodwin, *Redemption Redeemed*, ch. 13, sec. 31, p. 333.

§ 13. That same learned man in another passage argues using the example of the traitor Judas. "Although he was at one time counted among the elect, he turned out to be a son of perdition, and so he was erased from the Book of Life,"[84] even from the one that I called the Lamb's Book. Goodwin concludes that Judas was among the elect from the fact that the statement was made to Judas, just the same as to the other apostles, that a throne had been prepared for him. "Truly I say to you who have followed me that at the renewal, when the Son of Man sits on His throne in glory, you will also sit on twelve thrones, exercising judgment over the twelve tribes of Israel" (Matt. 19:28). Notice that there are twelve thrones, so not even one is missing for someone to sit on. I will dodge his sword thrust if I am able. And I think I can do so if I deny that these thrones signify the prize of eternal life, because the Savior only means that it will come to pass that, in that day, the tribes of Israel will be judged by what the twelve apostles preached in Judea. For in this precise sense, and no other, will the apostles be judges. Yet because the things Judas taught were identical to and just as sound as the other apostles' lessons, so then Judas was also assigned a throne. But this was only as regarded his doctrine, not his person. Johannes Gerhard says that "we must carefully note that this promise takes into account not so much the persons as the apostolic office."[85]

But to lend my opponents a somewhat sharper weapon—one that Goodwin himself does not wrest from this passage—the statement coming from the Savior's mouth in the evangelist Luke strikes a more forceful blow. Something more complete is promised here. It indicates an assured, heavenly glory, and it belongs only to those we call the elect. These are Christ's words: "You are they who have remained with Me in my temptations. But I covenant with you a kingdom, just as My Father covenanted with Me, that you may eat and drink at My table and sit upon thrones, judging over the twelve tribes of Israel" (Luke 22:28–30). Note that, in addition to thrones, there is a kingdom, and there is reclining at table with Christ the Lord in that kingdom. But I answer that we should not understand Judas as included here. There is no mention of the whole number, as there was in the previous passage I cited, where Christ discusses twelve thrones. Here the only specific statement he makes is, "You will sit upon thrones." The promise does not apply to all the apostles but only to those who had remained with Christ in His temptations. That wretched man did not do so. For at the very moment these comments were made, Judas had agreed to betray Him. In fact, if one consults the sequence of the gospel history, I believe it

---

84. Ἀπολύτρωσ., cap. 14 § 15. & cap. 15 § 9.] Goodwin, *Redemption Redeemed*, ch. 14, sec. 15, p. 361; ch. 15, sec. 9. pp. 373–74.

85. Harmon Evang c. 173.] Gerhard, *In Harmoniam Historiae Evangelicae.*

is evident that Judas was not present when Christ made these comments. The Lord had said a little bit before in verse 21, as is obvious from verse 22 of the same chapter of Luke, "Behold the hand of the one who betrays Me is with Me at the table." At that moment, moreover, the little piece of bread was offered to Judas. When he had taken it, "he immediately went out," as John records (John 13:30). If Judas's departure took place before those words were said (it is extremely likely that is how it happened), then Christ's promise applies only to the eleven who were present, not to Judas who had left. So that no one thinks I am alone in this interpretation, allow me to cite a fairly respectable writer from among the Romanists. I am referring to Martin Eisengrein, who first said, "Christ the Lord revealed to His disciples that they were elect and that, after this life, they would receive the gift of eternal happiness, when He said to them, 'Rejoice because your names are written in heaven.'" Then he adds, "He also revealed this to the apostles specifically when Judas was no longer with them. He promised them the Holy Spirit to abide with them forever. And likewise, when He said to them, 'You are the ones who have remained with Me in My temptations,' and, 'I am preparing for you a kingdom, just as My Father prepared one for Me.'"[86]

§ 14. We have not yet completely finished explaining the whole reward that Christ the Lord promised to the members of the church at Sardis, provided they showed themselves victors. There is still one final short clause to unpack as briefly as possible: καὶ ἐξομολογήσομαι τὸ ὄνομα αὐτοῦ ἐνώπιον τοῦ πατρός μου, καὶ ἐνώπιον τῶν ἀγγέλων αὐτοῦ [Rev. 3:5].[87]

The words ὁμολογεῖν and ὁμολογεῖσθαι represent two different actions. The first one means *acknowledgment*, as Beza explains when he comments on Christ's statement in Matthew, Πᾶς ὅστις ὁμολογήσει ἐν ἐμοὶ ἔμπροσθεν τῶν ἀνθρώπων, ὁμολογήσω κἀγὼ ἐν αὐτῷ ἔμπροσθεν τοῦ Πατρός μου, τοῦ ἐν οὐρανοῖς (Matt. 10:32).[88] Beza renders his own translation and then defends it like this: *Quisquis agnoscet me coram hominibus, agnoscam & ego eum coram Patre meo qui est in coelis.*[89] The second word means *commendation*, a meaning the Apostle uses in Hebrews. "Through Him let us ceaselessly raise to God a sacrifice of praise"—namely, καρπὸν

---

86. De certitud. gratiae tractat. Apologetic. p. 139. & 140.] Eisengrein, *De Certitudine Gratiae*, pp. 139, 140.

87. "And I will confess His name before My Father and before His angels."

88. "Whosoever acknowledges Me before men, him I will acknowledge before My Father in heaven."

89. Beza, *Annotationes Maiores*, sub loc. Matt. 10:32.

χειλέων ὁμολογούντων τῷ ὀνόματι αὐτοῦ ("the fruit of lips that extol his name"; Heb. 13:15).

The saints offer each of these actions to Christ. The first one is found in Song of Songs, where the bride, after a metaphorical description of Christ is given, immediately shouts, "He is my delight and my friend, O daughters of Jerusalem" (Song 5:16). The second one is found in Revelation, where the four living creatures and the twenty-four elders fall down before the face of the Lamb and sing a new song, saying, "You are worthy to take the scroll and to open its seals because You were slain, and You have redeemed us for God through Your blood, from every tribe, tongue, people, and nation. And You have made us to be kings and priests to our God, and we will reign on earth" (Rev. 5:8–10). Christ will give both of these as a reward at the last day to those who conquer. Yes, He will not only acknowledge them and name them the blessed ones of His father but will add in words of praise in addition, saying, "You fed Me when I was hungry; you gave Me drink when I was thirsty; I was a stranger, and you took Me in; I was naked, and you clothed Me; I was sick, and you visited Me; I was in prison, and you came to Me" (Matt. 25:34–36). In that very same chapter, we find the happy statement, "Well done, good and faithful servant" (Matt. 25:21). To receive praise from those who have been praised, and in the presence of those who are about to be praised, this is really genuine praise. This will come to us from the Lord Jesus and occur "in the presence of the Father and His angels." Plutarch tells us that Themistocles arrived at the stadium while the Olympic Games were underway. The spectators ignored the competitors and extolled Themistocles alone. For a whole day, they kept their eyes fixed on him. He became so filled with joy that he said to his friends, "I have received enough reward for the suffering I endured for Greece."[90] Will the Christian regret that he struggled to the point of sweat—no, to the point of shedding his blood—when, in that great assembly of angels and the elect, he will realize that everyone has acknowledged him, everyone has accepted him? The same very famous writer tells us that Alexander proclaimed that Achilles was blessed "because while he was alive, he found a faithful friend," meaning Patroclus. "And after he died, he found a great spokesman for his deeds"—namely, Homer.[91] O Christian, you who have God as your friend, who will someday enjoy Christ as the herald of your praises, how blessed you are! Another leading spokesman among the pagans held that

---

90. *Plutarch.* in *Themistocle.*] Plutarch, *Themistocles*, in *Omnium Quae Exstant*, vol. 1 (Frankfurt, 1620).

91. Id. in *Alexandro.*] Plutarch, *Alexander*, in *Omnium Quae Exstant*, vol. 1 (Frankfurt, 1620).

this was the best kind of prayer: "While I am living, I want others to find me acceptable, and when dead, I want to be praised."[92] I salute you, soldier of Jesus, for your courage (or, rather, for the courage of the one whose soldier you call yourself). Go on boldly to the final victory, and surely the Lord Himself will praise you at the final judgment with higher acclaim.

---

92. This statement is attributed to Piscennius Niger, r. 193–194, Roman Emperor, from *Scriptores Historiae Augustae*, 11.

CHAPTER III

An Explanation of Some Apostolic Ἐπινίκια[1]

Sections 1–2: The first ἐπινίκιον[2] is taken from Romans 8. An exposition of the clauses in verses 35 and 37, particularly of the verb ὑπερνικῶμεν. Sections 3–4: Election and justification are laid down as the two foundations of Christian victory from God's perspective, and we inquire in passing whether the elect are actually justified from eternity. Section 5: The foundations of that same victory on the part of Christ are laid down—that is, His death, resurrection, session at the right hand of the Father, and intercession. Section 6: An explanation of the present feeling of divine love on the part of believers as plainly shown by the trials of Paul, Arnolph, and Pomponius Algerius. Sections 7–8: The sure conviction of future love. The treatment of this theme in the last two verses of Romans 8 raises the question, first, What is the love of God in Christ Jesus? and second, Who are the persons or the things in that passage whose authority to separate the elect from that love has been removed? Section 9: The second ἐπινίκιον is in 1 Corinthians 15 near the end. The discussion of the identity of death and hell. Section 10: What it means that sin is called death's sting, and the law, sin's power. Section 11: Our victory over death through Christ. The examples of Gerard (Bernard's brother) and Wolfgang Musculus. Section 12: Hell, which is opposed to ψυχοπαννυχία.[3] A successful defense of the parable in Luke 16. Section 13: Censure of Castellio and commendation of Spanheim. Section 14: The law. An exegesis of Colossians 2:13–14. Section 15: The third ἐπινίκιον is taken from 2 Timothy 4:6–8. What the Pauline expression σπένδομαι[4] means there and in Philippians 2:17. The meaning of ἀνάλυσις. Euphemisms for death. Sections 16–17: What the phrases τὸν καλὸν ἀγῶνα ἀγωνίζεσθαι, δρόμον τελεῖν, and πίστιν τηρεῖν mean in the Timothy passage.[5] What the phrase τρέχειν ὡς οὐκ ἀδήλως[6] means in 1 Corinthians 9:26. What

---

1. "Victory-hymns."
2. "Victory hymn."
3. "Soul-sleep."
4. "I am poured out as a drink offering."
5. "Fight the good fight," "finish the race," and "keep the faith."
6. "Run not aimlessly."

ὄγκον *and* εὐπερίστατον ἁμαρτίαν[7] *mean in Hebrews 12:1. Section 18: Why the heavenly prize, the crown, has a name inscribed on it. Sections 19–20: Christ's righteousness by which we obtain the crown for us, and God's righteousness that bestows that crown upon us. Section 21: Where this crown is stored for believers and whether it can be lost. A careful examination of Revelation 3:11.*

§ 1. The ἐπινίκια[8] found in the Old Testament generally apply to political and external victories. Those in the New Testament are spiritual. I intend to select some of these from Paul's letters and, by explaining them, try to illustrate more clearly their main purpose. I gladly begin with this, because in the very last section of chapter 8, Paul sets out for us an incredibly extensive victory hymn of the saints, together with the same hymn's foundations resting partly on God, partly on Christ, and partly on believers. The words themselves sound the victory note right at the beginning: Ἐν τούτοις πᾶσιν ὑπερνικῶμεν ("In all these things we are more than conquerors"; Rom. 8:37).

Here the context is the sufferings that just a little before Paul had listed like this: affliction, hardship, persecution, hunger, nakedness, danger, and death (Rom. 8:35). Sometimes all of these threats were piled up on the heads of the same Christians because of the tyrants that raged against the church in her infancy. Just as grains of wheat are crushed by repeated blows during threshing, so Christians were pummeled by these increased afflictions. This is what θλῖψις means [Acts 14:22]. They were squeezed into such a tight spot that they did not know how to even turn around. This is the meaning of στενοχωρία [2 Cor. 6:4]. And yet they were forced to turn around. According to Fischer, this is the meaning of διωγμός in this passage. It refers to the tyrannical violence of men who drove the righteous into exile so that they did not even have any place to rest. Now found in exile, they suffered famine with nakedness and, from this, danger.[9] Finally, they were struck with the sword, as the passage cited from the psalm shows: "For your sake we are killed all day long; we are counted as sheep destined for slaughter" (Rom. 8:36).

[**§ 2.**] Paul does not merely say νικῶμεν[10] but ὑπερνικῶμεν,[11] we are more than conquerors. That is, we overcome in a spectacular or impressive fash-

---

7. "Weight" and "entangling sin."

8. "Victory-hymns."

9. Piscator, *Epistolae Pauli Ad Romanos*, sub loc. Rom. 8:35.

10. "We conquer."

11. "We more than conquer."

ion. Or, as Cyprian once translated it, we "superconquer."[12] This means the following:

First, we overcome our butchers even while dying. Commonly in battle, it is not the victors but the vanquished whose casualties are counted up. The Apostle here in one breath, so to speak, says θανατούμεθα and ὑπερνικῶμεν, "we are put to death" and "we more than conquer." Lactantius writes, "Our children and little wives (to say nothing of the men) silently overcome their torturers; and not even fire can wring from them a groan."[13] And Cyprian says, "It turns out a woman is braver than the men torturing her."[14] And in another passage: "The tortured stood there with more bravery than those torturing them. Their whipped and torn limbs conquered the instruments of torture that whipped and tore at them."[15] But I think hardly anything else in this category is more famous than what Gregory Nazianzus recorded about an old man named Marcus Arethusius.[16] Nazianzus described him as he suffered under Julian:

> He was superior to those who imprisoned him and, thus, indifferent to his pains and troubles. Really, it was as if he were simply observing someone else's ruin and as if he considered the torment a parade, not a disaster. As he watched, the man holding the office of lieutenant[17] could not bear the increased torture and how the man endured it. He supposedly spoke freely to his commander, "Are we not ashamed, commander, to be so inferior to all these Christians that we cannot even overcome one old man who has undergone every kind of torture device? Isn't it an outright disaster that we should leave, defeated by someone so inconsequential and undistinguished?"[18]

Second, victors escape without any notable loss. Sometimes in common military life, an insignificant victory comes at a great cost. After King Pyrrhus of Epirus[19] defeated the Roman army with immense loss to his own troops, he reportedly said to someone congratulating him on the outcome, "Yes, we have won. But if we gain another such victory, we will be

---

12. *Supervincimus.*

13. Lib. 5. c. 13.] Lactantius, *Divinarum Institutionum*, 5.13, p. 334.

14. De habitu virgin.] Cyprian, *De Habitu Virginum*, in *Opera* (Basel, 1558), p. 107 (*tractatus* 2).

15. De Lapsis.] Cyprian, *Martyribus Et Confessoribus*, in *Opera* (Basel, 1558), p. 43 (*epistola* 6).

16. Marcus Arethusius, fl. AD 359, Christian author and martyr.

17. *Hyparchi.*

18. Orat. adversus. *Julian.* 1. p. 89. & 90.] Gregory Nazianzus, *Adversus Iulianum*, pp. 89, 90 (*oratio* 3).

19. Pyrrhus, 319–272 BC, r. 307–302 BC, 297–272 BC, king of Epirus.

wiped out completely."[20] Christian soldiers are not the true, genuine vintage unless they suffer the same loss, toiling under the cross as gold does in a furnace. It only destroys the dross. Or we could say they suffer the same as the natural body after the proper application of purgatives, as these only destroy noxious humors. The prophet bears witness to this when he says of the cross of God's people, "Jacob's wickedness is atoned for by this, and this is its whole fruit: to remove his sin" (Isa. 27:9).

Third, after winning, the victors profit handsomely and generally return loaded with extravagant plunder. These, of course, are holiness and righteousness, as the Apostle states with great brilliance: "God disciplines us for our own good so that we might become sharers in His holiness. But every discipline for the moment does not seem like joy, but sorrow. Yet later it reaps a peaceful harvest of righteousness for those trained by it" (Heb. 12:10–11). The final words here are ὕστερον δὲ καρπὸν εἰρηνικὸν τοῖς δι᾽ αὐτῆς γεγυμνασμένοις ἀποδίδωσι δικαιοσύνης ("Later it reaps a peaceful harvest of righteousness for those trained by it" [Heb. 12:11]). These words had so great an effect on Peter Faber[21]—a man of consummate skill in all those allusions in sacred Scripture and anywhere else that deal with physical training—that he conjectured it is referenced here also. Crowns were usually fashioned from the wild olive tree and bestowed on victors in the Olympic Games. The olive was understood as a symbol of peace, which is the source of Vergil's well-known line,

> The branch by hand he now extends of peaceful olive fair.[22]

Faber says, "From these preliminary comments, I have absolutely no doubt that the blessed Paul understood by the word *olive crown* the peaceful harvest prepared for those trained in athletics (the subject he had previously discussed). And he intended to apply this concept to eternal rewards in Hebrews 12."[23]

§ 3. The foundations of this incredibly extensive victory are built, for God's part, upon two things: election and justification. "Who will bring charges against God's elect. It is God who justifies" (Rom. 8:33). The bringing of charges (specifically called διαβάλλειν) was and is a major part of the Devil's scheme. Our countryman Jewel, right near the beginning of his "gem-encrusted" *Defense*, notes that "we can scarcely find any period in all

---

20. Plutarch, *Pyrrhus*, in *Omnium Quae Exstant*, vol. 1 (Frankfurt, 1620).

21. Pierre Favre (Peter Faber), 1506–1546, cofounder of the Jesuits.

22. Aeneid. 8.] Vergil, *Aeneidos*, bk. 8 (line 116).

23. *Pet. Fabri* Agonistic. l. 2. cap. 22. p. 182.] Faber, *Agonisticon* (Lyon, 1592), bk. 2, ch. 22, p. 182.

previous history, when the faith began to grow, when it was established, or when it was reborn, that men did not treat truth and integrity with despicable, excessive scorn."[24]

Then a little bit later, he writes,

> Who is ignorant of the reproaches hurled at our fathers when they first began to acknowledge and profess Christ's name? That they were "conspiring against the state and launching secret plans," and that this is why they met in darkness in the early morning hours? That they "murdered babies, feasted on human flesh, and drank human blood in a savage ritual, etc."?[25]

There is hardly any more ready antidote for accusations like this than to remember our election and justification. This is why in Zechariah the Lord raised up Joshua as a priest when Satan stood at his right hand as an accuser. In rebuking the Devil, he very pointedly mentions election. "Jehovah rebuke you, O Satan, Jehovah who has chosen Jerusalem rebuke you" (Zech. 3:1–2). In a similar fashion, Tertullian mentions our justification at the very end of his *Defense of Christians against the Gentiles*. These are the closing words: "Although you condemn us, God forgives us."[26]

§4. But to humor here a little the cause of contentious theology, I note that some men conclude from the passage in Romans, which states that God justifies the elect, that they are justified when they are elected. And they hold that justification occurs at the same time as election, which they acknowledge is eternal. Because this controversy today has caused much trouble among our theologians, it will not be superfluous to append here a short digression on this question: Are the elect actually justified from eternity?

Let this be our first thesis: God's eternal design in deciding to justify this man or that should not be taken as actual justification, no more than His plan to create the world can be called creation or His plan to send Christ in the flesh can be called the incarnation.

Second thesis: every elect person can undergo justification in two ways conceptually, and actual justification applies to that person in both respects. The first respect is that which refers to the person they all hold in common—that is, Christ, who is the head of the elect and their surety. And so all those whom the Father had given to His Son from eternity would seem to have acquired justification, and in fact actual justification, when Christ Himself was justified in the Spirit—that is, when He rose from the dead and was released from all the guilt that He carried as our bond and bail. "Christ is

---

24. Jewel, *A defence of the Apologie of the Churche of Englande*, ch. 1, div. 1, p. 4.
25. Jewel, *A defence*, ch. 1, div. 1, p. 5.
26. Tertullian, *Apologeticus*, ch. 50.

called justified," Parker says, "when He rose again, 1 Timothy 3:16. And we were justified in His rising again, Romans 4:25, because that loosening—that is, the Father's resuscitating Him—was actual justification. He was released from the sins of others for whom He had made satisfaction. But we were released from the particular sins for which Christ gave Himself as collateral."[27]

Third thesis: the second respect is the one that refers to the individual person. And so a twofold, actual justification attaches to every individual elect person: one declarative and the other formal. Declarative justification is defined as that by which the elect are justified, whether in the court of the world before men or in the court of conscience before themselves. Formal justification is defined as that by which the elect are justified in the court of heaven before God.

Fourth thesis: this thesis has to be understood in terms of the recently posed question, according to the rule of the Scholastics: *An analogy taken by itself is understood in terms of the most important thing to which it is analogous.* Now the most important sense is the one that Paul shows in his letters to the Romans and Galatians, where he argues beyond any doubt that a sinner's formal justification is through and because of Christ, who was received by faith. He is not talking about declarative justification, because what takes place in the court of the world is before men, and it is by works and not by faith. The justification that takes place in the courtroom of the conscience is not so much before God as it is before ourselves.

After dispensing with these appetizers, such as they are, I now assert a little more boldly that the elect are actually justified not from eternity but in time. The following are my reasons. First reason: formal justification happens by faith. "And we believe in Jesus Christ," says the Apostle, "that we may be justified through faith in Christ" (Gal. 2:16). And so faith precedes justification, which is the major part of sanctification. But all admit that justification is latent in the rational creature as it now actually exists. For however the object suffices for election in the known being, nevertheless, the object is required for sanctification in the physical being just the same as in the known one.

Second reason: the elect are actually justified not from eternity but in time, because justification, in the order of nature, follows effectual calling, just as Paul testifies in this very passage where he takes great pains, as it were, to assign its own natural order to supernatural blessings. "Whom He

______

27. De descensu ad inferos lib. 3. § 30 p. 59.] Hugh Sanford, d. 1607, English servant of the earl of Pembroke, *De Descensu Domini Nostri* (Amsterdam, 1611), bk. 3, sec. 30, p. 59. Probably Robert Parker, 1564–1614, Puritan theologian. Parker seems to be the coauthor of the work cited along with Sanford.

predestined, these He also called. Whom He called, these He also justified. Whom He justified, these He also glorified" (Rom. 8:30). Now in point of fact, nobody would say that effectual calling is measured by eternity, but by time, in keeping with this statement: "I have heard you in a favorable time, and in the day of salvation I came to help you. Behold, now is the acceptable time; behold, now is the day of salvation" (2 Cor. 6:2).

Third reason: no transient action[28] exists from eternity. This is the way in which it differs from something immanent. Justification is a transient action of God. Here I call my countryman Wotton as witness:

> We must understand that of all God's actions pertaining to our salvation, predestination is the one immanent action in God. The other actions—justification, sanctification, adoption, and the redemption that encompasses almost all of these—are numbered among God's transient actions. For all of these individually assume something that is physical, or at least moral, and this would have been justified, adopted, and redeemed. But in the case of predestination, in the schools it is a truism that it supposes nothing in the one predestined.[29]

Fourth reason: if justification were from eternity, then all the elect would be justified at one and the same time. This is because in eternity, there is no prior and posterior. But we know that one man was justified earlier, and another man later. He who is "in Christ" before another man is justified before another man. Unquestionably, being "in Christ" means becoming a partaker in that righteousness by which we are considered just, as is evident from Romans 5. The Apostle, moreover, says of Andronicus and Junia οἳ καὶ πρὸ ἐμοῦ γεγόνασιν ἐν Χριστῷ (Rom. 16:7).[30]

§5. The foundations from the perspective of Christ that have been established are reviewed in verse 34 of the same chapter: "Who is it that condemns? Christ is the one who was dead, in fact, who also rose again, who is at the right hand of God, who also intercedes for us" [Rom. 8:34]. There are four important points here.

First: Christ's death. As it has great power to overcome other disasters mentioned elsewhere, so it does with respect to the one specifically mentioned here. As the waters of Marah turned sweet when wood was added [Exod. 15:22–26], so through the wood of the cross, our most bitter sufferings become sweet. The cross of Christ, laid hold of by faith, swallows

---

28. In Thomistic metaphysics, a distinction is drawn between God's immanent and transient *actiones*.

29. De Reconcil. peccator. part. 1. lib. 1. c. 3. § 12. & 16.] Wotton, *De Reconciliatione Peccatoris*, part 1, bk. 1, ch. 3, sec. 12, p. 11.

30. "Were in Christ before me."

up our crosses just like Aaron's staff easily devoured the sorcerers' [Exod. 7:12]. Notice please, reader, the remarks I made on this subject in book II, chapter VI, paragraph 6.

Second: Christ's resurrection. In many different instances, the sacred Scriptures make His resurrection the prototype and earnest of our own resurrection from the miseries that usually assail the church. Two passages in particular make this clear. The first is from Hosea: "Come, let us return to Jehovah. He Himself will restore us to life after two days" (Hos. 6:1–2). This means, as van den Driesche interprets it, "You will call us back from death's disasters to a pleasant and peaceful life, free from all troubles."[31] "On the third day He will raise us up, and we shall live in His presence" [Hos. 6:2]. Some interpreters philosophize at length about the third day, when the wounds of the injured generally start to hurt the most. An example is the men of Shechem after their foreskins were removed (Gen. 34:25). Doctors call the third day the critical day, when those struggling with disease start to pray for their recovery to begin. But the prophetic reference rises up higher and points to the Messiah's coming resurrection on the third day. The stone the Jews rolled in place could not prevent it, nor the seal placed on the tomb and the guard detachment keeping vigil. Similarly, after a short period of time, after maybe a day or two, the church will rise again from the tomb of her calamities. Another prophet represents the church talking about this: "Do not triumph over me, my enemy. Because though I die, I shall rise again. Though I sit in shadows, the Lord shall be my light" (Mic. 7:8).

The second passage which makes this clear occurs in Revelation, in a discussion of the witnesses that were cut off: "After three and a half days, the living Spirit of God entered them, and they stood upon their own feet. And great fear came upon all who saw them" (Rev. 11:11). There is absolutely no doubt that this is a reference to Christ's death and resurrection:

> His death is calculated to have lasted for three days, with portions of the days included by synecdoche. If the night in which He was captured and betrayed to the Jews is added to the total, then one will be able to reach the sum of three and a half days. Then when He was restored to life by the Spirit, the Lord frightened the guards at his tomb, etc. Because His vivification is the source of each of ours, the prophet took these words and adapted them for his purpose.

These are Clüver's comments in his *Apocalyptic Dawn.*[32]

---

31. Drusius, *Commentarius In Prophetas Minores*, sub loc. Hos. 6:2.

32. Tom. 3. p. 61.] Clüver, *Diluculum Apocalypticum*, vol. 3 (Lübeck, 1647), pp. 60–61.

Third: Christ's session at the right hand of God. Because it is at the right hand and identified as the power of God in the Evangelist (Luke 22:69) and as the majesty of God in the Apostle (Heb. 1:3), this proves that Christ was sitting there with an equally extensive majesty and authority. This majesty and authority is more than enough to protect His dependents and to shatter His church's enemies. I would like to compare here the first verse of Psalm 110, "The Lord said to my Lord, sit at My right hand until I make Your enemies a footstool for Your feet" [Ps. 110:1], with verse five of the same hymn, "The Lord sits at Your right hand, smashing kings on the day of His wrath." It should also be taken with the last and second to last verse of Psalm 109: "I will earnestly praise Jehovah with my mouth, and in the midst of the assembly I will extol Him. Because He stands at the right hand of the one in need to preserve him from those who would take his life" [Ps. 109:30–31]. Whoever you are, poor in spirit, Christian soldier, although Satan may stand at your right hand as he once stood at the right hand of the high priest (Zech. 3:1), because the one who sits at the right hand of God condescends to stand at the right hand of the one in need, you must be of good cheer. All things shall remain safe, and you as victor shall at last sit on Christ's throne as He Himself has promised, saying, "Whoever overcomes, to him I will grant to sit with Me on My throne, just as I have conquered, and I sit with My Father on His throne" (Rev. 3:21).

This reminds me of a particularly noble deed of Alexander the Great. When his army (as Curtius tells us) was wandering through the woods almost frozen solid from the cold, and exhausted bodies lay strewn on the ground here and there, by chance a rank-and-file soldier named Macedo finally reached the camp, barely supporting himself and his weapons. The king saw him, and although at that very moment he was trying to keep his own limbs warm by sitting near the fire, he jumped from his seat and ordered the numb and almost senseless soldier to take off his equipment and sit in his own chair. Macedo for a long time did not know where he was resting nor who had welcomed him. After finally recovering warmth, when he saw the royal chair and the king, he jumped up in terror. Alexander looked at him and said, "Do you understand, soldier, how much better your condition is than what the Persians enjoy under their king? It would mean death for them to sit on the king's throne. For you, it was salvation."[33] Surely, we will find it just as much a cause of honor as it is our salvation to sit on the throne of Christ.

Fourth: Christ the Savior's intercession with the Father. If Queen Esther's intervention successfully repelled from the heads of all those people

---

33. Curtius, *De Rebus Gestis Alexandri Magni*, bk. 9, pp. 282–84.

the butchery that threatened the entire Jewish nation, is there any destruction, or even harm, that the beloved Son's intercession with His Father in heaven will not deflect from the church? Christ is said "to appear for our sakes" (Heb. 9:24). Nevertheless, He did so in such a way that now nothing servile should be attributed to Him in His exalted state, now that He has put off the form of a servant. With this in mind, to prevent the reader from perhaps conceiving of Christ the Lord's intercession in some less than appropriate way, I would like to tack on here the following eight lines of verse that D'Espence quotes from the poem of a certain Hildebert:

> By this prayer on our behalf by ceaseless intercession,
> Christ prays angels' help depart, though in His deepest passion.
> What help it wins us with the Father none can truly know,
> The presence of our flesh assumed, incarnate here below.
> His pleas though silent still surpass what once the Levite prayed,
> No matter what their form or time, nor with what fervor made.
> By His prayers the Father's wrath and judgment are forgotten,
> Now recalled alone the Father's love for His begotten.[34]

§6. The foundations as concerns believers still remain, and these correspond to two main points. One is a present sense of divine love; the other, a sure conviction of future affection. We may identify the first in the very clause that contains the extensive victory: "We are more than conquerors," he says, "through Him who loved us." And in the preceding words, "Who will separate us from the love of Christ?" This means "from the love of God who loved us in Christ."

> The Apostle explained it that way in the last verse. But again, by "love" understand "the feeling of love." For we must hold to the Apostle's purpose, which is to comfort believers. Now believers only recognize consolation from God's love and that of Christ in the cross if they feel it in their hearts.

So says Fischer in his *Scholia*.[35] If this feeling is missing, we hardly—and not even hardly—overcome. But if it is there, ὑπερνικῶμεν.[36] Paul should be our example. He says, "Let us boast in trials, knowing that affliction produces perseverance; and perseverance, character; and character, hope. Hope, moreover, does not put us to shame, since the love of God has overflowed in our hearts through the Holy Spirit who has been given to us" (Rom. 5:3–5).

---

34. Digress. de Christo Mediatore p. 284.] Hildebert of Lavardin, 1056–1133, archbishop of Tours, quoted in d'Espence, *In Posteriorem Ad Timotheum*, dig. 2, ch. 8, p. 223.

35. Piscator, *Epistolae Pauli Ad Romanos*, sub loc. Rom. 8:35.

36. "We more than overcome."

After Paul, Arnulphus[37] should come forward, a man who served as a soldier of Christ around the time of Bernard. The following story is told of him in a book that describes famous men of the Cistercian order:

> He quite often suffered severe indigestion and was convulsed with a kind of stomach worm. After he had lain mute for a long time, he suddenly shouted aloud and kept repeating the same words over and over: "Everything You have said, Lord Jesus, is true." Those who stood near him began to think he was out of his mind. When Arnulph sensed that they were whispering, he said, "I am absolutely in my right mind, brothers. Therefore, I repeat what I said before: Everything that Jesus said is true." When the brothers kept asking him why he said that, Arnulphus replied, "The Lord in the gospel promises one hundred fold in this life to those who have left father, mother, and the world for Him. And He promises eternal life after this. I am now realizing the truth of this promise. The pains of this illness completely overwhelm me with their sweetness because of the increase of divine compassion that lies beneath them. Not only that, but if I am defiled by so many sins, I am awash with such great happiness in the midst of these pains, as though I am set between the anvil and the hammer. Are there any joys that the righteous and perfect will not experience to the full? Therefore, spiritual joys, even a single one, truly surpass by a hundred thousand times—even a joy grasped only by hope—all the joys of this world, and to a very great extent."[38]

Following Arnulphus, Pomponius Algerius,[39] that distinguished witness to the truth of the gospel, in the letter he wrote from the orchard of the Leonine Prison July 12, 1555, presented us with these very elegant words (the letter contains his ὑπογραφή):[40]

> What I'm about to reveal to you is unbelievable. I have found a honeycomb deep down within the "lion." Within the deepest pit, I have found a pleasant place. In the location of bitterness and death, I have found calm repose and the hope of life. In the bottomless pit, I have found happiness. Where others weep, there I have found joy. Where everyone else is afraid, there I have found strength, etc. The sweet and merciful hand of God has provided me all these things. Behold, He who was once far off from me is now with me. Him that I once in some way felt, I now more openly see. The one I sometimes spotted far off, now I embrace Him up close. I used to thirst for Him, but now He holds my hand, etc. The burning heat has become for me a cool shade. Winter is a fresh spring in the Lord. I who

---

37. Perhaps Arnolfus Lexoviensis, d. 1184.

38. Jacobus Canisius, 1584–1647, German Jesuit, hagiographer, and professor of philosophy, *Ars Artium* (Cologne, 1630), part 4, ch. 16, sec. 2, pp. 305–6.

39. Pomponius Algerius, d. 1555, Italian Protestant martyr.

40. "Signature."

do not fear the flame, shall I tremble at the burning heat? Does the one who is on fire with the love of the Lord suffer the freezing cold? Yes, this prison is a rough place for guilty men. But for me, innocent, it flows with sweet honey.[41]

§7. A little further on, in the final two, brief verses, we find these words: "For I am convinced that neither death nor life, neither angels nor principalities, nor powers, neither present, nor future, not height, nor depth, nor anything else created can separate us from the love of God that is in Christ Jesus our Lord" [Rom. 8:38–39]. I have already explained at length some of the words of this pericope in book II.IX. But I must give a complete answer to two knotty questions, to clarify everything more fully. First, What does the Apostle mean by "the love of God that is in Christ Jesus"? Here is my answer: this does not mean either the στοργή[42] by which God embraces all creatures or the φιλανθρωπία[43] by which He embraces all men. Instead, if one may speak this way, it is ἐκλεκτοφιλία[44]—that is, a specific love that the Lord exercises toward all and only those who, from all eternity past, He has given to Christ to be redeemed. So the best interpreters, like Calvin, write:

> Electing love is in Christ—that is, it is that of which Christ is the bond. For He is the beloved Son in whom the Father is well pleased. So then, if we are joined to the Father through Him, we are assured of God's unbending and unfailing goodwill toward us. Paul has established that there is a fountain of love in the Father and states that it flows from Christ to us.[45]

Cajetan writes, "In the phrase 'separate us,' the pronoun 'us' means 'the elect.' 'From the love of God' is, of course, His active love that is in Christ Jesus our Lord, as though in the mediator and executor of that very love of God toward us. So we understand that in the mystery of Jesus Himself, His work, suffering, resurrection, etc., God's love toward the elect is fulfilled."[46]

Moreover, we must know—so as not to pass over such an important idea with a lighter step than is warranted—that God's saving benefits that flow down from this love are not confined to one class. One category is that which displays the image of a fountain—namely, election. The second is the image of the smaller streams that flow forth from it. Now all these accrue to us not only in Christ but also through Christ and because

---

41. Foxe, *Actes and monuments of matters most speciall and memorable*, pp. 142–43.
42. "General affection."
43. "General love for mankind."
44. "Love for the elect."
45. Calvin, *Commentarii*, sub loc. Rom. 8:39.
46. Cajetan, *Epistolae Pauli*, fol. 31v (sub loc. Rom. 8).

of Him. This is not something one should rashly claim when it comes to election. For although we were elected in Christ as the head of the elect, nevertheless, it was not because of the merit of Christ as the foundation of election. If, however, one has in view the goal of election (i.e., the grace and glory appointed for us in that decree), then Christ must be taken as the meritorious cause. Nevertheless, insofar as one considers the action of electing, then there is no consideration of the antecedent cause but only of the consequent effect. Aquinas's formula is well known: "God desires something because of that thing, but it is not because of it that God desires something."[47] Thus, keeping in mind Aquinas's rule, we may reach the following conclusion on our subject: *God decreed from eternity to save the elect because of Christ's merit. But it was not because of Christ's merit that He so decreed from eternity.* Or we could say, *God wills grace and glory for us because of Christ, but it is not because of Christ that He so wills.* If I am not mistaken, Paul Ferry summed it up very nicely when he said in his work *The Pattern of Scholastic Orthodoxy,*

> God decreed apart from the merit of Christ to communicate His glory to us because of the merit of Christ. He did this by referring it without merit to the decree and by referring it because of merit to the act of communicating. And so Christ is the meritorious cause for God's communicating His glory in time; He is not the reason why God decreed to communicate it.[48]

But as soon as the Remonstrants hear such remarks and ones like them, they immediately start shouting that our theologians have completely excluded Christ Himself as Mediator from election (though they meanwhile seem to acknowledge election as love's first fruit). Nothing is more mistaken than this conclusion! Let us listen to some of their own representatives, for it is not fair to bury them beneath the weight of their own slanders without a hearing. Wallaeus: "Certainly no orthodox individual will ever deny that Christ's mediation, as the foundation and proximate cause of our salvation, is contained in the decree of election under salvation."[49] Ames writes: "It is false to say that we exclude consideration of Christ as mediator in men's election. It is true that we deny consideration of Christ as the meritorious cause of the actual act of election, but not as the head and source from

---

47. Thom. part. 1ª. qu. 19. artic. 5. in corp.] Aquinas, *Summa Theologiae*, in *Opera Omnia*, vol. 10 (Venice, 1593), 1.19.5.

48. Cap. 23. parag. 10.] Paul Ferry, 1591–1669, French Reformed theologian, *Specimen Orthodoxi Scholastici* (Geneva, 1616; 2nd ed., John Lambert: Leyden, 1630).

49. Respons. ad censuram *Arnoldi*, p. 552.] Walaeus, *Responsio Ad Censuram Ioannis Arnoldi Corvini*, vol. 1 (Leiden, 1625), ch. 25, p. 552.

which we will derive the blessings of election."[50] The Leyden professors say in their *Synopsis of Purer Theology*,

> Although Christ's merit is not the cause of our election, because even the very merit of Christ comes from election, nevertheless, our election was not executed with respect to Christ's future merit. This is because Christ's future merit and the whole of His mediation are among the objects of this election and, at the same time, are the foundation of all those benefits that have been appointed to us through election.[51]

Do we need any further citations? If anyone should voice the objection that our theologians—who teach that God's most simple decree is one and the same with respect to the end and the means and also that, among those means, first and foremost is the mediation of Christ our Lord (as our theologians constantly assert)—exclude Christ from election, such a person deserves to be regarded not so much as a determined disputant as an obnoxious slanderer.

§ 8. The second question to ask is this: What are those items, whether persons or things, that have been stripped of their authority to separate the elect from God's love—that is, of so corrupting and destroying them that when they have fallen from divine favor, they fall into His everlasting hatred? To be sure, all of these concepts are explained in different ways, and there are almost as many opinions as interpreters. Still, I think there will be room for me to glean a little after the very rich harvest of others.

By the word *death* it seems we can understand the greatest of all terrors. In fact, in Aristotle, the word *death* is defined as φοβερῶν φοβερώτατον,[52] and in the book of Job, "the king of terrors" (Job 18:14). By *life* we understand the greatest pleasures that the living experience and by which many are enticed. This is the way that both sacred and profane authors typically understand *to live*—namely, as substitutes for *enjoying* and *delighting in*. Paul writes, "Now we live if you stand fast in the Lord" (1 Thess. 3:8). And Martial:

> Tomorrow's life comes much too late, live today, don't hesitate.[53]

---

50. Antisynod. c. 10. parag. 4.] Ames, *Anti-synodalia Scripta* (Amsterdam, 1633), ch. 10, p. 125.

51. Disput. 24. thes. 29.] Johannes Polyander, 1568–1646, Dutch Calvinist theologian and Counterremonstrant, Rivet, Walaeus, and Thysius Sr., *Synopsis Purioris Theologiae* (Leiden, 1652), disp. 24, thes. 29, p. 282.

52. Ethic. lib. 3.] Aristotle, *Ethicorum*, 3.6. "The most frightening of fears."

53. Martial, *Epigrammata*, 1.15.

Another says, "While we still live, let us live."[54] Cajetan, in his typical way, says, "Life is the greatest thing desirable; and death, the last of all that could frighten us. These two words contain everything else that we could seek and reject."[55] By *angels* I do not think that we are to understand those blessed spirits that—as the Apostle explains—are dispatched to minister to those who will be heirs of salvation. Instead, I believe that he means the enemy spirits whose entire purpose (as Estius here notes)[56] is to separate believers in Christ from salvation. Moreover, there are very frightening attacks of the Devil, especially the ones found to be stronger than either natural emotions or carnal lusts. Nature drove David to tears and to the most bitter lamentation conceivable at the premature death of his son Absalom (2 Sam. 19). Still, Joab by his admonition pulled David back from them. The same Joab strenuously sought to restrain that same David from taking a census of the people, but to no avail. David advanced all the more aggressively toward this crime as Satan provoked him. "Satan rose up," Scripture says, "and incited David to number Israel" (1 Chron. 21:1).

Principalities (ἀρχαί) are those governmental authorities who, at the time and afterward, held sway over human affairs and, in keeping with that malevolence toward the Christian religion with which they had been endowed, tried to drive many toward apostasy, partly by slaughter, partly by deceit. The book of Revelation is testimony to this: "Behold the great red dragon that has seven heads and ten horns and, on its head, seven crowns. And its tail dragged across one third of the stars of heaven and sent them to earth" (Rev. 12:34). The Holy Spirit Himself should be His own interpreter here: "The seven heads are the seven mountains upon which the woman sits. The ten horns, moreover, are ten kings" (Rev. 17:9, 12). Now this is how we are to understand the passage, if we consider Johannes Clüver trustworthy:

> While the dragon—that is, the Devil—holds sway through the gentile emperors, the crowns are worn on Rome's seven heads or hills. But after Caesar's head was cut down in death, the crowns were transferred to the horns—that is, to the kings of princes and nations, which before were subject to one emperor. They entrusted their crowns (a terrible thing to describe) to the dragon so that he could himself abuse those crowns to harm God's church. Or it could mean that on Rome's seven hills, cruel edicts were forged against Christians, and the ten kings executed these edicts.[57]

---

54. Anonymous.

55. Cajetan, *Epistolae Pauli*, sub loc. Rom. 8, fol. 31v.

56. Estius, *In Omnes Beati Pauli* (Paris, 1623), sub loc. Rom. 8:38.

57. Dilucul. Apocalypt. Tom. 3. p. 83.] Clüver, *Diluculum Apocalypticum*, vol. 3, p. 83.

The particular tools the tyrants used were their military forces. These are what we are to take the next word, *powers* (δυνάμεις) to mean. Johannes van den Driesche, a very famous man, is quite intent on proving that the word δυνάμεις regularly means *army*, with clearly the same meaning that we English use in saying *forces*.[58] Indeed, in the Septuagint, the Lord of Hosts is called Κύριος δυνάμεων. In 1 Maccabees as well, chapter 3, where ἀποστεῖλαι ἐπ’ αὐτοὺς δύναμιν is written; this is translated correctly as "To send an army against them." Just as I believe (according to van den Driesche) that what we read in the same chapter, καὶ ἔδωκεν ὀψώνια ταῖς δυνάμεσιν αὐτοῦ, should be translated "He gave rations to his troops." Somewhere else he cites Theodoret, who says in his *Epitome of Divine Dogmas*, τὸ δὲ Κύριος σαβαώθ, κύριος τῶν δυνάμεων ἑρμηνεύεται ἢ κύριος στρατιῶν. οὕτω γὰρ παρ’ Ἕλλησι τὰ στρατιωτικὰ τάγματα καλοῦνται.[59] May I add that in the *Thesaurus* of Henri Estienne, there occur some citations from Greek writers that demonstrate beyond all doubt the same meaning of the word.[60] But even the ancient sorcerers, along with their tricks that once troubled the Christian cause considerably, are referred to as δυνάμεις. Examples include Simon Magus, whom Luke describes in *Acts*; Apollonius Tyaneus, according to Philostratus; and Peregrinus the Cynic and Alexander Paphlagus, whom Lucian records. The people shouted of Simon Magus that οὗτος ἐστίν ἡ δύναμις τοῦ Θεοῦ ἡ μεγάλη (Acts 8:10).[61] Justin Martyr described the same man as δυνάμεις ποιήσας μαγικάς.[62] Paul assigns the advent of the son of perdition to Satan's power: ἐν πάσῃ δυνάμει καὶ σημείοις καὶ τέρασι ψεύδους (2 Thess. 2:9).[63] Christ presents the reprobate as speaking like this: τῷ σῷ ὀνόματι δυνάμεις πολλὰς ἐποιήσαμεν (Matt. 8:22).[64] I do not here establish any rule, but rather leave it open. I acknowledge that I am very ready to yield to those who might teach something more accurate. In the meantime, let us move on as quickly as possible to touch on the remaining items.

---

58. Praeterit p. 53. 208. 211. & Observat. sacrar. lib. 10. cap. 14.] Drusius, *Annotationes In Totum Jesu Christi Testamentum* (Amsterdam, 1632), pp. 53, 208, 211; Drusius, *Observationum Sacrarum* (Franeker, 1594), pp. 223–24. "Forces" is one of four English words that occur in this work.

59. Theodoret, *Haereticarum Fabularum*, in *Opera Omnia*, vol. 4 (Paris, 1642), bk. 5, ch. 3, p. 260. "The phrase 'Lord of Hosts' is interpreted as 'Lord of Powers,' or 'Lord of Soldiers.' For this is what companies of soldiers are called among the Greeks."

60. Henri Estienne (Stephanus), 1531–1598, French printer and classical scholar, *Thesaurus Graecae Linguae* (Geneva, 1572), sub loc. δύναμις, col. 1057.

61. "This is the power of God, a great one."

62. Apologet. 2°.] Justin Martyr, *Apologeticus*, 2. "Working magical miracles."

63. "With every miracle and signs and false wonders."

64. "We did many miracles in your name."

Cajetan holds that the heavenly bodies are designated by the word ὕψωμα;[65] and lower bodies, by the word *depth*.[66] Pareus holds the same view, that all of the elements both above and below are summarized by these two terms.[67] Other interpreters think that this means the pinnacle of worldly happiness and the abyss of temporal misery. I would prefer (if there is room for a humble suggestion) to mention here ideas more suited to our salvation. Thus, by the word ὕψωμα I understand haughtiness and hubris of the mind, like Hezekiah underwent when he reportedly cast himself down ἀπὸ τοῦ ὕψους τῆς καρδίας ("from his haughtiness of heart"; 2 Chron. 32:16). Paul also borrowed this meaning: Πᾶν ὕψωμα (2 Cor. 10:5).[68] And by βάθος, or *depth*, I think we should understand the spiritual abandonment the psalmist endured when he prayed, "Out of the depths I cried to You, Jehovah." Or as the Septuagint renders it, ἐκ βαθέων ἐκέκραξά σοι, Κύριε (Ps. 130:1). "'Out of the depths,' that is, from the pressing fear of condemnation for my sins. It is such a fear and so overwhelming that I think I am already going to be swallowed up in despair, the same as if I already sat in deep waters, afraid that even now I was swallowed up and going to be suffocated." So writes John Fischer.[69]

So far as concerns the final little clause (οὔτε τις κτίσις ἑτέρα [Rom. 8:39]),[70] I think that one of the more recent, not at all contemptible Romanist writers has skillfully hit the mark:

> Why does he call forth another creature, why does he appeal to a new one, why mention another more powerful creation? The soul of him who loves rightly and properly is so far above everything that it calls forth what is not because it has already overcome that which is. The Apostle, because he does not acknowledge the world as an equal competitor, contemplated something outside the world. The soul, powerful with God as its fellow soldier, is so internally strong that by itself it superabounds in all things that are and that could be. It is greater than things that are and things that are not; than things that are and that could be; that is, in a twofold manner it is greater than this world and another.

Thus writes Juan Eusebio Nieremberg.[71]

---

65. "Height."

66. Cajetan, *Epistolae Pauli*, probably sub loc. Rom. 8, fol. 31v.

67. Pareus, *In Divinam S. Pauli Apostoli Ad Romanos*, sub loc. Rom. 8, pp. 571–72.

68. "All haughtiness."

69. Piscator, *In Librum Psalmorum Commentarius* (Herborn, 1611), sub loc. Ps. 130:1.

70. "Or any other created thing."

71. De Arte voluntat. lib. 1. cap. 29. p. 40.] Nieremberg, *De Arte Voluntate*, 1.29, p. 40.

§ 9. A second ἐπινίκιον follows, taken from 1 Corinthians 15: "Where, O death, is your sting? Where, O grave, is your victory? The sting of death is sin, but the power of sin is the law. Thanks be to God, who gives us the victory through our Lord Jesus Christ" [1 Cor. 15:55–56]. Tertullian's famous statement is as well known as it is highly accurate—namely, that "Christians' confidence is the resurrection of the dead."[72] And so it is no surprise that the Apostle labors long to establish this dogma and heaps up numerous, significant arguments. He remembered the triumph that will be consummated after the resurrection is finally accomplished, and said, "When this corruptible body puts on the incorruptible, and this mortal body puts on the immortal, then will come to pass what is written in the Scripture, 'Death was swallowed up in victory' (κατεπίθη ὁ θάνατος εἰς νῖκος)" (1 Cor. 15:54). It is no surprise if—after meditating on this type of birth and by faith gaining a foretaste of all the glory that age holds—the Apostle immediately, joyfully broke out in that ἐπινίκιον I mentioned, ποῦ σου, Θάνατε, τὸ κέντρον; Ποῦ σου, ᾅδη, τὸ νῖκος;[73]

No one can doubt what θάνατος, or *death*, is. But when it comes to the word *hades*, which our theologians render in various places as *tomb*, there is no clear consensus. The famous Jesuit Delrio, in his *Sacred Adages on the Old Testament*, sets down two axioms, as he calls them. The first is, "There are many passages in the sacred books where one cannot interpret the Hebrew word שְׁאוֹל or the Greek word ᾅδης[74] as 'tomb,' or as a state of the dead generally, or as meaning anything besides a holding place for the dead, by metonymy at least, without doing harsh violence to the text." The second: "There is no passage found in sacred Scripture where we are forced to interpret שְׁאוֹל or ᾅδης as 'tomb,' etc."[75] Delrio produces many texts from both Testaments to prove each claim and, in fact, tallied up as many as eighty-seven. But as a very learned man (and one to whom I am quite attached by the tightest bond of friendship) noticed in his review of the first claim, the usually quite careful Jesuit made absolutely no mention of one particular passage in Job.[76] There is no way Delrio could have, by any machinations, forced this passage to fit his position. I refer to this one: "If only You would hide me in שְׁאוֹל"—which the Septuagint takes as in

---

72. De Resur. carn. c. 1.] Tertullian, *De Resurrectione Carnis*, in *Opera Quae Hactenus Reperiri*, vol. 3 (Cologne, 1617), ch. 1, sec. 1.

73. "Where, O death, is your sting? Where, O grave, is your victory?"

74. "Sheol" and "hades."

75. Adag. 197. pag. 213. 239.] Delrio, *Adagialia Sacra Veteris Et Novi Testamenti* (Lyon, 1614), pp. 213, 239.

76. D. *Ant. Tuckney*, conc. funebri in 1 Cor. 15.55. p. 5.] Anthony Tuckney, 1599–1670, Church of England clergyman and college head, *Funeral Oration* (London, 1654), p. 4. *Summa…Necessitudine.*

ᾅδης—"and would hide me away until Your anger passes by" (Job 14:13). But who could ever believe Job had grown so delirious that he hoped to hide from God's anger in Gehenna or Tartarus, where that anger burns more hotly than anywhere else? So allow me to note here that Delrio, in his explanation of his second axiom, almost completely ignores this text—I mean the one right before us. He merely promises, in his exegesis of that passage in Hosea referenced here,[77] that he will develop his thoughts further when explaining the Pauline passage. I do not really know whether he ever made good on that promise.

Doubtless, one cannot take ᾅδης in Job as a reference to the prison of the damned. This is because, although the tomb will give up its dead at the resurrection and those who have suffered the state of separation will then experience the state of reunion, Gehenna will, nevertheless, never be deprived of the victory once gained. It is irrelevant that the Romanists blather on that the soul of their touted Falconilla was freed from hell through the supplications of some martyr or another and that Trajan's soul was freed by Pope Gregory's prayers. Our theologians, with good reason, explain ᾅδης in various places as the tomb, the state of separation, or as a holding place for the dead who are under the power of death. Profane authors used the term in a similar fashion. The iambic verses of Philemon are well known:

> Καὶ γὰρ καθ᾽ ᾅδην δύο τρίβους νομίζομεν,
> Μίαν δικαίων, χἀτέραν ἀσεβῶν ὁδόν
>
> By *Hades* we hold two paths are intended:
> The just take the first, the wicked the second.[78]

If ᾅδης is taken to mean the tomb or the state of the dead, these are all true. But if it is taken as the hellish penitentiary, then it is false to hold that it applies to both classes of the human race, since only the reprobate are detained there.

§ 10. But so no one can miss what exactly the Apostle means here by the sting of death, he goes on to introduce two very weighty theological principles. The first is this: τὸ δὲ κέντρον τοῦ θανάτου ἡ ἁμαρτία [1 Cor. 15:56].[79] By sting of death (following Augustine's remark) Paul means the sting "by which death was caused, not the sting that death caused. For by

---

77. I.e., in exegeting Hosea, del Rio mentions that he will develop his thoughts further when he reaches the 1 Corinthian passage, as Paul references Hosea in Corinthians.

78. Philemon, 368/360–267/263 BC, New Comedy poet, from his *Charites* as quoted in Justin, *De Mon.*, 3.137.

79. "The sting of death is sin."

sin we die, it is not by death that we sin."[80] We can borrow a metaphor from snakes. Serpents, especially the various venomous ones equipped with fangs, usually use their fangs to strike and inflict a lethal wound. But if, by chance, their fangs are removed, they have no more power to harm. In the same way, death uses sin like a weapon to pierce and destroy people. But without sin, death is unarmed. Ambrose puts it nicely: "We have nothing to fear in death, if our life has committed no crime that we should fear. It is true that death separates soul and body. The soul is freed, the body is dissolved. The soul rejoices in its release; the body, when dissolved into dust, feels nothing, knows nothing."[81]

This is the second theological principle: ἡ δὲ δύναμις τῆς ἁμαρτίας ὁ νόμος [1 Cor. 15:56].[82] This, of course, is because the law reveals sin. "Through the law came knowledge of sin" (Rom. 3:20), Paul says. And again, "The law came in so that the trespass might abound" (Rom. 5:20). This is just like blemishes and wrinkles that were at first hidden on the face. They do not arise when one faces the mirror, but are simply brought to light. Next, the law makes one liable to punishment. For where the law does not exist, there is no transgression (Rom. 4:15). Finally, the law provokes us to sin. "Sin," says the Doctor of the Gentiles, "taking hold of the opportunity provided by the commandment κατειργάσατο ἐν ἐμοὶ πᾶσαν ἐπιθυμίαν" (Rom. 7:8).[83] And so just as death through sin became more deadly, so sin through the law became more sinful: καθ᾽ ὑπερβολὴν ἁμαρτωλὸς ἡ ἁμαρτία διὰ τῆς ἐντολῆς (Rom. 7:13).[84] Pareus argues, "It is not by guilt that the law restrains, refutes, and condemns sin. But it is by the guilt of a vitiated nature that one is carried along with a greater impulse toward what has been forbidden. It is just like a horse: the more stubborn it is against the reins, the more it is restrained by a sharp-toothed bridle." I add this: it is like when a river swells over an obstacle placed in its way, or when a chain thrown over a Molossian hound makes it fiercer, not by introducing any new ferocity but by drawing out what is already there. The truth of this observation is so completely obvious that long ago the following verses became proverbial:

---

80. De peccat. merit. & remiss. l. 3. c. 11.] Augustine, *De Peccatorum Meritis Et Remissione*, 3.11.20.

81. Lib. de bono mortis.] Ambrose, *Liber De Bono Mortis*, in *Omnia Quae Extant Opera*, vol. 4 (Basel, 1567), ch. 8, p. 237.

82. "The power of sin is the law."

83. "Produced all covetousness in me."

84. "Sin through the commandment became exceedingly sinful."

We always seek forbidden fruit and lust for what's denied.
What is allowed displeases, but what's not burns hot inside.[85]

§ 11. Now that he has finished with these meditations, the blessed Apostle finally pours out his whole being in gratitude. With consummate delight, he adds these words: "Thanks be to God, who gives us the victory through our Lord Jesus Christ" [1 Cor. 15:57]. God in Christ is the one to whom alone this prize of valor is due and is offered. What once produced in the Corinthians, as Paul writes, true happiness cannot help but produce abundant comfort each day as the Spirit brings it to mind. "God is faithful, through whom you have been called into communion with His Son, Jesus Christ our Lord" (1 Cor. 1:9). Yes, we are sharers in communion with Christ the Lord, not only in His offices—as it is written, "He has made us kings and priests to His God and Father" (Rev. 1:6)—but also in His privileges. The voice from heaven proclaimed that He was the beloved Son of God in whom the Father was well pleased. The sacred Book proclaims that we are beloved and His sons. Nor is He pleased with us only in the midst of conflicts, according to the well-known statement, "That I may know Him and share in his sufferings, while I am conformed to His death" (Phil. 3:10). But He is also pleased with us in our victories. He says, "I have overcome the world" (John 16:33). "And this is that victory," says the apostle, "that overcomes the world—namely, our faith" (1 John 5:4). He has conquered and tamed death and hades, sin and the law (which are mentioned here). And God through Christ has granted that we receive a very splendid victory over all these enemies, and He will give it.

The first is victory over death. "How blessed is the death of those," John Knox once said, "who have become partakers in Christ's death."[86] Bernard personally heard and saw his brother Gerard on his deathbed "reveling in death and insulting it. Where is your victory, death? Where is your sting? Now there is no sting but a cry of joy" Bernard overheard him praying, "Father, into Your hands I commit my spirit." And Bernard heard him groaning repeatedly, "Father, Father." And he even heard him shouting, "What a great privilege that He is the Father of men. How great is the glory for men to be sons and heirs of God!" For if we are sons, then we are also heirs. This is why that honey-sweet priest, right in the middle of recounting this victory, turned toward death and said:

You are dead, O death, by that pierced Hook you carelessly swallowed, by
that phrase mentioned in the prophet: "O death, I shall be your death."

---

85. Ovid, *Amorum*, bk. 3, *elegia* 4; bk. 2, *elegia* 19.

86. Histor. reformat. Eccles. Scotic.] Knox, *The Historie of the Reformation of the Church of Scotland* (London, 1644), sig. a4r.

By that pierced Hook, I say, you open up for the faithful a wide and happy exit. So they travel right through your center and out toward life. Gerard is not afraid of you, ghastly spook! Gerard is passing right through the center of your jaws to his homeland, not just safe but even filled with joy and thanksgiving.[87]

I would like to add some devout comments here, filled with the savor of a great theologian. I am referring to the poems of Wolfgang Musculus. These were composed just a few months before his death, and in them he speaks to his own soul:

> Now leave behind this wretched home soon falling to its fate,
> This too the faithful hand of God will quickly reinstate.
> Your sin cries out? I know, and yet all those who trust in Him,
> Christ by His blood does fully cleanse of all their foul sin.
> Death frightens sore? Yes, I admit but 'tis so near to life,
> Christ's steadfast grace calls you to this from out the endless strife.
> Christ is present, triumphing o'er Satan, sin and death,
> So then to Him pass on with speed along the winged path.[88]

§ 12. Second, there is victory over hades, whether we interpret the word to mean the tomb or the state of separation. To be sure, Christ deigns to recognize as brother the one who has God, in Christ, as Father. This is consistent with the statement "He will not be ashamed to call them brothers" (Heb. 2:11). Such a person shall be able, with a calm mind at least, if not with a joyous one, to borrow Job's words: "The tomb is my home, and in the shadows I have made my bed. I have said to the rotting of my flesh, 'You are my father,' and to the worms, 'You are my mother and my sister'" (Job 17:13–14). Whatever Christ has suffered, this He has sanctified to us. "He has made poverty rich," to borrow Luther's words. "He has turned shame into glory, has brought death to life."[89] Why should I not also say that He has robbed the grave of its stench and has made it so pleasing to His people that, in the end, the righteous can no longer look upon its residents— rottenness and worms—as enemies but as intimates and friends, parents and sisters? So far as concerns the state of separation, this is also a status filled with profit and happiness for those dead in Christ the Lord.

---

87. *Bernard. Serm.* 26. in Cant.] Bernard of Clairvaux, *In Cantica Canticorum*, sec. 15 (*sermo* 26).

88. *Melch. Adam.* Vit. Theol. German. p. 385, 386.] Adam, *Vitae Germanorum Theologorum*, pp. 385–86.

89. This quotation is attributed to Luther (also without citation) in other early modern texts. Cf. the similarly dated William Strong, *Select Sermons* (London, 1656), p. 591.

I recognize that for a long time there have been people, and even today there are many, who hold a contrary opinion. But I am absolutely certain that, no matter their number, they are all mistaken. So far as I can myself determine, Vigilantius[90] was more or less the first person who introduced into the church the disgusting doctrine of soul sleep, a dogma that persists to this very day. The ancient authors deservedly called him by the name "Dormitantius."[91] Several years after his death, this notion began to pollute the papal throne during the reign of John XXII.[92] John reportedly defended the notion and transmitted it to the Paris theologians. They then taught this exact position both in the schools and in their churches. Beyond that, they refused to confer theology degrees on anybody who would not first swear to defend this deadly tenet. No matter how very strenuously Bellarmine tries to come up with excuses for John XXII, he cannot free him from guilt.[93] Next the Anabaptists arose and doggedly held to the same doctrine. Calvin had words for their captains in that golden pamphlet he wrote in 1534 entitled *Psychopannychia*: "Those babblers have hunkered down into their own positions so stubbornly that they have dragged several thousand men with them into the same madness."[94] Next the issue has arisen with the Socinians. They call into question almost every doctrine orthodox theologians teach concerning the state of souls after death, together with the Socinian-Remonstrant preacher Heinrich Slatius. These are his words: "We don't know whether souls remain alive after death, or at least it is indiscernible."[95] They also side with Smalcius, who argued thus against Frantzius: "We seriously doubt whether the spirit that returns to God and has been separated from the body is endowed with any sense and whether it enjoys any pleasure before Christ's return and before it has been joined anew with the glorified body that God will at some point give believers." They either seriously doubt, or, with the same Smalcius, completely deny, the state of the soul after death in the very next words: "In point of fact, we believe that the circumstance is quite different; namely, that inasmuch as a body without a spirit is a mere cadaver, so in turn, a spirit without a body can perform no actions."[96] Or finally, they mock the notion, along with those swindlers

---

90. Vigilantius, fl. ca. AD 400, presbyter of Aquitaine.

91. I.e., "Sleepy," the opposite of his name's etymology, i.e., "wakeful."

92. John XXII, 1249–1334, *p.* 1316–1334.

93. De Beatitud. Sanctor. lib. 1. cap. 1, & 2.] Also in Bellarmine, *De Controversiis Fidei Christiani* (Ingolstadt, 1588), tom. I, bk. 4, ch. 14.

94. Calvin, *Psychopannychia* (Strasbourg, 1545), sig. a1v (*praefatio*).

95. *Apud Peltium*, p. 257.] Henricus (Heinrich) Slatius, 1580–1623, German Arminian preacher. Probably in Johannes Pelt, 1600–1642, Reformed, *Harmonia Remonstrantium Et Socinianorum* (Leiden, 1633).

96. Pag. 409.] Smalcius, *Refutatio Thesium*, p. 409.

who, in the unpublished *Acts of the Racovian Colloquy*, as quoted by Beckmann, say, "The notion that anyone went to hell and is tortured there or reclines in Abraham's bosom, these are obvious fabrications and just like the fables the poets tell about Ixion, Sisyphus, and Tantalus."[97] How disgusting, how shamelessly these men innovate!

But far be it from us to allow ourselves to be budged an inch from this passage's true meaning, toward which we are driving, by irreligious sarcasm. Although theology based on a parable, as it is called, should not be the basis of an argument, nevertheless, one can with full justification and great force argue from a parable's purpose. The purpose of the parable in Luke where the rich man and Lazarus are brought on stage (Luke 16:29) seems to be exactly this: to present before our eyes the completely disparate condition of the righteous and unrighteous man after each has died—that is, in the state of separation preceding the final judgment. Because in that passage Moses and the prophets are mentioned as providing useful service to those who were still alive on earth at the time, it should be clear that once the resurrection has taken place, they no longer teach men. But there, in the very heart of the parable, when he died, Lazarus was immediately carried by the angels to Abraham's bosom and there found comfort (Luke 16:22–25). Here, as is quite often the case elsewhere, the metaphor of a banquet is used in a discussion of the saints' happiness enjoyed after death. This is a common occurrence among sacred writers (as the passages that I have noted in the margin reveal: Matt. 8:11; Luke 22:30) and is also found in pagan authors. The Stoics, for example, used to say that their sages μετὰ θεῶν ἐστιάσθαι.[98] Epictetus expressly mentions this in that passage where he describes the character of the wise man as ἄξιος τῶν θεῶν συμπότης.[99] So the metaphor is a banquet, I say, in which the πρωτοκλισία [100] is assigned to Abraham as father of the faithful. But the rest are described as reclining in his bosom. That is how Lazarus is described here, and I would like to quote a few words from Heins on his comparison with the rich man. He says, "At this banquet, the man who was constantly feasting[101] now sees the beggar feasting and actually positioned right next to Abraham in the kingdom of God—that is, in his bosom. But the rich man himself is

---

97. Exercitat. 25. p. 488.] Christianus Becmannus (Beckmann), 1580–1648, German Reformed theologian, *Exercitationes Theologicae* (Amsterdam, 1644), *exerc.* 24, p. 488. Ixion, Greek king punished by Zeus by being tortured on a spinning, fiery wheel. Sisyphus, Greek king punished to roll a stone up a hill forever only for it immediately to roll back down. Tantalus, king of Lydia who suffered the punishment of perpetual thirst and hunger.

98. "Feasted with the gods."

99. Epictetus, *Enchiridion*, ch. 21, p. 10. "A worthy drinking buddy of the gods."

100. "Foremost seat of honor."

101. I.e., the rich man.

now a beggar and desperate for water and asks that someone provide him with it."[102]

§ 13. The third is a victory over sin, but gradually. Here is the comparison: Christ advances *conquering* and *in order to conquer*—that is (as our countryman Mede translates it), "He has not yet conquered completely but has laid the foundations of victory, and then the victory will be more and more complete."[103] Likewise, Christians, in their own victory gained over sin, advance a little bit at a time. They advance conquering first in their conversion. But this is so that they might conquer in the remaining course of their life and finish off the victory in death. The comment typically made on another subject applies here: "Daughter has swallowed up mother." For sin gave birth to death, and sin cannot be devoured before death. If death existed apart from sin, death never would have entered the world. If sin existed apart from death, sin would never leave the world. This deadly shaft sticks in its side and cannot be completely removed before death. Says Bernard, "I tell you that this kind of sin that bothers me so much—I mean lustful thoughts[104] and evil desires—surely must and can be held in check by God's grace so it does not rule over us. But only in death is it fully dislodged."[105]

Now Sebastian Castellio, in his treatise *Justification*, pompously mocks these and similar judicious conclusions our theologians draw: "I ask you, where did you learn that sin is abolished at death? Reason loudly objects to this. The holy writings also loudly object and, in different places, shout that it happens in this life. If you deny this, I can bury you in countless citations, some of which I have already supplied above."[106] You really mean that? But tell me, if you please, my good man, what exactly are these proofs of yours? "Some of them," you claim, "I have already supplied above." I went back to check, and in that treatise, I find nothing I could even drag by the throat and force to this purpose. But in another treatise you wrote, *The Obedience We Must Offer God* (here you croak at us the same old tune), I find a passage of Paul you cited from Titus 2: "The grace that brings salvation has taught us how to live soberly, justly, and with righteousness ἐν τῷ νῦν αἰῶνι (in the present age)" [Titus 2:12].[107] Therefore, you conclude that we are perfected

---

102. Vid. D. *Heinsium* exercit. l. 3. cap. 14. & cap. 19.] Heins, *Sacrarum Exercitationum*, bk. 3, ch. 14–15, pp. 171, 181.

103. Apoc. 6.2.] Mede, *The key of the Revelation* (London, 1650), sub loc. Rev. 6.

104. *Concupiscentias*.

105. Serm. 6. de advent. Dom.] Bernard of Clairvaux, *Sermones Per Annum*, in *Opera Omnia*, vol. 2 (Cologne, 1641), *sermo* 6, sec. 2.

106. Pag. 37.] Castellio, *De Iustificatione* in *Dialogi IV*, p. 37.

107. Pag. 240.] Castellio, *Dialogi IV*, p. 240.

in this life. Here's my answer, which I give not to satisfy you, since you are already dead (if only in death you were purged of the filth of your errors)! No, I respond in order to satisfy your followers. First, the saints do live in this age soberly, justly, and with righteousness. Yet their sobriety, justice, and righteousness are not exercised adequately according to the standard of divine law, such that their perfection lacks nothing. Second, I hold that this happens *in the present age* because it takes place during the transition before the soul becomes an inhabitant of another world. You say,

> I will ask you, Does Christ put to death the old man by faith, by death, or by employing neither of these? The answer cannot be "By faith," because I have demonstrated above that there is no faith in death. If you say, "By death," then you join death to Christ as an ally even though He hates it. The one who came to abolish death is neither able nor willing to abolish sin except through death's help. But if you say, "By employing neither of these," the result is that we must not ascribe salvation to faith. And yet you more than all men claim that men are saved by faith.[108]

Those are his comments; here is my answer. I do not hold that this happens entirely *by death* but *in death*, nor does it happen so much *by faith* working at the very moment of death, since the believer is hardly in control of himself— no, not even hardly. No, it is more by that faith with which the soul first rested upon Christ, who helps it as it struggles in its dying moments. Or instead, it is by the indwelling Spirit of Christ who refuses to abandon the soul at the final moment of agony.

As for the rest of my answer, I will explain it not in my own words but in those of the renowned Spanheim:

> It is likely that our life and sanctification have the same endpoint. As the soul begins to be infected with sin at the moment of its conjunction with the body—as soon as it begins to be a human being—likewise, when through death the human being ceases to be a human being, the soul is perfectly sanctified at its separation from the body. Thus it can stand spotless before God. Nor is it an ἔνστασις[109] that either the living or dead mortal is completely sanctified.[110] If we hold that the living human being is completely sanctified, we learn that sanctification is completely accomplished in this life. If we hold that the dead mortal is sanctified, then the human being is not sanctified, but only a portion of him. Neither position is absurd, either that sanctification is completed with this life or in this life or that part of the human being—but a particular part—is sanctified at the time of its separation from the body. Naturally, to this

---

108. *Castell.* de Justificat. p. 37.] Castellio, *De Iustificatione* in *Dialogi IV*, p. 37.
109. "Valid objection."
110. I.e., it is a false dichotomy that these are the only two options.

part alone is granted immediate access to heaven at its departure from the body. But the whole human being will receive such access when the entire person shall be conducted into the joy of his Lord. More speculative positions can be discussed and argued, but by the same token, they cannot be proven.[111]

§ 14. The fourth is victory over the law. If we have any indemnity from the law's hostility, we owe it to Christ alone as an inheritance. The Apostle teaches in Colossians, "God made you alive together with Christ, pardoning all your sins, and voiding what was written against us in the legal requirements, which was opposed to us. He removed it completely, nailing it to the cross" (Col. 2:13–14). That most distinguished interpreter of this letter, John Davenant, writes,

> Paul also wanted us to understand here the moral law. He explains that what was "written by hand in legal requirements" refers to the power of the moral law that binds to perfect obedience, condemns because of any deficiency, and is freighted with ceremonial rituals down to the smallest little pieces and parts. The passage also shows very clearly that Paul, in a very beautiful rhetorical climax, took the greatest care here for frightened consciences. He was not content with the notion that all our sins are pardoned. He connected to this the fact that the written record itself was erased. Or maybe it is not so much that it was erased, as though a new law could be introduced later. So he adds that, what is more, it has been removed. But perhaps the law is stored away somewhere, hidden, and later on will be reintroduced? "No," Paul says, "it was nailed to the cross"—that is, it was torn in shreds and divided up into tiny pieces with the same spikes by which Christ was nailed and shredded on the cross.

Thus Davenant.[112] It will not be out of place to add here Grotius's note on the passage: "It was customary, of course, among certain nations to post canceled decrees in public. Perhaps this practice was followed in Asia, and Paul references it here."[113]

Obviously, although believers are freed from the moral law in that respect, they still embrace it as a guide. However, they do not perceive the moral law as something that provokes them to sin, as under the prior state. Nor do they fear it as something that condemns, because they rely on their victory through Christ. I will quote here just one witness to make my point, but he is a lion. I am referring to Luther, who wrote these words: "When I feel your terrors and threats, O law, I plunge my conscience into Christ's

---

111. Dub. Evang. part. 3. Dub. 141. parag. 7.] Spanheim, *Dubia Evangelica* (Geneva, 1639), part. 3, 141.7, pp. 829–30.

112. Pag. 273. & 275.] Davenant, *Ad Colossenses*, sub loc. Col. 2:14, pp. 273, 275.

113. Grotius, *Annotationes In Novum Testamentum*, sub loc. Col. 2:14.

wounds, blood, death, resurrection, and victory. He is all I want to see and hear distinctly."[114] And Luther also has this to say about a famous verse in Galatians—namely, "But I mean that the law, which came 430 years afterward, does not abolish the covenant God previously ratified with respect to Christ, so as to render the promise useless" (Gal. 3:17). Luther writes:

> Of course, you should get used to the idea of separating law from promise even temporally. So when the law comes and accuses your conscience, you should say, "Mrs. Law, you are not arriving at a good time but are actually very late. Stay here for 430 years, and then once those years are up, you can come back. But then, of course, you will arrive much, much too late, because the promise arrived 430 years before you! I concur with the promise and rest comfortably in it. So I have no more business with you, and I'm not listening to you. I am already alive with Abraham who believes. Or rather, I live after Christ, the one who is my righteousness, was exhibited. He rendered you void, law, and cancelled you."[115]

§ 15. The third and final ἐπινίκιον (more could have been added if respect for the readers' rising boredom had not restrained me) will be the one in 2 Timothy 4:6–8. "I am now poured out as a drink offering, and the appointed time of my departure (or migration) is at hand. I have fought the good fight, I have finished the course, I have kept safe my deposit. Now what remains is this, a crown of righteousness stored up for me." Within the compass of these words one can see the blessed Apostle's threefold perspective.

First, he appears to be looking downward and gazing at the tomb into which he feels he will soon descend. For he says, ἐγὼ γὰρ ἤδη σπένδομαι.[116] Under the old covenant, in addition to sacrifices from living creatures, there were routinely oblations from inanimate things. These were partly from dry substances, sacrifices the Hebrews described as מִנְחָה. And they were partly of liquids, which are known in Greek as σπονδαί and in Latin as *libamina*. Hesychius says that λοιβὴ σπονδή, θυσία οἴνου.[117] Moschopholus says λοιβὴ δι᾽ ὑγρῶν θυσία.[118] One could readily believe that Paul here used the word σπένδομαι to show that he foresaw the type and manner of his own

---

114. Tom. 4. fol. 119. B.] Luther, *Commentarius In Epistolam Pauli Ad Galatas*, sub loc. Gal. 4:4.

115. Comment. in epist. ad Gal. e *Lutheri* praelect. concin. p. mihi 226.] Luther, *Commentarius in Epistolam Pauli Ad Galatas*, sub loc. Gal. 3:17.

116. "I am already being poured out as a drink offering."

117. "A drink offering is a pouring out, a sacrifice of wine." Hesychius of Alexandria, *Hesychii Alexandrini Lexicon* (1521).

118. "A drink offering is a sacrifice through liquids." Probably Manual Moschopulus, 1265–1316, Byzantine grammarian, *Grammaticae Artis Graecae Methodus* (Basel, 1540).

death—namely, that it would be joined with the shedding of blood like wine. Scultetus asks, "What is the death of the martyrs? It is the pouring out a drink offering on God's altar. But for the one who pours it out, it is glorious, and for the church, it is fruitful."[119] Grotius comments on this passage, "The victims under the law are antetypes of the martyrs. Therefore, the souls of the martyrs are under the altar (Rev. 6:7) because victims' blood used to be poured out under the altar (Lev. 1:5, 15; 3:28)."[120] But the *libamina* I just mentioned were sometimes offered separately but were also very often joined to the sacrifices and victims as supplements. This happened with the Jews, as we read in Numbers 28, and also among the pagans. Thus, we have this familiar epigram:

> Chew on, Ram, the vine for now; yet from it when you stand
> At the altar on your horns there could be placed a strand.[121]

When the Apostle references this custom in a different passage, he uses the same word. "Εἰ καὶ σπένδομαι ἐπὶ τῇ θυσίᾳ (If I am poured out as a drink offering) upon the sacrifice of the ministry of your faith, I rejoice and am glad for you all. You likewise must rejoice and be glad with me" (Phil. 2:17–18). Quistorp interprets this verse as follows:

> While through my ministry I offered you to God as a sacrificial victim, you must also offer yourselves and your bodies as a living sacrifice, holy and pleasing to God. I also (as was common in the Old Testament, when a libation of wine or oil was poured upon the victims) shall pour out my own blood with joy and true delight, that you may be drenched with that as with the victim's libation. Really, you also must take joy from this and congratulate me, if, for this reason, I am slaughtered and killed.[122]

These are the words that follow: καὶ ὁ καιρὸς τῆς ἐμῆς ἀναλύσεως ἐφέστηκεν [2 Tim. 4:6].[123] Some read this as, "The time when I shall be undone is at hand," or, "The time when I shall be released is drawing near." But these words are a little more sober than what the sacred Scriptures usually employ. When expressing something quite weighty, the Scriptures usually lessen death's bitterness with more mild phrasing. So Christ's death is termed a "departure" (Luke 9:31) and a "lifting up" (John 3:14). The death of Christians is called "sleeping" (John 11:11) and "sowing seed" (1 Cor. 15:42–43). Peter's death is deemed "putting off the tabernacle"

---

119. Observat. in 2^{am} ad Tim. cap. 20.] Scultetus, *Divi Pauli Epistolae Ad Singulares*, ch. 20, p. 91.

120. Grotius, *Annotationes In Novum Testamentum*, sub loc. 2 Tim. 4:6.

121. Ovid, *Fastorum*, bk. 1.

122. Quistorp, *In Divinam S. Apostoli Pauli Ad Philippenses* (Rostock, 1636), p. 43.

123. "And the time of my dissolution has arrived."

(1 Peter 1:14). Both here and elsewhere, Paul's death is referred to as an ἀνάλυσις (Phil. 1:23).[124] Other interpreters prefer to render the term "departure," "migration," "return," or at least "dismissal," so that it represents not destruction of body and soul so much as their dismissal from the world.[125] By this dismissal, the Christian man is granted return to his heavenly fatherland. Clearly the word ἀναλύειν is used to mean *go back, return home*. The same pattern is found in sacred and profane authors alike, in the passages cited by the very learned scholars Camerarius and Scultetus.[126]

§ 16. Second, the Apostle looks back and joyfully considers the life he lived before as very good. Doubtless, the Latin epigrammatist expressed this idea with consummate skill:

> The good man makes his span of life to last for twice as long,
> For this is living twice: that one can savor days bygone.[127]

That man is described as truly enjoying his previous life when memory of it persists:

> There is no day he wishes whole to blot from out his mind.[128]

It is indeed quite probable, judging from verse 7, that our dear Paul experienced this very thing from the moment he began to profess the Christian faith. In that verse, he is overwhelmed, so I think, with exquisite happiness and continues, saying: "I have fought the good fight, I have finished the course, I have kept safe my deposit" [2 Tim. 4:7]. The first two metaphors are borrowed from athletes in physical competitions, and the third is perhaps taken from the world of banking.

The Lacedaemonians—as Peter Faber teaches us from Aelian[129]— used to say, καλῶς ἀγωνίσασθαι,[130] when they were describing men who had died in battle. For this act, they were wreathed with olive and other branches and lifted to the gods with praises. Paul had not yet died. He

---

124. "Dissolution."

125. Vid. *Ludov. de Dieu* & *Grotium* in locum hunc ad Tim.] De Dieu, *Animadversiones In D. Pauli Apostoli* (Leiden, 1646), sub loc. 2 Tim. 4:6; Grotius, *Annotationes In Novum Testamentum*, sub loc. 2 Tim. 4:6.

126. *Camerar.* in Luc. 12.36. & *Scultet.* Exerc. Evang. lib. 1. c. 62.] Joachim Camerarius, Sr., 1500–1574, Lutheran humanist and theologian, *Iesu Christo Domini Nostri Novum Testamentum* (Cambridge, 1642), sub loc. Luke 12:36, this work is a collection of New Testament annotations by Roger Daniel at Cambridge in 1642, including quotes from Beza and Camerarius; Scultetus, *Exercitationes Evangelicae*, 1.62, p. 157.

127. Martial, *Epigrammata*, 10.23.

128. Martial, *Epigrammata*, 10.23.

129. Agonist. l. 3. c. 10. pag. 268.] Faber, *Agonisticon*, bk. 3, ch. 10, p. 268.

130. "They fought valiantly."

dared, however, as he was so close to death, to confess that τὸν ἀγῶνα τὸν καλὸν ἠγώνισμαι.[131] Of course, in these words, he refers to the contest that elsewhere he calls τὸν καλὸν ἀγῶνα τῆς πίστεως (1 Tim. 6:12),[132] while he was preserving the Christian faith against others' monstrous sentiments. And he preserved practices that were consistent with the Christian faith against the introduction of hostile vices. Thus, as he played the boxer, he never struck the air but always his opponent, as he makes clear in 1 Corinthians 9: οὕτως πυκτεύω ὡς οὐκ ἀέρα δέρων (1 Cor. 9:26).[133] Many people as they box strike the air with pointless blows, leaving their opponent meanwhile untouched. The blows Paul landed were much more effective. Many times when he was dealing with heretics, Paul followed the very instructions he gave Titus: ἔλεγχε αὐτοὺς ἀποτόμως (Titus 1:13).[134] He struck even to the point of cutting! Very often Paul did not gently rebuke his own flesh but (I will borrow his own words) he "pummeled [his] own body and brought it into submission" (1 Cor. 9:27).

The little clause that follows shows the blessed Apostle was an extraordinary runner, and in fact Olympic level (if we can take Olympus to stand for heaven). In another passage, Paul had said that he was running ὡς οὐκ ἀδήλως (1 Cor. 9:26),[135] but with direction and progress. He said, "Not aimlessly" (this is what ἀδήλως means), to make it clear he not only kept moving in his religious course but also streaked past all the spectators and even himself. He felt he was improving daily and drawing nearer the heavenly finish line. Here, with the end of his life approaching, he says, τὸν δρόμον τετέλεκα ("I have finished the course"). This is in keeping with the pattern of his Lord Jesus Christ, who said to the Father, "I have glorified You on earth. I have completed the task that You gave me to do. Now then, You glorify Me, Father, with You" (John 17:4–5).

§ 17. Finally, Paul had fulfilled his own command (if it truly was his) as given in Hebrews 12.1: ὄγκον ἀποθέμενοι πάντα καὶ τὴν εὐπερίστατον ἁμαρτίαν, δι' ὑπομονῆς τρέχωμεν τὸν προκείμενον ἡμῖν ἀγῶνα [Heb. 12:1].[136] Ὄγκος is typically rendered *weight* or *burden* and is explained as either the pleasures or the cares of this present age that tend to slow down those who run. But some more recent critics take the word to mean *arrogance* and *haughtiness*, following Hesychius. "Ὄγκος," he said, "means

---

131. "I have fought the good fight."
132. "The good fight of faith."
133. "So I land blows not like one beating the air."
134. "Rebuke them sharply."
135. "Not like someone without purpose."
136. "Throwing aside every weight and the sin that entangles us, let us run with perseverance the race that lies before us."

φύσημα, ὑπερηφανία, 'to be puffed up.'"[137] Or they follow Estienne in his gloss, where he says that ὄγκος is a tumor, and ὀγκοῦμαι means *I swell*.[138] And some of them follow Plutarch, who somewhere explains that those ὄγκου καὶ φρονήματος γέμοντας[139] are useless when it comes to learning new skills. The eminent Daniel Heinsius think it is this very arrogance that is censured in this passage: "Clearly, there is no greater hindrance to running a race than when someone thinks he has already arrived at a point he has not yet reached."[140] Paul carefully separates himself from this arrogance when he writes to the Philippians, "Brothers, I do not think that I myself have yet reached the goal. But one thing I do know: forgetting those things that are behind I press on to those things that lie before me, striving ahead toward the goal, toward the prize of the upward call of God in Christ Jesus" (Phil. 3:13–14). Louis de Dieu also understands this as haughtiness, but of a plainly different variety. He says:

> I admit that ὄγκος means more like *swelling* and should be taken here as mental haughtiness, as it always means in good authors. I understand by this word not the conviction by which one rashly believes he has already reached the finish line. Instead, it is the conviction by which someone, giving himself too much credit, asserts that his afflictions are beneath him. For nothing is more opposed to τῇ ὑπομονῇ [Heb. 12:1][141] than such haughtiness. If anyone thinks himself so immensely important that he is unwilling to suffer like the people whose examples Paul had recounted in chapter 11 and δὶ ὑπομονῆς τρέχειν τὴν προκείμενον ἀγῶνα,[142] the Apostle concludes that this is actually ὄγκος—that is, it is revealing one's own haughtiness. This haughtiness must be laid aside in order to complete the race properly.

Those were his comments.[143] But if this is the right meaning of the passage, then one cannot deny that Paul has also put off this arrogance. For doing such was absolutely consistent with his sufferings, so that he said, "I am content in weaknesses, in insults, in hardships, in persecutions, and difficult circumstances for the sake of Christ" (2 Cor. 12:10).

There is no doubt that in addition to the word ὄγκος that I have discussed at sufficient length, the same passage of Hebrews commands us to

---

137. Hesychius of Alexandria, *Hesychii Alexandrini Lexicon*.

138. Estienne, *Thesaurus Graecae Linguae*, sub loc. ὄγκος, col. 550.

139. Plutarch, *De Auditione*, in *Omnium Quae Exstant*, vol. 2 (Frankfurt, 1620). "Swollen with a sense of their own importance."

140. Heins, *Sacrarum Exercitationum*, bk. 16, ch. 8, p. 548.

141. "Endurance."

142. "To run the race set before us with endurance."

143. De Dieu, *Animadversiones In D. Pauli*, sub loc. Heb. 12:1.

lay aside τὴν εὐπερίστατον ἁμαρτίαν [Heb. 12:1].[144] There is not yet any clear consensus among interpreters as to what this means. A very accomplished English paraphraser and scholiast recently hammered out a new exegesis of this passage.[145] I will explain his exegesis and illustrate it here for the sake of foreigners unfamiliar with the English language. Even though this interpretation is very recent, I do not think one should at all dismiss it. The word περίστασις[146] properly means *circumstance*. Orators talk about a θέσις ἀπερίστατος—that is, a *bare proposition*, one presented with no other attendant conditions. So then, this author thinks that εὐπερίστατον ἁμαρτίαν means sin that, under a beautiful but deceptive guise and through a variety of enticing circumstances, is so appealing to the heart that it strongly draws the heart toward it. And in terms of its cost, it surpasses all other vices by comparison.[147] Certainly theologians, especially those concerned with application, have much to say about a "sin of delight," or as we Englishmen call it, "a bosom sin."[148] Unless this is laid aside, it is impossible for anyone to run happily from the starting blocks to the finish line in a race of sincere piety. Although nature's corruption cannot be completely destroyed so long as man walks among the living, certainly any bosom sin can be set aside and typically is among the truly regenerate. The venerable Beza, however, very faithfully exegetes this passage as follows. He says that there can be no doubt that ἁμαρτίαν means *corruption of our nature*, and this is affirmed by the addition of the perfectly suitable epithet εὐπερίστατον.[149] I call David as a witness, who, with the common disposition of the regenerate, said, "I am blameless and have preserved myself from my iniquity" (Ps. 18:23). But the vice that enticed the Christians of that age[150] and wormed its way into them more than other vice, seeing that it was totally supported by the many alluring circumstances around them, is syncretism with the Jews, with the Judaizing followers of Christ. Paul showed that he kept himself quite removed from whatever they had done and thus, without interruption, finished his own race. The passage in Galatians that deals with the brothers falsely introduced is aimed at this subject. He says, "They had been secretly introduced to spy on our freedom that we have in Christ, to reduce us to servitude. I did not yield to them in submission even

---

144. "The sin that easily entangles."

145. D. H. H.] Probably Hammond, *Deuterai Phrontides*, sub loc. Heb. 12, pp. 236–37.

146. A. begins to discuss this word because it is the basis of the compound εὐπερίστατον that appears in verse 1 of Hebrews 12, modifying ἁμαρτίαν.

147. Hammond, *Deuterai Phrontides*, sub loc. Heb. 12, pp. 236–37.

148. A. gives three English words, "a bosome sin."

149. Beza, *Annotationes Maiores*, sub loc. Heb. 12:1.

150. I.e., in the time that Paul wrote 2 Timothy.

for a moment, so that the truth of the gospel would remain among you" (Gal. 2:4–5).

Now only the last little clause of this verse remains—namely, τὴν πίστιν τετήρηκα [2 Tim. 4:7].[151] We must understand that Christ and Christians are mutually creditors to one another. The Christian entrusts his very soul to Christ, while He entrusts His truth to the Christian. As though by the one Spirit, the Apostle remembers each deposit in 2 Timothy: "I know whom I have believed, and I am persuaded that He is able to keep safe my deposit until that day" (2 Tim. 1:12). Just after that, he says, "I have kept safe that worthy deposit through the Holy Spirit who lives in us" (2 Tim. 1:14). Christ had preserved Paul's soul in the midst of a thousand dangers. Paul had kept the truth of Christ safe and in good condition up to that point. And so, as he was soon about to die, he faithfully and joyfully said, "I have kept the faith." Epaminondas,[152] the Theban general, when he was pierced through by a spear, first looked around to see whether his shield was intact and, next, whether the enemy had been completely vanquished. When other soldiers assured him of both, he said, "This is not the end of my life, dear fellow soldiers, but a better and more abundant beginning has arrived. For now your friend Epaminondas is born, because thus he dies."[153] These words are not at all beneath the dignity of the Christian man to use at the moment of his own death, when Satan has been routed, truth defended, and assurance is strong in that faith that, in my previous discussions, I have compared to a shield.

§ 18. And finally, the Apostle turns his eyes upward and, beholding heaven, speaks the last portion: "The crown of righteousness has been laid up for me. The Lord will give it to me at the last day, as the just judge" [2 Tim. 4:8]. Because the purpose of athletics is to promote military readiness (this is why Dionysius Halicarnassus says that ὁ τρόπος τῆς ἀγωνίας χρήσιμος πρὸς τὴν ἀνδρείαν τὴν ἐν τοῖς πολέμοις),[154] and the *Agonistica* presents athletics as the picture of martial conflict, so likewise Plato called warriors "soldier-athletes." So it is no surprise that the Apostle, when discussing Christian warfare and victory, quite often makes reference to the Greek games. That is, without a doubt, what he does in this passage, likening

---

151. "I have kept safe my deposit." A. gives the Greek phrase with no Latin gloss.

152. Epaminondas, d. 362 BC, Theban general and statesman.

153. *Valer.* maxim. lib. 3. cap. 2.] Valerius Maximus, *Factorum Et Dictorum Memorabilium*, bk. 3, sec. 5, pp. 278–79.

154. Apud *Fabrum* Agonistic. pag. 2.] Dionysius Halicarnassus, ca. 60–ca. 7 BC, Greek historian and literary critic, quoted in Faber, *Agonisticon*, bk. 1, ch. 1, p. 2. "This kind of training is highly conducive to military strength."

himself to the victor, Christ to the one who presides over the games, and eternal life to the crown bestowed as a prize.

The Olympian, Pythian, Isthmian, and Nemean games were the most popular of the Greek sporting events. In all of them, it was common practice for the presenters to distribute crowns as the prize for the winners. But these were of different kinds. In the Olympic Games, the crowns were made of olive branches; in the Pythian, from myrtle. The Isthmian games distributed crowns of pine, and in the Nemean, they were made of parsley. This is precisely why the reward of eternal life—bestowed by the great presider on those who are the true conquerors (i.e., on righteous and victorious Christians)—is called a crown. In another passage, Paul says, "Contend for that good fight of the faith. Lay hold of eternal life" (1 Tim. 6:12). James writes, ὅτι δόκιμος γενόμενος λήμψεται τὸν στέφανον τῆς ζωῆς (James 1:12).[155] These lines found among the *Sybilline Oracles* sound the same note:

Ἁγνὸς γὰρ Χριστὸς τούτοις τὰ δίκαια βραβεύσει;
Καὶ δοκίμους στέψει[156]

Furthermore, the word *crown* has two meanings when applied to eternal life. First, it means the glory of the prize itself. There is nothing in these realms below more glorious than a crown or a diadem, and that is why, in different places in Revelation, the very best persons are marked off with crowns. And second, it indicates the fullness of that glory. Just as the head is encircled completely with a crown, so the entire man is crowned with heavenly glory. The Lord is described as crowning the year with His abundance (Ps. 65:11), because each of the individual seasons of the year are loaded with God's fruits and blessings toward us. Likewise, when the inhabitant of heaven puts on both robes, his individual faculties and every part of his body will drink heavenly glory to the absolute depths, and thus, the whole man shall be crowned.

§ 19. The crown of righteousness is described by two titles, both because it is shared with us and acquired for us through Christ's righteousness and because it has been given to us from God's righteousness. With respect to the first, Christ's righteousness is threefold if considered very broadly: *personal, official,* and *collateral. Personal* righteousness is that essential and

---

155. "Blessed is the man who stands firm under temptation, because when he has stood the test, he will receive the crown of life."

156. *Sibyllina Oracula* (Paris, 1599), 2.45–46.

"So Christ the Lamb shall full repay the righteous for their works,
    And He shall crown those who o'ercome…"

infinite righteousness that belongs to Christ, as such, as the second person of the Trinity. And as it is God's righteousness, so He is God. I term that righteousness *official* that Christ demonstrated by taking upon Himself that most distinguished and, at the same time, most difficult office of mediator, according to the command and law the Father had passed regarding that subject. The Lord remembered this law in the psalmist: "Behold, I have come. I am pleased, my God, to do Your will. Your law is in my inmost being" (Ps. 90:8–9).[157] We hear of this commandment again and again in the evangelist John, when Christ readied Himself for His suffering: "I have received this commandment from my Father, just as my Father has commanded me, so shall I do. Rise up, etc." (John 10:18; 14:31).

I call the third kind of righteousness *collateral*. This is the righteousness that Christ, after He took upon Himself the mediatorial office of mediator, fulfilled in executing that office. He offered *official* righteousness to God the Father as an obedient Son. He offered *collateral* righteousness to God the judge as pledge and surety. Through *official* righteousness, He fulfilled the special law that bound no one except Him (for to which of the angels did God say, "Be a mediator between men and Me"?). Through *collateral* righteousness, He fulfilled the moral law, by whose bond all of Adam's posterity are held fast, just as Adam himself was once held, as rational creatures. Finally, Christ discharged *official* righteousness on His own behalf, *collateral* righteousness on our behalf. Inasmuch as He had been placed over the moral law by virtue of the hypostatic union, He was Lord of the whole Decalogue as well as of the Sabbath. Nevertheless, He submitted Himself to the whole law to become our surety, after He had voluntarily taken upon Himself that obligation.

But although collateral righteousness alone would be sufficient for our justification—inasmuch as it is an inescapable effect of Christ's total obedience—this obedience ought to be described by a single word, *activo-passiva*, rather than being divided into active and passive, as though into distinct units. This is because Christ the Lord, in all His sufferings, acted resolutely (He willingly and with the highest pleasure underwent punishment and laid down His life). He revealed Himself passively in His mediatorial actions. Even if not all of those sufferings brought pain, nevertheless, they individually manifested a far greater emptying and humiliation than the highest monarch in the world would show if he were to stoop down from his throne in order to raise up the poor and if he were to live in the filthiest latrine. Even though this *collateral* righteousness by itself, I repeat, when imputed to us would suffice for our salvation, nevertheless,

---

157. Read, Ps. 40:7–8.

the whole remainder of Christ's righteousness, regardless of how extensive it is, is needed to win for us full salvation and the crown of eternal life. Because if it had taken place without the whole of His righteousness, there is no way possible that grace could reign through righteousness unto eternal life through Jesus Christ our Lord (Rom. 5:21).

§ 20. As for the second part, that we have said this crown is bestowed from God's righteousness, the Scholastics customarily ask whether strict righteousness can be assumed between God and man. I answer in the negative because, as Lessius teaches, righteousness has two components: "What is owed and equality."[158] And as Thomas holds, "The principle of righteousness consists in this: rendering to another what he is owed" and doing so "according to the principle of equality."[159] From God's side, the debt of obligation is not rendered through the means of strict right, nor on man's side is there equality of what is given and received. There is a common expression among legal experts that "it is discourteous to say God owes anyone." There is also this statement of Bernard: "Human merits are not the sort of thing for which humans are rightly owed eternal life or that God would be committing some wrong if He did not grant it. For all God's merits are gifts, and man, because of these very merits, is more God's debtor than is God to man."[160] No matter what the ungrateful Sophists may chatter, we must firmly believe that men contribute nothing on the basis of what is not owed or that God accepts anything as gain. Rather, it is true that there is no principle of equality between what we grant by means of obedience and what we receive from God by means of reward. Our Savior said very explicitly, "When you have done everything that you have been commanded, say, 'We are unprofitable servants, because we have done what we were supposed to do'" (Luke 17:10). "What benefit is it to God if you are righteous?" Eliphaz said in the book of Job, "or what do you contribute to Him if your path is spotless?" (Job 22:3). And Elihu also said, "If you live justly, what will you give to God, or what will He receive from your hand?" (Job 35:7).

I add here an excellent remark of Macarius, who was able to speak correctly about that office that Christians will possess by hereditary right: εἰ ἕκαστος, ἀφ᾽ οὗ ἐκτίσθη ὁ Ἀδὰμ ἕως τῆς συντελείας τοῦ κόσμου,

---

158. De perfect. divin. l. 13. c. 1.] Leonardus Lessius, 1554–1623, Flemish Jesuit moral theologian, *De Perfectionibus Moribusque* (Paris, 1620), bk. 13, ch. 1, sec. 1, p. 352.

159. Aquin. 2ᵃ 2ᵃᵉ. qu. 80. artic. 1. in corpore.] Aquinas, *Summa*, 2-2.80.1.

160. *Bern.* Serm 1 de Annunciat.] Bernard of Clairvaux, *In Festo Annunciationis*, in *Opera Omnia*, vol. 2 (Cologne, 1641), *sermo* 1, sec. 2.

ἐπολέμει πρὸς τὸν Σατανᾶν, καὶ ὑπέμεινε τὰς θλίψεις, οὐδὲν μέγα ἐποίει πρὸς τὴν δόξαν, ἣν μέλλει κληρονομεῖν.[161]

These considerations, however, are no barrier to recognizing that there is also a twofold debt owed directly to God. One is a debt of propriety; the other, of faithfulness. It is in respect to these that God is called righteous in the bestowal of this crown. In terms of the formal cause for the crown, it is not, of course, by strict justice, as it would be when dealing with someone other than God, as Aquinas teaches.[162] But because "this is the promise," according to John, "that He Himself has promised us—namely, eternal life" (1 John 2:25). And according to James, "The Lord has promised the crown of life" (James 1:12). Now every promise implies a debt. Augustine says, "The Lord Himself has made Himself our debtor not by receiving anything from us but by promising."[163] And again, "You repay what is owed, although You owe no one. You make loans but suffer no loss."[164] In another passage, Augustine writes, "It is just that God repays because He owes. But He owes because He has promised from grace and not from something owed." And because God is a debtor to Himself to act with propriety and in a way fitting and congruous with His goodness, as He cannot deny Himself, so He must not do anything that is unworthy of Himself. Davenant, as usual, expresses this with brilliance and clarity:

> Righteousness in God is the divine will under the control of the first rule determining itself to act according to the propriety of His own goodness. Therefore, God's righteousness is not so much directed toward another, like human righteousness, as it is toward Himself, as if He were another. And when God gives eternal life to Peter or Paul, the divine will is not paying a debt to a creature but to itself only.

A little further on, Davenant writes, "We must acknowledge that all of that right to eternal life that we are said to have depends on this, that God is, as it were, a debtor to Himself to act in conformity with both the propriety of His goodness and the faithfulness of His own promise."[165]

§ 21. Finally, the Apostle boasts about this crown stored up for him, even though it has not yet been placed upon his head. This is because it is kept safe in heaven according to Peter's comment: "God has given us new birth

---

161. *Macar.* homil. 15. p. m. 206.] Macarius of Egypt, *Homiliae Spirituales*, p. 206 (*homilia* 15). "If anyone, from the time that Adam was created right down to the world's consummation, could struggle against Satan and endure his afflictions, he would accomplish nothing significant with respect to the glory that he will attain."

162. 2ᵃ 2ᵃᵉ qu. 58. artic. 2.] Aquinas, *Summa*, 2-2.58.2.

163. In Ps. 83.] Augustine, *Psalmi Enarratio*, sub loc. Ps. 83:12, 16.

164. Confess. l. 1. c. 4.] Augustine, *Confessiones*, 1.4.4.

165. De Justit. habit. & actual. p. 640.] Davenant, *De Iustitia Habituali*, ch. 66, p. 640.

into an inheritance that can neither spoil nor fade, kept safe for us in heaven" (1 Peter 1:3–4). And so it has been put in a safe place. More than that, as the Savior bears witness, the treasure deposited in heaven cannot perish or be snatched away, because "there neither worm nor rust corrodes, and thieves do not sneak in and steal" (Matt. 6:20).

Nevertheless, because some people hold that this crown can be lost—based on their reading of a statement in Revelation, "Hold on to what you have so no one takes your crown" (Rev. 3:11)—I must offer a brief corrective. Although we grant—but do not concede—that this passage really does refer to the crown of life the Lord has stored up for His elect in heaven, it will not follow from this that the crown can be lost. Instead, we must understand that our very indulgent Father is driving us on with these kinds of admonitions and making them work to create in us perseverance so as not to lose the crown. But if this statement refers to a much different crown, then there is no impact whatsoever on the controversy's main point. And the Lord actually seems to mean another crown in this statement. If anyone said that this was the "crown of ministry," it could almost be taken in the following sense: "Be watchful over yourself, angel of Philadelphia"—the letter was written to an angel—"and over your office. Otherwise, if you reveal that you are slothful or a steward of bad faith, when you are rejected, another will take your place." Or it could be taken to mean the crown of gospel truth and doctrine that the false apostles were trying to steal from the angel and the church, as if the Lord had said, "ὑποτύπωσιν ὑγιαινόντων λόγων.[166] This is a representation, for you and your people, of that most glorious crown. See to it that you keep it in good repair and that it does not fall into the hands of thieves." I actually think that Hebrew practice favors this interpretation, especially when seen in light of Revelation 12:12. The context there is the woman robed with the sun, under whose feet was the moon and on whose head was a crown of twelve stars. The gospel preached throughout the world by the twelve apostles is likened to a crown encircling her head. The Hebrew practice favors this interpretation, I say, as they habitually referred to the law of God as a crown. Among others, there is the notable statement in a certain Rabbi Simeon. "There are three kinds of crowns. There is the crown of the law, the crown of the priest, and the crown of the kingdom. But the crown of a good reputation surpasses them all."[167] If anyone would like more proof, he should consult, if he desires, the *Sacred and Profane Offhand Remarks* of Luigi Novarini. The references can be found at the very beginning of the first book. I must now go on to weave another web.

---

166. "Hold onto the pattern of sound words."

167. Rabbi Simeon, quoted in Novarini, *Schediasmata Sacro-Prophana* (Lyon, 1635), bk. 1, ch. 1, sec. 1, p. 1.

CHAPTER IV

A Modest Σκιαγραφία[1] of the Heavenly Triumph

Sections 1–2: Revelation 7 describes the triumph we are going to celebrate in our fatherland. A multitude and variety of those victors will celebrate this triumph. This multitude and variety, however, does not imply universal redemption. Sections 3–5: A description of the setting and the raiment. An action is required for the formal blessedness of each faculty. White garments represent the dignity, purity, and joy that all inhabitants of heaven owe Christ. The palm branches stand for victory. Sections 6–7: The shouting of the saints proclaims God's goodness and reveals three sources of salvation. Romans 9:21–22 is explained. The mediation of Christ in His two natures is affirmed against Francesco Stancaro. Section 8: The angelic chorus' twofold posture, ministering and adoring. The meaning of the word ἀνακεφαλαίωσις in Ephesians 1:10. What adoration properly understood means. Section 9: A catholic resolution of the wide-reaching dispute over grace and free will. Sections 10–13: The Sacred Pleiades in the angels' doxology—that is, the εὐλογία[2] of the words Δόξα Σοφία Ἐυχαριστία Τιμή Δύναμις Ἰσχύς[3] are each treated in order. Sections 14–15: An epilogue to the angelic anthem and the entire work.

§1. Up to this point, I have been cast into a deep ocean of subjects and words. I can now see the land, or rather heaven, where my long argument must come to an end. Heaven is where the triumph takes place. Victors usually celebrate their triumph both in enemy territory and after they return to their own homeland. Christians dwell in enemy territory so long as they fulfill military service in the world. But just as the Romans στεφανώσαντες[4] Horatius Cocles[5] and ἀπέφερον εἰς τὴν πόλιν ὑμνοῦντες ὡς τῶν ἡρώων

---

1. "Sketch."
2. "Praise."
3. "Glory, wisdom, thanksgiving, honor, power, strength."
4. "Crowned."
5. Horatius Cocles, legendary Roman hero.

ἕνα,[6] so Christians are led triumphant after they say goodbye to the world through death, are wreathed with their crowns, and decorated with songs of praise. They come to the "city of the living God, the heavenly Jerusalem, ten thousands of angels"—to introduce here the Apostle's very welcome words—"the universal throng, the assembly of the firstborn enrolled in heaven, and to God the judge of all things, to the spirits of those made righteous, to Jesus the mediator of a new covenant, to the blood of sprinkling that speaks things better than Abel's blood" (Heb. 12:22–23). The loftiness of this language and the majesty of the mere words so overwhelm and affect my heart that I see clearly that I lack the strength to paint this heavenly triumph in its proper colors. Its excellence and beauty surpass human eloquence and require angelic speech. I shall try, nevertheless, to demonstrate, in some fashion or another, a sort of σκιαγραφία.[7] I will follow the contours of a particular passage in Revelation. Although some people think it applies to the church militant, all acknowledge that its final fulfillment comes in the church triumphant. The passage is found in the very center of chapter 7 and reads as follows:

> I looked, and behold, there was a great multitude beyond what anyone could count from every nation, tribe, people, and language. They were standing before the throne in full view of the Lamb, robed in white apparel, and had palm branches in their hands. And they were shouting with a loud voice, saying, "Salvation is from our God who sits upon the throne, and from the Lamb." All the angels, moreover, were standing in a great arc before the throne and the elders and four living creatures. And they threw themselves down on their faces before the throne, and worshipped God, saying, "Amen. Blessing and glory and wisdom and thanks and honor and power and strength be to our God forever and ever. Amen." (Rev. 7:9–12)

After I had decided to explain this passage just quoted as my essay's final section, I happened upon the statement of a certain famous man while reading. It would not be responsible for me to hide it from the reader now. I am referring to Johannes Clüver. I have cited him several times in the preceding pages. In the second volume of his *Apocalyptic Dawn*, as soon as he reached this passage, he wrote,

> The consensus opinion is that this vision concerns the blessed spirits of the saints. It, therefore, gives such abundant happiness and comfort to all destined for the heavenly fatherland that I don't really know whether

---

6. *Dionys. Halicarn.* Antiq. lib. 5.] Dionysius Halicarnassus, *Antiquitates*, in *Dionysii Halicarnassei Quae Extant, Omnia* (Frankfurt, 1586), bk. 5, ch. 25, sec. 1. "Carried him back to their city, singing his praises as one of their heroes."

7. "Sketch."

there is any other more brilliant passage like this in all Scripture. Therefore, because I personally love this passage beyond measure, I seek to
persuade my brothers to value it as a most precious possession.[8]

§ 2. I think that these words, though not very numerous, set before us in
summary the whole countenance, so to speak, of the church triumphant.
Here is God, together with the Lamb, whom we must gaze upon in beatific
vision. And here are the blessed men and women, together with the elect
angels, glorifying with shouts and doxologies of praise the inexpressible
divine presence. Meanwhile, I hope Christ and the Christian reader alike
shall forgive me as I stammer to express these difficult and recondite subjects. Paul made the same request when he wove for himself this defense:
"When I was a child, I spoke like a child, I had the wisdom of a child, I
reasoned like a child" (1 Cor. 13:11).

Now the starting point of our discussion ought to be the vast array
of the blessed that appears first. It is described here as comprised of many
parts. First, it is from a *multitude*. "Behold there was a great multitude
beyond what anyone could count." God once said to Abraham, the father
of the faithful, "Now look up toward heaven, and count the very stars, if
you really can number them. This will be your offspring" (Gen. 15:5). In the
same way, he said to Jacob, "I shall make your seed as numerous as the sand
of the seashore that cannot be counted for its great size" (Gen. 32:12). John
here received in a revealed vision what each of the patriarchs got as promises. And it truly results in God's honor, who had this fixed purpose for all
eternity past, "to bring many sons to glory" (Heb. 2:10). Solomon testifies
to this as well: "The king's glory depends on the multitude of his people"
(Prov. 14:28). But it also results in the comfort of the blessed, whose happiness, of course, increases in proportion to their number. Therefore, Christ,
as He was about to leave, warmed the hearts of His disciples by reminding them of the "many mansions in heaven" (John 14:2). Nature dictates
the sentiment, and Seneca is her secretary: "Without a friend, there is no
joy in owning something good."[9] Certainly, in heavenly blessing, when our
companions are multiplied, no category of good is missing. Why do I say
missing? Every category of delightful enjoyment must be there. It is absolutely impossible for it not to be.

Second, the blessed is comprised of a variety of those same people,
"from every nation, tribe, people, and language." This is in keeping with the
statement that "wisdom" (which the eternal Son of God adopts as His title)
"rejoiced in the whole habitable world, and it was her delight to dwell with

---

8. Pag. 280.] Clüver, *Diluculum Apocalypticum*, vol. 2, ch. 7, p. 280.
9. Epist. 6.] Seneca, *Epistolae, epistola* 6.

the sons of men" (Prov. 8:31). From this we can conclude that no habitable part of the world exists or has existed but that Christ has had, does have, or shall have within it some sons of men who are His delight. However widely the world extends, to that part of the world also extends the election of some. This is why the Lord wanted to be born not in a private home but in a guesthouse, a place of public lodging, because He received travelers from every nation. And He suffered not within the walls of Jerusalem but "outside the gate" (Heb. 13:12). Perhaps He did this to indicate that He suffered death not only for the Jews but also for His elect from every nation and people. We know that twelve gates are assigned to the new Jerusalem, positioned so that there are three on the east, the same number on the north, three on the south, and the same number again on the west (Rev. 21:12–13). So it is very obvious that the elect have a wide-open entrance to stream into heaven and into the church triumphant from all sides, from whatever point on earth they come. This fact plainly serves to significantly increase the praise due Christ our Lord. He also takes praise from that new song that the author of Revelation mentioned a little before, in an address directed to the Lamb: "You are worthy to take the book and open its seals. Because You were slain and have redeemed us for God by Your blood, from every tribe, tongue, people, and nation" (Rev. 5:9).

The position the Remonstrants and others so noisily jabber on about, however—that is, universal redemption—does not at all follow from the diversity of the redeemed. As if Christ had laid down His own life equally for all persons and individuals! As if that were true because the contour of personal election and effectual redemption—according to some—is the same, and the works of the Most Holy Trinity—the Father in electing, the Son in redeeming, and the Holy Spirit in converting—are commensurate! Therefore, the Son only redeems without exception those whom the Father elected, and the Holy Spirit only converts without exception those whom the Son redeemed. I myself quite agree with this statement: "By Christ's death some good things come to all men, and all good things come to some men (i.e., to the elect and to them alone)." But discussing this topic here at any length would take me well beyond the playing field. I will only cite two distinguished statements, disregarding some people's penchant for knitting together paradoxes. One statement is Augustine's: "Everyone redeemed by the blood of Christ is a human being. But not every human being has been redeemed by the blood of Christ."[10] The second comes from Scotus: "As the Word foresaw the suffering He was going to offer to the Father for the elect, so He also efficaciously offered it in its effect. The whole Trinity

---

10. De adulterin. conjug. lib. 1. c. 15.] Augustine, *De Adulterinis Coniungiis Ad Pollentium*, in *Omnium Operum*, vol. 6 (Basel, 1528), 1.15.

efficaciously accepted His suffering in place of the elect, and it was not offered efficaciously or from eternity accepted for any other persons."[11]

§ 3. Third, the blessed are described in terms of their location. They stood before the throne and in the presence of the Lamb. It is the duty of those who minister to stand at attention, and verse 15 teaches us that this duty was incumbent upon them. "So they are before the throne of God, and they worship Him day and night in His temple. And the one who sits on the throne shall protect them with His shadow." Standing before the throne of God and in the presence of the Lamb means the highest happiness. The queen of Sheba once said to Solomon, "Blessed are your men, and blessed are your servants who stand before you always and listen to your wisdom" (1 Kings 10:8). How much more blessed must all those be who contemplate God's countenance in Christ face-to-face and forever! What pinnacle of blessedness could they fail to reach? There is quite widespread agreement about *objective* blessedness. And "nothing makes a man happy except God who made man," as all theologians after Augustine acknowledge. But there is certainly dispute among the Scholastics concerning *formal* blessedness— I mean that principal act by which the blessed mind is carried along toward its object as it beatifies it. Thomas strongly contends for the vision of God as formal blessedness; Scotus, for the love of God; and Bonaventure, for both. I think that such an important dispute can be resolved once three statements have been made.

First, those who say that happiness consists in the vision of God have a strong thesis, provided they do not mean by this merely vision. The Scripture says, "We now see through a mirror darkly, then face-to-face. When He shall appear, we shall be like Him, because we will see Him as He is. Blessed are the pure of heart, because they shall see God" (1 Cor. 13:12; 1 John 3:2; Matt. 5:8). The fathers—for example, Augustine—say, "Contemplation is the reward of faith, and hearts are cleansed to receive this reward by faith."[12] Irenaeus: "Eternal life comes to each person because he sees God."[13] Even the more sober philosophers understood this. Aristotle says, ἔστιν ἡ εὐδαιμονία θεωρία τις.[14] Or as Steuco translates it, "The contemplation of God."[15] Seneca, at the end of letter 102, among other things well worth reading, writes, "Through these delays of mortal life, we receive a preview of

---

11. In tertiam Sententiar. Distinct. 19. qu. unica.] Duns Scotus, *Quaestiones In Lib. III. Sententiarum*, vol. 1 (Lyon, 1639), dist. 19, qu. 1, p. 415.

12. De Trin. l. 1. c. 8.] Augustine, *De Trinitate*, 1.8.17.

13. Contra haeres. l. 4. c. 37.] Irenaeus, *Adversus Haereses*, bk. 4, ch. 37.

14. "Happiness is a kind of vision." Quoted as Aristotle (without citation) in Steuco; this seems to be a paraphrase of *Nicomachean Ethics*, bk. 10, 1178a8.

15. De peren. philosoph. lib. 4. c. 11.] Agostino Steuco, 1497–1548, Italian humanist,

that better and longer life to come. We cannot yet endure heaven except at arm's length. Sometimes nature's secrets will reveal themselves to you"—I think he means the creating nature—that is, God. "That black cloud will be shattered, and clear light will break through on all sides. No shadow will disturb our peace."[16]

Second, perhaps those hold a better opinion who think that blessedness resides in love of God, provided they do not exclude vision. This blessedness resides absolutely in the final and highest perfection. It is clear that the love of God is perfection from the fact that hating God is worse than not knowing Him. It is, to be sure, the worst of all things that can befall creatures. Therefore, by the law of contraries, loving God is better than seeing Him and is the best action by far. From this we can conclude that it is the last perfection, because love follows vision. The blessed do not love God in order to see Him, but they see Him in order to love Him. Here, no doubt, that statement is very applicable: ἐκ τοῦ ὁρᾶν τὸ ἐρᾶν.[17] Furthermore, no reasonable person will deny that happiness resides in the enjoyment of God. But according to Augustine, enjoyment means "clinging to anything for its own sake through love."[18] This occurs most fully in our homeland where the affection is at rest in God and, as the same father says, "the appetite of the one who is filled with longing becomes the love of the one who enjoys."[19]

Third, those men philosophize best and most accurately who hold that blessedness consists in both at the same time, in the vision and love of God. Some derive this principle from certain Davidic expressions, such as this one: "Taste and see that Jehovah is good" (Ps. 34:8). Hugh of Saint Victor says of this passage, "In the command 'Taste' is delight; in the command 'See' is knowledge."[20] There is also this passage: "You shall make them drink from the stream of Your pleasures" [Ps. 36:8]. Look, here is the kindling for love's true fire: "Because in Your presence is the fountain of life, and in Your light we shall see light" [Ps. 36:9–10]. Essential blessedness must be based upon possessing God. But by the action of both faculties—namely, the will and the intellect equally—the blessed will come to possess God in principle

---

Old Testament scholar and counter-Reformer, *De Perenni Philosophia* (Basel, 1542), bk. 3, ch. 11, p. 233.

16. Seneca, *Epistolae, epistola* 102.

17. "Love is born from sight," a Platonic sentiment without attribution.

18. De Doctrin. Christian. cap. 4.] Augustine, *De Doctrina Christiana*, 1.4.

19. De Trinit. l. ult.] Augustine, *De Trinitate*, 15.26.47.

20. In cap. 7. *Dionys.* de coelest. hierar.] Hugh of St. Victor, *Annotationes Elucidatoris In Caelestem Hierarchiam*, in *Opera Omnia*, vol. 1 (Mainz, 1617), bk. 7, ch. 7, p. 388.

and without mediation. This is the position of Jacob de Bay.[21] Gregory de Valencia, citing Boethius, argues very forcefully that blessedness is

> the state brought to perfection by an accumulation of everything good. Therefore, it must consist in the operations of both rational faculties. Because if the vision of God were missing, as the first truth, or the enjoyment of Him through love, as the highest good, the mind would remain restless. But restlessness and happiness are mutually exclusive.[22]

But if then one should ask why—this being the case—both the sacred texts and theologians so often insist on vision when they describe the condition of the blessed, and speak so sparingly about love, perhaps we can respond with this: it is completely appropriate to maintain that it happened this way not because a clear vision of God is *per se* either complete blessedness or a significant part of that blessedness but rather because it is only by vision that pilgrims are distinguished from those who have laid hold of blessedness. No doubt there is very little difference between them with respect to love. After all, both of them love God with the same love Paul said "never fails" [1 Cor. 13]. But there is a very great difference between them with respect to vision. For the former walk "by faith," the latter "by sight" [2 Cor. 5:7]. But if one continues to be puzzled as to how blessedness, a single entity, could reside in multiple aspects, it is common to say that multiple things merge into one formal element. Please heed, dear reader, Livio Galante, in his work *A Comparison between Christian and Platonic Theology*:

> In the fatherland, love is vision's immediate goal, just as, along the journey, the goal of the commandment is love. Vision is a function of understanding and is also the foundation of blessedness. Enjoyment and love are functions of will and are the goal of that same will. Therefore, there are two partial causes of blessedness that produce one complete, formal cause. Blessedness is an operation of the intellect with respect to its origin, when conceived in terms of its starting point. Blessedness is also a function of the will with respect to its goal, when conceived in terms of its completion.[23]

To sum up: *the happiness of man undoubtedly consists in vision, but in a vision characterized by love; and it consists in love, but in a love endowed with perfect vision.*

---

21. Instit. Relig. Christian. l. 1. c. 371. p. 291.] Jacob de Bay, 1545–1614, Belgian Roman Catholic theologian, *Institutionum Religionis Christianae Libri IV* (Antwerp, 1624), bk. 1, ch. 371, p. 291.

22. In 1ᵃᵐ 2ᵃᵉ Disp. 1. qu. 3. punct. 4.] Gregory de Valencia, *Commentariorum Theologicorum*, vol. 2, disp. 1, qu. 3, punct. 4, pp. 49ff. is cit. 5.

23. Lib. 17. p. 423.] Livio Galante, fl. 1617–1627, Italian professor of theology and philosophy, *Christianae Theologiae Cum Platonica Comparatio* (Bologna, 1627), bk. 17, p. 423.

§4. Fourth, the blessed are described in terms of their clothing, and this in two ways. "They are dressed in white robes and carry palm branches in their hands." The whiteness of the robes means three things. First, dignity, a meaning it had among all peoples. Among the various adornments attributed to the Roman senator by Martial is this:

And a toga to outshine the whitest snow unsoiled.[24]

The leading citizens among the Jews were called חוֹרִים (1 Kings 24:8; Neh. 4:14, 19). This is the origin of the Greek word ἥρως, and it means literally *white*, because of the whiteness of their garments.[25] When Joseph was elevated among the Egyptians to the highest pinnacle of dignity, he put on linen garments at Pharaoh's command (Gen. 41:42). Likewise, Mordechai among the Persians left the king's presence dressed in a royal garment of sapphire blue and white (Esth. 8:15).

Second, the white robe indicates purity. It was customary for those who sought some political office at Rome to wear white, and this is why they were called *candidates*. The point of this practice was for them to display the integrity of character that the republic's laws demanded from such a magistrate. Beyond that, the ancient Christians dressed the recently baptized in white robes to show the cleanness of their hearts. Lactantius took note of it in this short line of verse:

The robe of white does signify as well their cleansed souls.[26]

One can also see the Lamb's wife in Revelation "robed in linen clean and bright." τὸ δὲ βύσσινον τὰ δικαιώματα ἐστίν τῶν ἁγίων (Rev. 19:8).[27] David prayed, "Cleanse me with hyssop that I may be clean, wash me that I may be white as snow" (Ps. 51:7). And in a certain passage, Prudentius recalls "the snow-white garment of righteousness."[28]

Third, the white garment indicates joy. Those who grieve usually dress in mournful gray; those who rejoice, in white, as at holiday celebrations. Thus, we have Horace's famous quote: "The man dressed in white should celebrate the holidays."[29] In addition, we have Solomon: "Eat your bread in joy, and drink your wine with gladness. Let your garments at all times be white" (Eccl. 9:7–8).

---

24. *Lib. 2. Epigram. 29.*] Martial, *Epigrammata*, 2.29.

25. This is a false etymology, as *heroes* is not derived from the Jewish word but from a Proto-Indo-European root meaning "to protect."

26. Lactantius, *Ad Felicem Episcopum*, in *Opera Quae Extant Omnia* (Leiden, 1652), p. 660.

27. "Fine linen is the saints' righteousness."

28. Prudentius, *Contra Symmachum*, bk. 1, fol. 119r.

29. Horace, *Satyra*, bk. 2.

All of these are very well suited to the saints as they triumph. In fact, they simultaneously acquire priestly and royal dignity. Among the Jews, white clothing signified both. That they obtain priestly dignity is evident from Maimonides, as quoted by Louis de Dieu: "Every priest, without exception, who has rejected his ancestral privilege puts on and wears black clothing and departs the atrium. But every priest found acceptable and upright dons white clothing and serves beside his fellow priests."[30] It is clear from comparing Luke in Acts with Josephus that the blessed also acquire royal dignity. Herod Agrippa is described as sitting upon his seat of judgment dressed in a royal garment (Acts 12:21). Josephus, in his *Antiquities*, comments, "He was dressed in a garment made entirely from silver with amazing workmanship. When it was struck by the rays of the rising sun, it gave off a kind of divine shimmer and struck everyone who saw it with a reverence mixed with awe."[31] The blessed also receive a purity that exceeds every possible conception of purity. Then truly they become godlike, or similar to God, as they are those who "see Him as He is" [1 John 3:2]. In the same fashion, they acquire a joy that exceeds every possible conception of joy. Augustine remarks, "O joy surpassing joy, joy that conquers all joy, beyond which no joy exists! When shall I enter into you, to see my God who dwells in you?"[32]

§ 5. In the meantime, the saints should acknowledge that they now owe all these blessings, and shall owe them forevermore, to our most blessed Mediator Jesus Christ. For a little later in this very chapter, the saints are described as those who "washed their robes and made them white in the blood of the Lamb" (Rev. 7:14). From this comes the connection between priestly and royal dignity through blood in chapter 1: "He who loved us and has washed us from our sins by His blood and made us to be kings and priests to God and to His Father" (Rev. 1:5–6). From this same fountain, the author of Hebrews derives purity: "If the blood of bulls and goats, and the ash of a heifer sprinkling those who were unclean, sanctified them in purity of the flesh, how much more shall the blood of Christ, who through the Holy Spirit has offered Himself blameless to God, completely cleanse your conscience from dead works to worship the living God?" (Heb. 9:13–14). What about the fact that the very word *holy*,[33] as Isidore attests, is derived from words that mean *dipped in blood*? This is because in antiquity,

---

30. Animadvers. in Apoc. 3.4.] Maimonides, quoted in de Dieu, *Animadversiones In D. Pauli*, sub loc. Rev. 3:4.

31. Lib. 19. c. 7.] Josephus, *Antiquitatum Iudaicarum*, bk. 19, ch. 7.

32. Augustine, *Soliloquiorum Animae Ad Deum*, ch. 35.

33. Isidore of Seville, ca. 560–636, bishop, grammarian, and exegete, *Etymologiae* (Venice, 1473). A. cites a spurious etymology that *sanctus* is a combination of *san[guine tin]ctus*.

those who desired purification were touched with the blood of the sacrificial victim. It is true that in political affairs, as the poet records, "one must strive by virtue, not blood."[34] But in theology, relying on one's own virtue is utterly vain. Instead, everything depends solely upon the blood of Christ. Some of the men who did this were martyrs and shed their own blood for Christ. Nevertheless, they made their garments white not with their own blood but with His.

So far as concerns joy, however great it is, the blessed attributed all the joy they had received to Christ the Lord and Him crucified. I think that it was perhaps as a memorial to this that the Italians established their famous military regiment—in Mantua, to be specific. They were called "Soldiers of the Blood of our Lord Jesus Christ," and the title was endorsed by Pope Paul V.[35] Around their neck is a pendant with two angels holding three drops of blood, and next to this emblem, the inscription "There is no sadness when one has Christ's blood."[36]

As for the rest, this crowd is described as carrying palms, and it is absolutely certain that this is a victory sign. Claudian gives us this poetic description:

As victory with verdant palm rejoiced, all dressed with spoils.[37]

And in Vergil, those preparing to fight receive, among other things,

> …sacred tripods and flowering crowns,
> And palms the prize for victors…[38]

Aulus Gellius gives a reason for this practice, and he gets it from Plutarch: "The wood of the palm tree does not break when people try to force and bend it. Even when it bears great weight, the palm does not bow nor bend in half. But it springs back against the weight, remains upright, and retains its original shape."[39] Grynaeus captured the whole idea with a short couplet in his letters published by Scultetus:

Though crushed beneath an awful load the palm still blossoms green.
So hearts fixed on their God below the cross ne'er lose their sheen.[40]

---

34. Claudian, *De IV Consulatu Honorii Augusti*, in *Quae exstant* (220).

35. Paul V, 1552–1621, *p.* 1605–1621.

36. According to tradition, the centurion who pierced Christ's side brought His blood to Mantua, Italy, where the relic resides.

37. Claudian, *De Laudibus Stiliconis*, in *Quae Exstant*, bk. 3.

38. Aeneid l. 5. carm. 110, 111.] Vergil, *Aeneidos*, bk. 5 (lines 110–11).

39. *Plutarch*. Sympos. l. 6. qu 4. *A. Gell.* Noctium Attic. l. 3. c. 6.] Plutarch, *Symposiacon*, in *Omnium Quae Exstant*, vol. 2 (Frankfurt, 1620), bk. 8, quaes. 4; Aulus Gellius, 125/128–180, Roman author and grammarian, *Noctes Atticae* (Geneva, 1609), bk. 3, ch. 6.

40. Lib. 2. Epist. 15. p. 475.] Johann Jakob Grynaeus, 1540–1617, Swiss Reformed theologian, *Epistolarum Selectarum* (Offenbach, 1612), bk. 2, p. 475 (*epistola* 15).

With good reason then, palm branches are distributed to those mentioned in this passage. For "they had come," as it says in the subsequent text, "out of great affliction" (Rev. 7:14). And at last, they attained the goal of their faith, the salvation of their souls. We read in the sacred Book that long ago, palms were carved on the holy of holies. The holy of holies beautifully represents the heaven of heavens, that is, the very highest heaven. Similarly, the inner courtyard, where the candelabras were placed, is star-studded heaven. In the courtyard of the gentiles, or the exterior courtyard, is heaven's lowest part (1 Kings 6:29). Palm branches are attached to the holy of holies because only those who conquer the world, the flesh, and Satan enter the third heaven this image represents.

§6. There next follows the shouting of these same blessed saints, and it immediately demands our special attention. "They were shouting with a loud voice, saying, ἡ σωτηρία τῷ Θεῷ ἡμῶν τῷ καθημένῳ ἐπὶ τῷ θρόνῳ καὶ τῷ ἀρνίῳ"[41] [Rev. 7:10]. These are not the words of men merely expressing what they desire but of men filled with praise. Nor do the words constitute a prayer but a confession. They do not say that "the majority of salvation" belongs to the one who is salvation itself. No. They ascribe all of it to Him. And these words teach us very explicitly that God in Christ is the one to whom alone we owe, right down to the uttermost, every aspect of salvation.

If this phrase concerns temporal salvation, it would be, "Salvation belongs to Jehovah," as David said (Ps. 3:8). Moses also said something like this to the people of Israel, when their backs were hard pressed against the wall: "Do not fear; stand firm, and see the salvation of Jehovah" (Exod. 14:13). That statement of Mezentius[42] in Vergil breathes a pure, unadulterated atheism:

My own right hand is all my God, and fleet spear that I heft.[43]

Pharaoh, not at all instilled with a knowledge of the true God, called Joseph by a new name, Zaphnath-Paaneah. Jerome translates this as *savior of the world*. For this was published in the text itself: "And he changed his name and called him, in the Egyptian language, 'savior of the world'" (Gen. 41:45). But Joseph personally explained to his brothers that, when it came to salvation, he understood clearly that God and not he was its author. He said, "God sent me here before you into Egypt for your salvation. God sent me ahead so you would be preserved on earth and you could get sustenance

41. "Salvation is from our God who sits upon the throne, and from the Lamb."
42. Mezentius, Etruscan king in Vergil's *Aeneid*.
43. Aeneid. l. 10.] Vergil, *Aeneidos*, bk. 10 (line 773).

to live. It was not by your plan but by the will of God that I was sent here" (Gen. 45:5, 7–8).

But if the passage deals with the spiritual salvation that finds its end-point in eternity, then the free gifts of God shine brightly on each of its individual steps. In election God has freely given us to Christ. As the Lord says to the Father, in John, "They were Yours, and You have given them to Me" (John 17:6). In redemption He has given us Christ, as we read in Isa-iah: "To us a child is born, to us a Son has been given" (Isa. 9:6). The faith by which we lay hold of Christ unto salvation is according to His gift. This is what Paul says: "By grace you have been saved through faith; this is not from yourselves but is the gift of God" (Eph. 2:8). The same is just as true of that obedience by which we testify to our faith, as he likewise asserts: "The grace that was conferred upon me was not in vain, but I worked harder than all the rest. Yet it was not I that labored but the grace of God with me" (1 Cor. 15:10). Yes, even the perseverance that makes obedience perfect is God's gift. For thus the Lord spoke through the prophet: "I shall put in them a heart to worship Me all their days, and I will implant reverence for Me in their minds so that they do not depart from Me" (Jer. 32:39–40). Finally, that very eternal life that crowns perseverance is God's gift. Listen to what Christ says: "Remain faithful unto death, and I shall give you the crown of life" (Rev. 2:10).

§ 7. But it is also from this shouting, moreover, that the primary sources of our salvation lay open to those who seek them. The first of these is that covenant of grace that the Lord condescended to enter into with us, and by the reasoning of which He is said to be peculiarly the God of those who are saved. The text says, τῷ Θεῷ ἡμῶν.[44] "I am Yours, save me," David says (Ps. 119:94). And in the book of Jeremiah, the church cries, "Behold, we have come to You, for You are the Lord our God. Truly in the Lord our God is Israel's salvation" (Jer. 3:22–23). That familiar passage of Daniel that mentions the Messiah suggests that this is not extended to everyone but ought to be considered the privilege of the elect alone: "He has established His covenant with many" (Dan. 9:27). The Septuagint translates it as δυναμώσει διαθήκην πολλοῖς.[45] Christ seems to have alluded to this passage in the institution of the Lord's Supper, when He addressed His disciples and explained the cup to them: "This is My blood of the new cov-enant, which is poured out for many for the remission of sins" (Matt. 26:28). And following Him, Paul said, "Through the obedience of one man, many (οἱ πολλοί) shall be made righteous" (Rom. 5:19). Evidently,

---

44. "To our God."

45. "Shall establish His covenant for many."

these "many" are those Daniel mentioned in his prophecy. If someone should ask who these many were, Fisher answers that we must take them to mean the elect. In Daniel the word is לְרַבִּים. He translates it as *the excellent ones* (i.e., the elect) and compares it with the statement in Isaiah. "By knowledge of Him, My righteous servant shall justify *Larabbim*," the excellent ones [Isa. 53:11]. If this interpretation is valid, then indeed we must say that the covenant of grace was not initiated with all men but with those many *excellent ones* (i.e., the elect). And we must say that the blood of the covenant was shed for them, and if not for them alone, at least for them in a particular way and purpose.

The second source of our salvation is God's supreme sovereignty, as expressed in these words: "Salvation is from God who sits on the throne." This is a characteristic of those with highest authority, as David explains: "The Lord, the King is enthroned forever" (Ps. 29:10). And again, "The Lord has prepared His abode in heaven, and His kingdom rules over all" (Ps. 103:19). It is God's prerogative, therefore, to elect whom He pleases and to lead whom He elects infallibly to salvation. Surely Christ derives distinguishing grace from God's supreme sovereignty when He addressed the Father like this: "I give You glory, Father, Lord of heaven and earth, because You have hidden these things from the wise and those with understanding, and You have revealed them to infants. Yes, Father, because it pleased You to do so" (Matt. 11:25–26). Paul spoke no differently when he thundered from heaven in his letter to the Romans. To stop the mouth of quarrelsome reason, he said, "O man, who are you to argue with God? There is no way the pot will say to the potter, 'Why did you make me like this?' Or does the potter not have authority over the raw clay to make from the same lump one vessel for honor and another for dishonor?" (Rom. 9:21–22). I do not want to wrap around this apostolic text the gloss of Calvin or Beza, much less that of Ames or Twisse. For now, let us listen to the Jesuit Leonard Lessius only. He says,

> The creature depends upon God alone for everything. And although, in many instances, God uses secondary causes, He Himself puts them all in place and does not need them. Yet the pot is not dependent upon the potter alone but needs the marl from which it is made, the water that softens it and makes it manageable, the wheel it is turned on, and the fire that bakes it. The pot is indebted to all these the same as to the potter, who alone applies these elements through spatial motion. He supplies, however, nothing independently. Now if the potter has this much authority over the pot because of the application of causes which he himself did not make and which do not take their efficacy from him, how much more right shall God have over His creatures, since He alone has, by His own

power, provided the material, the shape, the potentialities, the qualities, and all the externalities?[46]

The third source of our salvation is the mediation of Christ our Lord. In this passage, salvation is also ascribed to the Lamb. We note this elsewhere too, in Peter, who states that we have been redeemed "not by silver or gold but by precious blood, yes, of a guiltless and unblemished Lamb, Christ" (1 Peter 1:18–19). A common question among the Scholastics is whether Christ was the mediator as God, as man, or as the Θεάνθρωπος.[47] Peter Lombard and, after him, Franco Stancaro[48] taught that the office of mediator does not apply to Christ except according to His human nature. Andreas Osiander,[49] the father of Lucas, held that His mediation did not apply except according to the divine nature. The consensus position of the church fathers and of Protestants is that the Lord was mediator according to both natures. Chamier thought that the very best of the fathers, Augustine, spoke a little too stridently on this topic, even in a way that was ἀκύρως.[50] But that very learned man[51] would not have spoken so rashly about Augustine's judgment if he had remembered what the "hammer of heretics" says in his *Homily* or *Book on the Sheep*, in volume 9, chapter 12 of his collected works: "Divinity without humanity is not a mediator. But Christ's human divinity and divine humanity is a mediator between divinity alone and humanity alone."[52] I do not know whether anything more appropriate than this could have been said. And Revelation itself (so as not to belabor the point) seems to favor this position very much. For here salvation is attributed to the Lamb, in His slaughtered state, and this word indicates a nature capable of suffering. But salvation is also attributed to the one who sits on the throne. Yet this is a divine honor Christ arrogates to Himself in the second to last verse of chapter 3: "I have overcome, and I am seated with My Father on His throne" [Rev. 3:21].

§ 8. Next follows the angelic chorus who, under the same head Christ (to whom they owe their στάσις, but not their ἀνάστασις,[53] as they have never fallen), constitute the second half of the church. Similarly, the

---

46. *Lessius* de perfect. divinis, l. 10. cap. 3. § 19.] Lessius, *De Perfectionibus*, bk. 10, ch. 3, sec. 19, p. 128.

47. "God-man."

48. Francesco Stancaro, 1501–1574, Italian Protestant theologian and Hebraist.

49. Andreas Osiander, 1498–1552, German Lutheran theologian.

50. *Panstrat.* tom. 2. lib. 7. cap. 6. § 16.] Chamier, *Panstratiae Catholicae*, vol. 2, bk. 7, ch. 6, sec. 16, p. 251.

51. I.e., Chamier.

52. Augustine, *De Ovibus Liber Sive Homilia*, in *Opera*, vol. 9 (Basil, 1528), ch. 14, p. 748.

53. "Position" and "restoration," respectively.

passage in Hebrews that I have commended above to the reader recounts the "ten thousands of angels, in addition to the spirits of the righteous men made perfect" [Heb. 12:23]. And in Ephesians, God is described as "ἀνακεφαλαιώσασθαι[54] in Christ all things, both those that are in heaven and those that are on earth" (Eph. 1:10). I believe that by the phrase τὰ ἐπὶ τῆς γῆς[55] Paul meant elect men who dwelt on earth before they were translated to the heavens above. And by the phrase τὰ ἐν τοῖς οὐρανοῖς[56] he meant the elect angels that were the native residents of heaven. And by ἀνακεφαλαιώσασθαι[57] [Eph. 1:10] he does not mean, in the rhetorical sense, a brief summation of many different arguments, but he meant it as a numerical idea—that is, as the sum of several different numbers. For when innumerable men are added to the blessed angels they constitute the total sum, as it were, of the one church triumphant. In the meantime, they love shouting! O song most sweet, surpassing all other songs, when God the Father of spirits embraces human and angelic spirits in His own bosom and created spirits are given new life by the Uncreated! When angels together with men harmoniously unite to celebrate the praises of the eternal Father, and, likewise, men together with angels, stirred up with mutual admonitions, enjoy as one the purest concord of heart!

Two different postures are attributed to these glorious spirits. The one is a posture of ministering: "All the angels stood in a great arc around the throne and the elders and the four living creatures." This echoes the passage in Daniel, where "the Ancient of Days sat on His throne, and thousands upon thousands of angels ministered to him, and ten thousand times ten thousand stood before him" (Dan. 7:9–10). The other posture is one of worship: "They threw themselves down before the throne on their faces καὶ προσεκύνησαν τῷ Θεῷ" [Rev. 7:11].[58] This means that they were attending to Him with religious worship. To identify this type of worship, we note that the Holy Spirit employed a word derived from gentile superstition. The pagans typically placed their hands over their mouths during worship. This is what the word προσκυνεῖν properly means, as it is from κύω, and from that, κυνέω, which means *to kiss*. "And the Latin word *adorare* has exactly the same meaning. It was formed not from *orare*, 'to pray' (as ignorant men suppose), but from the action of moving the hand toward the mouth." So says Grotius.[59] It is clear from Job's statement that this was a very ancient

---

54. "Gathering together summarily."

55. "Those that are on earth."

56. "Those that are in heaven."

57. "Gathering together summarily."

58. "And worshipped God."

59. In explicat. Decalog. ad 2ᵃᵐ praecept.] Grotius, *Explicatio Decalogi* (Amsterdam, 1640), p. 39.

worship practice: "If I saw the sun when it shone and the moon coming on clearly, and my heart within was glad, and I kissed my hand with my own mouth" (Job 31:26–27). Quite some time ago, the very knowledgeable scholars Drusius and Lipsius produced a large number of additional testimonies to prove this claim. Those who have the free time and desire should consult them.[60] I thought it helpful to add just one that I especially like from Lipsius, a man very familiar with the writings of both Senecas. It is not his original observation, or if it is, not one he produced from a passage that deals specifically with this religious rite. I do not know whether he is quoting from another author. The quote is excerpted from book 8, the second controversy, like this:

> The Elians borrowed Phidias[61] from the Athenians to make the Zeus at Olympia for them, after they agreed that they would either return Phidias or 100 talents. When the statue of Zeus was completed, the Elians said that Phidias had stolen the gold, and they cut off his hand as a kind of violation of the oath. Then they sent him back mutilated to the Athenians. The Athenians demand their 100 talents and argued against the Elians: "We made a contract with Phidias for his hands. Do you expect us to take Phidias back without the very thing that, were it missing, you yourselves would not accept him? We loaned you a man who could make gods. We have gotten back someone who cannot even worship them."[62]

§ 9. Next, these figures[63] are introduced as saying "Amen. Blessing and glory and wisdom and thanks and honor and authority and strength be to our God forever and ever. Amen" [Rev. 7:12]. We must understand the word *amen* to refer to the foregoing shout of the saints. Then, we take it as referring to the angels who approve the statement as with a vote. Grotius, therefore, comments on this passage that "here the angels sing in harmony with those making their confession as citizens of one kingdom."[64] Look closely, Christian reader, at that noble controversy the church triumphant now resolved. It is a controversy that constantly ripped apart the church militant. In this controversy, a significant motive of the mischief makers is the sectarian zeal of different parties. Not too long ago, Spanheim said that "we are all born Pelagians, or actually with Pharisaical arrogance. This

---

60. *Drus.* Observat. l. 1. c. 20.] Drusius, *Observationum Libri XII* (Antwerp, 1584) bk. 1, ch. 20, p. 32.

61. Phidias, fl. ca. 490–430 BC, Greek sculptor.

62. *Lips.* Elector. l. 2. cap. 6.] Lipsius, *Electorum Liber* (1580), II.6.

63. I.e., angels, elders, and four living creatures.

64. Grotius, *Annotationes In Novum Testamentum*, sub loc. Rev. 7:11. There is an error, so verse 12 is not present, and this line appears under verse 11.

character trait is almost impossible to destroy."[65] And so this is a tendency we all share: we try to join ourselves to God, and our will with His grace, in the whole business of human salvation. We do this even though the entire church of heaven has eloquently ruled on this point, that God in Christ is the one to whom alone, fundamentally, we owe salvation in every fine detail. She says, "Salvation is from our God, who sits upon the throne, and from the Lamb." The saints in glory shout this out loud; the elect angels agree in one accord: "Amen!" [Rev. 7:10–12].

Although I recognize—to the extent I am able to grasp these mysteries (which doubtless always stretch to the utmost the greatest intellects)—that we must credit both divine grace and human will as causally concurrent in the sinner's return to God and his acquisition of salvation, nevertheless, they are in no way coordinated as equal causes. They neither function equally as concurrent with respect to the effect, like two horses pulling a chariot with equal effort. Nor do they function unequally, like a giant and a child engaged in trying to lift the same heavy object. Instead, this is the proper way to understand it: the much lighter portion rests upon the child, the greater burden upon the giant, but all subordinated to him, as I will explain. At the first moment of conversion, when the Holy Spirit comes to dwell in the soul and pours into it His life-giving principle, the elect grace of God presents itself as the acting principle, the human will as the recipient subject in which the Spirit works as He pleases. But at the second moment and those that follow, when the freed will is freely carried along to its chief end, God still remains as the acting principle. The will is subordinated to it as an instrument. It is not, to be sure, an unthinking instrument, but a rational one that acts and produces the life-giving operations of believing and loving that grace determines for it. Meanwhile, God both moves and determines the person, and the person goes and determines himself. It is not, however, a twofold motion, one from man, the second from God. It is the same motion from both of them: from God as the first cause, from man as the second, but from the former cause antecedently by nature, in that He directs this motion to its second cause by His causation. Thus, both God and man, as complete causes, directly act concurrently to produce the same actions. God acts in His own genus by subordinating the second cause to Himself. Man in his own genus acts like an instrument by moving under the first cause.

§ 10. The remaining words of the angels constitute their actual doxology. These words display before us, as I would say, the Sacred Pleiades, assigning

---

65. Praefation. ad Lectorem praefix. Exercit. de gratia Universali.] Spanheim, *Exercitationes*, vol. 1, sig. ***8r (*praefatio*).

to God seven perfections or special privileges. All of them flash forth with the greatest brilliance in the task of human salvation (the context strongly suggests that this is its point of reference).

First is ἡ εὐλογία (blessing). The voice of nature herself proclaims that God must receive blessing. Consequently, the pagans established hymns to sing praise to their gods at their altars. Orpheus[66] and others wrote such hymns. The voice of Scripture also makes this clear. We see it especially in the Psalms, where Psalm 145 delights in this title, "David's Song of Praise," and the whole song is a eulogy to God derived from His attributes.[67] The rabbis thought this psalm was so significant that they said whoever recited it three times a day would be safe the rest of his life. Kimchi tried to soften this statement a bit, because it was somewhat clumsy.[68] He said one must not take it as applying to the man who only recites with his mouth but to the man who recites with mouth and heart. Five additional psalms throughout the psalter begin as well as end with the word *hallelujah*. This means *praise the Lord*, and ancient Christians apparently used it no matter their circumstance or age. Jerome, in his letter to Laeta,[69] strongly approves of the fact that "your little girl's tongue, though chattering, still cries, 'Hallelujah.'"[70] And in his letter to Marcella,[71] he says, "The ploughman, while gripping his plough handle, chants out, 'Hallelujah.'"[72] No one should be surprised if, since nature and Scripture lead the way like this, the voice of the universal church commends this practice in its own unique way. "Praise awaits You, or befits You, O God in Zion," says the psalmist (Ps. 65:1). Here he expressly mentions Zion.[73] The Apostle adds his voice: "To Him who, by His all-surpassing power, is able to do all things, far beyond what we ask or think, according to His might at work in us, to Him be glory in the church, through Christ Jesus" (Eph. 3:20–21). Again, here we have expressly stated "in the church" and "through Christ Jesus," who is made known only to the church.

The second of the seven is ἡ δόξα (glory). This is properly attributed to persons or things whose excellence shines brighter than other items in the same category. Among inanimate objects, the stars are the most excellent; and among the stars, the sun and moon. Therefore, we read, "The glory of

---

66. Orpheus, mythical Greek musician.

67. *Muis* in locum.] De Muis, *In Omnes Psalmos*, p. 335.

68. Radack (Radaq, Rabbi David Kimhi/Kimchi), 1160–1235, rabbi and biblical commentator.

69. Laeta, fl. ca. AD 403, cousin of Marcella.

70. Jerome, *Opera Divi Hieronymi Stridoniensis*, vol. 1, *epistola* 7.

71. Marcella, d. AD 410, Roman aristocrat.

72. Jerome, *Opera Divi Hieronymi Stridoniensis*, vol. 1, *epistola* 18.

73. I.e., meaning the church.

the sun is ἄλλη δόξα;[74] that of the moon, another; and still another for the stars. For star διαφέρει ἐν δόξα" (1 Cor. 15:41).[75] Kings surpass commoners by a wide margin, and angels surpass kings, as they do all the other innumerable creatures endowed with understanding. Therefore, the sacred texts attribute glory to each. When the Lord spoke of lilies, he said that "King Solomon in all his glory" was not dressed like one of them (Luke 12:27). Likewise, John bears witness that "the kings of the earth will bring their glory and honor to the new Jerusalem" (Rev. 21:24). In the same fashion, the angels are described as possessing cherubic glory. So it is no surprise that the one who outshines stars, kings, angels, and everything else—the most exalted and uncreated being, beyond anything that can be named—is called the God of glory. And it is no surprise if any person of the Godhead should be marked out by the same attribute. So the Father is called "Father of glory" (Eph. 1:17); the Son, the "Lord of glory" (1 Cor. 2:8); the Holy Spirit, the "Spirit of glory" (1 Peter 4:14). And it is no surprise if the angels once sang in their birthday song, "Glory to God in the highest" (Luke 2:14), or if the churches in their liturgies sing, "Glory to the Father, and to the Son, and to the Holy Spirit."

§ 11. The third of the seven is ἡ σοφία (wisdom). In one passage, Paul joins to this the word φρόνησις.[76] "In Christ," Paul says, "we have redemption through His blood, according to His divine grace, ἐπερίσσευσεν εἰς ἡμᾶς ἐν πάσῃ σοφίᾳ καὶ φρονήσει" (Eph. 1:7–8).[77] Grotius comments that "it was a mark of wisdom to find means for healing the human race and of prudence to distribute them."[78] In another passage, Paul connects wisdom with γνῶσις.[79] We find it in that very famous passage in Romans 11: "O the deep riches καὶ σοφίας καὶ γνώσεως τοῦ Θεοῦ![80] How unsearchable are His judgments and His paths beyond finding out!" (Rom. 11:33). Ἡ σοφία here seems to refer to God's secret κρίματα, decrees. Nothing except divine wisdom is sufficient to search these out. Γνῶσις (knowledge) means the paths of God's providence adminstering all things according to these decrees. Such paths are very well known to God but impenetrable to human reason. Paul himself is stunned at this and shouts, ὦ βάθος! [Rom. 11:13].[81] Even before Paul, David was captivated by an equal amazement,

---

74. "Of one kind."
75. "Excels star in its glory."
76. "Prudence."
77. "Which He has showered upon us with all wisdom and prudence."
78. Grotius, *Annotationes In Novum Testamentum*, sub loc. Eph. 1:8.
79. "Knowledge."
80. "Both of the wisdom and the knowledge of God."
81. "O the depth!"

so much that he said, "Your knowledge is too wonderful for me. It is lofty, I shall not reach it" (Ps. 139:6). Simone de Muis interprets this to mean, "Your knowledge, by which You know all things, is so marvelous that I can in no way comprehend it; so lofty, that I cannot at all attain it. For although I know that You know all things, still I do not know how You can understand such different and diverse things at once with perfect simultaneity, instead of one at a time."[82]

A modern writer put it brilliantly:

God's incomprehensible wisdom cannot be compressed within the narrow confines of human reason. Moreover, in this mystery, human reason must be humbled beneath the piety of faith. For that is what was appropriate, and the order of our restoration demanded this. And God's image, twisted through reason's arrogance, in the mystery of our redemption had to be reformed through humiliation of reason.[83]

The fourth of the seven is ἡ εὐχαριστία (thanksgiving). When the prophet was discussing Zion, he said, "Joy in happiness shall be found in her, thanksgiving and the sound of praise" (Isa. 51:3). All Zion's inhabitants must offer thanksgiving, whether they are pilgrims on the way or are already at rest in the fatherland. And they do this first from a debt of honesty. A familiar expression among the Hebrews is that the Lord must be praised in even the least significant matter. He must be magnified in the elephant, in the sun, the moon and adored in the rest of the stars. Let us also say that it is honorable and beautiful to fill up the measure of our thanksgiving according to the measure of the grace we have received. And so, as we have received eternal salvation, we owe eternal gratitude.

Second, they offer thanksgiving from a debt of righteousness. For this aspect of gratitude is, as it were, a kind of poll tax and specific obligation (as the experts in law call it) that God imposes on all His beneficiaries, proportional to their acknowledgment of His supreme sovereignty. Those who refuse to pay the beneficiary excise, so to speak, are rightly put out of the people. Bernard piously comments,

What shall I render to the Lord for all the benefits He has bestowed upon me? For if I owe my whole being to God for making me, what should I add now that He has remade me? The first thing He did, doubtless, was to give me myself, and the second was to give me Himself. And when He gave me Himself, He restored me to myself. So then, since I have been given and regiven, I owe Him myself for myself, and so I am twice in

---

82. De Muis, *In Omnes Psalmos*, sub loc. Ps. 138:6.

83. *Jo. Euseb.* Neieremberg. Theopoliticus. p. 9.] Nieremberg, *Theopoliticus* (Antwerp, 1641), bk. 1, ch. 1, pp. 8–9.

debt. What shall I offer God in return for Him? For even if I should spend myself a thousand times, what am I worth to God?[84]

Good God! As repayment of such a massive debt, how very small a thing is our thanksgiving! Nevertheless, someone has called this the key of God's tender mercies. For it routinely unlocks those mercies, abundantly distributing all manner of good things to those who perform this duty properly.

§ 12. The fifth is ἡ τιμή (honor). Heins notes that in several Pauline passages, this word connotes not so much an honor offered as evaluation of another person, how one appraises them.[85] The standard of measurement is humility. It brings a person so low that he places someone else before himself. Heins tried to gain support and credibility for his position by comparing this apostolic statement in Romans 12:10, τῇ τιμῇ ἀλλήλους προηγούμενοι,[86] with Philippians 2:3, ἀλλὰ τῇ ταπεινοφροσύνῃ ἀλλήλους ἡγούμενοι ὑπερέχοντας ἑαυτῶν.[87] Now if we accept this interpretation as accurate, we could not say that anyone honors God with a debt of honor except the one who values Him above everything else and worships Him (as the Scholastics say) "at His proper worth." Of course, the psalmist was once led by the same Spirit and, through Him, shouted, "Whom have I in heaven except You? And on earth nothing pleases me except You!" (Ps. 73:25). And Hannah says, "No one is holy like Jehovah, for there is none beside You, and there is no rock like our God" (1 Sam. 2:2). I think that a writer of great devotion not long ago beautifully sketched out this feeling of a pious mind in an oration:

O Lord, great God, how wonderful You are! Not only do You have no equal but You have no one that can know You and Your perfections as they are! You far surpass our knowledge. And although we are right to call You wise, good, powerful, and lovely, still we are right to say that You are not wise, not good, not powerful, not lovely precisely in the way in which we conceive You, because You are beyond wise, beyond good, beyond powerful, beyond lovely, beyond being. Let all weakness of created intellect bow before Your glory, and may it always recognize that it is unequal to the task of comprehending that glory. Let us struggle to feel this properly, let us cling to our small understanding. Our good consists in this, that even what we perceive properly of You is far from accurate.[88]

---

84. Tractat. de diligendo Deum.] Bernard of Clairvaux, *Tractatus De Diligendo Deo*, in *Opera Omnia*, vol. 4 (Cologne, 1641), ch. 5.

85. Exercit. sac. lib. 6. cap. 7.] Heins, *Sacrarum Exercitationum*, bk. 6, ch. 7, p. 341.

86. "Surpassing one another in honor."

87. "But with humility count others better than yourselves."

88. *Caspar Tauchius* in lib. cui titulus Fontes Salvatoris, pag. 372.] Caspar Tausch, 1594–1645, *Fontes Salvatoris* (Antwerp, 1643), sec. 12, p. 372.

The sixth is ἡ δύναμις (power).[89] Theologians distinguish in God a threefold principle of acting. One is a directing action, which is His intellect. The second is ruling, which is His will. The third is an executing principle, which is His power. Whatever action the divine intellect conceives and the divine will commands, this is offered to divine power for execution. These words of Job demonstrate these relations: "I know You can do all things, and You cannot be deterred from fulfilling Your purpose" (Job 42:2). The psalmist has this in mind as well: "The Lord in heaven, on earth, on the sea, and in all the depths of the earth has done all things whatsoever that He has purposed" (Ps. 135:6). Paul likewise: "By His all-surpassing power, He is able to do all things, far beyond what we ask or think" (Eph. 3:20). I would like to add to these a citation from Plutarch, which is all the more noteworthy as it comes so close to the Christian spirit and style:

ὑπ᾽ εὐνοίας καὶ φιλίας πρὸς τὸν Θεὸν ἄγαν ἐμπαθῶς ἔχουσι μέγα πρὸς πίστιν ἐστὶ τὸ θαυμάσιον, etc. That is, God's majesty greatly reinforces the faith of those who honor him for his tremendous goodwill and love, as he is one who surpasses human strength by these aspects of his divine power. It is not irrational for God to do what we ourselves cannot do and to accomplish what we are not strong enough to accomplish. Actually, in point of fact, as he is dissimilar to us in all respects, he is even more removed and separate in his works. But divine qualities surpass our knowledge by a wide margin (as Heraclitus said) because of their implausibility.[90]

Plutarch argues his points like a skilled theologian.

But for this topic we are currently discussing, I would like us to understand not so much God's power in its total extent but in a particular instance. This is evident in the conversion of sinners and preservation of the regenerate. One can read about this in Psalm 110: "Jehovah will send the scepter of His strength from Zion. And His people will be willing in the day of His power" [Ps. 110:2–3]. Likewise, in 1 Peter 1: "You are kept safe by God's defending might and power, through faith to salvation" [1 Peter 1:5].

§ 13. The seventh is ἡ ἰσχύς (strength). The verb ἰσχύειν means, among other things, *to be strong*. We see this in the phrase πολὺ ἰσχύειν[91] (James 5:16). Jacob, pouring out prayers and tears as the prophet relates, ἐνίσχυσεν

---

89. A. uses here the Greek word with Latin gloss *potentia*. In his Latin translation of the Revelation 7 passage earlier in the chapter, he uses *potestas*, which typically stands for authority, ἐξουσία, whereas *potentia* is usually taken as a synonym for δύναμις. Therefore, it is clear he is using the terms synonymously.

90. *Plutarch.* in Coriolano non procul a fine.] Plutarch, *Coriolanus*, in *Omnium Quae Exstant*, vol. 1 (Frankfurt, 1620).

91. "Prayer prevails much with God."

πρὸς Θεόν (Hos. 12:3).[92] I would understand the word ἰσχύν here to mean the efficacy of converting grace by which God prevails with a man. As Augustine says, "His grace intervenes with him who is unwilling to make him will, and it pursues the one who was willing so that he does not will in vain."[93] Or perhaps it refers to that power God exercised in drawing the sinner to Christ. The Savior said of this, "No one can come to Me unless the Father who sent Me drew him" (John 6:44). The hammer of the Pelagians, whom I just praised, notes, "The Lord did not say, 'Unless My Father led him.' Leading is a quality of one who first is willing. But the Lord said, 'Unless the Father drew him.' This applies to one who is not first willing; it is meant to show that our will does not precede God's motion but quite the contrary."[94] If God's efficacious motion depended on our will, as some speculate, it would be *antecedent*, and man would not be drawn by God but would instead draw God to himself. That vigorous champion of grace adds, "Man, by marvelous ways, is drawn so that he is willing, drawn by the one who knows how to work in the deepest areas of men's hearts. He does this not so that, though unwilling, they believe but so that they are changed from unwilling to willing."[95] That passage of the Apostle in Ephesians makes me a little more dogged in this interpretation, where he proclaims, with marvelous and lofty eloquence, the power of converting grace. He there mentions ἰσχυν. He says, Τί τὸ ὑπερβάλλον μέγεθος τῆς δυνάμεως αὐτοῦ εἰς ἡμᾶς τοὺς πιστεύοντας κατὰ τὴν ἐνέργειαν τοῦ κράτους τῆς ἰσχύος αὐτοῦ ἣν ἐνήργησεν ἐν τῷ Χριστῷ ἐγείρας αὐτὸν ἐκ νεκρῶν (Eph. 1:19–20).[96] Look, here he is exerting δύναμις, ἰσχύς, ἐνεργία at work in all those who are led to faith.[97] It is not just any kind of δύναμις but a superabounding one, ὑπερβάλλον μέγεθος τῆς δυνάμεως.[98] And it is not an average ἰσχύς but τὸ κράτος τῆς ἰσχύος.[99] Not a common ἐνεργία but that very omnipotent might that God exercised in raising Christ from the dead. Prosper expresses this with the greatest charm and clarity:

---

92. "Struggled with God." This is v. 4 in the Septuagint.

93. Enchirid. cap. 32.] Augustine, *Enchiridion Ad Laurentium*, ch. 32.

94. Vid. *Nugno* in 3[am] Thomae qu. 62. p. 64.] Quotation in Diego Nuño Cabezudo, 1550–1614, Spanish Dominican theologian, *Commentarii Et Disputationes In Tertiam Partem D. Thomae Aquinatis* ([Valladolid], 1601).

95. Augustine, *Contra Duas Epistol. Pelag. Lib.* i. *cap.* 19.

96. "What is the all-surpassing greatness of His power toward us who believe, according to the working of the great might of His strength, which He has worked in Christ Jesus, raising Him from the dead."

97. "Power," "strength," and "might," respectively.

98. "All-surpassing greatness of His power."

99. "Might of His strength."

> When almighty grace saves man by herself,
> She finishes work once begun.
> No time does she waste but always attends,
> To will and complete what she's done.
> Grace brooks no delay, 'tis not in her trade,
> Nor gives up her causes, not one.[100]

And yet no one should conclude from this that violence is done to the will, because in every state, it is free from coercion. Nothing is more certain than that, through grace operating "powerfully and persuasively"—as Bernard says[101]—or "with omnipotent ability"—as Augustine says[102]—the will is truly impelled by such an efficacious motion that it freely follows where grace leads. I do not say the will is acted upon irresistibly in all things but just that it is "without resistance" in the here and now. This happens in such a way, meanwhile, that the will acts freely and follows grace's leading, and so as the will is inclined, it turns inexorably where grace steers it. I say that the will is *impelled* but not *compelled*. Fulgentius expresses it quite well: "By God's grace the human will is not obviated but healed. It is not removed but corrected; not removed but eliminated. It is not emptied of all meaning but aided."[103]

§ 14. Finally, as I get ready momentarily to draw in my sails, the angels ascribe all these traits to their God: εἰς τοὺς αἰῶνας τῶν αἰώνων [Rev. 7:12].[104] Hemmingsen interprets the phrase from the end of Ephesians 3, εἰς πάσας τὰς γενεὰς τοῦ αἰῶνος τῶν αἰώνων [Eph. 3:21],[105] in these words: "In this world, until judgment, and then after the resurrection for all eternity."[106] Daniel Fessel says, "When the conjunction of this age and the coming age is mentioned in the sacred Scriptures, it is called αἰῶνες τῶν αἰώνων."[107] Now the subject of this very doxology stands at the same time both in heaven and on earth, throughout the course of both ages. Chrysostom aptly calls praise and thanksgiving μελλούσης ζωῆς τὰ προοίμια,

---

100. Lib. de Ingratis c. 15.] Prosper of Aquitaine, *De Ingratis Contra Pelagianos*, in *Opera* (Cologne, 1630), ch. 15, p. 557.

101. Bernard of Clairvaux, *Apologia De Vita Et Moribus*, in *Opera Omnia*, vol. 4 (Cologne, 1641), ch. 3.

102. Augustine, *Epist.* 107.

103. De Verit. praedestinat. lib. 2.] Fulgentius, *De Incarnatione Et Gratia Domini*, in *Opera Quae Extant Omnia* (Basel, 1587), bk. 1, ch. 20, p. 764.

104. "Forever and ever."

105. "To all generations forever and ever."

106. Niels Hemmingsen, 1513–1600, Danish Lutheran theologian and professor, *Commentaria in Omnes Epistolas Apostolorum* (Frankfurt, 1579), sub loc. Eph. 3:21.

107. Adversar. Sacror. lib. 3. c. 2. p. 232.] Daniel Fessel, 1599–1674, German Lutheran court preacher, *Adversariorum Sacrorum* (Wittenberg, 1650), bk. 3, ch. 3, p. 232. "Ages of ages."

or "opening stanzas of eternity."[108] There is nothing more appropriate for saints warring in this world than to begin earnestly and, in season, to do the very thing they will do forever.

Finally, the blessed spirits put a seal on their song with a second "Amen." This word has a variety of meanings in the sacred Book. Sometimes it should be taken as a noun. Then it means simply *truth*, as when the text says, "The Amen says these things, he is a witness faithful and true" (Rev. 3:14). Sometimes it should be taken as an adverb and so translated *truly* or *certainly*. This is the more common usage in John: "Truly, truly, I say to you" (John 3:3, 5). In still other instances, it should be taken as a verb, meaning *I assert* or *it is so*. This is the usage at the end of the individual gospels. Or it could be taken as a hope, as in *may it be so*, the usage found at the end of the Lord's Prayer. This little tiny word we have labored over so much begins with an assertion and ends with a hope. The angels say to themselves, "So it is. May everything we have recounted be ascribed to our God forever."

§ 15. Now for what remains, my dear fellow soldiers, we must immediately arm ourselves—though we are still mere mortals—for the study of God's attributes that, in the state of immortality, without even the slightest fatigue, we shall eternally celebrate. Right now, let us learn some skill in praising our Lord, a skill we must put to use through endless ages. As the trophies of Miltiades[109] once drove on Themistocles, so may the victories of those in heaven spur us on. Let us remember the example of David Pareus, who used to encourage those zealous to know something intimately to recall Jerome's advice to Paulinus: "May we on earth learn those things whose knowledge will stay with us in heaven!"[110] This also applies to the theology classroom, where every day Pareus taught the sacred Scriptures and commented on them, as his own son tells us. Let us remember Leonard Lessius. When he was on the very brink of bidding this world farewell, he completed a treatise, *God's Fifty Names*, and added the final touch to it four or five days before his death. In that work, he frequently said he found so much light and spiritual joy—amid the bitterest pain from kidney stones—that he far preferred this little volume to all the commentaries on Aquinas's *Summa* he considered merely unfinished.[111] And let us not forget Monica, who for so long discussed the heavenly kingdom with her son Augustine. She told him

---

108. In Psal. 144.] Chrysostom, *Opera*, vol. 5 (Paris, 1836), p. 563. "Introductions to the life to come."

109. Miltiades, fl. fifth century BC, Athenian aristocrat and general.

110. *In Vita patris sui.*] Jerome, quoted in Pareus, *Narratio Historica*, p. 167.

111. *De vita & moribus Leon. Lessi*, § 25. pag. 43. *& in Epistola praefixa ipsius tractatui de 50 Nominibus Dei.*] Lessius, *De Vita Et Moribus* (Paris, 1644), ch. 6, sec. 25, p. 43; Lessius, *De L Nominibus Dei* (Leuven, 1643), sig. 6r.

what the future life would be like, though we cannot feel or conceive it with our eyes or our ears. We cannot really even imagine it with our thoughts. After long conversation, she said, "As for me, my son, there is nothing in this life that could please me more. What am I doing here?"[112]

I now conclude all of this with the words of the prophet David. He gasped for heaven and spoke to God with a longing so very sweet. I present his words in the verse of George Buchanan, from his paraphrase of the Psalms (Ps. 36:8–10):

> While my mind lay chained, within this corp'ral prison fastened,
> As a bird that shelters 'neath her wings all of her fledglings,
> So sure hope of your defense does loose us from all evils.
> But the soul, an exile freed by death will seek her homeland,
> The starry threshold and its doorway soon to tread once more.
> There all want and sorrows cast outside to utter darkness,
> No one forced to suffer things that brute upon his wishes.
> Pleasures far surpassing, purest joys strewn o'er the landscape,
> These and fair delights the brook of gen'rous flow delivers.
> There eternal life streams forth, its headlands in a fountain,
> Life ne'er to be shortened by death's heavy hand of sorrow.
> There the thickset clouds that darken minds shall flee at morning,
> Cares that once our heavy hearts weighed down beneath their shadows.
> By the impulse of your shining face its ray diffusing,
> On the light of your pure knowledge we shall feast forever.[113]

The End

---

112. Augustine, *Confessiones*, 9.10.26.

113. George Buchanan, 1506–1582, Scottish humanist poet and historian, *Psalmorum Davidis Paraphrasis Poetica* (Leipzig, 1595), p. 69 (sub loc. Ps. 36).

APPENDICES

Dedication to the 1700 Edition

*To the most excellent, renowned, and learned man
master Heinrich Hüls,
doctor of sacred theology and professor ordinarius of the same
at Teutoburg University, most prolific translator of sacred literature,
and distinguished patron:[1]*

Your unique and well-known philanthropy, my good man, could have all by itself urged me to dedicate this work to you. The charm of your countenance promises such generosity to all who observe, and your polished character and easygoing nature make it evident to everyone. The joy of your personal deportment does as well, and the services you have rendered me proclaim it aloud. They urge me to offer these firstfruits of my labor to your name as a symbol of a grateful heart and a pledge of my respect. For this work, although it is but a trifling gift, gives some warrant that it should not be spurned but rather received, as is the custom, with a calm smile. And yet there are also more serious reasons. For men who have served the church with distinction wanted these *Sacred Strategies* entrusted to no other commander than that exacting bishop of the sacred Pallas, the tireless doctor of heavenly truth and hammer of errors. The most learned Arrowsmith, if he still enjoyed this life, would demand no one else as his patron. These martial topics (obviously I speak figuratively—not of blood and brutality but of the victor's salvation as he lounges upon the grass) call for no other man as their calm yet bold and very shrewd, defender of true wisdom.

Therefore, since these works demand that you take them into your safekeeping and care,[2] it will be easy to permit my labor, whatever it is worth, to rejoice in your protection. This is my confidence. That the truth, the

---

1. Heinrich Hüls (Hulsius), 1654–1723, Reformed professor of theology at Duisburg (Teutoburg).

2. Solmans uses *clientelam* here, which plays on his earlier use of *Patronum*. Hulsius as patron is to receive A.'s work as a client, a common analogy taken from Roman political life.

church, the academy, and all good men receive its fruit more abundantly, I humbly beseech our triune,[3] most great, and most glorious God to preserve Your Eminence unharmed for a long time.

I, the most careful guardian of your most exalted reputation, Engelbert Solmans,[4] wrote this at Amsterdam, December 26, 1699.

---

3. Solmans has *Ter*, "threefold."
4. Engelbert(us) Solmans, fl. ca. 1701–1709, Amsterdam printer.

Preface to the 1700 Edition

PREFACE

The first edition of this little volume, published at Cambridge in the year of our Lord 1657, was not for sale at the booksellers in Holland for several years and could not be acquired at public auctions for a reasonable price. This was due to the extreme scarcity of copies. (Quite often it went for 6 or 7 florins, and even then, the buyer was pleased.) Consequently, for the benefit of the reader, this work has been sent back to the press and now brought again to light. The bookseller was emboldened to this step all the more as soon as certain men offered him reasons he could not ignore. They persuaded him that our author was discussing a most agreeable subject—namely, the whole spiritual armor—as well as shedding light on many passages of Holy Scripture that deal with that topic (especially Ephesians 6). Such passages diffuse the aroma of the ancient practices or rites of warfare. No matter the reader's circumstance, the bookseller has decided to roll the dice and not spare any expense[1] in publishing this little work. He hopes he has offered you, reader, something you welcome and, thus, will provide an incentive, Lord willing, to publish other learned works he has written. But before I put the finishing touch on this preface, I must first briefly say what is noteworthy in this edition. First, it features a better cover and one more decorated than before. There is also set before you a catalogue of the authors mentioned in this work. The typographical errors that the author himself noted in the previous edition have all been fixed, especially those that escaped his eye, as can be demonstrated from several passages. Various dividing and punctuation marks that the typesetter or even the author himself perhaps sloppily inserted have been very carefully excised. Even many learned men deserve censure when, because they neither have the craft of marking a text nor, in keeping with their disposition, learn it, carelessly prove that old proverb, "That one does ably teach who ably divides twixt each." Such negligence is evident in their manuscripts and published works.

---

1. I.e., print a quality edition whether or not there will be buyers.

If the reader notices certain persistent faults anywhere in this second edition, through the typesetter's carelessness and indolence, it will be very easy to edit them out of the attached catalogue and index. But allow me to conclude with the author's own words, found on the last page of the previous edition:[2]

> Finally, dear reader, may we enjoy your indulgence when it comes to pardoning mistakes of little significance, like the kind occurring in punctuation, numbering, breathing marks, and accents. Allow me to add as a defense the words written long ago by Joannes de Cartagena in the preface to his *Catholic Homilies*: "'One must remember Macrobius 5.3, that the ancients once noted that there are three famously impossible tasks: to separate Hercules[3] from his club, Jupiter from his lightning, and Homer from his verse."[4] This remark makes very clear that the art of proofreading had not yet been invented. Had it already been in full swing then, the ancients would doubtless have added a fourth task: separating proofreading from its errors. I would dare say that experience has sufficiently proven this remark, that a completely clean manuscript gone to press is
>
> > A bird unknown in all the earth
> > Like to a swan all black from birth.[5]
>
> If there is any bird more rare, it is the phoenix. Yet even if typesetters and proofreaders had better vision than John's animals[6]—filled with eyes in front and behind—or than the shepherd Argus, whom Ovid mentions and who abounded in one hundred eyes, still, there is no way this work would be published error-free.[7]

These were his comments. Farewell.

---

2. Solmans cites the *errata* page in A., *Tactica Sacra* (Cambridge, 1657), p. [367].

3. Hercules, Roman equivalent to Greek Heracles, demigod son of Jupiter.

4. Macrobius, *Saturnalia*, bk. 5, ch. 3.

5. Juvenal, *Satires*, VI.165.

6. Rev. 4:8.

7. Juan de Cartagena, 1563–1618, Spanish Jesuit theologian, reader's preface in *Homiliae Catholicae* (Paris, 1616), 2v (†iiii, 2v).

Scripture Index

Subject Index